Handbook of Gerontology

Evidence-Based Approaches to Theory, Practice, and Policy

Edited by
James A. Blackburn, PhD
Catherine N. Dulmus, PhD

BICENTENNIAL
1807
WILEY
2007
BICENTENNIAL

John Wiley & Sons, Inc.

Library of Congress Cataloging-in-Publication Data:

Handbook of gerontology : evidence-based approaches to theory,
    practice, and policy / edited by James A. Blackburn, Catherine N.
    Dulmus.
        p. ; cm.
    Includes bibliographical references.
    ISBN-13: 978-0-471-77170-8 (cloth : alk. paper)
    1. Geriatrics—Handbooks, manuals, etc.   2. Gerontology—Hand-
books, manuals, etc.   3. Evidence-based medicine—Handbooks,
manuals, etc.   I. Blackburn, James A., Ph. D.   II. Dulmus,
Catherine N.
    [DNLM: 1. Aging—physiology.   Aging—psychology.
3. Geriatrics—methods. 4.   Health Policy.   5. Health Services for
the Aged.   WT 104 H2343 2007]
    RC952.55.H395   2007
    618.97—dc22

                                                    2006027614

Printed in the United States of America.

10 9 8 7 6 5 4 3 2 1

To our baby boomer colleagues who are educating the next generation of gerontologist researchers and practitioners.
Teach them well . . . they will be taking care of all of us.

Contents

Preface

THIS BOOK BEGAN by a conversation between the two editors regarding the need for a comprehensive and readable gerontology handbook that could serve as a primary or secondary text for undergraduates and graduate students across disciplines, as well as a resource to practitioners. We conceptualized a book that would cover the current state of knowledge related to evidence-based theory, practice, and policy in gerontology. Our esteemed authors from around the globe embraced our vision for the book and delivered state-of-the-art chapters. We thank them. We also thank our editors at Wiley. Tracey Belmont was there as we conceptualized the project and Lisa Gebo shepherded us through the development and delivery of the finished product. A good editor is essential for the successful fruition of any book and we were fortunate to have two.

The study of adulthood and aging has emerged as a totally new field of study; its organization is wholly new and so is the greater part of its content. After all, it can fairly be argued that the field of adult development and aging is moving forward at a great pace. Bibliographic references have increased over the past 20 years along with an increase in the number of journals and books devoted to this narrow yet broad field of study. Not only do we have far more data; we also have a more substantial base for an inclusive perspective. Such consideration led us to begin consolidating the knowledge base in the field of adulthood and aging through the book's 20 chapters that summarize the latest research findings on a broad range of topics.

Whatever our biases, we hope that we do not include a preference for any one discipline's (e.g., legal, medical, psychological, social work) approach to the issues and challenges of adulthood and aging. We cannot conceive of formulating any of the central issues presented throughout the book in terms of any one discipline alone. An interdisciplinary approach to the further development and implementation of evidence-based theory, practice, and policy is not only essential, but imperative.

With over 600 million elderly persons living around the globe, this book is timely. It is comprehensive, practical, well researched, and very readable. Everyone with a serious interest in adulthood and the aging years should read it. Our hope is that this book will serve as a resource in seeking to move various national and international agendas as they relate to the later years of life, and be deemed a valuable addition to our knowledge base in the field of human development and aging.

JAMES A. BLACKBURN
CATHERINE N. DULMUS

About the Editors

James A. Blackburn, PhD is professor in the School of Social Work at Hunter College in New York City. A noted gerontology expert, he came to Hunter in 2004 from the University of Wisconsin at Milwaukee, where he was active in promoting and generating multidisciplinary research both within the University and in cooperation with other institutions. During his 12 years as dean, Dr. Blackburn worked with state and federal governments and private donors to provide major funding opportunities for research and faculty positions in the areas of gerontology, child welfare, addiction, and behavioral health. He spearheaded the efforts to bring in the largest gift ever received by the University of Wisconsin at Milwaukee. Dr. Blackburn also has been active in the national social work arena. He has served the Council of Social Work Education in various active roles including service on the Board of Directors, the Commission on Education Policy, and the Commission on Accreditation. He is currently a member of the Gerontological Society of America, the National Council on Family Relations, and a number of other professional organizations.

Catherine N. Dulmus, PhD is associate dean for research and director of the Buffalo Center for Social Research in the School of Social Work at the University at Buffalo. She received her baccalaureate degree in social work from Buffalo State College in 1989, the master's degree in social work from the University at Buffalo in 1991 and a doctoral degree in social welfare from the University at Buffalo in 1999. Dr. Dulmus's research focuses on child mental health, prevention, and violence. She has authored or coauthored several journal articles and books, and has presented her research nationally and internationally. Dr. Dulmus is co-editor of *The Journal of Evidence-Based Social Work: Advances in Practice, Programming, Research, and Policy*, co-editor of *Best Practices in Mental Health: An International Journal*, associate editor of *Stress, Trauma, and Crisis: An International Journal*, and sits on the editorial boards of the *Journal of Human Behavior in the Social Environment*, *Victims and Offenders: Journal of Evidence-Based Policies and Practices*, and the *Journal of Health and Social Policy*. Previous books she has co-authored or co-edited that have been published by John Wiley and sons include *Social Work and Human Services Treatment Planner*, *Essentials of Child Welfare*, *Handbook of Preventive Interventions with Children*, and the *Handbook of Preventive Interventions with Adults*. In addition, she is co-editor of the *Handbook of Social Work and Social Welfare* that is currently in development. Prior to obtaining her doctorate, her social work practice background encompassed almost a decade of experience in the fields of gerontology, mental health, and school social work.

Contributors

Gretchen E. Alkema, MSW, LCSW
University of Southern California
Ethel Percy Andrus Gerontology
    Center
Los Angeles, California

Paul B. Baltes, PhD
Max Planck Institute for Human
    Development
Berlin, Germany

Jill Bradshaw, MSW
University of Connecticut
School of Social Work
West Hartford, Connecticut

Linda J. Brock, PhD
Texas Woman's University
Department of Family Sciences
Family Therapy Program
Denton, Texas

Patricia Brownell, PhD
Fordham University
Graduate School of Social Services
New York, New York

Benjamin P. Chapman, PhD
University of Rochester Medical Center
Rochester, New York

Natalie C. Ebner, PhD
Max Planck Institute for Human
    Development
Berlin, Germany

Susan M. Enguidanos, PhD, MHP
Research Center Partners in
    Care Foundation
San Fernando, California

Anna C. Faul, PhD
University of Louisville
Kent School of Social Work
Louisville, Kentucky

Alexandra M. Freund, PhD
University of Zurich
Institute of Psychology
Zurich, Switzerland

Jan Steven Greenberg, PhD
University of Wisconsin
School of Social Work
Madison, Wisconsin

Robert O. Hansson, PhD
University of Tulsa
Department of Psychology
Tulsa, Oklahoma

Leslie Hasche, LCSW
Washington University
George Warren Brown School of
    Social Work
St. Louis, Missouri

Bert Hayslip Jr., PhD
University of North Texas
Department of Psychology
Denton, Texas

Akira Homma, MD
Tokyo Metropolitan Institute of Gerontology
Department of Psychiatry
Tokyo, Japan

Glen Jennings, EdD
Texas Woman's University
Department of Family Sciences
Family Therapy Program
Denton, Texas

Waldo C. Klein, PhD
University of Connecticut
School of Social Work
West Hartford, Connecticut

Karl Kosloski, PhD
University of Nebraska
Gerontology Department
Omaha, Nebraska

Ute Kunzmann, PhD
International University
Bremen, Germany

Mary Ann Leitz, PhD, RN
Tarleton State University
Social Work, Sociology and
    Criminal Justice
Stephenville, Texas

Elizabeth Lightfoot, PhD
University of Minnesota
School of Social Work
St. Paul, Minnesota

Rhonda J.V. Montgomery, PhD
University of Wisconsin, Milwaukee
Helen Bader School of Social Welfare
Milwaukee, Wisconsin

Rebecca Morgan, JD
Stetson University College of Law
St. Petersburg, Florida

Nancy Morrow-Howell, PhD
Washington University
George Warren Brown School of
    Social Work
St. Louis, Missouri

Laura J. Pankow, OD, PhD
University of Chicago
Pritzker School of Medicine
Windermere Senior Health Center
Chicago, Illinois

Hwa-Ok Hannah Park, PhD
Kangnam University
School of Social Welfare
Yongin, South Korea

Gina R. Rosich, MSW
George Daley House
New York, New York

Noell L. Rowan, PhD
University of Louisville
Kent School of Social Work
Louisville, Kentucky

Jeannine M. Rowe, MSW
University of Wisconsin-Milwaukee
Helen Bader School of Social Welfare
Milwaukee, Wisconsin

William S. Rowe, DSW
University of South Florida
School of Social Work
Tampa, Florida

Susanne Scheibe, PhD
Max Planck Institute for Human
    Development
Berlin, Germany

Masahiro Shigeta, MD
Tokyo Metropolitan University
Health Sciences
Tokyo, Japan

Jeffrey M. Solotoroff, MSW
University of Chicago
Pritzker School of Medicine
Windermere Senior
    Health Center
Chicago, Illinois

Karen M. Sowers, PhD
University of Tennessee
College of Social Work
Knoxville, Tennessee

Debra A. Street, PhD
University at Buffalo
Department of Sociology
Buffalo, New York

Margaret S. Stroebe, PhD
Utrecht University
The Netherlands

Jeanette C. Takamura, PhD
Columbia University
School of Social Work
New York, New York

Kathleen H. Wilber, PhD, LCSW
University of Southern California
Ethel Percy Andrus Gerontology Center
Los Angeles, California

Jay Wolfson, DrPH, JD
University of South Florida
Public Health and Medicine
Tampa, Florida

PART I

INTRODUCTION

CHAPTER 1

Global Aging

KAREN M. SOWERS and WILLIAM S. ROWE

THE WORLD IS experiencing dramatically increased numbers of people living to an advanced old age. Often referred to as "the graying of the planet," this dramatic increase represents the most significant population shift in recent history (Obaid & Malloch-Brown, 2002). Population aging may be considered one of humanity's major achievements while posing a major challenge for much of the world. This chapter provides an overview of global aging, shifts in the aging population, discusses similarities and differences among the elderly, and provides some suggestions for how you can become involved in promoting the well-being of the aged.

Aging is defined by the World Health Organization (WHO, 1999) as the process of progressive change in the biological, psychological, and social structure of individuals. According to the U.N. definition, persons 60 years and over are considered elderly (United Nations, n.d.).

GLOBAL DEMOGRAPHICS

Globally, the total population is growing at a rate of 1.2% annually. In 2000, the percentage of older persons was as follows:

Africa	5%	Europe	20%
Asia	9%	North America	16%
Latin America and Caribbean	8%	Oceania	13%

More than 600 million persons in the world are 60 years of age or older. This represents about 10% of the world's population. However, by the year 2050, 21% of the world's population is expected to be 60 years old or over. In less than 50 years, one person in five will be over 60. Other basic facts about global aging include:

- The increased life expectancy is a product of improved public health, sanitation, and development.
- In 1950, 8 out of every 100 people were over 60. By 2050, 22 out of every 100 people will be over 60.
- Life expectancy worldwide is expected to increase by 11 years, from 65 in 1995 to 2000 to 76 in 2045 to 2050, despite the impact of HIV/AIDS.
- Most of the world's older people live in developing countries.
- Even in the poorest countries, life expectancy is increasing and the number of older people is growing. In 2000, there were 374 million people over 60 in developing countries—62% of the world's older people. In 2015, there will be 597 million older people in developing countries—67% of the world's older people.
- In 2005, 1 in 12 people in developing countries were over 60. By 2015, 1 in 10 people in developing countries will be over 60 and, by 2050, 1 in 5 people in developing countries will be over 60.
- In every region, the rate of population increase for the 65-and-over age group is higher than for the under-14 age group and the 15 to 64 age group.

Many older people in developing countries live in poverty:

- 80% of older people in developing countries have no regular income.
- At best, older people live on between one-third to a half of average incomes.
- Poverty rates in households with older people are up to 29% higher than in households without older people.
- Over 100 million older people live on less than a dollar a day.
- Lack of food is a serious cause of ill health in older people.
- Older widows are among the poorest and most vulnerable groups in developing countries.

Older women outnumber older men:

- In 2005, there were 83 men for every 100 women over 60 worldwide.
- In developing countries, the gap is less wide: there are 91 men for every 100 women over 60. However, this gap is increasing—by 2015, there will be 89 men for every 100 women and, by 2030, 86 men for every 100 women.

Older people care for people with HIV/AIDS and orphans:

- Older people are the primary caregivers for orphaned and vulnerable children affected by HIV/AIDS and those living with HIV/AIDS.

DEVELOPMENTAL ASPECTS OF AGING

Aging begins before we are born, is a lifelong process and continues throughout life. Throughout the life course, differing life experiences influence our capabilities and well-being in our later years. The functional capacity of our biological systems increases during the first years of life, reaches its peak in early adulthood and naturally declines thereafter (WHO, 1999). Throughout most countries (but not all), persons experience a long childhood and a long old age. These two lengthy developmental spans have provided great utility. Throughout history, it has enabled older persons to educate the younger and pass on values to them. The young are provided opportunities to learn from older persons when the elderly are in the home, the neighborhood, and in all forms of social life (International Federation on Ageing, n.d.). There is substantial evidence around the world that indicates that many older persons can and do lead productive lives and contribute financially, in child care and in emotional support to the family.

Gender does appear to effect the way people age. Throughout the world, women live longer than men. Eastern Europe, the Baltic States, and Central Asia have the largest differences in the life spans between men and women. Female life expectancy at birth ranges from just over 50 years in the least developed countries to well over 80 in many developed countries. As a result, the oldest people in most parts of the world are mostly women. Although women may live longer than men, they are affected more by disabling diseases in later life than are men. In fact, overall, the patterns of health and illness in women and men are markedly different. Because of women's longevity, they are more likely to suffer from chronic diseases associated with old age. These include osteoporosis, diabetes, hypertension, incontinence, and arthritis (WHO, 1999). Many of these chronic disabling diseases significantly impact quality of life. To date, there is little scientific understanding of the life expectancy differences or the differences in relative health during the aging process (WHO, 1998).

Much of the developmental research to date has focused on the social and intellectual growth of children. But, as life expectancy increases, researchers are beginning to turn their attention to adult development and aging and as a result we are now beginning to understand how memory and learning abilities change over the lifespan, what types of memory decline, and what types are sustainable. Researchers are also beginning to study multiple related issues such as how social and family interactions contribute to successful aging, problems relating to work and retirement, and issues relating to living arrangements. But we urgently need for science to do more. It is critical for research to catch up to the worldwide aging phenomenon. For instance, we still need to know more about the factors conducive to achieving a satisfying and productive old age, how to improve and maintain memory and learning in later life, and how to best address sensory problems connected with failing vision and hearing and how these sensory impairments impact cognitive and social functioning (Canadian Psychological Association, n.d.).

What is known is that some life course factors which influence health and aging are modifiable by the individual. Research presents new opportunities for wellness promotion because people are able to influence how they age by adopting healthier life styles and by adapting to age-associated changes (WHO, 1999). Because the problems associated with development and aging are ones that all societies face, there is a critical need for interdisciplinary collaboration between the helping professions to apply current research findings to existing problems, identify the gaps in the knowledge base, and create new knowledge to better understand the developmental process of aging.

COMMON ELEMENTS OF GERONTOLOGY PRACTICE ACROSS THE GLOBE

Despite the many societal and cultural differences between countries, there does appear to be a common set of characteristics to gerontological practice. Those elements that appear to be fairly common across all countries include the areas discussed next.

ELDER MALTREATMENT

Abuse of the elderly is found in almost all countries of the world. According to the World Health Organization (n.d.), elder abuse is expected to continue to increase, particularly as many countries experience rapidly aging populations. Throughout the world, both elderly men and women are at high risk of abuse, neglect, and exploitation. Although older men are at risk of abuse in about the same proportion as women, elderly women are at higher risk of abuse, neglect, and exploitation in cultures where women are devalued (Sowers & Rowe, 2006).

The World Health Organization (n.d.) estimates that between 4% to 6% of the elderly have experienced abuse in the home and that elderly are also at risk of abuse in institutions such as hospitals, nursing homes, and other long-term care facilities. Cultural and socioeconomic factors also appear to play an important role in elder abuse (Sowers & Rowe, 2006). According to the World Health Organization (n.d.) cultural and socioeconomic factors influencing abuse among the elderly include:

- The depiction of older people as frail, weak, and dependent
- Erosion of the bonds between generations of a family
- Restructuring of the basic support networks for the elderly
- Systems of inheritance and land rights, affecting the distribution of power and material goods within families
- Migration of young couples to other areas, leaving elderly parents alone, in societies where older people were traditionally cared for by their offspring

SOCIAL SERVICES

Countries that deliver social services to the elderly most commonly do so through existing health and social services networks. These generally include medical, legal, psychological, and financial help, as well as help with housing and other environmental issues. Because older persons who are more socially integrated enjoy a higher quality of life and better health, there is an emphasis on providing the elderly with the emotional and practical resources known to positively impact the aging process. These often include social clubs, religious activities, and family-based activities (WHO, n.d.).

ECONOMIC SERVICES

Across the globe, the impact of population aging is increasingly evident in the old-age dependency ratio, the number of working-age persons (aged 15 to 64) per older persons (65 years or older) that is used as an indicator of the so-called dependency burden on potential workers. The rising dependency burden is most pronounced in Europe and Japan and least pronounced in Africa and the Middle East, but is a reality in nearly all countries (World Bank, n.d.). The United Nations (n.d.) estimates that between 2000 and 2050 the old-age dependency ratio will double in more developed regions and triple in less developed regions. In addition to the escalating dependency burden ratio, in many countries, traditional family support mechanisms are being eroded due to declining family size, rural to urban migration, urbanization, and declining co-residence, and in some countries younger family members dying of HIV/AIDS. As a result, many older people, and particularly older women, are faced with isolation, abandonment, loneliness, and no means of financial support. The potential socioeconomic impact on society that may result from an increasing old-age dependency ratio and other social shifts is an area of growing concern (Sowers & Rowe, 2006).

Pension systems play an important role in the economic stability of countries and the security of their aging populations. They serve to reduce poverty, eliminate the risk of rapidly falling standards in retirement, and protect vulnerable elderly people from economic and social distress. The World Bank (n.d.) suggests that the projected increase in the dependency burden ratio has two main implications: (1) They contend that pension systems that collect taxes from one generation to provide benefits to their parents will need to be adjusted to address the realities that elderly people live longer lives today than was anticipated when the systems were first designed. (2) They suggest that pensions systems be more flexible in the future to provide incentives for older workers to delay their retirement until later life in order to maintain a sufficient workforce. While calling for more flexible pension systems, the World Bank also notes that because countries have a number of different combination of elements that can impact their pension system that each country must develop their own pension system tailored to the needs of their specific country.

HEALTH SERVICES

Chronic and infectious diseases, many of which are direct results of life course events, influence the quality of life in older age. The types of conditions older people experience vary by country or region, economic status, gender, race, and ethnicity. In general, however, throughout the world those older persons with higher incomes report their health as being much better than do older people with less income (Dunkle & Norgard, 1995; Sowers & Rowe, 2006).

Long-term care for the elderly has been a challenge for all countries around the globe and the challenge will increase substantially in the years to come. In all developed nations, including the United States, the overwhelming majority of long-term care received by persons with disabilities of all ages is provided by informal caregivers, family members, or a combination of caregivers and family members. The United States does not have a comprehensive long-term care system. In general, the nation relies on Medicaid, a state administered safety net, as the primary source of financing for long-term care. Of the 29 nations that have older populations than the United States, most do not have strong or effective long-term care systems. Some, however do, for example, Germany and Japan have implemented comprehensive social insurance systems for long-term care. They cover a wide range of benefits in the home and community in addition to nursing home care. Many Scandanavian nations, as well as Austria, Japan, and Germany, have universal long-term care programs. These programs reach large numbers of their older populations and persons with disabilities. It may be useful to look to these countries that can serve as "natural laboratories" for tracking the impact of long-term care policy changes on coverage, cost, quality of care, and quality of life (Gibson, 2003).

Long-term health care for the elderly is problematic even in those countries that have traditionally placed a high value on the elderly. Most East Asian governments promote care for the aged as a family responsibility. As a result, they have not developed a sufficient number of long-term care facilities for frail older people (Choi, 2002; Ngan, 2004; Phillips, 1999). In China, there is a long-time tradition of children supporting their elderly parents. As a result, many families experience undue stress and financial strain (Choi, 2002; MacKenzie & Beck, 1991). Because of the rising incidence of suicide among the elderly as well as other family problems, many Asian governments are now exploring the need to introduce national policies on aging and long-term care to augment the traditional system (Howe & Phillips, 2001; Ngan, 2004). Japan, South Korea, Hong Kong, Singapore, and Taiwan are beginning to plan for a major increase in long-term care services (Ngan, 2004).

TRENDS IN GERONTOLOGICAL PRACTICE

COMMUNITY-BASED CARE

To meet the needs of older people most countries have moved toward community-based care (Higgins, 1989) as a means of providing adequate and cost-effective care. Community-based care focuses around an integrated and more comprehensive approach to the special needs of older persons, their families, and the community. This type of model involves and requires interorganizational collaboration and interdisciplinary cooperation. A community-based approach in social services and in health care is a strategic approach to meet the mounting demands for integrated health and social services for the elderly (Zimmerman, Sloane, & Eckert, 2001). Community health care usually includes both the health and social services sectors. Typically, self-care, informal care, and formal care are provided within this approach and the care often includes prevention, curative care, rehabilitation, palliative care, and terminal care. These integrated services may be delivered in a variety of settings including home or residential care settings (World Health Organization Centre for Health Development, n.d.).

FILIAL SUPPORT

In many places throughout the world, families are faced with increasing pressure to provide care for their elderly family members (Sowers & Rowe, 2006). As a result, several countries, including some states in the United States (George, 1997) have adopted filial support legislation. In China, filial support is mandated in the Marriage Laws of 1982 (Barusch, 1995), and the government of Singapore offers incentives for families to care for elderly parents (Teo, 1994). However, recent research indicates that policies that require or encourage relatives to provide care may have adverse consequences for elderly people and their families (Barusch, 1995). As a result, it appears that policies and interventions that provide universal access to a continuum of care alternatives that facilitate rational health care decision making by families and that empower and sustain family members who choose to care for elderly relatives may be a more effective approach than legislating caregiving. In fact, a new approach that gives the elderly or their family members the power to hire, train, supervise, and fire workers assigned to them for home and community-based services may provide better quality of life care for the elderly (Tilly & Weiner, 2001).

THE RIGHTS OF OLDER PERSONS

Over the past 60 years, many documents, including the 1948 Universal Declaration of Human Rights, have addressed the rights of all persons. But it was not until the Declaration on Social Progress and Development in 1969 that the human rights of the elderly were specifically mentioned in an international rights document (Office of the United Nations High Commissioner for Human Rights, n.d.). The United Nations adopted the first International Plan of Action on Ageing in 1987 and the General Assembly of the United Nations adopted the Principles for Older Persons in 1991. The four main themes of the latter were independence, participation, care, and self-fulfillment and dignity. In 1995, the Committee on Economic, Social, and Cultural Rights adopted General Comment No. 6 on the economic, social, and cultural rights of older persons. The United Nations declared 1999 to be the International Year of Older Persons and developed a conceptual framework based on four priority areas, including (1) the situation of older persons; (2) individual lifelong development; (3) the relationship between generations; and (4) the interrelationship of populations, aging, and development. In 2002, the Madrid Plan of Action seriously addressed the situation of older persons and the Commission for Social Development was given the charge to implement the plan (International Association of Gerontology, 2005).

Believing that these precedents were not enough to give older persons their rights or to recognize their contribution to society, the International Association of Gerontology and other nongovernmental organizations (NGO) called on the Commission on Human Rights to adopt a Declaration on the Rights of Older Persons. In their appeal to the commission, they called for a declaration recognizing that older persons have rights, including intergenerational rights, and that elders need protection but also make an important contribution to social peace and cohesion. They further urged that a Declaration on the Rights of Older Persons be based on the situation of older persons; individual lifelong development; the relationship between generations; and the interrelationship of population, aging, and development (International Association of Gerontology, 2005).

ADVOCATING FOR THE ELDERLY

The International Plan of Action on Ageing is the first international advocacy instrument on aging. It influences the development and implementation of policies and programs affecting the elderly. It was endorsed by the U.N. General Assembly in 1982, having been adopted earlier the same year at the World Assembly on Ageing at Vienna, Austria. It is often referred to as the "Vienna Plan" or the "International Plan." It aims to "strengthen the capacities of governments and civil society to deal effectively with the aging of populations and to address the developmental potential and dependency needs of older persons. It promotes regional and global cooperation. The plan also seeks to ensure that people everywhere will age with security and dignity, and continue to participate in their societies as citizens with full rights" (United Nations, n.d.). The top priorities include:

- Involving older persons in the development process
- Advancing health and well-being into old age
- Ensuring supportive environments that enable older persons to have choices

Core themes of the plan include:

- Recognition of the needs of older women;
- The desire of older people to stay active and engaged; and
- The need to create intergenerational solidarity.

These themes demonstrate how the global community shares a common vision of a better future for older persons (United Nations, n.d.). It includes 62 recommendations for action addressing research, data collection and analysis, training, and education as well as the following:

- Health and nutrition
- Protection of elderly consumers
- Housing and the environment
- Family
- Social welfare
- Income security and employment
- Education

The plan is part of an international framework of standards and strategies developed by the global community in the past few decades (International Federation on Ageing, n.d.). The United Nations Principles for Older Persons encourage governments to incorporate the following principles into their national programs:

Independence
- Older persons should have access to adequate food, water, shelter, clothing, and health care through the provision of income, family and community support, and self-help.
- Older persons should have the opportunity to work or to have access to other income-generating opportunities.
- Older persons should be able to participate in determining when and at what pace withdrawal from the labor force takes place.
- Older persons should have access to appropriate educational and training programs.
- Older persons should be able to live in environments that are safe and adaptable to personal preferences and changing capacities.
- Older persons should be able to reside at home for as long as possible.
- Older persons should remain integrated in society, participate actively in the formulation and implementation of policies that directly affect their well-being, and share their knowledge and skills with younger generations.

- Older persons should be able to seek and develop opportunities for service to the community and to serve as volunteers in positions appropriate to their interests and capabilities.
- Older persons should be able to form movements or associations of older persons.

Care

- Older persons should benefit from family and community care and protection in accordance with each society's system of cultural values.
- Older persons should have access to health care to help them to maintain or regain the optimum level of physical, mental, and emotional well-being and to prevent or delay the onset of illness.
- Older persons should have access to social and legal services to enhance their autonomy, protection, and care.
- Older persons should be able to utilize appropriate levels of institutional care providing protection, rehabilitation, and social and mental stimulation in a humane and secure environment.
- Older persons should be able to enjoy human rights and fundamental freedoms when residing in any shelter, care, or treatment facility, including full respect for their dignity, beliefs, needs, and privacy, and for the right to make decisions about their care and the quality of their lives.

Self-Fulfillment

- Older persons should be able to pursue opportunities for the full development of their potential.
- Older persons should have access to the educational, cultural, spiritual, and recreational resources of society.

Dignity

- Older persons should be able to live in dignity and security and be free from exploitation and physical or mental abuse.
- Older persons should be treated fairly regardless of age, gender, racial, or ethnic background, disability, or other status, and be valued independently of their economic contribution.

NEW TRENDS AND CHALLENGES IN GERONTOLOGICAL PRACTICE

INCREASED INTERDISCIPLINARY COLLABORATION

Aging is a development issue. By 2050, the number of persons aged 60 and over is projected to increase from 600 million to almost 2 billion. If countries are to meet the challenges and opportunities that will accompany the demographic transition and the epidemiological revolution that is taking place worldwide, they must start now to build the infrastructure that will enable them to deliver a sufficient supply of appropriate health care, housing, income support, transportation, and other elements necessary for quality of life for their older populations. This will require researchers, educators, practitioners, planners, and administrators to collaborate effectively based on emerging knowledge and best practices. They will need to look beyond their traditional disciplines and strategies to develop and implement an infrastructure that will positively support the burgeoning elderly population.

DEVELOPMENT OF CULTURALLY RELEVANT PRACTICE

The form of gerontological practice that develops in any society is shaped by the prevailing social, economic, and cultural forces. But most cultures around the world are responding to the challenges of rapidly changing social and economic forces in their countries. Extreme cultural fluctuations, such as intercultural migration, interethnic marriages, reduced family size, and individual mobility are impacting gerontological practice. Practitioners, researchers, and educators must develop methods that build on and reinforce those cultural values that promote the well-being of the elderly from all cultural and ethnic groups. Working out an understanding of human beings and personal development that incorporates cultural conception and beliefs is critical to effective practice with the elderly, particularly in a global context. Making gerontological services more accessible by working with informal care-giving resources can enhance culturally relevant and appropriate practice.

PROMOTION OF HEALTHY AND ACTIVE AGING

Recent research clearly indicates that individuals do have some control over the aging process. Healthy and active lifestyles throughout the lifespan do contribute positively to the aging process. And, it appears that it is never too late to introduce a healthy and active lifestyle with positive benefits. As a result, the field of gerontology is beginning to try to change the concept of old age from a period of loss to a time of enjoyment, from a time of disease and incapacity to days of benefiting from a healthy and active lifestyle. It is expected that in this century of aging, there will be a greater emphasis on promoting the aging population to be healthy and active, despite limitations. We can expect to see more programs develop that provide education and opportunities for living and aging well.

CHALLENGES FOR THE FUTURE

Persons are living longer and healthier lives. Older people increasingly want to remain economically active and make a contribution to society. Societies need to recognize the strengths of older persons and empower them (Sowers & Rowe, 2006). Human rights, sustainable human development, poverty eradication, and improved health care programs must be developed, designed, and monitored at all levels, with older people playing an active role (Obaid, 2002). A number of significant challenges require the introduction of policies and programs that respond to older peoples' needs. These challenges include:

- Promoting lifelong education and training, and healthy and active aging
- Recognizing and supporting the care-giving services provided by older persons, especially women, to grandchildren orphaned by the effects of HIV/AIDS

- Eliminating violence and other crimes against older persons who are caught in conflict and other complex humanitarian situations
- Supporting gender-sensitive research on population aging
- Strengthening social protection schemes for older persons, particularly the long-term care of the frail and poor (Obaid & Malloch-Brown, 2002)

This book's combined expertise is timely. Each chapter provides the latest research findings to address a myriad of challenges facing older persons in this new century. Such information is critical as the world experiences the dramatic increase in numbers of people living to an advanced old age.

RESOURCES: INTERNATIONAL ORGANIZATIONS ON AGING

ALZHEIMER'S DISEASE INTERNATIONAL

Alzheimer's Disease International is the umbrella organization of Alzheimer associations around the world, which offer support and information to people with dementia and to their caregivers (for more information see http://www .alz.co.uk).

AMERICAN ASSOCIATION OF RETIRED PERSONS

Founded in 1958, the American Association of Retired Persons (AARP) provides global resources for information and advocacy on major issues affecting aging populations. Through its Office of International Affairs, AARP works with numerous governmental and nongovernmental organizations, promotes communication and the exchange of ideas, and establishes and communicates best practices in aging concerns worldwide. The AARP has consultative status as a nongovernmental organization at the U.N. Economic and Social Council. With this status, AARP is able to submit statements and make recommendations to ensure that the interests of people over 50 are addressed in major international initiatives and documents. The AARP's International Visitor Program provides informational briefings and reports to government officials, business leaders, NGO representatives, and researchers who visit AARP from around the world to learn more about policies, programs, and activities. In the United States and abroad, AARP seeks to lead positive social change and enhance the quality of life for people over 50. They seek to promote the concerns of the elderly through social policy, communications, advocacy, community service, and group buying arrangements. The AARP is dedicated to bettering the situation for aging people so they can live longer, healthier, more financially secure, and more productive lives (for more information see http://www.aarp.org).

INTERNATIONAL FEDERATION ON AGEING

The International Federation on Ageing (IFA) informs, educates, and promotes policies, programs, and practices to improve the quality of life of older persons around the world. Their mission includes:

- Building, facilitating, and strengthening bridges between governments, service providers, practitioners, and individuals concerned with improving the quality of life of older people around the world
- Strengthening nongovernment organizations across the regions of the world through linking together for a common purpose

The IFA focuses on three key areas:

1. *Policy:* working with and disseminating information from governments across the world committed to developing policies for an aging society and today's older people
2. *Practice:* sharing best practice from organizations committed to providing quality programs and services for older people
3. *Impact:* working with older people to understand the impact that policies, programs, and practices has on the lives of older people

The IFA also advocates for member organizations and older people globally within the United Nations, WHO, U. N. Educational Scientific and Cultural Organization (UNESCO), the U. N. Economic and Social Commission for Asia and the Pacific (UNESCAP), and the Council of Europe, though consultative status.

The IFA maintains a knowledge bank on aging issues and best practices to influence, advocate, and promote change that affects the lives of older people (for more information see http://www.ifa-fiv.org).

HELPAGE INTERNATIONAL

HelpAge International is a global network of members and partner organizations working in over 80 countries on practical and policy issues. Its mission is to improve the lives of disadvantaged older people (for more information see http://www.helpage.org).

INTERNATIONAL ASSOCIATION OF GERONTOLOGY AND GERIATRICS

The mission of the International Association of Gerontology and Geriatrics (IAGG) is to promote the highest levels of achievement of gerontological research and training worldwide, and to interact with other international, intergovernmental, and nongovernmental organizations in the promotion of gerontological interests globally and on behalf of its member associations. The IAGG aims to promote the highest quality of life and well being of all people as they experience aging at individual and societal levels. (For more information see http://www.iagg.com.)

REFERENCES

Barusch, A. S. (1995). Programming for family care of elderly dependents: Mandates, incentives and service rationing. *Social Work, 40*(3), 315–322.

Canadian Psychological Association. (n.d.). *Human development and ageing.* Retrieved July 17, 2006, from http://www.cpa.ca.

Choi, S. J. (2002). National policies on aging in Korea. In D. R. Phillips & A. Chan (Eds.), *Aging and long term care: National policies in the Asia-Pacific* (pp. 68–106). Singapore: Institute of Southeast Asian Studies.

Dunkle, R. E., & Norgard, T. (1995). Aging overview. In R. L. Edwards & J. G. Hopps (Eds.), *Encyclopedia of social work* (19th ed.). Washington, DC: NASW Press.

George, J. (1997). Global graying: What role for social work? In M. C. Hokenstad & J. Midgley (Eds.), *Issues in international social work: Global challenges for a new century.* Washington, DC: NASW Press.

Gibson, M. J. (2003, October). *Long-term care in developed nations: A brief overview* (Issue paper #2003-13, AARP Public Policy Institute). Washington, DC: American Association of Retired Persons.

Higgins, J. (1989). Defining community care: Realities and myths. *Social Policy and Administration, 23*(1), 3–16.

Howe, A., & Phillips, D. R. (2001). *National policies on aging: Why have them?* Paper presented at the World Congress of Gerontology, a meeting of the International Association of Gerontology, Vancouver, British Columbia, Canada.

International Federation on Ageing. (n.d.). *Part of a world wide revolution.* Retrieved July 30, 2006, from http://www.ifa-fiv.org.

MacKenzie, P. A., & Beck, I. (1991). Social work practice with dementia patients in adult day care. In M. Holosko & M. D. Feit (Eds.), *Social work practice with the elderly* (pp. 191–217). Toronto: Canadian Scholars Press.

Ngan, R. (2004). Long-term care for older people and the social welfare system in East Asia: Is the East Asian welfare model a myth? *Social Development Issues: Alternative Approaches to Global Human Needs, 25*(3), 74–86.

NGO Committee on Ageing. (2005). *Ageing and the righs of older persons: Statement for the Human Rights Commission.* Retrieved February 5, 2007, from http://ngo.fawco.org.

Obaid, T. A. (2002, April). *Statement at the Launch of HelpAge International's State of the World's Older People.* Madrid, Spain.

Obaid, T. A., & Malloch-Brown, M. (2002). *Joint statement to the Second World Assembly on Ageing.* April 8–12, 2002, Madrid, Spain.

Office of the United Nations High Commissioner for Human Rights. (n.d.). *Declaration on social progress and development, 1969.* Retrieved July 18, 2006, from http://www.ohchr.org.english/law/progress.htm.

Phillips, D. R. (1999). Aging in the Asia-Pacific region: The impact of the aging and development report. *Hong Kong Journal of Gerontology, 13*(2), 44–53.

Sowers, K. M., & Rowe, W. S. (2006). *Social work and social justice: From local to global perspectives.* Belmont, CA: Thomson Learning.

Teo, P. (1994). The national policy on elderly people in Singapore. *Ageing and Society, 14,* 405–427.

Tilly, J., & Weiner, J. M. (2001). *Consumer-directed home and community services: Policy issues.* Washington, DC: Urban Institute.

United Nations. (n.d.). *Ageing is society-wide.* Retrieved July 30, 2006, from http://www.un.org/esa/socdev/ageing.

World Bank. (n.d.). *Pensions: Overview.* Retrieved July 22, 2006, from http://web Worldbank.org.

World Health Organization. (n.d.). *Abuse of the elderly.* Retrieved July 13, 2004, from http://www.who.org.

World Health Organization. (1998). *Social determinants of health: The solid facts.* Geneva, Switzerland: Author.

World Health Organization. (1999). *World health day: Active ageing makes the difference.* Retrieved July 20, 2006, from http://www.who.int/docstore/world-health-day/en/pages1999.

World Health Organization Centre for Health Development. (n.d.). Retrieved July 14, 2004, from http://www.who.or.jp/ageing/researches/index.html.

Zimmerman, S., Sloane, P. D., & Eckert, J. K. (Eds.). (2001). *Assisted living: Needs, practices, and policies in residential care for the elderly.* London: Johns Hopkins University Press.

PART II

EVIDENCE-BASED THEORY

CHAPTER 2

Biological Aspects and Theories of Aging

LAURA J. PANKOW and JEFFREY M. SOLOTOROFF

THIS CHAPTER DESCRIBES the biology and biological theories of aging. Biology is the science that studies life. This is a complex process with many variables! In this chapter, we present evidence for the discoveries that have been made about the biology of aging. However, the biology of aging is in the early days of study. The assimilation of evolution, a basic tenet of biology, and gerontology has been a process fraught with problems, which led to missed opportunities for aging research, as described by Gavrilov and Gavrilova (2002). However, preconceived notions are being uprooted and the disciplines of gerontology and biology are embarking on a new appreciation of what each has to offer the other.

DEFINING AGING

Although the topic of aging has been the subject of fascination and research for hundreds of years, such a vast topic can be confusing in terms of accurate definition and description. Several authors (Arking, 1998; Spence, 1989; Wickens, 1998) have written of the challenges inherent in defining aging and the numerous attempts that have been made to do so. There are also several definitions that are central to the understanding of aging.

Aging is a popular, general term that describes advancing through the life cycle, beginning at birth and ending at death. Aging is commonly used by the general population to describe the process of getting older. As such, aging can include the developmental stages of preadulthood. Scientifically, however, aging is the process of gradual decline that occurs beginning in middle adulthood and continuing to death. As a result, many gerontologists prefer the more descriptive term *senescence.* Comfort (1979, p. 21) has defined senescence as

> a deteriorative process. What is being measured, when we measure it, is a decrease in viability and an increase in vulnerability. Senescence shows itself as an increased

probability of death with increasing chronological age: the study of senescence is the study of the group of processes, different in different organisms, which lead to this increase in vulnerability.

It is crucial to differentiate between chronological and biological age. *Chronological age* refers to a measurement, expressed in temporal terms such as months and years, of the time that has passed since the birth of the organism. Determination of accurate chronological age depends on accurate determination of the time of the individual's birth, usually recorded on a birth certificate. It can be difficult to ascertain correct chronological age if an individual's time of birth was not recorded. As there are countless instances of inaccurate or nonexistent birth records, it is often difficult to compile a complete record of the age of the human species. Determination of accurate chronological age in humans is therefore more difficult than for certain plants and animals that have markings or other signs of chronological age.

Biological age refers to an individual's position along the life span, according to the level of development or deterioration of his or her biological organs and systems. Because organisms develop and decline at different rates regardless of chronological measures, biological age can differ significantly from chronological age. Whereas increase in chronological age is inevitable and proceeds along a predictable scale, biological age can vary greatly among individuals of a species, depending on the rate of changes in each individual's development.

Longevity has been defined by Hayflick (1994, p. 15) as "the period of time that an animal can be expected to live, given the best of circumstances." Two longevity measurements are commonly used: mean longevity and maximum longevity. *Mean longevity* is the average number of years that members of a given species population live; it is also referred to as *life expectancy. Maximum longevity* is the age that the longest living member of the species population has reached at the time of death. The current estimate of the maximum human life expectation is 115 years. This has remained stable for thousands of years. What has changed is that due to medical advances, an increased number of humans reach maximum life expectation.

Death can be defined as the event that concludes the individual's life span. Death is frequently linked to age, although this is not always the case. For example, death can occur as the result of childhood illnesses or accidents that are unrelated to the aging process. Due to the availability of medical care and improved standard of living, however, death among the majority of the population will occur as the result of age-related diseases or events.

LIFE SPANS OF LIVING ORGANISMS

We have mentioned the challenges inherent in estimating human life expectancy, primarily due to problems with accurate record keeping. The task of estimating life spans for animals can be even more daunting, for several reasons. Accurate measurement of animal life span is dependent on human knowledge, which is often anecdotal and affected by limited ability to study a large enough sample of animals to make an accurate determination. In addition, many animals are killed for food, sport, or clothing, adding to the inaccurate measurement of life span. Additional difficulty is due to the challenges inherent in studying a given animal species sample of sufficient size to obtain reliable data. For this reason, some of the most reliable records about animal longevity are produced by zoos with a sample size capable of yielding such data.

Longevity data are readily available for domestic animals, but maximum life spans are also accessible for wild species. A sampling of animals and their life spans is shown in Table 2.1.

ANIMALS THAT DO NOT AGE

Examples of animals that do not age are lobsters, many but not all fish (i.e., flounder), amphibians (i.e., alligators), and reptiles (i.e., Galapagos tortoise; Comfort, 1979). These animals are more primitive species than humans, all other mammals, and birds, which do age. All animals that do not age have the common trait of a peak in physiological function after sexual maturity. However, as they continue to grow, physiological performance does not wane. There are lobsters measured at 44 pounds that are probably between 50 and 100 years old. These lobsters clasp their claws at the same rate as much smaller, "younger" lobsters (Hayflick, 1994, p. 22).

When nonaging animals are put in zoos or aquariums, their growth and physiological function continue in a manner similar to the same animals in the wild. Some animals that live in colonies, such as sea anemones and coral, were once thought to be immortal. However, it is now known that individual cells in these colonies die, but the colony does not die because new cells are consistently being formed (Jones, 1982).

Each year following sexual maturity, nonaging animals have the same chance of dying. The animal will grow each year after sexual maturation but will eventually die. It may seem odd that mammals, a highly evolved animal group, has a

Table 2.1
Animal Life Expectancies

Animal	Years
Chimpanzee	53
Gorilla	54
Domestic cat	28
Domestic dog	34
House mouse	3
Gray squirrel	24
Eagle owl	68
Golden eagle	46
Galapagos tortoise	>100
Bullfrog	16
Halibut	>60
Guppy	6

Adapted from *Ageing: The Biology of Senescence*, by A. Comfort, 1964, New York: Holt, Rinehart and Winston; and "Ageing" (pp. 43–103), by M. J. Lamb, in *The Genetics and Biology of Drosophila* (Vol. 2C), M. Ashburner and T. R. F. Wright (Eds.), 1978, London: Academic Press; and updated in 1997 by Steven N. Austad (personal communication to R. Arking).

more limited life expectancy than more primitive animal groups that do not age. It seems that mammals pay for their sophistication by having a life expectancy that is more limited than that of fish (Hayflick, 1994, p. 29).

ANIMALS THAT REGENERATE

Some animals are able to regenerate body parts. Regeneration, like lack of decline in physiological function, is limited to more primitive animals in the evolutionary timetable. When organs regenerate many times, some body parts are older than others, making it difficult to determine an individual animal's age. Examples include earthworms, starfish, and jellyfish (Brockes, Kumar, & Velosos, 2001), salamanders (Kato, Orii, Watanabe, & Agata, 2001), spiders and sponges (Uetz, McClintock, Miller, Smith, & Cook, 1996).

REPRODUCTION AND AGING IN ANIMALS

In some animals, aging happens quickly and immediately following an energy spurt associated with reproduction. After spawning, Atlantic and Pacific salmon develop a back hump, patches of fungus that penetrate the skin, and deterioration of virtually every body organ, leading to death. Spawning occurs in the river of the salmon's birth. Migration from the ocean to the river of origin occurs approximately 2 to 3 years after birth (Robertson & Wexler, 1962).

HOW PLANTS AGE

Plants and animals differ in how they age. Trees, for example, have developed the ability to amass and heap frames of dead cells. Retention of the dead cells of the tree's trunk and limbs serves the functional purpose of elevating the living cells to a height that affords the tree a competitive advantage for obtaining sunlight crucial to photosynthesis and continued life. In contrast, animals do not retain their dead cells, which are shed by the millions daily (Nooden & Leopold, 1988).

The chronological age of woody trees is determined by counting their growth rings. However, most of the cells in these rings are dead. The living cells of these trees are located in a band between the dead outer bark and the dead internal annual rings. From a biological age standpoint, it is the cell lineage that is very old in these trees, not the living cells in the trees. The number of cells in a tree is not a measure of its age (Nooden & Leopold, 1988).

In plants that can breed by cutting, age is very difficult to determine. Because it develops a new root system, the rerooted cutting can live longer than the plant from which it was cut. Plants that promulgate in this manner, cabernet sauvignon grapevines, for example, have proliferated through serial cuttings for more than a thousand years (Nooden & Leopold, 1988).

AGING OF PLANTS THAT PROLIFERATE VIA ROOTS AND SHOOTS

Other plants breed by sprouting new plants from roots that propagate underground. Aspen and elm trees as well as some types of prairie grass spread in this manner and can do so for centuries. Determining the biological age of these plants is difficult (Nooden & Leopold, 1988).

AGING IS NOT DISEASE

As the focus of this chapter is on biological theory, we do not cover the numerous and often complex biological changes that occur during the aging process; other texts contain this information (Arking, 1998; Hall, 1984; Morrison & Meier, 2003; Schneider & Rowe, 1995; Spence, 1989). There are general concepts useful for understanding the differences between aging as a "normal" process and the diseases that often accompany the aging process.

Aging is a process that occurs throughout the life cycle, not just in later adulthood. Although society tends to limit aging to a process occurring in the later years of life, in truth the aging process, the gradual wearing down of the body, begins in early adulthood. Hall (1984, p. 4) has outlined criteria for examining the process of aging: (a) Aging may be apparent throughout life but is more noticeable in the postreproductive period; (b) aging lowers the functional capacity of cells, organs, and entire organisms; (c) aging results in the degradation of structural elements within the body; (d) aging lowers the effectiveness of the response of the organism to internal and external factors; and (e) aging increases the likelihood of ultimate dysfunction: death.

Although older adults often experience several medical conditions, Hayflick (1994) draws an important distinction between "normal" aging and age-related diseases. Normal aging is simply the aging process. There is no "abnormal" aging; there are no defects related to aging in the way there are birth defects. It is important to note that both the aging process and age-related diseases produce impairments or limitations in an individual's optimal functioning. However, age-related changes are not diseases; they are changes that occur in the body, including a decrease in strength and muscle tone, short-term memory loss (not related to dementia), menopause, and declines in vision and hearing. These conditions occur as the result of numerous changes as we age, changes whose underlying process is not perceptible by the human eye. It is estimated that thousands of changes occur in organs and tissues, in their component cells and molecules, and in the cement that holds cells together. Individually, these changes are unnoticeable, but taken together, they manifest in the changes that are associated with aging.

The aging process does not necessarily lead to illness; however, it does make humans more vulnerable to diseases that a younger adult can defend against due to a stronger immune system. These diseases include cancer, cardiovascular disease, Alzheimer's disease, and strokes, conditions that, perhaps contrary to popular belief, are not part of older adulthood.

Just as aging is a process, dying is a process, one that leaves the individual vulnerable to various diseases that are predominant at the time of death and are listed as the cause of death on the person's death certificate. Although popular thinking views the diseases as the cause of a person's death, in reality the dying process—that is, the changes that leave the human vulnerable to such diseases—are the true cause of death.

Often, there is confusion about the exact cause of death. This is especially true when an autopsy is not performed, or in those patients who have multiple medical conditions at the time of death. Historically, physicians often attributed death to "natural causes," which was often used as a general term for those situations in which the physician could not identify the specific cause of death. There are also cases in which a physician who is not clear about the exact cause of death will take an educated guess, which is recorded on the death certificate but is not necessarily accurate. In addition, most medical research is directed toward the various diseases that are present at the time of death and not toward the vulnerability of the individual, which leads to the person acquiring the disease. Hayflick (1994, pp. 45–46) asserts that even if all diseases were curable, humans would die as a result of physiological losses, a normal part of later life.

There can be ambiguity in discussing age-related illnesses, in part because many of the changes related to aging also can produce disease. For example, menopause, which is a natural part of aging for women, can increase the risk of diseases such as osteoporosis and atherosclerosis. In men, enlargement of the prostate, again a normal part of aging, can result in cancer. Hayflick (1994) makes a further distinction between disease, which generally occurs at the molecular level, and aging, which occurs at the higher levels of cells, tissues, and organs. This is particularly significant because aging occurs in all members of society, making it a universal experience, as opposed to disease, which occurs only in certain individuals. A distinction can also be made between individual aging and population aging.

ACTUARIAL AGING

Research about age-related issues is not limited to biologists or gerontologists. In particular, the insurance industry produces and utilizes research on life expectancy and survival rates for particular groups. This aspect of research is commonly known as *actuarial aging.* Hayflick (1994, p. 63) has defined actuarial aging as "the sum of the biological changes or functional losses that increase the likelihood of dying." It is important to note that actuarial aging provides valuable statistical and demographic data related to aging. However, it does not address underlying biological processes that produce aging-related physiological changes.

Actuarial research began in 1825 with the work of Benjamin Gompertz (1779–1865). A self-educated man, Gompertz developed a method utilizing calculus as a means of measuring life expectancy and presented it to the Royal Society of London for the Improvement of Natural Knowledge in 1820. In his 1825 publication, he demonstrated that rate of mortality increased geometrically throughout the life span. This has been plotted logarithmically, with a straight line (known as the Gompertz function) illustrating the rate of mortality. Through his efforts, Gompertz was the first person to demonstrate that probability of death increased exponentially in human adults. He was appointed actuary of the Alliance Assurance Company in 1824, and his findings greatly influenced the growth of the life insurance field. More than 150 years later, in a research article, Boxenbaum (1991) wrote of the Gompertz scale as an extraordinarily useful variable in the investigation, analysis, and evaluation of survival data generated in the fields of aging and toxicology.

Data gathered by actuaries increase understanding of aging's statistical, not biological, aspects. Gompertz (1825) found that, beginning at age 30, rate of mortality doubles every 8 years. Thus, a human at 50 is twice as likely to die as one at 42. Gompertz's formula is:

$$qx = (q_0)\,(e_x)$$

where q_0 = Further expectation of life at time of birth, or the y intercept
$\quad qx$ = Further expectation of life at the beginning of age interval x
$\quad\ x$ = The slope constant

Wickens (1998, pp. 7–8) described limits to Gompertz's scale; for example, it does not seem to apply to individuals younger than 30 or over 90. In fact, data show that rates of death tend to *decrease* after 90; it is speculated that this is because those humans who survive past 90 are particularly hardy and are able to survive at a greater rate than those who succumbed to death at an earlier age. Wickens also writes of attempts to apply the Gompertz scale to the life spans of nonhuman animals. Many of them did not fit the Gompertz pattern, in part due to the potential environmental hazards resulting in significant accidental death rates. He does, however, discuss an 1867 attempt by W. H. Makeham of the British Museum to apply the Gompertz scale to the animal kingdom while accounting for accidental death. This produced a pattern more fitting with Gompertz's scale for humans. However, the adaptability of the Gompertz scale for nonhuman animals remains unclear.

Pearl and Pearl (1934) introduced the Total Immediate Ancestral Longevity index to determine survival rates of individuals. They established the likelihood of achieving longevity if an individual had long-lived ancestors. Their writing, along with Gompertz's work, has stimulated research by life insurance companies.

Life Tables and Survival Curves

Life insurance companies that make use of actuarial measurements rely on display models, including life tables and survival curves. Arking (1998, p. 28) has defined a life table as "a concise and standardized summary of the survival statistics in relation to age." A life table breaks the life span down into age intervals. For each age interval, additional data are provided; the most common data, described by Arking (p. 28), and shown in by Table 2.2, are the following:

x = The age interval, with the time units specified by the person constructing the table
$l(_x)$ = The number of organisms alive at the beginning of each interval
$d(_x)$ = The number of animals dying during each age interval
$q(_x)$ = The age-specific death rate, or the proportion of the animals alive at the beginning of the age interval that die during that interval
$L(_x)$ = The average number of animals alive during the age interval x
$T(_x)$ = The total number of organism age units to be lived by the total number of organisms alive at the beginning of the age interval
$e(_x)$ = The mean further expectation of life at the beginning of the age interval x

When data are plotted graphically, a survival curve is the result. Survival curves plot survival rates over a given longitudinal period.

Table 2.2
Life Table for the Total Population: United States, 2002

Age	Probability of Dying between Ages x to x + 1 $q_{(x)}$	Number Surviving to Age x $l_{(x)}$	Number Dying between Ages x to x + 1 $d_{(x)}$	Person-Years Lived between Ages x to x + 1 $L_{(x)}$	Total Number of Person-Years lived above Age x $T_{(x)}$	Expectation of Life at Age x $e_{(x)}$
0–1	0.006971	100,000	697	99,389	7,725,787	77.3
1–2	0.000472	99,303	47	99,279	7,626,399	76.8
2–3	0.000324	99,256	32	99,240	7,527,119	75.8
3–4	0.000239	99,224	24	99,212	7,427,879	74.9
4–5	0.000203	99,200	20	99,190	7,328,667	73.9
5–6	0.000176	99,180	17	99,171	7,229,477	72.9
6–7	0.000144	99,163	14	99,155	7,130,306	71.9
7–8	0.000142	99,148	14	99,141	7,031,151	70.9
8–9	0.000152	99,134	15	99,127	6,932,009	69.9
9–10	0.000145	99,119	14	99,112	6,832,883	68.9
10–11	0.000151	99,105	15	99,097	6,733,771	67.9
11–12	0.000153	99,090	15	99,082	6,634,674	67.0
12–13	0.000186	99,075	18	99,065	6,535,592	66.0
13–14	0.000225	99,056	22	99,045	6,436,526	65.0
14–15	0.000266	99,034	26	99,021	6,337,481	64.0
15–16	0.000346	99,008	34	98,990	6,238,460	63.0
16–17	0.000573	98,973	57	98,945	6,139,470	62.0
17–18	0.000680	98,917	67	98,883	6,040,525	61.1
18–19	0.000849	98,849	84	98,807	5,941,642	60.1
19–20	0.000942	98,765	93	98,719	5,842,835	59.2
20–21	0.000934	98,672	92	98,626	5,744,116	58.2
21–22	0.000985	98,580	97	98,532	5,645,490	57.3
22–23	0.000939	98,483	93	98,437	5,546,958	56.3
23–24	0.000949	98,391	93	98,344	5,448,521	55.4
24–25	0.000948	98,297	93	98,251	5,350,177	54.4
25–26	0.000930	98,204	91	98,158	5,251,927	53.5
26–27	0.000953	98,113	94	98,066	5,153,768	52.5
27–28	0.000913	98,019	90	97,974	5,055,703	51.6
28–29	0.000940	97,930	92	97,884	4,957,728	50.6
29–30	0.000994	97,838	97	97,789	4,859,845	49.7
30–31	0.001024	97,740	100	97,690	4,762,056	48.7
31–32	0.001063	97,640	104	97,588	4,664,365	47.8
32–33	0.001061	97,536	104	97,485	4,566,777	46.8
33–34	0.001185	97,433	115	97,375	4,469,293	45.9
34–35	0.001251	97,317	122	97,257	4,371,917	44.9
35–36	0.001369	97,196	133	97,129	4,274,661	44.0
36–37	0.001454	97,063	141	96,992	4,177,532	43.0
37–38	0.001568	96,922	152	96,846	4,080,540	42.1
38–39	0.001718	96,770	166	96,686	3,983,694	41.2
39–40	0.001913	96,603	185	96,511	3,887,008	40.2
40–41	0.002072	96,419	200	96,319	3,790,497	39.3
41–42	0.002236	96,219	215	96,111	3,694,178	38.4
42–43	0.002357	96,004	226	95,890	3,598,067	37.5
43–44	0.002634	95,777	252	95,651	3,502,177	36.6
44–45	0.002826	95,525	270	95,390	3,406,525	35.7
45–46	0.003061	95,255	292	95,109	3,311,135	34.8
46–47	0.003301	94,964	313	94,807	3,216,026	33.9
47–48	0.003509	94,650	332	94,484	3,121,219	33.0
48–49	0.003888	94,318	367	94,135	3,026,735	32.1
49–50	0.004134	93,951	388	93,757	2,932,600	31.2
50–51	0.004422	93,563	414	93,356	2,838,843	30.3
51–52	0.004822	93,149	449	92,925	2,745,487	29.5
52–53	0.005003	92,700	464	92,468	2,652,563	28.6
53–54	0.005549	92,236	512	91,980	2,560,094	27.8

Table 2.2 *Continued*

Age	Probability of Dying between Ages x to $x + 1$ $q_{(x)}$	Number Surviving to Age x $l_{(x)}$	Number Dying between Ages x to $x + 1$ $d_{(x)}$	Person-Years Lived between Ages x to $x + 1$ $L_{(x)}$	Total Number of Person-Years lived above Age x $T_{(x)}$	Expectation of Life at Age x $e_{(x)}$
54–55	0.005845	91,724	536	91,456	2,468,114	26.9
55–56	0.006719	91,188	613	90,882	2,376,658	26.1
56–57	0.006616	90,576	599	90,276	2,285,776	25.2
57–58	0.007621	89,976	686	89,634	2,195,500	24.4
58–59	0.008344	89,291	745	88,918	2,105,866	23.6
59–60	0.009429	88,546	835	88,128	2,016,948	22.8
60–61	0.009747	87,711	855	87,283	1,928,820	22.0
61–62	0.010877	86,856	945	86,384	1,841,536	21.2
62–63	0.011905	85,911	1,023	85,400	1,755,153	20.4
63–64	0.012956	84,888	1,100	84,338	1,669,753	19.7
64–65	0.014099	83,789	1,181	83,198	1,585,414	18.9
65–66	0.015308	82,607	1,265	81,975	1,502,217	18.2
66–67	0.016474	81,343	1,340	80,673	1,420,242	17.5
67–68	0.018214	80,003	1,457	79,274	1,339,569	16.7
68–69	0.019623	78,545	1,541	77,775	1,260,295	16.0
69–70	0.021672	77,004	1,669	76,170	1,182,520	15.4
70–71	0.023635	75,335	1,781	74,445	1,106,350	14.7
71–72	0.025641	73,555	1,886	72,612	1,031,905	14.0
72–73	0.027663	71,669	1,983	70,678	959,294	13.4
73–74	0.030539	69,686	2,128	68,622	888,616	12.8
74–75	0.033276	67,558	2,248	66,434	819,994	12.1
75–76	0.036582	65,310	2,389	64,115	753,560	11.5
76–77	0.039775	62,921	2,503	61,670	689,444	11.0
77–78	0.043338	60,418	2,618	59,109	627,775	10.4
78–79	0.047219	57,800	2,729	56,435	568,666	9.8
79–80	0.052518	55,071	2,892	53,624	512,230	9.3
80–81	0.057603	52,178	3,006	50,676	458,606	8.8
81–82	0.062260	49,173	3,061	47,642	407,930	8.3
82–83	0.071461	46,111	3,295	44,464	360,288	7.8
83–84	0.073437	42,816	3,144	41,244	315,825	7.4
84–85	0.084888	39,672	3,368	37,988	274,581	6.9
85–86	0.093123	36,304	3,381	34,614	236,593	6.5
86–87	0.101914	32,923	3,355	31,246	201,979	6.1
87–88	0.111270	29,568	3,290	27,923	170,733	5.8
88–89	0.121196	26,278	3,185	24,686	142,810	5.4
89–90	0.131694	23,093	3,041	21,573	118,125	5.1
90–91	0.142761	20,052	2,863	18,621	96,552	4.8
91–92	0.154390	17,189	2,654	15,862	77,931	4.5
92–93	0.166569	14,535	2,421	13,325	62,069	4.3
93–94	0.179282	12,114	2,172	11,028	48,744	4.0
94–95	0.192507	9,942	1,914	8,985	37,716	3.8
95–96	0.206215	8,028	1,656	7,201	28,730	3.6
96–97	0.220375	6,373	1,404	5,671	21,530	3.4
97–98	0.234947	4,968	1,167	4,385	15,859	3.2
98–99	0.249887	3,801	950	3,326	11,474	3.0
99–100	0.265146	2,851	756	2,473	8,148	2.9
100+	1.000000	2,095	2,095	5,675	5,675	2.7

Source: "United States Life Tables," by E. Arias, 2004, *National Vital Statistics Reports, 53*(6), retrieved February 23, 2006, from www.cdc.gov/nchs/data/nvsr53/nvrs53_06.html.

D. W. E. Smith (1993), comparing survival curves for Americans during the twentieth century, noted three significant developments: (1) the increase in mean life expectancy at birth; (2) changes in the shape of the survival curve to a more rectangular form, reflecting this increase in life expectancy; and (3) a particular increase in survival rates for older adults, beginning after the middle of the century.

ACCELERATED AGING IN HUMANS

Several medical disorders, all of them extremely rare, occur in humans and exhibit an acceleration of the aging process. These include progeria, Werner syndrome, Cockayne's syndrome, and Down syndrome.

Progeria has its onset in childhood. A patient with progeria displays the characteristics of biological aging early in life: slowed growth, disfigurement of facial features, development of heart disease and atherosclerosis, increased levels of blood pressure and cholesterol, thinning and wrinkling of skin, and hair loss. Mental capacity is normal. The progeria patient generally dies due to heart attack or stroke around the age of 12. The disease affects both sexes equally, with no predilection for particular races or nationalities. There is no proven cause of progeria. Although progeria mimics the aging process, it does not include all the signs of aging, and therefore there is no evidence that it is truly accelerated aging.

Werner syndrome has its onset in adolescence; incidence is about twice as high as progeria. Symptoms include cataracts, loss and whitening of hair, and a wasting away of the skin. It occurs due to a genetic anomaly and is recessively inherited from both parents. Cockayne's syndrome is often accompanied by changes in facial expression that mimic older adulthood.

Down syndrome is caused by a chromosomal abnormality. Symptoms of Down syndrome include physical characteristics such as muscle hypotonia, flat facial profile, hyperflexible joints, dysplastic ear, and an upward slant to the eyes (National Down Syndrome Society, www.ndss.org). Down syndrome is the most frequently identified cause of mental retardation and causes higher rates of death than in the general population. Yang, Rasmussen, and Friedman (2002) have reported that the median age of death for Down syndrome patients increased from 25 years in 1983 to 49 years in 1997. As a result, older individuals with Down syndrome, particularly those in their 40s, can develop dementia, a disease that affects the general population at a much higher age.

Hayflick (1994) has disputed the degree to which these conditions compare to aging. They do cause degenerative changes similar to those found in older adults; however, Hayflick has argued that progeria and similar conditions tend to *mimic* aging, rather than represent the full aging process.

LONGEVITY AND HEALTH

Longevity represents a chronological measurement of a person's length of life. Longevity is affected by advances in medical care and social conditions. The resulting decrease in incidence of causes of death has increased longevity. In addition, these advances can also affect the leading causes of death. For example, in 1900, the leading cause of death came from infectious diseases; with medical and social improvements, infectious diseases are no longer a major cause of death. Vascular disease, stroke, and cancer have taken their place (Hayflick, 1994).

A large body of research has focused on lifestyle adjustments involving biological interventions that could be used to delay death. This section addresses interventions related to exercise, diet, and temperature.

EXERCISE

Research has shown that exercise can improve quality of life (Gersten, 1991; Oberman, 1984). Exercise can be physically challenging as humans age, due to decreases in muscle strength, aerobic capacity, and motivation to exercise. Despite the proven benefits of exercise, people tend to exercise less as they get older (Belza et al., 2004).

Hayflick (1994) has argued that despite proven benefits to general health and well-being that exercise provides, there is no conclusive evidence that it directly prolongs life. It does not alter the normal process of aging, nor does it lengthen the life cycle. The benefits of exercise mainly stem from its ability to modify the disease process, particularly in the area of cardiovascular disease. There is evidence that exercise can reduce or postpone the occurrence of heart attack and other diseases, that it might affect cholesterol levels, and that it can produce a sense of well-being and decreased emotional stress. However, there is no definitive proof that it directly affects the aging process in humans or in laboratory animals. Even when there appears to be some correlation between exercise and longevity, it can be difficult to pinpoint exercise as the causative factor in longevity.

DIET

Studies of diet and its effect on longevity are based largely on research begun in 1934 by McCay, Maynard, Sperling, and Barnes (1939) at Cornell University. This research was based on the concept of "undernutrition without malnutrition," or "caloric restriction." Laboratory rats were fed a diet that restricted calories but otherwise provided normal amounts of nutrients. McCay found that this diet slowed the animals' development without affecting the attainment of developmental milestones, thereby lengthening the life span. Hayflick (1994) acknowledges McCay's success in proving that caloric intake affected longevity, however not in the way that McCay described.

Additional research on diet and aging was provided by the Baltimore Longitudinal Study of Aging (Shock et al., 1984). This study challenged many previously used actuarial tables regarding correlations between "ideal" height and weight and longevity, largely because these tables were based on a population of life insurance policy holders that did not fit the profile of the general population. Indeed, research from the 1980s showed that whereas being mildly to moderately overweight had been emphasized as a risk factor for early death, and that this pattern was true for both sexes, being slightly overweight in middle adulthood could actually increase longevity. This runs counter to the prevailing theory that extolled the benefits of caloric restriction. It is believed that the previously used tables were possibly based on society's ideal that emphasized slimness and therefore perceived risk or undesirability in overweight (Hayflick, 1994; Shock et al., 1984).

TEMPERATURE

Efforts to control aging through use of temperature are based on the concept that biological reactions occur at a reduced rate at colder temperatures. This grew out of the research of Loeb and Northrup (1917) and later Raymond Pearl (1928). Research in this area has shown that cold-blooded animals that are placed at temperatures several degrees lower than their natural habitat can experience rates of longevity that are double or triple their normal rate. It has also been proved that certain cold-blooded animals (e.g., certain reptile and frog species) can survive while in a frozen state. However, later research called into question the relationship between temperature and rate of living. In addition, efforts to control temperature to increase longevity would not apply to humans or other warm-blooded animals.

AGING AT THE CELLULAR LEVEL

Cell cultures were established in the late 1800s and transformed biological research. The technique consisted of placing a cell released from a fragment of living animal tissue with supplemental nutrient solution into laboratory glass and keeping it at the animal's body temperature in an incubator. The cell grew and divided, increasing the number of cells.

In the early 1900s, Alexis Carrel of the Rockefeller Institute placed a bit of chick heart tissue in a culture. The tissue fragment was fixed to the culture materials with a blood clot consisting of a drop of chick blood plasma (blood excluding red and white blood cells) on top of the tissue sample and a drop of chick embryonic fluid extract. The embryo extract and plasma contained nutrition necessary for growth of cells in the tissue scrap. When the culture was placed in an incubator at normal chick body temperature, the cells increased in number in approximately 1 week. Once the cells had grown to the edge of the clot, they ceased dividing; the cell mass was then divided and each portion moved to a new culture tube with a new affixing clot to start the process anew. Carrel and his colleagues claimed to have maintained continual growth of cells from the original heart tissue sample for 34 years (Carrel & Ebeling, 1921).

Carrel died in 1944, and his colleague Albert Ebeling performed the majority of the cell movements from one culture plate to another. Ebeling discarded the cells in 1946. Due to the huge number of cultures resulting if a sample of tissue doubled in size in a week, was halved, and placed in another culture plate for 34 years, only a few cultures were kept from each cell transfer.

Carrel's experiment showed that animal cells could be grown indefinitely in cultures outside of the animal (in vitro), which meant that normal animal cells did not age. They were immortal! If these cells did not age outside of the body, the cause of aging had to be the material that connected cells in the body or a chemical external to the cell in the body—hormones, for example.

In the 1940s and 1950s, a few cultures of tissue fragments from rodents and humans were grown and appeared to demonstrate this same immortality in culture. The first immortal human cell culture was developed from cancerous cervical cells of a female patient at Johns Hopkins University. They were termed HeLa cells in honor of the woman from whom they were obtained, Henrietta Lacke (Gey, Coffman, & Kubicek, 1952). To preserve her anonymity, the name Helen Lane was used in the publication.

Carrel's experiment and these follow-up studies dominated cell culture science through the 1940s and 1950s. However, the claim of immortality of cultured cells soon died as the result of a discovery made at Wistar Institute in Philadelphia by Leonard Hayflick and Paul Moorhead (1961). In the 1950s these scientists were working to identify potential cancer viruses in cell samples from legally aborted Swedish human embryos. They received cells cultured without the use of blood clots. Techniques had modernized since Carrel's time, and trypsin, a pancreatic digestive enzyme, was used to release cells individually. The cells were then suspended in a growth medium that contained many substances necessary for cell growth. Because not all nutrients for different species' cells are known, some type of blood is required in the medium. Human cells have a preference for culture media with beef blood.

After the cells were placed in the culture vessel, a tube containing the culture medium and blood, they were incubated at human body temperature. The individual cells attached to the floor of the tube, so no blood clot was required. The cells divided; when they covered the tube's floor, they stopped dividing. The limiting factor was that cells stop dividing when they come into contact with neighboring cells. If additional cells are needed, the cells can be divided and placed in another culture medium tube in a process called *subculturing* (Hayflick, 1994).

The cells stuck on the floor of the culture tube were moved to the trypsin to separate them. The culture medium was discarded, and the cells were moved from the trypsin, in equal portions, into two new culture medium tubes. The process was repeated every 2 or 3 weeks until a sufficient number of research cells were obtained. Moorhead and Hsu (1956), experts in human chromosomes, ran a test to determine that the cells obtained from Sweden and grown in the lab were not cancerous. Normal cells do not continue to grow if they are injected into appropriate laboratory animals; cancer cells will. When the Swedish cells grown in the laboratory were injected into laboratory animals, they did not grow. However, when cells from the "immortal" cultures of the human cells from Johns Hopkins were injected, they formed tumors in the laboratory animals! The cells from Sweden were limited in the ability to divide in a culture medium. They were mortal! As the work on the Swedish human cells continued, the scientists noticed that the longer the cell culture was retained, the more likely there would be cell death.

Curious about these findings, the scientists cultured "old" cultured human male cells and "young" cultured human female cells in the same culture dish because it was easy to distinguish the older and younger cells by looking for the presence or absence of a Y chromosome. They also had a dish with "old" and "young" cultured female cells. After 30 subcultivations, the mixed male and female dish had only female cells, and the culture of mixed "old" and "young" female cells was still thriving. The scientists reversed the experiment, using "old" human female cells mixed with "young" human male cells and a culture plate of mixed "old" and "young" human male cells. The results were that the younger male cells survived but the older female cells did not, eliminating the possibility of a difference in mortality between male and female cells.

When the scientists raised this issue with senior colleagues, they were accused of "mishandling" the cells, causing cell death. These colleagues were challenged by Hayflick and Moorhead to perform their own cultures of the "older" and "younger" cells from Hayflick and Moorhead's subcultures. Several senior scientists took the challenge and had the same results of cell death approximately 4 months later. Hayflick and Moorhead submitted a paper reporting their findings. After being rejected by the *Journal of Experimental Medicine* with the criticism that their assertions were "rash," the scientists submitted the paper to *Experimental Cell Research*, where it was published. The paper is a classic (Hayflick & Moorhead, 1961).

There is an obvious disparity between the results of Hayflick and Moorhead's cell cultures and those of Carrel. Several discoveries since Carrel's experiment have shed light on this disparity. First, in 1960s cancer research, it was determined that normal cells could be turned into abnormal cells through radiation exposure or contact with cancer-causing chemicals or cancer-causing viruses. However, it is unlikely that such causative agents could have affected Carrel's cultures. It is also implausible that the cells in Carrel's culture became immortal spontaneously. Hundreds of scientists have tried to replicate Carrel's immortal cell culture since it was extinguished in 1946. The scientific community has come to the conclusion that Carrel's immortal cell culture was the result of an error. The extract from the chick embryo that Carrel used to attach the heart tissue to the floor of the culture vessel appears to be the cause.

The chick embryo extract was centrifuged to move whole and broken cells to the bottom of the centrifuge tube. The upper portion of the tube should then contain only cell free fluid. However, in Carrel's experiment, centrifuges were ineffective in total cell removal, yielding broken and whole cells in virtually every drop of extract used to feed the cultures and in the clots used to affix tissue fragments to new cultures. Thus, new chick cells were introduced into the culture every time feeding or cell transfer to a new culture occurred. One of Carrel's technicians later confirmed that this was the case (Hayflick, 1994). Carrel is dead, so there will always be debate concerning fraudulent publications emerging from Carrel's lab.

Because human cells live about 8 months before reaching 50 doubling divisions (Hayflick's limit) and dying, a way to freeze them was developed to avoid the monotonous task of starting new strains every 8 months. Cells are kept alive by placing them in a glass container stored in liquid nitrogen. A chemical is added to keep ice from forming on the cells by slow freezing them. Cell thawing must be rapid.

Once it was discovered that a single human cell strain could be kept alive for a considerable period of time by freezing, a question arose: If human cells were frozen at different stages of development, what number of doubling stages would a cell go through after thawing? The answer was that the cells have a "memory" of where they were in the doubling process and move on from the point at which they were frozen.

As human cells have their last few division stages, changes including but not limited to enzyme activity, synthesis of carbohydrates, fats, and protein, cell size, and DNA occur. Cells extracted from species with greater longevity undergo more doubling stages than those extracted from animals with shorter longevity. As previously noted, human cells divide 50 times; cells of the Galapagos tortoise, with a maximum longevity of 175 years, divide 110 times (Goldstein, 1974). In humans with progeria (aging at an abnormally young age), far fewer cell divisions occur (Salk, Au, Hoehn, & Martin, 1981).

When Hayflick and Moorhead conducted their studies, 2% oxygen (O_2) was the standard concentration for cell cultures. When the O_2 culture content is increased to 3%, closer to conditions in the human body, the cell division number of cultured human fibroblast cells increases by 20 divisions (Chen, Tsai, & Wu, 1995). Fibroblasts are the most frequently dividing cells in vitro and are the cement holding tissue together, providing arrangement and organization. In contrast, muscle and nerve cells never divide. Aging of both fibroblasts and muscle and nerve cells is dependent largely on genetic programming (Hayflick, 1994).

Disparately, when O_2 content of a culture is increased above 20%, other types of human cells undergo fewer divisions and growth arrest is hastened (Alaluf, Muir-Howie, Hu, Evans, & Green, 2000). In contrast, this effect does not occur in human tumor cells (Saito, Hammond, & Moses, 1995). O_2 concentration >50% kills normal human cells (Horikoshi, Balin, & Carter, 1991). Other sources of damage due to oxidation injury are ethyl alcohol and radiation. These oxidative stressors can affect cell function based on a single contact or repeated short contacts with stressors.

Another factor is that different species vary in optimum culture conditions. Mouse fibroblast cells are affected by partial pressure of O_2 and increased O_2 thwarts division of mouse cells in culture (in vitro; Parrinello et al., 2003). The results of these studies may be reflecting differences in O_2 sensitivity within a species rather than demonstrating optimum O_2 in different species for cell division (Toussaint et al., 2002). Because there is a positive correlation between animal size and longevity, it may be that cells taken from long-lived animals tolerate more cell divisions than those of smaller, shorter-lived animals due to their larger size, not their long life span.

The link between aging and cell division stopping is obscure. In centenarian cell donors, studies showed that there was no difference in the number of cell divisions remaining when compared to donors of younger ages (Cristofalo, Allen, Pignolo, Martin, & Beck, 1998; Tesco et al., 1998). These differences between human cells in culture and those in the human body (in vivo) raise questions about differences in the way genes are expressed in vivo compared to in vitro (Takeda, Gosiewska, & Peterkofsky, 1992).

The ends of the chromosomes consist of hundreds of repeating subunits in an area called the telomere. With each cell division the telomere loses some of these repeating subunits. The reduction in the length of the telomere may serve as a clock for the cell. Immortal cells have found a way to prevent their telomeres from shortening (Wibe & Oftebro, 1974).

When tissue is placed in cultures, the cells grow out from the tissue scrap. The older the scrap donor, the longer the time needed for cell growth to begin. This phenomenon is termed the *latent period,* and it occurs in all species. The latent period is due to fewer cells in the dividing process, not because time for division is longer (Karatza & Shall, 1984; Ponten, Stein, & Shall, 1983). However, the latent period effect has been questioned since Cristofalo et al. (1998).

As human cells age, they undergo a string of characteristic changes termed *biomarkers* that define the aging process (Campisi, 1999). These biomarkers include the following:

- Cell division ceases (Cristofalo & Sharf, 1973; J. R. Smith & Whitney, 1980).
- Diversity in cell size and shape (morphology) increases as the number of old cells increases in a cell population (Bayreuther et al., 1988).

- ß-galactosidase (an enzyme, a substance increasing the rate of a chemical re-action), normally active in an acidic environment of pH 4 in a younger human cell, is active at pH 6, a more basic environment in older human cells (Dmiri et al., 1995). A hypothesis is that increased presence of ß-galactosidase in aging cells may contribute to increased digestion of the cells' organelles (autophagy; Gerland et al., 2003).
- Normal human cells, with the exceptions of eggs and sperm, contain two copies of each chromosome. Errors in the DNA of the cell's mitochondria, the cell's energy organelle, also occur as human cells age, but at low levels (Tanhauser & Laipis, 1995).
- Old human cells have decreased capacity to express heat shock proteins in cultures (Blake, Udelsman, Feulner, Norton, & Holbrook, 1991) and in the body (Bonelli et al., 1999).
- The level of gene expression changes as human cells age in the body (Cristofalo, Volker, Francis, & Tresini, 1998).
- Telomeres, areas where DNA does not code for proteins at the tips of chromosomes, shorten as cultured human cells age (Harley, Futcher, & Grieder, 1990), and it is postulated that the same process occurs in the body in aging human cells (Allsopp et al., 1992).

Old cells and their associated biomarkers are found in vivo and are most commonly found in human tissue that is prone to stress. When fibroblasts are cultured from the lower legs of patients with venous reflux, which occurs prior to venous ulcers, the culture grows cells that have the characteristics of old (senescent) cells (Mendez et al., 1998). Senescent cells have also been found in fibroblasts from areas of atherosclerosis (Minamino et al., 2002) and benign prostatic hyperplasia (noncancerous prostate enlargement; Castro, Giri, Lamb, & Ittmann, 2003). Conversely, it has also been postulated that cells that stop dividing as a result of aging actually stop dividing due to a buildup of error-producing gene expression that changes the O_2 concentration in surrounding cell division (Ly, Lockhart, Lerner, & Schultz, 2000).

A positive correlation between stress resistance and longevity also appears to exist. Cells cultured from patients with progeria are less resistant to stress than cells of people who do not have progeria (Gebhardt et al., 1988). Human senescent fibroblasts are also less stress-resistant than fibroblasts from younger human beings (Yuan, Kanako, & Matsuo, 1996). Whether stress resistance is related to the rate of aging is unknown at this time. However, aging and resistance to stress appear to be negatively correlated.

In vivo, old human cells can be found without telomere shortening (Melk, 2003). It has been hypothesized that cell division cessation does not occur in the human body and that stress factors, outlined previously, are responsible for in vivo cell aging. The cells of even very old people continue to divide (Cristofalo, 2001; Tesco et al., 1998). The probability that cell division cessation occurs in vivo is improbable. With human fibroblasts dividing 50 times, 2^{50} are more than enough cells to last a human life span, as Hayflick espoused in 1994. Although it has been suggested that even a small number of cells not undergoing cell division could interfere with the function of human tissue (Shay & Wright, 2000), cell division cessation to any large extent in vivo would be mathematically impossible during any potential human lifetime.

There are some lines of cells that never reach senescence. These lines of cells are termed "immortal" and include embryonic stem cells and most cell lines that are derivatives of tumors. It has been hypothesized that the purpose of cellular aging is to be a mechanism to prevent cancer (Wynford-Thomas, 1999). Stem cells are nonspecialized cells that undergo long periods of cell division, which, under physiologic or experimental conditions, can be induced to take on a specialized cell function (Stem Cell Basics, 2006); they are found throughout the human body and the bodies of other animals. They contribute to the body's ability to maintain physiological stability (homeostasis) by replacing the differentiated cells of a given tissue that have died. This replacement function makes stem cells a topic of interest in the study of cellular aging. Human stem cells can emit telomerase, an enzyme that overcomes shortening of the telomere that occurs with aging (Sugihara et al., 1999). It is interesting that in the first 2 decades of life there is a correlation between mean telomeres and age in human muscle satellite cells, but not after age 20 (Decary et al., 1997). One hypothesis is that human body cells can divide only a limited number of times but are continually restocked by stem cells, which can actively and accurately divide and differentiate to replace them. However, several studies with mice have shown that stem cell senescence influences aging of the organism (de Haan & Van Zant, 1999; Snyder & Loring, 2005). Currently, this is pure speculation (citations on cellular senescence obtained from the website of Joao Pedro de Magalhaes, www.senescence.info/cells.html). The doctrine of the immortal germplasm states that germ cells are immortal and can divide eternally (Kirkwood, 1977; Weismann, 1889). A corollary of this doctrine is based on a correlation between stress resistance and cell repair mechanisms (Kirkwood, 1977). However, experimental evidence does not support this corollary in all animals. There is no difference in sensitivity to radiation between germ cells in male mice and bone marrow cells (van Loon et al., 1993). However, there is also increased DNA repair in male mouse germ cells compared to other body cells (Walter et al., 1994). In *Drosophila* (genus of the fruit fly), germ cells (soma) are more susceptible to mutations (errors in DNA replication) than other types of cells (Vogel & Ziljstra, 1987). At this point, germ cells having improved DNA repair and thus avoiding senescence is still disputable (Walter, Walter, & McCarrey, 2003).

BIOLOGICAL THEORIES OF AGING

Before embarking on a discussion of biological theories of aging, we want to express the impossibility of describing and discussing all of them in a book chapter; there are far too many. Instead, we explore an assortment to various degrees that represent the broad diversity of theories. We encourage further investigation of the vast diversity of biological theories of aging and their support and lack thereof by empirical research.

To dismiss weaker theories, Strehler (1986) proposed that an acceptable biological theory of aging include (a) biological causes of loss of physiological function; (b) an explanation of why these losses are gradual (progressive); (c) an explanation of why the losses cannot be corrected; and (d) an explanation of why the losses occur in all members of a species given the chance. These guidelines are valuable for they define biological aging very accurately. They also exclude other factors with biological aging is often confused, such as *disease*.

Recall the difference between normal aging and the diseases of "old age." Many diseases are progressive, inherent, and deleterious, but unlike age changes, none of them occurs in all species' members. The difference between longevity and aging must also be remembered: A species' longevity is generally held to be genetically determined; aging changes occurring from sexual maturity to death are credited to an array of factors outlined in the following theories.

There are two wide-ranging categories of biological aging theories: those having an a priori assumption of a preexisting master plan (theories based on purposeful events) and those based on random events. Before embarking on the discussion of these two categories of more modern theories of biological aging, we first discuss earlier theories of aging, their precursors.

BIOLOGICAL THEORIES OF AGING BASED ON PURPOSEFUL EVENTS

Vital Substance Theory   The history of thought on aging has informed biological theories by which gerontology operates. One of the early aging theories was *the vital substance theory*. The theory postulates that animals are born with a restricted amount of an undefined essential life substance. As the substance is consumed, lack of energy occurs. The person dies when the substance is totally gone. This substance was thought to be an array of *humors* controlling all of human biology. This theory continues to be prevalent.

Francis Bacon, barrister and Lord of the Seal of Elizabeth I, is the father of inductive reasoning. He challenged the vital substance theory in the sixteenth century, postulating that if repair processes (healing after skin is bruised or cut) that occurred in human beings and animals could be flawless, the life of humans and animals would be eternal (Ugalis, 1996).

A modern version of this theory contends that each animal has a limited number of heartbeats or breaths. Once these are used up, death ensues. The problem with this theory, regardless of which version, is its total lack of empirical support.

Genetic Mutation Theory   Mutations (changes in DNA) were discovered in the early 1900s, and genetics became the dominant focus in aging in the 1950s. Human embryonic deleterious mutations are thought to cause the high rate of spontaneous abortions (occurring a few weeks into pregnancy and unable to be discriminated from late menstruation). Mutation drives evolution and natural selection, prompting diversity and environmental adaptation. Mutation is therefore a strong candidate for being the major factor in longevity and aging.

Early evidence supporting the hypothesis of mutations as a cause of aging came from animal experiments showing that radiation, already known to cause mutations, concurrently hastened aging. However, it was subsequently observed that the changes occurring after radiation exposure only *appeared* to be related to aging, similar to progeria, considered by some aging experts to have selected characteristics of aging, but not being true aging. Further supportive evidence for the differentiation between true aging and changes due to radiation exposure was acquired with the demonstration that the amount of radiation needed to generate a lifetime's worth of mutations does not result in a shorter life span in rats (Sacher, 1982). In fact, George Sacher (1982) discovered that moderate doses of radiation increased rat life span. More evidence for nonsupport of the hypothesis that radiation causes aging was attained when Clark studied wasps, which uniquely occur in two normal forms, one with one set of chromosomes (haploid) and the other with two (diploid). Each form has the same life span (Clark & Kelly, 1950). Clark postulated that if both forms of wasp were exposed to the same dose of radiation, the form with only one set of chromosomes should have a shorter life span than the form with two. He reasoned that a spare set of genes should provide a superfluous set of genetic material to the animal. The experiment showed that wasps with two sets of chromosomes did have longer life spans than those with one (Clark, Gould, & Graham, 1971). Both forms of wasp not exposed to radiation had the same life span, leading Clark to conclude that background radiation exposure in daily life did not affect longevity.

Australian F. McFarlane Burnet (1974) proposed a curl on the mutation hypothesis: that precursor cells (basic primitive cells in many tissues) may be mutation's origin. He argued that precursor cells produce millions of self-duplicates as a tissue matures and could produce a lifetime of mutations. There is no experimental evidence to support this unique explanation of mutation as a cause of aging.

Reproductive Exhaustion Theory This theory postulates that animals and plants expend enormous energy during their reproductive years and then rapidly age and die when they are incapable of propagating. Fish such as the Pacific salmon and some perennial and annual plants do exhibit this pattern, as discussed earlier. However, this is not a universal pattern in aging. Humans, for example, can give birth many times, and women characteristically live for many years after menopause. Remember that Strehler (1986) said a credible aging theory must be universally applicable. Although this theory maintains its followers, there is a lack of empirical evidence to support it.

Aging by Design Theory The theory of aging by design assumes a master plan preceding life. The American anatomist Charles Sedgwick Minot (1907) is the Harvard scientist credited with expressing the tenets of this theory. He purported that aging is simply the last stage of biological development. He also contended that aging changes always result in senility, a claim now known to be false. The immense amount of dementia research conducted over the past 3 decades has demonstrated that the majority of humans are not destined to experience senility. Despite this, Minot's theory is fortified by the fact that body weight never increases in such great proportion as it does from conception to birth. Humans grow from one cell to billions of cells during this time period. In the early 20s human growth stops. Minot held that when the growth rate begins to decline at birth, aging starts.

Aging experts at odds with Minot take a less traditional view of the aging process. They say that aging commences when mortality has its weakest influence on the human population, the "actuarial prime of life" (Hayflick, 1994, p. 230). For humans this age is 7.

The promotion of programmed aging in this theory is appealing because it is well correlated with programmed cell death, an observable, experimentally proven fact with universal acceptance by biologists. Discrete fingers and toes develop in human embryos due to the programmed death of healthy cells between these digits at a specific time in development, enabling their formation. Scientists know that cell death is determined by genetics, but do not know that it accounts for aging.

The modern hypothesis using Minot's ideas is that DNA has the encoded plan for a human lifetime. It is enticingly simple because the individual's DNA, in accordance with current tenets, controls all complex body processes. A major problem with this hypothesis, though, is that it is in conflict with evolutionary theory. Historically, insufficient surviving older members of a species' population prevented evolution's "natural selection" of aging. Biological gerontologists ostracized the age by design theory in preference for overwhelming evidence for evolution. The Pacific salmon and some higher order animals may be part of a unique group of plants and animals programmed to die shortly after reproduction. Annual plants such as corn and wheat flower and produce seeds only when they approach death. Older seeds do not sprout as well as younger seeds. However, history has recorded several examples of seeds that have survived for numerous years in tombs, and some seeds that were placed underground in ancient times have germinated within the past century (Toole, 1986). Regardless of these examples, aging as a cause of death is questionable.

Neuroendocrine Theory   Neuroendocrine cells produce and store hormones, chemical messengers, in the ductless endocrine glands for release directly into the blood and other body fluids when needed (Campbell, 1996, pp. 913–914). These organs and their hormones regulate body functions, including metabolism and reproduction. Large amounts of hormones can accelerate some aging processes and retard others. Hormones have been used experimentally as rejuvenation agents since 1889 (Everitt & Meites, 1989).

Animals giving birth to litters show diminished litter size prior to total loss of propagation ability. Changes in reproductive ability are controlled by the neuroendocrine system augmented by biological clocks. These are persuasive reasons to examine the neuroendocrine system as a prospective aging cause. Studies have shown that the pituitary gland and ovaries, both endocrine glands, are not responsible for halting the estrogen cycle in older female rats. Estrogen cycle cessation is initiated in the brain's hypothalamus (Meites, 1991). Rapid acceleration of a hypothetical biological clock may explain why gray hair and diminished physiological ability occurred after severe head trauma in a few medical case reports.

The hormone dehydroepiandrosterone (DHEA), secreted by the adrenal gland, was studied for cause of aging. Very little was known about this hormone with the exception of its presence in high levels in younger humans and its presence at significantly decreased levels as humans age. In mice, DHEA decreased breast cancer, delayed immune system dysfunction, increased longevity, and gave a younger appearance. Mice treated with DHEA also ate less. It may be that increased longevity was due to the decreased eating, known to increase longevity.

There is no doubt that the neuroendocrine system performs many complex and necessary physiological functions for the human body. Few body parts act in seclusion. Disturbing nerve cell activities or hormone secretion can profoundly affect health and possibly aging. The register of aging processes associated with neural or hormonal factors is huge. Menopause, for example, is an age-related hormonally caused physiological change that affects the entire body. However, there is no direct evidence that the neuroendocrine system is the source of all aging changes. Although men have decreases in levels of some hormones as they age, they continue to have the capacity to actively reproduce while they are aging, whereas women do not.

A discussion of purposeful event biological theories of aging is incomplete without tackling the question "Do human beings lose nerve cells as they age?" (Hayflick, 1994, p. 233). The more sophisticated question is "Do humans lose cells as they age, not just nerve cells?" (p. 233). The brain decreases in weight in normal human aging, as is true of several other human organs. Brain weight decreases by 10%, the coiled appearance of the brain's surface narrows, and spaces between the convolutions widen. The decrease in size may be caused by loss of water or neurons or both. The significance of these changes is a point of considerable debate in the scientific community. The tenet is that central nervous system neurons cannot reproduce. However, experiments with songbirds (Alvarez-Buylla, Theelen, & Nottebohm, 1990; Barnea & Nottebohm, 1994) and other animals (Galea & McEwen, 1999; Kempermann, Kuhn, & Gage, 1998; Radmilovich, Fernandez, & Trujillo-Cenoz, 2003) show that they go through seasonal cycles of death and reproduction of brain neurons.

A 1980s proposal was that all aging is the result of brain changes. This postulation received considerable media attention but showed weak to no supportive evidence. The theory purported that the brain produced a "death hormone." The hormone, termed *decreasing oxygen consumption hormone,* was supposedly produced by the pituitary gland. Denckla (1975) offered some support for this hypothesis, but no other researchers have pursued this topic and Denckla no longer studies it.

The brain remains a serious contender for the organizer of aging. Experiments have shown that pituitary gland removal can rejuvenate animals fortunate enough to survive the surgery.

BIOLOGICAL THEORIES OF AGING BASED ON RANDOM EVENTS

Wear-and-Tear Theory   Wear-and-tear theory was introduced by August Weisman, a German biologist, in 1882. As its name implies, the theory postulates that daily living activities can negatively affect the body's biochemical processes. Because cells, tissues, and organs are not able to regenerate indefinitely, the repeated erosion of bodily components leads to breakdown and, ultimately, to death.

Arking (1998) has explained limitations of the wear-and-tear theory. While acknowledging that the theory can be applied to minor changes in the body, he identifies three reasons for the failure of the theory:

> First, animals raised in an environment that protects them from such minor insults and pathologies not only still age but also fail to show any improvement in their maximum life span. Second, many of the minor damages postulated by the wear and tear hypothesis are time dependent changes only, and while they can certainly increase the probability of death for any individual, they cannot logically serve as a causal mechanism of the aging process. A lost tooth does not initiate aging. Finally, and most important, the theory is outdated. Advances in our knowledge of cell and molecular biology have generated the need to explain cellular and organismic aging in more precise terms. (p. 378)

Rate-of-Living Theory   Rate-of-living theory was also developed in Germany, by physiologist Max Rubner (1908 referenced in Hall, 1984; Arking, 1998; Hayflick, 1994). Rubner compared metabolism rates for several animals (including humans) and found that, with the exception of humans, the animals studied expended between 30 and 55 million calories of energy over the course of a lifetime. Rubner postulated that an animal's life span was based on the rate at which it used this energy. The theory states that animals are born with limited biological capacity, which is used and exhausted at different rates. The rate of use determines the rate of aging; thus, in an organism that uses this capacity quickly, death will occur at an earlier stage than in an organism with a slower rate. As Hall (1984, p. 21) writes:

> Both man and mouse expend about 2.9 kJ/g of tissue throughout their lives, but the *rate* at which this is expended by the mouse is roughly 30 times greater than that for man. The mouse lives 2–3 years as opposed to the man 60–90.

Loeb and Northrop (1917) published research supporting Rubner's rate-of-living theory. Their work was largely based on their ability to expand the life of fruit flies by raising them in different temperatures. Being cold-blooded creatures, the fruit flies responded to the cold weather by slowing their rate of metabolism, and thus increasing their life span. Additional research, performed on other cold-blooded animals, indicated a similar result.

The theory was further advanced by Raymond Pearl at Johns Hopkins University. He coined the phrase "rate of living" in 1928. Pearl found that placing fruit flies in warmer temperatures served not only to accelerate their metabolism and decrease their life span, but also stimulated development; thus, general growth, development of eggs, and the aging process occurred more quickly, leading to a shorter life span. Pearl (1928, pp. 150–151) summarized his findings, and the theory, by stating, "The duration of life varies inversely as the rate of energy expenditure during its continuance. In short, the length of life depends inversely on the rate of living."

In the 1970s, Cutler (1976, 1978, 1979) performed several studies that established a relationship between maximum life-span potential (MLP) and specific metabolic rate (SMR) and combined these into a single product (MLP x SMR). This established maximum life-span potential calorie consumption (MCC), a new measure of life capacity, to Jerison's (1973) encephalization quotient (EQ), which is the degree of development over and above the amount required for normal bodily function. Maximum life-span potential is calculated from Sacher's (1959) formula, which established a close correlation between the combination of brain weight and body weight with life span:

$$MLP = 10.839 \times (\text{brain weight})^{0.636} \times (\text{body weight})^{-0.225}$$

Cutler calculated SMR from Brody's (1945) equation:

$$SMR = 442.74 \times (\text{body weight g})^{-0.266}$$

and calculated EQ from Jerison's (1973) equation:

$$EQ = 8.33 \times (\text{brain weight g}) \times (\text{body weight g})^{-0.666}$$

Through his research, Cutler (1979) demonstrated that values for both MLP and MCC increased for individual families of the animal kingdom during their evolutionary development.

Despite the success of these early studies in supporting rate-of-living theory, subsequent research has challenged its validity. John Maynard-Smith (1962) of University College in London published research that appeared to contradict Pearl's theory. In his research, Maynard-Smith raised fruit flies at a colder temperature and then moved them to a warmer temperature for the second half of their life; he subsequently raised fruit flies at a warmer temperature and then moved them to a colder one. He found that these flies had life spans that were similar to the ones that had spent their entire lives in the temperature that the study flies had lived in during the second half of their lives. Maynard-Smith accounted for this by downplaying the role of metabolism and focusing on what he termed *vitality:* the ability of the animal to cope with physiological stresses such as changes in temperature. Additional research by Walford, Harris, and Weindruch (1987), while reinforcing rate-of-living theory, also called into question the effect that controlling metabolism has on the life span. In addition, it is difficult to apply this theory to the study of humans and other warm-blooded animals. Hayflick (1994) has pointed out the limitations of rate-of-living theory: the fact that the biological capacity that the theory addresses is unknown, and there is little evidence—even anecdotal—that it exists.

Waste Production Accumulation Theory   According to this theory, aging occurs due to buildup of waste products, inert and reactive, not eliminated by the organism and thus accumulating in body cells and disrupting normal cell function, ultimately resulting in cell death. Spence (1989) terms this cellular garbage theory. The theory is based on anabolism, building simple substances into more complex compounds, and catabolism, breaking down complex molecules into simpler elements. These processes can produce waste that the organism must eradicate to ensure optimum function.

The theory is supported by the fact that waste accumulation does occur in the body. These wastes include free radicals, aldehydes, histones, and lipofuscin. Lipofuscin, also referred to as "age pigment," is a substance that accumulates in cells as animals, including humans, age. Lipofuscins are chemically inert and composed of inseparable, cross-linked molecules. However, there is no evidence that lipofuscin interferes with normal cell function.

Cross-Linking Theory   Cross-linking theory was developed by Bjorksten in 1942, with revisions made in 1974 and 1990. This theory purports that as the organism ages, certain proteins become increasingly cross-linked and may interfere with metabolic processes by blocking nutrient passage into cells. Bjorksten (1942, p. 868) wrote:

> The aging of living organisms I believe is due to the occasional formation by tanning [cross-linking], of bridges between protein molecules, which cannot be broken by the cell enzymes. Such irreparable tanning may be caused by tanning agents foreign to the organism, or formed by unusual biological side reactions, or it may be due to the formation of a tanning bridge in some particular position in the protein molecules. In either event, the result is that cumulative tanning of body proteins, which we know as old age.

Cross-linkages can affect the physical and chemical properties of the linked molecules, which decreases their ability to carry out their biological function. As cross-linkages can occur as the result of free radicals, this theory is closely tied to free-radical theory.

A common protein is collagen. Hayflick (1994, p. 243) has written that collagen is "the skeleton of soft tissues, and in bone it has been compared to the reinforcement bars in concrete," and has estimated that close to one-third of all protein in the human body is composed of collagen. Collagen protein consists of parallel molecules connected by cross-links.

As the organism ages, proteins like collagen are subject to increasing numbers of cross-links that impede normal passage of nutrients and wastes. This occurs primarily on an extracellular level, in contrast to waste-product theory, occurring mainly intracellularly. An example of cross-linking in collagen occurs in skin, characterized by decrease in pliability and increased wrinkling. Cross-linking can also appear in nucleic acids, which make up genes.

Free-Radical Theory   Free-radical theory was proposed by Denham Harman in 1956 and focuses on the chemical composition of the organism. The majority of chemical compounds are composed of electrons that are paired with each other; they are moderately reactive and require a reaction outside of themselves to produce a chemical reaction with other substances. A molecule containing a free radical, by contrast, becomes highly reactive in an attempt to pair off its free electron (Arking, 1998, p. 399). Spence (1989, p. 22) has defined a free radical as "cellular chemicals containing an unpaired electron [that] are formed as by-products of various normal cellular process involving interactions with oxygen." Although they have extremely short periods of existence—generally less than a second—they can still interact with cell membranes or chromosomes in a way that alters the functioning of the cell. Free-radical theory suggests that age-related changes occur as the result of accumulation of free radicals in cells until they exceed threshold concentrations. In addition, free radicals are self-propagating; thus, they can rapidly multiply in number and do increased damage to the cell. It is believed that the production of free radicals can be impeded by the ingestion of antioxidants, which would prevent oxidation from occurring.

A recent study (Ahluwalia et al., 2004) challenged free-radical theory, claiming that free radicals are not the cause of cellular damage, as originally thought. The researchers discovered that enzymes triggered by intracellular potassium, digest foreign substances, causing cellular damage.

Immune System Theory   Immune system theory, also referred to as autoimmune theory, postulates that, as the individual ages, the immune system becomes less functional, thereby leading to breakdown. To understand this theory, it is necessary to recall that the immune system becomes operative when an antigen—a foreign substance—enters the body. At that point, the immune system works to destroy the antigen and thus restore the body to optimal health. Immune system theory proposes that the immune system erroneously begins to attack healthy cells, thus leading to aging. There are two categories of immune system theory. The first states that new antigens appear later in life, possibly the result of mutations of altered proteins due to alterations to RNA or DNA. Because these altered proteins are not recognized by the body's immune system, the immune system interprets them as new antigens and attempts to rid the body of them. The second category states that, as changes occur in antibody molecules, autoimmune reactions will increase. The antibodies then stimulate the body's immune system.

Accumulation-of-Errors Theory   This theory is closely tied to protein synthesis, the process by which cell development occurs. This is particularly true with proteins that are produced by enzymes that facilitate cellular activity. If there exists an error in the structure of the enzyme, it could produce a protein that is unable to function normally; such cases could result in abnormal functioning of the cell.

Order-to-Disorder Theory   This theory has been studied primarily by physicists, particularly those involved in the branch of physics known as thermodynamics. The theory states that, during development, the body functions in an orderly way to guarantee arrival at sexual maturity. Once this has been accomplished, the body no longer is able to do the constant work necessary to maintain the orderliness, and disorder results. On a physical level, this results in deterioration of the body's component parts, leading to aging.

Evolutionary Theories of Aging   Gavrilov and Gavrilova (2002) at the University of Chicago have reported that evolutionary theories of aging provide a broader view of aging than current research strategies focused on the molecular level of aging. However, the authors also explain that evolutionary theories of aging have limitations because they apply only to organisms that reproduce. Also, rather than theories, they are a set of thoughts requiring amplification and corroboration.

Initially, biological evolution of aging was studied from only a theoretical standpoint (no hypothesis testing) by August Weismann (1882), Peter Medawar (1946), and George Williams (1957), among many others. An early criticism of evolutionary theories of aging was that they contained only theoretical conjecture with limited and indirect evidence to give evolutionary validation to Orgel's (1963) error catastrophe theory, hypothesizing that aging was the results of a failure in accuracy of protein synthesis in somatic cells. Orgel's theory ultimately failed, so even indirect evolutionary justification of a futile theory did not meet with a welcome scientific reception! There are three major evolutionary theories of aging: (1) theory of programmed death, (2) mutation accumulation theory, and (3) antagonistic pleiotropy theory.

THEORY OF PROGRAMMED DEATH   August Weismann (1834–1914), a German, was one of the first biologists to explain aging using evolution. He theorized a specific death mechanism designed through natural selection to eradicate the "old," providing space and resources for the young.

Weismann (1882) suggested that the mechanism by which death programming occurred was specific limits to the number of cell divisions. Hayflick's (1994) limit is specified in the classic publication proving Weismann's purely theoretical speculation. Gavrilov and Gavrilova (1991) contend that the work of H. Earle Swim at Case Western Reserve University is relatively unknown. Swim (1959), Swim and Parker (1957), and Haff and Swim (1956) published similar findings in rabbit, chick, and human cellular fibroblast division limits that Hayflick and Moorhead reported with human cells in 1961. Gavrilov and Gavrilova (1991) have argued that Hayflick's limit should be attributed to Weismann, Swim, and Hayflick for their historic discoveries made at various points in time. This topic has been the subject of heated debate between the authors and Hayflick (Gavrilov

& Gavrilova, 1994). However, Weismann's foreshadowing of the discovery of limits to cell divisions did nothing to support his theory of programmed death. When the cells stopped dividing, no programmed cell death occurred. In fact, the cessation of cell division actually seems to benefit organism survival as a means of cancer protection.

Gavrilov and Gavrilova (2002) report that Weismann's perspective on the evolution of aging itself evolved as he aged. In his own old age he considered old organisms "neutral," not "harmful" for the biological species. This significant change in his own theory went unnoticed by the majority of scientists. His revised theory never received the attention that his earlier theory did.

Experimental tests of the theory of programmed death were performed. Resulting evolutionary theories of aging were then tested on fruit flies (*Drosophila melanogaster*) in the laboratory (Luckinbill & Clare, 1985) and on guppy populations (*Poecilia reticulosa*) in nature (Reznick, Buckwalter, Groff, & Elder, 2001). Findings were that life spans evolve in subsequent generations of species in a theoretically predictable way as a function of specific conditions of nature. Offspring born later in life to mothers artificially selected for breeding predictably produced fruit flies with longer life spans in the laboratory. However, animals in the natural environment with a greater number of surrounding mortality sources had a shorter offspring life span. If death is programmed, the differences in life span between these two populations should not significantly vary, so Weismann's theory was not supported. This same experiment was repeated with chaffinches (Comfort, 1964; Paevsky, 1985), field voles (Fenyuk & Sheikina, 1940), and chimpanzees (Hill et al., 2001), with similar results. The same conclusion is reached in analysis of data regarding human life span when comparing developed and underdeveloped countries.

Another way to test the validity of the theory of programmed death is to study age as the independent variable that affects the dependent variable, death. If this theory is correct, age-dependence of death rate should demonstrate a dramatic change at some critical age in later life when this programmed death phenomenon is activated. A group of genetically identical animals in a species could be studied in the laboratory to determine if and where this dramatic change occurred. Hundreds of published life tables were analyzed for dramatic age-dependent death changes. However, all plots of death as a function of age were very smooth curves, with no dramatic changes. Finally, a programmed death would have no benefit to an individual's survival or the survival of his or her offspring via parental protection (Gavrilov & Gavrilova, 2002).

MUTATION ACCUMULATION THEORY OF AGING   Mutation accumulation theory, originally proposed by Peter Medawar (1952), sees aging as a side effect of natural selection. This theory considers aging a nonadaptive trait endorsed by natural selection because beyond a certain age, increased life span does not promote reproduction probability. Detrimental mutations that occur at a young age are selected against in a forceful way because they have a deleterious effect on reproduction. However, detrimental mutations occurring after the age of reproduction do not have this profound negative response from natural selection because they do not affect reproduction of individuals or their offspring.

In relation to humans, people with many detrimental mutations have less probability of reproducing the earlier in human development these mutations are expressed. An example is people with progeria, having a life span of about 14 years (Turker, 1996). These individuals are unlikely to pass their genes on to offspring due to their short life span. Progeria is the result of a new mutation in offspring, not a mutation passed on by the parents. People having mutations expressed later in life have already reproduced prior to the detrimental effect's expression. For example, genes for Alzheimer's disease are not removed from the human gene pool as promptly as are genes for progeria. These examples show that the mutation accumulation theory expects the frequency of genetic diseases to increase at older ages.

Mutation accumulation theory has produced several testable hypotheses. One is that dependence of offspring life span on parental life span is not linear, as is almost every other observable numeric trait in humans (e.g., height). The nonlinear relationship between offspring and parental life span is the result of the theory's prediction that detrimental mutations expressed later in life are not selected against as effectively and efficiently as detrimental mutations expressed in youth. The graph of offspring life span dependence on parental life span should be a regression line with an increased slope for the dependence of offspring life span on the long life span of long-lived parents.

The theory would also predict that variability in genes for life span would increase with age. If mutation increases with age, gene variance must increase with age. This expectation can be studied by comparing the ratio of additive genetic variance to observed gene expression variance (phenotype). This comparison can be estimated by doubling the slope of the regression line for the dependence of offspring life span on parental life span mentioned in the preceding paragraph. If age of death is determined by accumulation of late-expression mutations, the slope will be steeper, with higher parental ages at death. This hypothesis has been tested through analysis of genealogical data on longevity of royal and noble families in Europe. These data are renowned for accuracy and reliability. The results were that the regression line slopes for dependence of offspring life span on parental life span increased with parental life span, as predicted by mutation accumulation theory. Gavrilov and Gavrilova (2002) are of the opinion that this theory is a productive working hypothesis awaiting further validation.

In contrast, John Bowles (2000) at the University of Chicago argues that Medawar's assertion that aging is accidental and could not have evolved precludes settlement of an increasing quantity of evidence signifying many evolved aging systems. Medawar used an analogy of glass test tubes with constant random breakage to characterize lethal forces in nature. Bowles argues that natural lethal forces such as famine and disease have unique effects on populations. He claims that predation is the only natural force that continually devises new ways to overcome victims' defenses, but ramparts for nonevolving lethal forces should develop quickly. He also points out that Medawar's test tube analogy fails to consider limited resource forces and disregards decreasing reproduction in aging species. He further asserts that Medawar's claim that there are not enough older individuals at any time to affect a species' gene pool is incorrect when variation in the age of reproductive cessation is brought into a population free of predators.

To correct deficiencies in Medawar's analogy, Bowles (2000) offers his analogy of competing strains of algae in a predator-free ocean and a series of environmental changes affecting their reproduction. In this analogy, aging evolved and maintains to keep enough genetic variability in the species' gene pool to enable rapid defense development to combat novel predators.

ANTAGONISTIC PLEIOTROPY THEORY OF AGING   This theory, also known as the "pay later" theory, was proposed by George Williams (1957). The theory of antagonistic pleiotropy is based on two assumptions: (1) A specific gene may have an effect on more than one trait in an organism (pleiotropy), and (2) these pleiotropic effects may affect individual health in opposite (antagonistic) directions. Williams noted that natural selection was biased toward youth over old age at any time that conflict of interest was present. He explained that natural selection of a gene advantageous to survival at one age and detrimental at another is a function of not only the extent of the effects, but also the points in life when the effects occur. For example, a gene giving the benefit of increased ability to reproduce during an individual's time of maximum propagation would increase the total reproductive probability of the species more than a similar ratio of later detriment would decrease reproduction. Thus, Williams proposes that natural selection commonly exploits energy in youth at the cost of energy in older age, yielding an energy decline during adult life. Williams's ideas were later expressed mathematically by Brian Charlesworth (1994). As an example of antagonistic pleiotropy, although cellular aging and division cessation are known to arrest malignant tumor development in youth (Itahana, Dimri, & Campisi, 2001; Krtolica, Parrinello, Lockett, Desprez, & Campisi, 2001), they promote cancer in later life when old cells kindle growth of precancer and cancer cells to propagate and form tumors (Krtolica et al., 2001).

This theory explicates why reproduction may come at a cost to a species' longevity. Any mutations enabling individuals to produce more offspring will be passed on to future generations even if they have detrimental effects in later life. The swap between reproduction—including energy, propagation, fitness, success, and longevity—is predicted from his theory and described by Williams (1957, p. 403) as "testable deductions from the theory." He postulated that rapid development should correlate with rapid aging because reproductive maturation is the most important milestone in the life cycle for the commencement of aging. This prediction has been tested in the fruit fly, but contrary to Williams's prediction, there was not a linear relationship between rate of development and longevity (Economos & Lints, 1986).

Another prediction from this theory is that "successful selection for increased longevity should result in decreased vigor in youth" (Williams, 1957). This prediction was tested in fruit flies. Fruit flies with later reproduction onset were selected for these experiments, and life span was increased as Williams predicted (Partridge, Prowse, & Pignatelli, 1991; Rose, 1991). However, selection of fruit flies with late reproduction onset also unintentionally selected for flies with longer life spans, so findings of increased longevity in these experiments were inconclusive (Zwaan, Bijlsma, & Hoekstra, 1995).

Another outcome was that increased longevity was accompanied by evolutionary decline in fertility early in adult life, confirming antagonistic pleiotropy theory's prediction (Partridge et al., 1999; Rose, 1991; Stearns, Ackermann, Doebeli, & Kaiser, 2000).

In another experiment with fruit flies, offspring of parents with low mortality rates showed increased longevity, longer development times, and decreased early reproductive maturity. Results of this experiment supported Williams's predicted association between increased longevity and decreased fitness in early life.

Experiments were also performed with round worms (*Caenorhabaitis elegans*). When worms with long-term mutations were nurtured with nonmutant individuals in standard cultures, neither demonstrated a viable benefit, contrary to the predictions of evolutionary theory (Johnson & Hutchinson, 1993; Walker, McColl, Jenkins, Harris, & Lithgow, 2000). When cultures were exposed to alternative starvation cycles attempting to mimic the species' natural environment, the worms without mutations outnumbered those with mutations (Walker et al., 2000). These findings lead to the conclusion that in harsh environmental conditions increasing life span may be advantageous, lending limited support to the antagonistic pleiotropy theory.

Human data collected to test Williams's predictions are less credible. One study showed that long-lived people (particularly women) did have impaired fertility, as Williams predicted (Westerdorp & Kirkwood, 1998), but following the publication of this study severe flaws in its methods were published (Gavrilov & Gavrilova, 1999; Gavrilova & Gavrilov, 1999). Furthermore, the study's findings were inconsistent with results of other researchers and historic demographers (Gavrilov & Gavrilova, 1999; Le Bourgh, 2001).

The study relied on a database containing 335 childless women. However, when the database was compared with others, 32% of the women the study authors claimed were childless had a child or children (Gavrilov & Gavrilova, 2003).

Furthermore, childlessness does not confirm inability to propagate. The fact that a woman does not have children in later life tells researchers nothing about her reproductive capacity when she was younger. Marriage to an infertile man says nothing about the woman's propagation ability. These explanations led Gavrilov and Gavrilova (2001a) to conclude that the evolutionary trade-off between human biological ability to propagate and human longevity may be an artifact caused by incomplete data and neglecting other, nonbiological explanations.

The intellectual aid given by evolutionary biology to gerontology was detrimental for aging studies due to evolutionary theory's being interpreted to mean that seeking single gene mutations with immense positive effects on longevity was a completely futile search destined for failure. In the past, researchers bought into Williams's (1957) theory of antagonistic pleiotropy, which stated that aging should always be considered a generalized decline and never due primarily to degeneration in one system. Wonderful opportunities for aging research were passed up until new and astounding discoveries were made of single gene mutants significantly extending longevity (Lin, Dorman, Rodan, & Kenyon, 1997; Lithgow, White, Melov, & Johnson, 1995), despite discouraging predictions and admonitions to the contrary from evolutionary influence.

One of these discoveries is that one single gene mutation (daf-2) more than doubles the life span of round worms (nematodes; Lin et al., 1997). Gavrilov and Gavrilova (2002) say that evolutionary theories of aging are helpful in opening new areas of research by offering testable hypotheses, but these theories should never be used to limit research.

Reliability Theory of Biological Aging   Like evolutionary theories of aging, the reliability theory of biological aging is a macroscopic theory originally presented as an explanation for failure in architectural kinetics (Barlow, Proschan, & Hunter, 1965). Posited by Gavrilov and Gavrilova, the reliability theory of biological aging is a body of ideas, mathematical models, and methods to predict, estimate, understand, and optimize the life span distribution of systems of biological species and their components (Gavrilov, 1978). The reliability function is $S(x)$, where S is the probability that a system (or component) will perform its task through time x (Ringdon & Basu, 2000). The reliability function evaluated at time x is the probability P that failure time X is later than time x.

Gavrilov and Gavrilova propose that failure time equals mortality force. Mortality force not increasing with age indicates a nonaging system (or component). Examples are atoms of radioactive elements and many wild animal populations with high mortality threats (Finch, 1990; Gavrilov & Gavrilova, 1991). The mathematical models used in this theory are beyond the scope of this text, but further information is in Gavrilov and Gavrilova (2001b).

In systems that age, the system (component) has a greater chance of failing as age increases. That mortality increases with age and that there is a subsequent mortality plateau are theoretical predictions of inevitability in all reliability models hypothesizing that aging is a continuous accrual of random damage. There is a detailed mathematical proof for these predictions in Gavrilov and Gavrilova (1991). Succinctly, if the destruction of an organism occurs in two or more sequential random phases, it is possible for mortality increase to occur and subsequently vanish as the organism ages. Each destruction phase corresponds to one of the organism's necessary life structures. In simple organisms with exclusive structures necessary for life, damage of this type usually leads to death; thus damage does not accumulate in these organisms. In higher order organisms with many structures necessary for life, significant surplus (redundancy) is present. In these organisms, damage accrues because injury does not result in death due to surplus. According to reliability theory, aging is a direct consequence of this surplus, which assures a longer life span and increased organism reliability. As the organism amasses defects, elements continue to fail to function and eventually disappear, resulting in exhaustion of surplus elements and death. No further defects can accrue, so the mortality rate levels off. Mathematical proofs for the reliability theory of aging for highly redundant systems replete with defects and the reliability theory of aging for partially damaged redundant systems are outlined by Gavrilov and Gavrilova (2001b).

Reliability theory enables prediction of age-related body structure failure. The theory explains why the majority of biological species weaken with age, why the probability of death increases with increasing age, and why some primitive organisms do not have a direct correlation between mortality rate and increased age (Gavrilov & Gavrilova, 2001b).

Both reliability theory and evolutionary theory of biological aging explain *negligible senescence,* but have completely difference explanations (Charlesworth, 1994; Gavrilov & Gavrilova, 2001b). Charlesworth posits that effective mechanisms of repair are the explanation for negligible aging rates in some species. He explains that one-cell organisms such as bacteria that multiply by simple division of one cell into two have increased their species' population for billions of years without aging. He concludes that aging cannot be an unavoidable consequence of accrued damage.

Reliability theory's answers to Charlesworth's (1994) charges are provoking questions as well as other points of contention: What are the actual death rates in species' populations with negligible aging? Are these death rates really negligible? That is, is there perfect repair in these species? Reliability theory explains (a) why mortality rate increases exponentially as age increases in some species, as specified by Gompertz's (1825) law; (b) why age-related mortality rate increase disappears at older ages; and (c) the relative mortality rate differences in compared populations with a known species decrease with age and mortality convergence observed due to their redundancy exhaustion (Gavrilov & Gavrilova, 2001b).

CONCLUSION

We have seen that the biology of aging is a large and varied field of study, lending itself to a variety of descriptions and theories. Numerous theories have been proposed to explain the process of aging, but only a limited number have proven to be sufficiently accurate to explain this complex process. These include theories based on programmed aging and those based on stochastic (random) events that lead to the aging of organisms. The field of actuarial aging, though not providing a biological explanation for the aging process, still provides demographic data that are useful for statistical analysis by researchers and industries such as the insurance field. Finally, advances in medical care and social conditions have contributed to an increase in life expectancy and attempts to further prolong life expectancy in future years.

REFERENCES

Ahluwalia, J., Tinker, A., Clapp, L. H., Duchen, M. R., Abramov, A. Y., Pope, S. (2004). The large-conductance Ca^{2+}-activated K^+ channel is essential for innate immunity. *Nature, 427*, 853–858.

Alaluf, S., Muir-Howie, H., Hu, H. H., Evans, A., & Green, M. R. (2000). Atmospheric oxygen accelerates the induction of a post-mitotic phenotype in human dermal fibroblasts: The key protective role of glutathione. *Differentiation, 66*, 147–155.

Allsopp, R. C., Vaziriki, H., Patterson, C., Goldstein, S., Younglai, E. V., Futcher, A. V., et al. (1992). Telomere length predicts replicative capacity of human fibroblasts. *Proceedings of the National H. Academy of Sciences, USA, 89*, 10114–10118.

Alvarez-Buylla, A., Theelen, M., & Nottebohm, F. (1990). Proliferation "hot spots" in adult avian ventricular zone reveal radial cell division. *Neuron, 5*, 101–109.

Arias, E. (2004). United States life tables, 2002. *National Vital Statistics Reports, 53*(6). Retrieved February 23, 2006, from www.cdc.gov/nchs/data/nvsr53/nvrs53_06.html.

Arking, R. (1998). *Biology of aging* (2nd ed.). Sunderland, MA: Sinauer Associates.

Barlow, R. E., Proschan, F., & Hunter, L. C. (1965). *Mathematical theory of reliability*. New York: Wiley.

Barnea, A., & Nottebohm, F. (1994). Seasonal recruitment of new neurons in the hippocampus of adult, free-ranging black-capped chickadees. *Proceedings of the National Academy of Sciences, USA, 91*, 11217–11221.

Bayreuther, K., Rodemann, H. P., Hommel, R., Dittmann, K., Albiez, M., & Francz, P. I. (1988). Human skin fibroblasts in vitro differentiate along a terminal cell lineage. *Proceedings of the National Academy of Sciences, USA, 85*, 5112–5116.

Belza, B., Walwick, J., Shiu-Thornton, S., Schwartz, S., Taylor, M., & LoGerfo, J. (2004). Older adult perspectives on physical activity and exercise: Voices from multiple cultures. *Preventing Chronic Disease, 1*, A09. Retrieved February 23, 2006, from www.cdc.gov/pcd/issues/2004/oct/04_0028.html.

Bjorksten, J. (1974). Crosslinkage and the aging process. In M. Rockstein, M. L. Sussman, & J. Chesky (Eds.), *Theoretical aspects of aging* (pp. 43–59). New York: Academic Press.

Bjorksten, J., & Champion, W. J. (1942). Mechanical influence upon tanning. *Journal of the American Chemistry Society, 64,* 868–869.

Bjorksten, J., & Tenhu, H. (1990). The crosslinking theory of aging: Added evidence. *Experimental Gerontology, 25,* 91–95.

Blake, M. J., Udelsman, R., Feulner, G. J., Norton, D. D., & Holbrook, N. J. (1991). Stress-induced heat shock protein 70 expression in adrenal cortex: An adrenocorticotropic hormone-sensitive, age-dependent response. *Proceedings of the National Academy of Sciences, USA, 88,* 9873–9877.

Bonelli, M. A., Alfieri, R. R., Petronini, P. G., Brigotti, M., Campanini, C., & Borghetti, A. F. (1999). Attenuated expression of 70-kDa heat shock protein in WI-38 human fibroblasts during aging in vitro. *Experimental Cell Research, 252,* 20–32.

Bowles, J. (2000). Shattered: Medawar's test tubes and their enduring legacy of chaos. *Medical Hypotheses, 54,* 326–339.

Boxenbaum, H. (1991). Gompertz mortality analysis: Aging, longevity hormesis and toxicity. *Archives of Gerontology and Geriatrics, 13,* 125–138.

Brockes, J. P., Kumar, A., & Veloso, C. P. (2001). Regeneration as an evolutionary variable. *Journal of Anatomy, 199,* 3–11.

Brody, S. (1945). *Bioenergetics and growth.* New York: Reinhold.

Burnet, F. M. (1974). *Intrinsic mutagenesis: A genetic approach to ageing.* Lancaster, CA: Medical and Technological Publications.

Campbell, N. A. (1996). *Biology* (4th ed.). Menlo Park, NJ: Benjamin/Cummings.

Campisi, J. (1999). Cell senescence, aging, and cancer. *Molecular Biology of Aging, Alfred Benzon Symposium, 44,* 112–118.

Carrel, A., & Ebeling, A. H. (1921). Age and multiplication of fibroblasts. *Journal of Experimental Medicine, 34,* 314–337.

Castro, P., Giri, D., Lamb, D., & Ittmann, M. (2003). Cellular senescence in the pathogenesis of benign prostatic hyperplasia. *Prostate, 55,* 30–38.

Charlesworth, B. (1994). *Evolution in age-structured populations.* Cambridge, England: Cambridge University Press.

Chen, P. F., Tsai, A. L., & Wu, K. K. (1995). Cysteine 99 of endothelial nitric oxide synthase (NOS-III) tetrahydrobiopterin-dependent NOS-III stability and activity. *Biochemical and Biophysical Research, 215*(Commun.), 1119–1129.

Clark, A. M., Gould, A. B., & Graham, S. F. (1971). Patterns of development among mosaics in Habrobracon juglandis. *Developmental Biology, 25,* 133–148.

Clark, A. M., & Kelley, E. M. (1950). Differential radiosensitivity of haploid and diploid prepupae and pupae of Habrobracon. *Cancer Research, 19,* 348–352.

Comfort, A. (1964). *Ageing: The biology of senescence.* New York: Holt, Rinehart and Winston.

Comfort, A. (1979). *The biology of senescence* (3rd ed.). New York: Elsevier.

Cristofalo, V. J. (2001). "I no longer believe that cell death is programmed . . . " (an interview with Vincent Cristofalo). *Biogerontology, 2,* 283–290.

Cristofalo, V. J., Allen, R. G., Pignolo, R. J., Martin, B. G., & Beck, J. C. (1998). Relationship between donor age and the replicative lifespan of human cells in culture: A reevaluation. *Proceedings of the National Academy of Sciences, USA, 95,* 10614–10619.

Cristofalo, V. J., & Sharf, B. B. (1973). Cellular senescence and DNA synthesis: Thymidine incorporation as a measure of population age in human diploid cells. *Experimental Cell Research, 76,* 419–427.

Cristofalo, V. J., Volker, C., Francis, M. K., & Tresini, M. (1998). Age-dependent modifications of gene expression in human fibroblasts. *Critical Review of Eukaryotic Gene Expression, 8,* 43–80.

Cutler, R. G. (1976). Nature of aging and life maintenance processes. *Interdisciplinary Topics in Gerontology, 9,* 83–133.

Cutler, R. G. (1978). Alteration with age in the informational storage and flow system of the mammalian cell. *Birth Defects, 14,* 463–498.

Cutler, R. G. (1979). Evolution of human longevity: A critical overview. *Mechanical Ageing and Development, 9,* 337–354.

Decary, S., Mouly, V., Hamida, C. B., Sautet, A., Barbet, J. P., & Butler-Browne, G. S. (1997). Replicative potential and telomere length in human skeletal muscle: Implications for satellite cell-mediated gene therapy. *Human Gene Therapy, 8,* 1429–1438.

de Haan, G., & Van Zant, G. (1999). Dynamic changes in mouse hematopoietic stem cell numbers during aging. *Blood, 93,* 3294–3301.

Denckla, D. W. (1975). A time to die. *Life Sciences, 16,* 31–44.

Dmiri, G. P., Lee, X., Basille, G., Acosta, M., Scott, G., Roskelley, C., et al. (1995). A novel biomarker identifies senescent human cells in culture and aging skin in vivo. *Proceedings of the National Academy of Sciences, USA, 92,* 9363–9367.

Economos, A. C., & Lints, F. A. (1986). Developmental temperature and life-span in Drosophila melanogaster: Pt. 1. Constant development temperature: Evidence for physiological adaptation in a wide temperature range. *Gerontology, 32,* 18–27.

Everitt, A., & Meites, J. (1989). Aging and anti-aging effects of hormones. *Journal of Gerontology, 44B,* 139–147.

Fenyuk, B., & Sheikina, M. (1940). Length of life of Microtus arvalis. *Microbiology, Epidemiology, and Parisitology, 19,* 571–589.

Finch, C. E. (1990). *Longevity, senescence and the genome.* Chicago: University of Chicago Press.

Galea, L. A., & McEwen, B. S. (1999). Sex and seasonal differences in the rate of cell proliferation in the dentate gyrus of adult wild meadow voles. *Neuroscience, 89,* 955–964.

Gavrilov, L. A. (1978). Mathematical model of aging in animals. *Proceedings of the National Academy of Sciences, USSR, 238,* 290–292.

Gavrilov, L. A., & Gavrilova, N. S. (1991). *The biology of life span: A quantitative approach.* New York: Harwood Academic.

Gavrilov, L. A., & Gavrilova, N. S. (1994). A question of history. From Leonid A. Gavrilov and Natalia S. Gavrilova. *BioEssays, 16,* 592–593.

Gavrilov, L. A., & Gavrilova, N. S. (1999). Is there a reproductive cost for human longevity? *Journal of Anti-aging Medicine, 2,* 121–123.

Gavrilov, L. A., & Gavrilova, N. S. (2001a). Biodemographic study of familial determinants of human longevity. *Population: An English Selection, 13,* 197–232.

Gavrilov, L. A., & Gavrilova, N. S. (2001b). The reliability theory of aging and longevity. *Journal of Theoretical Biology, 213,* 527–545.

Gavrilov, L. A., & Gavrilova, N. S. (2002). Evolutionary theories of aging and longevity. *Scientific World Journal, 2,* 339–356.

Gavrilova, N. S., & Gavrilov, L. A. (1999). Data resources for biodemographic studies on familial clustering of human longevity. *Demographic Research, 1,* 1–48.

Gebhardt, E., Bauer, R., Raub, U., Schinzel, M., Ruprecht, K. W., & Jonas, J. B. (1988). Spontaneous and induced chromosomal instability in Werner syndrome. *Human Genetics, 80,* 135–139.

Gerland, L. M., Peyrol, S., Lallemand, C., Branche, R., Magaud, J. P., & French, M. (2003). Association of increased autophagic inclusions labeled for beta-galactosidase with fibroblastic aging. *Experimental Gerontology, 38,* 887–895.

Gersten, J. W. (1991). Effect of exercise on muscle function decline with aging. *Western Journal of Medicine, 154,* 579–582.

Gey, G. O., Coffman, W. D., & Kubicek, M. T. (1952). Tissue culture studies of the proliferative capacity of cervical carcinoma and normal epithelium. *Cancer Research, 12,* 264–265.

Goldstein, S. (1974). Aging in vitro: Growth of cultured cells from the Galapagos tortoise. *Experimental Cell Research, 83,* 297–302.

Gompertz, B. (1825). On the nature of the function expressive of the law of human mortality and on a new mode of determining the value of life contingencies. *Philosophical Transactions of the Royal Society of London, 115,* 513–585.

Haff, R. F., & Swim, H. E. (1956). Serial propagation of 3 strains of rabbit fibroblasts: Their susceptibility to infection with Vaccinia virus. *Proceedings of the Society of Experimental Biological Medicine, 93,* 200–204.

Hall, D. A. (1984). *The biomedical basis of gerontology.* Boston: Wright-PSG.

Harley, C. D., Futcher, A. B., & Grieder, C. W. (1990). Telomeres shorten during aging of human fibroblasts. *Nature, 345,* 458–460.

Harman, D. (1956). Aging: A theory based on free radical and radiation chemistry. *Journal of Gerontology, 11,* 298–300.

Hayflick, L. (1994). *How and why we age.* New York: Ballantine Books.

Hayflick, L., & Moorhead, P. S. (1961). The serial cultivation of human diploid cell strains. *Experimental Cell Research, 25,* 585–621.

Hill, K., Boesch, C., Goodall, J., Pusey, A., Williams, J., & Wrangham, R. (2001). Mortality rate among wild chimpanzees. *Journal of Human Evolution, 40,* 437–450.

Horikoshi, T., Balin, A. K., & Carter, D. M. (1991). Effects of oxygen tension on the growth and pigmentation of normal human melanocytes. *Journal of Investigative Dermatology, 96,* 841–844.

Itahana, K., Dimri, G., & Campisi, J. (2001). Regulation of cellular senescence by p53. *European Journal of Biochemistry, 268,* 2784–2791.

Jerison, H. J. (1973). *Evolution of the brain and intelligence.* New York: Academic Press.

Johnson, T. E., & Hutchinson, E. W. (1993). Absence of strong heterosis for life span and other life history traits in Caenorhabditis elegans. *Genetics, 134,* 465–474.

Jones, M. I. (1982). Longevity of captive animals. *Zoological Garden, N. F. Jena, 52,* 113–128.

Karatza, C., & Shall, S. (1984). The reproductive potential of normal mouse embryo fibroblasts during culture in vitro. *Journal of Cell Science, 66,* 401–409.

Kato, K., Orii, H., Watanabe, K., & Agata, K. (2001). Dorsal and ventral positional cues required for the onset of planarian regeneration may reside in differentiated cells. *Developmental Biology, 233,* 109–121.

Kempermann, G., Kuhn, H. G., & Gage, F. H. (1998). More hippocampal neurons in adult mice living in an enriched environment. *Nature, 386,* 493–495.

Kirkwood, T. B. (1977). Evolution of aging. *Nature, 270,* 301–304.

Krtolica, A., Parrinello, S., Lockett, S., Desprez, P. Y., & Campisi, J. (2001). Senescent fibroblasts promote epithelial cell growth and tumorigenesis: A link between cancer and aging. *Proceedings of the National Academy of Sciences, USA, 98,* 12072–12077.

Lamb, M. J. (1978). Ageing. In M. Ashburner & T. R. F. Wright (Eds.), *The genetics and biology of Drosophila* (Vol. 2C, pp. 43–103). London: Academic Press.

Le Bourgh, E. (2001). A mini-review of the evolutionary theories of aging: Is it the time to accept them? *Demographic Research,* 1–28.

Lin, K., Dorman, J. B., Rodan, A., & Kenyon, C. (1997). Daf-16: An HNF-3/forkhead family member that can function to double the life-span in Caenorhabolitis elegans. *Science, 278,* 1319–1322.

Lithgow, G. J., White, T. M., Melov, S., & Johnson, T. E. (1995). Thermotolerance and extended life-span conferred by single-gene mutations and induced by thermal stress. *Proceedings of the National Academy of Sciences, USA, 92,* 7540–7544.

Loeb, J., & Northrup, J. H. (1917). On the influence of food and temperature on the duration of life. *Journal of Biological Chemistry, 32,* 103–121.

Luckinbill, L. S., & Clare, M. J. (1985). Selection for life span in Drosophila melanogaster. *Heredity, 55,* 9–18.

Ly, D. H., Lockhart, D. J., Lerner, R. A., & Schultz, P. G. (2000). Mitotic misregulation and human aging. *Science, 287,* 2390.

Makeham, W. H. (1867). On the law of mortality. *Journal of Insurance Actuaries, 13,* 325–358.

Maynard-Smith, J. (1962). Review lectures on senescence: Pt. I. The causes of aging. *Proceedings of the Royal Society of London, Series B, 157,* 115–127.

McCay, C. M., Maynard, L. A., Sperling, G., & Barnes, L. L. (1939). Retarded growth, life span, ultimate body size and age changes in the albino rat after feeding diets restricted in calories. *Journal of Nutrition, 18,* 1–13.

Medawar, P. B. (1946). Old age and natural death. *Modern Quarterly, 1,* 50–56.

Medawar, P. B. (1952). *An unsolved problem of biology.* London: H. K. Lewis.

Meites, J. (1991). Role of hypothalamic catecholamines in aging processes. *Acta Endocrinology, 125*(Suppl.), 98–103.

Melk, A. (2003). Senescence of renal cells: Molecular basics and clinical implications. *Nephrology Dialysis Transplantation, 11,* 444–453.

Mendez, M. V., Stanley, A., Phillips, T., Murphy, M., Menzoian, J. O., & Park, H. Y. (1998). Fibroblasts cultured from distal lower extremities in patients with venous reflux display cellular characteristics of senescence. *Journal of Vascular Surgery, 28,* 1040–1050.

Minamino, T., Miyauchi, H., Hoshida, T., Ishida, Y., Yoshida, H., & Komuro, I. (2002). Endothelial cell senescence in human atherosclerosis: Role of telomere in endothelial dysfunction. *Circulation, 105,* 1541–1544.

Moorhead, P. S., & Hsu, T. C. (1956). Cytologic studies of HeLa, a strain of cervical carcinoma III. *Journal of the National Cancer Institute, 12,* 1047–1066.

Minot, C. S. (1907). The problem of age, growth and death: A study of cytomorphosis. *Popular Science Monthly, 71,* 97–120, 193–216, 359–377, 455–473, 481–496.

Morrison, R. S., & Meier, D. (Eds.). (2003). *Geriatric palliative care.* New York: Oxford University Press.

National Institutes of Health. (2006). *Stem cell basics.* Available from www.stemcells.nih.gov/info/basics/default.asp. Accessed January 23, 2007.

Nooden, L. C., & Leopold, A. C. (Eds.). (1988). *Senescence and aging in plants.* San Diego, CA: Academic Press.

Oberman, A. (1984). Healthy exercise. *Western Journal of Medicine, 141,* 864–871.

Orgel, L. E. (1963). The maintenance of the accuracy of protein synthesis and its relevance to aging. *Proceedings of the National Academy of Sciences, USA, 49,* 517–521.

Paevsky, V. A. (1985). *Demografia ptits* [Demography of birds]. Moscow: Nauka.

Parrinello, S., Samper, E., Krtolica, A., Goldstein, J., Melov, S., & Campisi, J. (2003). Oxygen sensitivity severely limits the replicative lifespan of murine fibroblasts. *Nature Cell Biology, 5,* 741–747.

Partridge, L., Prowse, N., & Pignatelli, P. (1999). Another set of responses and correlated responses to selection on age at reproduction in Drosophila melanogaster. *Proceedings of the Royal Society of London, Series B, 266,* 255–261.

Pearl, R. (1928). *The rate of living: Being an account of some experimental studies on the biology of life duration.* New York: Knopf.

Pearl, R., & Pearl, R. D. (1934). *The ancestry of the long-lived.* Baltimore: Johns Hopkins University Press.

Ponten, J., Stein, W. D., & Shall, S. (1983). A quantitative analysis of the aging of human glial cells in culture. *Journal of Cell Physiology, 117,* 342–352.

Radmilovich, M., Fernandez, A., & Trujillo-Cenoz, O. (2003). Environment temperature affects cell proliferation in the spinal cord and brain of juvenile turtles. *Journal of Experimental Biology, 206,* 3085–3093.

Reznick, D. N., Buckwalter, G., Groff, J., & Elder, D. (2001). The evolution of senescence in natural populations of guppies (Poecilia reticulata): A comparative approach. *Experimental Gerontology, 3,* 791–812.

Ringdon, S. E., & Basu, A. P. (2000). *Statistical manual for repairable systems.* New York: Wiley.

Robertson, O. H., & Wexler, B. C. (1962). Histological changes in the pituitary gland of the pacific salmon (genus Oncorhynchus) accompanying sexual maturation and spawning. *Journal of Morphology, 110,* 171–185.

Rose, M. (1991). *The evolutionary biology of aging.* New York: Oxford University Press.

Rubner, M. (1908). *Das problem der levensdauer und seine beziehungen zum wachstom und ernahrung.* Munich: Oldenbourg.

Sacher, G. A. (1959). Relation of lifespan to brain weight and body weight in mammals. In G. E. W. Wolstenholme & M. O'Connor (Eds.), *Ciba Foundation colloquia on ageing* (Vol. 5). London: Churchill.

Sacher, G. A. (1982). Evolutionary theory in gerontology. *Perspectives in Biology and Medicine, 25,* 339–353.

Saito, H., Hammond, A. T., & Moses, R. I. (1995). The effect of low oxygen tension on the in vitro-replicative life span of human diploid fibroblast cells and their transformed derivatives. *Experimental Cell Research, 217,* 272–279.

Salk, D., Au, K., Hoehn, H., & Martin, G. M. (1981). Effects of radical-scavenging enzymes and reduced oxygen exposure on growth and chromosome abnormalities of Werner syndrome cultured skin fibroblasts. *Human Genetics, 57,* 269–275.

Schneider, E. L., & Rowe., J. W. (Eds.). (1995). *Handbook of the biology of aging.* New York: Academic Press.

Shay, J. W., & Wright, W. E. (2000). Hayflick, his limits, and cellular ageing. *National Review of Molecular and Cellular Biology, 1,* 72–76.

Shock, N. W., Greulich, R. C., Andres, R., Arenberg, D., Costa, P. T., Lakatta, E. G., et al. (1984). *Normal human aging: The Baltimore Longitudinal Study of Aging* (NIH Publication 84–2450). Washington, DC: U.S. Government Printing Office.

Smith, D. W. E. (1993). *Human longevity.* New York: Oxford University Press.

Smith, J. R., & Whitney, R. G. (1980). Intraclonal variation in proliferative potential of human diploid fibroblasts: Stochastic mechanism for cellular aging. *Science, 207,* 82–84.

Snyder, E. Y., & Loring, J. F. (2005). A role for stem cell biology in the physiological and pathological aspects of aging. *Journal of the American Geriatrics Society, 53*(Suppl.), S287–S291.

Spence, A. P. (1989). *Biology of human aging.* Englewood Cliffs, NJ: Prentice-Hall.

Stearns, S. C., Ackermann, M., Doebeli, M., & Kaiser, K. M. (2000). Experimental evolution of aging, growth, and reproduction in fruit flies. *Proceedings of the National Academy of Sciences, USA, 97*, 3309–3313.

Strehler, B. L. (1986). Genetic instability as the primary cause of human aging. *Experimental Gerontology, 21*, 283–319.

Sugihara, M., Ohshima, K., Hakamura, H., Suzumiya, J., Nakayama, Y., Kanda, M., et al. (1999). Decreased expression of telomerase-associated RNAs in the proliferation of stem cells in comparison with continuous expression in malignant tumors. *International Journal of Oncology, 15*, 1075–1080.

Swim, H. E. (1959). Microbiological aspects of tissue culture. *Annual Review of Microbiology, 313*, 141–176.

Swim, H. E., & Parker, R. F. (1957). Culture characteristics of human fibroblasts propagated serially. *American Journal of Hygiene, 66*, 235–243.

Takeda, K., Gosiewska, A., & Peterkofsky, B. (1992). Similar, but not identical, modulation of expression of extracellular matrix components during in vitro and in vivo aging of human skin fibroblasts. *Cell Physiology, 153*, 450–459.

Tanhauser, S. M., & Laipis, P. J. (1995). Multiple deletions are detectable in mitochondrial DNA of aging mice. *Journal of Biological Chemistry, 270*, 24769–24775.

Tesco, G., Vergelli, M., Grassilli, E., Salomoni, P., Bellesia, E., Sikora, E., et al. (1998). Growth properties and growth factor responsiveness in skin fibroblasts from centenarians. *Biochemical and Biophysical Research, 244*, 912–916.

Toole, V. K. (1986). Ancient seeds: Seed longevity. *Journal of Seed Technology, 10*, 1–23.

Toussaint, O., Dumont, P., Remacle, J., Dierick, J. F., Pascal, T., Frippiat, C., et al. (2002). Stress-induced premature senescence or stress-induced senescence-like phenotype: One in vivo reality, two possible definitions? *Scientific World Journal, 2*, 230–247.

Turker, M. (1996). Premature aging. In J. E. Birren (Ed.), *Encyclopedia of gerontology: Age, ageing and the aged* (Vol. 2, pp. 342–354). Orlando, FL: Academic Press.

Uetz, G. W., McClintock, W. J., Miller D., Smith, E. I., & Cook, K. K. (1996). Limb regeneration and subsequent asymmetry in a male secondary sexual characteristic influences sexual selection in wolf spider. *Behavioral and Ecological Sociobiology, 38*, 233–257.

Ugalis, B. (1996). *Selected 16th century through 18th century philosophers.* Retrieved January 23, 2007, from http://oregonstate.edu/instruct/phl302/philosophers.html.

van Loon, A. A., Sonneveld, E., Hoogerbrugge, J., van der Schans, G. P., Grootegoed, J. A., Lohman, P. H., et al. (1993). Induction and repair of DNA single-strand breaks and DNA base damage at different cellular stages of spermatogenesis of the hamster upon in vitro exposure to ionizing radiation. *Mutation Research, 294*, 139–148.

Vogel, E. W., & Ziljstra, J. A. (1987). Somatic cell mutagenicity in Drosophila melanogaster in comparison with genetic damage in early germ-cell stages. *Mutation Research, 180*, 189–200.

Walford, R. L., Harris, S. B., & Weindruch, R. (1987). Dietary Restriction and Aging: Historical Phases, Mechanisms, and Current Directions. *Journal of Nutrition, 117*, 1650–1654.

Walker, D. W., McColl, G., Jenkins, H. L., Harris, J., & Lithgow, G. J. (2000). Evolution of lifespan in *C. elegans. Nature, 405*, 296–297.

Walter, C. A., Lu, J., Bhakta, M., Zhou, Z. Q., Thompson, L. H., & McCarrey, J. R. (1994). Testis and somatic Xrec-1 DNA repair gene expression. *Somatic Cell Molecular Genetics, 20*, 451–461.

Walter, C. A., Walter, R. B., & McCarrey, J. R. (2003). Germline genomes: A biological fountain of youth? *Science of Aging Knowledge and Environment, 8*, PE4.

Weismann, A. (1882). *Ober die Dauer des Lebens.* Jena, Germany: Verlag von Gustav Fisher.

Weismann, A. (1889). The duration of life. In J. B. Poulton (Ed.), *Collected essays upon heredity and kindred biological problems* (pp. 8–156). Oxford: Clarendon Press.

Westerdorp, R. G. J., & Kirkwood, T. B. L. (1998). Human longevity at the cost of reproductive success. *Nature, 396,* 743–746.

Wibe, E., & Oftebro, R. (1974). Inactivation by the mitotic inhibitor NY 3170 of human cells in vitro. *British Journal of Cancer, 40,* 222–227.

Wickens, A. P. (1998). *The causes of aging.* Amsterdam: Harwood Academic.

Williams, G. C. (1957). Pleiotropy, natural selection and the evolution of senescence. *Evolution, 11,* 398–411.

Wynford-Thomas, D. (1999). Cellular senescence and cancer. *Journal of Pathology, 187,* 100–111.

Yang, Q., Rasmussen, S. A., & Friedman, J. M. (2002). Mortality associated with Down's syndrome in the USA from 1983 to 1997: A population-based study. *Lancet, 359,* 1019–1025.

Yuan, H., Kanako, T., & Matsuo, M. (1996). Increased susceptibility of late passage human diploid fibroblasts to oxidative stress. *Experimental Gerontology, 31,* 465–474.

Zwaan, B. J., Bijlsma, R., & Hoekstra, R. F. (1995). Direct selection on life-span in Drosophila melanogaster. *Evolution, 49,* 649–659.

CHAPTER 3

Cognitive and Affective Theories of Adult Development

BERT HAYSLIP JR. and BENJAMIN P. CHAPMAN

THIS CHAPTER EXPLORES a variety of cognitive theories that have played important and meaningful roles in shaping our ideas about how older adults function. At both a conceptual and an everyday, functional level, concerns about the veracity of the notion of cognitive decline with age have been voiced for easily 3 decades, reflecting a great deal of research into the memory, intellectual, problem-solving, information-processing, and decision-making capacities of older adults. Our purpose here is to examine the major approaches to aging viewed from within a cognitive lens. We do so with regard to those theories whose impact has been substantial and for which there is a substantial amount of empirical evidence on which to base an evaluation of their potential to guide clinical practice and shape social policy. The importance of this issue is underscored by the public's concerns about Alzheimer's disease: its origins, treatment, and the impact of the disease on family caregivers. More broadly speaking, concerns about normative aging-related declines in cognitive functioning and everyday competence and their potential remediation underscore the public's views about older individuals who are capable of continued cognitive growth, as persons who can continue to live independently, or as persons who must face the specter of the inevitable loss of their skills. In this chapter, we discuss the following cognitive theories as they apply to the aging process: cognitive-behavior theory, information-processing theory, and modern theories of emotional development and regulation such as socioemotional selectivity theory, cognitive affective developmental theory, differential emotions theory, and discrete emotions functionalist theory. These approaches all share a common emphasis on some aspect of cognition: how one thinks about or evaluates his or her experiences or those of others. Indeed, most approaches to healthy, successful, and productive aging (e.g., Morrow-Howell, Hinterlong, & Sherraden, 2001;

Rowe & Kahn, 1998; Vaillant, 2002) either implicitly or explicitly identify the maintenance of one's cognitive skills or how one thinks about oneself as key components in aging well.

COGNITIVE-BEHAVIORAL THEORY

Reflecting its popularity in psychology more generally, it is not surprising to find that a cognitive-behavioral approach to aging has become popular and virtually universally accepted as a framework in which to examine change in later life. This approach is derived from the cognitive-behavior therapy tradition defined principally by Albert Ellis (1962), Aaron Beck (1987), and Donald Meichenbaum (1977, 1985, 1989). Ellis and Beck focus on a rational analysis of the individual's belief system; Meichenbaum stresses altering the "inner dialogue" of the individual to achieve more adaptive functioning. In general, however, cognitive-behavior therapists believe that the way a person thinks largely determines the way he or she feels. In other words, thought causes emotional response. Reflecting the very positive approach to aging that can be realized via the application of cognitive-behavior theory, it is worth noting that former president Jimmy Carter (1998, p. xi) stated in his book *The Virtues of Aging*, "I'm old, but it's good!"

The application of cognitive-behavior theory, cognitive-behavior therapy, is an attempt to help persons change their maladaptive thinking habits to relieve emotional disturbances such as depression, anger, and anxiety, and to more generally facilitate everyday adjustment. Ellis (1962) views this process in an A-B-C-D fashion. A is designated as the event that the client thinks is causing the anxiety, depression, and so on. The emotional disturbance lies at point C. An older client might believe that, for example, her depression (C) is being caused by her getting old (A). Ellis insists that age (A) is not causing the depression (C). Instead, the depression (C) is attributed to the woman's belief (B) about her own aging; this belief about aging is the culprit. In this case, the woman might erroneously believe that being old means that she is a person unworthy of respect or love. This false belief may lead to behavior (D) that is either maladaptive per se, for example, isolating oneself from others and avoiding social interactions, or that leads to other maladaptive behaviors, such as disturbances in eating and sleeping, a lack of physical self-care, or self-abusive behaviors such as drinking or substance use.

A concrete application of this approach to the emotional and mental health of older persons has been taken by Ellis and Velton (1998), who stress the relationship between activating events (e.g., a change in one's health, retirement, a lack of financial resources), (B) core irrational cognitions and thoughts, and (C) consequences (e.g., depression, anxiety, impaired everyday cognitive or social-interpersonal functioning). The essence of change involves substituting more rational thoughts and cognitions for irrational ones, wherein the latter have an either/or quality to them. Such thoughts must be examined rationally and actively disputed if they are to be translated into different ways of feeling and behaving. Ellis and Velton urge older persons to dispute such irrational "musts," "have to's," or "shoulds" (e.g., I must always be liked by others, I have to appear young, I must never appear to be unhealthy) and to act on the rational ways of thinking about oneself and others. Such irrational thinking is frequently overlearned and elicited "automatically" in situations involving other persons that activate feelings of fear, inferiority, failure, or threat. Differentiating healthy from unhealthy emotions, approaching one's thinking scientifically (e.g., evaluating the evidence), accepting responsibility for oneself, ignoring the past, and, perhaps most important, failing to buy into the myths of aging are key elements in cognitive change for older adults, who must deal with changes in their physical and cognitive capacities, retirement, age discrimination, relocation, and the loss of family and friends through death.

Elderly persons, perhaps lacking realistic feedback about themselves from others, often make "thinking errors" that are not realistic (Hayslip & Caraway, 1989). For example, irrational assumptions about one's age or about the loss of skills one once had may lead to feelings of self-depreciation. These feelings can lead to anger, guilt, and depression. Cognitive techniques are available to instruct the elder to substitute more rational thoughts for these irrational ones (Hayslip & Caraway, 1989). These techniques have been discussed extensively in the context of cognitive restructuring and reframing by Knight (2004), and more generally within a cognitive-behavioral framework by Laidlaw, Thompson, Dick-Siskin, and Gallagher-Thompson (2003).

Of particular importance, such changes can be presented to older persons as changes that they are entirely capable of making, that engender feelings of control over, not what happens, but how one thinks about what happens to oneself. This distinction parallels that between primary control (control over objective events and the environment) and secondary control (control over how one reacts to, processes, or thinks about such events and experiences; Schulz & Heckhausen, 1996).

The principles underlying cognitive-behavior therapy (CBT) are perceived as practical, understandable, and applicable to their everyday lives by most older persons, especially if techniques that engender their active involvement in the process of cognitive and behavior change are employed, that is, conducting a rational analysis of one's thinking patterns via the provision of homework (see Hayslip, 1989; Laidlaw et al., 2003). In many cases, a strictly behavioral component is combined with the cognitive emphasis to provide a diversified package of acquirable skills. This behavioral component involves the monitoring of one's daily moods and emotions in light of specific positive and negative events, whereby activity levels associated with pleasant events are increased over time relative to those associated with negative events. To facilitate such effects, progressive muscle relaxation techniques are often beneficial for older adults who are physically able to utilize them (Hayslip, 1989; Laidlaw et al., 2003).

Specific techniques are available for this purpose and have been discussed in detail by Thompson et al. (1991), Zeiss and Steffen (1996), and most recently by Laidlaw et al. (2003) as they relate to the treatment of depression, anxiety and mood/panic disorders, insomnia and sleep disorders, physical illness and disability, poststroke depression, and depression among dementia caregivers. Indeed, the meta-analysis of CBT research with older persons by Laidlaw et al. as well as a recent review of the efficacy of such techniques by Knight, Kaskie, Shurgot, and Dave (2006) as they apply to depression, anxiety, sleep disorders, the enhancement of cognitive and emotional functioning in mildly demented older persons, and depression related to health difficulties suggests CBT to be effective. In contrast, interventions, some of which have a CBT component, appear to be less successful in increasing caregiver well-being and reducing burden (Knight et al., 2006), though work by Mittelman et al. (1995) is more positive in this regard.

Although not explicitly labeled cognitive-behavioral in nature, there is nevertheless extensive research substantiating a link between older persons' beliefs about themselves and others and their behavior, particularly in the context of (a) the activation of ego-threatening aging stereotypes, (b) their internalization by the older person, or (c) the stereotypic consistent attitudes and behaviors of others (Hess, 2006). Moreover, there is a powerful connection between emotion and cognition (see Carstensen, Mikels, & Mather, 2006) via the selective allocation of cognitive resources to emotionally salient persons and situation as predicted by socioemotional selectivity theory (see later discussion). For example, Hess, Auman, Colcombe, and Rahhal (2003) found impaired memory performance to be associated with exposure to negative age stereotypes regarding memory decline, and Levy (1996) and her colleagues (e.g., Levy, Hausdorff, Hencke, & Wei, 2000) have demonstrated that the activation of negative and positive age stereotypes had predictably negative and positive effects, respectively, on cognitive performance, reactions to stress, walking speed, and handwriting (see Hess, 2006).

Although the similarities outweigh the differences in cognitive therapy with younger versus older adults, there are a few aspects of cognitive-behavioral therapy that are unique to older adults (Thompson et al., 1991; Zeiss & Steffen, 1996). For example, the therapist must be more flexible, special attention should be given to cohort differences in education and interests, an assessment of one's physical history must be made, and a conference with the client's physician and family should be arranged. In addition, the therapist may have to be more active with older clients, keeping them focused on the issue at hand, and should expect the pace of therapy to be slower, due to fatigue or resistance in giving up long-held assumptions about self or others (Hayslip & Caraway, 1989; Thompson et al., 1991).

Cognitive-behavioral approaches to therapy have been successfully utilized to treat a variety of cognitive and emotional problems in the aged, that is, depression, memory loss, test anxiety, performance on intellectual tasks, and response slowness (Zeiss & Steffen, 1996). Kooken and Hayslip (1984) and Hayslip (1989) have used a cognitive-behavioral approach emphasizing both stress inoculation (cognitive) and relaxation training to modify test anxiety and intellectual performance in older persons. Puder (1988) used cognitive-behavior therapy to successfully treat the side effects of chronic pain, that is, medication use, coping ability, in older people. The research by Thompson, Gallagher, and Breckenridge (1987) and by Gallagher-Thompson, Hanley-Peterson, and Thompson (1990) are excellent examples of the potential of cognitive-behavioral interventions with elderly persons in dealing with depression. As the name suggests, they use both cognitive and behavioral approaches to treat the client. These authors, however, qualify their support for this method in noting that it works best with people who experience depression that is exogenous (a reaction to recent stress) versus depression that is endogenous (depression that is lifelong in nature; see Thompson et al., 1987). In this respect, Thompson, Coon, Gallagher-Thompson, Sommer, and Koin (2001), working with less severely depressed older persons, found CBT alone to be as effective as CBT plus drug (desipramine) treatment, and each to be more effective than mediation alone. Although persons who are suffering from mild dementia can benefit, suicidal or severely depressed clients do not seem to respond as well to cognitive-behavioral techniques (see Knight, 2004; Thompson et al., 1991).

COGNITIVE-BEHAVIORAL ASPECTS OF EVERYDAY COGNITION IN LATER LIFE

Fillenbaum (1985) found that 20% to 30% of community-residing elderly persons report having difficulty with at least one of the seven domains of independent living, though to a certain extent, these estimates vary by age, gender, and the nature of the instrumental activity of daily living (IADL) considered. Indeed, Schaie (1996) has found IADL performance to decline over time. Overall, estimates of some degree of IADL disability range from 5% to 15% among community-residing elderly (Jette, 1995), yet there remains that proportion of the elderly population who do not accurately report the extent of their difficulty with IADLs (they either over- or underestimate). This very bias in estimating one's cognitive or everyday living skills (see Marsiske & Margrett, 2006) underscores the relevance of one's beliefs about whether declines in one's skills are inevitable or not, the consequences attached to such declines, as well as one's beliefs about whether such declines are remediable.

For many elderly individuals, the loss of everyday competence may stem from a variety of sources. Notable among the antecedents of decrements in independent living skills is the presence of disease (Jette, 1995; S. L. Willis, 1991). From a cognitive-behavioral perspective, however, an awareness of losses in everyday competence (e.g., answering the telephone, being able to understand medicine labels and instructions, being able to understand schedules and forms) is a prerequisite for conscious, deliberate efforts at compensation (Bäckman & Dixon, 1992; Salthouse, 1995). As deficits in IADLs are often associated with mild or early dementia (Kemp & Mitchell, 1992), remediating skills that one may have possessed at a higher level of competence earlier in life may not only alleviate fears of dependency and eventual institutionalization among community-residing elderly adults, but also enhance self-efficacy, life satisfaction, and quality of life. In this light, persons whose self-esteem is closely linked to their ability to remain independent may be especially prone to anxiety about the loss of everyday living skills. Such persons may be more likely to benefit from stress inoculation training (Brockner, 1983; Hayslip, 1989), as they, paradoxically, have already invested great effort into maintaining their skills as a function of their concerns about losing such skills. For older individuals, then, the management of their anxiety about the loss of their everyday living skills may represent a means of compensating for physical losses, contributing to a sense of everyday competence, that is, the capacity to apply one's cognitive skills in naturalistic or everyday situations that are complex or multidimensional (S. L. Willis & Schaie, 1993).

Such gains in self-competence may also be important for the oldest old, who are more likely to report needing assistance with IADLs and who are more likely to suffer from chronic illnesses interfering with independent living skills (Jette, 1995; S. L. Willis, 1991). Persons who live alone or who lack functional or social-emotional support may also benefit from stress inoculation training. In stress inoculation training, external supports are replaced by internal cognitive strategies by which to deal with uncertainty, everyday performance anxiety, or a lack of everyday self-efficacy. Significantly, depression is as common a determinant or correlate of disability and deficits in everyday skills as are impaired cognitive skills (Kemp & Mitchell, 1992). Indeed, IADLs may be more impacted by depression (and other affective states influencing the ability and desire to perform IADLs) than are activities of daily living (ADLs). Kemp and Mitchell state that the "higher" or more skilled the activity is (i.e., the extent to which intact skills are crucial), the more easily it is disrupted by affective dysfunction. Thus, it would be likely that IADLs would be more strongly influenced by worry, anger, anxiety, denial, or distortion (representing the manner in which older adults assess the extent of their everyday skills or the consequences of declines in such skills) than would ADLs. The accurate estimation and processing of such skills might be especially disrupted, for example, if one suffered from a chronic illness or lived alone; that is, worry and anxiety or depression may mediate the relationship between poor health and isolation and everyday skills.

As Park and Gutchess (2000) have pointed out with regard to driving, one must not assume that declines in everyday skill levels are necessarily mediated by declines in basic cognitive skills. As persons become less proficient in the performance of everyday skills that were once more intact, more effortful processing (see discussion of information processing theory) may be required to process task requirements and execute appropriate behaviors. As the efficient allocation of emotional resources to deal with the real or perceived difficulty in performing well (due to a lack of practice or novel requirements for responses to everyday tasks, as might occur when one moves, purchases a new stove, microwave, or VCR, or when one must drive an unfamiliar route because one has moved or when there is road construction) becomes more salient, the effortful processing of elderly persons might be further impaired. This is significant in light of the fact that such resources do decline in older persons (Ackerman, 1986, 1987). Thus, it may be argued that emotional distress or anxiety over poor performance or future declines dictates the shift to the effortful processing of formerly automatically processed and overlearned everyday skills. This further interferes with such effortful processing via the reallocation of attention or effort that might otherwise be directed to successful task performance. Having failed in carrying out an everyday task they had formerly been quite skilled at, individuals may either avoid such tasks, self-handicap (e.g., claiming that poor health prevents them from cooking), or engage in "defensive pessimism," wherein low performance expectations are a priori set, protecting the individual from failure (Norem & Cantor, 1986). Confronting such tasks thus becomes linked to motives to avoid failure or cope with anxiety linked to such failures.

In understanding the development of belief systems and associated behaviors that may undermine individual efforts to maintain everyday competence, acknowledging the powerful role that age stereotypes (i.e., that with aging comes dependence) as well as the older person's personal goals (i.e., to avoid becoming dependent on others by maintaining independent living skills) is critical to successful efforts in enhancing skill levels in later life (Bieman-Copland, Ryan, & Cassano, 1998). Indeed, the evocation of age stereotypes has been demonstrated to have a powerful effect on behavior and self-perceptions in later life (see review by Hess, 2006). Such an approach by the older individual to declines in everyday skill in changing behavior (involving the past, present, and future selves) might be termed assimilative in nature (Whitbourne, 1987).

In her review of everyday competence, S. L. Willis (1991) points out that there is little basis for understanding why individuals may or may not perceive themselves to be no longer competent to function independently in daily life. Diehl (1998) indicates that there is little research to reveal how an awareness of everyday performance deficits motivates compensatory behaviors, nor is it known how awareness affects performance or well-being. Indeed, Diehl (1995) cites preliminary findings based on a sample of older rehabilitation patients that suggests that persons who are unaware of their deficits have greater deficits in their independent living skills. In this light, the longitudinal findings of S. Willis, Jay, Keihl, and Marsiske (1992) suggest that one of the outcomes of everyday competence is enhanced self-efficacy. Viewed recursively (S. L. Willis, 1996), enhanced self-efficacy can be both a determinant and a consequence of improvements in everyday skill.

Krause (1997) has stressed that everyday competence needs to be understood not only in terms of physical health status and cognitive functioning, but also in terms of the perceptions and behaviors of others (or in this case, one's perceptions of others' perceptions and behavior) as well as the elder's self-perceptions. Such components are critical to understanding and changing elderly persons' perceptions of their everyday skills as well as behaviors that promote competence in the context of fears about others' reduced expectations of them and fears about becoming dependent or incapacitated (see also Bäckman & Dixon, 1992).

Everyday skills are often directed to maintaining an environment that is personally meaningful and stable (e.g., one's home, everyday tasks and routines). Such skills might also be employed in responding to changes in this environment, such as when one moves from one residence to another. In this respect, everyday skill reflects the pragmatics of intelligence versus its mechanics (Baltes, 1993, 1997). Labouvie-Vief (1992) argues that everyday competence is best thought of in terms of postformal reasoning, emphasizing one's sensitivity to the socioemotional context in which such skills are expressed. Thus, the emotional salience of the everyday problems one faces is an important dimension of everyday skill (Blanchard-Fields, 1986; Labouvie-Vief, 1992). Even if everyday cognition in part depends on the intactness of underlying cognitive abilities, its expression and functional significance is nevertheless impacted by contextual and personological variables (see Poon, Welke, & Dudley, 1993). In this light, the perspective of person-environment fit on everyday competence would be consistent with the attention necessary to be given to individuals' perceptions of the demandingness of the task, the perceived fit between one's skills and the everyday task, and the real and perceived consequences of success and failure (e.g., incapacitation, dependence on others or institutionalization).

As one's emotional state may codefine everyday performance (see S. L. Willis & Schaie, 1993), studying and altering everyday cognitive skills from a cognitive-behavioral perspective is advantageous in light of the emotionally salient and functional importance older adults may attach to their everyday skills. This is especially true if it can be assumed that among older adults who reside in the community, minimal levels of intactness of one's everyday functional skills (i.e., IADLs) are necessary to remain independently functional in the community (e.g., driving, grocery shopping, paying one's bills, getting health care). Such individuals have long-established histories in which the criteria for determining the extent to which these skills are intact have been defined, and failures in performance can serve to motivate individuals to learn new skills, develop compensatory strategies, seek help from others, or become dysfunctionally anxious about such failures and subsequently avoid tasks at which they sense they are no longer as proficient as they once were. Thus, decrements (real and perceived) in everyday skill can be both a cause of and a consequence of emotional concern, the anticipation of decline, or changes in perceived social support linked to such declines. Such a perspective on the enhancement of functioning also reflects an emphasis on the study of the aging mind in context by studying older persons' motives to maintain their skills.

Data collected by the first author (Hayslip, Servaty, & Ward, 1996; Hayslip, Servaty, Ward, & Blackburn, 1995) support the contention that the use of everyday skills is indeed related to perceptions of one's competence to carry out such tasks. Nearly 400 community-residing elderly rated 100 task examples along the dimensions of worry, intellectual vitality, everyday relevance, and competence. Such ratings are stable over time (Hayslip & Thomas, 1999). Not only were such ratings differentially related to level of education, health, and gender, but they also were differentially yet predictably related to measures of intellectual self-efficacy, needs for cognitive stimulation or activity, self-rated everyday cognitive difficulties, locus of control, and anxiety (Hayslip et al., 1995). This suggests that older persons worried *more* ($p < .05$) about their ability to perform everyday tasks, which tapped IADLs such as cooking, shopping, cleaning, money management, driving, accessing public transportation, dealing with health and legal matters, using the telephone, and remembering names, faces, figures of an everyday character. Moreover, they also ascribed *more* everyday importance (functionality) to such tasks, deemed them to be *more* critical to their intellectual health and vitality, and, surprisingly, felt *more* competent in their ability to complete such tasks well. All of these judgments were contrasted with nonecological measures of short-term memory, crystallized ability (Gc), and fluid ability (Gf). Moreover, additional data examining personality-ability relationships (Hayslip, 1988) and relationships between psychoneuroimmunological indicators of stress (cortisol, Epstein Barr virus) and intellectual performance or intellectual self-efficacy (Kelly & Hayslip, 2000; Kelly et al., 1998; Kelly, Hayslip, & Servaty, 1997; Kelly, Hayslip, Servaty, & Ennis, 1997) reinforce the conclusion that older adults do experience stress or anxiety when confronted with tasks that are either unfamiliar or difficult. These data also suggest that older persons are concerned about losing those skills that are intact at present. These studies involved community-residing samples of older persons who were in varying degrees worried about the loss of their skills.

The studies by Hayslip et al. (1995, 1996) in particular suggest that, relative to nonecological tasks, older persons not only estimate their everyday skills to be greater than they are, place more value on being able to perform such tasks well, and associate feelings of intellectual vitality with being able to perform such tasks. Individuals also worry more about being able to perform such tasks. Consequently, they are more concerned about skills that they place a greater value on in both an intellectual and an everyday sense, despite the fact they rate their ability to perform such tasks positively. This could easily also reflect an awareness of the fact that although their skills are still intact, older persons nevertheless worry about no longer being as skilled in the future.

More direct evidence regarding the relationship between anxiety and everyday skill has been gathered by the first author (Hayslip, Elias, Barta, & Henderson,

1998), who studied 77 community-residing older adults. The study found that persons who had greater concerns about their current and future levels of everyday functioning scored more poorly on several subscales of the Educational Testing Service (ETS) Basic Reading Skills, had lower self-rated IADLs, scored ($p <$ .01) more poorly on the Independent Living Scale (a performance-based measure of everyday skill; Loeb, 1996), and reported more everyday cognitive failures. Such persons also were more depressed, were more state anxious, and reported less intellectual self-efficacy. For persons with higher self-rated everyday task efficacy, these relationships were in the opposite direction.

In a separate study of 30 VA outpatients (Hayslip et al., 2000), these relationships were essentially replicated: Persons with more everyday task concerns and less everyday task self-efficacy performed more poorly on the Independent Living Scale (ILS), had lower self-reported IADLs, were more state anxious, and reported more everyday cognitive failures ($p < .05$). Collectively, these studies substantiate the basis for the relationship between concerns about everyday competence and everyday task performance among older persons, and provide a rationale for the implementation of a noncognitive intervention to enhance everyday skills.

Viewed from a cognitive-behavioral perspective, evidence for the impact of such interventions on everyday skills in older persons has been gathered by Hayslip, Galt, et al. (1998) who contrasted five-session ($1\frac{1}{2}$ hours/session) stress inoculation ($n = 39$) training with a waiting-list control condition ($n = 38$) regarding their impact on everyday skill, as assessed by ETS Basic Reading Skills Test, the ILS, and the Older Social Resources Scale (OARS) IADL scale (Fillenbaum, 1985). Hayslip, Elias, et al. (1998) found that the extent to which persons concerned about present and future declines in everyday functioning were anxious or depressed or self-efficacious interacted with the efficacy of stress inoculation (SI) rather than benefiting from practice. In this respect, it is important to note that the direction of such findings varied by whether everyday skill was assessed via self-reported IADLs (where ANOVAs indicated that persons in the SI condition with less perceived everyday skill evidenced improvement; see Galt, 1999). Moreover, persons in the SI group who had more present concerns about everyday skills reported improvements in IADLs; such persons also reported fewer everyday cognitive failures with training (Galt, 1999). In a hierarchical regression analysis, it was found that for some subtests of the ETS and the ILS (performance-based), an opposite pattern of training benefit was observed as it interacted with such individual differences (Hayslip, Elias, et al., 1998). In addition, for persons who were younger, male, less healthy, and less highly educated, training gains were greater (Hayslip, Galt, et al., 1998).

Regarding stress inoculation, some findings (Hayslip, Galt, et al., 1998) indicated that persons who, for example, are more depressed or preoccupied with decline may not utilize the cognitive restructuring and relaxation techniques as effectively as they might, and therefore do not evidence the same degree of everyday skill improvement. For such persons, more intensive training, a longer training program, or the provision of booster or supplemental training may be beneficial. In contrast, these results in part also suggest that some persons paradoxically may be more attuned to the possibility of decline in their everyday skills, and perhaps have taken steps to deal with such feelings (e.g., enrolling in a stress inoculation program). These persons may benefit more from such training.

Interestingly, there was some limited evidence to suggest that persons in the training group gained ($p < .07$) to a greater extent regarding an index of everyday self-efficacy (being able to teach others) relative to controls. There was also some evidence ($p < .09$) indicating that gains in generalized self-efficacy were greater in the training group. Retest effects were also substantial for present and future concerns about everyday competence.

Collectively, these data reinforce the salience of older persons' beliefs about the adequacy of their skills as an important correlate or determinant of not only more basic cognitive abilities, but also everyday living skills crucial to health and well-being. As such, they represent an important and meaningful extension of the CBT work as it applies to the treatment of depression, derived from the seminal work of Beck, Ellis, and Meichenbaum. As the Baby Boomer generation ages, education about the aging of one's skills and the development of accurate and rational, adaptive ways of thinking about one's skills are likely to be critical dimensions of future efforts to enhance the quality of life that such persons hopefully will enjoy as they age.

BEHAVIORAL INTERVENTIONS

As noted earlier, behavioral techniques are often used in concert with those that are cognitive in nature in the context of CBT. Obviously, the use of behavioral methods of intervention is not unique to older persons. Behaviorally oriented therapy focuses on the immediate, observable consequences of stimulus-response contingencies in the environment (Hoyer, 1973) and is most often used in an institutional, inpatient setting, where control over reinforcers (rewards) and those behaviors one wants to change is more likely. According to this approach, application of a behavioral strategy requires three primary tasks be carried out: (1) a definition and assessment prior to intervention of the desired target behavior; (2) a reinforcer, defined as a stimulus, whose impact makes the desired behavior more frequent or of longer duration must be identified; this reinforcer may be self-administered, or administered by the therapist; and (3) the establishment of specific behavior-reinforcer contingencies.

Positively reinforcing stimuli, which lead to pleasurable events, negatively reinforcing stimuli, which provide relief from aversive events, or punishing stimuli, which decrease the frequency of a behavior by providing unpleasant consequences, may all be used for the purpose of defining such contingencies. Zarit and Zarit (1998) note the appeal of behavior therapy to older persons in terms of identifying definable outcomes and the ease in implementing behavior change in gradual, incremental steps, each of which are readily understandable to most older persons. Behavior therapy has proven useful in treating a variety of problem difficulties that involve both excesses (wandering, agitation, incontinence) and deficits (isolation, lack of self-care, exercise; see Knight, 2004; Zarit & Zarit, 1998). Another technique that can be utilized by the behaviorist involves positively reinforcing a behavior that competes with the unwanted target behavior (e.g., rewarding self-care behaviors that compete with aggressive behaviors). Contracting is a form of behavior modification; the older client and therapist arrive at a mutually agreed upon, clearly specified goal. Being able to jointly define this goal may in itself promote a sense of control and independence for some elderly persons (see Zarit & Zarit, 1998).

Extensive discussions of behavioral techniques with the aged can be found in Hussian (1986) and Zeiss and Steffen (1996); they demonstrate that benefits can be readily documented and measured. Behavior therapy can be readily carried out and understood by staff if they are trained in its use (Zeiss & Steffen, 1996). Relative to drug therapy and aversive behavioral interventions (e.g., time-out procedures), positive behavioral interventions, such as reinforcing the individual if an inappropriate behavior has not occurred, are more acceptable to older persons (Burgio & Sinnott, 1990). Behavior therapy can also be tailored to the individual patient. Behavioral procedures are relatively brief and economical; however, they require a great deal of expertise to use effectively, and their use can create some ethical questions, particularly when used with impaired, institutionalized or isolated older adults. Indeed, there is ample, well-designed research to support the efficacy of behavioral techniques in dealing with a variety of behavior problems (Smyer, Zarit, & Qualls, 1990; Zeiss & Steffen, 1996). For example, and as noted earlier, overly dependent interactions with other elderly persons as well as with nursing home staff, incontinence, assertive behavior, withdrawal, inappropriate sexual behavior, wandering, anxiety, and poor self-care can all be treated behaviorally (Smyer et al., 1990). Many of these behaviors are a consequence of being institutionalized; they have been termed *excess disabilities* (Kahn & Miller, 1978).

INFORMATION PROCESSING

The information processing (IP) perspective (Sternberg, 1985) views the older person as an active processor of information contained in a problem or in the real world. Individuals develop logical operations and strategies by which to understand and analyze information presented to them. Those who support this approach focus on component processes that are a function of the interaction between task influences and person influences (Salthouse, 1992). Examples of component processes are encoding, storage, retrieval, rule formation, and pattern analysis. In addition to specific component processes, IP approaches assume the existence of an executive processor, which selects and supervises the use of these processes, and processing resources, referring to the energy or space available within the person to carry out cognitive operations or processes (Salthouse, 1992). Impairments with age in terms of speed or accuracy of performance may exist in each of these components required to process information. Generally speaking, age declines in intelligence (see Schaie, 2005), viewed from an IP perspective, are seen in terms of the speed, capacity, and efficiency of central processing resources (e.g., working memory, attention, processing speed; Salthouse, 1998). Ideally, by using an IP approach to intelligence, we may discover and foster the component skills that individuals of all ages may use on an everyday basis.

Sternberg (1985) argues that three aspects of intellectual functioning underlie our adaptive behavior, termed a triarchic theory of intelligence. The metacomponents of intelligence, which are executive processes, enable persons to plan what they are going to do, monitor while they are doing it, and evaluate it after it is done. More specific to the task are performance components, which are the actual mental operations (e.g., encoding, making inferences, making comparisons) people use to solve specific problems. A last dimension of intelligence is the knowledge acquisition component, which helps persons gain new knowledge. Separating new from old and relevant from irrelevant information in solving a problem and being able to form new knowledge by combining specific bits of information into a new "whole" are aspects of knowledge acquisition. For example, surgeons and lawyers must learn to recognize what is important and be able to put things together to form a theory about a legal case or make a diagnosis. Berg and Sternberg (1985) found younger adults to be superior in most metacomponents of intelligence a well as in the performance components. Older adults have more difficulty defining problems to be solved, managing their attention to solve problems, and monitoring solutions effectively. These skills may, however, improve with practice. Likewise, making inferences and combining and comparing information are impaired in older persons. It may be that the knowledge acquisition components that are based on experience do not decline with age, especially if they are critical in helping people to cope with new situations (Cunningham & Tomer, 1991).

The empirical literature on cognition viewed from an information processing perspective is extensive. In this context, a number of major explanations for declines in cognitive performance have been offered: (a) a slowing of the speed at which information is processed, (b) declines in working memory function, (c) increased inability to inhibit one's attention (and thus the allocation of one's processing processes) to irrelevant information, (d) sensory loss (see Park, 2000; Salthouse, 1999, 2006), and (e) impaired ability to refresh (rehearse) recently acquired information (Johnson, Reeder, Raye, & Mitchell, 2002; see Carstensen et al., 2006). Slowness in processing information, for example, is explained in terms of interference from efforts directed to process earlier tasks, on the assumption that information is processed in serial fashion (Salthouse, 1992). Thus, judgment and decision making may be impaired because older persons retrieve less information or process it less efficiently. Declines in working memory reflect the inability to actively process distinct types of sources of information that are presented simultaneously; the encoding, storage, and retrieval of such information suffers because both sources and tasks cannot be thoroughly and accurately processed together, leading to declines in performance on both. This basic deficit in processing resources is most apparent when material is presented quickly, when the task is complex, when multiple tasks must be solved simultaneously, when the efficient allocation of one's attention is critical, when stimuli (people, tasks, voices) or previously acquired associations that interfere with active processing (e.g., inhibiting a particular sequence of turns when one must take a new route to work), and when effortful processing (of new or complex material) is required (see Park, 2000; Salthouse, 1999, 2006). Tasks that minimize speed of processing, that are familiar to the older person (thereby minimizing inhibition of what is irrelevant), or that require less active or effortful processing (computation, recall, allocation of attention, necessary attention to detail) yield better performance. Impairments in sensory function with age (Lindenberger & Baltes, 1994) impact the initial registration of incoming information (e.g., raising the threshold beyond which information must pass to be further processed).

Taking an IP approach to intellectual functioning in late life, the Adult Development and Enrichment Project (ADEPT; Baltes & Willis, 1982) has demonstrated that the fluid ability (Gf) performance of older persons can be enhanced via cognitive skill training, emphasizing as criteria a hierarchical pattern of training transfer and its maintenance over time. In this respect, a study by Hayslip (1989) explored alternative means by which to enhance Gf performance, utilizing both ADEPT induction training and stress inoculation (see earlier discussion of CBT) approaches to changing Gf performance. This research suggested that (a) induction training and stress inoculation were both effective in enhancing Gf scores; (b) the range of training transfer to other measures of Gf was very narrow; and (c) training effects for the stress inoculation intervention seemed to vary with the difficulty of the task and persons' willingness to access the anxiety-coping techniques they had been taught to use with the Gf tasks. Underutilization of experimenter-provided strategies has been a problem in much memory training research (e.g., Hill & Vandervoort, 1992; Scogin & Bienias, 1988). These findings therefore suggest that both an information processing and a cognitive-behavioral perspective may be valuable in understanding how persons deal with losses in function with increased age.

THEORIES OF EMOTIONAL DEVELOPMENT AND EMOTIONAL REGULATION

Our awareness of our emotions, our ability to report them, and our skill in regulating them in the context of our own well-being and relationships with others are an important form of cognitive activity in later life. In this respect, the literature and interest in emotional development and emotional self-regulation are relatively recent, in contrast to that reflecting a cognitive-behavioral or information processing perspective on aging.

Emotional development across the life span has given rise to a large and complex literature. Like cognition and behavior, the bulk of this literature concurs that whereas some aspects of the emotion system remain stable, other dimensions of the experience and regulation of affect change to some extent with increasing age, with considerable interindividual variation possible in intraindividual trajectories. Three primary theories address the changing dynamics of emotion with age: Carstensen's (1995) socioemotional selectivity theory (SST), Labouvie-Vief's (1997) cognitive-affective developmental theory (CADT), and Magai's (Magai & Nussbaum, 1996) discrete emotions functionalist theory (DEFT), which is an adaptation and extension of differential emotions theory (Izard, 2004). We review here each of these three primary theories in the context of aging, assess the empirical support for each, and draw conclusions about their commonalities. Finally, we comment on other important contributions to emotional development in later life, including Lawton's research on affective experience in old age (e.g., Lawton, Kleban, Rajagopal, & Dean, 1992), Schulz and Heckhausen's (1997) control theory of emotion, and recent examinations of the emotional intelligence (EI) construct from a life span perspective (Chapman & Hayslip, in press; Kafetsios, 1994).

SOCIOEMOTIONAL SELECTIVITY THEORY

Carstensen's (1992, 1995) SST was originally formulated as a nonpathological alternative to disengagement theory (Cumming & Henry, 1961) and attempts to make explicit the links between social motives and affect regulation over the life span. Rather than viewing withdrawal from broad social involvement in later life as a sign of overall decline or depression, SST suggests that the narrowing of social networks in later years reflects an adaptive and normal aging pattern that is tied to emotional regulatory efforts. The theory proposes that social interaction across the life span is driven by three primary motives: information seeking, the development and preservation of self-esteem, and emotion regulation (Carstensen, 1992, 1995). Though all three motives are present throughout the life span, the relative importance of each changes at different points in life, resulting in corresponding changes observed in social patterns.

Early in life, individuals have had relatively fewer experiences and less time to acquire knowledge. Thus, one important role of social relationships through childhood and young adulthood is to provide one with access to novel experiences. As a result, social networks may consist of a broad array of acquaintances, and time and effort may be allocated to cultivating and maintaining a relatively wide range of social relationships (Carstensen, 1995). Not every member of this range of social contacts constitutes a deeply intimate or emotionally meaningful relationship, but maintaining a broad array of social contacts assures that new knowledge may be gleaned from the variety of unique experiences and viewpoints to which one has access. The development and maintenance of self-esteem assures throughout this time that select closer relationships, such as those with primary caregivers and influential mentors, will also be cultivated.

By midlife, however, SST postulates that the relative importance of knowledge acquisition goals subsides in relation to the importance of emotion regulation (e.g., Carstensen, 1995). Social networks may thus be pared down, with less time spent meeting new people or maintaining more superficial acquaintances. Coincident with this pruning of one's social network, the depth of existing close relationships is optimized, with relatively greater time devoted to intimate friendships and family relationships. This shift is thought to occur for at least two reasons: First, by midlife, many adults have gained a broad knowledge base about the world, both through their own and through others' life experiences; second, by midlife, individuals' perceptions of time shift subtly as they become more aware of a foreshortened future. Time begins to be framed in the context of years left to live, rather than years lived.

The narrowing of social networks and corresponding deepening of a select group of close relationships occurs in the service of the third primary social motive posited by SST: emotional regulation. Emotion regulation is successful to the extent that positive emotions are optimized and negative emotions minimized (Carstensen, 1995). With increased age, individuals spend more time and personal resources on relationships that optimize positive emotions and spend relatively less time on relationships that provoke or maintain negative moods, such as conflict-ridden relationships. Such relationships may be minimized or discarded. Shifts in the way information is sought out and processed may also occur, with relatively greater attention given to information likely to maintain or enhance positive affect, and selective inattention to or avoidance of information or situations likely to provoke negative apprehension, sadness, or other negative emotions (Löckenhoff & Carstensen, 2004).

Empirical evidence supports many of the tenets of SST. At a broad level, some longitudinal evidence suggests that positive affect may increase slightly with age (Mroczek, 2001; Mroczek & Kolarz, 1998), although the magnitude of such increases may be small at the population level. A large experience-sampling study found that older adults reported less negative affect than younger adults (Carstensen, Pasupathi, Mayr, & Nesselroade, 2000), and that positive affect persisted longer, whereas negative affect diminished more quickly, with age.

Although this study involved repeated measures over a week, the age comparisons were cross-sectional and thus may be partially explainable by cohort as well; this qualification applies to many of the studies reviewed in this section, the bulk of which have been cross-sectional. Studies on specific emotions indicate that older adults report less depression, anxiety, hostility, and shyness and greater contentedness than middle-aged or young adults (Lawton, Kleban, & Dean, 1993), although a study controlling for socially desirable reporting found that older adults scored lower than other ages only with respect to anger (Gibson, 1997). These studies, and others reviewed later, indicate only that affect is optimized in older individuals, without direct tests of the mechanisms through which this is achieved.

Other studies have specifically linked age-related differences in affective valence and emotion regulation to future time perceptions (FTP) and the characteristics of social networks. Indeed, the breadth versus depth of one's social network may be more specifically related to FTP than to chronological age, though the two clearly covary. For instance, when younger individuals are asked to imagine a foreshortened future, their preference is for similar rather than novel social partners, perhaps reflecting a greater priority for emotion regulation through close relationships rather than information acquisition (Carstensen & Fredricksen, 1998). Similarly, HIV-positive men further along in disease progression prioritized emotion-related over information-related social goals (Carstensen & Fredrickson, 1998). Other evidence suggests that asking older individuals to imagine themselves benefiting from a life-extending medical advance, and therefore extending FTP, may cause information-related goals to assume a higher level of importance (Fung, Carstensen, & Lutz, 1999). Thus, the relative primacy of emotion-regulatory versus information-seeking goals appears to be largely related to future time perception.

Empirical results also support the notion that differences in the balance of emotional to informational goals translate into meaningful differences in the size of one's social network. A 4-year longitudinal study of elderly individuals reported that close relationships were maintained with greater consistency than casual or novel relationships, and that individuals who perceived their own death as imminent preferred to spend time with family and close friends over other relationships (Lang, 2000). Lang and Carstensen (2002) found in a large cross-sectional study of German individuals ranging in age from young to late adulthood that perceptions of limited FTP were associated with smaller and more emotionally satisfying social networks; when individuals perceived considerable future time, less social strain was associated with social partners thought to convey greater knowledge. Of particular importance, FTP was highly correlated with chronological age, and therefore the same pattern of results obtained when using age, rather than FTP, as the primary predictor. Pasupathi and Carstensen (2003) also report that in the same 1-week experience-sampling study mentioned earlier, when participants engaged in mutual reminiscing, age was associated with greater positive affect, though the effect appeared specific to reminiscing about positive events.

On the whole, SST has accumulated a fairly broad evidence base, particularly for its more general hypothesis of affect optimization. However, extant evidence supports the notion that relationships serve a greater emotion regulatory function with age, and that changes in the size and depth of social networks with age reflect greater priority of emotionally meaningful goals.

Cognitive-Affective Developmental Theory

Labouvie-Vief's (1997) CADT conceptualizes changes in the experience and regulation of affect as a function of increasing cognitive sophistication and ego development. The emotional regulation and coping styles of young adults are largely influenced by social and culture conventions of appropriate behavior, a phase of development roughly paralleling Piagetian formal operations. However, as individuals approach middle age, their mode of emotional regulation becomes increasingly influenced by contextual factors, relativistic rather than absolutistic, and self-determined. Emotions become more salient and at the same time better modulated, a process both resulting from and driving increasing intrapsychic differentiation and self-integration (Labouvie-Vief, 1997).

Cognitive-affective developmental theory is similar to SST in predicting that age brings with it increased abilities to optimize positive affect, but it focuses somewhat more on coping and defensive styles as opposed to social networks (although changes in information processing of the sort that might inform coping and defensive processes are also posited to underlie age-related increases in emotional regulation in SST [e.g., Löckenhoff & Carstensen, 2004], and CADT also recognizes the effect of social, contextual, and relational factors on age-related optimization of positive emotion). This theory also deals with two primary modes of affect regulation. One involves optimizing positive emotions and minimizing negative ones. This ability does, indeed, appear to increase with age (Labouvie-Vief & Medler, 2002) and is related to the age-related increases in the use of more mature coping strategies that permit the tolerance of ambiguity, restrain maladaptive impulses, and involve less reality distortion (Diehl, Coyle, & Labouvie-Vief, 1996). In this respect, Labouvie-Vief's work coincides with a fundamental premise of SST but represents an explication of the emotional processes coinciding with at least three noteworthy psychodynamic theorists. Cognitive-affective developmental theory notes the increasing maturity of ego defenses across the life span documented by George Vaillant (1993), is similar to Loevinger's (1976) theory of ego development in its conception of movement from socially conventional to integrated and autonomous self-regulation, and adopts Haan's (1977) distinction between coping processes (adaptive responses) and defensive processes (maladaptive or reality-distorting responses). However, CADT does note that affect optimization is not strictly an intrapsychic process, as it is strongly tied to relationship quality (Labouvie-Vief & Medler, 2002).

The second primary mode of emotion regulation involves increases in cognitive-affective complexity (Labouvie-Vief, 1997). Such increasing complexity consists of simultaneously tolerating competing or differentially valenced affects, experiencing the blending of different affects, and implementing flexible self-regulation strategies that permit the tolerance of ambiguity. These skills coincide with greater cognitive complexity. This process may peak at midlife, with declines in affective complexity in old age (Labouvie-Vief, Chiodo, Goguen, Diehl, & Orwoll, 1995; Labouvie-Vief, Diehl, Chiodo, & Coyle, 1995). Considerable individual differences may exist in the extent to which individuals successfully develop or tolerate greater cognitive-affective complexity.

Several studies have accumulated from the work of Labouvie-Vief and her colleagues supporting the tenets of CADT. An early qualitative study of the narratives of young and middle-aged adults suggested that younger individuals implement more crude affect strategies in managing their affect, and middle-aged adults were more tolerant of complex blends of feelings and less governed by social norms and conventions (Labouvie-Vief, DeVoe, & Buka, 1989). As noted earlier, subsequent empirical work found peaks in affective complexity in middle age (Labouvie-Vief, Chiodo, et al., 1995; Labouvie-Vief, Diehl, et al., 1995) and increasing sophistication and maturity of coping and defenses with age. Evidence also exists that affect optimization and affect complexity are separate but related modes of affect regulation influenced respectively by relational and socioeconomic status and education (Labouvie-Vief & Medler, 2002). These data also suggest that cognitive-affective integration is tied to cognitive complexity; the former is associated with family variables, the latter primarily with education.

On the whole, these studies provide support for the notion that aging may involve increases in cognitive-affective complexity that are at least partially attributable to cognitive maturation, and that this intrapsychic differentiation, along with affect optimization, improves the maturity, flexibility, and effectiveness of coping. Labouvie-Vief and colleagues' work is often elegantly complex, attempting to measure and model relations between many elements of psychic and interpersonal functioning.

DIFFERENTIAL EMOTIONS THEORY AND DISCRETE EMOTIONS
FUNCTIONALIST THEORY

Differential emotions theory (DET; Izard, 2004) and its elaboration, discrete emotions functionalist theory (DEFT; Magai & Nussabaus, 1997; Magai & Halpern, 2001; Magai & Haviland-Jones, 2002; Malatesta & Wilson, 1988), each arrive at conclusions about age-related increases in the complexity of emotional experience similar to SES and CADT, but begin from a different focal point. Differential emotions theory was first introduced by Carol Izard to explain the building blocks and functional mappings of human emotions, rooted in Tompkins's (1962, 1963) affect theory and espousing some of the same principles of emotion originally articulated by Darwin (1872/1965). Although DET dealt extensively with early developmental processes, its adult development and aging component was relatively less emphasized, with some exceptions (Dougherty, Abe, & Izard, 1996; Izard & Ackerman, 1997). Carol Magai (Magai & Haviland-Jones, 2002; Magai & Nussbaum, 1997; Malatesta & Wilson, 1988) developed DEFT as a life span-oriented extension of DET, focusing on the dynamics and longitudinal course of discrete emotions, particularly as they pertain to personality organization and change.

Differential emotions theory taxonomizes human emotional experience by distinguishing interest, joy, anger, sadness, fear, surprise, and disgust as seven qualitatively discrete emotional states that exist practically since birth and therefore are originally independent of cognitive development (Izard, 2004). Each emotion has a neural-evaluative component, involving the physiological structures and functions necessary for the production and recognition of that emotion, an expressive component that involves the vocal, facial, and other nonverbal characteristics of each particular emotion, and an experiential component that includes cognition and motivational properties associated with each emotion. Four emotions develop slightly later because they are more contingent on early, basic cognitive operations such as self-other distinctions: contempt, shame, shyness, and guilt.

These discrete emotions serve important motivational processes, which, from an evolutionary perspective, are adaptive (Malatesta & Wilson, 1988). For instance, fear is elicited by the perception of danger and prompts fight or flight. Anger is elicited by the frustration of goals and motivates actions intended to remove the offending impediment. Surprise serves to alert an organism to the presence of novel or previously unencountered stimuli and motivates curiosity and exploratory behavior. Commensurate with cognitive development, such specific affects become attached to certain thoughts, forming ideoaffective structures. Complex emotional states may be characterized by blends of discrete emotions and multiple interacting ideoaffective structures. For example, social anxiety may be a combination of fear, shame, shyness, and the bundle of thoughts, memories, and images associated with each. Depression may involve a blend of sadness and guilt, possibly with an absence of joy. The absence or surfeit of certain affect(s) in various forms of psychopathology are considered by Malatesta and Wilson in considerable detail, along with their developmental antecedents and consequents.

As individuals age, the fundamental experience or feeling state of basic emotions remains constant, but the network of associations, thoughts, and memories associated with each discrete emotion—the ideoaffective structures—grow more complex (Dougherty et al., 1996). In this sense, DET dovetails with CADT's emphasis on increasing cognitive-affective complexity with age. The former emphasizes, however, that the motivational properties and valence of given emotions remain stable as a means of preserving the coherence of experience. This constancy thus has an adaptive value for older persons, because the same class of stimuli will elicit the same emotion, which in turn retains the same conative properties at different points throughout the life span (Dougherty et al., 1996).

Premised on DET, DEFT articulates the developmental implications of the functional, motivational, and organizing properties of specific emotions from the perspective of dynamic systems theory (Magai & Nussbaum, 1997). Beginning from early childhood, certain external stimuli that reliably elicit certain specific affects tend to be experienced more frequently than others, leading to the repeated experience of selected specific affects more often (and possibly with greater intensity) than others. For instance, the repeated expression of parental contempt may elicit chronic shame, and the frequent experience of danger—as in the case of an unsafe or abusive environment—may elicit recurring fear. These affects, and the ideation associated with them, begin to grow entrenched in conscious experience, and their habitual presence motivates corresponding behavioral responses. These behavioral routines become repeatedly linked to ideoaffective structures and can help to perpetuate the experience of specific emotions. For instance, habitual fear and shyness may galvanize socially inhibited behavior, which becomes stable and reinforces further fear and shyness. As a result of this repetitive experience, certain discrete emotions become crystallized within personality itself, come to organize experience, and maintain personality coherence (Magai & Nussbaum, 1997; Malatesta & Wilson, 1988).

When added to DET's emphasis on the constancy of the valence or basic qualitative feeling state of specific emotions, DEFT's propositions about personality coherence seem to imply increasing stability, with age, of specific affects and the personality structures ultimately maintained by them. Indeed, the crystallization of discrete emotions within the personality system, if it proceeds uninterrupted, may result in highly stable enduring affects throughout the life span (Malatesta & Wilson, 1988). However, although certain affects may predominate consciousness by virtue of their habitual or chronic elicitation and experience, the increasing complexity of ideoaffective structures also permits increasing sophistication in the management of negative affects with age. Discrete emotions functionalist theory also articulates a set of mechanisms through which such stability may be interrupted and with which dynamic change in personality may occur, even into later life.

Based on the principles of dynamic systems theory, DEFT proposes that the equilibrium of personality may be interrupted by sudden changes within an individual self-system that, even if apparently small, may have far-reaching effects (Magai & Nussbaum, 1997). More important, these changes are typically characterized by a high intensity of emotional experience, are often interpersonal in nature, and may result in sudden, discontinuous, or salutatory—rather than gradual—personality change. A classic example is sudden religious conversion, which is characterized by an intensely moving episode of personal clarity, followed by a thorough reevaluation of core organizing beliefs and attendant alteration in behavior.

According to DEFT, such radical changes in personality are likely to occur in the presence of an intense atypical experience and are closely linked to the specific emotion of surprise (or shock, a variant of surprise; Magai & Haviland-Jones, 2002; Magai & Nussbaum, 1997). Although the experience eliciting surprise or shock may be negative, such as in the case of a trauma, experiences evoking intense positive emotions may also catalyze a "phase shift" in the personality system. However, a highly salient, affectively charged experience alone is not enough to instigate sudden change. The experience must, according to DEFT, also be followed by the temporary suspension of thoughts and beliefs typifying one's old worldview. Subsequent to this, an individual must experience a period of exploration in which alternative worldviews, self-views, and perceptions are entertained. These events must occur in an interpersonal context conducive to change, such as a supportive social network, if such change is to be sustained. Finally, openness to change and the capacity to introspect facilitate this process. Thus, whereas sudden personality reorganization is the product of an initial affective perturbation of great magnitude, sequelae of this perturbation include one's cognitive and interpersonal systems. Magai and Haviland-Jones provide an interesting and explicit exploration of this dynamic-systems conceptualization with respect to both personality change induced by psychotherapy and general personality change.

In addition to allowing for precipitous change in personality, DEFT also suggests that personality change may be gradual, but is again catalyzed by emotional experience. In the case of gradual change, the capacity to introspect and reflect on one's emotional experience is still seen as critically important. A supportive interpersonal context remains essential to gradual change, and major life events that are interpersonal—regardless of whether they are experienced as positive or negative—may hold greater power as catalyzing agents of personality change than noninterpersonal events.

At least three studies provide some support for the theses of DET and DEFT. With respect to the increasing ideoaffective complexity supposed by DET, in addition to some of Labouvie-Vief's work, the Carstensen et al. (2000) experience-sampling study found evidence at least for increasing complexity in emotional experience with age. Although it was cross-sectional, intraindividual factor analyses of specific emotions over a weeklong period found that more factors were required to characterize the emotional experience of older individuals. Substantively, this suggests that age (or cohort), on average, brings with it a greater complexity of affective experience, although the study did not attempt to assess ideoaffective structures per se.

Another study tested DET's postulate of the stability of discrete emotions. Izard, Libero, Putnam, and Haynes (1993) found a strong degree of rank-order stability in the 11 basic emotions during a 3-year period after childbirth in a group of middle-class mothers, with stability coefficients for all emotions except guilt above .69 or .70. Guilt evidenced a stability coefficient of .50. Note that these stability coefficients likely underestimated the true degree of stability, because they include measurement error and therefore have, as an upper bound, the test-retest reliability of the scale itself (cf. McCrae & Costa, 2003). As measurement error attenuates stability correlations, these results are even more supportive of the notion that discrete emotions remain relatively stable, in rank order within a population, over time. Although the mothers were on average on 30.1 years old, this degree of stability at such an early point in the life span suggests, if anything, greater stability in later years, given that the leveling off of personality change does not begin until midlife (Roberts & DelVecchio, 2000). In Izard and colleagues' study, however, mean levels of disgust, contempt, shyness, and shame decreased steadily from the period right after childbirth to a period 2 years later. The authors note the considerable social and hormonal changes associated with childbirth which may have affected these emotions, but in the broader context of DET, one might interpret this as evidence of small increments in emotion regulatory ability, given that all four emotions are aversive and decreased in frequency over time. Finally, with respect to emotion-personality correlations, positive emotions tended to be strongly associated with the trait of extraversion and negative emotions strongly associated with neuroticism. Izard and colleagues interpreted this as support for the thesis that personality traits are organized around the experience of specific affects.

Thus, the overall findings from this complex study suggest that discrete emotions accounted for large amounts of variance in the neuroticism and extraversion traits, that specific emotions have a high degree of stability within a sample of relatively younger women for 3 years after a significant event, and that this rank-order consistency is combined with mean level decreases in certain negative emotions. Indeed, these emotions may have been heightened by the childbirth experience and regressed toward their mean by the follow-up period. From the perspective of DEFT, childbirth may have represented a systemic perturbation accompanied by relatively more intense affect, although this was not the focus or interpretation of Izard et al. (1993).

Finally, Malatesta-Magai (1999) conducted an 8-year longitudinal study in which she assessed several emotional dispositions, other elements of personality, and individuals' perceptions of emotionally significant life events in a sample of 63 late-middle-age adults (mean age of 63). Again, stability coefficients for emotions of anxiety, depression, interest, anger, and aggression suggested moderate stability, particularly given the 8-year range of the study and attenuating effect of measurement error; they ranged from .47 to .75. Changes in personality were associated with significant interpersonal events such as marriage and divorce, but not with major changes such as career shifts in which close relationships were not involved. This study offers some support for DEFT's notion that personality change can occur, even well into later life (a finding now supported by groups formerly suggesting strong stability; cf. Terraciano, McCrae, Brand, & Costa, 2005), and that such changes are a function of emotionally significant events with interpersonally meaningful components.

OTHER CONTRIBUTIONS TO EMOTIONAL DEVELOPMENT IN LATER LIFE

Other researchers have also presented informative theory and data about emotional development in later life. Richard Schulz and Jutta Heckhausen (1997) proposed a control theory of emotion predicated on the notion that people desire, at a fundamental level, to have control over their environment throughout the life span. However, they distinguish between two types of control: primary and secondary. Primary control strivings involve instrumental activities designed to change, maintain, or arrange the exterior world in a desired way. Secondary control strivings involve altering one's internal perspective in an effort to adapt to external circumstances. Both forms of control may operate in a selective fashion, directing individuals toward certain modes of acting on the environment (primary) or viewing goals (secondary control), or in a compensatory form such as seeking assistance from another person when faced with an external problem (primary), or making the decision to disengage from the pursuit of a goal (secondary).

Primary and secondary control strivings are elicited in different measure and in different forms by emotional experience and affectively salient events (Schulz & Heckhausen, 1997). Emotions may vary in kind, intensity, general valence, duration, or any combination of these, evoking varying types and degrees of primary and secondary control efforts. In general, primary control efforts increase throughout childhood and adolescence, peaking in early adulthood, and then begin to decline in old age, when physical and functional limitations may decrease one's ability to act instrumentally on one's environment. Secondary control efforts continue to rise gradually throughout the life span, increasing into old age at the same time primary control strivings decline. Schulz and Heckhausen suggest that around middle age, the relative preference for primary over secondary control begins to shift gradually, with secondary control being preferred gradually more and more as one progresses through the second half of one's life.

M. Powell Lawton published a series of empirically driven papers on emotion across the life span in the early 1990s that lend general support to the consensus among SES, CADT, and DEFT that emotional regulation probably improves over the life span. For instance, Lawton, Kleban, Rajagopal, et al. (1992) found that older adults reported better emotional control and more stable moods than middle-aged or younger adults, and less physiological responsiveness than these two groups. However, two additional studies conducted by Lawton's group suggest interesting specific patterns of emotion in older adults. Lawton, Kleban, Dean, Rajagopal, and Parmelee (1992) examined the factor structure of a brief measure of positive and negative affect, the Philadelphia Geriatric Center Positive and Negative Affect scales, finding that comparable positive and negative affect factors characterized healthy young, middle-aged, and older adults. But differences emerged between healthy and sick older adults in the factor structure of their measure. This suggests that the pattern of correlation between affect terms such as anxious, depressed, elated, and content varied meaningfully in older adults of differing health status. Substantively, the implication is that illness in old age may impact the interrelations between different specific emotions. Lawton, DeVoe, and Parmelee (1995) had 79 residents of a nursing home complete their affect measure and record daily events for a 30-day period. Findings indicated that affect varied over time as a function of events, with events of different valence producing mood-congruent fluctuations. This event-mood congruent variation characterized both the depressed and the nondepressed elders. In sum, Lawton's work supports the thesis that emotion regulation improves with age but offers at least two important qualifications: First, that the structure of affect in elderly persons may vary as a function of physical illness, and second, that despite reports of general improvement in mood regulations, older adults in a nursing home setting do experience expected variation in positive and negative affect commensurate with daily events, whether they are depressed or not.

A final relevant area that has only recently begun to be integrated into the general literature on emotional development in adulthood and later life is emotional intelligence (EI). Emotional intelligence was originally proposed as an individual differences construct pertaining to the skill or ability with which one could appraise, regulate, and perceive one's own and others' emotions (Salovey & Mayer, 1990). A torrent of research and theory followed, with suggested applications typically outstripping evidence at the same time EI researchers often failed to incorporate other relevant "non-EI" emotion literatures into their work; Matthews, Zeidner, and Roberts (2002) provide a review of these developments from 1990 to 2002, and Matthews, Roberts, and Zeidner (2004) objectively summarize the state of EI research. One of the central tenets of EI theory was that EI skills would improve with age as a function of life experience and socialization, but the focus of this proposition had been largely confined to the period from childhood through young adulthood until Werner Schaie (2001) called for research on EI later in the life span, and at midlife in particular. Subsequently, Kafetsios (1994) conducted a cross-sectional study in which he reported that middle-aged to late-middle-aged adults scored higher on a quasi-objective performance task of EI than young adults in the areas of understanding and managing emotions, as well as using emotions to facilitate cognition. In another study, Chapman and Hayslip (in press) found that, contrary to the differentiation sometimes observed for cognitive ability at midlife, the same dimensional structure of emotion appraisal, optimistic mood regulation, and emotional utilization characterized both middle-aged and younger adults' responses to a self-report EI instrument, but that older adults reported greater use of optimistic thinking to regulate their mood than did younger adults, controlling for measurement error. This difference existed even when the affectively oriented personality traits of neuroticism and optimism were controlled and, as they note, is generally consistent with SES, CADT, and DEFT indications of improved mood regulatory ability with age.

Despite these two studies, much research remains to be done on the life span developmental antecedents and consequents of the EI construct, and considerable work must occur to integrate EI research in the broader framework of aging and emotion throughout the life span.

In light of the relative newness of this emerging application of cognitive theory to later life, though the intricacies of SST, CADT, DET, and DEFT may vary, it is interesting that some higher order consensus exists with respect to age-related improvements in affect regulation, and possibly in the complexity or sophistication of emotion. Broadly speaking, most empirical work supports such a consensus. The literature on adult development and aging in emotion is complex and varied, however. The interested reader is referred to more detailed discussions, in chapter form, in Magai and Halpern (2001), and in volume form in Schaie and Lawton (1997) and Magai and McFadden (1996).

REFERENCES

Ackerman, P. (1986). Individual differences in information processing: An investigation of intellectual abilities and task performance during practice. *Intelligence, 10,* 101–139.

Ackerman, P. (1987). Individual differences in skill learning: An integration of psychonomic and information processing approaches. *Psychological Bulletin, 102,* 3–27.

Bäckman, L., & Dixon, R. A. (1992). Psychological compensation: A theoretical framework. *Psychological Bulletin, 112,* 259–283.

Baltes, P. B. (1993). The aging mind: Potential and limits. *Gerontologist, 33,* 580–594.

Baltes, P. B. (1997). On the incomplete architecture of human ontogency: Selection, optimization, and compensation as foundation of developmental theory. *American Psychologist, 52,* 366–380.

Baltes, P. B., & Willis, S. L. (1982). Plasticity and enhancement of intellectual functioning in old age: Penn State's Adult Development and Enrichment Project (ADEPT). In F. I. M. Craik & S. E. Trehub (Eds.), *Aging and cognitive processes* (pp. 353–389). New York: Plenum Press.

Beck, A. T. (1987). Cognitive models of depression. *Journal of Cognitive Psychotherapy: An International Quarterly, 1,* 5–37.

Berg, C., & Sternberg, R. (1985). A triarchic theory of intellectual development during adulthood. *Developmental Review, 5,* 353–389.

Bieman-Copland, S., Ryan, E., & Cassano, J. (1998). Responding to the challenges of late life: Strategies for maintaining and enhancing competence. In D. Pushkar, W. Bukowski, A. Schwartzman, D. Stock, & D. White (Eds.), *Improving competence across the life span* (pp. 141–158). New York: Plenum Press.

Blanchard-Fields, F. (1986). Reasoning in adolescents and adults on social dilemmas varying in emotional saliency: An adult developmental perspective. *Psychology and Aging, 1,* 325–333.

Brockner, J. (1983). Low self-esteem and behavioral plasticity. In L. Wheeler & P. Shaver (Eds.), *Review of Personality and Social Psychology, 4,* 237–271.

Burgio, L., & Sinnott, J. (1990). Behavioral treatments and pharmacotherapy: Acceptability ratings by elderly individuals in residential settings. *Gerontologist, 30,* 811–816.

Carstensen, L. L. (1992). Social and emotional patterns in adulthood: Support for socioemotional selectivity theory. *Psychology and Aging, 7,* 331–338.

Carstensen, L. L. (1995). Evidence for a lifespan theory of socioemotional selectivity. *Current Directions in Psychological Science, 4,* 151–156.

Carstensen, L. L., & Fredrickson, B. (1998). Influence of HIV status and age on cognitive representations of others. *Health Psychology, 17,* 494–503.

Carstensen, L. L., Mikels, J., & Mather, M. (2006). Aging and the intersection of cognition, motivation, and emotion. In J. E. Birren & K. W. Schaie (Eds.), *Handbook of the psychology of aging* (6th ed., pp. 343–362). San Antonio, TX: Academic Press.

Carstensen, L. L., Pasupathi, M., Mayr, U., & Nesselroade, J. R. (2000). Emotional experience in everyday life across the adult life span. *Journal of Personality and Social Psychology, 79,* 644–655.

Carter, J. (1998). *The virtues of aging.* New York: Ballantine Books.

Chapman, B. P., & Hayslip, B. (in press). Emotional intelligence in young and middle adulthood: A cross sectional analysis of latent structure and means. *Psychology and Aging.*

Cumming, E., & Henry, W. E. (1961). *Growing old: The process of disengagement.* New York: Basic Books.

Cunningham, W. R., & Tomer, A. (1991). Intellectual abilities and age: Concepts, theories, and analysis. In E. Lovelace (Ed.), *Aging and cognition: Mental processes, self awareness, and interventions* (pp. 379–406). Amsterdam: North Holland.

Darwin, C. E. (1965). *The expression of emotion in man and animals.* Chicago: University of Chicago Press. (Original work published 1872)

Diehl, M. (1995, November). *Everyday competence in later life: What we know and don't know.* Paper presented at the Gerontological Society of America Conference, Los Angeles.

Diehl, M. (1998). Everyday competence in later life: Current status and future directions. *Gerontologist, 38,* 422–433.

Diehl, M., Coyle, N., & Labouvie-Vief, G. (1996). Age and sex differences in strategies of coping and defense across the life span. *Psychology and Aging, 11,* 127–139.

Dougherty, L. M., Abe, J. A., & Izard, C. E. (1996). Differential emotions theory and emotional development in adulthood and later life. In C. Magai & S. H. McFadden (Eds.). *Handbook of emotion, adult development, and aging* (pp. 27–41). San Diego, CA: Academic Press.

Ellis, A. (1962). *Reason and emotion in psychotherapy.* New York: Lyle Stuart.

Ellis, A., & Velton, E. (1998). *Optimal aging.* Beru, IL: Open Court Publishing.

Fillenbaum, G. G. (1985). Screening the elderly: A brief instrumental activities of daily living measure. *Journal of the American Geriatrics Society, 33,* 698–706.

Fung, H. H., Carstensen, L. L., & Lutz, A. M. (1999). Choosing social partners: How old age and anticipated endings make people more selective. *Psychology and Aging, 14,* 595–604.

Gallagher-Thompson, D., Hanley-Peterson, P., & Thompson, L. W. (1990). Maintenance of gains versus relapse following brief psychotherapy for depression. *Journal of Consulting and Clinical Psychology, 58,* 371–374.

Galt, C. (1999, August). *Impact of stress inoculation on performance efficacy linked to instrumental activities of daily living.* Unpublished doctoral dissertation, University of North Texas.

Gibson, S. J. (1997). The measurement of mood states in older adults. *Journal of Gerontology: Psychological Sciences, 52B,* P167–P174.

Haan, N. (1977). *Coping and defending, processes of self-environment organization.* New York: Academic.

Hayslip, B. (1988). Personality-ability relationships in the aged. *Journal of Gerontology, 43,* 79–84.

Hayslip, B. (1989). Alternative mechanisms for improvements in fluid ability performance in older adults. *Psychology and Aging, 4,* 122–124.

Hayslip, B., & Caraway, M. (1989). Cognitive therapy with aged persons: Implications for research design for its implementation and evaluation. *Journal of Cognitive Psychotherapy, 3,* 255–271.

Hayslip, B., Elias, J., Barta, J., & Henderson, C. (1998, April). *Perceptions of everyday skill and everyday task performance in older adults.* Paper presented at the biannual Cognitive Aging Conference, Atlanta, GA.

Hayslip, B., Galt, C., Lambert, P., Kelly, K., Elias, J., Barta, J., et al. (1998, November). *The impact of anxiety reduction training on everyday skill among older adults.* Paper presented at the annual scientific meeting of the Gerontological Society of America, Philadelphia.

Hayslip, B., Ratliff, L., Galt, C., Lane, B., Lane, M., Radika, L., et al. (2000, April). *Perceptions of everyday skill and everyday task performance in older adults: A replication.* Paper presented at the biannual Cognitive Aging Conference, Atlanta, GA.

Hayslip, B., Servaty, H., & Ward, A. (1996, April). *Perceptions of everyday and psychometric intelligence and ability performance among older adults.* Paper presented at the sixth annual Cognitive Aging Conference, Atlanta, GA.

Hayslip, B., Servaty, H., Ward, A., & Blackburn, J. (1995, November). *Toward a definition of cognition in later life.* Paper presented at the 1995 Gerontological Society of America Conference, Los Angeles.

Hayslip, B., & Thomas, P. (1999, August). *Stability of perceptions of intelligence among older adults.* Paper presented at the annual convention of the American Psychological Association, Boston.

Hess, T. (2006). Attitudes toward aging and their effects on behavior. In J. E. Birren & K. W. Schaie (Eds.), *Handbook of the psychology of aging* (6th ed., pp. 379–406). San Antonio, TX: Academic Press.

Hess, T., Auman, C., Colcombe, S., & Rahhal, T. (2003). The impact of stereotype threat on age differences in memory performance. *Journal of Gerontology: Psychological Sciences, 58B,* P3–P11.

Hill, R. D., & Vandervoort, D. (1992). The effects of state anxiety on recall performance in older learners. *Educational Gerontology, 18,* 597–605.

Hoyer, W. (1973). Application of operant techniques to the modification of elderly behavior. *Gerontologist, 13,* 18–22.

Hussian, R. A. (1986). Severe behavior problems. In L. Teri & P. Lewinsohn (Eds.), *Geropsychological assessment and treatment* (pp. 121–143). New York: Springer.

Izard, C. E. (2004). *The psychology of emotions.* New York: Plenum Press.

Izard, C. E., & Ackerman, B. P. (1997). Emotions and self-concepts across the life span. In M. P. Lawton (Series Ed.) & K. W. Schaie (Vol. Ed.), *Annual review of gerontology and geriatrics: Focus on emotion and adult development* (Vol. 17, pp. 1–26). New York: Springer.

Izard, C. E., Libero, D. Z., Putnam, P., & Haynes, M. O. (1993). Stability of emotion experiences and their relations to traits of personality. *Journal of Personality and Social Psychology, 64,* 847–860.

Jette, A. (1995). Disability trends and transitions. In R. Binstock & L. George (Eds.), *Handbook of aging and social sciences* (pp. 94–117). San Antonio, TX: Academic Press.

Johnson, M. K., Reeder, J. A., Raye, C. L., & Mitchell, K. J. (2002). Second thoughts versus second looks: an age-related deficit in reflectively refreshing just activated information. *Psychological Science, 15,* 208–214.

Kafetsios, K. (1994). Attachment and emotional intelligence abilities across the life course. *Personality and Individual Differences, 37,* 129–145.

Kahn, R., & Miller, N. (1978). Assessment of altered brain function in the aged. In M. Storandt, I. Siegler, & M. Elias (Eds.). *The clinical psychology of aging* (pp. 43–69). New York: Plenum Press.

Kelly, K., & Hayslip, B. (2000). Gains in fluid ability performance and their relationship to cortisol. *Experimental Aging Research, 26,* 153–158.

Kelly, K., Hayslip, B., Hobdy, J., Servaty, H., Ennis, M., & Pavur, R. (1998). The relationship of cortisol to practice-related gains in intelligence. *Experimental Aging Research, 24,* 217–230.

Kelly, K. S., Hayslip, B., & Servaty, H. (1997). Psychoneuroendocrinological indicators of stress and intellectual performance among older adults: An exploratory study. *Experimental Aging Research, 22,* 393–401.

Kelly, K., Hayslip, B., Servaty, H., & Ennis, M. (1997). Physiological indicators of stress and intellectual performance among anxious older adults. *Educational Gerontology, 23,* 69–79.

Kemp, B. J., & Mitchell, J. (1992). Functional assessment in geriatric mental health. In J. E. Birren, R. B. Sloane, & G. D. Cohen (Eds.), *Handbook of mental health and aging* (pp. 672–698). New York: Academic Press.

Knight, B. (2004). *Psychotherapy with older adults.* Thousand Oaks, CA: Sage.

Knight, B., Kaskie, B., Shurgot, G., & Dave, J. (2006). Improving the mental health of older adults. In J. E. Birren & K. W. Schaie (Eds.), *Handbook of the psychology of aging* (6th ed., pp. 407–424). San Antonio, TX: Academic Press.

Kooken, R., & Hayslip, B. (1984). The use of stress inoculation in the treatment of test anxiety in older students. *Educational Gerontology, 10,* 29–38.

Krause, N. (1997). The social context of competence. In S. L. Willis, K. W. Schaie, & M. Hayward (Eds.), *Societal mechanisms for maintaining competence in old age* (pp. 83–93). New York: Springer.

Labouvie-Vief, G. (1992). A neo-Piagetian perspective on adult cognitive development. In R. Sternberg & C. Berg (Eds.), *Intellectual development* (pp. 197–228). New York: Cambridge University Press.

Labouvie-Vief, G. (1997). Cognitive-emotional integration in adulthood. In M. P. Lawton (Series Ed.) & K. W. Schaie (Vol. Ed.), *Annual review of gerontology and geriatrics: Focus on emotion and adult development* (Vol. 17, pp. 207–237). New York: Springer.

Labouvie-Vief, G., Chiodo, L. M., Goguen, L. A., Diehl, M., & Orwoll, L. (1995). Representations of self across the life span. *Psychology and Aging, 10,* 404–415.

Labouvie-Vief, G., DeVoe, M., & Buka, D. (1989). Speaking about feelings: Conceptions of emotions across the life span. *Psychology and Aging, 4,* 425–437.

Labouvie-Vief, G., & Diehl, M. (2000). Cognitive complexity and cognitive-affective integration: Related or separate domains of adult development? *Psychology and Aging, 15,* 490–504.

Labouvie-Vief, G., Diehl, M., Chiodo, L. M., & Coyle, N. (1995). Representations of self and parents across the life span. *Journal of Adult Development, 2,* 207–222.

Labouvie-Vief, G., & Medler, M. (2002). Affect optimization and affect complexity: Modes and styles of regulation in adulthood. *Psychology and Aging, 17,* 571–588.

Laidlaw, K., Thompson, L., Dick-Siskin, L., & Gallagher-Thompson, D. (2003). *Cognitive behavior therapy with older people.* Hoboken, NJ: Wiley.

Lang, F. R. (2000). Endings and continuity of social relationships: Maximizing intrinsic benefits within personal networks when feeling near to death? *Journal of Social and Personal Relationships, 17,* 157–184.

Lang, F. R., & Carstensen, L. L. (2002). Time counts: Future time perspective, goals, and social relationships. *Psychology and Aging, 17,* 125–139.

Lawton, M. P., DeVoe, M. R., & Parmelee, P. (1995). Relationship of events and affect in the daily life of an elderly population. *Psychology and Aging, 10,* 469–477.

Lawton, M. P., Kleban, M. H., & Dean, J. (1993). Affect and age: Cross-sectional comparisons of structure and prevalence. *Psychology and Aging, 8,* 165–175.

Lawton, M. P., Kleban, M. H., Dean, J., Rajagopal, D., & Parmelee, P. A. (1992). The factorial generality of brief positive and negative affect measures. *Journal of Gerontology: Psychological Sciences, 47,* P228—P237.

Lawton, M. P., Kleban, M. H., Rajagopal, D., & Dean, J. (1992). Dimensions of affective experience in three age groups. *Psychology and Aging, 7,* 171–184.

Levy, B. (1996). Improving memory in old age by implicit self-stereotyping. *Journal of Personality and Social Psychology, 71,* 1092–1107.

Levy, B., Hausdorff, J., Hencke, R., & Wei, J. (2000). Reducing cardiovascular stress with positive self-stereotypes of aging. *Journal of Gerontology: Psychological Sciences, 55B,* P205–P213.

Lindenberger, U., & Baltes, P. (1994). Sensory functioning and intelligence in old age: A strong connection. *Psychology and Aging, 9,* 339–355.

Löckenhoff, C. E., & Carstensen, L. L. (2004). Socioemotional selectivity theory, aging, and health: The increasingly delicate balance between regulating emotions and making tough choices. *Journal of Personality, 72,* 1395–1423.

Loeb, P. (1996). *Independent Living Scales.* San Antonio, TX: Psychological Corporation.

Loevinger, J. (1976). *Ego development: Conceptions and theories.* San Francisco: Jossey Bass.

Magai, C., & Halpern, B. (2001). Emotional development during the middle years. In M. Lachman (Ed.), *Handbook of midlife development* (pp. 310–344). New York: Wiley.

Magai, C., & Haviland-Jones, J. M. (2002). *The hidden genius of emotion.* Cambridge, England: Cambridge University Press.

Magai, C., & McFadden, S. H. (1996). *Handbook of emotion, adult development, and aging.* New York: Academic Press.

Magai, C., & Nussbaum, B. (1996). Personality change in adulthood: Dynamic systems, emotions, and the transformed self. In C. Magai & S. H. McFadden (Eds.), *Handbook of emotion, adult development, and aging* (pp. 403–419). San Diego, CA: Academic Press.

Malatesta, C. Z., & Wilson, A. (1988). Emotion cognition interaction in personality development: A discrete emotions, functionalist analysis. *British Journal of Social Psychology, 27,* 91–112.

Malatesta-Magai, C. (1999). Personality change in adulthood: Loci of change and the role of interpersonal processes. *International Journal of Aging and Human Development, 49,* 339–352.

Marsiske, M., & Margrett, J. (2006). Everyday problem solving and decision making. In J. E. Birren & K. W. Schaie (Eds.), *Handbook of the psychology of aging* (6th ed., pp. 315–342). San Antonio, TX: Academic Press.

Matthews, G., Roberts, R. D., & Zeidner, M. (2004). Seven myths about emotional intelligence. *Psychological Inquiry, 15,* 179–196.

Matthews, G., Zeidner, M., & Roberts, R. D. (2002). *Emotional intelligence: Science and myth.* Cambridge, MA: MIT Press.

McCrae, R. R., & Costa, P. T. (2003). *Personality in adulthood.* New York: Guilford Press.

Meichenbaum, D. (1977). *Cognitive-behavior modification: An integrative approach.* New York: Plenum Press.

Meichenbaum, D. (1985). *Stress inoculation training*. New York: Pergamon Press.

Meichenbaum, D. (1989). *Stress inoculation training*. New York: Pergamon Press.

Mittelman, M., Ferris, S., Schulman, E., Steinberg, G., Ambinder, A., Mackell, J., et al. (1995). A comprehensive support program: Effect on depression in spouse caregivers of AD patients. *Gerontologist, 35,* 792–802.

Morrow-Howell, N., Hinterlong, J., & Sherraden, M. (2001). *Productive aging: Concepts and challenges.* Baltimore: Johns Hopkins University Press.

Mroczek, D. K. (2001). Age and emotion in adulthood. *Current Directions in Psychological Science, 10,* 87–90.

Mroczek, D. K., & Kolarz, C. M. (1998). The effect of age on positive and negative affect: A developmental perspective on happiness. *Journal of Personality and Social Psychology, 75,* 1333–1349.

Norem, J. K., & Cantor, N. (1986). Anticipatory and post hoc cushioning strategies: Optimism and defensive pessimism in "risky" situations. *Cognitive Therapy and Research, 10*(3), 347–362.

Park, D. (2000). The basic mechanisms accounting for age-related decline in cognitive function. In D. Park & N. Schwarz (Eds.), *Cognitive aging: A primer* (pp. 3–22). Philadelphia: Taylor & Francis.

Park, D., & Gutchess, A. (2000). Cognitive aging and everyday life. In D. Park & N. Schwarz (Eds.), *Cognitive aging: A primer* (pp. 217–232). Philadelphia: Taylor & Francis.

Pasupathi, M., & Carstensen, L. L. (2003). Age and emotional experience during mutual reminiscing. *Psychology and Aging, 18,* 430–442.

Poon, L., Welke, D., & Dudley, W. (1993). What is everyday cognition? In J. M. Puckett & H. W. Reese (Eds.), *Mechanisms of everyday cognition* (pp. 19–32). Hillsdale, NJ: Erlbaum.

Puder, R. (1988). Age analysis of cognitive behavioral group therapy for chronic pain outpatients. *Psychology and Aging, 3,* 204–207.

Roberts, B. W., & DelVecchio, W. F. (2000). The rank order consistency of personality from childhood to old age: A quantitative review of longitudinal studies. *Psychological Bulletin, 126,* 3–25.

Rowe, J. W., & Kahn, R. L. (1998). *Successful aging.* New York: Pantheon.

Salovey, P., & Mayer, J. D. (1990). Emotional intelligence. *Imagination, Cognition, and Personality, 9,* 185–211.

Salthouse, T. A. (1992). The information processing perspective on cognitive aging. In R. Sternberg & C. Berg (Eds.), *Intellectual development* (pp. 261–277). New York: Cambridge University Press.

Salthouse, T. A. (1995). Refining the concept of psychological compensation. In R. Dixon & L. Bäckman (Eds.), *Compensating for psychological deficits and declines* (pp. 21–34). Mahwah, NJ: Erlbaum.

Salthouse, T. A. (1998). Cognitive and information processing perspectives on aging. In I. Nordhus, G. VandenBos, S. Berg, & P. Fromholt (Eds.), *Clinical gerontology* (pp. 49–60). Washington, DC: American Psychological Association.

Salthouse, T. A. (1999). Pressing issues in cognitive aging. In N. Schwarz, D. Park, B. Knauper, & S. Sudman (Eds.), *Cognition, aging, and self reports* (pp. 185–200). Philadelphia: Taylor & Francis.

Salthouse, T. A. (2006). Theoretical issues in the psychology of aging. In J. E. Birren & K. W. Schaie (Eds.), *Handbook of the psychology of aging* (6th ed., pp. 3–13). San Antonio, TX: Academic Press.

Schaie, K. W. (1996). *Intellectual development in adulthood: The Seattle Longitudinal Study.* New York: Cambridge University Press.

Schaie, K. W. (2001). Emotional intelligence: Psychometric status and developmental characteristics—Comment on Roberts, Zeidner, and Matthews. *Emotion, 1,* 243–248.

Schaie, K. W. (2005). *Developmental influences on adult intelligence.* New York: Oxford University Press.

Schaie, K. W., & Lawton, M. P. (1997). *Annual review of gerontology and geriatrics: Vol. 17. Focus on emotion and adult development.* New York: Springer.

Schulz, R., & Heckhausen, J. (1996). A life span theory of successful aging. *American Psychologist, 51,* 702–714.

Schulz, R., & Heckhausen, J. (1997). Emotion and control: A life-span perspective. In M. P. Lawton (Series Ed.) & K. W. Schaie (Vol. Ed.), *Annual review of gerontology and geriatrics: Focus on emotion and adult development* (Vol. 17, pp. 185–205). New York: Springer.

Scogin, F., & Bienias, J. (1988). A three-year follow-up of older adult participants in a memory-skills training program. *Psychology and Aging, 3,* 334–337.

Smyer, M., Zarit, S., & Qualls, S. (1990). Psychological intervention with the aging individual. In J. E. Birren & K. W. Schaie (Eds.), *Handbook of the psychology of aging* (pp. 375–404). New York: Academic Press.

Sternberg, R. (1985). Cognitive approaches to intelligence. In B. B. Wolman (Ed.), *Handbook of human intelligence: Theories, measurements, and applications* (pp. 59–118). New York: Wiley.

Terraciano, A., McCrae, R. R., Brand, L. J., & Costa, P. T. (2005). Hierarchical linear modeling analyses of the NEO-PI-R scales in the Baltimore Longitudinal Study of Aging. *Psychology and Aging, 20,* 493–506.

Thompson, L. W., Coon, D. W., Gallagher-Thompson, D., Sommer, B., & Koin, D. (2001). Comparison of desipramine and cognitive/behavioral therapy in the treatment of elderly outpatients with mild to moderate depression. *American Journal of Geriatric Psychiatry, 9,* 225–240.

Thompson, L. W., Gallagher, D., & Breckenridge, J. (1987). Comparative effectiveness of psychotherapies for depressed elders. *Journal of Consulting and Clinical Psychology, 55,* 385–390.

Thompson, L. W., Gantz, F., Florsheim, M., Del Maestro, S., Rodman, J., Gallagher-Thompson, D., et al. (1991). Cognitive-behavioral therapy for affective disorders in the elderly. In W. Myers (Ed.), *New techniques in the psychotherapy of older clients* (pp. 3–20). Washington, DC: American Psychiatric Press.

Tompkins, S. S. (1962). *Affect, imagery, consciousness: Vol. 1. The positive affects.* New York: Springer.

Tompkins, S. S. (1963). *Affect, imagery, consciousness: Vol. 2. The negative affects.* New York: Springer.

Vaillant, G. E. (1993). *The wisdom of the ego.* Cambridge, MA: Harvard University Press.

Vaillant, G. E. (2002). *Aging well.* Boston: Little, Brown.

Whitbourne, S. K. (1987). Personality development in adulthood and old age: Relationships among identity style, health, and well-being. In K. W. Schaie & C. Eisdorfer (Eds.), *Annual review of gerontology and geriatrics* (pp. 189–216). New York: Springer.

Willis, S., Jay, G., Keihl, M., & Marsiske, M. (1992). Longitudinal change and prediction of everyday task competence in the elderly. *Research on Aging, 14,* 68–91.

Willis, S. L. (1991). Current issues in cognitive training research. In E. A. Lovelace (Ed.), *Aging and cognition: Mental processes, self-awareness and interventions* (pp. 263–280). Amsterdam: North-Holland.

Willis, S. L. (1996). Everyday competence in elderly persons: Conceptual issues and empirical findings. *Gerontologist, 36,* 595–601.

Willis, S. L., & Schaie, K. W. (1993). Everyday cognition: Taxonomic and methodological considerations. In J. M. Puckett & H. W. Reese (Eds.), *Mechanisms of everyday cognition* (pp. 33–53). Hillsdale, NJ: Erlbaum.

Zarit, S., & Zarit, J. (1998). *Mental disorders in older adults: Fundamentals of assessment and treatment.* New York: Guilford Press.

Zeiss, A., & Steffen, A. (1996). Behavioral and cognitive behavioral treatments: An overview of social learning. In S. Zarit & B. Knight (Eds.), *A guide to psychotherapy and aging* (pp. 35–60). Washington, DC: American Psychological Association.

CHAPTER 4

Personality Theories of Successful Aging

NATALIE C. EBNER and ALEXANDRA M. FREUND

IN THIS CHAPTER, we combine an action-theoretical view with a life span-developmental perspective on personality and successful aging to examine the role of goals and goal-related processes for adaptive development. One of the basic assumptions of this integration is that goals and goal-related processes motivate, organize, and direct behavior and development over time. By setting, pursuing, and maintaining goals, persons can actively shape their development in interaction with their given physical, cultural-historical, and social living context. This renders goals and goal-related processes central to personality and successful development across the life span as they constitute a link between the person and his or her life contexts over time.

We start this chapter by defining the concept of *successful development and aging.* Then we outline the concept of *personality* underlying our approach using McAdams's (1990, 1995) model of levels of personality. This model integrates dispositional traits, personal concerns and goals, and life narratives as three levels of personality. We discuss the notion of goals as personality-in-context by describing goals as dynamic aspects of personality reflecting the interaction of a person with his or her environment over time. Finally, to highlight the role of personal goals for successful development, we present three prominent conceptual frameworks of developmental regulation: the model of selection, optimization, and compensation (P. B. Baltes & Baltes, 1990), the dual-process model of coping (Brandtstädter & Renner, 1990), and the model of primary and secondary control (Heckhausen & Schulz, 1995).

WHAT IS SUCCESSFUL DEVELOPMENT?

On a very broad level, current life span-developmental psychology often describes adaptive (or successful) development as a lifelong process of generating new resources as well as adjusting to physical, social, and psychological changes with the overall aim to simultaneously maximize developmental gains and minimize developmental losses (M. M. Baltes & Carstensen, 1996; P. B. Baltes, 1997; P. B. Baltes & Baltes, 1990; Brandtstädter, 1986; Labouvie-Vief, 1981). At present, however, the literature offers no commonly accepted set of criteria that defines successful aging on a more specific level. As elaborated by Freund and Riediger (2003), different authors make different suggestions regarding criteria for successful development in general and successful aging in particular. P. B. Baltes and Baltes, for example, list as criteria for successful aging longevity, physical and mental health, cognitive functioning, social competence, productivity, perceived personal control, and life satisfaction. Similarly, Lawton (1983) proposes to combine perceived life quality such as subjective satisfaction with various life domains, psychological well-being (e.g., happiness or goal achievement), behavioral competence with respect to health, motor behavior, and cognition, and objective environmental conditions such as financial or living situation as measures of "the good life." One of the shortcomings of such lists, however, is that they leave open how these criteria should be combined, whether a different weight should be attached to one over the other, and whether the lists should be considered comprehensive or simply a collection to which criteria could be added or from which criteria could be deleted.

Freund and Riediger (2003) distinguish two approaches to defining successful development: (1) Criteria-oriented approaches focus on characteristics constituting success as an end point or outcome of development; the guiding question of these approaches is *What is successful development?*; (2) process-oriented approaches to defining successful development focus on the question *What are the processes and conditions that foster developmental success over time?* These approaches are dynamic in that they view individuals as continuously adapting to changing environmental situations, acting on and creating environments to fit their needs, and generating new resources (Lawton, 1989; Lerner & Busch-Rossnagel, 1981). They emphasize the balance or fit between a person's needs and capabilities on the one hand and environmental opportunities and constraints on the other (Lawton & Nahemow, 1973; Thomae, 1976).

There is general agreement that a comprehensive characterization of successful development entails multiple criteria instead of one specific, single criterion. Most empirical research, however, still follows the single-criterion approach that employs the individual's global sense of well-being as the only criterion for successful aging and adaptive developmental regulation. Therefore, to understand the concept of successful aging as often conceptualized in empirical studies it is necessary to reflect on the notion of *subjective well-being*.

As is true for the concept of successful development, there is no single definition of subjective well-being. Often, subjective well-being is seen as indicating that the person successfully manages his or her life and ages well (Neugarten, Havighurst, & Tobin, 1961). Kunzmann (1999) distinguishes between "broad" and "narrow" conceptualizations on the basis of the number of defining facets. Broad definitions encompass various facets of well-being (e.g., Lawton, 1975). Ryff (1989, 1995; Ryff & Keyes, 1995), for instance, stresses the importance of going beyond happiness to define positive psychological functioning. Her conception takes six dimensions into account: self-acceptance, environmental mastery, positive interpersonal relations, purpose in life, personal growth, and autonomy. Narrower conceptualizations typically distinguish between two dimensions of subjective well-being: a cognitive dimension (life satisfaction) and an emotional dimension (encompassing positive and negative affect; Bradburn, 1969; Campbell, Converse, & Rodgers, 1976; Diener, 1984; Veenhoven, 1991). These dimensions can be either used in a domain-general way or applied to specific life domains.

One of the critiques of subjective well-being as the main or even sole criterion for successful development is that it does not explicitly take environmental conditions into consideration that support successful aging or the successful interaction between a person and his or her life context (Havighurst, 1963; Lawton, 1989). A multiple-criteria approach, in contrast, aims at an integration of subjective indicators (e.g., personal life satisfaction and happiness) and more objective indicators (e.g., everyday instrumental competence). These criteria can be either short term (e.g., last week's happiness) or long term (e.g., meaning and purpose in life), domain-specific (e.g., satisfaction with financial situation) or general (e.g., overall life satisfaction), as well as static and with a definite end point (e.g., life satisfaction at a given point in time) or dynamic (e.g., change in life satisfaction over time; Freund & Riediger, 2003).

Taken together, we distinguish four main approaches to conceptualizing successful development and aging: criteria-oriented, process-oriented, single-criterion, and multi-criteria approaches. Table 4.1 summarizes these four outlined approaches.

As we pointed out, there is currently no agreement as to which single criterion or combination of criteria best defines successful development. One of the reasons for this lack of consensus is that there is no generally agreed-upon model of successful development and aging that could serve as the basis for such a definition. Instead, there are numerous theoretical approaches to successful development and even more empirical findings pertaining to more or less specific factors contributing to adaptive development. Integration of these findings is difficult because studies use different indicators for successful aging.

It is beyond the scope of this chapter to offer a comprehensive, integrative model of successful development. Instead, we aim at approaching the topic of successful aging on different levels of personality, focusing on the level of personal goals and taking different criteria and dimensions into account.

Table 4.1
Approaches to Conceptualizing Successful Development and Aging

Approach	Aim of Approach (Leading Question)
Criteria-oriented	Description of characteristics constituting success as an outcome of development ("What *is* successful development?")
Process-oriented	Perspective on individuals as in continuous interaction with their environment ("What are the *processes* and *conditions* that foster developmental success over time?")
Multiple criteria	Integration of subjective and objective indicators ("How can *subjective and objective indicators* be integrated into one index of successful development?")
Single criterion	Assessment of a person's global or domain-specific subjective well-being ("How can *subjective well-being* as one indicator of successful development be assessed [general or domain-specific, once or repeatedly]?")

Endorsing the life span-developmental view (P. B. Baltes, 1987, 1997) that (a) development from birth to death has no clear end point and that developmental trajectories, (b) are multidirectional (i.e., encompass both gains and losses), and (c) are multifunctional (i.e., most developmental processes and outcomes serve more than one function), we favor a process-oriented approach. This approach focuses on *how* people interact with their environment in adaptive ways (M. M. Baltes & Carstensen, 1996). As we will elaborate in more detail, we posit that *personal goals* are particularly well suited for understanding the processes of successful developmental regulation (Freund & Riediger, 2006). Before elaborating on the role of goals for successful aging, however, we embed the concept of personal goals into a broader conceptualization of personality in terms of three levels, as proposed by McAdams (1996).

LEVELS OF PERSONALITY

How is personality related to successful development and aging? To address this question, we first need to clarify what we mean by *personality*. Following Freund and Riediger's (2006) approach to the relationship between personality and successful aging, we use a model of personality by McAdams (1995, 1996) comprising three levels of personality. Level I refers to *dispositional traits*. Traits are conceptualized as broad, decontextualized, and relatively nonconditional dispositions that generalize across a variety of situations and show considerable stability over time. Level II constructs are *personal concerns*. Personal goals are a prototypical instance of such Level II constructs. Other personality descriptions on this level are personal strivings, life tasks, defense mechanisms, coping strategies, and a wide range of other motivational, developmental, and strategic constructs. These concepts contextualize a person's life in time, place, and/or social roles. Level III pertains to people's identity, that is, to how they integrate and internalize their *life stories* as narrations of their personal reconstructed past, perceived present, and anticipated future. According to McAdams (2001), most adults who live in modern societies seek to provide their lives with unity, purpose, and meaning by constructing internalized and evolving life narratives, including specific settings, scenes, characters, plots, and themes. Level III of personality is seen as being embedded in and echoing cultural, political, economic, and social environments. As these contexts change, so does the life story of a person. Moreover, the flexibility of life stories is also evident in the notion that "people offer different stories about themselves in different contexts" (McAdams, 1996, p. 307). Identity is not merely the sum of all of these life narratives but the overall story that binds together high and low points in life, chance encounters, critical life events, and social relations. The following sections elaborate on these three levels of personality.

LEVEL I: STABLE ASPECTS OF PERSONALITY

On Level I, personality can be described in terms of basic personality traits, that is, behavioral dispositions that are independent of the context and stable across time and situations (see Costa & McCrae, 1994, for a strong version of the stability argument; but see also Srivastava, John, Gosling, & Potter, 2003, for a softer version of the "plaster" hypothesis). The main question of research on personality traits refers to the identification of a universal structure of personality, individual differences, and the extent of longitudinal stability (Costa & McCrae, 1994, 1995).

There is consensus that personality can be well described by the Big Five personality traits: extraversion, agreeableness, conscientiousness, neuroticism, and openness to new experiences. These five factors have been identified by means of factor analysis across various instruments and samples. Cross-sectional as well as longitudinal evidence on the structural invariance of the Big Five exists for adulthood and into old age (Costa & McCrae, 1994; Small, Hertzog, Hultsch, & Dixon, 2003). Moreover, according to a meta-analysis by Roberts and DelVecchio (2000), the rank-order stability of the Big Five increases across the life span. These results were recently supplemented with regard to old and very old age by longitudinal aging studies (Mroczek & Spiro, 2003; Small et al., 2003).

Contrary to some trait personality theorists' view that personality is "set like plaster" after the age of 30 (Costa & McCrae, 1994), cross-sectional as well as longitudinal evidence on mean levels of personality show changes in some of the Big Five characteristics across adulthood. Neuroticism, for example, decreases across adulthood (Mroczek & Spiro, 2003) and shows some increase again in very old age (Small et al., 2003). Moreover, in addition to becoming more neurotic, elderly people tend to become less open to new experiences and less extraverted (Costa, Herbst, McCrae, & Siegler, 2000), whereas they tend to become slightly more agreeable and conscientious (Helson & Kwan, 2000).

Summarizing this empirical evidence based on trait as well as growth models of personality clearly suggests that personality development in adulthood and old age is characterized by both stability and change. Regarding the relationship of the Big Five to subjective indicators of aging well, neuroticism is typically found to be negatively associated with measures of subjective well-being, whereas extraversion shows a positive relation to well-being. For instance, Isaacowitz and Smith (2003) demonstrated that in old and very old age (70 to 102 years), neuroticism is linked to higher negative and lower positive affect. The opposite pattern was found for extraversion (negative correlation with negative affect, positive correlation with positive affect). Note, however, that this pattern also holds for younger age groups (e.g., Diener, 1984) and thus does not seem to constitute a *developmental* phenomenon.

JUMPING TO LEVEL III: PERSONAL IDENTITY

In contrast to dispositional traits, life narratives are heavily influenced by specificities of the context and are subject to change across situations and time. McAdams (1990) argues that a unified or integrated life story, however, provides individuals with an identity and allows them to maintain a coherent self-concept across the entire life span (Cohen, 1998). Life stories are told to different audiences with different purposes: A life story told to a future spouse might look very different from the life story told to a future employer, not because the narrator becomes a different person in between the two events but because different aspects of a biography seem important and merit elaboration in these two contexts. According to McAdams, identity is not derived from *one* (veridical) life story but from the very act of meaning-making and integration of different aspects of a life into one coherent story (albeit possibly a different one each time it is told).

The concept of autobiographical memories is closely related to the concept of life stories (see also Habermas & Bluck, 2000). Some theories on autobiographical memory (e.g., Pillemer, 1992) hold that it can serve three broad functions: directive (planning for present and future behaviors), self (self-continuity, psychodynamic integrity), and social (social bonding, communication; Bluck & Alea, 2002). The directive function involves using the past during conversations to guide present and future thought and behavior such as problem solving, developing opinions and attitudes, or providing flexibility in the construction and updating of rules. The self-function provides the ability to support and promote continuity and development of the self and preserves a sense of being a coherent person over time. This function serves to explain oneself to others (and to oneself). The social (intimacy or bonding) function, finally, is important for developing, maintaining, and nurturing social relationships. This makes us a more believable and persuasive partner in conversations, provides the listener with information about ourselves, and allows us to better understand and empathize with others.

Life stories can be related to successful development and aging in multiple ways. As pointed out by Erikson (1968), life review becomes a major developmental task in old age. This life stage, according to Erikson, is characterized by the two opposite poles of "integrity" and "despair." Following Erikson, wisdom emerges when people are able to accept both the positive and negative events of their lives and do not simply gloss over disappointments and failures but are able to integrate them in a coherent life story together with positive aspects of their past lives. If one understands successful aging as reaching this point, one might argue that positivity of the life story should not be a criterion of aging well. Interestingly, already at midage, it is the theme of redemption (i.e., turning a negative event into a positive one), not a smooth life path filled with positive events, that is, for instance, related to generativity (i.e., giving to the next generation in some way; McAdams, 2001) as a possible indicator of successful development.

Another argument could be made for continuity of the life story as a milestone of successful development and aging (Bluck & Alea, 2002). As it turns out, however, continuity of a life story over time is not necessarily related to positive functioning in old age. In a study by Coleman, Ivani-Chalian, and Robinson (1998), a substantial percentage of their sample of older adults (> 80 years) did not conceive of their life story as a coherent one, but were not necessarily dissatisfied with their present life.

The specific autobiographical memories that are most accessible at a given time may largely depend on a person's goals. As goal-relevant information is more important than information not related to personal goals, it is also more likely to be activated and accessible at a certain time point (Conway & Pleydell-Pearce, 2000). As we will see, personal goals can change over the life span. As a consequence, a set of memories that was once goal-related and self-defining may no longer be so at a later point in life (Singer & Salovey, 1993). Abandoned earlier goals, however, can define one's "past self" and thereby provide a psychological history of changes in the self. In this way, changes in goals can contribute to life narratives ("What did I use to want in the past, and how did it change over time?").

People construe their self and their identity partially around their personal goals because goals can offer a sense of purpose and meaning in life (Little, 1989) and provide the possibility for integration of otherwise unconnected behaviors into one unifying frame (Freund, 2006b). As will be elaborated more in the next sections, personal goals can therefore be seen as part of the binding thread that links the person with his or her context (Freund, 2006b; Little, 1989; McAdams, 1996). This will then clarify how personal concerns and personal goals as Level II constructs link Level I and Level III.

PERSONAL GOALS: PERSONALITY-IN-CONTEXT

From early on, personality psychology has conceptualized goals as building blocks of personality (Freund & Riediger, 2006). In his dynamic theory of personality, Allport (1937, pp. 320–321) regards

> motives as personalized systems of tensions, in which the core of impulse is not to be divorced from the images, ideas of goal, past experience, capacities, and style of conduct employed in obtaining the goal. Only individualized patterns of motives have the capacity to select stimuli, to control and direct segmental tensions, to initiate responses and to render them equivalent, in ways that are consistent with, and characteristic of, the person himself.

Personal goals are often defined as consciously accessible cognitive representations of states a person wants to achieve, maintain, or avoid in the future (Emmons, 1996). They are relatively consistent across situations and over time. Cantor (1990) suggests locating goals at an intermediate level of personality, the level between "being" (i.e., personality traits, basic dispositions) and "doing" (i.e., behavioral responses in a given situation), a distinction introduced by Allport (1937). That is, goals are not as broad and comprehensive as personality traits, although they may be influenced by them. They are also not as specific as behaviors. Rather, they motivate, structure, and direct behavior over time and situations into meaningful action units (Baumeister, 1991; Emmons, 1986; Ford, 1987; Gollwitzer, 1990; Klinger, 1977) and favor the acquisition and use of resources to obtain the goals (cf. Boesch, 1991; Freund, 2003). Goals can focus attention on those stimuli and actions in a given situation that are goal-relevant (Bargh & Ferguson, 2000; Gollwitzer & Moskowitz, 1996; Kruglanski, 1996; Pervin, 1989). As a consequence, they reduce situational complexity and facilitate interaction with the environment.

As goals are inherently content- or domain-specific, Little (1989) called this Level II of personality the "personality-in-context." According to Little, the notion of personality-in-context is based on the idea of an interaction between the person and his or her environment over time. Personal goals reflect the interface between the person's basic personality traits and the specific environment in which he or she lives. Specifically, the content a goal refers to as well as the goal-related processes that specify how people select, pursue, and disengage from goals are crucial in this regard. Addressing the issue of successful development and aging in the present context, we do not focus on the content of goals (see Freund & Riediger, 2006, for a recent overview) but on the motivational processes that accompany and underlie goal-related processes and their relations to successful development.

DEFINING CONTEXT

Context can be broadly defined as the set of circumstances that surrounds a person, such as culture, historical time, family, social relations, and geographical environment. It does not only serve as a background for the behavioral expression of personality, but also plays an important role in shaping personality. Cultural, social, or geographic conditions may represent limitations as well as chances and opportunities in that they exclude or allow certain possibilities of whether and how a person can express his or her basic personality traits. For example, growing up with older siblings may render a person more agreeable because only by being more agreeable might the younger child, constantly lagging behind the older siblings regarding verbal, cognitive, and motor skills, be able to achieve his or her goals. Contextual constraints fulfill an important function in that they specify the boundaries without which personality development would be impossible, as the space of possible developmental trajectories would be too vast and unstructured otherwise.

Life span-developmental psychology (P. B. Baltes, 1987, 1997) provides a useful framework for understanding how person and context interact over time. This theoretical framework regards development as a lifelong process of flexible adaptation to changes in opportunities and constraints on biological, social, and psychological levels (P. B. Baltes, Lindenberger, & Staudinger, 2006; P. B. Baltes, Reese, & Lipsitt, 1980; Brandtstädter & Lerner, 1999; Bronfenbrenner, 1988; Lerner & Busch-Rossnagel, 1981). This assumption has two implications: (1) Individuals exist in environments that create and define possibilities and limiting boundaries for individual pathways; (2) individuals select and create their own living contexts and thus can play an active part in shaping their lives.

How to Interact with One's Context: Goals and
Goal-Related Processes

Goals and the basic regulatory processes of goal selection, pursuit, and disengagement are central aspects that help to explain an individual's interaction with his or her environment (Brandtstädter, 1998; Chapman & Skinner, 1985; Emmons, 1986; Freund, 2003, 2006b; Freund & Baltes, 2000; Gollwitzer & Bargh, 1996; Heckhausen, 1999). Goals emerge from and determine the nature of people's transactions with the surrounding world. Experiencing the effects but also the limitations of goal-directed action can feed back to the individual's view of the world, the self, personal goals, beliefs and wishes, and further goal-directed actions. Thus, there is an interplay among goals, goal-directed actions, and developmental contexts (Brandtstädter, 1998).

Addressing the contextual nature of goals, Freund (2003) distinguishes two interacting levels of representation: social expectations and personal goals. Social expectations are reflected in social norms that inform about age-graded opportunity structures. Age-related social norms can define opportunities and limitations for developmental trajectories of a person's life course. For example, they indicate the appropriate time to marry and to have children. Thereby, age-related social expectations or norms can also give an indication about the availability of resources in certain life domains for specific age groups (Freund, 2003; Heckhausen, 1999). Setting personal goals in accordance with social norms and expectations may help to take advantage of these available resources. Through social sanctions as well as approval or disapproval by the society, social expectations can serve as an orientation or standard for the development, selection, pursuit, maintenance, and disengagement of personal goals (Cantor, 1994; Freund, 1997; Nurmi, 1992). Social expectations are also reflected in personal beliefs about the appropriate timing and sequencing of goals, and personal beliefs incorporate individual values and experiences. Together, social and personal expectations directly influence behavior and also the personal goals an individual selects and pursues. This influence can be conscious or unconscious, as, in addition to consciously represented goals, automatized goals and unconscious motives impact on behavior and development (Bargh & Ferguson, 2000).

In sum, goals can be viewed as the building blocks of personality, person-context interactions, and lifelong development. The concept of personal goals seems particularly well suited for a developmental approach to personality theories of successful aging as it allows integrating motivational processes into a life span context and furthers our understanding of both the *direction* of development and of interindividual differences in the *level* of functioning in various life domains over time. Of particular importance in this regard is the selection of goals from a pool of possible alternatives and the investment of resources into the pursuit and maintenance of goals, also in the face of setbacks and losses. Goal selection and pursuit can improve individual competences and generate new resources, which can then be used for further goal attainment.

One of the basic assumptions of joining an action-theoretical with a life span-developmental perspective in personality theories of successful aging is that, in interaction with a given physical, cultural-historical, and social context, people actively shape their own developmental context (Brandtstädter & Lerner, 1999; Ford, 1987; Freund & Baltes, 2000; Lerner & Busch-Rossnagel, 1981). Goals link the person to his or her life contexts and thus are central to personality and development across the life span. In the following, we introduce three approaches that consider goal selection, initiation of goal-related actions, and the investment of goal-related resources as crucial for achieving desired developmental outcomes.

THE ROLE OF GOALS AND GOAL-RELATED PROCESSES FOR SUCCESSFUL DEVELOPMENT

By nature, human beings are goal-oriented organisms. They organize their lives around the pursuit of goals that reflect their fundamental needs (e.g., autonomy, competence, relatedness; Ryan, 1995). Goals provide persons with standards and ideal outcomes against which they can evaluate their actual level of functioning, their progress in the direction of higher levels of functioning, and the effectiveness of their goal-related behaviors (Carver & Scheier, 1990). Empirical evidence has shown that personal goals are positively related to well-being (Emmons, 1986; Omodei & Wearing, 1990; Palys & Little, 1983; Sheldon & Elliot, 1999). What are the mechanisms underlying this relation? That is, how do goals and goal-related processes influence well-being and successful aging?

There are different views on how goals affect well-being. It is often argued that successful development implies that individuals succeed in progressing toward their goals or reaching desired states (M. M. Baltes & Carstensen, 1996; Maslow, 1954; McClelland, 1987). Humanistic psychology proposes that a person's sense of well-being depends on the person's progress toward his or her goals, especially when these are in accord with "organismic" or "innate" needs (Maslow, 1954; Rogers, 1963; Ryan, 1995; see also Brunstein, Schultheiss, & Grässman, 1998). Other authors argue that having goals can in itself be a predictor of life satisfaction (Brunstein, Schultheiss, & Maier, 1999; Emmons, 1996). Still others posit that not goals themselves but rather the availability of goal-related resources is positively related to life satisfaction (Diener & Fujita, 1995). Finally, Brandtstädter and Rothermund (2002) maintain that goals can ambivalently affect well-being. They argue that neither goals nor resources themselves bring about goal attainment or successful development. In fact, unattainable goals can lead to dissatisfaction and depression if they are not abandoned or readjusted.

Thus, setting and pursuing challenging but attainable goals and standards are important self-regulatory processes conducive to successful aging (Brandtstädter & Renner, 1990; Carver & Scheier, 1981, 1982; Freund & Baltes, 2000; Heckhausen,

1999). In addition, disengaging from goals that are no longer attainable, restructuring goals, and reallocating goal-related resources into alternative goals and goal domains are facets of adaptive functioning (Klinger, 1975; Wrosch & Heckhausen, 1999).

To elaborate further on the idea that personal goals and goal-related processes are central for successful development and to understand better the underlying mechanisms of the relationship between goals and well-being, we introduce three current self-regulatory theories of adaptive development in the following part of this chapter. All three theories view development as multidirectional, comprising gains and losses across the entire life span. They refer to personal goals and basic goal-related processes such as setting, pursuing, reformulating, and disengaging from goals as means to successfully shape individual development. All three frameworks converge in their assumption that resources are limited throughout life, and increasingly so in old age, and that successful developmental regulation requires suitable mechanisms for allocation of these limited resources. The three theories vary, however, in their particular focus (e.g., on life span strategies and personal goals, coping processes, and control processes), in their particular characteristics of the proposed mechanism of resource allocation, as well as in their postulated generality. Table 4.2 summarizes the three theoretical frameworks.

Table 4.2
Goal-Related Theories of Successful Aging

Theoretical Framework	Central Strategies	Specific Examples
Model of Selection, Optimization, and Compensation	Selection	Focusing on Spanish as a foreign language
	Optimization	Investing more time to improve Spanish-language skills
	Compensation	Hiring a translator when traveling in Spain
Dual-Process Model of Assimilative and Accommodative Coping	Assimilative coping	Altering dietary habits to attain the desired bodily appearance
	Accommodative coping	Accepting your physical state and giving up the goal to run the marathon after knee surgery
Model of Optimization in Primary and Secondary Control	Selective primary control	Seeing each other more frequently to improve the relationship
	Compensatory primary control	Seeing a marriage guidance counselor to improve the relationship
	Selective secondary control	Regarding the current partner as the "only love of life"
	Compensatory secondary control	Regarding the former partner as a "wrong choice" after the relationship ends

THE MODEL OF SELECTION, OPTIMIZATION, AND COMPENSATION: A GENERAL, METATHEORETICAL FRAMEWORK FOR UNDERSTANDING ADAPTIVE DEVELOPMENT

THEORETICAL ASSUMPTIONS

The model of selection, optimization, and compensation (SOC) constitutes a general, metatheoretical framework for understanding human development (e.g., P. B. Baltes, 1997; P. B. Baltes & Baltes, 1980, 1990; P. B. Baltes, Freund, & Li, 2005). It assumes a dynamic between developmental gains and losses across various stages of life (childhood, adolescence, adulthood, old age) that is represented at different levels of analysis (e.g., neuronal, behavioral) and within and across different domains of functioning (e.g., physical or cognitive development, emotion regulation). In the context of SOC theory, life span development is a process of resource generation and regulation. This theory describes general developmental processes by addressing both the *direction* of development and the *level* of functioning. As such, SOC is a model of successful development, specifying processes that help to manage changing resources over the life span. In particular, the theory proposes three fundamental and universal processes of successful development: *selection, optimization*, and *compensation*. All three processes are proposed to have various possible phenotypic realizations depending on functional domains (e.g., cognition, social), sociocultural contexts, and person-specific features that vary along the dimensions active-passive, internal-external, and conscious-unconscious (Freund, Li, & Baltes, 1999).

At the most general level of definition, *selection* refers to the process of specialization or canalization of a particular pathway or set of pathways of development. Selection includes the delineating and narrowing down of a range of possible alternative developmental trajectories. Selection also serves the management of limited resources by concentrating resources on delineated domains. Only through this concentration can specification occur and certain skills and abilities evolve. Thus, selection is a general-purpose mechanism to generate new resources (P. B. Baltes et al., 2005). Selection can occur *electively* or as a response to losses in resources (i.e., *loss-based*).

Optimization refers to the acquisition, application, coordination, and maintenance of internal and external resources (means) involved in attaining higher levels of functioning (Freund & Baltes, 2000). Optimization is important for achieving higher levels of functioning, as has been shown in the literature on expertise. Expertise, a high skill level in a selected functional domain, can be achieved only through a substantial amount of deliberate practice (Ericsson, Krampe, & Tesch-Römer, 1993; Krampe & Baltes, 2003).

Compensation refers to the investment of means to avoid or counteract losses in functions in previously available resources. Given that development entails both gains *and* losses across the entire life span (P. B. Baltes, 1987), a model of successful aging needs to take processes of managing losses into account. The SOC model does this by including loss-based selection (referring to reorientation after encountering a loss) and compensation (aimed at the maintenance of functioning in the face of losses).

The SOC theory can be approached from many different theoretical perspectives, such as social, behavioral-learning, cognitive, and neuropsychological (M. M.

Baltes & Carstensen, 1996; P. B. Baltes et al., 2005; P. B. Baltes & Singer, 2001). Freund and Baltes (2000) propose an action-theoretical conceptualization of SOC. This approach embeds SOC in the context of active life-management and refers to developmental regulation through the selection, pursuit, and maintenance of *personal goals.*

From an action-theoretical perspective, *selection* denotes processes related to *goal setting. Elective selection* refers to developing and choosing a subset of goals out of multiple options. Given the finite nature of resources, selection needs to take place to realize developmental potentials. *Loss-based selection* refers to adapting existing or developing new goals to fit losses in resources. Restructuring one's goal hierarchy by exclusively focusing on the most important goal, lowering one's aspiration level, or finding a substitution for unattainable goals are possible manifestations. From an action-theoretical perspective, optimization and compensation refer to processes of *goal pursuit,* that is, the investment of resources into obtaining and refining goal-relevant means. *Optimization* refers to means for achieving desired outcomes and aims at coordination, acquisition, and generation of new resources or skills, serving the growth aspect of development. *Compensation,* from an action-theoretical perspective, addresses the regulation of loss or decline in means and goal-relevant resources that threatens the maintenance of a given level of functioning. When previous goal-relevant means are no longer available, compensation can involve substitution of lost means. It thus denotes a strategy for managing and counteracting losses by changing goal-relevant means to attain a certain goal instead of choosing another goal (as in loss-based selection). The use of hearing aids to counteract hearing losses is one example. Phenotypically, the strategies used for optimization and compensation, such as acquisition and practice of skills, energy and time investment, or activation of new or unused resources, can overlap.

The theory states that the use of SOC strategies changes over the life span as a function of available resources. The expected peak of expression of all three regulatory principles is in adulthood, with elective selection and compensation increasing in importance with advancing age when resource losses become more salient (Freund & Baltes, 2002b).

ADAPTIVE DEVELOPMENT AS ENDORSEMENT OF THE MODEL OF SELECTION, OPTIMIZATION, AND COMPENSATION THROUGHOUT LIFE

Several studies provide evidence for the role of SOC in the description, explanation, and modification of development and support their impact on adaptive life-management (see P. B. Baltes et al., 2005, for an overview). Evidence suggests that the relative prevalence of using and coordinating SOC changes with age and that people who engage in SOC behaviors show more positive outcomes. The existing research comprises different empirical specifications referring to global levels and specific life contexts. It encompasses different assessment levels such as self-report measures (P. B. Baltes, Baltes, Freund, & Lang, 1999), behavior observation (e.g., M. M. Baltes, 1996), and experimental studies (e.g., Li, Lindenberger, Freund, & Baltes, 2001). Some approaches simultaneously investigate all three components of SOC as well as their orchestration (e.g., Riediger, Li, & Lindenberger, 2006), whereas others focus on some of the processes only (e.g., Ebner, Freund, & Baltes, 2006; Freund, 2006a).

Addressing the question whether there exists cultural and individual knowledge of SOC as strategies of successful development, Freund and Baltes (2002a) identified a body of proverbs reflecting SOC. This suggests that SOC strategies are represented in cultural knowledge about pragmatic aspects of everyday human life as expressed in proverbs. Selection, for instance, is expressed in the proverb "You can't have the cake and eat it too." In a series of studies, these proverbs were used to examine whether younger and older adults' lay conceptions of, or preferences for, life-management behaviors were consistent with the SOC model. In a choice-reaction time task, participants were asked to match SOC-related and alternative proverbs to sentence stems indicative of everyday life-management situations. Both age groups chose SOC-related proverbs both more frequently and faster than alternative proverbs. Consistent with the SOC theory, these preferences for SOC-related proverbs over alternatives existed only in tasks referring to goals and success, but not in contexts involving relaxation or leisure. This suggests that both younger and older adults have a preference for SOC-related proverbs over alternatives in everyday life-management situations and that their judgment of the adaptive use of these life-management strategies is in line with what the SOC model proposes.

To investigate the impact of a person's self-reported engagement in SOC on adaptive life-management and successful aging, several studies used versions of the SOC questionnaire developed by P. B. Baltes et al. (1999). Freund and Baltes (2002b) investigated a heterogeneous sample of younger, middle-aged, and older adults and found that participants who indicated high engagement in SOC behaviors reported more positive emotions and higher levels of subjective well-being. The associations remained stable after controlling for self-regulation variables such as tenacious and flexible goal pursuit as well as for person characteristics such as neuroticism, extraversion, and openness to new experiences. As expected, SOC-related strategies were most strongly expressed in middle adulthood; that is, middle-aged adults showed higher endorsement of SOC than younger and older adults. One exception was elective selection, which showed a positive age trend. This suggests that older adults are more selective but report less use of optimization and compensation. This weakening of self-reported optimization and compensation in older ages could be due to the fact that these two strategies are effortful and resource demanding. Both strategies may exceed resources available in late life. This is especially true for the oldest old and for people suffering from severe illness (P. B. Baltes & Smith, 2003; Jopp, 2002). Using the SOC questionnaire in the context of the Berlin Aging Study, Freund and Baltes (1998) showed that SOC is effective well into very old age. They found that older adults between 72 and 102 years who reported more engagement in SOC-related strategies also showed higher expressions of subjective well-being such as positive affect, satisfaction with aging, lack of agitation, and absence of loneliness.

Wiese and colleagues (Wiese, Freund, & Baltes, 2000, 2002) applied the SOC model to goal pursuit in the work and family domains. In a cross-sectional questionnaire study, Wiese et al. (2000) measured self-reported use of SOC behaviors of younger to middle-aged professionals in general as well as domain-specifically. Higher endorsement of general and work- and family-related SOC strategies was positively related to various indicators of well-being. Longitudinal data replicated these positive associations between self-reported engagement in SOC behaviors and global as well as work-related subjective well-being

(Wiese et al., 2002). Moreover, participants with primarily work-oriented goals reported higher levels of general and work-related well-being than those who engaged in both work and family goals. These findings underscore the importance of selecting goals and setting priorities as adaptive regulatory mechanisms in personal goal involvement and development.

Taken together, the summarized self-report studies support a positive association between the endorsement of SOC-related strategies and indicators of global and domain-specific well-being. Similar findings supporting the adaptive use of SOC are reported by Lang, Rieckmann, and Baltes (2002; see also M. M. Baltes & Lang, 1997). Thus, SOC seems to contribute to successful development and aging throughout the adult years and into old and very old age.

Taking a more process-oriented approach, a number of studies addressed the question of *what aspects of* and *how* selection, optimization, and compensation are related to positive functioning across life. A life span-developmental perspective argues that the overall dynamic between optimization or approach goals (i.e., goals directed at approaching positive outcomes) and compensation or avoidance goals (i.e., goals directed at preventing negative outcomes) should change with age. Given the increase of losses and the decrease of gains over the life span, goals are hypothesized to shift from a gain orientation (i.e., optimization, approach) in young adulthood to an orientation toward maintenance or loss avoidance (i.e., compensation, avoidance) in later life (Ebner, 2005; Freund & Baltes, 2000; Freund & Ebner, 2005; Staudinger, Marsiske, & Baltes, 1995). If such an age-related shift in goal orientation is adaptive for managing successfully the changing balance of gains and losses, younger adults should profit more from adopting goals that aim at optimizing their performance and older adults more from working on goals that are geared toward compensating losses in previously available means. Using a behavioral measure of persistence, namely, time, on a simple sensorimotor task that was framed in terms of either (a) optimizing performance or (b) compensating for losses, Freund (2006a) found evidence for age-differential motivational effects of optimization versus compensation. Compared to younger adults, older adults were more persistent when pursuing the goal to compensate for a loss and less persistent when pursuing the goal to optimize their performance.

In a similar vein, a series of studies by Ebner et al. (2006) propose that goals can be directed toward the improvement of functioning, toward the maintenance of functional levels, and toward avoidance or regulation of loss. In a multimethod approach (self-report, preference-choice behavior), as well as different life contexts (cognitive and physical functioning), Ebner et al. found age-group differences in goal orientation and in the associations between goal orientation and subjective well-being. As expected and in line with the results by Freund (2006a), younger adults showed a primary goal orientation toward growth, whereas goal orientation toward maintenance and loss prevention became more important in old age. This age-related difference was shown to be related to perceived availability of resources. Moreover, loss prevention was negatively related to general well-being in younger but not older adults. Interestingly, in old age, orienting goals toward maintaining functions was positively associated with general subjective well-being. Together, the studies by Freund and Ebner et al. suggest that shifting one's goal orientation from the promotion of gains toward maintenance and loss prevention from early to late adulthood constitutes one mechanism of adaptive goal selection.

A study by Riediger, Freund, and Baltes (2005) addressed the nature of inter-goal relations as possible characteristics differentiating between more and less adaptive aspects of goal selection. Specifically, Riediger et al. examined the question whether the relationship among multiple personal goals affects goal pursuit in everyday life and subjective well-being. The first notable finding of their study was that older adults reported more facilitation between their goals and less conflict than younger adults. This finding can be interpreted as indicating that the competence to select personal goals so that they form a coherent, congruent, and nonconflicting goal system increases across adulthood. Moreover, the authors found that intergoal conflict was negatively related to indicators of psychological well-being in everyday life over time. Intergoal facilitation, in contrast, was associated with higher involvement in goal pursuit and an increased likelihood of goal attainment over time. This study underscores the importance of taking multiple goals into account when studying the complex way goals affect behavior and subjective well-being.

Several studies demonstrate the relevance of SOC as adaptive life-management strategies on the behavioral level. For instance, Wiese and Schmitz (2002) provided evidence for the relationship between self-reported SOC and behavioral outcomes in the context of study success. In a sample of college students, Wiese and Schmitz found that students high in self-reported SOC behaviors spent more time studying than students low in self-reported SOC behaviors. Additionally, students low in self-reported selection and optimization were more likely to skip their exams.

Several experimental studies identified SOC processes and demonstrated age-related differences in these processes in the context of dual-task paradigms (Kemper, Herman, & Lian, 2003; Krampe, Rapp, Bondar, & Baltes, 2003; Li et al., 2001; Lindenberger, Marsiske, & Baltes, 2000; Rapp, Krampe, & Baltes, 2006). Different from self-selected goals, as assessed in most studies reported earlier, that allow individuals to pursue one goal after the other, a dual-task situation is characterized by the necessity to manage two tasks (provided for by the experimenter) at the same time. Li et al., for example, conducted work on the role of SOC in coordinating cognitive and sensorimotor behavior (i.e., simultaneous performance of memorizing and walking). Older adults showed greater costs when performing both tasks concurrently. As expected on the basis that the body is the primary domain where aging losses occur and serious risks exist, older adults selected walking over memorizing as the primary target of resource allocation. Moreover, older adults showed more compensatory strategies (i.e., using a handrail) to keep their balance and to maintain higher levels of performance, whereas younger adults showed more compensatory strategies in the domain of thinking (i.e., slowing down the speed of presentation for words to be remembered). These age-associated effects of differential use of SOC in favor of motor over cognitive tasks were stronger when the behavioral system was tested at its limits by increasing task difficulty.

Taken together, these findings supplement the relevance of SOC on the behavioral level. Older adults engage in selection (i.e., prioritizing walking over thinking) and compensation (i.e., use of a handrail) to preserve their walking performance when at risk. This preference of older adults to allocate their resources primarily to motor behavior (such as keeping one's balance) rather than to solving a memory problem is an example of highly automatized and largely subconscious SOC processes. Rapp et al. (2006) obtained similar results with cognitive information processing and motor balance as competing tasks. Bondar, Krampe, and Baltes (2003) showed that younger and older adults could be instructed to allocate resources to different task requirements. In the case of a motor behavior situation that entailed the risk of falling, however, older adults were unable to flexibly adjust their resources. Their differential allocation system manifested itself as robust and asymmetrical, which seems to be adaptive to maintaining stability.

This selective review of empirical findings on SOC suggests that there exists cultural and individual knowledge about SOC-related strategies and that SOC is related to specific and general well-being in younger, middle-aged, and older adults. Moreover, the use of SOC changes over the life span. Whereas younger adults are more oriented toward optimizing and increasing gains, older adults show a higher orientation toward maintenance of functioning and counteracting losses. Studies using a dual-task paradigm suggest that older adults direct their resources to those domains of functioning that have high priority for their survival.

In summary, self-report, observational, and experimental research strengthens the assumption that the SOC strategies constitute adaptive developmental processes. Given this broad empirical support, the SOC model can be regarded as a general framework for investigating and understanding life span development. It characterizes a system of strategies that permits individuals to master the general tasks of life. Focusing primarily on *coping* with age-related changes in goal-relevant resources, the dual-process model of assimilative and accommodative coping by Brandtstädter and colleagues (e.g., Brandtstädter & Renner, 1990), also places a strong emphasis on the role of goal-related processes for successful development. This model is presented next.

THE DUAL-PROCESS MODEL OF ASSIMILATIVE AND ACCOMMODATIVE COPING

THEORETICAL ASSUMPTIONS

Whereas SOC theory provides a general, metatheoretical framework to understand adaptive development with an emphasis on resource generation and real-location in the face of loss, the dual-process model of assimilative and accommodative coping proposed by Brandtstädter and colleagues (e.g., Brandtstädter & Greve, 1994; Brandtstädter & Renner, 1990; Brandtstädter & Rothermund, 2002; Brandtstädter & Wentura, 1995) focuses on two distinct but complementary self-regulatory strategies to cope with discrepancies between actual and desired courses of individual development when faced with difficulties or loss: *assimilative* (e.g., tenacious goal pursuit) and *accommodative modes of coping* (e.g., flexible goal adjustment). Specifically, the assimilative tendency involves active and intentional efforts to change life circumstances and the adjustment of developmental situations to personal preferences and goals. Assimilative means refer to active instrumental, self-corrective, optimizing, and compensatory activities. An example is intentionally changing one's lifestyle, such as altering dietary habits to adapt one's body appearance to the desired body self. The accommodative strategy implies the adjustment of personal preferences, goals, or standards and changes in action resources to situational constraints. Accommodative reorientations involve downgrading, or disengagement from, barren goals, revising evaluative standards, lowering aspiration levels, rescaling criteria of success, or even selecting new, feasible goals. Accommodation includes emotional and cognitive reappraisal; it cannot be initiated intentionally, but shapes the selection of goals, and thus constitutes a basic mechanism of action regulation in the face of loss.

The model specifies differential situational conditions that selectively activate or inhibit the two modes of coping. Assimilative tendencies dominate as long as people feel able to actively change a given situation. When experiences of loss increase or assimilative attempts to change the situation are ineffective and action-outcome expectancies become low, accommodative tendencies are activated. This is also the case when assimilative modes are inefficient from the outset. Thus, people often first employ assimilative coping efforts to actively overcome obstacles that block their goals. If these attempts are unsuccessful, a gradual shift to accommodative processes of goal adjustment occurs, which is modulated by personal and situational factors (e.g., goal importance; Brandtstädter & Wentura, 1995).

According to the model, goal attainment leads to positive affect. Negative emotions arise when losses of goal-relevant resources lead to unattainability of goals and one falls short of one's ambitions and personal standards. Discrepancies between actual states and desired outcomes become especially salient in later phases of life when irrevocable losses and uncontrollable events cumulate. Brandtstädter and colleagues (Brandtstädter, 1999; Brandtstädter & Greve, 1994; Brandtstädter & Renner, 1990) maintain that in old age this growing impact of negative events on personal development favors an age-related shift from an active, assimilative to a more accepting, accommodative coping. As the aim of accommodative coping is to make the given situation appear less negative and more acceptable, this strategy may help individuals to maintain positive developmental perspectives into old age. With declining resources, as is especially the case in old age, it may not be possible to maintain the highest standard in multiple domains (Brandtstädter & Wentura, 1995). Accommodative coping therefore becomes particularly effective to protect against decline in well-being and favors adaptive development in later life (see also Heckhausen & Schulz, 1995). Thus, the dual-process model of coping characterizes successful aging primarily as a shift from actively counteracting the onset of age-related losses to cognitively restructuring personal goals and standards.

ADAPTIVE DEVELOPMENT AS SHIFTING FROM ASSIMILATIVE TO ACCOMMODATIVE COPING THROUGHOUT LIFE

Empirical evidence supports the expectation of age-related differences in the employment of assimilative and accommodative coping strategies. In a self-report study with younger, middle-aged, and older adults, Brandtstädter and Renner (1990) found that self-reported tenacious goal pursuit and flexible goal adjustment were complementarily associated with age. There was an age-graded gradual shift from active, tenacious goal pursuit to accepting, flexible goal adjustment. In addition, the study demonstrated a buffering effect of flexible goal adjustment with regard to the impact of perceived deficits on dissatisfaction with personal development. This finding suggests that flexibly adjusting one's goals helps to maintain a sense of well-being and satisfaction despite the actual experience of loss.

In a large sample of older adults, Rothermund and Brandtstädter (2003) found that accommodative strategies to overcome functional impairments had a curvilinear, inverted U-shaped relationship to age. The strategies increased up to the age of 70 years; with decreasing availability and efficiency of action-related resources beyond this age, accommodative coping then decreased again. Rothermund and Brandtstädter explain their results by arguing that the increasing limitation of action-related resources in very old age limits the usage and efficiency of accommodative coping strategies.

Brandtstädter, Rothermund, and Schmitz (1997) used structured interviews with elderly people to explore how accommodative thoughts are expressed in biographical narratives and how they relate to attitudes toward age and aging. They found that participants who were more prone to express accommodative thoughts reported greater satisfaction with aging, had a more positive attitude toward their biography, and found more continuity and meaning in their life.

Summarizing the empirical evidence, there is a general shift from assimilative to accommodative coping and an increasing adaptiveness of the latter in later adulthood when losses become more widespread and resources necessary for tenacious goal pursuit in the face of obstacles decline (Brandtstädter & Renner, 1990; Brandtstädter, Wentura, & Greve, 1993). Accommodative coping strategies become more salient in later adulthood, a phase characterized by increasing losses in temporal, social, and physical resources that enforce adjustments of goals and priorities. Accommodative processes seem to help the person to cope with irreversible losses and constraints and to come to terms with developmental outcomes that diverge from originally selected goals. In this sense, the dual-process model of coping lends support to the idea that balancing gains and losses as a function of aging-related changes in goal-related resources across the life span constitutes one aspect of successful development. Similarly, the model of optimization in primary and secondary control by Heckhausen and Schulz (1995) aims at explaining how people can successfully navigate the decline in goal-related resources in adulthood.

THE MODEL OF OPTIMIZATION IN PRIMARY AND SECONDARY CONTROL

THEORETICAL ASSUMPTIONS

The model of optimization in primary and secondary control (OPS) by Heckhausen and Schulz (1995) is another prominent theory of adaptive developmental regulation. This theory is based on two assumptions (Heckhausen, 1997, 1999): (1) A person tries to actively influence his or her development by selecting goals, and (2) he or she tries to adapt to the constraints of a given developmental ecology. Individuals are seen as highly motivated to enact control over their lives. In line with SOC theory, OPS theory conceptualizes *selectivity* and *compensation* as the two central principles for successful developmental regulation (Heckhausen, 1999; Schulz, 1986; Schulz & Heckhausen, 1996). Different from the SOC model, however, selectivity in the context of OPS theory refers to the focused investment of resources into selected goals (corresponding to what P. B. Baltes and Baltes, 1990, termed "selective optimization"). In accordance with the definition in the action-theoretical approach to the SOC theory, compensation implies the use of alternative strategies to attain goals when goal-relevant resources are insufficient or loss has occurred. In the OPS framework, optimization is the higher order regulatory process that balances selectivity and compensation (Heckhausen & Schulz, 1998).

Similar to the dual-process model of assimilative and accommodative coping, the OPS model particularly emphasizes the role of perceived personal control for developmental regulation. It assumes that humans have a basic need for control, that is, to protect themselves in the face of difficulties and setbacks. The primary way to achieve control is by modifying the environment according to one's goals by making instrumental efforts (i.e., *primary control*). If such primary control efforts are not available or fail, *secondary control* takes place, that is, modifying one's goals and standards or engaging in self-protective attributions and favorable social comparisons. Secondary control aims at focusing and protecting motivational resources for primary control and buffers negative effects of failing in primary control strivings. The theory posits a primacy of primary over secondary control strategies. According to the model, people aim at maximizing primary control. Secondary control strivings serve to bolster primary control. They are the second-best strategy after primary control strivings fail or are not available.

Two forms of primary and secondary control strategies are distinguished: *selective* and *compensatory*. Selective primary control comprises actions that are directly aimed at goal achievement. It denotes the focused investment of resources into the pursuit of a chosen goal. Examples are time investment or investment of effort and skills into pursuing one's goals. Compensatory primary control refers to the investment of external resources. It involves the recruitment of external help or technical aids for the attainment of a chosen goal. It comes into play when internal resources for goal achievement are insufficient or depleted. Examples are employing the help of others or applying new, alternative resources. Selective secondary control is directed at the internal world to promote the volitional commitment to a chosen goal. It subsumes metavolitional strategies to keep oneself focused on the pursuit of selected goals, for example, by avoiding distractions. Examples are boosting the value of a chosen goal or the perception of personal control. Finally, compensatory secondary control refers to cognitive reframing of goals such as down-regulating the desirability of a blocked goal or disengaging from it. It serves as a buffer for negative effects of failure. It involves strategies such as disengagement from unattainable goals, downward social comparison, and external causal attributions.

According to the authors, none of these four strategies is functional per se. Rather, a higher order optimization process is postulated that coordinates control strivings such that the potential for primary control is maximized across life. Consistent with this proposition, empirical evidence indicates that self-protective compensatory strategies (compensatory secondary control) become more prevalent and more adaptive in later adulthood and when opportunity structures for goal attainment are unfavorable (Wrosch & Heckhausen, 1999), whereas continued involvement in primary control efforts is maladaptive in such situations (Chipperfield, Perry, & Menec, 1999; Heckhausen, Wrosch, & Fleeson, 2001).

According to the OPS model, maximization of primary control potential characterizes adaptive functioning. This, however, becomes particularly difficult in older ages when losses become more prominent and less under personal control and when declines in goal-relevant resources make the achievement of resource-intensive goals increasingly difficult (Schulz, 1986). As a consequence, with advancing age, compensatory primary and secondary control strategies gain increasing importance for successful life management. The use of secondary control strategies is theorized to contribute to a long term increase in primary control in that it buffers negative motivational effects of failure and maintains self-efficacy and well-being. Therefore, these strategies should be employed more frequent in old age (cf. Heckhausen & Schulz, 1995). However, OPS theory argues that it is not the four control strategies separately that bring about adaptive development but rather their orchestration in line with developmental opportunities and constraints. The following section provides empirical support for these assumptions.

ADAPTIVE DEVELOPMENT AS SHIFTING FROM PRIMARY TO SECONDARY CONTROL STRATEGIES THROUGHOUT LIFE

In a self-report study, Heckhausen, Schulz, and Wrosch (1998) observed that the use of control strategies increased from early to late adulthood. Unexpectedly, however, compensatory secondary control did not show a positive age trend. Positive associations between all four types of control strategies and self-esteem supported the role of primary and secondary control strategies for adaptive functioning. Wrosch and Heckhausen (1999) demonstrated that disengaging from unobtainable goals and reallocating resources to alternative domains (i.e., compensatory secondary control) is functional when goal-relevant resources decline and opportunity structures for goal attainment become less favorable. The authors examined goals in the partnership domain in recently committed or separated adults in early adulthood and late midlife. Younger separated adults mentioned more partnership goals and reported more primary control strivings for attaining their goals. In contrast, older separated adults reported more secondary control actions such as goal deactivation. They disengaged from partnership goals and invested their resources into alternative social domains. Moreover, younger separated adults reported a decline in positive affect over a time period of 15 months when they disengaged from their partnership goals, whereas for older separated adults goal deactivation proved beneficial. One explanation is that the objective chances to remarry are lower for people in late middle age compared to young adulthood. The age-related change in opportunities for attaining the partnership goal, then, is reflected in a shift in importance and functional impact of this goal. These findings can be viewed as evidence supporting the notion that individuals activate and deactivate developmental goals in accordance with age-graded changes in opportunities for goal achievement.

Similarly, Heckhausen et al. (2001) investigated developmental regulation before and after the developmental deadline for childbearing. Younger and middle-aged women with or without children were compared with regard to various indicators of primary and secondary control striving for goal attainment versus goal disengagement and self-protection. Women approaching the developmental deadline for childbearing were actively engaged in the goal of bearing a child. In contrast, women who had passed the deadline disengaged from the goal. These differences were evident in the number and type of goals nominated as well as the salience of information related to children. Moreover, women who had passed the deadline but for whom child-related information was still more salient were more prone to negative affect. Thus, a selective responsiveness to information relevant for an obsolete developmental goal appears to have negative implications for well-being.

Taken together, the findings in the context of OPS theory provide evidence that the endorsement of control strategies favors successful aging as they help to balance developmental gains and losses. Specifically, the use of compensatory control strategies increases in importance with positive effects on well-being and adaptive developmental regulation when goal-related resources are lost or become increasingly threatened, as is often the case in late adulthood. As is true for the SOC model and the dual-process model of coping, the OPS model supports the fruitfulness of approaching successful aging by investigating personality-in-context in terms of personal goals and goal-related processes. In the next and final section, we address this briefly.

SUMMARY, FUTURE OUTLOOK, AND PRACTICAL RELEVANCE

This chapter combined an action-theoretical with a life span-developmental perspective on personality and successful aging. This integration allows an understanding of goals as dynamic aspects of personality that reflect the person-environment interaction over time. All three theoretical frameworks presented in this chapter (the SOC model, the dual-process model of coping, and the OPS model) argue that individuals can actively shape their development through the motivating, organizing, and directing functions of personal goals and goal-related processes, and they all empirically support the role of goals and goal-related processes for adaptive development. Moreover, they all stress that the management of resource changes from a dominance of gains to increasing losses is a key to successful aging. They differ, however, with regard to the specific processes proposed to best serve the management of resources across adulthood. There exists good evidence supporting each of these models. As of yet, no integration or systematic comparison of the models has been attempted (Freund & Riediger, 2003; for exceptions, see Freund & Baltes, 2002a, 2002b, for positive associations of SOC and assimilative and accommodative coping). We believe that it will be a fruitful next step in future research on successful aging to close this gap.

Another future research direction in this field should be to investigate the practical relevance of the three models. As various studies have shown that work-related goals are most central for younger adults and goals related to health issues become most prominent in older adults (Nurmi, 1992; Rapkin & Fischer, 1992), our practical examples and speculations about the role of goals and goal-related processes for successful aging refer to the domains of health and work.

Research has demonstrated that framing health messages in terms of gains and losses has a differential effect on health-related goal adoption and goal pursuit when implementing health programs in younger and older adults. Gain-framed messages emphasize benefits gained (e.g., becoming more attractive through a regular physical workout), whereas loss-framed messages emphasize the avoidance of benefits lost (e.g., preventing weight gain through regular physical activity; Brendl, Higgins, & Lemm, 1995). When individuals perceive themselves as highly vulnerable to certain health risks, as is often the case in old age, loss-framed messages are more effective, whereas gain-framed messages become more effective when perceived vulnerability is low, as is typically the case at younger ages (Lee & Aaker, 2004). Framing a health program with an emphasis on benefits lost, as opposed to benefits gained, might therefore be more persuasive for older adults. As a consequence, elderly people might be more persistent in pursuing the program and might manage to improve their physical and cognitive functioning and, in this sense, age more successfully. The opposite should be true for younger adults. But not only the direction of goals might have practical implications but also the underlying motivation of goals. Riediger (2001) showed, for instance, that goals related to attractiveness and fitness are central for younger adults, whereas health in itself becomes the main motivation for regular physical activity in older adults. Taking this into consideration when setting up successful training concepts for younger and older adults appears to be of great importance.

The second example of the possible applied consequences of this research is motivation at the workplace. With demographic changes (a combination of lower birth rates and more people becoming older in much better cognitive and physical conditions; e.g., P. B. Baltes, 1997), it is likely that retirement age will increase to keep well-educated and highly experienced people in the workforce. Here, it will become an important task of the future to take into account how goals and goal-related processes in the work domain might change over adulthood. In contrast to younger people, older adults might simply not be primarily motivated to achieve new and higher outcomes, but instead focus on maintenance and prevention of losses. Providing younger as well as older adults with work tasks that meet their underlying motivation and that are framed in age-appropriate ways (i.e., gain frames for younger adults and loss frames for older adults) may increase their work-related performance as well as their personal satisfaction with work in young but also in old age. Moreover, encouraging accommodative coping styles and providing opportunities for primary control even and especially when resources decline will likely help older adults to derive meaning and satisfaction from their workplace.

In sum, we believe that conceptualizing successful aging using a framework of person-in-context fosters our understanding of the processes underlying aging well and will ultimately also help shape environments in a more age-friendly way to support the strengths of old and very old age and to maintain positive functioning even in the face of decreasing resources.

REFERENCES

Allport, G. W. (1937). *Personality: A psychological interpretation.* New York: Hogrefe.

Baltes, M. M. (1996). *The many faces of dependency in old age.* New York: Cambridge University Press.

Baltes, M. M., & Carstensen, L. L. (1996). The process of successful aging. *Ageing and Society, 16,* 397–422.

Baltes, M. M., & Lang, F. R. (1997). Everyday functioning and successful aging: The impact of resources. *Psychology and Aging, 12,* 433–443.

Baltes, P. B. (1987). Theoretical propositions of life-span developmental psychology: On the dynamics between growth and decline. *Developmental Psychology, 23,* 611–626.

Baltes, P. B. (1997). On the incomplete architecture of human ontogeny: Selection, optimization, and compensation as foundation of developmental theory. *American Psychologist, 52,* 366–380.

Baltes, P. B., & Baltes, M. M. (1980). Plasticity and variability in psychological aging: Methodological and theoretical issues. In G. E. Gurski (Ed.), *Determining the effects of aging on the central nervous system* (pp. 41–66). Berlin, Germany: Schering.

Baltes, P. B., & Baltes, M. M. (1990). Psychological perspectives on successful aging: The model of selective optimization with compensation. In P. B. Baltes & M. M. Baltes (Eds.), *Successful aging: Perspectives from the behavioral sciences* (pp. 1–34). New York: Cambridge University Press.

Baltes, P. B., Baltes, M. M., Freund, A. M., & Lang, F. R. (1999). *The measurement of selection, optimization, and compensation (SOC) by self-report: Technical report 1999.* Berlin, Germany: Max Planck Institute for Human Development.

Baltes, P. B., Freund, A. M., & Li, S.-C. (2005). The psychological science of human aging. In M. Johnson, V. L. Bengtson, P. Coleman, & T. Kirkwood (Eds.), *The Cambridge handbook of age and aging* (pp. 47–71). New York: Cambridge University Press.

Baltes, P. B., Lindenberger, U., & Staudinger, U. M. (2006). Life-span theory in developmental psychology. In W. Damon & R. M. Lerner (Eds.), *Handbook of child psychology: Vol. 1. Theoretical models of human development* (6th ed., pp. 569–664). New York: Wiley.

Baltes, P. B., Reese, H. W., & Lipsitt, L. P. (1980). Life-span developmental psychology. *Annual Review of Psychology, 31,* 65–110.

Baltes, P. B., & Singer, T. (2001). Plasticity and the ageing mind: An exemplar of the biocultural orchestration of brain and behaviour. *European Review: Interdisciplinary Journal of the Academia Europaea, 9,* 59–76.

Baltes, P. B., & Smith, J. (2003). New frontiers in the future of aging: From successful aging of the young old to the dilemmas of the fourth age. *Gerontology, 49,* 123–135.

Bargh, J. A., & Ferguson, M. J. (2000). Beyond behaviorism: On the automaticity of higher mental processes. *Psychological Bulletin, 126,* 925–945.

Baumeister, R. F. (1991). *Meanings of life.* New York: Guilford Press.

Bluck, S., & Alea, N. (2002). Exploring the functions of autobiographical memory: Why do I remember the autumn? In J. D. Webster & B. K. Haight (Eds.), *Critical advances in reminiscence work* (pp. 61–75). New York: Springer.

Boesch, E. E. (1991). *Symbolic action theory and cultural psychology.* Berlin, Germany: Springer.

Bondar, A., Krampe, R. T., & Baltes, P. B. (2003). *Balance takes priority over cognition: Can young and older adults deliberately control resource allocation?* Unpublished manuscript, Max Planck Institute for Human Development, Berlin.

Bradburn, N. M. (1969). *The structure of psychological well-being.* Chicago: Aldine.

Brandtstädter, J. (1986). Personal control over development and development-regulating action: Considerations and results concerning a neglected research topic. *Zeitschrift für Entwicklungspsychologie und Pädagogische Psychologie, 18,* 316–334.

Brandtstädter, J. (1998). Action perspectives on human development. In W. Damon & R. M. Lerner (Eds.), *Handbook of child psychology: Vol. 1. Theoretical models of human development* (5th ed., pp. 807–863). New York: Wiley.

Brandtstädter, J. (1999). The self in action and development: Cultural, biosocial, and ontogenetic bases of intentional self-development. In J. Brandtstädter & R. M. Lerner (Eds.), *Action and self-development: Theory and research through the life span* (pp. 37–65). Thousand Oaks, CA: Sage.

Brandtstädter, J., & Greve, W. (1994). The aging self: Stabilizing and protective processes. *Developmental Review, 14,* 52–80.

Brandtstädter, J., & Lerner, R. M. (Eds.). (1999). *Action and self-development: Theory and research through the life span.* Thousand Oaks, CA: Sage.

Brandtstädter, J., & Renner, G. (1990). Tenacious goal pursuit and flexible goal adjustment: Explication and age-related analysis of assimilative and accommodative strategies of coping. *Psychology and Aging, 5,* 58–67.

Brandtstädter, J., & Rothermund, K. (2002). The life-course dynamics of goal pursuit and goal adjustment: A two-process framework. *Developmental Review, 22,* 117–150.

Brandtstädter, J., & Rothermund, K., & Schmitz, U. (1997). Coping resources in later life. *European Journal of Applied Psychology, 47,* 107–114.

Brandtstädter, J., & Wentura, D. (1995). Adjustment to shifting possibility frontiers in later life: Complementary adaptive modes. In R. A. Dixon & L. Bäckman (Eds.), *Compensating for psychological deficits and declines: Managing losses and promoting gains* (pp. 83–106). Hillsdale, NJ: Erlbaum.

Brandtstädter, J., Wentura, D., & Greve, W. (1993). Adaptive resources of the aging self: Outlines of an emergent perspective. *International Journal of Behavioral Development, 16,* 323–349.

Brendl, C. M., Higgins, E. T., & Lemm, K. M. (1995). Sensitivity to varying gains and losses: The role of self-discrepancies and event framing. *Journal of Personality and Social Psychology, 69,* 1028–1051.

Bronfenbrenner, U. (1988). Interacting systems in human development: Research paradigms—Present and future. In N. Bolger & A. Caspi (Eds.), *Person in context: Developmental processes—Human development in cultural and historical contexts* (pp. 25–49). New York: Cambridge University Press.

Brunstein, J. C., Schultheiss, O. C., & Grässman, R. (1998). Personal goals and emotional well-being: The moderating role of motive dispositions. *Journal of Personality and Social Psychology, 75,* 494–508.

Brunstein, J. C., Schultheiss, O. C., & Maier, G. W. (1999). The pursuit of personal goals: A motivational approach to well-being and life adjustment. In J. Brandtstädter & R. M. Lerner (Eds.), *Action and self-development: Theory and research through the life-span* (pp. 169–196). Thousand Oaks, CA: Sage.

Campbell, A., Converse, P. E., & Rodgers, W. L. (1976). *The quality of American life: Perceptions, evaluations, and satisfactions.* New York: Russell-Sage.

Cantor, N. (1990). From thought to behavior: "Having" and "doing" in the study of personality and cognition. *American Psychologist, 45,* 735–750.

Cantor, N. (1994). Life task problem solving: Situational affordances and personal needs. *Personality and Social Psychology Bulletin, 20,* 235–243.

Carver, C. S., & Scheier, M. F. (1981). *Attention and self-regulation: A control theory approach to human behavior.* New York: Springer.

Carver, C. S., & Scheier, M. F. (1982). Control theory: A useful conceptual framework for personality, social, clinical, and health psychology. *Psychological Bulletin, 92,* 111–135.

Carver, C. S., & Scheier, M. F. (1990). Origins and functions of positive and negative affect: A control-process view. *Psychological Review, 97,* 19–35.

Chapman, M., & Skinner, E. A. (1985). Action in development: Development in action. In M. Frese & J. Sabini (Eds.), *Goal directed behavior: The concept of action in psychology* (pp. 200–213). Hillsdale, NJ: Erlbaum.

Chipperfield, J. G., Perry, R. P., & Menec, V. H. (1999). Primary and secondary control-enhancing strategies: Implications for health in later life. *Journal of Aging and Health, 11,* 517–539.

Cohen, G. (1998). The effects of aging on autobiographical memory. In C. P. Thompson, D. J. Herrmann, D. Bruce, D. J. Read, D. G. Payne, & M. P. Toglia (Eds.), *Autobiographical memory: Theoretical and applied perspectives* (pp. 105–123). Hillsdale, NJ: Erlbaum.

Coleman, P. G., Ivani-Chalian, C., & Robinson, M. (1998). The story continues: Persistence of life themes in old age. *Ageing and Society, 18,* 389–419.

Conway, M. A., & Pleydell-Pearce, C. W. (2000). The construction of autobiographical memories in the self-memory system. *Psychological Review, 107,* 261–288.

Costa, P. T., Herbst, J. H., McCrae, R. R., & Siegler, I. C. (2000). Personality at midlife: Stability, intrinsic maturation, and response to life events. *Assessment, 7,* 365–378.

Costa, P. T., & McCrae, R. R. (1994). Set like plaster? Evidence for stability of adult personality. In T. F. Heatherton & J. L. Weinberger (Eds.), *Can personality change?* (pp. 21–40). Washington, DC: American Psychological Association.

Costa, P. T., & McCrae, R. R. (1995). Domains and facets: Hierarchical personality assessment using the Revised NEO Personality Inventory. *Journal of Personality Assessment, 64,* 21–50.

Diener, E. (1984). Subjective well-being. *Psychological Bulletin, 95,* 542–575.

Diener, E., & Fujita, F. (1995). Resources, personal strivings, and subjective well-being: A nomothetic and idiographic approach. *Journal of Personality and Social Psychology, 68,* 926–935.

Ebner, N. C. (2005). *Striving for gains and preventing losses: Multi-method evidence on the differences in personal goal orientation in early and late adulthood.* Doctoral dissertation, Free University of Berlin.

Ebner, N. C., Freund, A. M., & Baltes, P. B. (2006). Developmental changes in personal goal orientation from young to late adulthood: From striving for gains to maintenance and prevention of losses. *Psychology and Aging, 21,* 664–678.

Emmons, R. A. (1986). Personal strivings: An approach to personality and subjective well-being. *Journal of Personality and Social Psychology, 51,* 1058–1068.

Emmons, R. A. (1996). Striving and feeling: Personal goals and subjective well-being. In P. M. Gollwitzer & J. A. Bargh (Eds.), *The psychology of action: Linking cognition and motivation to behavior* (pp. 313–337). New York: Guilford Press.

Ericsson, K. A., & Krampe, R. T., & Tesch-Römer, C. (1993). The role of deliberative practice in the acquisition of expert performance. *Psychology Review, 100,* 363–406.

Erikson, E. H. (1968). *Identity: Youth and crisis.* New York: Norton.

Ford, D. H. (1987). *Humans as self-constructing living systems: A developmental perspective on behavior and personality.* Hillsdale, NJ: Erlbaum.

Freund, A. M. (1997). Individuating age-salience: A psychological perspective on the salience of age in the life course. *Human Development, 40,* 287–292.

Freund, A. M. (2003). The role of goals for development. *Psychologische Rundschau, 54,* 233–242.

Freund, A. M. (2006a). Differential motivational consequences of goal focus in younger and older adults. *Psychology and Aging, 21,* 240–252.

Freund, A. M. (2006b). Levels of goals—Understanding motivational processes across adulthood. In B. R. Little, K. Salmela-Aro, & S. D. Phillips (Eds.), *Personal project pursuit: Goals, action and human flourishing.* Mahwah, NJ: Erlbaum.

Freund, A. M., & Baltes, P. B. (1998). Selection, optimization, and compensation as strategies of life management: Correlations with subjective indicators of successful aging. *Psychology and Aging, 13,* 531–543.

Freund, A. M., & Baltes, P. B. (2000). The orchestration of selection, optimization and compensation: An action-theoretical conceptualization of a theory of developmental regulation. In W. J. Perrig & A. Grob (Eds.), *Control of human behavior, mental processes, and consciousness* (pp. 35–58). Mahwah, NJ: Erlbaum.

Freund, A. M., & Baltes, P. B. (2002a). The adaptiveness of selection, optimization, and compensation as strategies of life management: Evidence from a preference study on proverbs. *Journal of Gerontology: Psychological Sciences, 57B,* 426–434.

Freund, A. M., & Baltes, P. B. (2002b). Life management strategies of selection, optimization and compensation: Measurement by self-report and construct validity. *Journal of Personality and Social Psychology, 82,* 642–662.

Freund, A. M., & Ebner, N. C. (2005). The aging self: Shifting from promoting gains to balancing losses. In W. Greve, K. Rothermund, & D. Wentura (Eds.), *The adaptive self: Personal continuity and intentional self-development* (pp. 185–202). Ashland, OH: Hogrefe & Huber.

Freund, A. M., Li, K. Z. H., & Baltes, P. B. (1999). Successful development and aging: The role of selection, optimization, and compensation in successful aging. In J. Brandt-städter & R. M. Lerner (Eds.), *Action and self-development: Theory and research through the life span* (pp. 401–434). Thousand Oaks, CA: Sage.

Freund, A. M., & Riediger, M. (2003). Successful aging. In R. M Lerner, M. A. Easter-brooks, & J. Mistry (Eds.), *Comprehensive handbook of psychology: Vol. 6. Developmental psychology* (pp. 601–628). Hoboken, NJ: Wiley.

Freund, A. M., & Riediger, M. (2006). Goals as building blocks of personality and development in adulthood. In D. K. Mroczek & T. D. Little (Eds.), *Handbook of personality development* (pp. 353–372). Mahwah, NJ: Erlbaum.

Gollwitzer, P. M. (1990). Action phases and mind-sets. In E. T. Higgins & R. M. Sorrentino (Eds.), *Handbook of motivation and cognition: Vol. 2. Foundations of social behavior* (pp. 53–92). New York: Guilford Press.

Gollwitzer, P. M., & Bargh, J. A. (Eds.). (1996). *The psychology of action: Linking cognition and motivation to behavior.* New York: Guilford Press.

Gollwitzer, P. M., & Moskowitz, G. B. (1996). Goal effects on action and cognition. In E. T. Higgins & A. W. Kruglanski (Eds.), *Social psychology: Handbook of basic principles* (pp. 361–399). New York: Guilford Press.

Habermas, T., & Bluck, S. (2000). Getting a life: The emergence of the life story in adolescence. *Psychological Bulletin, 126,* 748–769.

Havighurst, R. J. (1963). Successful aging. In R. H. Wiliams, C. Tibbitts, & W. Donahue (Eds.), *The process of aging: Vol. 1. Social and psychological perspectives* (pp. 299–320). New York: Atherton Press.

Heckhausen, J. (1997). Developmental regulation across adulthood: Primary and secondary control of age-related changes. *Developmental Psychology, 33,* 176–187.

Heckhausen, J. (1999). *Developmental regulation in adulthood: Age-normative and sociostructural constraints as adaptive challenges.* New York: Cambridge University Press.

Heckhausen, J., & Schulz, R. (1995). A life-span theory of control. *Psychological Review, 102,* 284–304.

Heckhausen, J., & Schulz, R. (1998). Developmental regulation in adulthood: Selection and compensation via primary and secondary control. In J. Heckhausen & C. S. Dweck (Eds.), *Motivation and self-regulation across the life span* (pp. 50–77). New York: Cambridge University Press.

Heckhausen, J., Schulz, R., & Wrosch, C. (1998). *Developmental regulation in adulthood: Optimization in primary and secondary control.* Unpublished manuscript, Max Planck Institute for Human Development, Berlin.

Heckhausen, J., Wrosch, C., & Fleeson, W. (2001). Developmental regulation before and after a developmental deadline: The sample case of "biological clock" for childbearing. *Psychology and Aging, 16,* 400–413.

Helson, R., & Kwan, V. S. Y. (2000). Personality development in adulthood: The broad picture and processes in one longitudinal sample. In S. Hampson (Ed.), *Advances in personality psychology* (Vol. 1, pp. 77–106). London: Routledge.

Isaacowitz, D. M., & Smith, J. (2003). Positive and negative affect in very old age. *Journals of Gerontology, 58B*, P143–P152.

Jopp, D. (2002). *Successful aging: On the functional interplay between personal resources and adaptive life-management strategies.* Doctoral dissertation, Free University of Berlin.

Kemper, S., Herman, R. E., & Lian, C. H. T. (2003). The costs of doing two things at once for young and older adults: Talking while walking, finger tapping, and ignoring speech or noise. *Psychology and Aging, 18*, 181–192.

Klinger, E. (1975). Consequences of commitment to and disengagement from incentives. *Psychological Review, 82*, 1–25.

Klinger, E. (1977). *Meaning and void: Inner experience and the incentives in people's lives.* Minneapolis: University of Minnesota Press.

Krampe, R. T., & Baltes, P. B. (2003). Intelligence as adaptive resource development and resource allocation: A new look through the lenses of SOC and expertise. In R. J. Sternberg & E. L. Grigorenko (Eds.), *Perspectives on the psychology of abilities, competencies, and expertise* (pp. 31–69). New York: Cambridge University Press.

Krampe, R. T., Rapp, M. A., Bondar, A., & Baltes, P. B. (2003). Allocation of cognitive resources during the simultaneous performance of cognitive and sensorimotor tasks. *Der Nervenarzt, 74*, 211–218.

Kruglanski, A. W. (1996). Goals as knowledge structures. In P. M. Gollwitzer & J. A. Bargh (Eds.), *The psychology of action: Linking cognition and motivation to behavior* (pp. 599–618). New York: Springer.

Kunzmann, U. (1999). *Being and feeling in control: Two sources of older people's emotional well-being.* Berlin, Germany: Max Planck Institute for Human Development.

Labouvie-Vief, G. (1981). Proactive and reactive aspects of constructivism: Growth and aging in life-span perspective. In R. M. Lerner & N. A. Busch-Rossnagel (Eds.), *Individuals as producers of their development: A life-span perspective* (pp. 197–230). New York: Academic Press.

Lang, F. R., Rieckmann, N., & Baltes, M. M. (2002). Adapting to aging losses: Do resources facilitate strategies of selection, compensation, and optimization in everyday functioning? *Journal of Gerontology: Psychological Sciences, 57B*, 501–509.

Lawton, M. P. (1975). The Philadelphia Geriatric Center Morale Scale: A revision. *Journal of Gerontology, 30*, 85–89.

Lawton, M. P. (1983). Environment and other determinants of well-being in older people. *Gerontologist, 23*, 349–357.

Lawton, M. P. (1989). Environmental proactivity in older people. In V. L. Bengston & K. W. Schaie (Eds.), *The course of later life: Research and reflections* (pp. 15–23). New York: Springer.

Lawton, M. P., & Nahemow, L. (1973). Ecology and the aging process. In C. Eisdorfer & M. P. Lawton (Eds.), *The psychology of adult development and aging* (pp. 619–674). Washington, DC: American Psychological Association.

Lee, A. Y., & Aaker, J. L. (2004). Bringing the frame into focus: The influence of regulatory fit on processing fluency and persuasion. *Journal of Personality and Social Psychology, 86*, 205–218.

Lerner, R. M., & Busch-Rossnagel, A. (1981). *Individuals as producers of their development: A life-span perspective.* New York: Academic Press.

Li, K. Z. H., Lindenberger, U., Freund, A. M., & Baltes, P. B. (2001). Walking while memorizing: Age-related differences in compensatory behavior. *Psychological Science, 12,* 230–237.

Lindenberger, U., Marsiske, M., & Baltes, P. B. (2000). Memorizing while walking: Increase in dual-task costs from young adulthood to old age. *Psychology and Aging, 3,* 417–436.

Little, B. R. (1989). Personal project analysis: Trivial pursuits, magnificent obsessions, and the search for coherence. In D. M. Buss & N. Cantor (Eds.), *Personality psychology: Recent trends and emerging directions* (pp. 15–31). New York: Springer.

Maslow, A. (1954). *Motivation and personality.* New York: Harper & Row.

McAdams, D. P. (1990). Unity and purpose in human lives: The emergence of identity as a life story. In A. I. Rabin, R. A. Zucker, R. A. Emmons, & S. J. Frank (Eds.), *Studying persons and lives* (pp. 148–190). New York: Springer.

McAdams, D. P. (1995). What do we know when we know a person? *Journal of Personality, 63,* 365–396.

McAdams, D. P. (1996). Personality, modernity, and the storied self: A contemporary framework for studying persons. *Psychological Inquiry, 7,* 295–321.

McAdams, D. P. (2001). The psychology of life stories. *Review of General Psychology, 5,* 100–122.

McClelland, D. C. (1987). *Human motivation.* New York: Cambridge University Press.

Mroczek, D. K., & Spiro, R. A., III. (2003). Modeling intraindividual change in personality traits: Findings from the Normative Aging Study. *Journals of Gerontology, 58B,* P153–P165.

Neugarten, B. L., Havighurst, R. J., & Tobin, S. S. (1961). The measurement of life satisfaction. *Journal of Gerontology, 16,* 134–143.

Nurmi, J.-E. (1992). Age differences in adult life goals, concerns, and their temporal extension: A life-course approach to future-oriented motivation. *International Journal of Behavioral Development, 15,* 487–508.

Omodei, M. M., & Wearing, A. J. (1990). Need satisfaction and involvement in personal projects: Toward an integrative model of subjective well-being. *Journal of Personality and Social Psychology, 59,* 762–769.

Palys, T. S., & Little, B. R. (1983). Perceived life satisfaction and the organization of personal project systems. *Journal of Personality and Social Psychology, 44,* 1221–1230.

Pervin, L. A. (1989). Goal concepts: Themes, issues, and questions. In L. A. Pervin (Ed.), *Goal concepts in personality and social psychology* (pp. 473–479). Hillsdale, NJ: Erlbaum.

Pillemer, D. B. (1992). Remembering personal circumstances: A functional analysis. In E. Winograd & U. Neisser (Eds.), *Emory Symposia in Cognition: Affect and accuracy in recall—Studies of "flashbulb" memories* (4th ed., pp. 236–264). New York: Cambridge University Press.

Rapkin, B. D., & Fischer, K. (1992). Framing the construct of life satisfaction in terms of older adults' personal goals. *Psychology and Aging, 7,* 138–149.

Rapp, M. A., Krampe, R. T., & Baltes, P. B. (2006). Adaptive task prioritization in aging: Selective resource allocation to postural control is preserved in Alzheimer disease. *American Journal of Geriatric Psychiatry, 14,* 52–61.

Riediger, M. (2001). *On the dynamic relations among multiple goals: Intergoal conflict and intergoal facilitation in younger and older adulthood.* Doctoral dissertation, Free University of Berlin.

Riediger, M., Freund, A. M., & Baltes, P. B. (2005). Managing life through personal goals: Intergoal facilitation and intensity of goal pursuit in younger and older adulthood. *Journals of Gerontology, 60B,* P84–P91.

Riediger, M., Li, S.-C., & Lindenberger, U. (2006). Selection, optimization, and compensation (SOC) as developmental mechanisms of adaptive resource allocation: Review and preview. In J. E. Birren & K. W. Schaie (Eds.), *Handbook of the psychology of aging* (6th ed., pp. 289–313). Amsterdam: Elsevier.

Roberts, B. W., & DelVecchio, W. F. (2000). The rank-order consistency of personality traits from childhood to old age: A quantitative review of longitudinal studies. *Psychological Bulletin, 126,* 3–25.

Rogers, C. (1963). The actualisation tendency in relation to "motives" and to consciousness. In M. R. Jones (Ed.), *Nebraska Symposium on Motivation* (Vol. 11, pp. 1–24). Lincoln: University of Nebraska Press.

Rothermund, K., & Brandtstädter, J. (2003). Coping with deficits and losses in later life: From compensatory action to accommodation. *Psychology and Aging, 18,* 896–905.

Ryan, R. M. (1995). Psychological needs and the facilitation of integrative processes. *Journal of Personality, 63,* 397–427.

Ryff, C. D. (1989). In the eye of the beholder: Views of psychological well-being among middle-aged and older adults. *Psychology and Aging, 4,* 195–210.

Ryff, C. D. (1995). Psychological well-being in adult life. *Current Directions in Psychological Science, 4,* 99–104.

Ryff, C. D., & Keyes, C. L. M. (1995). The structure of psychological well-being revisited. *Journal of Personality and Social Psychology, 69,* 719–727.

Schulz, R. (1986). Successful aging: Balancing primary and secondary control. *Adult Development and Aging News, 13,* 2–4.

Schulz, R., & Heckhausen, J. (1996). A life-span model of successful aging. *American Psychologist, 51,* 702–714.

Sheldon, K. M., & Elliot, A. J. (1999). Goal striving, need satisfaction, and longitudinal well-being: The self-concordance model. *Journal of Personality and Social Psychology, 76,* 482–497.

Singer, J. A., & Salovey, P. (1993). *The remembered self.* New York: Free Press.

Small, B. J., Hertzog, C., Hultsch, D. F., & Dixon, R. A. (2003). Stability and change in adult personality over 6 years: Findings from the Victoria Longitudinal Study. *Journals of Gerontology, 58B,* P166–P176.

Srivastava, S., John, O. P., Gosling, S. D., & Potter, J. (2003). Development of personality in early and middle adulthood: Set like plaster or persistent change? *Journal of Personality and Social Psychology, 84,* 1041–1053.

Staudinger, U. M., Marsiske, M., & Baltes, P. B. (1995). Resilience and reserve capacity in later adulthood: Potentials and limits of development across the life span. In D. Cicchetti & D. Cohen (Eds.), *Developmental psychopathology: Vol. 2. Risk, disorder, and adaptation* (pp. 801–847). New York: Wiley.

Thomae, H. E. (1976). *Patterns of aging.* Basel: Karger.

Veenhoven, R. (1991). Questions on happiness: Classical topics, modern answers, blind spots. In F. Strack, M. Argyle, & N. Schwarz (Eds.), *Subjective well-being: Vol. 2. An interdisciplinary perspective* (pp. 7–26). Oxford: Pergamon Press.

Wiese, B. S., Freund, A. M., & Baltes, P. B. (2000). Selection, optimization, and compensation: An action-related approach to work and partnership. *Journal of Vocational Behavior, 57,* 273–300.

Wiese, B. S., Freund, A. M., & Baltes, P. B. (2002). Subjective career success and emotional well-being: Longitudinal predictive power of selection, optimization and compensation. *Journal of Vocational Behavior, 60,* 321–335.

Wiese, B. S., & Schmitz, B. (2002). Action regulation at university: Application of a developmental meta-model. *Zeitschrift für Entwicklungspsychologie und Pädagogische Psychologie, 34,* 80–94.

Wrosch, C., & Heckhausen, J. (1999). Control processes before and after passing a developmental deadline: Activation and deactivation of intimate relationship goals. *Journal of Personality and Social Psychology, 77,* 415–427.

CHAPTER 5

Wisdom, Life Longings, and Optimal Development

SUSANNE SCHEIBE, UTE KUNZMANN, and PAUL B. BALTES

IN THIS CHAPTER, we present theoretical and empirical work on two relatively novel constructs relevant for life span development: wisdom and *Sehnsucht* (life longings). Both deal with positivity in its radical form, akin to psychological utopias. Our work on these constructs was guided by the search for "new" developmental constructs that are holistic (dealing with the overall or systemic evaluation and conduct of life) and life span-integrative (dealing simultaneously with the past, the present, and the future). Our hope is that this line of inquiry aids in capturing the complexity of lifelong development, as well as essential components of the structure and function of psychological identity (P. B. Baltes, Lindenberger, & Staudinger, 2006).

In the search for such holistic and life span-integrative constructs, we were informed not only by related psychological work, but also by the nature of public discourse in everyday life and the contents of studies in the humanist tradition (*Geisteswissenschaften;* see Groffmann, 1970). We considered these traditions not so much for making psychological analysis more humanist in method; rather, we assumed that in these traditions there were themes and topics that psychological research had shied away from because of their complexity and method constraints.

BACKGROUND

In the selection of themes and topics we considered as we attempted to identify unchartered territory of life span development, wisdom was the first example

The theoretical and empirical work presented here combines insights from two projects initiated and directed by Paul B. Baltes who passed away shortly before this book was published. We owe many thanks especially to the following colleagues who served as coprincipal investigators during the various phases of the two projects, in historical order: Freya Dittmann-Kohli, Roger A. Dixon, Jacqui Smith, Ursula M. Staudinger, and Alexandra M. Freund.

(e.g., P. B. Baltes, 2004; P. B. Baltes & Smith, 1990; P. B. Baltes & Staudinger, 2000; Dittmann-Kohli & Baltes, 1990; Dixon & Baltes, 1986; Kunzmann & Baltes, 2005). Similar to others (Clayton & Birren, 1980; Sternberg, 1990), we worked on a conceptualization of wisdom as a utopian, ideal end point of human development. In more recent formulations (P. B. Baltes & Staudinger, 2000), we labeled wisdom the perfect integration of mind and virtue.

During the past few years, we were influenced by the emerging topic of the chronic incompleteness of life (P. B. Baltes, 1997a, 2006; P. B. Baltes & Smith, 2003). To explore this state, we added the topic of *Sehnsucht* (German for "longing, yearning") to our research agenda. The observation that themes of longing and desire for remote or unattainable ideals often appear in fairy tales and myths, in literature and art, in philosophical and political writings, as well as in personal conversations suggested to us that *Sehnsucht* is another candidate that deserves attention when trying to capture the deep core elements of life span continuity and change in personality (P. B. Baltes, Freund, & Scheibe, 2002; Scheibe, Freund, & Baltes, in press). In German culture, reference to *Sehnsucht* is omnipresent. However, although we are inclined to think that the experience of *Sehnsucht* can be found in most other cultures, including the American, we need to note at the outset that there is no fully equivalent word in the English language. We have therefore suggested the term "life longings" as a translation. It is meant to denote a psychological phenomenon that deals with the search for and management of a holistic and life span-integrative sense of an optimal life.

We do not claim that topics such as wisdom and life longings have been completely ignored by psychological researchers, yet up to recent times, they have not taken center stage. For the topic of wisdom, this situation seems to be changing (see the recent handbook by Sternberg & Jordan, 2005). One likely reason for this omission or long-term ignoring is the comprehensive and elusive nature of such topics, which may lead many to believe that they cannot be studied systematically and with the standards of normative psychological science. In this chapter, we hope to convince the reader that these concepts, though certainly elusive and difficult to study, have the potential to become part of scientific psychology. Efforts in that direction, we argue, advance our understanding of optimal human development, particularly of the ways individuals deal with the potentials, constraints, and contextual variations of life. As such, they also contribute to the emerging picture of adulthood and old age as a period that is characterized not only by loss and decline in various domains of functioning, but also by stability and potential for further growth. In short, we are convinced—and have started to show in our research—that wisdom and *Sehnsucht can* be studied empirically and make a meaningful, if not necessary, contribution to a science of psychological aging (P. B. Baltes, Freund, & Li, 2005).

In the following, we focus on two interrelated propositions of life span theory that suggest the theoretical and empirical significance of topics such as wisdom and life longings: the search for optimization (optimality) and its intimate connection with the notion of chronic incompleteness as a key feature of modern life. Next, we present our work on wisdom and life longings, focusing on their definition, defining characteristics, and operationalization. We also review evidence on their development across the life span. Subsequently, we discuss whether the two phenomena can be a route to optimal human development, that is, to approaching the utopia of life. We end the chapter with a discussion of how the two lines of re-search can be integrated to stimulate new, fruitful hypotheses about their inter-play in the promotion of successful development and personal growth.

THE INTERPLAY BETWEEN STRIVING FOR OPTIMALITY AND THE CHRONIC INCOMPLETENESS OF MODERN LIVES

There are at least two essential and interlocking propositions associated with life span theory (P. B. Baltes, 1997a; P. B. Baltes et al., 2006; P. B. Baltes & Smith, 2004) that suggest the theoretical and empirical significance of topics such as wisdom and life longings: first, the search for perfection (see also Tetens, 1777) and sec-ond, the notion that modern lives are marked by a continuing and perhaps grow-ing sense of imperfection and incompleteness (P. B. Baltes, 1997a).

The first component, the search for optimization (growth) or excellence, has been a hallmark topic of developmental psychology (P. B. Baltes et al., 2006), espe-cially in its child developmental tradition (Brandtstädter & Schneewind, 1977; Lerner, 2002, 2006). For Germans, the classic historical source is the two-volume milestone work of Tetens (1777; Groffmann, 1970; Lindenberger & Baltes, 1999). The leading concept of Tetens was the "perfectability of man," where he assigned the idea of perfectability both to historical social-cultural contexts and to opti-mizing expressions of individual lives and ontogenies.

The second component, the growing sense of the incompleteness of life, has at least two major sources. One is the nature of ontogeny, with its shifting age gradients of plasticity. The other likely results from a number of historic shifts in the contexts of human development that are associated with both gains and losses. Among the important historic trends that can be identified are in-creased longevity, rapid technological change, and globalization (e.g., P. B. Baltes & Freund, 2002).

First, the average length of life has substantially increased during the past cen-tury, from about 45 years in 1990 to about 80 years in 2000 (e.g., Vaupel, 1997). Historically speaking, therefore, "old age is young" (P. B. Baltes, 1997a, p. 367). Although the increase in longevity is usually regarded as a positive accomplish-ment of medical and cultural progress, there is one less obvious drawback. As P. B. Baltes noted, neither biological nor cultural evolution has had sufficient op-portunity to develop a satisfactory basis or scaffolding for the later parts of adult-hood. Thus, the aging body is not very well equipped for the challenges of old age. At the same time, many older adults have the desire for—and societal norms de-mand—a continued active and productive participation in social life. The increas-ing discrepancy between personal preferences and social norms on the one hand, and the declining resources of older adults on the other, is reflected in the in-creasing gap between the desired and actual age of older adults. When asked about the age at which they would have liked to remain, 70-year-olds report an age about 15 years below their actual age, and 90-year-olds report an age about 25 years below their actual age (Smith & Baltes, 1999).

Second, modern life is marked by accelerating technological change. New tech-nologies that permit more efficient ways of producing new or better products and services emerge at an unprecedented pace. The impact of technological change is not restricted to occupational life, but also affects social relationships and leisure activities. For example, changes in telecommunications infrastructure and the expansion of the Internet have led to new forms of communication in social relationships. This likely leads to a general sense that everything is changing and that existing knowledge and skills are less and less useful. To participate efficiently in society, lifelong learning is required, including the selective unlearning of skills that are no longer needed, as well as the acquisition of new knowledge and skills.

An increasing trend toward globalization is a third feature of modern life. Globalization denotes the increasing connectivity and interdependence of the world's markets and businesses and has been promoted by technological advances that make it easier for people to travel, communicate, and do business internationally. As economies and nations become more connected to each other, they have increased opportunity but also increased competition. Not everybody will be able to keep up with the increased competitive pressure and thus may be deprived of important resources that are available to others who win the competition. Aging is associated with a decrease in the plasticity necessary to adapt to changing environments (e.g., Kliegl, Smith, & Baltes, 1989). Therefore, older people may be at risk to be in the group who fail to keep up with the competitive pressure.

As emphasized earlier and according to the proposition that there is no gain without loss and no loss without gain (P. B. Baltes, 1997a; Brandtstädter, 1984; Labouvie-Vief, 1981), the three historical changes do not entail only progress. On the one hand, freedom and choice options have increased dramatically. Presumably, there are many more opportunities for active self-regulation and self-directed personal growth throughout the life span than was true in earlier historical times (Wrosch & Freund, 2001). Persons can nowadays choose among multiple possible developmental pathways rather then following predefined developmental tracks. On the other hand, this may go along with a loss in individuals' sense of security and mastery. Instead of knowing exactly what is right or wrong, persons are under permanent pressure to select the best options and endlessly acquire new information and skills. As P. B. Baltes and Freund (2002) note, developmental acquisitions and outcomes are never final, but need to continuously demonstrate their adaptive fitness. Lifelong learning is required. This is especially difficult with an aging body that is not well equipped for the challenges of rapid change.

The result is a sense of a permanent incompleteness and imperfection of human lives (P. B. Baltes, 1997a). As individuals move through life, they increasingly realize that many goals either cannot be pursued, can be reached only partly, or require disengagement. In addition, as people live longer and longer, it becomes increasingly clear that development does not stop when people reach adulthood. New tasks and problems emerge over the course of life that need to be confronted and solved. Moreover, individuals engage in a continuing search for personal improvement throughout the life course. As a result, the status quo is mentally contrasted with a *utopia of life.*

KNOWING ABOUT THE POTENTIALS AND CONSTRAINTS OF LIFE: WISDOM

Many psychological researchers value the investigation of individual characteristics and processes that help adults deal with the challenges of an increasingly complex world, including emotional intelligence, social competence, and self-regulation (e.g., Carstensen & Turk-Charles, 1998; Freund & Baltes, 2000; Salovey, Mayer, & Caruso, 2002; Sternberg, 1999). Wisdom is a candidate that we have considered in our own work (P. B. Baltes & Kunzmann, 2003; P. B. Baltes & Smith, 1990; P. B. Baltes & Staudinger, 2000; Dittmann-Kohli & Baltes, 1990; Dixon & Baltes, 1986). At the core of this concept is the notion of a perfect, perhaps utopian integration of knowledge and character, mind and virtue (P. B. Baltes & Kunzmann, 2003; P. B. Baltes & Staudinger, 2000). Although the psychology of wisdom is a relatively new field, several promising theoretical and operational definitions of wisdom have been developed (for reviews see P. B. Baltes & Staudinger, 2000; Kramer, 2000; Kunzmann & Baltes, 2005; Sternberg, 1990, 1998). In these models, wisdom is thought to be different from other human strengths in that it facilitates an integrative and holistic approach toward life's challenges and problems—an approach that embraces past, present, and future dimensions of phenomena, values different points of views, considers contextual variations, and acknowledges the uncertainties inherent in any sense-making of the past, present, and future.

A second important feature of wisdom is that it involves an awareness that individual and collective well-being are tied together so that one cannot exist without the other. In this sense, wisdom has been said to refer to time-tested knowledge that guides our behavior in ways that optimize productivity on the level of individuals, groups, and even society (e.g., Kramer, 2000; Sternberg, 1998).

Finally, given that wisdom has been linked to the ancient idea of a good life at all times, its acquisition during ontogenesis may be incompatible with a hedonic life orientation and a predominantly pleasurable, passive, and sheltered life. Given their interest in self-realization and the maximization of a common good, wiser people are likely to partake in behaviors that contribute to, rather than consume, resources (Kunzmann & Baltes, 2003a, 2003b; Sternberg, 1998). Also, an interest in understanding the significance and deeper meaning of phenomena, including the blending of developmental gains and losses, most likely is linked to emotional complexity (Labouvie-Vief, 1990) and to what has been called "constructivistic" melancholy (P. B. Baltes, 1997b).

Although there appears to be considerable agreement on several important ideas about the definition, development, and functions of wisdom, all existing psychological wisdom models encompass their unique features. On an abstract level of description, there are two ways of studying wisdom in psychological research (P. B. Baltes & Kunzmann, 2004). One is to focus on the nature of wise persons, that is, their intellectual, motivational, and emotional characteristics. This work is grounded in research on social and personality psychology (e.g., Ardelt, 2004; Erikson, 1980; Wink & Helson, 1997). An approach that we have pursued has been to define wisdom as a body of highly developed knowledge on the basis of relevant psychological and cultural-historical wisdom work (e.g., P. B. Baltes & Smith, 1990; P. B. Baltes & Staudinger, 2000). This approach proceeds from the idea that a comprehensive definition of wisdom requires going beyond the individual and his or her characteristics, simply because wisdom is an ideal rather than a state of being.

THE BERLIN WISDOM MODEL

Integrating work on the aging mind and personality, life span-developmental theory, and cultural-historical work on wisdom, in the Berlin paradigm, wisdom has been defined as highly valued and outstanding expert knowledge about dealing with fundamental, that is, existential, problems related to the meaning and conduct of life (e.g., P. B. Baltes & Kunzmann, 2003; P. B. Baltes & Smith, 1990; P. B. Baltes & Staudinger, 2000; Dittmann-Kohli & Baltes, 1990; Dixon & Baltes, 1986). These problems are typically complex and poorly defined and have multiple, yet unknown, solutions. Deciding on a particular career path, accepting the death of a loved one, dealing with personal mortality, and solving long-lasting conflicts among family members exemplify the types of problems that call for wisdom-related expertise. In contrast, more circumscribed everyday problems can be effectively handled by using more limited abilities. To solve a math problem, for example, wisdom-related expertise usually is not particularly helpful.

Five criteria were developed to describe this body of knowledge in more detail. Expert knowledge about the meaning and conduct of life is thought to approach wisdom if it meets *all* five criteria. Two criteria are labeled basic because they are characteristic of all types of expertise: (1) rich factual knowledge about human nature and the life course and (2) rich procedural knowledge about ways of dealing with life problems. The three other criteria are labeled metacriteria because they are thought to be unique to wisdom and, in addition, carry the notion of being universal: (3) life span contextualism, that is, an awareness and understanding of the many contexts of life, how they relate to each other and change over the life span; (4) value relativism and tolerance, that is, an acknowledgment of individual, social, and cultural differences in values and life priorities; and (5) knowledge about handling uncertainty, including the limits of one's own knowledge.

To test for wisdom, participants are instructed to think aloud about hypothetical life problems. One might be: "Imagine that someone gets a call from a good friend who says that he or she cannot go on anymore and wants to commit suicide." Another problem reads: "A 15-year-old girl wants to get married right away. What could one consider and do?" Trained raters evaluate responses to those problems by using the five criteria that were specified as defining wisdom-related knowledge. The assessment of wisdom-related knowledge on the basis of these criteria exhibits satisfactory reliability and validity. For example, middle-aged and older public figures from Berlin nominated as life experienced or wise by a panel of journalists—independently of the Berlin definition of wisdom—were among the top performers in laboratory wisdom tasks and outperformed same-age adults who were not nominated (P. B. Baltes, Staudinger, Maercker, & Smith, 1995).

THE DEVELOPMENT OF WISDOM ACROSS THE LIFE SPAN

The Berlin research program on wisdom has addressed a broad range of questions concerning the development of wisdom, including individual and social factors that facilitate or hinder its acquisition and refinement (for reviews, see P. B. Baltes & Staudinger, 2000; Kunzmann & Baltes, 2005; Staudinger, 1999). Some of the major findings are the following.

First, and consistent with the idea that wisdom is an ideal rather than a state of being, high levels of wisdom-related knowledge are rare. Many adults are on the way to wisdom, but very few people approach a high level of wisdom-related knowledge as measured by the Berlin wisdom tasks.

Second, wisdom-related knowledge seems to begin to develop during late adolescence to young adulthood. Investigating a sample of 14- to 20-year-olds, Pasupathi, Staudinger, and Baltes (2001) reported that wisdom-related knowledge considerably increased in this life period. Studying older adults, however, did not evince marked further changes for the average case. Specifically, in four studies with a total sample size of 533 individuals ranging in age from 20 to 89 years, the relationship between wisdom-related knowledge and chronological age was virtually zero and nonsignificant (P. B. Baltes & Smith, 1990; Staudinger, 1999). Within the limitations of cross-sectional data, this evidence suggests that, on a group-level analysis, wisdom-related knowledge remains stable over the adult years into the 60s and 70s. Although age-comparative studies on wisdom have been limited to what has been called the third age (i.e., young old adults), the evidence suggests that, given the absence of pathology such as dementia, some older adults will continue to perform well on wisdom tasks beyond their 70s (for reviews, see Kunzmann & Baltes, 2005; Staudinger, 1999).

Third, for wisdom-related knowledge and judgment to develop during the second half of life, factors other than age are critical. The evidence suggests that it takes a complex coalition of expertise-enhancing factors from different domains, ranging from a person's social-cognitive style (e.g., social intelligence, openness to experience) over this person's immediate social context (e.g., presence of role models) to societal and cultural conditions (e.g., exposure to societal transitions). Past prediction studies of wisdom suggest that neither academic intelligence nor basic personality traits play a major role in the development of wisdom-related knowledge during adulthood. General life experiences, professional training and practice, certain motivational preferences, such as an interest in understanding and helping others, and social-emotional competencies, such as empathic concern, seem to be more important (Kunzmann & Baltes, 2003a, 2003b; Smith, Staudinger, & Baltes, 1994; Staudinger, Lopez, & Baltes, 1997; Staudinger, Smith, & Baltes, 1992). If such a coalition of facilitating factors is present, some individuals may continue a developmental trajectory toward higher levels of wisdom-related knowledge. Therefore, simply getting older is not a sufficient condition for the development of higher levels of wisdom-related knowledge, and yet, older adults are among the top performers in wisdom-related tasks.

In sum and as graphically presented in Figure 5.1, wisdom can be regarded as a highly developed body of knowledge about the meaning and conduct of life. Wisdom-related knowledge involves an awareness of the strong interrelatedness of self and others, and it considers both the potentials and the constraints of life.

EXPERIENCING PERSONALLY THE POTENTIALS AND CONSTRAINTS OF LIFE: TOWARD A DEVELOPMENTAL PSYCHOLOGY OF LIFE LONGINGS

Whereas wisdom involves generalized knowledge about human nature and the life course, *Sehnsucht* (life longings) can be regarded as personalized, experiential knowledge, and awareness of the fundamental conditions of life, including the incompleteness and imperfection of life. It is the recurring, strong desire for ideal, alternative states and experiences coupled with a profound feeling that life is

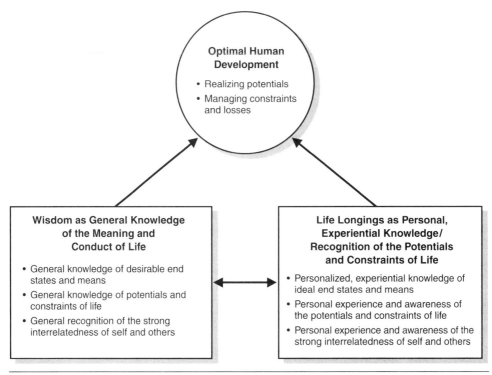

Figure 5.1   Theoretical Model of the Interrelations among Optimal Human Development, Wisdom, and Life Longings.

incomplete. It is often assumed that *Sehnsucht* is associated simultaneously with joy and sadness, producing a unique mixture of positive and negative feelings.

Sehnsucht is a prominent concept in everyday culture and the humanities, particularly in the German-speaking world. Its meaning structure is strongly influenced by German literature, especially from the time of Romanticism (around 1800). Romantic poets and painters cultivated the feeling of *Sehnsucht*; they regarded it as the primary route to gaining insight into themselves and the world (Danzer, 1998; Hogrebe, 1994). In literary circles in general, it is common to interpret novels or biographies by reference to a particular *Sehnsucht* as that guiding theme of the work or its main character. The popularity of *Sehnsucht* is illustrated by a recent public contest of the "most beautiful German word" called by the German Language Council: *Sehnsucht* was the third most often nominated (Spiegel Online, 2004). Its popularity is further illustrated by the existence of a tea called Moments of Longing available on the German market. The tea promises to produce a mood of longing for a distant place, for new fascinating experiences, as "nothing is more seductive than what seems unreachable."

The theme of *Sehnsucht* and longing has also been a subject of philosophical theorizing about the human condition. Philosophers often argue that experience itself is a desire, longing, or hope for utopian conditions (e.g., Bloch, 1959; Fichte, 1794/1962; Hegel, 1807/1927; for a discussion of longing in philosophy, see Danzer, 1998; Hogrebe, 1994; Ravicz, 1998). For example, the German philosopher Bloch posited that individuals are unfinished and animated by utopian dreams of a better life. According to this position, individual and collective hopes and longings are one of the driving forces behind personal, cultural, and historical developments.

Such popularity indicates the importance that is allocated to emotional and mental representations of peaks of life and unfulfilled desires, and it reflects thoughts about the unrealizability of dreams and chronic incompleteness as core features of lived lives. Clearly, *Sehnsucht* seems to be a topic of public interest that deserves attention by psychological theory and research.

A Psychological Conceptualization of Life Longings: A Framework of Six Structural Characteristics

When attempting to define and operationalize a new concept that is central in everyday culture and the humanities, it is important to keep these perspectives in mind. Thus, a psychological conceptualization should be sufficiently similar to the general use of the term in everyday language and the humanities. In the dictionary, *Sehnsucht* is defined as "a high degree of intense and often painful desire for something, particularly if there is no hope to attain the desired or when its attainment is uncertain, still far away" (Grimm & Grimm, 1854–1871/1984). Similar to *Zeitgeist, Sehnsucht* is difficult to translate into English. We have therefore suggested the term "life longings" to emphasize the holistic character of *Sehnsucht*, as well as its extension across multiple domains and times of life (Scheibe et al., in press).

Moving toward a psychology of life longings, we tried to integrate the dictionary definition of *Sehnsucht* with the general framework of life span psychology, that is, the central assumptions and propositions about lifelong development that have been formulated (e.g., P. B. Baltes, 1987). We also reviewed the existing (mostly conceptual) work on the topic, including the works of Boesch (1998), Holm (1999), Palaian (1993), Ravicz (1998), Vogt (1993), and Belk, Ger, and Askegaard (2003). While reviewing these different perspectives, six core characteristics repeatedly emerged. In a first study with 299 adults ages 18 to 91 years, we were able to show that these six characteristics are a useful description of the experiential gestalt or structure of life longings (Scheibe et al., in press).

The first characteristic is the observation that a central aspect of the experience of life longings is *a feeling of incompleteness and a sense of imperfection* of one's life. Life longings mean that something is missing that appears essential for a meaningful life and that, if attained, would make life more complete (Boesch, 1998; Holm, 1999). Thus, life longings can be regarded as the experiential awareness that human life is an ongoing process that in reality is never perfect and complete.

The second aspect is related to the sense of incompleteness and refers to the observation that life longings are directed at an idealized alternative to the imperfect present, that is, a *personal utopia* of desired alternative expressions of life. In other words, the imperfect present is mentally contrasted with experienced, imagined, and often counterfactual alternatives of one's life that are idealized and unrestricted by the limits of reality. They may represent individuals' memories or expectations of highly positive developmental states and conceptions of their own ideal life course or self. These utopian ideals can be approximated, but they cannot be fully attained (Boesch, 1998).

A third characteristic that repeatedly emerged in the literature, and that is consistent with a life span perspective, is that life longings extend beyond the present into the past and future. We termed this characteristic the "ontogenetic tritime focus" of life longings. Life longings can be directed at memories of past peak experiences (e.g., moments of intense joy, positive feelings associated with a past life phase or place) that one desires to reexperience in the present and future. Life longings can also be directed at peak experiences envisioned for the future. Thus, retrospection, concurrent evaluation, and prospection are expected to operate together in creating the experience of life longings (Vogt, 1993). This does not imply that life longings necessarily exists for or encompasses the whole life span from childhood to old age, but they are assumed to always extend beyond the present into the past and future.

The fourth proposed characteristic of life longings is their *emotional ambivalence.* In the existing literature, life longings are often described as "enjoyable discomfort" or "fervent desire" that may include pleasure, excitement, hope, and energetic feelings, but also the pain of loss, frustration, and regret (Belk et al., 2003; Boesch, 1998; Palaian, 1993). Emotional ambivalence is consistent with an attribute fundamental to life span theory: that development is multifunctional and always involves both gains and losses (e.g., P. B. Baltes, 1987; Brandtstädter, 1984; Labouvie-Vief, 1981). Therefore, the emotional quality of life longings is postulated to be inherently ambivalent or bittersweet. For example, life longings probably are pleasurable or sweet because they involve pleasant fantasies; at the same time, they probably are unpleasant and bitter because these fantasies are out of reach, thus producing an ambivalent, bittersweet emotional quality.

The fifth proposed characteristic of life longings is that they elicit reflective and evaluative processes. We assume that life longings are associated with the evaluation of one's actual developmental state, relative to one's lifetime and relative to personal or social standards of life quality. Self-critical reflection on the past, present, and (expected) future, as well as an exploratory search for optimal ways of living, are therefore expected to be part of the experience of life longings.

Finally, we assume with Boesch (1991, 1998) that life longings are rich in symbolic meaning. Symbolic richness implies that life longings are more than a specific, concrete behavior or experience. Instead, specific objects or targets of life longings should be linked to more encompassing mental and emotional representations for which they stand. A specific longing (e.g., for an embrace by a loved one) becomes relevant for our consideration of life longings only if the mental and emotional representations associated with this desired state are linked with a broader configuration of thoughts and feelings that are relevant for multiple domains or times of life.

Considering these six characteristics as a whole clarifies that life longings are not fully equivalent with existing psychological concepts, such as goals, regret, hope, or possible selves. Life longings might share single characteristics with these other concepts, but the overlap does not extend to all six characteristics. For example, both life longings and goals target desired states and provide a sense of directionality in life. Different from goals, however, the object of life longings is principally unattainable, its emotional tone is inherently ambivalent, and the desired state is less concrete. Accordingly, goals are more controllable and have a stronger influence on the structuring of everyday life (Mayser, Scheibe, & Riediger, 2006). Life longings, in contrast, are probably more important during times of intensified life reflection, evaluation, and planning. As elaborated later in the chapter, it seems to have important functions for giving directionality for future development and managing losses and nonrealizability. We therefore argue that the concept of life longings is unique and is not adequately captured by existing psychological concepts.

ASSESSMENT OF LIFE LONGINGS

Based on the framework of the six life longing characteristics, our research group developed a self-report procedure to assess life longings in young, middle-aged, and old adults (Scheibe, 2005; Scheibe et al., in press). This procedure combines idiographic and nomothetic techniques. In the idiographic part, participants are asked to generate a list of life longings defined as "strong wishes for persons, things, events, or experiences from your personal past, present, or future that are intense, enduring, and not easily attainable at present." This task is supported by a "guided mental journey through life," in which participants visualize different life phases from their past, present, and future (childhood, youth, young adulthood, middle adulthood, old age) by imagining significant persons, places, or experiences from each life phase. The procedure requires participants to reflect on their whole life, including memories of the past and expectations and fantasies about the future. After visualizing each life phase, participants are asked to report life longings related to this phase if they have any that are still relevant today. Subsequently, they select their three most important life longings.

Table 5.1 lists examples of life longings from different life domains reported in the study by Scheibe et al. (in press). The reported life longings were highly stable across a time interval of 5 weeks. When asked to generate their life longings again after 5 weeks, 85% of participants regenerated their most important life longing, 75% regenerated their second most important life longing, and 72% regenerated their third most important life longing. These data are a first indication that life longings are not fleeting phenomena, but are part of persons' self-concept and their "personal utopia of life."

In the nomothetic part of the task, participants rate each of their three selected life longings on a self-report questionnaire (Scheibe et al, in press; see Table 5.2 for sample items). The questionnaire contains scales covering the six characteristics defined as central for the experience of life longings (personal utopia, sense of incompleteness, ontogenetic tritime focus, ambivalent emotions, life reflection and evaluation, and symbolic richness) and other important characteristics (frequency and intensity, functional significance, and controllability of life longings). All scales evince acceptable internal consistencies and substantial retest stabilities across 5 weeks (Scheibe et al., in press).

THE DEVELOPMENT OF LIFE LONGINGS ACROSS THE LIFE SPAN

When in the life course do life longings emerge, and how do they change with advancing age? The concept of life longings outlined in the present conceptualization is a complex phenomenon with cognitive, affective, and motivational components. Such a phenomenon is likely to involve abilities that become fully available only in middle to late adolescence. For example, the emotionally ambivalent quality of life longings requires an understanding that multiple, and

Table 5.1

Examples of Life Longings in Different Life Domains

Percentage	Life Domain	Reported Life Longing
41	Family	To found a family, without ever worrying about money, divorce, and so on
40	Self-image/ State of mind	Lightheartedness (not having to care about anything; being without worry, just like a child)
33	Partnership/ Intimacy/ Sexuality	A partner who is with me for the rest of my life, who gives me warmth and security, and who sticks by me through rough times
23	Health	A life without pain that allows me to be active again
23	Leisure/ Hobbies	A journey through Europe along with the spring! This has been my unfulfilled dream ever since I can remember
20	Work/ Occupation	Earn a doctoral degree and become head of a company (achieve a high level of education, work independently, and lead others)
16	Living situation/ Location	The house of my dreams with a garden and a sun terrace
15	Friendships	A friend, who became a soldier during the war. I miss him. I have never seen him again.
14	Past or future life phase/ Death and dying	My first love, apprenticeship, work: to relive these times with the wisdom I have today
14	Financial situation	To get back to a life without worry about debts and payments
14	Political/ World situation	That all people of this world live together peacefully and respect human dignity

Note: The sample included 299 adults, 19 to 81 years of age. Reported life longings were assigned to life domains by two independent raters (Cohen's $\kappa = .87$). On an anonymous follow-up checklist, 35% ($n = 99$) of participants reported having additional, "more private" life longings. Most important categories (in descending order) were sexual experiences ($n = 56$), own death ($n = 22$), infidelity ($n = 18$), revenge ($n = 15$), and death of others ($n = 13$), among others (multiple endorsements were possible).

sometimes opposite, feelings can be directed at the same target or situation, an ability that emerges in early adolescence (Saarni, 1999). Other components of life longings, including symbolic richness, tritime focus, and reflection and evaluation, require autobiographical reasoning and memory, abilities that become fully available only in middle to late adolescence (e.g., Bluck & Habermas, 2001; Pasupathi et al., 2001; Staudinger, 2001). Therefore, we assume that the developmental origin of life longings as defined by the six characteristics lies before adulthood, presumably in late adolescence or early adulthood. For the majority of individuals, the basic structure of life longings should be established by the time adulthood is reached.

Similar to the developmental course of wisdom (P. B. Baltes & Staudinger, 2000), we would not expect any major age-related changes in the basic structure

Table 5.2
Sample Items From the Life Longing Questionnaire

Scale (Number of Items)[a]	Sample Item[b]
Structural Elaboration	
Personal utopia (3 × 3)	I am longing for something too perfect to be true.
Incompleteness (3 × 3)	My longing means that something essential is missing in my life.
Tritime focus (2 × 3)	My longing has to do with people, things, experiences, or events . . . from my past/present/future.[c]
Ambivalent emotions (4 × 3)	My longing is a bittersweet feeling.
Reflection (4 × 3)	My longing makes me think a lot about the meaning of my life.
Symbolic richness (3 × 3)	What I am longing for is heavily filled with meaning.
Salience (4 × 3)	My longing appears . . . *very rarely* (0)/*very often* (5).
Subjective Developmental Function	
Directionality (3 × 3)	My longing gives direction to my life.
Managing nonrealizability (3 × 3)	Experiencing my longing partially compensates for something I cannot have in reality.
Perceived Controllability	
Control over life longing experience (3 × 3)	I can always control my feelings of longing very well.
Control over life longing realization (3 × 3)	I am sure that I can fulfill my longing sometime.

[a] This index indicates the number of differently worded items multiplied by the three life longings, as persons rated each item for each of their three life longings.
[b] Responses ranged from 0 (does not apply at all) to 5 (applies very much), except for Salience.
[c] The indicator was derived by calculating the mean of the three items.

of life longings across the ages of adulthood. Instead, subsequent adult changes should be determined more by factors other than chronological age, such as personality, cognitive style, motivational orientations, and life experiences. Whereas the structure of life longings should be invariant, the *content* of life longings (i.e., the objects that persons are longing for, such as persons, places, events, or experiences) are expected to change as individuals move through the stages and settings of life. In addition, it is possible that adult age groups vary in terms of the more quantitative aspects of life longings, such as its frequency and intensity, and a sense of controllability.

Results from our study with young, middle-aged, and old adults are largely consistent with these predictions about the developmental course of life longings (Scheibe et al., in press). In terms of mean levels, five of the six core characteristics of life longings (personal utopia, ontogenetic tritime focus, ambivalent emotions, life reflection and evaluation, and symbolic richness) were invariant across adult age groups. In contrast, feelings of the incompleteness of life associated with life longings decreased with age, indicating that older adults have fewer feelings that life is incomplete or imperfect. This is consistent with the finding that older adults "shift horizons" by approximating their ideal and actual views of themselves (Ryff, 1991). Stability across age groups was also found in terms of the covariance structure of the six characteristics (Scheibe, 2005). Considering the age trajectories of the six core characteristics, it can be concluded that the basic, experiential structure of life longings is largely stable across the ages of adulthood.

What about content differences? One possible framework to organize the contents of life longings are the age-specific themes described by Erikson (1980) or the developmental tasks outlined by Havighurst (1948). According to this framework, identity is the primary topic in adolescence. Social connectedness, establishing a partnership, and occupational development are in the foreground for young adults. Work and family, as well as the balance between the two, are in the focus in middle adulthood, and older adults are expected to deal primarily with health and generativity-related themes (e.g., family members, politics, and the society at large).

For each of these tasks, our assumption is that life longings become relevant as individuals wrestle with incompleteness and imperfection in achieving these goals, and as they review, manage, and plan their lives as a whole. Accordingly, life longings are expected to deal with current and past developmental themes. The example of partnership may serve to explain this point. Finding a partner is an important developmental task in young adulthood. This task can be expressed as a concrete, controllable, and action-relevant goal that stimulates active goal striving. At the same time, young adults may have a utopian and symbolically rich image of an ideal partner that is less concrete, not fully attainable, and possibly accompanied by ambivalent emotions and reflective processes, that is, a life longing. Thus, goals and life longings can exist simultaneously in the same life domain. In addition, life longings may be directed at *past* developmental tasks that have not been (fully) achieved. Being single in middle or late adulthood may lead to strong feelings of failure and incompleteness and, given the lower probability of establishing a satisfactory partnership in later phases of adulthood, may give rise to a partnership-related life longing.

Age differences obtained in the Scheibe et al. (in press) study are largely consistent with both of these views. Participants rated the extent to which their three life longings were related to each of 13 thematic categories, such as health, partnership, and work/education. All age groups reported that their life longings were most strongly related to physical well-being, probably because it is the precondition for an active and self-determined life. Age group differences emerged, however, in the ranks obtained for the remaining content domains. Among the next most important content domains of life longings reported by younger adults (19 to 39 years) were, in descending order, personal characteristics/identity, family, and partnership. For middle-aged adults (40 to 59 years), these were family, partnership, and personal characteristics. Hence, personal characteristics became somewhat less important and received a lower rank. In older adults (60 to 81 years), family, health, and friendships obtained ranks 2, 3, and 4, respectively. Further age differences emerged in the domains of work/education and politics/world situation. Work/education was ranked 8 and 7 in young and middle-aged adults, respectively, but ranked only 12 in older adults, indicating the decreasing importance of occupational development with age. Politics/world situation moved from rank 12 in young and middle-aged adults to rank 10 in older adults, suggesting older adults' increasing generative interest in the society at large. These results suggest that life longings are mostly directed at current developmental themes. However, as the prevalence of identity themes in young adults and the prevalence of partnership themes in middle-aged adults suggests, life longings can also be directed at developmental tasks of earlier life periods.

Finally, we tested age differences in the more quantitative elements of life longings, such as intensity, frequency, and controllability. There were no age differences in intensity and frequency of life longings: across age groups, participants reported experiencing life longings equally frequently and intensely. Interesting age differences emerged with regard to a sense of control over life longings. We found that, compared to younger adults, older adults felt more able to regulate their experience of longing (indicated by a positive age correlation), but less able to actually fulfill their longings (indicated by a negative age correlation). These findings are in conformity with the emerging picture of stable or even improved emotional functioning and emotional control in later periods of adulthood (e.g., Isaacowitz, Charles, & Carstensen, 2000), yet a reduced capacity to shape the external environment according to own desires and preferences (e.g., Brandtstädter & Renner, 1990; Lachman & Weaver, 1998).

To summarize, we have offered a developmental conceptualization of the phenomenon of *Sehnsucht,* or life longings, which was identified as a central yet understudied concept in everyday culture and the humanities. This conceptualization defines life longings as recurrent, emotionally rich mental representations of ideal, alternative states and realizations of life with six core characteristics. Life longings involve (1) utopian (unattainable) conceptions of ideal development; (2) a sense of the incompleteness and imperfection of life; (3) a conjoint focus on the personal past, present, and future (tritime focus); (4) ambivalent emotions; (5) a sense of life reflection and evaluation; and (6) richness in symbolic meaning. These characteristics were derived from a review of previous literature on longing and *Sehnsucht,* as well as basic assumptions of life span theory. We have described a self-report assessment procedure based on this conceptualization. Using this assessment procedure, we have provided evidence that, similar to wisdom-related knowledge, the basic structure of life longings is largely stable across the ages of adulthood. The specific targets or contents of life longings are not fully invariant across adulthood, however. Whereas themes of identity and occupational development are more important in younger adults, family, health, and generativity-related themes come to the foreground in later stages of adulthood.

Coming back to our integrative model presented in Figure 5.1, life longings can be regarded as personalized, experiential knowledge of ideal end states and means, the personal experience and awareness of the potentials and constraints of life, and the personal experience and awareness of the strong interrelatedness of self and others.

WISDOM AND LIFE LONGINGS: A ROUTE TO PERSONAL GROWTH AND SUCCESSFUL DEVELOPMENT?

Can wisdom and life longings contribute to successful development, the maximal realization of potentials, and the optimal management of constraints and losses?

Before turning to this question, it will be useful to reflect on the criteria of successful development.

Successful development has been operationalized in many ways, including with subjective and objective, short- and long-term, and specific and global criteria (e.g., P. B. Baltes & Baltes, 1990; Freund & Riediger, 2003). Among the subjective criteria, subjective well-being, persons' feelings about and evaluations of the quality of their lives, is considered as one of the most important criteria. Recently, it has become common to distinguish between two different facets of subjective well-being, one related to personal growth and the other related to happiness. For example, McGregor and Little (1998) distinguish between happiness, which they relate to efficacy and the successful accomplishment of goals, and meaning, which they view as integrity and the consistency of goal pursuits with the self-concept. Helson and Srivastava (2001), in analogy to Ryff (1989), have made a distinction between environmental mastery and personal growth. Whereas environmental mastery emphasizes mastery and smooth functioning within society, personal growth involves intrapsychic differentiation, self-actualization, and independence of social norms. Kunzmann, Stange, and Jordan (2005) have proposed a similar distinction between hedonic and growth-related lifestyles. People with hedonic lifestyles value pleasure, consumption, and entertainment. In contrast, people with growth-related lifestyles are more likely to partake in behaviors that contribute to, rather than consume, resources; they consider the welfare of others important and have an interest in personal development. In the realm of affect regulation, Labouvie-Vief and Medler (2002) propose two similar regulatory strategies: affect optimization (the constraint of affect to positive values) and affect complexity (the amplification of affect in search of differentiation and objectivity). Ideally, the two aspects of subjective well-being, happiness and growth, can be integrated; however, in everyday life, we expect that individuals often prioritize one aspect over the other given that the behaviors involved in the pursuit of happiness are often incompatible with the behaviors involved in a growth-related lifestyle and vice versa.

We propose that wisdom and life longings should be more strongly related to the personal growth aspect of subjective well-being than to happiness. As outlined before, both phenomena deal with the potentials *and* constraints of life. Persons high on wisdom-related knowledge are presumably motivated to understand the complex and sometimes paradoxical nature of life; they view events and experiences from multiple perspectives; and they simultaneously consider the gains and losses inherent in any developmental change (Kunzmann & Baltes, 2003b). Similarly, life longings involve at the same time ideal conceptions of self and development (i.e., personal utopias of life) and a sense of incompleteness and imperfection. Therefore, persons with moderate- to high-level expressions of life longings may be highly self-critical and have high ideals and seek to attain them. It is therefore unlikely that wiser persons and persons with strong life longings have an abundance of pleasant feelings. Nevertheless, it is possible that wisdom and life longings contribute to personal growth.

THE RELATION BETWEEN WISDOM AND SUCCESSFUL DEVELOPMENT

Empirical evidence from our laboratory is consistent with the idea that wisdom is knowledge about ways of developing oneself, not only without violating others' rights but also with coproducing resources for others to develop (Kunzmann &

Baltes, 2003a, 2003b). In a questionnaire study we assessed wisdom-related knowledge by our standard procedure and, in addition, measured several motivational and emotional dispositions such as value orientations (i.e., preference for a pleasurable life, personal growth, insight, well-being of friends, environmental protection, societal engagement), preferred modes of conflict management (i.e., dominance, submission, avoidance, cooperation), and affective experiences (pleasantness, positive involvement, and negative affect).

As mentioned earlier, our specific predictions were based on the notion that wisdom-related knowledge requires and reflects a joint concern for developing one's own and others' potential (see also Sternberg, 1998). In contrast, a predominant search for self-centered pleasure and comfort should not be associated with wisdom. Accordingly, people high on wisdom-related knowledge should report (a) a profile of values that is oriented toward personal growth, insight, and the well-being of others, rather than a pleasurable and comfortable life; (b) a cooperative approach to managing interpersonal conflicts rather than a dominant, submissive, or avoidant style; and (c) an affective structure that is process- and environment-oriented rather than evaluative and self-centered.

The findings reported in Kunzmann and Baltes (2003b) were consistent with our theory-guided predictions. As depicted in Figure 5.2, people with higher levels of wisdom-related knowledge reported less preference for values revolving around a pleasurable and comfortable life. Instead, they reported preferring self-oriented values such as personal growth and insight, as well as a preference for other-oriented values related to environmental protection, societal engagement, and the well-being of friends. People with high levels of wisdom-related knowledge also showed less preference for conflict management strategies that reflect

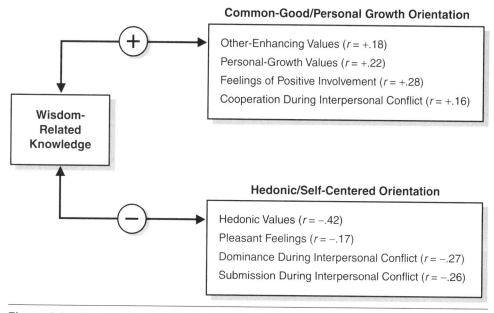

Figure 5.2   Wisdom-Related Knowledge and Its Association with Values, Affect, and Interpersonal Behavior. *Note:* The evidence suggests that wisdom is incompatible with a hedonic and self-centered life orientation.

either a one-sided concern with one's own interests (i.e., dominance), a one-sided concern with others' interests (i.e., submission), or no concern at all (i.e., avoidance). As predicted, they preferred a cooperative approach reflecting a joint concern for one's own and the opponent's interests. Finally, people with high levels of wisdom-related knowledge reported that they less frequently experience self-centered and hedonic pleasant feelings (e.g., happiness, amusement) but more frequently process-oriented and environment-centered positive emotions (e.g., interest, inspiration). Together our findings are consistent with the notion that wisdom-related knowledge involves complexity and modulation rather than pleasure, as well as a joint commitment to the well-being of oneself and others (e.g., P. B. Baltes & Staudinger, 2000; Kramer, 2000; Sternberg, 1998). Nevertheless, our findings can be considered only a first step toward understanding how people with different degrees of wisdom-related knowledge differ on the behavioral level in specific interpersonal situations. Given the limitations of questionnaire approaches to studying behaviors (e.g., selective memory or interpretative biases), we share the view that experimental research is needed in which people's actual behaviors are observed.

THE RELATION BETWEEN LIFE LONGINGS AND SUCCESSFUL DEVELOPMENT

Do life longings have any functional significance for the planning, evaluation, and management of life development, and thus contribute to successful development? Although we are far from having a systematic theoretical account of the functional role of life longings, we assume that this is the case. For example, we assume that life longings may give a general sense of *directionality* to development by outlining ideal life trajectories and producing powerful incentives to act toward the realization of these ideals. In this sense, life longings may help to select the most suitable developmental tracks, in which environmental demands and support systems converge with individual motivations, skills, and biological capacity—an essential aspect of adaptive and active self-regulation (P. B. Baltes & Baltes, 1990; Freund & Baltes, 2000).

In addition, life longings may help to *regulate (irreversible) losses and unrealizable life paths.* We assume that experiences of life longings often occur together with the insight that not all desirable goals of life can be realized. Some personal goals that are perceived as being unlikely to be achieved may be transformed into life longings. They have less reality status but may continue to operate on the imaginary level as occasional dreamlike motivators and states of consumption. In this sense, life longings may serve as a mechanism of managing conditions of loss, failure, and unattainability.

Empirical data are consistent with this view (Scheibe et al., in press). Specifically, participants with high-level expressions of life longings reported that their life longings gave them a high degree of directionality to their future development (a key item read: "My life longing gives a direction to my life") and helped them to regulate losses and incompleteness ("Experiencing my life longing partially compensates for something I cannot have in reality"). The latter function was more strongly endorsed by older adults. Certainly, later stages of life bring more and more threats to the realization of personal goals, as aging is associated with accumulating losses (P. B. Baltes & Smith, 2003) and a shortening in the lifetime left to live (Lang & Carstensen, 2002). Therefore, using life longings as a strategy to manage loss and unattainability may become increasingly important with advancing age.

Given that life longings have at least two important functions for the planning, evaluation, and management of life, one would expect them to be related to more general positive developmental outcomes, such as subjective well-being. However, too much of life longings could also be an indicator of chronic incompleteness and melancholy and the perception that important aspirations were not and never will be reached. This should be particularly true for persons who have low control over their life longings. In this vein, life longings may have costs in the happiness aspect of subjective well-being. Expectations would be different for personal growth. Because life longings entail the imaginary anticipation of highly positive psychological states that surpass the status quo and elicits processes of self-critical reflection about oneself and the human condition, they may promote self-knowledge, creativity, and wisdom. Such links have been suggested in previous writings on life longings (Boesch, 1998; Hogrebe, 1994; Vogt, 1993).

In our previous empirical work, we started to explore the relationship between life longings and what may be considered aspects of happiness. Specifically, we considered correlations with subjective well-being, negative affectivity, and a desire for change in different life domains. We obtained negative associations: Persons with high-level expressions of life longings reported lower happiness and psychological well-being, more desire for change, and higher negative affectivity (Scheibe et al., in press). These negative associations were lower in persons who reported that they were able to influence the onset, course, and end of life longing-related thoughts and emotions (i.e., have a high degree of subjective control over their life longings). In fact, the negative correlations reached the range of zero associations when a high degree of control was reported. Such a finding reinforces the important role that a sense of control plays in the conduct and evaluation of life (M. M. Baltes & Baltes, 1986; Lachman & Bertrand, 2001).

So far, little attention has been paid to the relationship between life longings and more typical aspects of personal growth, such as self-knowledge and creativity. Self-knowledge, for example, includes knowledge about personal preferences and values, goals and motives, abilities and achievements, and rules and strategies for regulation behavior (Markus, 1983). It is reflected in the complexity and differentiation of self-representations (Labouvie-Vief, Chiodo, Goguen, Diehl, & Orwoll, 1995). Life longings may promote self-knowledge because it directs attention to neglected needs and motives and makes people reflect about their present and ideal realities of life. Research on self-knowledge and other facets of personal growth therefore will shed light on the possible multifunctionality of life longings for optimal development, comprising both benefits and costs.

Do Wisdom and Life Longings Conjointly Contribute to Successful Development? First Speculations

Can the two lines of inquiry on wisdom and life longings be integrated to stimulate new, fruitful hypotheses about their interplay in the promotion of personal growth? It is possible that the experience of and reflection on one's life longings may promote the development of wisdom-related knowledge. Dreaming about ideals and highest potentials on the one hand, and experiencing the impossibility of their (complete) fulfillment and the limits of life on the other, may help persons to acquire knowledge about the potentials, contexts, limits, and uncertainties of life. This type of knowledge does not remain pure theory, but is connected with emotionally meaningful personal experiences. In fact, several wisdom researchers have argued that wisdom can be acquired only through learning from one's own experiences, not vicariously through reading books or through others' instructions (e.g., Sternberg, 1998). In this sense, the experience of longing might facilitate the acquisition of wisdom, especially if longings are of moderate intensity and the emotions accompanying them are controllable.

On the other hand, it is possible that wisdom may promote the development of mature and adaptive forms of life longings. Based on theoretical considerations and our research on the relation between life longings and subjective well-being, we consider life longings to be adaptive if they have a moderate expression and are perceived to be under control. In contrast, frequent, intense, and uncontrollable life longings likely are an indicator of chronic incompleteness and a lack of perceived developmental progress and success. Wisdom-related knowledge about the contexts, limits, and uncertainties of life may help to put one's own experiences and life reality in perspective. As a result, it may be easier to accept that one cannot have everything in life, and that one always has to make choices, thus facilitating more positive feelings toward one's life longings.

One avenue for future research is to gain a better understanding of how life longings and wisdom-related knowledge might be interrelated. Given that our knowledge is quite limited, one could conduct a laboratory study in which adults with high versus low levels of wisdom-related knowledge are asked to relive a life longing and to subsequently reflect on it. Our prediction is that adults with low versus high levels of wisdom-related knowledge will differ in terms of the longing experience itself and the reflective processes. For example, wiser persons may be better able to grasp the deeper meaning of their longing experience and integrate this experience in more mature ways into the self.

Taken together, life longings may facilitate the acquisition of wisdom-related knowledge, and wisdom-related knowledge might help individuals to shape and make sense of their life longings. Given this reciprocal relationship, it is likely that experiencing personally the potentials and constraints of life (life longings) and knowing about the potentials and constraints of life (wisdom) may conjointly foster a successful development, particularly in personal growth.

CONCLUSION

In this chapter, we introduced wisdom and life longings as two developmental concepts that have been added to the agenda of life span researchers only relatively recently. Both deal with positivity in its most radical form, that is, as psychological utopia. Our general approach was to identify major topics of public and humanist discourse about life and life development that so far have not been studied from a psychological perspective, probably because of their complexity and method constraints. We hope that we were able to convince the reader that these concepts can and should be part of research on aging because they offer important insights into processes of successful lifelong development and make a meaningful contribution to a science of psychological aging.

Both concepts reflect an awareness of the notion that life span development is characterized by a search for perfection and a continuing sense of incompleteness, that is, the feeling and insight that development never comes to a standstill and has to remain incomplete and imperfect (P. B. Baltes, 1997a). This awareness may be especially critical in times of fundamental societal change. As we have argued, increased longevity, rapid technological change, and globalization are societal processes that constitute a challenge to adults living in today's world. Knowing and accepting that life is inherently incomplete may help individuals to make the most out of the potential gains that come with any societal transition and to deal with the potential losses constructively.

Consistent with this idea is evidence for a link between wisdom-related knowledge and positive developmental outcomes reflecting an interest in self-actualization and helping others grow. As we have reviewed, life longings have important developmental functions as well, including the provision of directionality in life and the management of loss and unattainability.

Despite their contributions to a meaningful and satisfying life, life longings and wisdom seem to also involve costs. Neither the insight that life is incomplete (wisdom-related knowledge) nor the experience of this incompleteness (life longings) seems to be compatible with feelings of joy, enthusiasm, and happiness.

One avenue for future research is to study the links between wisdom-related knowledge and life longings on the one hand and multiple developmental outcomes on the other hand more systematically and from a process-oriented perspective. For example, in what ways does the experience of life longings and the availability of wisdom-related knowledge help people deal with concrete life situations characterized by uncertainty and incompleteness so that they will grow and help others grow? Addressing this and related questions will also provide evidence about the interplay of life longings and wisdom in promoting successful development. As we have argued, wisdom-related knowledge about the potentials and constraints of life may help adults develop mature and adaptive forms of life longings; at the same time, personally experiencing the potentials and constraints of life may promote the acquisition of theoretical, wisdom-related knowledge.

Wisdom and life longings are two phenomena that may be particularly relevant for the period of adulthood and old age. They do not evince the typical pattern of aging-related decline that can be found in many other domains of functioning (e.g., cognitive, physical), but continue to be relevant and may even develop further with age and life experience. The evidence reviewed in this chapter suggests that older adults are performing at levels equal to that of younger adults in wisdom-related knowledge and experience structurally equivalent, and possibly more mature, forms of life longings (as indicated by a stronger sense of controllability and a stronger sense that life longings help to deal with loss and nonattainability). Certainly, older adults face many disadvantages when it comes to being successful in today's world. Whereas young adults can respond to the challenges of rapid technological change and globalization with increased flexibility, adaptability, and effort, these strategies are less available to older adults. Wisdom and life longings may be routes to cope with these fundamental societal changes that are particularly suited to older adults. In this sense, wisdom and life longings help us to arrive at a balanced picture of old age as a period with both gains and losses.

REFERENCES

Ardelt, M. (2004). Wisdom as expert knowledge system: A critical review of a contemporary operationalization of an ancient concept. *Human Development, 47,* 257–285.

Baltes, M. M., & Baltes, P. B. (1986). *The psychology of control and aging.* Hillsdale, NJ: Erlbaum.

Baltes, P. B. (1987). Theoretical propositions of life-span developmental psychology: On the dynamics between growth and decline. *Developmental Psychology, 23,* 611–626.

Baltes, P. B. (1997a). On the incomplete architecture of human ontogeny: Selection, optimization, and compensation as foundation of developmental theory. *American Psychologist, 52,* 366–380.

Baltes, P. B. (1997b). Wolfgang Edelstein: Über ein Wissenschaftlerleben in konstruktivistischer Melancholie [Wolfgang Edelstein: A scientific life in constructivistic melancholy]. In Max Planck Institute for Human Development Berlin (Ed.). *Reden zur Emeritierung von Wolfgang Edelstein: Speeches on the Occasion of Wolfgang Edelstein's Transition to Emeritus* (pp. 9–28). Berlin, Germany: Max Planck Institute for Human Development.

Baltes, P. B. (2004). *Wisdom: The orchestration of mind and virtue.* Unpublished manuscript, available at http://www.mpib-berlin.mpg.de/en/institut/dok/full/baltes/orchestr /Wisdom_compl.pdf.

Baltes, P. B. (2006). Facing our limits: Human dignity in the very old. *Daedalus, 135,* 33–39.

Baltes, P. B., & Baltes, M. M. (1990). Psychological perspectives on successful aging: The model of selective optimization with compensation. In P. B. Baltes & M. M. Baltes (Eds.), *Successful aging: Perspectives from the behavioral sciences* (pp. 1–34). Cambridge, England: Cambridge University Press.

Baltes, P. B., & Freund, A. M. (2002). Human strengths as the orchestration of wisdom and selective optimization with compensation. In L. G. Aspinwall & U. M. Staudinger (Eds.), *A psychology of human strengths: Fundamental questions and future directions for a positive psychology* (pp. 23–35). Washington, DC: American Psychological Association.

Baltes, P. B., Freund, A. M., & Li, S.-C. (2005). The psychological science of human ageing. In M. L. Johnson (Ed.), *The Cambridge handbook of age and ageing* (pp. 47–71). Cambridge, England: Cambridge University Press.

Baltes, P. B., Freund, A. M., & Scheibe, S. (2002). *Developmental psychology of Sehnsucht (longing): Central propositions and outlook for a new project.* Unpublished planning paper, Max Planck Institute for Human Development, Berlin, Germany.

Baltes, P. B., & Kunzmann, U. (2003). Wisdom: The peak of human excellence in the orchestration of mind and virtue. *Psychologist, 16,* 131–133.

Baltes, P. B., & Kunzmann, U. (2004). The two faces of wisdom: Wisdom as a general theory of knowledge and judgment about excellence in mind and virtue versus wisdom as everyday realization in people and products. *Human Development, 47*(5), 290–299.

Baltes, P. B., Lindenberger, U., & Staudinger, U. M. (2006). Life span theory in developmental psychology. In R. M. Lerner (Ed.), *Handbook of child psychology: Vol. 1. Theoretical models of human development* (6th ed., pp. 569–664). Hoboken, NJ: Wiley.

Baltes, P. B., & Smith, J. (1990). The psychology of wisdom and its ontogenesis. In R. J. Sternberg (Ed.), *Wisdom: Its nature, origins, and development* (pp. 87–120). New York: Cambridge University Press.

Baltes, P. B., & Smith, J. (2003). New frontiers in the future of aging: From successful aging of the young old to the dilemmas of the fourth age. *Gerontology, 49,* 123–135.

Baltes, P. B., & Smith, J. (2004). Lifespan psychology: From developmental contextualism to developmental biocultural co-constructivism. *Research in Human Development, 1*(3), 123–143.

Baltes, P. B., & Staudinger, U. M. (2000). Wisdom: A metaheuristic (pragmatic) to orchestrate mind and virtue toward excellence. *American Psychologist, 55,* 122–136.

Baltes, P. B., Staudinger, U. M., Maercker, A., & Smith, J. I. (1995). People nominated as wise: A comparative study of wisdom-related knowledge. *Psychology and Aging, 10*(2), 155–166.

Belk, R. W., Ger, G., & Askegaard, S. (2003). The fire of desire: A multisited inquiry into consumer passion. *Journal of Consumer Research, 30,* 326–351.

Bloch, E. (1959). *Das Prinzip Hoffnung* [The principle of hope]. Frankfurt, Germany: Suhrkamp.

Bluck, S., & Habermas, T. (2001). Extending the study of autobiographical memory: Thinking back about life across the life span. *Review of General Psychology, 5,* 135–147.

Boesch, E. E. (1991). *Symbolic action theory and cultural psychology.* New York: Springer.

Boesch, E. E. (1998). *Sehnsucht: Von der Suche nach Glück und Sinn* [Longing: About the search for happiness and meaning]. Bern, Switzerland: Huber.

Brandtstädter, J. (1984). Personal and social control over development: Some implications of an action perspective in life-span developmental psychology. In P. B. Baltes & O. G. Brim Jr. (Eds.), *Life-span development and behavior* (Vol. 6, pp. 1–32). New York: Academic Press.

Brandtstädter, J., & Renner, G. (1990). Tenacious goal pursuit and flexible goal adjustment: Explication and age-related analysis of assimilative and accommodative strategies of coping. *Psychology and Aging, 5,* 58–67.

Brandtstädter, J., & Schneewind, K. A. (1977). Optimal human development: Some implications for psychology. *Human Development, 20,* 48–64.

Carstensen, L. L., & Turk-Charles, S. (1998). Emotion in the second half of life. *Current Directions in Psychological Science, 7,* 144–149.

Clayton, V. P., & Birren, J. E. (1980). The development of wisdom across the life span: A reexamination of an ancient topic. In P. B. Baltes & J. O. G. Brim (Eds.), *Life-span development and behavior* (Vol. 3, pp. 103–153). New York: Academic Press.

Danzer, G. (1998). Versuch über die Sehnsucht [About longing]. In I. Fuchs (Ed.), *Eros und Gefühl: Über den emotionalen Wissenskern des Menschen.* Eros and Feelings: About the emotional core of the human being (pp. 179–203). Würzburg, Germany: Königshausen und Neumann.

Dittmann-Kohli, F., & Baltes, P. B. (1990). Toward a neofunctionalist conception of adult intellectual development: Wisdom as a prototypical case of intellectual growth. In C. Alexander & E. Langer (Eds.), *Higher stages of human development: Perspectives on adult growth* (pp. 54–78). New York: Oxford University Press.

Dixon, R. A., & Baltes, P. B. (1986). Toward life-span research on the functions and pragmatics of intelligence. In R. J. Sternberg & R. K. Wagner (Eds.), *Practical intelligence: Nature and origins of competence in the everyday world* (pp. 203–235). Cambridge, England: Cambridge University Press.

Erikson, E. H. (1980). *Identity and the life cycle.* New York: Norton.

Fichte, J. G. (1962). *Johann Gottlieb Fichte's nachgelassene Werke, Herausgegeben von I. H. Fichte* [Johann Gottlieb Fichte's writings, edited by I. H. Fichte]. Leipzig, Germany: De Gruyter. (Original work published 1794)

Freund, A. M., & Baltes, P. B. (2000). The orchestration of selection, optimization and compensation: An action-theoretical conceptualization of a theory of developmental regulation. In W. J. Perrig & A. Grob (Eds.), *Control of human behavior, mental processes, and consciousness: Essays in honor of the 60th birthday of August Flammer* (pp. 35–58). Mahwah, NJ: Erlbaum.

Freund, A. M., & Riediger, M. (2003). Successful aging. In R. M. Lerner, M. A. Easterbrooks, & J. Mistry (Eds.), *Handbook of psychology: Vol. 6. Developmental psychology* (pp. 601–628). Hoboken, NJ: Wiley.

Grimm, J., & Grimm, W. (1984). Deutsches Wörterbuch Bd. 1–33. [German dictionary Volumes 1–33]. Munich, Germany: Deutscher Taschenbuchverlag. (Reprinted from German Dictionary by J. Grimm & W. Grimm, 1854–1871, Leipzig: Hirzel.)

Groffmann, K. J. (1970). Life-span developmental psychology in Europe. In L. R. Goulet & P. B. Baltes (Eds.), *Life-span developmental psychology: Research and theory* (pp. 54–68). New York: Academic Press.

Havighurst, R. J. (1948). *Developmental tasks and education.* Chicago: University of Chicago Press.

Hegel, G. W. F. (1927). *Phänomenologie des Geistes* [The phenomenology of the mind]. Stuttgart, Germany: Frommann. (Original work published 1807)

Helson, R., & Srivastava, S. (2001). Three paths of adult development: Conservers, seekers, and achievers. *Journal of Personality and Social Psychology, 80,* 995–1010.

Hogrebe, W. (1994). *Sehnsucht und Erkenntnis: Antrittsvorlesung an der Friedrich-Schiller-Universität Jena am 11.11.1993* [Longing and gaining insight: First lecture at the Friedrich Schiller University, Jena, on November 11, 1993]. Erlangen, Germany: Palm und Enke.

Holm, O. (1999). Analyses of longing: Origins, levels, and dimensions. *Journal of Psychology, 133,* 612–630.

Isaacowitz, D. M., Charles, S. T., & Carstensen, L. L. (2000). Emotion and cognition. In F. I. M. Craik & T. A. Salthouse (Eds.), *The handbook of aging and cognition* (2nd ed., pp. 593–631). Mahwah, NJ: Erlbaum.

Kliegl, R., Smith, J., & Baltes, P. B. (1989). Testing-the-limits and the study of adult age differences in cognitive plasticity of a mnemonic skill. *Developmental Psychology, 25,* 247–256.

Kramer, D. A. (2000). Wisdom as a classical source of human strength: Conceptualization and empirical inquiry. *Journal of Social and Clinical Psychology, 19,* 83–101.

Kunzmann, U., & Baltes, P. B. (2003a). Beyond the traditional scope of intelligence: Wisdom in action. In R. J. Sternberg, J. Lautrey, & T. I. Lubart (Eds.), *Models of intelligence: International perspectives* (pp. 329–343). Washington, DC: American Psychological Association.

Kunzmann, U., & Baltes, P. B. (2003b). Wisdom-related knowledge: Affective, motivational, and interpersonal correlates. *Personality and Social Psychology Bulletin, 29,* 1104–1119.

Kunzmann, U., & Baltes, P. B. (2005). The psychology of wisdom: Theoretical and empirical challenges. In R. J. Sternberg & J. Jordan (Eds.), *Handbook of wisdom* (pp. 110–135). New York: Cambridge University Press.

Kunzmann, U., Stange, A., & Jordan, J. (2005). Positive affectivity and lifestyle in adulthood: Do you do what you feel? *Personality and Social Psychology Bulletin, 31,* 574–588.

Labouvie-Vief, G. (1981). Proactive and reactive aspects of constructivism: Growth and aging in life-span perspective. In R. M. Lerner & N. A. Busch-Rossnagel (Eds.), *Individuals as producers of their development: A life-span perspective* (pp. 197–230). New York: Academic Press.

Labouvie-Vief, G. (1990). Wisdom as integrated thought: Historical and developmental perspectives. In R. J. Sternberg (Ed.), *Wisdom: Its nature, origins, and development* (pp. 52–83). Cambridge, England: Cambridge University Press.

Labouvie-Vief, G., Chiodo, L. M., Goguen, L. A., Diehl, M., & Orwoll, L. (1995). Representations of self across the life span. *Psychology and Aging, 10,* 404–415.

Labouvie-Vief, G., & Medler, M. (2002). Affect optimization and affect complexity: Modes and styles of regulation in adulthood. *Psychology and Aging, 17,* 571–588.

Lachman, M. E., & Bertrand, R. M. (2001). Personality and the self in midlife. In M. E. Lachman (Ed.), *Handbook of midlife development* (pp. 279–309). Hoboken, NJ: Wiley.

Lachman, M. E., & Weaver, S. L. (1998). Sociodemographic variations in the sense of control by domain: Findings from the MacArthur studies of midlife. *Psychology and Aging, 13,* 553–562.

Lang, F. R., & Carstensen, L. L. (2002). Time counts: Future time perspective, goals, and social relationships. *Psychology and Aging, 17,* 125–139.

Lerner, R. M. (2002). *Concepts and theories of human development.* Mahwah, NJ: Erlbaum.

Lerner, R. M. (2006). Developmental science, developmental systems, and contemporary theories of human development. In R. M. Lerner (Ed.), *Handbook of child psychology: Vol. 1. Theoretical models of human development* (6th ed., pp. 1–17). Hoboken, NJ: Wiley.

Lindenberger, U., & Baltes, P. B. (1999). Die Entwicklungspsychologie der Lebensspanne (Lifespan-Psychologie): Johann Nicolaus Tetens (1736–1807) zu Ehren [Life span psychology: Honoring Johann Nicolaus Tetens (1736–1807)]. *Zeitschrift für Psychologie,* 299–323.

Markus, H. (1983). Self-knowledge: An expanded view. *Journal of Personality, 51,* 543–565.

Mayser, S., Scheibe, S., & Riediger, M. (2006). *(Un)reachable: An empirical differentiation of goals and life longings.* Unpublished manuscript, Max Planck Institute for Human Development, Berlin, Germany.

McGregor, I., & Little, B. R. (1998). Personal projects, happiness, and meaning: On doing well and being yourself. *Journal of Personality and Social Psychology, 74,* 494–512.

Palaian, S. K. (1993). The experience of longing: A phenomenological investigation (emotion, desires; Doctoral dissertation, The Union Institute, 1993). *Dissertation Abstracts International, 54,* 1678B.

Pasupathi, M., Staudinger, U. M., & Baltes, P. B. (2001). Seeds of wisdom: Adolescents' knowledge and judgment about difficult life problems. *Developmental Psychology, 37,* 351–361.

Ravicz, L. (1998). The experience of longing (desire, yearning; Doctoral dissertation, University of Tennessee, Knoxville, 1998). *Dissertation Abstracts International, 60,* 2958B.

Ryff, C. D. (1989). Happiness is everything, or is it? Explorations on the meaning of psychological well-being. *Journal of Personality and Social Psychology, 57,* 1069–1081.

Ryff, C. D. (1991). Possible selves in adulthood and old age: A tale of shifting horizons. *Psychology and Aging, 6,* 286–295.

Saarni, C. (1999). *The development of emotional competence.* New York: Guilford Press.

Salovey, P., Mayer, J. D., & Caruso, D. (2002). The positive psychology of emotional intelligence. In C. R. Snyder & S. J. Lopez (Eds.), *Handbook of positive psychology* (pp. 159–171). New York: Oxford University Press.

Scheibe, S. (2005). *Longing ("Sehnsucht") as a new lifespan concept: A developmental conceptualization and its measurement in adulthood.* Doctoral dissertation, Free University, Berlin, Germany. Retrieved from http://www.diss.fu-berlin.de/2005/159.

Scheibe, S., Freund, A. M., & Baltes, P. B. (in press). Toward a developmental psychology of Sehnsucht (life longings): The optimal (utopian) life. *Developmental Psychology.*

Smith, J., & Baltes, P. B. (1999). Trends and profiles of psychological functioning in very old age. In P. B. Baltes & K. U. Mayer (Eds.), *The Berlin Aging Study: Aging from 70 to 100* (pp. 197–226). New York: Cambridge University Press.

Smith, J., Staudinger, U. M., & Baltes, P. B. (1994). Occupational settings facilitating wisdom-related knowledge: The sample case of clinical psychologists. *Journal of Consulting and Clinical Psychology, 62,* 989–999.

Spiegel Online. (2004, October 25). *"Habseligkeiten" ist schönstes deutsches Wort* ["Belongings" is most beautiful German word]. Retrieved from http://www.spiegel.de/kultur /gesellschaft/0,1518, 324670,00.htm.

Staudinger, U. M. (1999). Older and wiser? Integrating results on the relationship between age and wisdom-related performance. *International Journal of Behavioral Development, 23,* 641–664.

Staudinger, U. M. (2001). Life reflection: A social-cognitive analysis of life review. *Review of General Psychology, 5,* 91–99.

Staudinger, U. M., Lopez, D. F., & Baltes, P. B. (1997). The psychometric location of wisdom-related performance: Intelligence, personality, and more? *Personality and Social Psychology Bulletin, 23,* 1200–1214.

Staudinger, U. M., Smith, J., & Baltes, P. B. (1992). Wisdom-related knowledge in a life review task: Age differences and the role of professional specialization. *Psychology and Aging, 7,* 271–281.

Sternberg, R. J. (Ed.). (1990). *Wisdom: Its nature, origins, and development.* New York: Cambridge University Press.

Sternberg, R. J. (1998). A balance theory of wisdom. *Review of General Psychology, 2,* 347–365.

Sternberg, R. J. (1999). The theory of successful intelligence. *Review of General Psychology, 3,* 292–316.

Sternberg, R. J., & Jordan, J. (Eds.). (2005). *Handbook of wisdom.* New York: Cambridge University Press.

Tetens, J. N. (1777). *Philosophische Versuche über die menschliche Natur und ihre Entwicklung [Philosophical essays on human nature and its development].* Leipzig, Germany: Weidmanns Erben und Reich.

Vaupel, J. W. (1997). The remarkable improvements in survival at older ages. *Philosophical Transactions of the Royal Society of London, Series B: Biological Sciences, 352,* 1799–1804.

Vogt, M. C. (1993). *Der anthropologische Zusammenhang zwischen Sehnsucht und Sucht* [The anthropological relationship between longing and addiction]. Unpublished doctoral dissertation, University of Zurich, Switzerland.

Wink, P., & Helson, R. (1997). Practical and transcendent wisdom: Their nature and some longitudinal findings. *Journal of Adult Development, 4,* 1–15.

Wrosch, C., & Freund, A. M. (2001). Self-regulation of normative and non-normative developmental challenges. *Human Development, 44,* 264–283.

CHAPTER 6

Sociological Approaches to Understanding Age and Aging

DEBRA A. STREET

TWO EMINENT GERONTOLOGISTS, one a sociologist, the other a social historian, wrote, "Aging may be a universal phenomenon but its impact and meaning are mediated by economic, structural and cultural factors" (Hendricks & Achenbaum, 1999, p. 22). What does it mean for individuals to age through time? How do the meanings of aging change over time? Which social roles and statuses involved in the experiences, continuities, and adjustments that individuals experience accompany advancing years? What impact do aging individuals have on the social institutions and societies in which their experiences are embedded?

Sociologists have sought to understand the processes and relationships involved in age and aging from the earliest days of their discipline, even before gerontology became an organized field of study (Hagestad, 1999). Sociologists have also long expressed concern about the underdevelopment of theories of aging (Bengston & Schaie, 1999; Birren & Bengston, 1988; Estes, 1979). The study of aging has been characterized by James Birren as "data rich and theory poor" (Birren & Bengston, 1988, p. ix) and by others as occasionally plagued by a lack of "gerontological imagination" (Estes, Binney, & Cuthbertson, 1992, p. 49). Hagestad describes an ongoing tension between sociology aimed at improved social scientific understanding of age and aging populations and social gerontology focused mainly on problem solving for aging individuals and societies (see Achenbaum & Levin, 1989, on "problems" in gerontology). Because advancing knowledge in sociology depends on testing and refining theories, from a disciplinary stance the more normative problem-focused gerontological studies of aging are regarded as overly descriptive rather than contributing to causal explanations of the interconnections between individual aging and the social, political, and economic structure favored by academic sociologists.

Tension between social gerontology and sociology has been one factor that has kept the study of aging at the margins of the discipline in sociology (Estes, Biggs, & Phillipson, 2003, p. 10; Maddox, 1979). In fact, the very interdisciplinarity of the study of aging has led a number of scholars—particularly sociologists who study

143

aging—to identify theoretical underdevelopment as an impediment to advancing gerontological studies (Bengston & Schaie, 1999). Tensions within sociology, between micro perspectives emphasizing individual actors and macro perspectives emphasizing the structure of society, have also played a part in the fragmentary nature of sociological contributions to theory and research on aging. Nonetheless, sociologists have always been centrally involved in social gerontological research and theorizing, despite the challenges. Recent developments in critical gerontology and life course theory hint of important sociological breakthroughs yet to come in terms of contributions to the evidentiary and explanatory basis for the study of age and aging.

Whether the purpose of research on aging is to identify practical knowledge, suggest effective clinical interventions, establish academic facts, build social scientific theories, or something else, all academic gerontological studies depend, in part, on assumptions or implicit viewpoints of optimal aging. Although the assumptions differ from study to study, they are usually conceptually consistent with the theoretical framework researchers use to frame their research. One important role for theory in research on aging, therefore, is the need for conceptual precision that attempts to make the underlying assumptions of particular theories used to study the aging process more explicit. Another is that formal statements of theory help researchers to integrate research findings and to systematically build knowledge in gerontology.

There are two dominant approaches to social science studies of aging. Identifying "old age" or "aging" as a *problem to be addressed*, a key feature of many multidisciplinary gerontological approaches to the study of aging, implies that characteristics and behaviors associated with some age other than "old" age are the appropriate benchmarks for assessing when individuals experience successful, normal, or positive aging. Deviations from these ideas of successful aging represent pathological aging or suboptimal problems to be addressed, either through policy interventions or clinical practices. The need to identify sources of the particular problems associated with old age inspires interdisciplinary studies attempting to devise evidence-based strategies to remedy them.

A more purely sociological approach is less attentive to potential interventions and more apt to explain social processes of age and aging as a *puzzle to be solved* within social systems, with careful attention to conceptual precision, theory testing, explanation, and links back to the discipline and other sociological theories (Bengston & Schaie, 1999). Like its more applied cousin, sociological research on aging depends in part on implicit (assumptions) or explicit (theoretically derived) ideal types or profiles of aging individuals and societies. Sociologists' research and theoretical concerns range from individual processes (micro theories) to large population-based ones (macro theories).

In practice, research on aging is often multidisciplinary or problem-focused; only occasionally is it more distinctively sociological and disciplinary in character. But whether research occurs at the problem-solving end of the spectrum, the puzzle-solving, or somewhere in between, sociologists seek evidence to explain individuals' lives through time and to explain both continuity and change in aging individuals and aging societies. The recent trend to practice public sociology (Burawoy, 2004; Light, 2005) reminds academic sociologists that pursuit of scientific knowledge derived from empirical tests of theories can also (and *should* also) produce socially relevant research.

Sociologists make their most important contributions to research on aging by explaining how institutions and social settings structure individual lives through time and how those settings and institutions are, in turn, shaped by individuals moving through adulthood to old age. Despite previous attempts to devise them, there are no general or grand theories of aging. Sociologists work within different theoretical frameworks that vary in terms of core focus, key conceptual categories, and units of analysis, depending on the problem or puzzle at issue. Some theories focus on aging individuals' social relationships, whether within families and friends or within other primary institutions of society such as education, work, or religion. Others are more concerned with aging societies, trying to understand how social structures enable and constrain individuals' choices and life chances. Gerontological theories can be classified in several different ways, such as normative versus interpretive theories (Hendricks, 1992; Marshall, 1996), macro versus micro approaches (Bengston, Parrott, & Burgess, 1996; Marshall, 1996), critical versus radical models (Marshall & Tindale, 1978; Phillipson, 1998), or as progressive generations of theories (Bengston, Burgess, & Parrott, 1997; Hendricks, 1992; Lynott & Passuth Lynott, 1996; Marshall, 1999). However, focusing on the level of analysis a theoretical framework takes as its central problematic, as in this chapter, orients readers to the differences in analytical focus and levels of explanation. This highlights the potential strengths and weaknesses of particular theoretical approaches, as well as the challenges of making linkages across levels of analysis.

Sociological researchers use different theoretical frameworks and methodological tools to design research to explain how individuals experience aging (micro level), how aging individuals relate to the social system (meso level), and how aging populations, institutions, and societies interact at the system level (macro level; also see Estes, 1999; Marshall, 1999). These three broad levels of analysis—micro, meso, and macro—have traditionally provided sociologists the analytic spaces to study aging individuals and their societies; they also organize the discussion in this chapter. A brief history of early sociological research relating to age sets the stage for a more detailed discussion of particular theories within each of the three levels of analysis, providing the theoretical foundations for sociologists' study of aging. Each perspective emerged within a particular historical moment so that aging theories developed in tandem with the main concerns of disciplinary trends at the time. Regardless of when initial theoretical developments occurred, however, sociological theories of aging continue to inform contemporary studies of aging, whether as the basis for research design or as a catalyst to further theoretical refinement. A selection of empirical findings and major critiques inspired by each theory are presented, followed by a conclusion that highlights recent developments in critical gerontology and life course studies and their potential to link concepts and concerns across theories sociologists use to explain aging.

SOCIOLOGICAL APPROACHES TO UNDERSTANDING AGE AND AGING

Nascent interest by sociologists in the formal study of aging—around the time that widespread interest in gerontology was crystallizing by the mid-twentieth century—focused on social psychological aspects of adjustment, life satisfaction, and the activities of individuals. Sociologists extended more general theoretical frameworks already used widely in the discipline, such as functionalism and symbolic interactionism, as foundations for development of what they hoped would be general theories of aging. Individuals were the unit of analysis, prediction centered around optimal and dysfunctional adjustment to old age (Hendricks & Achenbaum, 1999), and social factors were taken for granted rather than analyzed in the models (Hendricks, 1992).

Empirically testing the competing micro-level theories created something of a growth industry in a spate of studies of aging individuals in the 1960s and 1970s; disparate findings and rival theoretical frameworks encouraged more careful theory building and launched increasingly sophisticated studies. As interest in social gerontology grew, accompanied by a growing awareness of the demographic phenomenon of aging populations and public policies geared toward meeting the needs of the elderly, sociologists recognized that exclusively micro-level theories offered an incomplete picture of social aging. They expanded their repertoire to develop meso-level (or middle-range) theories that explored the linkages between individuals and society, and macro-level theories that specified the structural relationships between society and individuals in the context of the changing age structure of national populations. The three analytic levels of analysis provided the foundations for the sociological study of aging, but more recently, critical gerontology and life course studies have shown potential for specifying linkages across levels of analysis. These overlapping critical and life course theoretical orientations, combined with new methodological techniques and the increasing availability of rich longitudinal data sets, show promise for the continued centrality of sociological contributions in the study of aging (e.g., O'Rand & Campbell, 1999).

As discussed earlier, one useful way to think about theories of aging is to classify them by what each takes as its central puzzle: the subject of research interest (individuals, relationships, institutions, or society) and the focus of each theory. For example, micro-level theories of aging, such as disengagement theory, activity theory, and continuity theory, center on the individual as the subject of interest and explore the psychosocial and sociological factors that improve understanding of variations in outcome for elderly individuals. Micro-level theories owe much to theories of psychological development (see Chapters 2 and 3) for their conceptual consistency and signal one family of sociological theories that bridge disciplines.

Meso-level theoretical approaches, such as subculture theory and exchange theory, incorporate concepts that specify the relationships between individuals and social systems. For example, formation of subcultural groups of old people can occur both through positive (e.g., similar interests, friendships) and negative (e.g., exclusion from social participation) social processes. In contrast, exchange theory emphasizes relationships modeled after microeconomic exchanges, characterizing the experiences and behaviors of aging individuals as efforts to maximize their rewards and minimize costs. Meso-level theories are, in one sense, bridging theories within the discipline (see Marshall, 1999), encompassing at least some of the core conceptual categories of both micro- and macro-level theories.

From a more structural vantage point, sociologists use macro-level theories to understand aging at the societal level. Early macro-level studies of aging included modernization theory and age stratification theory. As another manifestation of sociology's midcentury project of devising grand or totalizing theories, modernization offered a general theory explaining how the social conditions experienced by elderly individuals changed as societies became less dependent on agrarian economies and family-centered production and entered the modern industrial age. By the late 1960s, attention to social inequalities had become central concerns for sociologists. Age stratification theory built on more general sociological theories of stratification (which focused on class and socioeconomic variation), analyzing how age structures and how aging is structured by institutional arrangements in modern societies.

More recently, critical sociologists have used theories of power and inequality to explore the experience of aging in modern societies. Some use a political economy framework to focus on social structural influences on aging, emphasizing how old age is defined and treated as a result of social struggles arising from power relationships (Estes, Linkins, & Binney, 1996; Phillipson, 1982; Street & Quadagno, 1993). Others have used feminist theories to emphasize the gendered nature of society generally, and aging individuals more specifically (Arber & Ginn, 1991, 1995; Calasanti & Slevin, 2001; Ginn, Street, & Arber, 2001; Harrington Meyer, 1996; McMullin, 1995). More sophisticated methodological techniques and the availability of longitudinal data sets have also contributed to increasing the use of life course perspectives to investigate the social relations of aging across a number of theoretical approaches (see, e.g., Mortimer & Shanahan, 2003). Combined with social constructionism (which explains how individuals and societies create social meanings of age through negotiation and discourse), critical and life course orientations suggest a fertile research agenda for sociologists studying aging, discussed in more detail at the end of this chapter.

This brief synopsis highlights just some of the varied ways sociologists study age and aging in modern societies. Despite the theoretical ambitions of mid-twentieth-century sociology for grand or all-encompassing theories of individuals and society, no single theory has emerged as adequate for fully predicting the scope and range of variation of aging individuals' relationships in society, or the impact of changing age structures and aging populations on societies. Rather, each family of sociological theories addresses a different level of analysis, a somewhat unique subject of interest, and focuses on different sets of relationships. Researchers often test competing or complementary theories, developing better explanations for experiences of aging. In the sections that follow, each theoretical family is described in greater detail, with similarities, differences, and overlaps in approaches highlighted and selected empirical findings based on theories presented in each section.

MICRO-LEVEL THEORIES

Micro-level sociological theories of aging focus on relatively intimate aspects of individuals' lives as social beings. As such, these sociological theories share much with theories in other social science disciplines, particularly psychology and anthropology, although sociologists focus somewhat more on the social rather than the exclusively psychological or cultural aspects of individual experiences. Although the micro theories predict different outcomes of the normal aging process, they all share a common component: an assumption of optimal aging, albeit one expressed in very different ways.

DISENGAGEMENT THEORY

In *Growing Old: The Process of Disengagement*, Elaine Cumming and William Henry (1961) described the first formal theory of aging. Unlike dominantly psychological theories, the more sociological take in disengagement theory shifted the conceptual focus from an exclusively individualistic one to relationships between individuals and the social systems they experienced (Lynott & Passuth Lynott, 1996). Decreasing levels of interaction between aging individuals and others in the social system (Cumming & Henry, 1961, p. 14) was regarded as a functional adjustment, benefiting both the individual and society. Because death is inevitable, individual withdrawal was theorized to represent a natural process that minimized disruption in the social system.

According to Cumming and Henry (1961), disengagement theory represented a corrective to the widespread "implicit theory" of normal aging, which assumed well-adjusted, satisfied, and happy individuals who remained active and socially involved. In opposition to such unexamined assumptions, they offered a theory of normal aging that involved a process of increasing and inevitable disengagement of aged individuals from their social world. Individuals who recognize that they have limited time left in their lives want to withdraw from many social interactions. Disengagement can be initiated either by an aging person or by society; regardless, the process becomes circular once initiated, weakening the norms of behavior shaping interactions as social interaction drops off. Individuals reduce the number and intensity of roles they play; society gives the individuals "permission" to withdraw, reinforcing the process of disengagement. Optimal aging, from a disengagement perspective, is aging in ways that are least disruptive both for individuals and for society.

What distinguished disengagement theory from exclusively psychological theories was its simultaneous focus on both the individual and the social system (Lynott & Passuth Lynott, 1996). The reciprocal process of disengagement—individuals withdrawing participation, society anticipating declining engagement—creates a *functional* outcome, permitting both the individual and the social system to experience death with little disruption to society. The disengagement approach was consistent with functional sociological theories that emphasized the smooth and efficient functioning of society and that interpreted individual activities within social systems as smoothing the way to socially functional outcomes (Parsons, 1942, 1951).

Critiques centered on whether disengagement was sufficiently comprehensive to represent a general theory of aging. Was disengagement a universal process, occurring in all historical times and societies? Was it inevitable, happening to everyone? Was it an intrinsic and natural component of aging, rather than a social process (Hochschild, 1975)? The next phase of psychosociological theory development directly challenged disengagement as a general sociological theory of aging.

ACTIVITY THEORY

Robert Havighurst formalized activity theory, the previously normative counterpoint to disengagement theory. Activity theory challenged the notion that elderly individuals' psychological or social needs were substantially different from those of middle-aged adults, or that most individuals had a propensity to withdraw from social life. Instead of disengagement, Havighurst and his colleagues (Havighurst, Neugarten, & Tobin, 1968) proposed that what was natural and normal for most aging individuals was to remain active—at levels of activity similar to those experienced in middle age—for as long as possible. When events beyond individual control intervened, such as a personal illness or frailty or when a family member died, optimal aging as predicted by activity theory suggested that individuals would actively resist shrinkage of their social world. As individuals aged, activity theory predicted they would use strategies that involved forging new social roles and relationships or intensifying existing ones to fill the gap rather than disengaging.

CONTINUITY THEORY

A distinctive theoretical contribution in its own right, continuity theory refined elements of both disengagement and activity theories of aging to develop a more encompassing theory that conceptualized normal life course experiences that intersected with the adjustment processes of aging individuals. The theory identifies key distinctions between internal and external continuities and aging processes and between normal and pathological aging (Atchley, 1989, 1999). Internal continuity reflects a variety of persistent individual experiences such as temperament, emotion, experience, preference, disposition, and skills (Atchley, 1989, p. 184). External continuity reflects the capacity of individuals to call upon the repertoire of skills, activities, roles, and relationships of middle age to successfully extend them into old age. In the continuity framework, sustaining usual activities and dispositions of middle-aged individuals into old age is the implicit gold standard of normal aging. From the personality and social bases of middle age, aging individuals readily incorporate change into their lives in ways that are adaptive, both in terms of their individual personalities and of preservation of social support systems.

Normal aging, according to continuity theory, occurs in the absence of mental or physical disease (Atchley, 1989, pp. 183–184) and distinguishes people who age normally—by meeting their own income, housing, health, and social needs (among others)—from others who age pathologically, by being so poor or disabled that they cannot meet their own needs. Under the rubric of continuity theory, disengagement can occur, but it is not the inevitable, functional process envisioned by disengagement theorists. Continuity theory regards disengagement as a process caused by a disruption in internal or external continuity, setting the stage for pathological outcomes. Continuity theory regards disengagement as a dysfunctional outcome, in contrast to the disengagement theory of functional social withdrawal. Continuity theory emphasizes that a foundation of earlier life experiences (skills, personality traits, dispositions, etc.) creates a repertoire of coping strategies that older individuals can call on to adapt to age-related changing circumstances.

THE CONTRIBUTION OF MICRO-LEVEL THEORIES

The rather contrarian positions of disengagement and activity theories, combined with additional refinements encompassed in continuity theory, fostered many studies designed to test which theory provided a better fit for general understanding of individual adjustment to aging. Evidence that normal aging meant remaining engaged in an active lifestyle well into old age mounted quickly, providing empirical support for activity and continuity theories. For example, in his study comparing the processes of individual aging in the United States and Japan, Palmore (1975) found that Japanese traditions contributed to higher levels of activity and involvement among Japanese elders, leading to better health and satisfaction in old age. Another study (Lemon, Bengston, & Patterson, 1972), this time of men and women in their 50s to 70s in California, showed that informal activities performed with friends contributed to higher levels of life satisfaction among older adults, but found no effect of formal (clubs, church) or solitary activities. Such findings helped to outline more specific contours of activity theory by demonstrating that activity alone did not necessarily predict better outcomes for older adults. Similar findings occurred in later studies of retirement communities in the Midwest (Longino & Kart, 1982).

However, just as a universal theory of functional disengagement proved empirically suspect, so too did activity theory founder as a general theory of aging. As continuity theory recognizes (although not without problems of its own), people grow old in myriad ways, influenced by social conditions, culture, and their own experiences and personalities.

The best way to think about the contributions of micro-level theories to evidence-based outcomes may be twofold: to appreciate the impetus they provided to more careful theorizing and empirical refinements to establish patterns of individual aging and adjustment, and to regard them as guiding frameworks for three potential pathways of adjustment in old age. Some individuals disengage, either by distancing themselves from others or by coming to terms with a smaller social world as very old age ensues and individuals become aware that time is finite (Johnson & Barer, 1992). Some individuals remain very active into old age, often acquiring new roles and activities, and at times become fiercely engaged with their social world (Savishinsky, 2000). Yet others tread a path to old age that represents the continuation of their social selves at earlier times in life—at least when good fortune preserves their mental and physical health and they have the resources in reserve to permit continuation—with very active and adaptive individuals continuing to remain so in old age, while individuals whose personalities or circumstances undermined their capacity to continue at the pace and complexity of their middle-age experiences participate in lower levels of activity and social engagement as they age. Differences in styles and timing of adjustment, focus on the conditions within which adjustment occur, and attention to the coping mechanisms individuals use to adapt to aging represent important contributions by micro-level sociological theories of aging.

Although the three approaches to micro-level theory differ in their assumptions of optimal aging, each shares a common concern for individual adjustment and provides rich intellectual fodder for ensuing studies based on the other microtheoretical frameworks. In small-scale studies, each theory usefully contributes to advancing at least partial explanations of the psychosocial processes of adjustment that aging individuals make. Within particular segments of aging populations, individuals whose dominant adjustment to aging is to disengage, to actively adapt, or to continue along a life course trajectory with skills and resources acquired earlier in life can be analyzed using conceptual tools from these microtheoretical frameworks.

Each micro-level theory also implies interventions that would be helpful to optimize individuals' aging experiences in theoretically consistent ways. For disengagement theory, identifying practices that foster gradual individual withdrawal from most social relations would be appropriate. In keeping with activity theory assumptions, creating broad-based interventions that provide opportunities for individuals to replace lost roles with new ones would be important; these reflect many of the practices that encourage senior participation in community activities, outgrowths of policies enacted by federal, state, and local governments. From a continuity perspective, interventions that help individuals acquire the coping skill set that enables them to sustain levels of activity and engagement at middle-aged levels into old age or that minimize the physical and resource limitations that undermine internal and external continuity would be important.

If aging and old age represent problems to be solved, however, many sociologists regard interventions targeted exclusively or mainly at individuals as inadequate. Psychosocial theories of aging are most appropriate for informing potential clinical or policy interventions at the individual level. Addressing issues of aging in a broader social context requires linkages between individuals and the social system. Researchers who explicitly incorporated such relationships into different theoretical models mounted the most serious challenges to the primacy of individually based theories for understanding the social implications of aging.

MESO-LEVEL THEORIES

Psychosocial explanations of aging that used disengagement, activity, and continuity theories provide important insights into personal adjustment in old age. One major critique of micro-level theories was that they attributed problems of aging to individual adjustment rather than to broader social structures (Townsend, 1981). Despite incorporating sociological concepts into such individualistic psychosocial theories, many other sociologists regarded the lack of attention to the more social aspects of aging and old age as another shortcoming. One way they addressed both individual and social system concerns was by developing meso-level theories of aging that linked the two together. Meso-level theories emphasize the quotidian relationships between individuals and the social systems they routinely experience. By explicitly incorporating the relationship between the individual and the social system into theories, sociologists moved beyond a predominantly individualistic focus into more socially oriented and, some would argue, sociological studies of aging. Among the examples of meso-level theories sociologists have used to frame their research on aging are theories of an aged subculture development and exchange theory. Each contributed in its own way to theory building that specified linkages between individuals and society in sociological research on aging.

Subculture Theory

One vein of sociological investigation in the late 1950s and early 1960s focused on the theoretical foundations and empirical expression of identifiable subcultures, such as beatniks or particular racial/ethnic groups, within mainstream society. In common with activity and disengagement theories, the aged-as-subculture theory also focused on role changes in later life. In contrast to the focus of activity and disengagement theories on the social psychological, the aged-as-subculture theory built on more general sociological theories of subcultural development to understand the relationship between old people and society. Subculture theorists identified two conditions that explained subculture formation. First, shared circumstances (interests, problems, concerns, friendships, etc.) could lead to a common "insider" identity. When this occurred, it created a sense of belonging for members of a cohesive subcultural group who regarded themselves as being distinctive in some way from broader society. Second, subculture formation could be catalyzed when the larger society excluded particular groups, such as members of racial or ethnic minority groups or the poor, from full social participation (Arnold, 1970). In those cases, subculture group formation represented an adaptation by disenfranchised groups in response to exclusion from broader society. Sometimes both conditions for subculture formation operated in tandem, making the virtue of shared identity a necessity when social exclusion occurred (Arnold, 1970).

Elderly people, according to Arnold Rose (1964, p. 47), simultaneously experienced an affinity for one another due to shared circumstances, including physical limitations and "common role changes and . . . common generational experiences." Further, as a group, elderly people were often excluded from social participation by younger people. Rose theorized that in the United States, diminishing social status often accompanied aging. Loss of status could in turn lead to isolation from younger people and to the experience of a shared common bond with older individuals. Theoretically, these twin processes created the conditions for an aged subculture. Mirroring social hierarchies in mainstream culture, within aged subcultures sociologically important hierarchies were theoretically possible, particularly distinctions based on good fortune combined with physical and mental health (p. 49).

Although the idea that any group as diverse as older people would form a single subculture based on age may appear naive (especially given other lifelong sources of affiliation such as family ties, hobbies, or religious identity), subculture theory makes important conceptual contributions to analyzing old people's experiences and lifestyles in age-segregated settings like assisted living facilities or retirement communities. For example, Arlie Hochschild's (1978) study of aged residents in a small California apartment building confirmed the hypothesis that health and good luck contributed to status rankings among subcultures of the aged. Unlucky residents, the "poor dears" Hochschild identified as occupying the bottom of the informal status hierarchy, had experienced the greatest losses in their social networks and the poorest health (p. 73). Given the growth of retirement communities and the assisted living industry, research on the subcultures of such aged communities has a theoretical tradition it can call on for the conceptual framework to advance additional studies of an increasingly common social phenomenon related to population aging.

In recent years, the idea that elderly people constitute an aged subculture due to their exclusion by younger people has given way to concern in some quarters that an aged subculture has the political clout to disadvantage younger citizens. Assertions that elderly people are a politically powerful age group that gets more than its fair share of resources from modern welfare states, a ubiquitous media characterization of elderly people in the United States, shares much in common with subculture theory. Rather than being excluded and marginalized, however, this more recent variant of the aged-as-subculture hypothesis emphasizes that age is a common bond that creates monolithic political preferences among elderly citizens and inspires their coordinated and bloclike political behavior. Although researchers have challenged the logic of monolithic age interests (Binstock & Quadagno, 2001; Street, 1993, 1997) and find scant empirical support for aged individuals exerting undue political influence or having political agendas much different from other age groups (Binstock & Quadagno, 2001; Street & Cossman, 2006a, 2006b), the stereotype of politically powerful elderly people often portrayed in the media owes much of its persuasive capacity to informal working hypotheses that elderly people actually do form an aged subculture.

EXCHANGE THEORY

Exchange theory involves the importation of concepts originated in microeconomics to the sociological study of relations between individuals in modern societies (Blau, 1961). Importing exchange theory into social gerontology permitted researchers to analyze how aging individuals maximized their rewards and minimized the costs of their social interactions (Dowd, 1975, 1980). Because the ability to benefit from an exchange depends on the resources an individual brings or is perceived to bring to an exchange, Dowd reasoned that most older adults had fewer resources—whether information, skills, strength, or endurance—than did younger individuals, and were thus disadvantaged in terms of what they could exchange. Exchanges (whether regarded as transactions or interactions) between young and old, decrease in the face of unequal resources between the two age groups—another potential explanation for disengagement among the elderly (Dowd, 1975).

A substantial body of literature contradicts exchange theory, noting the importance of "nonrational" exchanges such as love, altruism, and kindness that may trump what otherwise seem to be "unequal" exchanges (Passuth & Bengston, 1996; Silverstein, 2006). While exchange theory evaluates trading in "spot" transactions, ones that happen in the moment and where most elderly people appear to be disadvantages, another critique of exchange theory notes the dynamic and intergenerational aspects of exchange, particularly within families (Attias-Donfut & Arber, 2000; Lewis, 1990). In fact, in most families until very old age ensues, resource transfers tend to be from parent to child, and not vice versa (Attias-Donfut & Arber, 2000; Lewis, 1990).

THE CONTRIBUTION OF MESO-LEVEL THEORIES

Meso-level theories offer one way to extend the reach of sociological research beyond predominantly individual accounts to consider the ways individuals are linked in relationships and social groups. Aged-as-subculture theory underscores that, even when older individuals may perceive themselves and behave in ways that are inconsistent with subculture formation, some parts of society may yet regard elderly people as having subcultural characteristics. Exchange theory reminds scholars and practitioners that individuals often take into account concepts such as "trading" and "exchanging" in relationships where issues of time, money, and concern come into play (Silverstein, 2006). When resources are scarce, as they often are for vulnerable elders, having little to exchange may lead to social exclusion, particularly if older persons withdraw from interactions or fail to seek help they need because they perceive an inability to fulfill reciprocity norms. Conditions of exchange, whether within families or in other relational circumstances, never occur independent of context. Choices are made within "social structures, political economies, and cultural contexts that constrain or enhance opportunities and incentives to engage in transfer behavior" (p. 175).

Concerns about the structures of intergenerational transfers and relationships, the role societies play in constraining and enabling human agency during lifetimes, and the social and political construction of old age are central concerns for macro-level theories of aging.

MACRO-LEVEL THEORIES

Micro- and meso-level sociological theories make essential contributions to the study of aging. How well the theories fit particular research problems depends on the unit of analysis and the social process researchers are seeking to explain. Micro- and meso-level theories, however, cannot account for changes in the process of aging or the experiences of older people from the perspective of the broad sweep of history and rapid social change. Sociologists developed macro-level theories that framed processes of aging and the experiences of elderly people in the historical processes and structures of societies that impacted aging individuals and populations. Early macro-level theories, such as modernization and age stratification theory, created the foundation for structural analyses of the processes of aging in modern societies. As such, they emphasized how structural elements of societies contributed to an explanation of aging processes and mirrored dominant concerns in sociology that focused on understanding large-scale social change and processes and outcomes of social stratification. More recent developments in macro-level theories, particularly contributions from political economy theories and feminist research, build on the early foundations of structural analysis to extend the explanatory power of these theories.

MODERNIZATION THEORY

One way sociologists sought to understand the effects of widespread social change on older people was by researching aging and old age in the context of modernization. From a theoretical perspective, modernization identifies large-scale social change and historical processes, such as technological advances and changes in modes of production, as the creators of new roles and statuses for people (including older people) and their families. Modernization theory explains how specific social and technological changes create particular social and cultural effects for older people (and others) as societies modernize over time (Street & Parham, 2002). The jumping-off point for modernization theory is the assumption that there was a golden age of the aged: preindustrial societies where elderly people were revered for their wisdom.

Modernization theory was formalized by sociologists Donald Cowgill and Lowell Holmes (1972). They regarded the shift from traditional farm and craft production within families to mainly industrial production in factories as an overarching modernizing process that diminished the status of older people. Later theoretical refinements (Cowgill, 1974) identified four specific aspects of modernizing societies that led to declines in the status of older people: health technology, economic and industrial technology, urbanization, and education.

Advances in medical practice and public health improved health and increased longevity, but with some negative effects for older people. In some traditional societies, older members controlled family production, but longer modern lives created more labor market competition, with industrial employers preferring younger, stronger workers who possessed new occupational skills. This forced older workers out of the labor market, causing loss of income, prestige, and honor, contributing to a decline in the status of older people. Advances in economic and industrial technology created new occupations; formerly valued traditional skills and knowledge held by older family members became outdated. As younger people moved to cities for factory jobs, societies experienced urbanization. This process relegated older people to less prestigious and increasingly obsolete jobs or left them behind in rural areas, undermining the relations of the traditional extended family and increasing social and spatial distance between the young and the old. Increased literacy rates, new emphasis on scientific over traditional forms of knowledge, and education targeted toward children created knowledge gaps among family members of different generations. Skills and traditional knowledge that previously contributed to the high status of older people were rendered irrelevant by developments in science and technology. Intergenerational relations were fundamentally altered, to the detriment of older people.

The general model of the relationship between modernization and aging predicts a linear relationship between the degree of modernization and the status of older people in particular societies. According to the theory, modernization would inevitably affect the entire social structure of societies, including the position customarily held by their elderly communities, regardless of when or where it occurred. Soon after Cowgill and Holmes's (1972) original work, Palmore and Manton (1974) tested modernization theory using data from 31 countries. Their findings suggested refinements to the theory, including taking the phase of modernization into account when exploring status changes among older people. They found that early in modernization older people's social status was relatively lower, but that the status decline leveled off and sometimes rose after a period of modernization, suggesting nonlinear change in response to modernization.

Critics of modernization theory observed that the theory was based on faulty assumptions about the historical status of older people, both representing an oversimplification of the effects of modernization and ignoring important variations arising from cultural experiences, family forms, and social statuses other than age. British historian Peter Laslett (1976) led the challenge to modernization theory, which he argued portrayed and formalized an assumed mythical "world we have lost." Laslett identified four specific problems related to the "golden age of the aged" myth: (1) poorly specified processes connecting the social outcomes of aging to modernization; (2) an assumption that traditional societies held older people in universal high regard; (3) whether traditional societies had specified and valued economic roles for most older people; and (4) the belief that older individuals lived in multigenerational households, cared for by their relatives. Other scholars supported elements of Laslett's critique. U.S. social historians Achenbaum (1978) and Fischer (1977) agreed that the status of the aged had declined over time, but they claimed that the decline began long before modernization and industrialization could have been the cause. They regarded cultural factors, not the social and economic changes emphasized in modernization theory, as most influential in determining the social position of older people in U.S. society. Quadagno (1982) observed that historical evidence showed significant variation in the treatment of older people both across and within different societies and over time. Historically, older people were not always universally revered. She found that modernization had both positive and negative effects on older people (Quadagno, 1982).

Critics of modernization as a general theory observed that the historical status of older people varies according to race, gender, social class, and culture. Modernization theory overlooked the diverse positions of older people across different societies and the diversity of elders across gender and racial/ethnic groups and economic classes within societies. In the decades since its original formalization, modernization theory has been challenged as an oversimplification of the effects of social change on the status of older people. However, as a springboard for further research, critiques of modernization theory were one impetus to social gerontological research attentive to issues of the timing and pace of change, the evolution in family forms, cultural values about aging and old age, diversity among the elderly, and the multiple statuses that people enjoy—and endure—as they age in a modern world.

AGE STRATIFICATION THEORY

Social institutions are organized, in part, by age, with levels of age segregation and integration varying across social institutions and over the life course. Age stratification theory formalized and elaborated the concept of social organization around different age strata (such as childhood, adulthood, and old age), including the ways interactions within and between age strata ordered social relations and how age grading sorted individuals into particular age strata that directed people into age-graded roles and opportunity structures (Riley, 1971; Riley, Johnson, & Foner, 1972). Key concepts in age stratification theory include *birth cohorts, age norms,* and *structural lag* (Riley, Kahn, & Foner, 1994).

Birth cohorts flow through the various age strata of populations over time, exerting their capacity to influence social change. As birth cohorts, such as the baby boom, work their way through the social structure, the cohort contributes to social change that accompanies its passage through historical time. *Age norms,* another key age stratification concept, are sets of social and cultural expectations about age-appropriate individual capacities and opportunities that are linked in age-graded ways to particular social institutions such as family, education, and employment. In age-stratified societies, individuals develop normative expectations (which are consistent with societal expectations) about the appropriate times to transition, for example, from school to work, or to marry and form families.

Age stratification theory also highlighted the relationship between advancing age and disadvantages that may arise due to the way social opportunities are structured within social systems. *Structural lag* occurs when social structures (e.g., incentives for early retirement) are out of synch with population dynamics (fewer young workers) and individual lives (increasing life expectancy, later onset of disabilities and frailty). The extent of structural lag varies across institutions (e.g., education, workplaces, governments, and families) as individuals influence—and are in turn influenced by—changes in social structures and institutions as they age through time (Riley, Foner, & Riley, 1999; Riley et al., 1994). Age stratification theory fits comfortably within mainstream sociology's functionalist theories, emphasizing social order accomplished by social roles and norms (Passuth & Bengston, 1996).

Despite offering a comprehensive template to consider how societies organized age-segregated and age-integrated institutions, age stratification theory offered little conceptual leverage into issues of power and social class relationships (Estes, 1986) that were key to understanding later life outcomes, or insights into sociological theories of conflict and social inequality (Passuth & Bengston, 1996). Because age stratification represents a mainly static model of social structures, there was scant analytic space to explore the impact of human agency (Dowd, 1987) or how political processes contributed to social inequality and patterns of institutionalized inequality developed and were perpetuated over time (Quadagno & Reid, 1999, p. 47). Despite the importance age plays in stratifying modern societies, uncritical analysis from an age stratification perspective overemphasizes how age contributes to the structure of social inequalities (distribution of risk and rewards; Street & Cossman, 2006a, 2006b) and offers little in the way of analytic power to understand differences experienced within birth cohorts (Dannefer & Uhlenberg, 1999), which often outweigh differences between them.

CONTRIBUTIONS OF FOUNDATIONAL MACRO-LEVEL THEORIES OF AGING

Social processes have profound effects on all people living in modernizing societies, not just people of advanced age. Industrialization changed the way goods and services were produced and where production occurred. The rise of mass education expanded literacy and exposed people to new ideas and practices in science and technology. Family forms, cultural values, and other social institutions changed. Despite its shortcomings, modernization as a conceptual framework provides one useful way to consider the impact of massive social changes over the past two centuries. Systematic consideration of the interrelationships between the types and pace of change provides insights into the effects of broad social transformations on societies and the people living in them.

Age stratification theory built on some of these insights, seeking to understand how the age structure of society, and the movement of birth cohorts through social systems, contributed to social change. Age stratification highlighted the impact of human agency on social systems; individuals were not merely affected by social transformations, they were implicated in them.

Critical gerontologists, many of whom are sociologists, sought to build on the insights of modernization and age stratification theories, but also to remedy their shortcomings as structural theories of aging, in a second generation of macro-level theories.

CRITICAL GERONTOLOGY AND THE LIFE COURSE

More recent trends in macro-level research, including political and moral economy theories and feminist perspectives, are dominated by sociologists working in the critical gerontology tradition of research on aging and old age (see Estes et al., 2003, for a comprehensive overview of critical gerontology). The critical turn in social gerontology paralleled a similar trend in sociology. Just as gerontologists were challenging the uncritical assumptions implicit in many early gerontology theories, sociologists were adopting a more critical stance toward the discipline's theory and methods. Functionalist theories and social psychological theories pursued with positivist research strategies, though still dominant in mainstream sociology, were confronted by renewed interest among critical sociologists in conflict and interpretivist theories arising from Marxian and Weberian traditions in sociology, overlaid by sociological studies of the burgeoning welfare states in modern industrialized democracies (e.g., Esping-Andersen, 1990; Myles, 1989; O'Connor, 1973). Coupled with feminist theories, these approaches pursued rich new veins of scholarship on aging.

Using the life course (Dannefer & Uhlenberg, 1999; Elder, 1994; George, 1993; Mortimer & Shanahan, 2003; Settersten 2003, 2006) and social constructionism (Gubrium & Holstein, 1999; Walker, 1999) as orienting frameworks and bridging mechanisms, critical approaches have become the dominant trend in recent sociological research on aging (Bengston, Burgess, & Parrott, 1997; Bengston & Schaie, 1999; Estes et al., 2003; Hendricks & Leedham, 1991; Marshall, 1996; Phillipson, 1998). The critical approach incorporates theorizing and research that challenges status quo theories and functionalist explanations for the experiences of elderly individuals in modern societies (Marshall & Tindale, 1978), emphasizing instead differences in power relationships and political arrangements (Street & Quadagno, 1993). Critical studies of aging grew, in part, out of recognition that the foundational social theories of gerontology, while important building blocks of knowledge about the processes of aging, often took for granted aspects of the aging experience—for instance, the unreflective acceptance of the biomedicalization of aging (Estes & Binney, 1989) or the marginalized role of elderly people in capitalist economies (Street & Quadagno, 1993; Townsend, 1981; Walker, 1981)—that could be more critically analyzed to explain how structural inequalities shape the everyday experiences of individuals aging through time (Estes et al., 2003).

Critical researchers study aging from several theoretical vantage points, explaining how inequalities beyond just those associated with age contribute to older individuals' positions in society. As such, structured inequalities and the potential bases for social solidarity are analytically central to critical gerontologists' research, as is the development of dynamic theories of institutionalized patterns of inequality and the capacity for individuals to challenge them. Key critiques of earlier studies were that theories were typically imported from other parts of the life course, or from other areas in sociology, creating generic assumptions of a "standard" adult ideal type that serves as the appropriate, or at least usual, benchmark for comparison (Calasanti, 1996; Estes et al., 2003; Ginn et al., 2001). The misplaced assumption that the standard adult was a working-age, White, Western male (Harrington Meyer, Street, & Quadagno, 1994; Orloff, 1993) spawned a series of studies that used political and moral economy theories along with feminist theories to explain how status differences such as class, gender, and race, accompanied by aging, often perpetuated or worsened social inequality in later life outcomes. Social construction and life course perspectives helped move critical research forward by providing theoretical and conceptual frameworks that can help transcend the boundaries that previously often frustrated the capacity for explanation across levels of analysis.

POLITICAL ECONOMY THEORY

Political economy theory takes as its point of departure that most problems elderly people face are socially constructed (Estes, 1979, 1991; Phillipson, 1982; Walker, 1981). As Caroll Estes observed:

What is done for and about the elderly as well as what we know about them, including knowledge gained from research, are products of our conceptions of aging. In an important sense, then, the major problems faced by the elderly are the ones we create for them. (1979 p. 1)

From a political economy perspective, inequality in old age is due mainly to political and economic forces. Social exclusion occurs when processes of "structured dependency" (Townsend, 1981)—inadequate social opportunities compounded by insufficient resources provided by inadequate public policies—relegate elderly people to the margins of modern society.

The late 1970s and the 1980s were a particularly fruitful time for the development of multilevel, multitheoretical critical perspectives that built the political economy perspective on aging. Pioneering work explained how capitalism and the state contributed to systems of domination that marginalized elderly people (Estes, 1979; Phillipson, 1982; Walker, 1981) and challenged mainstream theories of aging with more radical perspectives (Marshall & Tindale, 1978), seeking to explain the relative poverty of elderly people in an era of prosperity. Close on the heels of this early work was continued elaboration of the political economy perspective, linking theories of aging to broader theories of the welfare state (Myles, 1989; Quadagno, 1988). As the size of national pension systems and other public policies for older citizens grew, sociologists devoted more attention to what John Myles (1989, p. 1) called "the welfare state for the elderly."

An extension of political economy theories of aging, moral economy, incorporates assessment of broadly held norms of obligation and reciprocity into analysis of political and economic arrangements of modern societies (Hendricks & Leedham, 1991; Minkler & Cole, 1991, 1999; Minkler & Estes, 1991, 1999). Partly a response to claims that the elderly used political power in ways that violated generational equity (e.g., Quadagno, 1989; Street, 1997), moral economy focused research on political and economic relationships affecting individuals of different ages on issues of distributive and economic justice and norms of reciprocity and generational equity.

Studies using a political economy framework have provided findings of significant interest for social gerontologists. By highlighting the ways societies structure social policies that shape later life income, access to health care, and the provision of long-term care, researchers in the political economy tradition underscore how welfare state policies often perpetuate rather than eliminate or minimize the social inequalities of earlier years.

Feminist Theories

Feminist approaches to the study of aging represent not so much a formal body of theory as a challenge to aging research that ignored differences between women's and men's experiences or assumed that ungendered social processes shaped aging and old age (Calasanti & Slevin, 2001). Gender relations are the main subject matter of feminist theories, which regard ideas of masculinity and femininity as socially constructed, emphasizing how men and women experience aging differently (Arber & Ginn, 1991, 1995). Researchers in the feminist tradition criticize existing research and theory that focuses on one sex to the exclusion of the other. For example, most research on the impact of the death of a spouse has focused on women who were widows, and most research on retirement focuses on men (Calasanti & Zajicek, 1993). Feminist scholars highlight this because most of the differences older men and women experience are not basic biological differences, but are organized by the social structure of societies and by gendered social definitions of reality.

The contributions of gender-sensitive scholarship to the study of aging are substantial. Examples include insights into men's and women's roles in caregiving, including their relationships with family and friends in social support networks (Antonucci, 1990; Antonucci & Akiyama, 1987); gendered experiences of work and retirement (Ginn et al., 2001; Harrington Meyer, 1996); and the gendered division of household labor (Calasanti & Slevin, 2001). Because women constitute the majority of elders in nearly every society and are disproportionately likely to be poor in old age, and because men continue to die at younger ages than women, gender-sensitive scholarship by sociologists makes a particularly important contribution to studies on aging.

LINKING THEORIES TOGETHER: LIFE COURSE PERSPECTIVES

Researchers of varying theoretical bents have used the *life course* as an orienting concept in their research, particularly over the past quarter century. Conceptually, life course studies in sociology are simultaneously a *theoretical orientation* (Elder, Johnson, & Crosnoe, 2003) toward research and a *methodological approach* to study that can be used within the conceptual frames of other theoretical approaches (Elder, 1994; George, 2003; Settersten, 2006). As such, the life course offers theorists new ways to conceptualize how individuals' lives are structured by the choices they make, constrained by the structure of the society in which they experience particular historical moments. Core topics in life course studies, including cohorts and the focus on lives lived through time, are also aspects of age stratification theory, but life course approaches make explicit linkages back to individuals and emphasize social dynamism and historical effects. Consequently, a life course theoretical orientation provides the capacity for conceptual enrichment as an overlay to other theoretical frameworks, enabling researchers to incorporate increased complexity into explanations about the relations between aging individuals and society by focusing attention on the implications of life course trajectories and transitions. Using a life course orientation has proved particularly useful in political economy, feminist, and other critical approaches to the study of aging.

Empirically, one particular way life course orientations have been used in sociological research on aging has been to focus on the relationships between role transitions and trajectories and outcomes in later life (George, 1993). A particularly strong vein of such research uses a life course perspective to explain processes of cumulative advantage and disadvantage. Age stratification theory, with its particular focus on how age grading contributed to social stratification, gave way to much more nuanced and comprehensive research projects exploring the relationships between aging and social stratification. According to cumulative disadvantage theory, stratification is not static or fixed; rather, stratification is a cumulative process that accrues over the life course of individuals, shaped by the structurally constrained life chances each person confronts in a lifetime (Dannefer, 1987; O'Rand, 2001, 2006). As such, theories of cumulative disadvantage often emphasize the role that public policies and practices, and not just individual circumstances, play in shaping life chances (Dannefer & Uhlenberg, 1999; O'Rand, 2006).

Researchers have shown that individuals experience cumulative advantage or disadvantage over their life course, shaped by earlier life experiences and conditioned by other statuses such as gender, race/ethnicity, and social class. Life course capital (resources such as social relationships, education, family supports) and life course risks (chances of experiencing adverse conditions or beneficial opportunities) are unequally distributed across populations and over the life course from birth to death (O'Rand, 2001, 2006). Ideally, understanding the processes that contribute to these inequalities may provide windows into interventions that could maximize life course capital and minimize life course risk.

Researchers have established that early disadvantage may compound over time, and on a number of dimensions, including most detrimentally to the health and wealth of individuals in old age. So too may early advantage accumulate, contributing to the "Matthew effect"—those who have more get more—a trickle of advantage surging to significant accumulations over the course of fortunate lifetimes (Dannefer, 1987). Theoretical development and research on cumulative (dis)advantage is consistent with sociological puzzle solving, but also fits comfortably within the problem-addressing strains of research on aging. Such life course theories highlight how outcomes in old age are conditioned by the incidence, timing, ordering, and duration of roles and life events (Moen & Spencer, 2006), underscoring the importance of individual and social turning points and the timing of transitions. Empirical findings from carefully designed studies of cumulative disadvantage underscore the inefficiency of designing interventions to implement only when individuals finally become elderly or disabled (see, e.g., Ferraro & Kelley-Moore, 2003). Understanding when in the life course interventions can be used to most effectively slow or halt the acquisition of disadvantage depends on continued refinements and methodological approaches applied to life course theories of cumulative advantage and disadvantage.

CONCLUSION

Sociologists and others who study aging have intersecting interests: the outcomes of age differentiation over the life course, how demographic and social change affects individual behavior, and how individual behavior contributes to social change. Population aging and changes in the demographic age structure in both developed and developing countries seem certain to inspire continued interest in understanding age-related processes. For sociologists, the centrality of age differentiation and aging populations impacts myriad sociologically important relationships. That, combined with the increasingly dominant role of public policies for elderly people, will likely keep sociological studies of aging on the front burner.

However, the tradition of academic work occurring within disciplinary silos makes it challenging to maximize the impact of sociological theory and research on interdisciplinary areas like social gerontology. The tension between building scientific understanding and solving the problems of old age and population aging (Hagestad, 1999) was laid out earlier in this chapter. Sociologists in particular have argued the need for more research of a theory-driven nature, rather than the more usual problem-solving kind. Sociologists have also recently expressed concern that social gerontology has exhibited a tendency to "microfi-cation"—a return to its roots of psychosocial processes and micro interactions—to the neglect of more macro-level processes (Hagestad & Dannefer, 2001). Pressures in this direction stem from several factors, including the contempo-rary emphases on individual agency and choice, the continued medicalization of old age, research funders' priorities for projects that address biomedical and so-cial pathological aspects of aging, and the persistence of the "social problem" perspective of old age (Hagestad & Dannefer, 2001). The problem with increas-ing microfication in social gerontology becomes especially worrisome when de-scriptive research at the micro level *seems* to provide evidence that individual interventions are called for, when in fact interventions at the macro level would make more difference in promoting most individuals' prospects for a "good" old age (see Gatz & Zarit, 1999; also George, 2006).

Estes et al. (1992, p. 50) have argued that the absence of a disciplinary core in gerontology has simultaneously contributed to both strength and weakness, in that gerontology is tokenized within traditional disciplines like sociology. Estes et al. (2003, p. 12) observe that relationship between social theory and gerontol-ogy has included a half century of "competition and struggle between para-digms . . . with sociological-critical perspectives . . . growing in influence." A critical sociological perspective requires that researchers focus not only on aging individuals, but on how lives, time, and place are interconnected in systematic ways and how individuals' aging lives are structured by the societies in which they live. From the beginnings of social gerontology as a formalized area of study, sociologists have been at the forefront of theorizing how age, human agency, and social structures interact to create later life outcomes.

Bengston and Schaie (1999, p. 16) wrote, "Applications of knowledge in geron-tology—whether in medicine, practice, or policy—demand good theory, since it is on the basis of *explanations* about problems that interventions should be made; if not they seem doomed to failure." Many formal theories have been developed, tested, rejected, and rehabilitated, all providing a rich foundation for the current generation of sociologists and gerontologists to extend their explanations of what it means to age in modern society. Yet Bengston and Schaie's point that theory building is critical for the integration and advancement of evidence-based re-search on aging is well taken. Knowing *why and how* particular outcomes occur, in all their complexity, is a product of robust theorizing, and critical for understand-ing the appropriateness and potential impact of interventions.

Criticisms that sociological theories, to date, insufficiently explain the processes of age and aging are fair ones, in that the complex processes and inter-action conditioning the status of older people in their social worlds are over-simplified and not always well incorporated into cohesive frameworks across lev-els of analysis. However, sociology is well suited to develop theories further (Estes et al., 2003). Although foundational theories used by sociologists were too general or too limited in scope to encompass the spectrum of aging experiences, they spurred thoughtful and sustained research agendas designed to prove or disprove their assumptions, to refine theories, and to extend explanations. Such work, building on the pioneering work of sociologists who early on launched for-mal studies of aging, has provided key findings that clarify the myriad and evolv-ing roles of elderly persons in modern societies and how societies have changed in response to them. Sociologists continue to build on this tradition, bringing continually more nuanced theories and more sophisticated analytic techniques and data to bear on the questions of aging in modern societies, aiming to improve our understanding of the complex interactions among changes in a society's social structure, people's racial/ethnic, gender, and cultural positions, and the outcomes that these complex social relationships generate. Accompanying confidence that methodological and data advances will improve prediction in sociology are reminders from prominent scholars in the field of the importance of investigating how age and the life course are structured in complex societies. In terms of cumulative disadvantage, O'Rand (2006) expresses considerable concern about the retrenchment of "equalizing institutions" such as quality public education and employment stability for ameliorating the effects of life course stratification. Accompanying these changes is de-institutionalization of the life course and evolving age and gender norms, creating more flexible options for life trajectories for men and women (Moen & Spencer, 2006). Will the more flexible men's and women's life options be a positive factor in the face of retrenching equalizing institutions? Such questions will provide rich terrain for macro-level research that uses the life course to help understand the reconstruction of aging and old age in the future.

Especially because helping professionals, policy makers, and politicians use models of aging (as they understand them) to influence and shape the behavior of and social attitudes toward older people (Biggs & Powell, 2001), it is critically important to fine-tune theories to get them "correct"—and then use evidence derived from them to get facts straight and interventions right. Sociologists have underscored the importance of understanding patterns of inequality within and between cohorts and social groups, and how such inequalities shape life chances. The critical turn in sociological theories of aging demonstrates that political and economic arrangements are implicated in constructing and reconstructing individual life courses in modern societies. The emphasis on structurally determined opportunities and constraints highlighted by political economy theory is tempered by the overlay of life course frameworks that attend also to human agency and individual life chances, shaping the recursive relationships between individuals and societies. Sociological theories provide some of the tools needed to understand both structural constraints and human agency as they influence aging. Continued refinement of sociological theories will offer more appropriate models to inform evidence-based interventions and decision making as new research techniques and data inform sociologists' research on aging.

REFERENCES

Achenbaum, W. A. (1978). *Old age in the new land.* Baltimore: Johns Hopkins University Press.

Achenbaum, W. A., & Levin, J. F. (1989). What does sociology mean? *Gerontologist, 29,* 393–400.

Antonucci, T. C. (1990). Social supports and social relationships. In R. H. Binstock & L. K. George (Eds.), *Handbook of aging and the social sciences* (3rd ed., pp. 205–226). San Diego, CA: Academic Press.

Antonucci, T. C., & Akiyama, H. (1987). Social networks in adult life: A preliminary examination of the convoy model. *Journal of Gerontology, 4,* 519–527.

Arber, S., & Ginn, J. (1991). *Gender and later life.* London: Sage.

Arber, S., & Ginn, J. (Eds.). (1995). *Connecting gender and aging: A sociological approach.* Buckingham, England: Open University Press.

Arnold, D. O. (1970). *Sociology of subcultures.* Berkeley, CA: Glendessary Press.

Atchley, R. C. (1989). A continuity theory of normal aging. *Gerontologist, 29,* 183–190.

Atchley, R. C. (1999). *Continuity and adaptation in aging: Creating positive experiences.* Baltimore: Johns Hopkins University Press.

Attias-Donfut, C., & Arber, S. (2000). Equity and solidarity across the generations. In S. Arber & C. Attias-Donfut (Eds.), *Myth of generational conflict: The family and state in aging societies* (pp. 1–21). London: Routledge.

Bengston, V. L., Burgess, E. O., & Parrott, T. E. (1997). Theory, explanation, and a third generation of theoretical development in social gerontology. *Journal of Gerontology: Social Sciences, 52B,* S72–S88.

Bengston, V. L., Parrott, T. E., & Burgess, E. O. (1996). Progress and pitfalls in gerontological theorizing. *Gerontologist, 36,* 768–772.

Bengston, V. L., & Schaie, K. W. (Eds.). (1999). *Handbook of theories of aging.* New York: Springer.

Biggs, S., & Powell, J. (2001). A Foucauldian analysis of old age and the power of social welfare. *Journal of Aging and Social Policy, 12*(2), 93–112.

Binstock, R. H., & Quadagno, J. (2001). Aging and politics. In R. H. Binstock & L. K. George (Eds.), *Handbook of aging and the social sciences* (5th ed., pp. 333–351). San Diego, CA: Academic Press.

Birren, J. E., & Bengston, V. L. (Eds.). (1988). *Emergent theories of aging.* New York: Springer.

Blau, Z. (1961). Social constraints on friendship in old age. *American Sociological Review, 26,* 429–439.

Burawoy, M. (2004). Public sociologies: Contradictions, dilemmas, and possibilities. *Social Forces, 82,* 1603–1618.

Calasanti, T. M. (1996). Gender and life satisfaction in retirement: An assessment of the male model. *Journal of Gerontology, 51B,* S18–S29.

Calasanti, T. M., & Slevin, K. F. (2001). *Gender, social inequalities, and aging.* Walnut Creek, CA: AltaMira Press.

Calasanti, T. M., & Zajicek, A. M. (1993). A socialist feminist approach to aging: Embracing diversity. *Journal of Aging Studies, 7,* 117–131.

Cowgill, D. O. (1974). Aging and modernization: A revision of the theory. In J. F. Gubrium (Ed.), *Communities and environmental policy* (pp. 124–146). Springfield, IL: Charles Thomas.

Cowgill, D. O., & Holmes, L. (Eds.). (1972). *Aging and modernization.* New York: Appleton Century-Crofts.

Cumming, E., & Henry, W. E. (1961). *Growing old: The process of disengagement.* New York: Basic Books.

Dannefer, D. (1987). Accentuation, the Matthew effect, and the life course: Aging as intracohort differentiation. *Sociological Forum, 2,* 211–236.

Dannefer, D., & Uhlenberg, P. (1999). Paths of the life course: A typology. In V. L. Bengston & K. W. Schaie (Eds.), *Handbook on theories of aging* (pp. 306–326). New York: Springer.

Dowd, J. J. (1975). Aging as exchange: A preface to theory. *Journal of Gerontology, 30*(5), 584–594.

Dowd, J. J. (1980). Exchange rates and old people. *Journal of Gerontology, 35,* 595–602.

Dowd, J. J. (1987). Reification of age: Age stratification theory and the passing of the autonomous subject. *Journal of Aging Studies, 1,* 317–335.

Elder, G. H. (1994). Time, human agency, and social change: Perspectives on the life course. *Social Psychology Quarterly, 57,* 4–15.

Elder, G. H., Johnson, M. K., & Crosnoe, R. (2003). The emergence and development of life course theory. In J. Mortimer & M. Shanahan (Eds.), *Handbook of the life course* (pp. 3–19). New York: Kluwer Academic/Plenum Press.

Esping-Andersen, G. (1990). *Three worlds of welfare capitalism.* Cambridge, England: Polity Press.

Estes, C. L. (1979). *Aging enterprise.* San Francisco: Jossey-Bass.

Estes, C. L. (1986). The politics of ageing in America. *Ageing and Society, 6*(2), 121–134.

Estes, C. L. (1991). The new political economy of aging: Introduction and critique. In M. Minkler & C. L. Estes (Eds.), *Critical perspectives on aging: The political and moral economy of growing old.* Amityville, NY: Baywood.

Estes, C. L. (1999). Critical gerontology and the new political economy of aging. In M. Minkler & C. L. Estes (Eds.), *Critical gerontology: Perspectives from political and moral economy* (pp. 17–35). Amityville, NY: Baywood.

Estes, C. L., Biggs, S., & Phillipson, C. (2003). *Social theory, social policy and aging: A critical introduction.* Buckingham, England: Open University Press.

Estes, C. L., & Binney, E. A. (1989). The biomedicalization of aging: Dangers and dilemmas. *Gerontologist, 29*(5), 587–596.

Estes, C. L., Binney, E. A., & Cuthbertson, R. A. (1992). The gerontological imagination: Social influences on the development of gerontology, 1945–present. *International Journal of Aging and Human Development, 35*(2), 49–65.

Estes, C. L., Linkins, K. W., & Binney, E. A. (1996). Bioethics in a disposable society: Health care and the intergenerational stake. In J. W. Walters (Ed.), *Choosing who's to live: Ethics and aging.* Urbana: University of Illinois Press.

Ferraro, K. F., & Kelley-Moore, J. A. (2003). Cumulative disadvantage and health: Long term consequences of obesity? *American Sociological Review, 68*(5), 707–729.

Fischer, D. H. (1977). *Growing old in America.* New York: Oxford University Press.

Gatz, M., & Zarit, S. H. (1999). A good old age: Paradox or possibility. In V. L. Bengston & K. W. Schaie (Eds.), *Handbook on theories of aging* (pp. 396–413). New York: Springer.

George, L. K. (1993). Sociological perspectives on life course transitions. *Annual Review of Sociology, 19,* 353–373.

George, L. K. (2003). What life-course perspectives offer for the study of aging and health. In R. A. Settersten Jr. (Ed.), *Invitation to the life course: Toward new understandings of later life* (pp. 161–190). Amityville, NY: Baywood.

George, L. K. (2006). Perceived quality of life. In R. H. Binstock & L. K. George (Eds.), *Handbook of aging and the social sciences* (6th ed., pp. 321–336). New York: Academic Press.

Ginn, J., Street, D., & Arber, S. (Eds.). (2001). *Women, work, and pensions: International issues and prospects.* Buckingham, England: Open University Press.

Gubrium, J. F., & Holstein, J. A. (1999). Constructionist perspectives on aging. In V. L. Bengston & K. W. Schaie (Eds.), *Handbook on theories of aging* (pp. 287–305). New York: Springer.

Hagestad, G. O. (1999). Gray zone? Meetings between sociology and gerontology. *Contemporary Sociology, 28*(5), 514–517.

Hagestad, G. O., & Dannefer, D. (2001). Concepts and theories of aging: Beyond microfication in social science approaches. In R. H. Binstock & L. K. George (Eds.), *Handbook of aging and the social sciences* (5th ed., pp. 3–21). San Diego, CA: Academic Press.

Harrington Meyer, M. (1996). Making claims as workers or wives: The distribution of social security benefits. *American Sociological Review, 61*(3), 449–465.

Harrington Meyer, M., Street, D., & Quadagno, J. (1994). The impact of family status on income security and health care in old age: A comparison of Western nations. *International Journal of Sociology and Social Policy, 14*(1/2), 54–83.

Havighurst, R. J., Neugarten, B. L., & Tobin, S. S. (1968). Disengagement and patterns of aging. In B. Neugarten (Ed.), *Middle Age and Aging: A Reader in Social Psychology.* Chicago: University of Chicago Press.

Hendricks, J. (1992). Generations and the generation of theory in social gerontology. *International Journal of Aging and Human Development, 35*(1), 31–47.

Hendricks, J., & Achenbaum, W. A. (1999). Historical development of theories of aging. In V. L. Bengston & K. W. Schaie (Eds.), *Handbook of theories of aging* (pp. 21–39). New York: Springer.

Hendricks, J., & Leedham, C. (1991). Dependency or empowerment? Toward a moral and political economy of aging. In M. Minkler & C. L. Estes (Eds.), *Critical perspectives on aging: The political and moral economy of growing old* (pp. 51–64). Amityville, NY: Baywood.

Hochschild, A. (1975). Disengagement theory: A critique and proposal. *American Sociological Review, 40,* 553–569.

Hochschild, A. (1978). *Unexpected community.* Berkeley: University of California Press.

Johnson, C., & Barer, B. (1992). Patterns of engagement and disengagement among the oldest-old. *Journal of Aging Studies, 6,* 351–364.

Laslett, P. (1976). Societal development and aging. In R. H. Binstock & E. Shanas (Eds.), *Handbook of aging and social sciences* (pp. 87–116). New York: Van Nostrand Reinhold.

Lemon, B., Bengston, V. L., & Patterson, J. (1972). An exploration of the activity theory of aging: Activity types and life satisfaction among in-movers to a retirement community. *Journal of Gerontology, 27,* 511–523.

Lewis, R. (1990). The adult child and older parents. In T. Brubaker (Ed.), *Family relationships in later life* (pp. 68–85). Beverly Hills, CA: Sage.

Light, D. W. (2005). Contributing to scholarship and theory through public sociology. *Social Forces, 83*(4), 1647–1654.

Longino, C., & Kart, C. (1982). Explicating activity theory: A formal replication. *Journal of Gerontology, 17,* 713–722.

Lynott, R., & Passuth Lynott, P. (1996). Tracing the course of theoretical development in the sociology of aging. *Gerontologist, 36*(6), 749–760.

Maddox, G. L. (1979). Sociology of later life. *Annual Review of Sociology, 5,* 113–135.

Marshall, V. (1996). The state of aging theory in aging and the social sciences. In R. H. Binstock & L. K. George (Eds.), *Handbook of aging and the social sciences* (4th ed.). San Diego, CA: Academic Press.

Marshall, V. (1999). Analyzing theories of aging. In V. L. Bengston & K. W. Schaie (Eds.), *Handbook of theories of aging* (pp. 434–455). New York: Springer.

Marshall, V., & Tindale, J. A. (1978). Notes for a radical gerontology. *International Journal of Aging and Human Development, 9,* 163–175.

McMullin, J. A. (1995). Theorizing age and gender relations. In S. Arber & J. Ginn (Eds.), *Connecting gender and aging: A sociological approach.* Philadelphia: Open University Press.

Minkler, M., & Cole, T. (1991). Political and moral economy: Not such strange bedfellows. In M. Minkler & C. L. Estes (Eds.), *Critical perspectives on aging: The political and moral economy of growing old* (pp. 37–49). Amityville, NY: Baywood.

Minkler, M., & Cole, T. (1999). Political and moral economy: Getting to know one another. In M. Minkler & C. L. Estes (Eds.), *Critical gerontology: Perspectives from political and moral economy* (pp. 37–49). Amityville, NY: Baywood.

Minkler, M., & Estes, C. L. (Eds.). (1991). *Critical perspectives on aging: The political and moral economy of growing old.* Amityville, NY: Baywood.

Minkler, M., & Estes, C. L. (Eds.). (1999). *Critical gerontology: Perspectives from political and moral economy.* Amityville, NY: Baywood.

Moen, P., & Spencer, D. (2006). Converging divergences in age, gender, health and well-being: Strategic selection in the third age. In R. H. Binstock & L. K. George (Eds.), *Handbook of aging and the social sciences* (6th ed., pp. 127–144). San Diego, CA: Academic Press.

Mortimer, J., & Shanahan, M. (2003). *Handbook of the life course.* New York: Kluwer Press Academic/Plenum Press.

Myles, J. (1989). *Old age and the welfare state* (Rev. ed.). Lawrence: University of Kansas Press.

O'Connor, J. (1973). *Fiscal crisis of the state.* New York: St. Martin's.

O'Rand, A. M. (2001). Stratification and the life course: The forms of life course capital and their interdependence. In R. H. Binstock & L. K. George (Eds.), *Handbook on aging and the social sciences* (5th ed., pp. 197–213). San Diego, CA: Academic Press.

O'Rand, A. M. (2006). Stratification and the life course: Life course capital, life course risks, and social inequality. In R. H. Binstock & L. K. George (Eds.), *Handbook on aging and the social sciences* (6th ed., pp., 145–162). San Diego, CA: Academic Press.

O'Rand, A. M., & Campbell, R. T. (1999). On reestablishing the phenomenon and specifying ignorance: Theory development and research design in aging. In V. L. Bengston & K. W. Schaie (Eds.), *Handbook on theories of aging* (pp. 59–78). New York: Springer.

Orloff, A. S. (1993). Gender and the social rights of citizenship: The comparative analysis of gender relations and welfare states. *American Sociological Review, 58*(3), 303–329.

Palmore, E. (1975). *Honorable elders: A cross cultural analysis of aging in Japan.* Durham, NC: Duke University Press.

Palmore, E. B., & Manton, K. (1974). Modernization and status of the aged: International correlations. *Journal of Gerontology, 29,* 205–210.

Parsons, T. (1942). Age and sex in the social structure of the United States. *American Sociological Review, 7,* 604–616.

Parsons, T. (1951). *Social system.* New York: Free Press.

Passuth, P., & Bengston, V. L. (1996). Sociological theories of aging: Current perspectives and future directions. In J. Quadagno & D. Street (Eds.), *Aging for the twenty-first century* (pp. 333–355). New York: St. Martin's Press.

Phillipson, C. (1982). *Capitalism and the construction of old age.* London: Macmillan.

Phillipson, C. (1998). *Reconstructing old age: New agenda in social theory and practice.* London: Sage.

Quadagno, J. (1982). *Aging in early industrial society: Work, family and social policy in nineteenth century England.* San Diego, CA: Academic Press.

Quadagno, J. (1988). *Transformation of old age security: Class and politics in the American welfare state.* Chicago: University of Chicago Press.

Quadagno, J. (1989). Generational equity and the politics of the welfare state. *Politics and Society, 17,* 360–376.

Quadagno, J., & Reid, J. (1999). The political economy perspective of aging. In V. L. Bengston & K. W. Schaie (Eds.), *Handbook on theories of aging* (pp. 344–358). New York: Springer.

Riley, M. W. (1971). Social gerontology and the age stratification of society. *American Sociological Review, 52,* 1–14.

Riley, M. W., Foner, A., & Riley, J. W., Jr. (1999). The aging and society paradigm. In V. L. Bengston & K. W. Schaie (Eds.), *Handbook of theories of aging* (pp. 327–343). New York: Springer.

Riley, M. W., Johnson, M. E., & Foner, A. (1972). *Aging and society: Vol. 3. A sociology of age stratification.* New York: Russell Sage Foundation.

Riley, M. W., Kahn, R., & Foner, A. (1994). *Age and structural lag: Society's failure to provide meaningful opportunities in work, family and leisure.* New York: Wiley-Interscience.

Rose, A. (1964). A current theoretical issue in social gerontology. *Gerontologist, 4,* 46–50.

Savishinsky, J. S. (2000). *Breaking the Watch: the Meanings of Retirement in America.* Ithaca, NY: Cornell University Press.

Settersten, R. A., Jr. (2003). Age structuring and the rhythm of the life course. In J. Mortimer & M. Shanahan (Eds.), *Handbook of the life course* (pp. 81–98). New York: Kluwer Press Academic/Plenum Press.

Settersten, R. A., Jr. (2006). Aging and the life course. In R. H. Binstock & L. K. George (Eds.), *Handbook of aging and the social sciences* (6th ed., pp. 3–19). San Diego, CA: Academic Press.

Silverstein, M. (2006). Intergenerational family transfers in social context. In R. H. Binstock & L. K. George (Eds.), *Handbook of aging and the social sciences* (6th ed., pp. 164–180). San Diego, CA: Academic Press.

Street, D. (1993). Maintaining the status quo: Old age interest groups and the Medicare Catastrophic Coverage Act of 1988. *Social Problems, 40*(4), 501–514.

Street, D. (1997). Special interests or citizens' rights? "Senior Power, Social Security, and Medicare" *International Journal of Health Services, 17*(4), 727–751.

Street, D., & Cossman, J. (2006a). Altruism or self-interest? Social spending and the life course. *Journal of Sociology and Social Welfare, 33*(3), 73–99.

Street, D., & Cossman, J. (2006b). Greatest generation or greedy geezers? Social spending preferences and the elderly. *Social Problems, 53*(1), 75–96.

Street, D., & Parham, L. (2002). Modernization and the status of older people. In D. J. Ekerdt (Ed.), *Macmillan encyclopedia of aging* (pp. 1332–1337). New York: Macmillan.

Street, D., & Quadagno, J. (1993). The state, the elderly, and the intergenerational contract: Toward a new political economy of aging. In K. W. Schaie & W. A. Achenbaum (Eds.), *Societal impact on aging: Historical perspectives* (pp. 130–150). New York: Springer.

Townsend, P. (1981). The structured dependency of the elderly: Creation of social policy in the twentieth century. *Aging and Society, 1*(1), 5–28.

Walker, A. (1981). Towards a political economy of old age. *Aging and Society, 1*(1), 73–94.

Walker, A. (1999). Public policy and theories of aging: Constructing and reconstructing old age. In V. L. Bengston & K. W. Schaie (Eds.), *Handbook on theories of aging* (pp. 361–378). New York: Springer.

PART III

EVIDENCE-BASED HEALTH PRACTICE

CHAPTER 7

Health Promotion

JILL BRADSHAW and WALDO C. KLEIN

T HINK ABOUT IT: health promotion; the idea of advancing good health. It would seem that the idea of health promotion should be one of those commonsense notions that would be clearly understood and heartily endorsed by all people. And yet, like common sense itself, neither the understanding of health promotion nor the endorsement of the many ways that it can be advanced are always readily apparent among older adults or even the professionals who provide service to them. We labor under the myth that the genetic material received from our parents is the most significant predictor of our longevity; in fact, it is the decisions that we make about our social and behavioral choices that are most influential with regard to health status and functioning (Ory, Hoffman, Hawkins, Sanner, & Mockenhaupt, 2003).

Contemporary life is filled with circumstances that run counter to health promotion. In many places, basic environmental conditions assault healthful living through the air we breathe or the water that hydrates our bodies. Social conditions, too, challenge health promotion through the stressors that manifest themselves as illness and injury, both physical and mental. Modern diets have moved away from traditions of whole foods toward highly processed food that often lacks basic nutrients. Of course, any diet cannot be evaluated without a simultaneous consideration of the physical exercise in which one is engaged. Work burns fuel; even when it is pleasant, exercise is work; food is fuel. We need to attend to a balance in this and in so many other areas to maximize health promotion.

Whether of their own choosing or externally imposed, the opportunities for older adults to ignore or avoid good health abound. Health promotion is, in short, the advancement of all things healthful. Health has been defined by the World Health Organization (1948) for nearly 60 years as "a state of complete physical, mental and social well-being and not merely the absence of disease or infirmity." When one considers the breadth of this definition, it is clear that although the fundamental notion of health promotion may ring true as common sense, in practice it involves an extensive array of social conditions and personal behaviors that interact in myriad ways.

HEALTH PROMOTION AS PRIMARY PREVENTION

This chapter approaches health promotion as an exercise in primary prevention. On their face, both health promotion and primary prevention seek to avoid the untoward consequences of illness, accidents, environmental stressors, and less than ideal personal habits. However, both health promotion and primary prevention must actively consider more than these negative influences that abound in contemporary life. Health promotion must be concerned with "well-being," not just the "absence of disease or infirmity." People do not present as simply a constellation of pathologies; they also bring to the table a range of important assets. These may include influences that coexist in the social and physical worlds, as well as the personal attributes and habits that contribute to individual well-being. To give full consideration to the "physical, mental and social well-being" of individuals that are incorporated into the definition of health by the World Health Organization (1948), along with both the assets and challenges that every individual carries, we have found it useful to apply a variation of a model of primary prevention as a mechanism for advancing health promotion.

Bloom's (1996, p. 2) configural equation to primary prevention is based on a definition of primary prevention that seeks "to prevent predictable problems, to protect existing states of health and healthy functioning, and to promote desired potentialities in individuals and groups in their physical and sociocultural settings over time." With health promotion in mind, this model highlights the simultaneous importance of avoiding conditions that may be anticipated to result in ill health, to protect those assets that individuals bring to their older adulthood, and, though too often neglected, to attend to those possibilities for the promotion of goals—for both individuals and macro social or physical environments—that serve the end state of health. The model has been previously applied as a guide for professional practice in the promotion of *successful aging* with older adults (Klein & Bloom, 1997).

Beyond the tripartite definition of primary prevention, this configural equation of primary prevention incorporates consideration of five levels of functioning. At the lowest level, the individual is recognized as being the central focus. The individual is embedded within a social structure that entails three additional levels. First, virtually every individual is a member of identifiable primary groups. These groups include family, close friends, and others for whom the relationship is characterized by face-to-face ongoing contact. The number of such groups may vary from individual to individual; the strength and salience of individual groups will also vary. However, most older adults have such primary social relationships. By the nature of primary relationships, it is among members of such groups that individuals turn for support, typically as both givers and receivers. Secondary groups exist for most older adults at a somewhat lower level of social connectedness. Secondary groups are characterized by a sense of membership but may lack regularized face-to-face contact. Larger membership organizations represent such relationships. Secondary groups are less likely to provide the personal-level relationships of primary groups, but they may provide other benefits in terms of supporting identity structures or connecting to other resources. Finally, all older adults are embedded in the macro sociocultural environment. Included here are the social institutions that create and define the responsibilities and entitlements of societal membership. Systems of law and regulation, cultural and ethnic influences, programs intended to provide services of support, and community values are all part of this system of influence. Above even these three levels of social engagement, all people live in some physical environment. To fully appreciate the role of the physical environment in health promotion, we must look beyond the natural physical environment (air, water, solitude, or the absence of any of these qualities) to include constructed systems of community infrastructure such as transportation systems, housing stock, and the other created physical realities that provide a forum for contemporary existence.

Within each of these levels, primary prevention—and, by extension, health promotion—may operate to reduce the limits or constraints that a person experiences, or to protect or enhance the positive conditions that a person carries in his or her health-promotive repertoire. Approaching health promotion from such a preventive orientation provides a structure for the organized study and application of health-promotive interventions that operate at any of these five levels. By intentionally drawing attention to the multiple levels at which life is played out, this approach to primary prevention offers a true ecological perspective. The interplay among these five levels and the opportunity for the prevention of predictable problems, the protection of existing strengths and resources, and the promotion of future goals and potentialities create a very rich stage for the expansion and application of health-promotive opportunities and interventions.

When we conceptualize health promotion in this way, it becomes much easier to see the relationship between modest, even subtle changes in the behavior of people and the impact that these changes can have collectively. The same power in numbers that has allowed the baby boom cohort to shape many other aspects of American social life can support their collective influence on macro health issues. Modest but widespread reductions in body weight, tobacco use, and alcohol consumption could potentially result in substantial reductions in heart disease, respiratory disease, and myriad costs associated with alcohol misuse. Simultaneous increases in exercise, health care screening, and stress management can produce parallel benefits at the collective level. In short, a preventive model of health promotion may yield huge benefits sorely needed by a dramatically aging society.

The reader may notice that the structure of this chapter differs somewhat from others in this book. Health promotion is exercised across a large number of activity areas, and consequently, the topics of trends, incidence, etiology, and prognosis do not provide neat and unique categories into which evidence-based health promotion interventions might be organized. We have tried to be responsive to the reasonable call for a uniform structure for the chapters of this book while accommodating the somewhat unique requirements of the proactive field of health promotion. To that end, each of the individual areas of health promotion is presented with content reflecting the common chapter themes incorporated as appropriate.

PREVENTIVE HEALTH CARE

When one first thinks about health promotion, it is perhaps the area of *preventive health care* that comes most easily to mind. After all, preventive health care is explicitly linked to health, and the idea of prevention is clearly connected to the notion of health promotion. We start this survey of the various areas in which one might practice health promotion with preventive health care for exactly those reasons. Preventive health care is about avoiding predictable problems as well as protecting the existing strengths—especially but not exclusively those of our physical bodies—as we move through time.

Even as the notion of preventive health care makes intuitive sense on its face, the actual practice of preventive health care within a society does not come without associated costs. Too often, individual consumers, as well as policy makers, fail to make the investment in prevention because the benefits to prevention are seen only in the *absence* of the negative outcomes that otherwise *may* occur. Unfortunately, the implicit assumption that seems to operate—that what we can't see (the *prevented* disease, or fall, or other avoidable catastrophe) won't hurt us—leads too many of us to precisely those deleterious outcomes that we fail to prevent. The opportunity to invest widely in prevention is the opportunity to avoid the often catastrophic costs associated with our failure to do so. It is a little like playing the lottery, but with *much better odds!*

There are a number of principal areas for direct action in preventive health care, including regular health screenings, appropriate use of vaccinations, and proper use of pharmaceuticals (prescribed as well as over-the-counter [OTC] drugs), that fall under the general rubric of medical health care. In addition to these, there are other areas of preventive health care that are clearly related to health promotion (e.g., exercise, nutrition, cessation of tobacco use) but that we do not choose to include in our narrower category of preventive medical health care. These nonmedical areas are addressed in the topical sections that this overview of preventive medical care provides.

Vaccinations

Clean water and vaccines rate among the top health interventions of human history. For the most part, issues of water quality have been satisfactorily addressed for older adults in American society. Access to and utilization of appropriate vaccines, however, continue to provide a challenge for those concerned with health promotion. In part, the lack of more widespread use of vaccinations stems from their very effectiveness. Since the development of the first vaccines over 200 years ago, their use has resulted in a radical diminution in many and virtual elimination of some diseases. With the ready threat of so many diseases removed, the motivation for becoming inoculated against them is also reduced. After all, why should we be vaccinated against a disease that almost nobody gets (the faulty logic goes)? In addition, some people are moved away from seeking inoculations by concerns about vaccination side effects or even acquiring the disease through the very vaccination intended to provide protection.

Two vaccinations stand out as essential features of preventive health care for older adults: influenza vaccine and pneumococcal vaccine. Influenza kills an average of 36,000 people in America each year, and over 90% of them are adults over age 65; an additional 3,400 older adults are estimated to have died of pneumococcal disease (Centers for Disease Control and Prevention [CDC], 2004b). The *Healthy People 2000* (U.S. Department of Health and Human Services [DHHS], 1991) initiative set targets for immunization of older adults to each of these diseases at 60% (for flu, the target was inoculation within the past year; for pneumococcal disease, it was ever having been inoculated), a goal that was successfully achieved. However, the *Healthy People 2010* initiative targets 90% for each of these (again, an annual inoculation for flu and ever having been inoculated for pneumococcal disease; DHHS, 2000). According to the Administration on Aging (n.d.), among non-nursing-home-residing older adults, flu shots reduce hospitalization and death by about 70% and 85%, respectively.

HEALTH SCREENINGS

Health screenings are not so much about *preventing* the likelihood that one experiences illness or disease as they are about enabling early detection so that subsequent treatments might be less invasive and more effective. Quite simply, the goal of health screenings is early detection, and early detection saves lives and reduces disability. The most common conditions for which older adults should be screened are high blood pressure, high cholesterol, diabetes, and a number of cancers. Depending on individual situations and circumstances, some of these screenings should be conducted with relative frequency; other screenings are recommended as infrequently as every 5 years. "Only one-third of older Americans receive all recommended screening measures. For example, 60% of Americans over age 65 have not had a sigmoidoscopy or colonoscopy in the past 5 years—two tests that can screen for colorectal cancer—even though Medicare covers both services" (American Public Health Association, 2005, p. 1).

Blood Pressure   Blood pressure should be screened at every health encounter for all adults. However, it must be appreciated that the condition of high blood pressure is not typically detected with a single test due to the normal fluctuations in blood pressure that are commonly experienced. Should an elevated blood pressure be detected, a second check should be performed during the same visit. Thus, it is best for older adults to take advantage of blood pressure screenings routinely—at least annually but more frequently if elevated blood pressure is detected. Generally the diagnosis of high blood pressure should be based on two or more elevated readings taken on two or more occasions. Through such a routine, individual norms for blood pressure may be established and used as a comparative basis to determine abnormalities. In the event that blood pressure higher than a moderate range is detected, the frequency of screening should be increased as indicated by a health professional. The combined affordability and availability of blood pressure screening to older adults suggests that this should be made a part of regular and ongoing preventive health care.

Cholesterol   High cholesterol and lipid disorders have been associated with coronary heart disease and cardiovascular disease in adults. The U.S. Preventive Services Task Force (2001) has made a strong recommendation that screening be conducted regularly (annually) among adults. The Task Force did not indicate an upper age limit for such screening; however, because lipid levels are not as likely to increase among older adults (> 65 years of age), the importance of continued screening diminishes for that group.

Diabetes   All older adults should be screened for diabetes every 3 years. The risk of diabetes increases with age, the presence of vascular disease, family history of diabetes, hypertension, and a body mass index of greater than 25. In addition,

Native Americans, African Americans, Hispanics, Asians, and Pacific Islanders are at increased risk of diabetes (International Diabetes Center, 2003).

Breast Cancer   Although recommendations vary somewhat for screening for breast cancer, it is well documented that regular mammography reduces death from breast cancer by approximately 30% in women between the ages of 50 and 69. After years of encouraging breast self-exam, the empirical evidence supporting this intervention is not so strong as to justify a continued recommendation one way or the other. Regular (every 1 to 2 years) mammography, which is a covered Medicare service, continues to be the recommended screening. However, the importance of such screening for women 70 years and older is less clear. Although older women experience a higher rate of getting and dying from breast cancer, they are simultaneously subject to higher risks of other causes of death as well. "Women with comorbid conditions that limit their life expectancy are unlikely to benefit from screening" (National Guideline Clearinghouse, 2005a).

Colorectal Cancer   Screening for colorectal cancer should be offered to men and women 50 years of age and older. The options for such screening vary widely and include home fecal occult blood testing, sigmoidoscopy, a combination of these two, colonoscopy, and double-contrast barium enema. Because each of these different screening methods carries different advantages and disadvantages—as well as costs and risks—providers should review the options with older adults and incorporate personal preferences of the consumer into the selection of a specific screen. The fecal occult blood testing (with samples collected at home) is recommended by the U.S. Preventive Services Task Force (2002a) annually, and the more invasive sigmoidoscopy is recommended on a 5-year schedule. When positive screening results are detected, further screening with a colonoscopy is recommended. Initial screening with a colonoscopy generally obviates the need for other screening procedures; however, both the inconvenience and the cost weigh against an automatic turn to colonoscopy as the screening procedure of choice (National Guideline Clearinghouse, 2005b).

Prostate Cancer   Although it has been recommended that all men age 50 and above receive annual screening for prostate cancer using either a prostate-specific antigen (PSA) test or a digital rectal exam, the U.S. Preventive Services Task Force (2002b) found inconclusive evidence that early detection actually improves health outcomes. In part, the difficulty arises from the proportion of false testing results. The PSA test is more sensitive than a digital rectal exam, but 10% to 20% of these tests yield false negatives. Naturally, as the threshold for assessment is made more stringent, an increased number of false-positive results occur. Negative factors associated with screening, including a high number of false positives, raise further questions about the benefits of population screening. African American men and men with a first-degree relative with a history of prostate cancer face an increased risk and therefore will derive greater benefit from routine screening, but even among this target population the benefits of biennial screening are likely to equal those of annual screening (National Guideline Clearinghouse, 2005c).

Osteoporosis   Osteoporosis is a disease characterized by reduced bone density. Although it occurs in both men and women, it predominates among women. The most serious effects of osteoporosis are spontaneous compression fractures of the spine and broken bones resulting from falls or other injury. Older women should receive regular screenings for osteoporosis. In fact, it would be ideal if women younger than 60 received a baseline screening for bone density against which to assess subsequent potential change. Risk factors for osteoporotic fractures include low body weight (<150 pounds), smoking, weight loss, a family history of osteoporosis, low calcium vitamin intake (either supplementary or dietary), and low physical activity.

PROPER USE OF PHARMACEUTICALS

"Take two aspirin and get plenty of rest." It seems like a simple enough instruction. But the reality of contemporary pharmacotherapy is not nearly so simple. Older adults take far more prescribed medications and OTC drugs daily than do younger adults. In 2001, Medicare beneficiaries accounted for about 14% of the community-residing population but consumed over 40% of the cost of prescribed drugs (Goulding, 2005). Add OTC medications to these prescriptions and the complexities of appropriately following administration guidelines increase exponentially. Some drugs are to be appropriately taken on any empty stomach, others with a meal; some should be taken specifically with milk, others with juice, but perhaps not a citrus juice. Following all of the directions to the letter can be daunting. Beyond the administration guidelines for multiple drugs, the potential interaction effects among multiple drugs are almost limitless. The effect of one drug might be potentiated, whereas another may be negated. Entirely new and often unanticipated interactive side effects occur. It is just not the simple world of two aspirin and plenty of rest.

Almost two-thirds of older adults take their prescriptions improperly, and of these about 140,000 die each year as a result of this medication mismanagement (American Public Health Association, 2005). The clear paradox here is that something with the power to have such a positive influence on health promotion, as well as treatment of acute and chronic conditions, can simultaneously create a health threat of such significant proportion. With perhaps 20 million older adults mismanaging their medications, the opportunity for health promotion through education and management is huge.

Practice Guidelines for Medicine Management　The practice guidelines for promoting good health by minimizing mismanagement of prescriptions and other drugs essentially entail creating avenues of clear communication and developing systems of support that provide cues for proper medicine administration. The booklet *Your Medicine: Play It Safe* (Agency for Healthcare Research and Quality, 2003) offers several steps aimed at older adults to reduce the likelihood of using medications inappropriately. These include the following:

- *Give your health care team important information.* Beyond the obvious benefit of providing other health-related information to providers, this step draws the older adult's attention to the fact that he or she is working with and is a part of a team. *Different* providers are not *independent* providers with regard to the individual client. They are intimately related through the interactive effects of their individual interventions in a shared client. Further, the client must *work with* these providers, not passively be *worked on*. To facilitate this

information exchange, the client should be prepared with a list of all medicines and supplements that are being taken.

- *Get the facts about your medicine.* Older adults must be educated to seek all the
relevant information about drugs that have been prescribed. Questions
about the name and purpose of the drug, dosage level and administration
schedule, side effects, interactions, and anticipated results should be prepared in writing and answered in full. Clients should feel comfortable in
taking notes while meeting with providers and should bring a friend or
family member to assist in recording this information if necessary. It is also
very beneficial to use a single pharmacy to fill prescriptions so that a single
record of all prescriptions can be maintained.
- *Stay with your treatment plan.* If the preceding steps have been followed, the required regimen should be clear; now it must be followed. Depending on individual needs, clearly understanding the requirements of administration may
be adequate. However, many people need assistance in managing their multiple medications on multiple schedules. At the very lowest level, a schedule list
may provide the structure that will support some people in meeting their
medication requirements. A variety of pill dispensers (with and without
timers) may address some needs; others may be better managed by friendly
reminder telephone calls. Still others will require explicit monitoring.
- *Keep a record of your medicines.* This final step serves to bring the list that
should have been presented to the health team in Step 1 up to date. Keeping
track of a range of different medications, each with its own schedule and set
of concerns, can be a daunting task. Mismanaging them can be fatal. Unfortunately, modern pharmaceutical miracles come packaged with a tremendous potential for mistakes, misapplication, and misery. The goals of health
promotion are served when a social worker or other supportive person can
provide the older adult with procedures, mental or mechanical, that minimize the opportunity for confusion and error.

SUMMARY OF PREVENTIVE HEALTH

Opportunities abound to exercise a preventive attitude toward the goal of health
promotion. Among these opportunities, keeping vaccinations up to date, attending to periodic and regular screenings for the common disease conditions of older
adulthood, and appropriately managing the multiple pharmaceuticals that are intended to bring the benefits of medical science *without* creating the quagmire of
drug interactive possibilities can do tremendous service in advancing good
health. But in each of these areas, the older adult or a responsible caregiver must
be proactively engaged in intentionally pursuing these preventive opportunities.
As with all efforts at primary prevention, the tendency is ever present to ignore
preventive opportunities in the absence of forceful personal evidence of need.
Alas, by the time that personal evidence is available to us, the opportunity for
prevention has often passed. Only through the good practice of intentional living
with an eye to prevention do we harvest these rich benefits.

EXERCISE

The health promotion activity that is widely believed to have the single greatest
impact on a person's overall health and well-being is physical activity. When

older adults increase their level of physical activity they significantly lower their risk of chronic diseases and conditions that often lead to premature death, while simultaneously improving their physical health, mental health, cognitive functioning, and quality of life.

SCOPE OF THE PROBLEM

Older adults are disproportionately affected by an array of chronic conditions and diseases that collectively account for more than 75% of deaths (CDC, 2005). The top three chronic diseases among Americans age 65 and older are heart disease, cancer, and stroke, accounting for 60% of all deaths in this age group (CDC, 2004b). Regular physical activity reduces one's risk for coronary heart disease, high blood pressure, colon cancer, diabetes, and overall risk of dying prematurely (CDC, 2004b; DHHS, 1996; Levkoff, Chee, & Noguchi, 2001; Rowe & Kahn, 1998). Regular physical activity can even negate the adverse effects of other risk factors associated with chronic disease, such as smoking, obesity, and high blood sugar (Rowe & Kahn, 1998). Adopting healthier behaviors, including regular physical activity, can dramatically reduce a person's risk for most chronic diseases.

The presence of chronic diseases in older adults is not only life-threatening, but also negatively impacts quality of life and functional status. "Chronic conditions limit activities for 12 million elderly individuals living in community settings; 25% of these affected individuals are unable to perform basic activities of daily living, such as bathing, shopping, dressing, or eating. Nearly one-third of adults over age 65 are disabled, compared to 18% of all Americans" (Center for the Advancement of Health, 2006, p. 9). By adopting healthier lifestyles, older adults can reduce and compress disability into a shorter period toward the end of life (Hubert, Bloch, Oehlert, & Fries, 2002)—the essence of health promotion.

In the surgeon's general report *Bone Health and Osteoporosis* (DHHS, 2004), it is suggested that the greatest benefit of physical activity for older adults is reduction in the risk of falling, discussed elsewhere in this chapter. "Physical activity is the only single therapy that can simultaneously improve muscle mass, muscle strength, balance, and bone strength. As a result, it may decrease the risk of fractures, in part by reducing the risk of falling" (p. 20). Approximately 20% of seniors who suffer a hip fracture die within a year of the fracture, and another 20% end up being placed in a nursing home within a year of the fracture. Maintaining bone health is critically important to the overall health and quality of life for all older adults, and regular exercise is the key to doing so.

Regular physical activity aids in weight control and is a key part of any weight loss effort. Maintaining a healthy weight improves one's overall mortality, as studies show that extra pounds can literally change DNA and accelerate the aging process (Yeager, 2005). In the ongoing 32-year research project at the Tulane School of Public Health (Yeager, 2005), researchers found that as people gained weight they became more insulin-resistant and their telomeres (strands of DNA on the tip of each chromosome that typically shorten with age) shrank, a clear sign that the aging process was accelerating in the overweight study volunteers.

In addition to the physical health benefits associated with regular physical activity, there are a number of mental health benefits. Moderate amounts of physical activity can help reduce depression, anxiety, and stress, while increasing feelings of self-confidence and self-esteem (CDC, 2004b; DHHS, 2000; Rowe & Kahn, 1998; Williams & Lord, 1995). People who get moderate amounts of exercise also report sleeping better and show lowered blood pressure reactivity to stress tests (DHHS, 2003). Those who participate in regular physical activity often report higher levels of social support, as well as higher levels of satisfaction with social relationships. Being physically active allows older adults to maintain their involvement in the community, thereby maintaining and building their social networks.

Despite the proven benefits of exercise and regular physical activity, 60% of the American public remains sedentary (Pescatello, 2001). Only 15% of adults participate in the recommended amount of regular physical activity. One third of adults age 65 and older do not engage in any leisure-time physical activities (CDC, 2004b). By age 75, 1 in 3 men and 1 in 2 women engage in no regular physical activity (DHHS, 2000).

EVIDENCE-BASED INTERVENTIONS

The surgeon general's report *Physical Activity and Health* (DHHS, 1996) concludes that people of all ages benefit from regular physical activity. It is recommended that people engage in moderate amounts of physical activity (e.g., 30 minutes of brisk walking or raking leaves, 15 minutes of running, or 45 minutes of playing volleyball) on most, if not all, days of the week. Traditionally it was recommended that the 30 minutes of moderate exercise be consecutive, but recent research concludes that accumulating several 5- to 10-minute bursts of physical activity over the course of the day provides the same beneficial effects as consecutive routines (Haber, 1999; Rowe & Kahn, 1998).

Physical activity is often thought to be synonymous with exercise, but exercise is really a subset of physical activity. The term *physical activity* is defined simply as the physical movements we participate in every day. Any body movement produced by the use of skeletal muscles that results in energy expenditure is considered physical activity. Rising from a seated position, standing, walking, bending to pick up the newspaper—these are all forms of physical activity and they all expend energy. *Exercise* is defined as planned, structured, repetitive body movements that use major muscle groups. The most beneficial physical activity is *planned* exercise that uses certain sets of muscles for certain periods of time, which provides maximum health benefits and minimal health risks for the least effort possible (Klein & Bloom, 1997).

Exercise is generally broken down into two classifications: aerobic and strength training. Aerobic activities are those that increase the flow of oxygen and improve cardiovascular functioning. Some examples of aerobic activities are walking briskly, jogging, dancing, hiking, cycling, and swimming. Aerobic exercises increase flexibility and overall endurance, but they generally do not significantly increase strength. Strength-training exercises involve resistance training (isometrics) or the use of weights; these exercises increase physical strength, muscle mass, muscle tone, balance, and bone density. Resistance training focuses on contracting muscles without moving joints, such as pushing against a wall and holding that pose. Weight training involves the use of free weights or machine weights.

The amount of exercise needed to produce health benefits is considerably less than the amount needed to improve physical fitness (Pescatello, 2001). The protective factors associated with moderate exercise are almost as significant as the protective factors associated with high levels of exercise. In an 8-year study of more than 13,000 people, walking for 30 to 60 minutes every day was almost as beneficial in reducing the overall death rate as jogging up to 40 miles per week (Blair et al., 1989).

The model of physical activity traditionally recommended by professionals was structured exercise routines, but the emphasis is slowly being shifted to models focused on increasing physical activity as part of one's everyday life. Over the past decade, research has begun to show that there are significant health benefits from engaging in low to moderate physical activity, and from this research the concept of "lifestyle physical activity" has emerged. "Lifestyle physical activity has deviated from traditional methods of exercise prescription by advocating accumulated, unstructured activities of daily living according to individual preferences and convenience" (Pescatello, 2001, p. 115). An increase in lifestyle physical activity is often an ideal fit for older adults who are predominantly sedentary and likely unable or unwilling to engaged in exercise programs.

There are potential risks involved in physical activity programs, but they are usually minor and can often be avoided by seeking advice from qualified medical professionals. Every older adult who is initiating an exercise program after being sedentary should receive a checkup by a physician to ensure that he or she is free from cardiac problems that may cause difficulty. Generally, it is advisable to start with a low-intensity exercise program and slowly build capacity and endurance for more vigorous exercise. Low-intensity exercises include balance exercise, tai chi, walking, gait training, and leg strength training. Instruction in the proper execution of any exercise is essential, and exercise should be initially supervised to ensure safety (Gill, DiPietro, & Krumholz, 2000).

Most older adults acknowledge that they understand what they should be doing to stay healthy and fit, yet fewer than half achieve even the minimum amount of recommended physical activity. From 1999 to 2003, the American Association of Retired Persons (AARP, 2004) conducted surveys and focus groups with some 15,000 Americans age 50 and over about attitudes and knowledge about exercise. Their research showed that lack of knowledge was not the primary challenge in addressing low levels of physical activity in older adults, but other barriers, both real and perceived, were deterring people from action. Some commonly noted excuses for not exercising are fatigue, fear of heart attack, trouble catching breath, need to relax, too old, bad back, and arthritis (Haber, 1999).

The AARP (2004) research found that imagery and tone of presentation were very important in motivating older adults to be physically active, but that photos of elite senior athletes made them feel discouraged or overwhelmed. "Some people discussed openly that images of very fit and toned people contributed to their discomfort and embarrassment about being physically active" (p. 6). The "no pain, no gain" message that is often used to motivate younger audiences to exercise is not motivating to seniors. The critical role of health care professionals was also noted, with the majority of research participants reporting that their doctor is their primary and most trusted source of health information. Focus group respondents who were most physically active consistently reported that they were following the recommendations of their doctor to exercise.

The transition from a sedentary lifestyle to one that involves regular physical activity is a struggle that requires both motivation and support. Research shows that older adults who are supported by friends and family are more likely to succeed in increasing their level of physical activity and in maintaining those lifestyle changes (AARP, 2004). In surveys conducted by the AARP, respondents suggested that motivational messages that encouraged lifestyle changes, while recognizing how difficult change can be, were most encouraging to older adults.

One of the barriers to regular physical activity that is often noted by older adults is the perception that exercise is painful and difficult, involves some level of skill that they do not currently possess, and is not enjoyable. Older adults seem more comfortable with the term and concept of physical activity rather than exercise, and can often provide several examples of physical activities that they find enjoyable, such as gardening and walking. Professionals working with older adults should carefully consider the language they are using when discussing recommended lifestyle changes, using realistic examples that are tailored to the individual's situation, needs, and desires.

For older adults to participate in exercise programs, they must have regular access to equipment, classes, and safe places to exercise. Many communities offer safe walking trails and parks, community centers with exercise groups specifically designed for older adults, community swimming pools, and some transportation services to and from these sites. Other communities offer very little in community resources; in those cases, opportunities for exercise within the home need to be available to older adults. Professionals supporting older adults should be aware of the resources in their community and be knowledgeable about home-based programs.

EVIDENCE-BASED PRACTICE GUIDELINES

In 2001, the *National Blueprint: Increasing Physical Activity among Adults Age 50 and Older* was released as a joint effort of many organizations interested in health promotion for older adults (Robert Wood Johnson Foundation, 2001). As part of the *Blueprint* project, a variety of national-level activities were initiated to identify programs that successfully increase seniors' level of physical activity. A few of those programs are highlighted next, with additional information available online at www.healthyagingprograms.org and www.agingblueprint.org.

The Lifetime Fitness program is a physical activity program that provides seniors with low-cost fitness classes taught by certified fitness instructors. The 1-hour classes meet three times per week in ongoing, 5-week sessions. The classes include strength training with wrist and ankle weights, as well as aerobics, stretching, and balancing exercises. The program is designed to be safe and effective for seniors with a wide range of physical abilities. Participants have shown a marked improvement in physical and social functioning, as well as a decline in areas such as pain, fatigue, and depression. Information about this program can be found at www.seniorservices.org/wellness/replication.htm.

The People with Arthritis Can Exercise (PACE) program was developed by the Arthritis Foundation specifically for older adults with arthritis. This program uses gentle activities to help increase joint flexibility and range of motion to maintain muscle strength. Two levels of PACE are available, basic and advanced, to address the varying levels of fitness and limitation among those with arthritis. Participants have experienced such benefits as increased functional ability, increased self-care behaviors, decreased pain, and decreased depression. Trained leaders are required to implement this course. More information about this program can be found at www.arthritis.org.

The National Institute on Aging has developed a manual and companion video that guides older adults through safe and effective exercises for increased endurance, strength training, balance, and flexibility. The program can be conducted in a group setting or individually. The manual is available online at no cost, and the video can be ordered for a cost of $7.00 (also available in Spanish). More information can be obtained at www.nia.nih.gov/exercisebook/index.htm.

In addition to community-based physical activity programs, a variety of exercise programs are designed to be done in the home on an individual basis. The Strong-for-Life program consists of a 35-minute videotaped program of 11 exercise routines performed by a trained leader (Jette et al., 1999). The program is developed specifically for older adults with some degree of physical disability. Additionally, there are literally hundreds of physical activity videos available at local retailers that provide video instruction of a variety of physical activities and exercises.

In addition to engaging older adults in specific physical activity programs, other strategies are recommended to help encourage older adults to maintain lifestyle changes. It has been estimated that between 22% and 76% of those who start exercise programs drop out within 6 months (Center for the Advancement of Health, 2006). Strategies proven to maintain or increase levels of physical activity in older adults include cognitive-behavioral approaches such as face-to-face meetings with health counselors, regular follow-up calls to check progress, group meetings, group exercise opportunities, and self-documentation of progress (Lachman & Jette, 1997; Williams & Lord, 1995).

Physicians are in a unique position to influence the potential lifestyle habits of older adults. More than 60% of older adults say that their primary care physician is their most trusted source of information about health care-related issues. When physicians have recommended lifestyle changes to their patients that include more regular physical activity, more than 50% of those patients followed those recommendations and increased their activity level. When physicians took the practice a step further and actually wrote a prescription for exercise, patients were even more likely to increase their level of exercise (Pfeiffer, Clay, & Conatser, 2001).

NUTRITION

It is essential to consider the role of nutrition when thinking about health promotion. Eating a healthy and well-balanced diet, along with taking supplemental vitamins and minerals as recommended by a physician, helps to ensure maintenance of a healthy body weight and good bone health while reducing one's risk of several nutrition-related problems, such as obesity, Type 2 diabetes, osteoporosis, and malnutrition.

Scope of the Problem

Approximately 65% of adults in the United States are overweight, and 30% are obese (Booth & Winder, 2005). The prevalence of obesity among adults age 65 and older is 19%, an increase from 12% in 1990 (CDC, 2004b; Rhoades, 2005). Being overweight or obese substantially raises one's risk of illness from high blood pressure, high cholesterol, Type 2 diabetes, heart disease and stroke, gallbladder disease, arthritis, sleep disturbances and problems breathing, and certain types of cancer. Obese individuals also often suffer from social stigmatization, discrimination, and lower self-esteem (DHHS, 2000). The effect of obesity on longevity has led many experts to believe that the steady rise in life expectancy during the past two centuries may soon come to an end (Olshanksy et al., 2005).

Type 2 diabetes is the fifth leading cause of death among adults in the United States, and 85% of all people with diabetes are overweight or obese (National Institute on Aging, 2000). Research shows that the majority of cases of Type 2 diabetes could be prevented by the adoption of a healthier lifestyle (Hu et al., 2001). The American Diabetes Association (n.d.) reports that having Type 2 diabetes increases your risk for many serious complications, including heart disease, blindness, nerve damage, and kidney damage. Several studies have also linked Type 2 diabetes to mild cognitive dysfunction in older adults (Hewer, Mussell, Rist, Kulzer, & Bergis, 2003).

The surgeon general's report on bone health and osteoporosis estimates that 10 million Americans over the age of 50 have osteoporosis, and another 34 million are at risk of developing osteoporosis (DHHS, 2004). Osteoporosis is often considered a "silent" condition, because so many people are unaware that their bone health is in jeopardy. "In fact, four times as many men and nearly three times as many women have osteoporosis than report having the condition" (p. 2). Each year, nearly 1.5 million people suffer a bone fracture related to osteoporosis. Hip fractures are the most serious type of fracture experienced by older adults. Hip fractures are the leading cause of death, disability, and a reduced quality of life in older adults (CDC, 2004b). Up to 25% of hip fracture patients die within a year, and those who survive often experience a reduced ability to remain independent.

Older adults are at greater risk for malnutrition than the general population, especially older adults who are hospitalized or institutionalized. Surveys conducted in nursing homes found malnutrition to be as high as 52% to 85% for all residents (Levkoff et al., 2001). Chandra's (1997) research found that almost one third of analyzed elderly were deficient in vitamins and trace elements. The Institute of Medicine (2000) reports that older adults are not getting adequate amounts of key nutrients such as calcium, vitamin D, magnesium, and phosphorus, which are nutrients associated with structural and muscular function, muscle metabolism, and bone health.

Eating healthfully has been shown to help lower people's risk for many chronic diseases, including heart disease, stroke, some cancers, diabetes, and osteoporosis. However, a large gap exists between recommended dietary habits and what Americans actually eat. An assessment by the U.S. Department of Agriculture (USDA) found that 74% of American diets need improvement (Center for the Advancement of Health, 2006). In 2003, only about 1 in 4 adults ate the recommended five or more servings of fruits and vegetables each day (CDC, 2005). Approximately 30% of Americans age 65 and older are underweight or malnourished (Haber, 1999).

EVIDENCE-BASED INTERVENTIONS

The *Dietary Guidelines for Americans 2005* (DHHS, 2005) recommends that people choose a healthful assortment of foods that includes vegetables, fruits, grains (especially whole grains), low-fat milk products, and fish, lean meat, poultry, or beans. A key recommendation is that people consume a variety of nutrient-dense foods and beverages within and among the basic food groups while choosing foods that are low in saturated fats and transfats, cholesterol, added sugars, salt, and alcohol.

The USDA developed the well-known *Food Guide Pyramid* to help people make healthy food choices. There are five major food groups, with specific recommendations on the amount of servings one should strive to eat from each food group on a daily basis: grains, 6 to 11 servings; vegetables, 3 to 5 servings; fruits, 2 to 4 servings; milk, yogurt, and cheese, 2 to 3 servings; and meat, poultry, fish, dry beans, eggs, and nuts, 2 to 3 servings. It is recommended that people limit their intake of fats, oils, and sweets. Consumers should note that the recommended pyramid servings are typically smaller than the serving sizes listed on nutritional labels of food products.

Although eating a wide variety of healthy foods is considered to be the ideal way to achieve nutritional goals, there is growing concern that the level of nutrients in the highly processed foods that many Americans eat may not be sufficient to ensure adequate nutrition.

Many physicians now recommend that older adults take a multivitamin containing modest amounts of vitamins and minerals (Haber, 1999). Older adults should always consult their doctor or a registered dietitian before taking any dietary supplements. Just like any other medication, there are potential side effects and drug interactions from taking dietary supplements, so patients should be encouraged to make their health care professional aware of all medications they are taking, as well as any medical conditions they may have.

Some vitamins and minerals are of significant concern to older adults in maintaining their health. Calcium is known to strengthen bones and decrease the risk of fracture in older adults, and vitamin D is essential to the absorption of calcium. The U.S. surgeon general recommends that the average adult consume about 1,000 mg of calcium and 200 IU of vitamin D per day (DHHS, 2004). The usual diet of most older adults includes only 700 to 800 mg of calcium daily, which means that older adults need to adjust their diet or consider taking a supplement (Rowe & Kahn, 1998). The surgeon general has identified other nutrients that may be potentially beneficial to bone health, including vitamins C and K, zinc, manganese, phosphorus, potassium, magnesium, and iron.

Older adults who are diagnosed with certain chronic diseases will often be required to follow specialized dietary guidelines specific to their diagnosis. For example, a person diagnosed with Type 2 diabetes will need to follow a dietary plan that limits intake of raw sugars and simple carbohydrates to maintain appropriate blood glucose levels. For overweight people diagnosed with Type 2 diabetes, a weight loss plan is a must for proper blood glucose control. When detected early, many older adults with Type 2 diabetes can keep their blood glucose levels near normal by controlling their weight, exercising, and following a sensible diet, sometimes making it possible for them to avoid taking medications (National Institute on Aging, 2000).

It is important for professionals to consider not only the specific nutritional needs of older adults, as assessed by their doctor or a registered dietician, but also environmental barriers that might prevent older adults from implementing dietary recommendations. Households with lower incomes are at greater risk for malnutrition, given the high costs of purchasing healthy food choices such as meats, dairy products, and fresh fruits and vegetables. Lack of physical ability or transportation to shop for food might present significant barriers to some older adults. Lack of family and social supports may also present a barrier to nutritional health, as studies show that older adults who eat alone are more likely to decrease their food intake (Center for the Advancement of Health, 2006).

EVIDENCE-BASED PRACTICE GUIDELINES

The USDA has created a new resource, called the MyPyramid Plan, which is designed to help individuals make better choices regarding their nutritional health. The plan is accessible online at www.mypyramid.gov. The plan allows a consumer to enter information about age, sex, and activity level, and it provides an easy-to-read estimate of what and how much should be eaten, including the total number of calories recommended per day. For those who are interested in a more detailed and daily assessment of diet quality and physical activity, there is a program called MyPyramid Tracker. This program allows one to assess food intake in terms of calories/energy and then subtracts the energy expended from activity, and it allows participants to monitor their progress online for up to a year.

The MyPyramid Plan website also has a teaching component designed for professionals who are interested in teaching others to better understand the federal food guidance program. The professional section includes a variety of resources to be used in teaching consumers about the concepts of the USDA's food pyramid, including Power Point slide presentations, sample menus, food intake patterns, calorie levels, and downloadable printed materials.

The American Diabetes Association (n.d.) has created its own version of the food pyramid for people with Type 2 diabetes, which can be accessed at www.diabetes.org. The website provides food exchange lists to help with meal planning. The website also provides a learning center for those who have been recently diagnosed, as well as answers to many commonly asked questions about treatment, complications, and other concerns. There is a great variety of educational programs throughout the country that have shown success in improving the health literacy and diet of older adults with Type 2 diabetes. The ADA website contains a state-by-state directory of educational programs that meet national standards for excellence in diabetes education.

An important national program aimed at improving the nutritional health of older adults is Meals on Wheels. Meals on Wheels delivers two nutritionally balanced meals per day to older adults who are home-bound and have limited incomes. Many communities have similar programs aimed at helping older adults to eat well. The Seattle Senior Farmers' Market Nutrition Program provides fresh, locally grown fruits and vegetables to low-income seniors. Research shows that seniors who participated in this program consumed more servings of fruits and vegetables (D. B. Johnson, Beaudoin, Smith, Beresford, & LoGerfo, 2004).

As with many health promotion activities, the primary care physician plays a critical role in effecting change in the nutritional habits of older adults. Physicians should conduct nutrition screenings with older patients to identify high-risk individuals. Physician counseling interventions aimed at adult patients at increased risk for diet-related chronic disease produced significant changes in the average daily intake of healthy foods (Center for the Advancement of Health, 2006).

REDUCING FALLS

Falling, or more particularly, the avoidance of falling, is an area of health promotion that deserves far more attention than it has received. Although the professional literature reflects an increasing recognition of the importance of preventing falling in regard to health maintenance for older adults, risk of injury from falling is frequently unrecognized by older adults (Baker et al., 2005). Yet both the risk of falling and the seriousness of injuries that may be sustained in falling represent major sources of ill health among older adults.

SCOPE OF THE PROBLEM

Over a third of seniors living in the community experience at least one fall annually, and as age increases, so too does the likelihood of falling (Center for the Advancement of Health, 2006). In considering all trauma patients over a 4-year period, falls were found to be the cause of injury 7 times more often among those older than 65 compared to younger adults: 48% versus 7% (Sterling, O'Connor, & Bonadies, 2001). The same study found falls to be the cause of death 7 times more frequently as well: 55% versus 7.5%. In fact, for adults 65 and older, unintentional falls are the leading cause of injury death, with 13,569 deaths in 2003, almost twice the number of motor vehicle traffic fatalities (CDC, 2006). Nearly 60% of all fatal falls among older adults occur in their home (Sattin, 1992), a finding that should not be surprising given the increased likelihood of both falling and spending more time in the home environment as one ages. White men over the age of 85 have the highest rate of death following falls (Sattin, 1992).

Beyond the cost of human suffering, falls result in a very significant financial cost to the society. These costs include out-of-pocket costs to the faller or his or her family, costs to insurance companies, and significant costs to both Medicare and Medicaid. Rizzo et al. (1998) report that the average health care cost of a fall was nearly $20,000, without including the cost of physician services. The collective cost of all fall-related injuries was estimated at $20 billion in 2000 (Center for the Advancement of Health, 2006) and has been projected to rise to over $27 billion by 2020 (Englander, Hodson, & Terregrossa, 1996).

RISKS FOR FALLING

Risk of falling is generally recognized as being multifactorial. The factors involved can be divided into those that are internal to the individual and those that are external or environmental. Intrinsic factors include balance, strength, and gait issues, cognitive impairment, the use of medications, and various disease states and illness. External or environmental factors "create challenges to balance that must be overcome to avoid falling" (King & Tinetti, 1995, p. 1150). The degree to which an external factor may actually result in precipitating a fall depends on the combination of the strength of the external risk balanced against the degree to which the older person is able to accommodate the risk and maintain balance. Thus, stairs, wrinkled rugs, poor lighting, misplaced furniture or other belongings, and a host of other conditions can present external risks for falling.

It is important to appreciate that the risk that each of these factors might represent can be evaluated only in the context of an individual older adult's *competence*, especially with regard to balance and strength, as suggested by Lawton and Nahemow's (1973) model of personal competence and environmental press. Following the logic of that model, it will be apparent that the risk of experiencing a fall increases as the number of risk factors present increases. Among the oldest old, it is common to find several risk factors—both internal and external—co-occurring, and it is this population that is at the highest risk of falling and of sustaining serious injury in doing so. A profile of older fallers would reflect that older White women who report more chronic disability, more medication use, less physical strength, lower muscle mass, and poorer balance and who are slower are at greatest risk of falling (de Rekeneire et al., 2003).

EVIDENCE-BASED INTERVENTIONS AND GUIDELINES

Clearly the risks for falling are not evenly distributed across the older population. Some people experience fewer internal and external risks, and some people have greater strength and balance to recover from a threat to balance and a potential fall. To that end, interventions to reduce falls and injury from falls should be designed specifically for either low- or high-risk individuals. Among low-risk older adults, there is mixed evidence in support of group delivery of fall risk education programs, exercise and balance improvement programs, strength training, and assessment of one's living environment for external risk factors. Although the evidence for such interventions is inconsistent, the low cost of incorporating many of these interventions into existing programs in senior centers, senior housing, and elsewhere probably justifies their use.

Among older adults who are known to be at high risk of falling, interventions are more appropriately tailored to the specific needs presented. Among this higher risk population, the evidence of intervention effectiveness is stronger. Starting with a comprehensive review of fall risk, successful interventions for fall prevention have included treatment of existing health problems (orthopedic, cardiovascular, and neurological), modification of medications to avoid interactive effects, removal of environmental risks, advice on the appropriate use of assistive devices, and physical therapy to improve strength, balance, range of motion, and gait problems (American Geriatrics Society, 2001; King & Tinetti, 1995).

There is evidence that targeted interventions to prevent falls are cost-effective as well. In a controlled group study, Rizzo, Baker, McAvay, and Tinetti (1996) tested an individualized prevention intervention with 153 older adults with an average age of nearly 78 years. The intervention cost an average of $905 to deliver (range: $588 to $1,346). Even with this fairly costly intervention, the health care costs of the intervention group averaged approximately $2,000 less than for the randomized control group. In short, fall prevention appears to be a financially viable opportunity for increased health promotion through prevention.

CESSATION OF NEGATIVE HABITS: SMOKING AND ALCOHOL CONSUMPTION

When we think of habits that result in potentially untoward consequences and that are widely practiced in contemporary society, two stand out as especially pernicious: smoking tobacco and misusing beverage alcohol. In both these cases, the behaviors are widespread, well-documented as physically addictive, and associated with a wide range of negative outcomes. Thus, we focus on tobacco smoking and alcohol misuse as examples of personal habits that represent the antithesis of health promotion.

TOBACCO USE: SCOPE OF THE PROBLEM

Tobacco use has been recognized as the foremost *avoidable* cause of death in the United States, accounting for approximately 430,000 deaths annually (CDC, 1997). Smoking among older adults is far less common than among adults younger than 65. In part, this certainly reflects the reduction by premature death of many smokers from tobacco-related illness. However, adult smoking has declined in the United States since the original surgeon general's warning of health risks in 1964, and only 10.1% of American older men and 8.6% of American older women continue to smoke cigarettes. The rates for older men have declined quite steadily since the mid-1960s, and after peaking in the mid-1980s, rates have declined for older women as well (CDC, 2004a). The downward trend seen in more recent years among older adults probably reflects the aging of a cohort that has been more steadily rejecting tobacco use over its adult lifetime.

Clearly, the use of tobacco is associated with a wide variety of disease outcomes, including a number of cancers, vascular diseases, pulmonary diseases, gastrointestinal diseases, and accidental burns. Most smokers see the value of quitting, yet older smokers among today's population face a number of obstacles. These include long-term behavioral habituation, physical addiction, and a fatalistic attitude that the damage from tobacco use has already been done and little benefit would be gained by quitting (Appel & Aldrich, 2003).

However, smoking cessation is beneficial to all age groups. "The benefits of smoking cessation are most clearly seen in coronary heart disease. One year after stopping smoking the excess risk of heart disease is reduced by 50% and after 10 to 15 years of abstinence the risk of heart disease is the same as for a person who has never smoked" (Gosney, 2001). Not only does smoking cessation improve health functioning, but it also provides an economic savings—in the purchase price of tobacco as well as health care copays and deductibles—that promotes economic well-being for many seniors.

Empirically Supported Interventions   There are a number of tobacco cessation interventions that have strong empirical evidence supporting their use. In 2000, the U.S. Public Health Service (Fiore et al., 2000), released an update to its 1996 *Smoking Cessation Clinical Practice Guideline No. 18* reflecting updates in current research. The new publication, *Treating Tobacco Use and Dependence* provides both brief and intensive interventions that were evaluated by a consensus panel of experts. Those interventions that were supported with multiple well-designed randomized clinical trials providing a consistent pattern of findings are reviewed in this chapter. Most important, based on this same standard of evidence, the consensus panel reported that age does not reduce the benefits of quitting smoking and that interventions that have been shown to be effective with the general population are also effective with older adults.

Brief tobacco cessations are those designed to be fitted into the very brief time that typifies physician appointments. As with brief alcohol interventions, discussed later, brief tobacco interventions basically take advantage of the patient-professional relationship to draw attention to the issue of quitting tobacco and motivating the patient to do so. Because a large majority of older smokers see a physician at least annually, the opportunity to employ brief interventions is widespread. For patients who indicate a willingness to quit tobacco use, the brief intervention may be represented by the "five As": *Ask* if the patient is willing to quit; *advise* the patient to quit in a "clear, strong and personalized manner"; *assess* the willingness to quit at this time; *assist* the patient in quitting by arranging counseling and pharmacotherapy; and *arrange* for follow-up (Fiore et al., 2000).

For patients who are unwilling to quit tobacco use at this time, the "five Rs" are recommended:

1. Encourage the older adult to indicate the *relevance* of quitting in his or her own life. This may include personal health concerns or social circumstances such as the health of others in the home.
2. Assist the older adult to articulate the *risks* of tobacco use, emphasizing those that are most relevant to the individual.
3. Encourage the older adult to identify the *rewards* of smoking cessation, again with attention to those that are most relevant to the individual.
4. Help the patient identify the *roadblocks* or barriers to successfully quitting and indicate the ways these barriers might be overcome.
5. *Repeat* these intervention steps whenever contact is made with the individual, acknowledging that many people make repeated attempts before achieving success.

In addition to these brief interventions, more intensive interventions involving counseling and pharmacotherapy are also recognized as having strong clinical support. Although much of the brief intervention research was conducted with physicians, there is encouraging research to suggest that these techniques are efficacious for use by *all clinicians*, including social workers. Further, when these procedures are employed by multiple clinicians in multiple settings, effectiveness is enhanced. Settings for which clinical evidence exists include proactive telephone counseling and group and individual counseling (Fiore et al., 2000).

Given the strong evidence indicating the deleterious effects of tobacco use and the equally strong support for these fairly easy to employ cessation interventions, every social worker and other human service professional should be assisting older adults who smoke to quit. Perhaps no other single action can have a more profound effect on health promotion.

ALCOHOL USE: SCOPE OF THE PROBLEM

The use of beverage alcohol among adults in American society is common. For older adults, problematic alcohol has been noted in a range of residential settings, including skilled nursing homes (Klein & Jess, 2002). Although its use decreases by age from young adulthood on, over 41% of older adults consume alcohol—about 52% of men and nearly 34% of women (CDC, 2004a). Certainly, it is noteworthy that in many social settings, including much retirement housing, utilization has been reported to be much higher (Mirand & Welte, 1996). Using community, hospital, and nursing home surveys, I. Johnson (2000) found prevalence rates for "problem drinking" among older adults ranging from 2% to 53%. This wide variance reflects both definitional and sampling differences. "Alcohol dependence" and "heavy drinking" (often defined as more than two drinks per day) are commonly in the range of 10% of older persons.

When considering alcohol use by older adults it is important to note that simple use does not constitute a problem in and of itself; indeed, there is empirical support for the claim that alcohol consumption may even convey health benefits (Barry, Oslin, & Blow, 2001). However, even modest use places the older drinker at risk for a number of reasons, including a reduction in retained body fluids, a thinning of the blood-brain barrier, a reduction in the capacity to process ethanol, and the degree of likely interactions with other appropriately used pharmaceuticals, prescribed and OTC (Klein, 2003). Thus, in addition to the risks represented by the consumption of alcohol itself, risk assessment must include the extensive array of independent factors with which even small amounts of alcohol may produce an interactive effect. At-risk drinking is simply "alcohol use that increases the risk of consequences from drinking" (Blow, 2000). Whereas clinical interventions are clearly appropriate for problematic drinking patterns, it is among so-called low-risk drinkers that health-promotive interventions hold the greatest promise—both because of the degree to which alcohol consumption is widespread among older adults, and because of the general success of interventions directed at reducing nonproblematic drinking. Although it might lean toward overgeneralizing, nonproblematic or *low-risk* drinking among older adults might be more productively conceptualized as *at-risk* drinking because of the preponderance of interaction potentials with negative health and social consequences.

Precise estimates of such drinking are even more difficult to obtain than for alcohol dependence or "problem drinking." In addition to the methodological challenges for these, low- or at-risk drinking carries a challenge that is common in preventive research: identifying the *potential* for an emergent problem, not the actual problem itself. The anticipated growth in the number of older adults who arrive in their senior years with more relaxed views concerning the use of alcohol and other drugs will only serve to exacerbate these potential problems (Patterson & Jeste, 1999).

Empirically Supported Interventions   The decision to intervene with an older drinker is complicated by the difficulties surrounding the identification of at-risk or other problem drinking behaviors. Many of the social controls that have operated to moderate drinking over one's lifetime are reduced or eliminated for older adults. Through retirement and increased social isolation, social contacts and workplace involvement may not operate to reduce opportunities for alcohol consumption. Further, many of the negative effects of alcohol consumption are commonly mistaken for normal aspects of the aging process, including forgetfulness, balance and gait problems, and depression. Many professionals incorrectly believe that the potential for developing problems with alcohol is substantially reduced by age 50 (Atkinson, 1993). In a nationally representative study of primary care physicians, less than 1% made a substance abuse diagnosis when presented with typical symptoms (National Center on Addiction and Substance Abuse, 1998). Social workers and other health care professionals are also hesitant to diagnose substance abuse problems among older adults (Googins, 1984; Ondus, Hujer, Mann, & Mion, 1999; Stewart & Oslin, 2001). The most recent *Clinician's Guide* of the National Institute on Alcohol Abuse and Alcoholism (2005) suggests a single screening question to distinguish problem drinkers from others: How many times in the past year have you had five (five for men; four for women) or more drinks in a day? Based on a client's response, interventions may range from the brief intervention discussed later to medically managed withdrawal and treatment.

Certainly among older adults who exhibit problematic drinking behaviors, general health is promoted by reductions in drinking or by complete abstinence. Traditional approaches, including counseling and pharmacotherapy, have been shown to be successful with older adults (Schonfeld & Dupree, 1990). Older adults respond particularly well to treatment utilizing age-segregated older adults groups (Atkinson, 1995; Blow, Walton, Chermack, Mudd, & Brower, 2000; Zimberg, 1996).

The most promising evidence-based intervention for drinking issues with nonproblematic older adults may well be the brief intervention. Clinical trials of the brief intervention have been impressive: 10% to 30% of nondependent problem drinkers reduced their drinking to moderate levels after a brief intervention (Babor & Grant, 1992; Fleming, Barry, Manwell, Johnson, & London, 1997). As implied by the name, brief intervention procedures incorporate assessment, negotiating and goal setting, behavioral modification techniques, self-help information, and follow-up reinforcement and are intended to be presented in one or two face-to-face interactions in the context of a health office setting (Fleming & Manwell, 1999). Flemming and Manwell present a review of over 20 empirical studies utilizing this method. As part of an overall strategy of health promotion, the bit of time required to reduce the risk that is inherent in alcohol consumption by older adults is a solid investment.

SOCIAL AND INTELLECTUAL ENGAGEMENT

One of the most commonly held myths associated with aging is that significant losses in mental functioning such as from dementia or Alzheimer's disease are an inevitable part of the aging process. Although it is true that there are some changes in mental ability associated with aging, the vast majority of older adults do not experience significant changes in their cognitive health. Current research shows that intellectual stimulation and social engagement, in combination with healthy lifestyle activities including regular physical activity and good nutrition, play a key role in maintaining cognitive health and preventing cognitive decline in older adults (Butler, Forette, & Greengross, 2004).

SCOPE OF THE PROBLEM

It is estimated that up to 10% of older persons have dementia, and at least 10% more have mild cognitive impairment (Rundek & Bennett, 2006). Estimates vary regarding the prevalence of Alzheimer's disease, mainly due to the fact that the disease cannot be diagnosed with certainty until the patient has died and the brain tissue is analyzed. It is estimated that approximately 10% of older adults over age 65 may have Alzheimer's disease (Rowe & Kahn, 1998).

EVIDENCE-BASED INTERVENTIONS

In a groundbreaking longitudinal study on healthy aging and dementia, Snowdon (2001) has followed 768 Catholic nuns between the ages of 75 and 107 since 1991. By analyzing the pathology of the brains of nuns who have died, as well as looking at their lifetime history, the study has made incredible advances in understanding why it is that a substantial number of the participants who showed mild to moderate stages of Alzheimer's disease pathology in postmortem examinations showed no symptoms of cognitive impairment prior to their death. The study suggests that it is possible to resist the genetic and pathological forces of Alzheimer's disease through lifestyle and environmental changes.

The Nun Study found that heart disease and stroke significantly increased a person's risk for dementia, and that the brain infarcts caused by strokes seem to "trip a switch," making the developing of dementia much more likely. Snowdon (2003) noted other conditions that may overwhelm the brain and trigger the clinical onset of Alzheimer's symptoms: brain trauma, depression, metabolic abnormalities, and specific nutritional deficits. Other researchers have found that cardiovascular risk factors such as high cholesterol, high blood pressure, smoking, and diabetes can also produce an increased risk of cognitive impairment (Almeida, Norman, Hankey, Jamrozik, & Flicker, 2006).

The greatest protective factors associated with the prevention of dementia and the development of the symptoms related to Alzheimer's disease are social engagement, intellectual engagement, and educational background. The Nun Study, as well as the work of others, has shown conclusively that the higher the level of schooling, the lower the risk of developing Alzheimer's disease (Raiha, Kaprio, Koskenvuo, Rajala, & Sourander, 1998; Rundek & Bennett, 2006; Snowdon, 2001). Routine engagement in cognitively stimulating leisure activities over one's lifetime, continuing into older adulthood, is strongly associated with a reduced risk of Alzheimer's disease (Wilson et al., 2002).

Regular social engagement is proven to reduce a person's overall mortality and risk for significant losses in cognitive functioning. In general, people who are married live longer than unmarried people, and people who are active members of religious or civic organizations live longer than people without such group affiliations (Rowe & Kahn, 1998). Although it is important to older adults to feel connected and involved with their immediate and extended families, research shows that social activities outside of the family may have a bigger impact on cognitive function than social contacts with family (Glei et al., 2005).

Several studies have found a clear link between physical activity and lower risks of cognitive impairment. The MacArthur Study reported that older men and women were more likely to maintain high cognitive capacity when they engaged in vigorous physical activity. A potential explanation was found in laboratory experimentation measuring the effects of exercise on the brains of rats. Increased exercise corresponded with increases in a nerve growth factor that promoted new brain cell growth (Rowe & Kahn, 1998). A study of over 18,000 women found that those who participate in regular moderate physical activity showed significantly better cognitive function than inactive women, and another study found that older men who walk more are less likely to develop dementia, including Alzheimer's disease (Center for the Advancement of Health, 2006).

EVIDENCE-BASED PRACTICE GUIDELINES

The well-known saying "Use it or lose it" applies to the brain and cognitive function just as much as it does to the rest of the body. Older adults should be encouraged to participate in an active lifestyle that includes frequent participation in a wide range of cognitively, physically, and socially engaging and challenging activities. Some of the specific leisure activities associated with reduced risk of dementia are reading, playing board games, playing musical instruments, and dancing (Verghese et al., 2003). Other recommended activities are memory games, crossword puzzles, walking, gardening, and simply socializing with others. "Interestingly, watching television was associated with approximately a 20% increased risk of developing cognitive impairments" (Rundek & Bennett, 2006, p. 795).

Older adults should be encouraged to participate in social groups that are meaningful to them. Most older adults can readily identify a circle of family and friends that provide support, but others may require encouragement and support from a professional to help them make connections in their communities (Rowe & Kahn, 1998). Many communities throughout the country have developed senior centers that provide regular opportunities for social contact and engagement, as well as involvement in cognitively and physically stimulating activities. Local parks and recreation departments often host social events and offer classes specifically designed for seniors, and some of these programs even offer transportation services.

Memory loss is not inevitable, and healthy older adults who are experiencing memory losses can participate in training and practice programs to improve their cognitive function. "Many people are amazed to learn that elderly men and women who have experienced some cognitive decline can, with appropriate training, improve enough to offset approximately 2 decades of memory loss" (Rowe & Kahn, 1998, p. 137). Even people who are diagnosed with dementia or Alzheimer's can still benefit from the protective factors of intellectual activity. A research study conducted with elderly patients with dementia found that cognitive stimulation therapy improved cognition and quality of life for participants (Spector et al., 2003). Day activity programs designed for older adults often offer stimulation therapy as part of their daily routine.

FUTURE RESEARCH DIRECTIONS

The most significant area for additional study in health promotion is almost certainly how to motivate older adults to initiate and sustain good practice with respect to those health-promotive activities that are already well understood. We know a great deal more about the practices that are reviewed in this chapter than is being practiced by most older adults. The *Healthy People 2010* (DHHS, 2000) targets for screening and inoculation are respectably high and would appear to be within reach. However, exercise patterns, nutritional habits, and the proclivity for falling all provide substantial room for improvement for most older adults. After 40 years of clear warnings about the hazards of smoking tobacco, use rates among older adults are dropping; perhaps similar warnings about the potential hazards associated with alcohol use—especially the indirect hazards through interaction with other drugs—will result in a more thoughtful use of beverage alcohol.

Future research aimed at documenting what works in health promotion should seek to identify the subgroups for whom particular approaches might be most beneficial. As with attention to cultural and ethnic variation in so much of the human services research, health promotion strategies should incorporate the subtleties and nuances that will make interventions more readily practiced among various groups of older adults. Similarly, we know that prevention efforts (e.g., for falls) are most effective when they are targeted to those at highest risk. Future health promotion research should seek further clarity about the preventive interventions that work best with specified high-risk groups.

CONCLUSION

It is our duty, my young friends, to resist old age; to compensate for its defects by a watchful care; to fight against it as we would fight against disease; to adopt a regimen of health; to practice moderate exercise; and to take just enough food and drink to restore our strength and not to overburden it. Nor, indeed are we to give our attention solely to the body; much greater care is due to the mind and soul; for they, too, like lamps grow dim with time, unless we keep them supplied with oil. (Cicero, c. 44 B.C./1946)

We do not agree with Cicero that we have a duty to resist old age; age is something that accumulates by the day. Each day should be celebrated. However, we agree with Cicero that the celebration of each day is made easier when we take good health into advanced age. Like the World Health Organization, Cicero draws our attention to psychological and spiritual dimensions of health rather than just an absence of disease. Even to the recommendations for exercise and moderation in our habits of consumption, Cicero anticipated some of the best contemporary advice for health promotion.

To be sure, contemporary life has brought new aspects to health promotion. On the positive side of the equation, modern health care has added the dimensions of health screening and vaccinations to a regimen of health promotion. Screening for common ailments has better enabled us to anticipate some of the conditions that assault our health and to initiate earlier treatment of those conditions so as to avoid more serious complications of delayed treatment. Vaccinations allow us to avoid other conditions completely, or nearly so. Yet, in part as a function of these successes, we have created new challenges to our health. As so many of us have commonly come to experience the frailties of our eighth and ninth decades, falls and chronic diseases have become increasingly present in our lives. But even as these challenges present themselves, a commitment to health promotion at both the personal and societal level works to mitigate many of the deleterious accompaniments. Exercise reduces the likelihood of falling; mental and social engagement moderates or delays some of the loss experienced from dementia. Such are the benefits of health promotion. The core principles of health promotion can be reduced to the fundamental principles of primary prevention with which we started this chapter. When we seek to avoid those problems of aging that can be anticipated, protect the strengths and resources that we are fortunate enough to carry into our advanced age, and seek always to promote forward-looking goals—both large and small—toward which our energies might be directed, we find ourselves promoting good health. Unfortunately, even rigorous attention to prevention and health promotion will not displace the role of remedial health care; however, both the costs and the inconvenience of ill health can be profoundly reduced. At every level—for individuals, families, communities, and the society as a whole—these opportunities should be pursued.

REFERENCES

Administration on Aging. (n.d). *Immunizations.* Retrieved March 12, 2006, from http://www.aoa.gov/eldfam/Healthy_Lifestyles/Vaccine/vaccine.asp.

Agency for Healthcare Research and Quality. (2003). *Your medicine: Play it safe* (AHRQ Pub. No. 03-0019). Washington, DC: U.S. Department of Health and Human Services.

Almeida, O. P., Norman, P., Hankey, G., Jamrozik, K., & Flicker, L. (2006). Successful mental health aging: Results from a longitudinal study of older Australian men. *American Journal of Geriatric Psychiatry, 14*, 27–35.

American Association of Retired Persons. (2004). *Synthesis of AARP research in physical activity: 1999–2003.* Washington, DC: Author.

American Diabetes Association (n.d.). *Type 2 diabetes.* Retrieved March 8, 2006, from http://www.diabetes.org/type-2-diabetes.jsp.

American Geriatrics Society. (2001). Guidelines for the prevention of falls in older persons. *Journal of the American Geriatrics Society, 49*, 664–672.

American Public Health Association. (2005, April 6). *Living stronger, longer through protection.* Washington, DC: Author.

Appel, D., & Aldrich, T. (2003). Smoking cessation in the elderly. *Clinics of Geriatric Medicine, 19*, 77–100.

Atkinson, R. (1993, November). *Late onset problem drinking in older adults.* Paper presented at the 46th annual scientific meeting of the Gerontological Society of America, New Orleans, LA.

Atkinson, R. (1995). Treatment programs for aging alcoholics. In T. Beresford & E. Gomberg (Eds.), *Alcohol and aging* (pp. 186–210). New York: Oxford University Press.

Babor, T., & Grant, M. (1992). *Project on identification and management of alcohol-related problems: Report on phase II—A randomized clinical trial of brief interventions in primary health care.* Geneva, Switzerland: World Health Organization.

Baker, D., King, M., Fortinsky, R., Graff, L., Gottschalk, M., Acampora, D., et al. (2005). Dissemination of an evidence-based multicomponent fall risk-assessment and management strategy throughout a geographic area. *Journal of the American Geriatrics Society, 53*, 675–680.

Barry, K., Oslin, D., & Blow, F. (2001). *Alcohol problems in older adults.* New York: Springer.

Blair, S., Kohl, W., Paffenbarger, R., Clark, D. G., Cooper, K. H., & Gibbons, L. W. (1989). Physical fitness and all-cause mortality: A prospective study of healthy men and women. *Journal of the American Medical Association, 262*, 2395–2401.

Bloom, M. (1996). *Primary prevention practices.* Thousand Oaks, CA: Sage.

Blow, F. (2000). Treatment of older women with alcohol problems: Meeting the challenge for a special population. *Alcoholism: Clinical and Experimental Research, 24*(8), 1257–1266.

Blow, F., Walton, M., Chermack, S., Mudd, S., & Brower, K. (2000). Older adult treatment outcome following elder-specific inpatient alcoholism treatment. *Journal of Substance Abuse Treatment, 19*, 67–75.

Booth, F. W., & Winder, W. W. (2005). Role of exercise in reducing the risk of diabetes and obesity. *Journal of Applied Physiology, 99*, 3–4.

Butler, R. N., Forette, F., & Greengross, B. S. (2004). Maintaining cognitive health in an aging society. *Journal of the Royal Society for the Promotion of Health, 124*(3), 199–121.

Center for the Advancement of Health. (2006, March). *A new vision of aging: Helping older adults make healthier choices* (Issue Brief No. 2). Washington, DC: Author.

Centers for Disease Control and Prevention. (1997). Perspectives in disease prevention and health promotion smoking attributable mortality and years of potential life lost—United States, 1984. *Morbidity and Mortality Weekly Report, 46*(20), 444–451.

Centers for Disease Control and Prevention. (2004a). *Health, United States, 2004* (DHHS Publication No. 2005-0152). Washington, DC: National Center for Health Statistics.

Centers for Disease Control and Prevention. (2004b). *The state of aging and health in America: 2004.* Washington, DC: U.S. Government Printing Office.

Centers for Disease Control and Prevention. (2005). *Physical activity and good nutrition: Essential elements to prevent chronic diseases and obesity.* Washington, DC: U.S. Government Printing Office.

Centers for Disease Control and Prevention, National Center for Injury Prevention and Control. (2006). *Web-Based Injury Statistics Query and Reporting System.* Retrieved March 30, 2006 from www.cdc.gov/ncipc/wisqars.

Chandra, R. (1997). Graying of the immune system: Can nutrient supplements improve immunity in the elderly? *Journal of the American Medical Association, 277,* 1398–1399.

Cicero, M. T. (1946). *De senectute* [On old age] (W. A. Falconer, Trans.). Cambridge, MA: Harvard University Press. (Original work c. 44 B.C.)

de Rekeneire, N., Visser, M., Peila, R., Nevitt, M., Cauley, J., Tylavsky, F., et al. (2003). Is a fall just a fall? Correlates of falling in healthy older persons. *Journal of the American Geriatrics Society, 53,* 841–846.

Englander, F., Hodson, T., & Terregrossa, R. (1996). Economic dimensions of slip and fall injuries. *Journal of Forensic Science, 41,* 733–746.

Fiore, M., Bailey, W., Cohen, S., Dorfman, S., Goldstein, M., Gritz, E., et al. (2000). *Treating tobacco use and dependence* (Clinical Practice Guideline). Washington, DC: U.S. Department of Health and Human Services.

Fleming, M., Barry, K., Manwell, L., Johnson, K., & London, R. (1997). Brief physician advice for problem alcohol drinkers: A randomized controlled trial in community-based primary care practices. *Journal of the American Medical Association, 277,* 1039–1045.

Fleming, M., & Manwell, L. (1999). Brief intervention in primary care settings: A primary treatment method for at-risk, problem, and dependent drinkers. *Alcohol Research and Health, 23*(2), 128.

Gill, T. M., DiPietro, L., & Krumholz, H. M. (2000). Role of exercise stress testing and safety monitoring for older persons starting an exercise program. *Journal of the American Medical Association, 284*(3), 342–349.

Glei, D. A., Landau, D. A., Goldman, N., Chaung, Y., Rodriguez, G., & Weinstein, M. (2005). Participating in social activities helps preserve cognitive functioning: An analysis of a longitudinal, population-based study of the elderly. *International Journal of Epidemiology, 34*(4), 864–871.

Googins, B. (1984). Avoidance of the alcoholic client. *Social Work, 29,* 161–166.

Gosney, M. (2001). Smoking cessation. *Gerontology, 47,* 236–240.

Goulding, M. (2005). *Trends in prescribed medicine use and spending by older Americans, 1992–2001* (Aging Trends, No. 5). Hyattsville, MD: National Center for Health Statistics.

Haber, D. (1999). *Health promotion and aging: Implications for the health professions.* New York: Springer.

Hewer, W., Mussell, M., Rist, F., Kulzer, B., & Bergis, K. (2003). Short-term effects of improved glycemic control on cognitive function in patients with Type 2 diabetes. *Gerontology, 49*(2), 86–92.

Hu, F. B., Manson, J. E., Stampfer, M. J., Colditz, G., Liu, S., Solomon, C. G., et al. (2001). Diet, lifestyle, and the risk of Type 2 diabetes mellitus in women. *New England Journal of Medicine, 345,* 790–797.

Hubert, H. B., Bloch, D. A., Oehlert, J. W., & Fries, J. F. (2002). Lifestyle habits and compression of morbidity. *Journal of Gerontology, 57*(2), 347–351.

Institute of Medicine. (2000). *The role of nutrition in maintaining health in the nation's elderly: Evaluating coverage of nutrition services for the Medicare population.* Washington, DC: National Academy Press.

International Diabetes Center. (2003). *Type 2 diabetes practice guidelines.* Minneapolis, MN: International Diabetes Center.

Jette, A. M., Lachman, M., Giorgetti, M. M., Assmann, S. F., Harris, B. A., Levenson, C., et al. (1999). Exercise: It's never too late—The Strong-for-Life program. *American Journal of Public Health, 89*(1), 66–72.

Johnson, D. B., Beaudoin, S., Smith, L. T., Beresford, S. A., & LoGerfo, J. P. (2004). Increasing fruit and vegetable intake in homebound elders: The Seattle Senior Farmers' Market Nutrition Pilot Program. *Preventing Chronic Disease* [Serial online]. Retrieved April 1, 2006 from http://www.cdc.gov/pcd/issues/2004/jan/03_00010a.htm.

Johnson, I. (2000). Alcohol problems in old age: A review of recent epidemiological research. *International Journal of Geriatric Psychiatry, 15*, 575–581.

King, M., & Tinetti, M. (1995). Falls in community-dwelling older persons. *Journal of the American Geriatrics Society, 43*, 1146–1154.

Klein, W. (2003). Substances, older adulthood: The prevention of problems with the use and misuse of alcohol among older persons. In T. Gullotta & M. Bloom (Eds.), *Encyclopedia of primary prevention* (pp. 1087–1093). New York: Kluwer Academic/Plenum Press.

Klein, W., & Bloom, M. (1997). *Successful aging: Strategies for healthy living.* New York: Plenum Press.

Klein, W., & Jess, C. (2002). One last pleasure? Alcohol use among seniors in nursing homes. *Health and Social Work, 27*, 193–203.

Lachman, M. E., & Jette, A. (1997). A cognitive-behavioral model for promoting regular physical activity in older adults. *Psychology, Health and Medicine, 2*(3), 251–262.

Lawton, M., & Nahemow, L. (1973). Ecology and the aging process. In C. Eisdorfer & M. P. Lawton (Eds.), *Psychology of adult development and aging* (pp. 619–674). Washington, DC: American Psychological Association.

Levkoff, S. E., Chee, Y. K., & Noguchi, S. (2001). *Aging in good health: Multidisciplinary perspective.* New York: Springer.

Mirand, A., & Welte, J. (1996). Alcohol consumption among the elderly in a general population, Erie County, New York. *American Journal of Public Health, 86*, 978–984.

National Center on Addiction and Substance Abuse. (1998). *Under the rug: Substance abuse and the mature woman.* New York: Columbia University Press.

National Guideline Clearinghouse. (2005a). *Guideline synthesis: Screening for breast cancer* (Rev. November 2005). Rockville, MD: Author. Retrieved December 28, 1998, from http://www.guideline.gov.

National Guideline Clearinghouse. (2005b). *Guideline synthesis: Screening for colorectal cancer* (Updated November 2005). Rockville, MD: Author. Retrieved June 7, 1998, from http://www.guideline.gov.

National Guideline Clearinghouse. (2005c). *Guideline synthesis: Screening for prostate cancer* (Updated September 2005). Rockville, MD: Author. Retrieved December 28, 1998, from http://www.guideline.gov.

National Institute on Aging. (2000). *Age page: Dealing with diabetes.* Washington, DC: U.S. Government Printing Office.

National Institute on Alcohol Abuse and Alcoholism. (2005). *Helping patients who drink too much: A clinician's guide.* Washington, DC: U.S. Department of Health and Human Services, National Institutes of Health.

Olshansky, S. J., Passaro, D. J., Hershow, R. C., Layden, J., Carnes, B. A., Brody, J., et al. (2005). A potential decline in life expectancy in the United States in the 21st century. *New England Journal of Medicine, 352*, 1138–1145.

Ondus, K., Hujer, E., Mann, A., & Mion, L. (1999). Substance abuse and the hospitalized elderly. *Orthopaedic Nursing, 18*, 27–34.

Ory, M., Hoffman, M., Hawkins, M., Sanner, B., & Mockenhaupt, R. (2003). Challenging aging stereotypes: Strategies for creating a more active society. *American Journal of Preventive Medicine, 25*(3Sii), 164–171.

Patterson, T., & Jeste, D. (1999). The potential impact of the baby-boom generation on substance abuse among elderly persons. *Psychiatric Services, 50,* 1184–1188.

Pescatello, L. S. (2001). Exercising for health: The merits of lifestyle physical activity. *Western Journal of Medicine, 174,* 114–118.

Pfeiffer, B. A., Clay, S. W., & Conatser, R. R. (2001). A green prescription study: Does written exercise prescribed by a physician result in increased physical activity among older adults? *Journal of Aging and Health, 13*(4), 527–538.

Raiha, I., Kaprio, J., Koskenvuo, M., Rajala, T., & Sourander, L. (1998). Environmental differences in twin pairs discordant for Alzheimer's disease. *Journal of Neurology, Neurosurgery, and Psychiatry, 65,* 785–787.

Rhoades, J. A. (2005). *Overweight and obese elderly and near elderly in the United States, 2002: Estimates for the noninstitutionalized population age 55 and older* (Statistical Brief No. 68). Rockville, MD: Agency for Healthcare Research and Quality.

Rizzo, J., Baker, D., McAvay, G., & Tinetti, M. (1996). Cost-effectiveness of a multifactorial targeted prevention program for falls among community elderly persons. *Medical Care, 34,* 954–969.

Rizzo, J., Friedkin, R., Williams, C., Nabors, J., Acampora, D., & Tinetti, M. (1998). Health care utilization and costs in a Medicare population by fall status. *Medical Care, 36,* 1174–1188.

Robert Wood Johnson Foundation. (2001). *National blueprint: Increasing physical activity among adults age 50 and older.* Princeton, NJ: Author.

Rowe, J. W., & Kahn, R. L. (1998). *Successful aging.* New York: Dell.

Rundek, T., & Bennett, D. A. (2006). Cognitive leisure activities, but not watching TV, for future brain benefits. *Neurology, 66,* 794–795.

Sattin, R. (1992). Falls among older persons: A public health perspective. *Annual Review of Public Health, 13,* 489–508.

Schonfeld, L., & Dupree, L. (1990). Older problem drinkers—Long-term and late-life onset abusers: What triggers their drinking? *Aging* (No. 361, pp. 5–11). Washington, DC: Administration on Aging.

Snowdon, D. (2001). *Aging with grace.* New York: Bantam Books.

Snowdon, D. (2003). Healthy aging and dementia: Findings from the nun study. *Annals of Internal Medicine, 139*(5), 450–454.

Spector, A., Thorgrimsen, L., Woods, B., Royan, L., Davies, S., Butterworth, M., et al. (2003). Efficacy of an evidence-based cognitive stimulation therapy programme for people with dementia. *British Journal of Psychiatry, 183,* 248–254.

Sterling, D., O'Connor, J., & Bonadies, J. (2001). Geriatric falls: Injury severity is high and disproportionate to mechanism. *Journal of Trauma, 50,* 116–119.

Stewart, D., & Oslin, D. (2001). Recognition and treatment of late-life addictions in medical settings. *Journal of Clinical Geropsychology, 7,* 145–158.

U.S. Department of Health and Human Services. (1991). *Healthy people 2000: National health promotion and disease prevention objectives.* Washington, DC: U.S. Government Printing Office.

U.S. Department of Health and Human Services. (1996). *Physical activity and health: A report of the surgeon general.* Washington, DC: U.S. Government Printing Office.

U.S. Department of Health and Human Services. (2000). *Healthy people 2010.* Washington, DC: U.S. Government Printing Office.

U.S. Department of Health and Human Services. (2003). *An overview of programs and initiatives sponsored by DHHS to promote healthy aging: A background paper for the Blueprint on Aging for the 21st Century Technical Advisory Group meeting.* Washington, DC: U.S. Government Printing Office.

U.S. Department of Health and Human Services. (2004). *Bone health and osteoporosis: A report of the surgeon general.* Washington, DC: U.S. Government Printing Office.

U.S. Department of Health and Human Services. (2005). *Dietary guidelines for Americans 2005.* Washington, DC: U.S. Government Printing Office.

U.S. Preventive Services Task Force. (2001). *Screening for lipid disorders in adults.* Retrieved January 23, 2007, from http://www.ahrq.gov/clinic/uspstf/uspschol.html.

U.S. Preventive Services Task Force. (2002a). *Screening for colorectal cancer.* Retrieved January 23, 2007, from http://www.ahrq.gov/clinic/uspstf/uspscolo.html.

U.S. Preventive Services Task Force. (2002b). *Screening for prostate cancer.* Retrieved January 23, 2007, from http://www.ahrq.gov/clinic/uspstf/uspsprca.html.

Verghese, J., Lipton, R. B., Katz, M. J., Hall, C. B., Derby, C. A., Kuslansky, G., et al. (2003). Leisure activities and the risk of dementia in the elderly. *New England Journal of Medicine, 348*(25), 2508–2516.

Williams, P., & Lord, S. R. (1995). Predictors of adherence to a structured exercise program for older woman. *Psychology and Aging, 10*(4), 617–624.

Wilson, R. S., Mendes de Leon, C. F., Barnes, L. L., Schneider, J. A., Bienias, J. L., Evans, D. A., et al. (2002). Participation in cognitively stimulating activities and risk of incident Alzheimer's disease. *Journal of the American Medical Association, 287*(6), 742–748.

World Health Organization. (1948). Preamble to the Constitution of the World Health Organization as adopted by the International Health Conference, New York, June 19–22, 1946 and entered into force on April 7, 1948. Retrieved January 23, 2007, from http://www.searo.who.int/EN/Section898/Section1441.htm.

Yeager, S. (2005). Weight gain speeds aging. *Prevention, 57*(10), 40.

Zimberg, S. (1996). Treating alcoholism: An age-specific intervention that works for older patients. *Geriatrics, 51*, 45–49.

CHAPTER 8

Disability

ELIZABETH LIGHTFOOT

T HE FIELDS OF aging and disability services and policy have traditionally been distinct. However, there is a growing awareness of the overlap between aging and disability, as many of the policy and practice issues are intertwined. Both fields have recently experienced a similar paradigm shift toward community-based services rather than institutional services and increasing consumer control over the types of services people receive. The disability field has been the leader in advocating for both community-based and consumer-controlled services, but both are now seen as desirable by many in both fields. Although the service delivery systems of aging and disability remain essentially separate, there are more and more instances in which the financing and delivery of such services are commingled. There has been a growing call for increased collaboration between the aging and disability sectors.

As people age, most desire to remain in their communities and in control of the services and supports they need. People with all types of disabilities have the same desire for remaining in their community, yet they may need unique supports and interventions, such as in the areas of health, housing, retirement, and later-life planning.

Many of the issues related to people aging with lifelong disabilities, such as people with Down syndrome disabilities, and people with disabilities acquired in later life, such as people with Alzheimer's disease, are similar. However, this chapter has a special focus on people aging with lifelong disabilities. In particular, this chapter presents information on trends, definitions, interventions, and practice guidelines for working with older people with lifelong disabilities.

The basis of this chapter is an evidence-based approach to working with older people with disabilities. There has not been a strong focus on evidence-based practice in the field of disability policy and services, particularly in comparison to some other fields, such as mental health services and policy. For example, an intervention common in both the fields of mental health and developmental disabilities is supported employment. Supported employment is considered an evidence-based practice for people with mental illness (Bond, 2004; Bond et al., 2001; Crowther, Marshall, Bond, & Husley, 2001; Twamley, Jeste, & Lehman, 2003), yet

there has been no attempt to establish this as an evidence-based practice for people with developmental disabilities (National Council on Disability, 2005). And although there is a growing trend for federally funded medical interventions
related to rehabilitation of people with disabilities to use evidence-based practice
guidelines (National Council on Disability, 2005), this is confined mainly to the
fields of medicine and supporting health professions, such as occupational therapy. Other types of disability interventions, such as supported living, education,
and employment, are far less focused on evidence-based guidelines. However,
there is a strong focus in these areas on outcomes and evaluation research of particular interventions and policies.

In fact, there is much skepticism in the field of disability as to the rise of evidence-
based practice (National Council on Disability, 2005). There are concerns that evidence-based practice is not focusing on indicators that might be important to an
individual with a disability, but rather focusing on a professional's view of appropriate outcomes. For example, Scherer, Coombs, and Hansen (2003) describe how a
person with a disability may view getting out of a house quickly using a wheelchair
and a ramp as more satisfying and having higher functional utility, yet a professional may find that getting out of a house by walking down the stairs with a cane,
albeit more time-consuming and tiring, is higher functioning. A related concern is
that because this model originated in the medical field, it portrays the medical
model approach to intervention (Muentz & Frese, 2001), which is viewed with great
trepidation by people within the disability movement. This attention on evidence-
based interventions rarely focuses on removing societal barriers, but rather on individual's rehabilitation to fit in with society. Further, there are concerns that the
focus on evidence-based practice is inherently intertwined with a cost-containment
mentality, and people with disabilities with great needs may end up getting services cut if they are not shown to have evidence of improvement (National Council
on Disability, 2005). Thus, this chapter, which describes current research in regard
to disabilities, consciously presents a social model approach to evidence and cautions practitioners to use a broad approach to evaluating and using evidence-based
interventions.

TRENDS AND INCIDENCE

The prevalence of disability among people over age 65 rapidly increased during
the twentieth century in the United States and other industrialized nations. According to the U.S. census, 54.7% of people over age 65 had a disability in 2000, approximately 18 million people (McNeil, 2001). The U.S. Census Bureau (1996)
projects that 20% of the total population will be over age 65 by the year 2030, and,
if disability rates remain constant, approximately 38 million people over age 65
will have a disability.

The growing number of people with disabilities over age 65 includes both a
growing number of people with lifelong disabilities who are living into later
years, and a growing number of people living longer and acquiring disabilities in
their later years. People with lifelong disabilities, such as intellectual or other developmental disabilities, rarely lived into adulthood at the beginning of the twentieth century (see Box 8.1). Currently there are about 641,000 people over age 65
with developmental disabilities in the United States, and this population is expected to rise to approximately 1,242,800 by the year 2030 (Heller, Janicki, Hammel, & Factor, 2002). Some of this growth is due to overall population growth of

---

Box 8.1
Intellectual Disability: A More Respectful Name

Intellectual disability is the preferred term worldwide for what some people in the United States still refer to as "mental retardation" (Sushila, Mammen, Russell, & Sudhakar, 2005). In the United States, many influential groups such as the President's Committee on Intellectual Disabilities (2003; formerly known as the President's Committee on Mental Retardation) and the Special Olympics have now officially substituted the term "intellectual disability" as a synonym for "mental retardation," and other professional groups are having ongoing debates about the terminology. The term mental retardation is becoming unpopular for two reasons. First, the term is sometimes confused with mental illness. Second, the word "retarded" or "retardation" has become a common slur (President's Committee on Intellectual Disabilities, 2003). Although many government and professional groups are still using the older term, it is falling into disfavor.

---

older adults, but the primary reason for these dramatic leaps is the growing life expectancy of people with intellectual or developmental disabilities. In 1930, the average life expectancy for a person with an intellectual disability was only about 20 years (Carter & Jancar, 1983). Currently, people with Down syndrome have a life expectancy of almost 60 years, and people with other developmental disabilities have a life expectancy approaching that of people without disabilities (Janicki, Dalton, Henderson, & Davidson, 1999; Warren, 1998). This older population of people with intellectual and developmental disabilities has essentially become a brand-new population, with needs for new types of supports and services to help them lead meaningful lives. As this population ages, they may experience new types of disabilities related to aging that require an increase in support, yet at the same time may now be outliving their parents who had previously been their sole source of support (Doka & Lavin, 2003). New services, supports, and interventions are needed to serve this emerging population.

Another sizable population of older people with disabilities is the growing number of people who have acquired a new disability as they age. The disability rate increases dramatically with age. According to U.S. census figures (McNeil, 1993), about 23.3% of people age 45 to 54 have a disability. This percentage increases to 41.4% for people 60 to 64 years old, and again to 58.7% for people age 75 to 80. For the oldest old, or people over age 85, approximately 84.2% report having a disability. The proportion of people with severe disability increases with age as well. Among people age 45 to 54, 10.6% have a severe disability and 12.7% have a nonsevere disability; among people ages 75 to 84, 41.5% report a severe disability and 22.2% a nonsevere disability (McNeil, 1993). As the disability rate rises as people age, and the overall longevity rate increases, we are seeing a quick rise in the older population with age-related disabilities. Researchers are noting that disability rates have actually been falling in recent decades among older people (Wolf, Hunt, & Knickman, 2005) as overall longevity is increasing, yet the total numbers of individuals with disabilities is still greatly expanding. These people with newly acquired disabilities may have little experience in receiving services and little familiarity with the disability system, and may not consider themselves to have a disability, despite having a functional limitation.

Older people with disabilities generally have the same wants and needs as people without disabilities. They desire to live at home in a community, to participate in activities of interest to them, and to have some level of control over the types of services they receive (American Association of Retired Persons [AARP], 2003). Older people with lifelong disabilities and those with newly acquired disabilities have some similar and differing barriers to living and participating in the community and needs for services. The following outlines the key trend in services over the past several decades that impacts older people with disabilities: the trend toward community-based and consumer-driven care for people with disabilities.

Trend toward Community-Based Care

The most significant paradigm shift in the area of disability services has been the trend toward providing community based care for people with disabilities. In the mid-twentieth century, most people with intellectual disabilities resided in institutions, and services to people with all types of disabilities were provided in institutions. The prevailing model viewed people with disabilities through the lens of the medical model. In the medical model, a person's impairment is viewed as a problem that must be treated. Persons with a disability were either rehabilitated to the extent that they could function in society, or else they were sent to segregated institutions to live. People with disabilities had little input into where and how they would live, with professionals alone determining their appropriate services and supports.

In the second half of the twentieth century there was a shift to community-based services for people with disabilities. It is now considered best practice for people with disabilities to live in a community-based setting rather than an institutionalized or formal setting and to have input into the types of services and supports they need. People with disabilities now live, work, and socialize in the community. They are not simply integrated into community settings, but rather are included in the community as full, valued members. "Disability" is now viewed less as a medical concept and more as a sociopolitical concept. This new view of disability fits with the social model of disability, a common philosophy in Europe and growing in the United States. In the social model, many of the problems associated with disability are viewed as caused by an inaccessible and oppressive society, rather than an individual and his or her impairment. Viewing disability through a social model lens brings attention to barriers in society, such as inaccessible buildings, lack of accessible transportation, segregated schools, and lack of residential options, which are significant problems for people with disabilities that must be alleviated.

Trend toward Consumer-Controlled Services

Along with services being community based, there is a co-occurring trend toward consumer-driven services. The consumer-controlled movement that is gaining steam in the aging network had its origins in the U.S. disability movement and goes hand in hand with the trend toward community inclusion. Beginning in the 1960s, the growing disability movement in the United States coalesced around the concept of independent living (Shapiro, 1993). People with disabilities, reacting against the paternalism of the disability service sector, the segregation that they experienced living and receiving services in isolated and subpar institutions, and general societal discrimination, formed a new movement in which they asserted control over their own destinies. There was a strong emphasis on controlling their own services, advocating for their rights, and eliminating societal, political, and structural barriers to their community participation and independence. A key aspect of the disability movement was a focus on determining the types of services they were going to receive, including hiring and firing their own staff and determining their own needs (Brisenden, 1986). This desire by people with disabilities has grown into formal programs today, funded through the federal government and private foundations, called consumer-controlled or consumer-directed services.

TREND TOWARD COLLABORATION BETWEEN AGING AND DISABILITIES FIELDS

There is a new recognition by those in the fields of aging and disability services and advocacy that there is considerable overlap between these two areas. Many of the key issues of older people and people with disabilities of all ages are similar, for example, family caregiving, residential options, consumer-directed services, and accessible transportation. This is especially evident for older people with disabilities, who often have to navigate a disjointed service system and would be better served through an integrated system. There is some beginning collaboration between the fields. For example, consumer-controlled service models currently target people with disabilities of all ages (Benjamin, Matthias, & Franke, 2000; Doty, 2000; Nadash, 1998); there have been joint policy efforts by disability and aging advocates for personal assistance services (Doty, Kasper, & Litvik, 1996; Eustis & Fischer, 1992); and the federal government, under the New Freedom Initiative (E.O. 13127, 1991), has just authorized states to develop Aging and Disability Resource Centers, which are jointly funded, to become a single point of entry for older people and people with disabilities into the state service system. However, much of the research, policy, practice, and advocacy efforts between these two fields are distinct.

DEFINITIONS AND ETIOLOGIES OF DISABILITY

Exploring the concept of definitions and etiologies of disability has become a frightfully political endeavor in the past several decades. This stems from the broad array of disciplines that study disability, including medicine, nursing, education, social work, economics, sociology, and recreation; the varying types of interventions related to disability, including health care, rehabilitation, behavioral, social service, housing, technological, and policy: the varying international conceptions of disability; the increased growth in a humanities approach to viewing disability as a social construction or a cultural group; the negative reaction by many people with disabilities toward labeling people based on disability; and the growing adoption of the social model of disability, which rejects the notion of focusing on personal impairment in general.

The World Health Organization (WHO, 2002) and representatives from across the world spent many years developing WHO's recently adopted International Classification of Functioning, Disability and Health (ICF). The ICF model reflects an intentional blending of the medical and social models, and it rests on what WHO calls a biopsychosocial model of disability (see Figure 8.1). Under the ICF, disability and functioning are seen as the result of the interactions between an individual's health conditions and contextual factors. Health conditions include diseases, disorders,

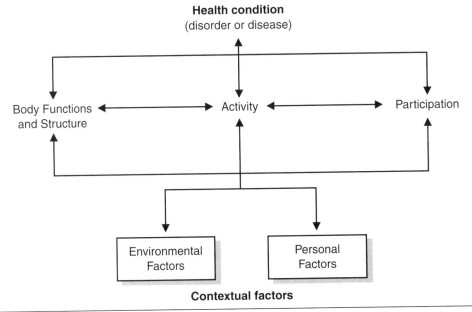

Figure 8.1   World Health Organization's Biopsychosocial Model of Disability as the Basis for WHO's International Classification of Functioning, Disability, and Health. *Source: Toward a Common Language for Functioning, Disability and Health: ICF*, by the World Health Organization, 2002, Geneva, Switzerland: Author. Reprinted with permission.

and injuries, and contextual factors include environmental factors, such as social attitudes and structural barriers, and personal factors, such as age, gender, socioeconomic status, geography, and coping skills. One of the purposes of this classification based on health and functioning is to allow for parity among disabilities, despite differing specific etiologies. The ICF outlines three levels of functioning: impairment, activity limitation, and participation restriction. A particular health condition can impact people in none, some, or all of these three areas, depending on both personal and contextual factors (see Table 8.1). The ICF is intended to help researchers and practitioners operate from a standard understanding of disabilities; it remains to be seen how the international community and those in the United States will actually use this model for developing an evidence base around disabilities.

In fact, there are literally hundreds of definitions of disability employed in the United States alone. Adler and Hendershot (2000) counted 43 programmatic definitions of disability among federal programs alone, and states, local governments, and other agencies can employ their own definitions. Disability has been variously defined based on individuals' specific impairments, their functional limitations, their receipt of disability benefits, their use of help for completing tasks, or general perceptions of disability (Adler & Hendershot, 2000). Numerous measurement problems result from these varied definitions, such as the lack of comparability between studies (Lightfoot & Lum, in press). In addition, the disability rate is an elastic concept, with people reporting disability at differing levels depending on a variety of factors, such as general economic conditions that influence their participation in the labor market or their receipt of disability benefits.

The two broadest definitions of disability among older adults is found in the Americans with Disabilities Act (ADA; 1990). The ADA uses a functional defini-

Table 8.1
WHO Classification of Disability, Functioning, and Health

Health Condition	Impairment	Activity Limitation	Participation Restriction
Spinal cord injury	Paralysis	Incapable of using public transportation	Lack of accommodations in public transportation leads to unemployment
Epilepsy	Seizures	None, controlled by medication	Does not go to school because of stereotypes about disease
Vitiligo	Facial disfigurement	None	Little participation in social activities because of discrimination
HIV	None	None	Denied housing because of fear of contagion

Adapted from World Health Organization. (2002). *Toward a common language for functioning, disability and health: ICF.* Geneva, Switzerland: Author.

tion of disability, which is broad enough to cover lifelong as well as newly acquired disabilities. The Act defines an individual with a disability as someone who "has a physical or mental impairment that substantially limits one or more of the major life activities, has a record of such impairment, or is regarded as having such impairment." The ADA does not include a list of physical or mental impairments, but rather focuses on the limitations that such impairment might have on activities of daily living. This focus on activities of daily living is common for measuring and comparing people with disabilities for both prevalence and severity.

The other federal definition of note is that of developmental disability, found in the Developmental Disabilities and Bill of Rights Act (DD Act, 2000). A developmental disability refers to a host of conditions that begin at birth or in childhood and cause a lifelong functional limitation:

A severe, chronic disability of an individual that:
- (i) is attributable to a mental or physical impairment or a combination of mental and physical impairments;
- (ii) is manifested before the individual attains age 22;
- (iii) is likely to continue indefinitely;
- (iv) results in a substantial functional limitation in 3 or more of the following areas of major life activity:
  - a. self-care,
  - b. receptive and expressive language,
  - c. learning,
  - d. mobility,
  - e. self-direction,
  - f. capacity for independent living,
  - g. economic self-sufficiency; and
- (v) reflects the individual's need for a combination and sequence of special, interdisciplinary or generic services, individualized supports, or other forms of assistance that are of lifelong or extended duration and are individually planned and coordinated.

Many people with lifelong disabilities, such as intellectual disability, cerebral palsy, Autism Spectrum Disorder, fetal alcohol syndrome, genetic and chromosomal disorders such as Down syndrome and Fragile X, and some sensory disabilities, fall under the category of developmental disability.

The etiologies of disability in older adults include everything from chromosomal abnormalities that cause impairments before birth that continue through an individual's life, to accidents or disease occurring in midlife, to age-related disabilities, such as Alzheimer's disease. Developmental disabilities, by definition, occur either at birth or during one's developmental years. There are hundreds of causes of developmental disabilities, including injuries and conditions in the brain before birth, during birth, or during childhood. Some developmental disabilities have a clear etiology, such as Down syndrome, resulting from a chromosomal abnormality; others have unknown etiologies or only inferred etiologies. For example, low birth weight is considered a risk factor for intellectual disability (Leonard & Wen, 2002), yet it does not meet the criteria for a cause of intellectual disability, as there is no clear causal pathway. Although most developmental disabilities cannot be prevented, there are some contextual characteristics that cause or influence developmental disabilities, such as poor nutrition, mother's excessive intake of alcohol or drugs before birth, injuries during birth, poor nutrition, and environmental exposure such as lead poisoning in childhood. When possible, knowledge of the etiology of an individual's disability, especially those with developmental disabilities, can be important for future screening for age-related comorbid conditions that are specific to a particular health condition.

Key Health Issues for Older Adults with Intellectual Disabilities

- Dementia
- Visual impairment
- Hearing impairment
- Thyroid conditions
- Osteoarthritis
- Oral health
- Obesity

The health conditions that cause impairment or activity limitations that people acquire over age 65 include visual loss, hearing loss, and arthritis, whose rates all rise dramatically as people age (Ettinger et al., 1994; National Center for Health Statistics, 1993). Other common age-related health conditions that may or may not cause activity limitations are diabetes, heart conditions, dementia, and hypertension (U.S. Census, 1996). Some disabilities in older age are related to organic conditions; contextual factors, such as smoking, poor diet, poor health care, and falls and accidents (Rubenstein, Robbins, Josephson, Schulman, & Osterweil, 1990), also can influence health conditions. Further, health conditions and activity limitations vary based on race, ethnic background, and socioeconomic status (Verbrugge & Jette, 1994).

EVIDENCE-BASED SUPPORTS FOR OLDER PEOPLE
WITH DEVELOPMENTAL DISABILITIES

Professionals caring for an older person with a disability should keep in mind several key factors. First, in the area of disability, the concept of professional intervention is more appropriately viewed as professional support for a person with a disability. Second, all professional supports offered to a person with a disability and his or her family should be based on the best evidence available, with an eye to improving or maintaining an individual's quality of life and inclusion into the community. Up until very recently people with disabilities had very limited civil rights, were regularly segregated or institutionalized, and were even used for medical and social experiments without informed consent. Using the best evidence available in designing and implementing professional supports for people with disabilities can be one way to respect these individuals. Third, professionals must recognize that the person with the disability and his or her family are always the experts on their individual situation and have the best assessment of their needs and desires. When intervening in an individual's life, the professional must assume the role of subordinate to the individual, and allow and encourage the person with the disability to make decisions based on evidence.

Professionals often collaborate with older people with disabilities to provide needed supports in the following broad life areas: health, residential and community living, life planning.

HEALTH

One reason the number of older people with disabilities is rapidly expanding is an overall improvement in health care, which has led to increased longevity for people with and without lifelong disabilities. People with developmental disabilities are also living longer because of greater access to health care and healthier and more active lifestyles that accompany community-based living, especially in comparison to living in an institution. People with developmental disabilities never used to live into old age, but with their increased life span they are now experiencing age-related health conditions. There is still extremely limited knowledge about age-related health conditions for people with developmental disabilities (Evenhuis, Henderson, Beange, Lennox, & Chicoine, 2000), though there are more studies and medical trials in process (Seltzer, 2004). However, it is clear that people with developmental disabilities have some age-related health conditions similar to those of people without disabilities, but also have unique health concerns. These can vary based on the specific etiology of the developmental disability; for instance, people with chromosomal syndromes, such as Down syndrome, have different age-related impairments than people with a central nervous condition, such as cerebral palsy.

The area with the most advanced research evidence is the health status of people aging with Down syndrome. People with Down syndrome have a shorter life expectancy than people with developmental disabilities. They also tend to experience age-related conditions earlier and have more significant age-related health conditions. Common age-related conditions of people with Down syndrome are adult-onset epilepsy, hearing loss, visual loss, hip disease, and thyroid disorder

(Dinani & Carpenter, 1990; Janicki, Heller, Seltzer, & Hogg, 1996; Puri, Ho, & Singh, 2001; Van Allen, Fung, & Jurenka, 1999). The most debilitating age-related condition is early-onset dementia. People with Down syndrome have a very high prevalence of early-onset dementia (Janicki & Dalton, 2000). Holland, Hon, Huppert, and Stevens (2000) found that personality and behavioral changes are indicators of early onset of dementia for people with Down syndrome; such conditions may begin in their 30s, with Alzheimer's disease following in their 40s or 50s. It appears that people with other types of developmental disabilities have no greater prevalence rate of dementia than people without disabilities (Zigman et al., 2004).

Diagnosis of many age-related conditions, such as dementia, can be complicated in people with developmental disabilities as it may be difficult to tease out the cognitive impacts of the disability from that of the dementia (Shultz et al., 2004). Further, there are few valid scales to measure common age-related conditions in people with developmental disabilities (Shultz et al., 2004). There is a new research focus on appropriate assessment of age-related health conditions in people with disabilities, particularly for dementia since the advent of antidementia drugs (Strydom & Hassiotis, 2003). For example, there is growing evidence that observer rater scales or instruments administered to informants have been found to be much more accurate for diagnosing dementia for people with Down syndrome than typical neuropsychological direct assessments (Deb & Braganza, 1999; Strydom & Hassiotis, 2003). Ball et al. (2004) found that an informant interview, specifically the Cambridge Mental Disorders of the Elderly Examination (CAMDEX) tool, is reliable and valid for assessing dementia. The most common tool, the Dementia Questionnaire for Persons with Mental Retardation, has been found to be both reliable and valid (Evenhuis, 1996), although there are still some concerns about sensitivity (Strydom & Hassiotis, 2003). The development of specific assessments such as these, which are modified to take into account the unique conditions of older people with developmental disabilities, are needed to appropriately diagnosis this population and begin to provide them appropriate treatment.

Another health-related concern for older people with developmental disabilities is health care providers' lack of general knowledge about their typical health and functioning levels (Messinger-Rapport & Rapport, 1997). In addition, health care providers may be unaware of the resistance some older people with disabilities may have toward the medical profession, relating to previous poor service received from untrained staff both in and outside of institutions (Seltzer & Luchterhand, 1994). Few medical professionals have been trained to work with older people with disabilities; there is a great need for combined training in the areas of geriatric medicine and intellectual and developmental disabilities (Janicki et al., 1999). A joint physician training program in aging and developmental disabilities has been developed at the Strong Center for Developmental Disabilities at the University of Rochester Medical Center (Program in Aging and Developmental Disabilities, 2006).

There are other accessibility barriers to receiving appropriate health care, including a complex bureaucracy and physical and societal attitudinal barriers. Many people with disabilities have complex cases and are receiving care from a multitude of sources, resulting in a very complex management of care as well as financial reimbursement problems. Case management by professionals with multidisciplinary training and expertise is necessary in these cases (Walsh, Kastner, & Criscione, 1997). A variety of other barriers, such as physically inaccessible services, must also be removed (Selzter & Luchterhand, 1994).

Along with improved health care, a healthier lifestyle associated with living in the community has helped to improve life expectancy for individuals with developmental disabilities. However, this population is still more likely to have a sedentary lifestyle and poor nutrition (Braunschweig et al., 2004; Heller et al., 2002) compared to people without disabilities. Health promotion activities can help them avoid conditions related to poor fitness and nutrition, such as Type 2 diabetes, osteoporosis, and coronary heart disease. Heller, Hsieh, and Rimmer (2004) found that adults with Down syndrome involved in fitness and health education training programs have improved attitudes toward exercise, as well as improved life satisfaction. Others have found that exercise and health training programs for adults with intellectual disabilities result in dramatically increased improvement in physical functioning and other fitness measures (Podgorski, Kessler, Cacia, Peterson, & Henderson, 2004; Rimmer, Heller, Wang, & Valerio, 2004). Key barriers to such participation are caregivers who perceive that physical fitness is not effective for adults with Down syndrome as well as access barriers (Heller, Hsieh, & Rimmer, 2002).

The overall increased longevity of people with disabilities has led to a new area of medical care that is just beginning to develop appropriate evidence for clinical, programmatic, and policy recommendations. There is a need for more evidence-based practice standards in the area of health care for older people with developmental and other disabilities, as well as more well-trained medical professionals who specialize in providing health care services to this population.

RESIDENTIAL AND COMMUNITY-BASED LIVING

Along with increased longevity, the other significant recent change for older people with disabilities has been the large shift toward residing in community-based settings. During the 1970s and 1980s, the philosophy of normalization (Wolfensberger, 1972) swept the field of disability services. Normalization meant that people with disabilities should no longer live in segregated facilities and lead segregated lives, but rather should lead "normal" lives in the community. This emphasis on normalization, which is related to more modern concepts of community integration and community inclusion, led to the closing of many large residential institutions and the deinstitutionalization movement in the United States and abroad. The majority of large institutions have now been closed in the United States, and most people with disabilities who are living outside their familial home live in small or medium-size community-based settings with paid staff, such as group homes or other shared living arrangements.

In the United States, federal policy has gradually shifted to support community-based options for people with disabilities. In 1981, 10 years after Medicaid began, Congress authorized states to use Medicaid to pay for home- and community-based services for older people and people with disabilities who would otherwise reside in or receive care from institutions (Omnibus Budget Reconciliation Act of 1981). The Home and Community-Based Services waiver is now the major source of funding for community living for older people with disabilities who receive funding for residential care. Currently, approximately 1.4 million people with disabilities receive services through Medicaid that support them to live at home (Harrington & Kitchener, 2003). Several years after the Medicaid waiver, the Nursing Home Reform Act was passed as part of the Omnibus Budget Reconciliation Act of 1987 (PL 100-203). This law was intended to prevent the inappropriate institutionalization of people with disabilities in nursing homes by requiring states to conduct a Preadmission Screening and Annual Resident Review of individuals with disabilities to ascertain if they actually needed skilled nursing care.

More recently, the *Olmstead* decision by the U.S. Supreme Court solidified the notion that people with disabilities should not be unnecessarily institutionalized (*Olmstead et al. v. L. C. et al.,* 1999). In this case, two women with intellectual disabilities and mental illness voluntarily admitted themselves to a state psychiatric hospital in Georgia. When the two women and their service providers determined that they were ready for discharge, the women were not discharged from the hospital because there were no "slots" available for them. The Atlanta Legal Aid Society filed a lawsuit on behalf of these two women, claiming discrimination under Title II of the Americans with Disabilities Act of 1990. The circuit court ruled in favor of the plaintiffs, and the U.S. Supreme Court upheld the ruling on the basis that unjustified institutionalization of people with disabilities is a form of discrimination under Title II of the Americans with Disabilities Act. States are now instructed to have comprehensive, effective working plans to ensure that individuals with disabilities receive services in the most integrated setting appropriate to their needs. The federal government signaled its support of *Olmstead* with President Bush's New Freedom Initiative of 2001. As part of the New Freedom Initiative, President Bush released Executive Order 13127 (June 2001), which ordered states to offer people with disabilities of all ages care in the least restrictive and most integrated setting possible and ordered federal agencies to work with states to ensure community-based alternatives to institution-based care.

There is ample evidence that people with lifelong disabilities, people with age-related disabilities, and their family members desire alternatives to nursing homes and other congregate care facilities. For example, in a 1999 survey by the AARP, 82% of people age 45 and older said that they would prefer to remain in their own home even if they needed help caring for themselves (Bayer & Harper, 2000). Similarly, a 1997 International Communications Research (ICR) survey asked people over age 50 where they would like to live if they had a disability that needed care 24 hours a day, rather than just help with everyday activities; only 23% responded that they would rather live in a congregate care facility. Both people aging with a disability and people with age-related disabilities demand such community-based services, and there is a growing acceptance in the professional fields of disability and aging services that community-based care is an appropriate and desired practice.

As a result of the philosophical and policy shifts relating to residential care and the ever-growing demand for community-based options, there has been a rapid expansion of home- and community-based living arrangements for older people with disabilities. Many residential providers, particularly in the field of developmental disabilities, have made large-scale changes in their provision of services, closing down large institutions and offering community-based residential options (Lightfoot, Hewitt, & Sauer, 2005). Unfortunately, the demand for such community-based living arrangements currently far exceeds the supply, with an estimated 75,000 people with intellectual and developmental disabilities alone on state waiting lists for such services (Prouty & Lakin, 1998). As the rate of older people with disabilities continues to grow rapidly, this supply problem may last far into the future.

Although philosophy, policy, and some programs have clearly shifted toward community-based living as the best arrangement for older people with disabilities, the research base is more mixed for people aging with developmental disabilities. For the most part, studies of middle-age and older individuals with developmental disabilities who moved from institutional to community-based care find that people living in the community fare better overall than those residing in institutions. Research has found that people with disabilities who have transitioned from institutions to community-based residential settings experience an increase in health (Heller, Factor, & Hahn, 1999; Litzinger, Duvall, & Little, 1993), activity levels (Barber, Cooper, & Owen, 1994), adaptive behavior (Donnelly et al., 1994; Heller et al., 1999; Larson & Lakin, 1989; Young, Ashman, Sigafoos, & Grevell, 2001), and level of community inclusion and integration (Barber et al., 1994; Heller et al., 1999).

However, several other studies have found that although certain aspects of the lives of people experiencing deinstitutionalization improved, the level of adaptive behavior either decreased (Barber et al., 1994) or showed no change (Young et al., 2001). Findings regarding the actual impact of the relocation have also been mixed, with some studies indicating that the relocation itself may cause some problems (Heller, 1988) and others finding no impact from the relocation (Heller et al., 1999).

There are a number of possible explanations for these mixed findings. It is more likely that age-related or other conditions of individuals living in a community setting will go undetected compared to those in an institutional setting. This points to a lack of access to health care for older people with disabilities in community settings, a lack of training and awareness on the part of health care and social service professionals, and less supervision and fewer behavior interventions in community settings (Carlsen, Galliuzzi, Forman, & Cavalieri, 1994; Rimmer, Braddock, & Marks, 1995). As mentioned earlier, there is a need for those working with older people with developmental disabilities, both as medical professionals and caregivers, to have training in the health needs of and provide comprehensive geriatric assessments for those with disabilities, particularly those residing in the community.

Although a large trend in the disability and aging field has been toward promoting community-based formal options for older people with disabilities, the most common living arrangement for adults with developmental disabilities remains living with their family of origin. Fujiura (1998) estimates that about 60% of adults with developmental disabilities live with their families rather than in group homes or other formal arrangements. These families receive little federal or state support in caring for their adult children with disabilities (Stancliffe & Lakin, 2004), and there are very long waiting lists for any supportive services, such as respite care, personal care assistance, and in-home health care, for these families (Davis, 1997). As there is so little state support for family caregivers, families end up spending large amounts of money caring for their adult children.

Fujiura, Roccoforte, and Braddock (1994) found that families spend approximately one fifth of their pretax annual income on expenses related to caring for their adult children. A survey of state units of aging regarding parent caregivers of adults with developmental disabilities found that respite care was their greatest unmet need (Factor, 2004).

Currently, over one fourth of the primary caregivers of adults with developmental disabilities are over age 60 (Braddock, 1999; Fujiura, 1998). The number of these "two-generation elderly families" (Davis & Berkobien, 1994) is expected to rise over the next decade, with the aging of the baby boom generation and increased life expectancies for all populations. These families often have not received any formal supports (Smith, Fullmer, & Tobin, 1994). Some may have an inherent distrust of the system and disability professionals if professionals advised these families to institutionalize their children at birth; some may not feel the need for supportive services (Smith, 1997). People in some ethnic and cultural groups may find natural supports, such as the extended family or community, rather than a formal support system (Magana, 1999). Others report a need for emotional and coping supports, such as support groups or counseling, but that these services are unavailable (Smith, Majeski, & McClenny, 1996). Hayden and Heller (1997) found that younger caregivers are more likely to seek supportive services and have higher expectations of the social service system to provide supportive services. As respite care use has been increasing by parents of older adults with developmental disabilities, and more people are likely to use such services in the near future both due to population growth and service-usage attitude, there will be a need for greatly increased provisions of respite care and other supportive services.

With increasing numbers of older adults with disabilities, including a new cohort of older adults with developmental disabilities, there is a dire need for new residential options for older people with disabilities. This is especially true for adults with lifelong disabilities who may need to transition at an older age to an alternative living arrangement when their family is no longer able to care for them because of family members' own declining health or death.

Because most people want to remain in their own homes, whether in their family home or in a long-term group home, there is a new focus on "aging in place" for older people with disabilities. Part of this movement focuses on the use of environmental modifications and assistive technology to help people remain in their own homes. This can include building ramps, modifying doorways, or using devices such as walkers, amplifiers, or call buttons that help people maintain their functioning level and independence (Hammel, Lai, & Heller, 2002). However, many older people with disabilities, especially those with cognitive functioning issues, may require paid staff to remain at home. For people who had been living with their parents, this could involve a move into the formal care system, which may not allow them to age in place. For those already living in a formal care arrangement, such as a group home, this may require changes to the rules and standards of the group home, and could require additional funding (Janicki, McCallion, & Dalton, 2002). Although aging in place is an attractive concept, the funding streams for older people with developmental disabilities have yet to make it a valid option for many.

There is also evidence that along with desiring community-based services, many people with disabilities would prefer to manage these services themselves, rather than having an agency do so. Several studies have shown that although older people with disabilities are less likely to desire consumer-controlled services than younger people with disabilities, there still are a significant percentage of people over age 65 who desire to control their own services. Mahoney et al.'s (1998) study of personal assistance recipients in New York found that 55% of people with disabilities under age 65 and 31% of those over age 65 desired a cash option. Similar results were obtained in studies by Eustis and Fischer (1992), who found that 33% of older clients showed evidence of participating in the control of their service, and Glickman, Brandt, and Caro (1994), who found that roughly 33% of older clients indicated willingness to become involved in controlling their services.

Older people with disabilities who are unaccustomed to the consumer-control model may be less likely to desire consumer-controlled services than younger people with disabilities; however, as the baby boomer population ages, it is likely that more people will desire consumer-controlled services (Batavia, 1998). Surveys of the aging baby boomer population have confirmed this growing desire. In the ICR (1997) survey of Americans over age 50, 76% of the respondents indicated that they would prefer to manage their own home care services if and when they acquired a disability. Furthermore, as evidence continues to grow that people with disabilities have higher satisfaction under consumer-controlled models (Beatty, Richmond, Tepper, & DeJong, 1998; Benjamin et al., 2000) with no harmful health or safety impacts, it is likely that older people with disabilities will increasingly desire to control their own services.

This move toward consumer-directed services has reached a degree of acceptance in aging and disability services, and there are a number of pilot consumer-directed services programs for people who are aging or have disabilities. For example, the Cash and Counseling Demonstration and Evaluation is testing consumer-directed services for people with disabilities of all ages on a large scale (Doty, 2000; Mahoney, Simone, & Simon-Rusinowitz, 2000).

LATER-LIFE PLANNING

Many parents do not plan for their adult child's later lives, due to lack of information, stress, worry, or denial (Heller & Factor, 1991; Kaufman, Adams, & Campbell, 1991). When later life planning does occur, the people with developmental disabilities themselves are often not included, consulted, or even informed of the plans (Heller, Miller, Ksieh, & Sterns, 2000; Sutton, Sterns, & Schwartz-Park, 1993). Further, the plans often only include arrangements for where the adult with disabilities will live in the future, without including other aspects of the individual's life that can impact his or her quality of life, such as financial matters, guardianship, retirement, and leisure activities (Reilly & Conliffe, 2002).

Residential planning is one of the key worries for people with lifelong disabilities and their families. This is particularly true for those who have not been involved in the formal service system and have been living at the family home. For these families, on the death of the parents the adult child may experience many significant transitions, coupled with grief at losing his or her parents, which can cause depression and confusion (Ludlow, 1999). Even those involved in the system usually experience some sort of transfer of care, either to a sibling or relative or into a formal system.

To support residential planning, families also need to financially plan for their adult child's future. Individuals and families have to determine the ability of the person to manage finances, estimate future costs, and work on estate planning (Davis & Berkobien, 1994). Families with limited incomes may have no choice but for their child to transfer to residential services paid through Medicaid. Coupled with financial planning is the need to plan for future guardianship, depending on the ability of the individual to make financial, medical, or other decisions (Davis & Berkobien, 1994).

Aside from residential and financial planning, there is also a need for planning for retirement and leisure activities as an adult with disabilities nears retirement age. Retirement is a relatively new option for older people with developmental disabilities. Some supported work programs and day programs for adults with disabilities are instituting new retirement programs, which allow for more leisure time. These programs may begin at an earlier age for people with some disabilities that have shorter life expectancies, such as Down syndrome, to allow them a chance for retirement. Some generic senior programs are also becoming more inclusive of older people with developmental disabilities.

Some people with disabilities are leery of the concept of retirement, as they like the structure and social interactions at their jobs, as well as the income (Janicki, 1992; Mahon & Mactavish, 2000). Currently, many people with developmental disabilities do not retire when they reach retirement age (Sutton et al., 1993). Many people with developmental disabilities and their families simply are unaware that retirement, even if still fairly limited, exists as an option for people working in supported employment or other work arrangements.

As planning is absolutely necessarily for adults with disabilities, many large and small agencies and advocacy organizations provide training sessions to families on this topic. However, there is evidence that training sessions where information is simply provided to family members about legal and financial information have not resulted in the development of actual plans by participants (Heller, Caldwell, & Factor, 2003). Person-centered planning is an approach that appears to fit the needs of people with developmental disabilities and their families. Person-centered family planning focuses on the desires of the person with a disability, with support and input from family members, friends, caregivers, and others (Abery & McBride, 1998). It is premised on the notion that the person with the disability should be the central focus of the plan, rather than a provider or the caregivers. Several studies of person-centered, later-life planning involving people with disabilities have found that such planning increases the knowledge of people with developmental disabilities with regard to possible later-life options, including work and retirement, residential options, and leisure activities; it also increases the life satisfaction of older people with disabilities (Hawkins, 1993; Mahon & Goatcher, 1999). Heller, Caldwell, and Factor (2000) found that family members who attended a series of five training sessions that provided legal and financial information through a person-centered planning approach were more likely to develop a letter of intent and a special needs trust and begin residential planning. Thus, a person-centered planning approach, in which people with disabilities and their families develop an expansive vision of the adult's later life, covering practical matters such as financial issues as well as quality of life issues, appears to be an effective way to engage families in later-life planning.

EVIDENCE-BASED PRACTICE GUIDELINES

Based on the discussion of best research available for supporting people with developmental disabilities as they age, evidence-based approaches to practice with this population can be derived. It should be noted that these guidelines are generally not generated from research that includes randomized controlled trials, but rather are based on the best possible evidence, coupled with the current policy framework for services. The following incorporates guidelines developed by WHO's series of reports *Healthy Aging—Adults with Intellectual Disabilities* (Evenhuis et al., 2000):

Health Guidelines

1. Health care providers should take a life span approach that recognizes the progression or consequences of various disabilities and appropriate interventions.
2. People with intellectual disabilities should be provided with training and supports to live healthy lives, including a focus on exercise, nutrition, and safety.
3. Health care providers should receive training on the unique health needs of older people with intellectual and developmental disabilities, including an introduction to appropriate assessment techniques.
4. Older people with intellectual and developmental disabilities should be regularly screened with an appropriate screening device for common age-related conditions related to their disability.

Community Living and Residential Support Guidelines

5. Older people with intellectual and developmental disabilities should live in community-based settings when at all possible.
6. Proper support should be provided to older people with disabilities when changing residence in later years, to prevent trauma related to the relocation.
7. People supporting older people with developmental disabilities in community residential settings should be trained in health and behavioral issues related to aging.
8. Older people with intellectual and developmental disabilities and their families should be given the option to control as much of their services and supports as they desire, depending on availability of such services.
9. Family caregivers of older people with developmental disabilities should be provided with respite care, peer support, counseling, and/or other culturally sensitive supports to help them in caring for their adult children.

Later-Life Planning for Older People with Intellectual and Developmental Disabilities

10. Later-life planning should take a person-centered approach, making the person with a disability central to the decision-making process.
11. Information on later-life planning should be introduced early and often to a person with a developmental disability and his or her family.

12. Later-life planning should be culturally sensitive, recognizing the diverse arrangements of family and community supports available for people with disabilities.
13. Older people with developmental disabilities and their families should be provided information about the range of retirement and leisure activities available.

Case Study and Evidence-Based Practice Application

The following case application involves a realistic but fictional composite of an older woman with Down syndrome. This case study illustrates how evidence-based practices relating to older people with intellectual disabilities can result in positive outcomes for older people with disabilities.

Susannah is a woman in her late 40s with Down syndrome. She is a vivacious, friendly woman, who fancies herself as having quite a green thumb and who loves plants and animals. When Susannah was born in the mid-twentieth century, the doctors told her parents that it would be best for the family if they institutionalized her in a large state facility for the retarded 140 miles away. Susannah's parents were among a small but growing number of parents in this era that refused to institutionalize their children with intellectual disabilities, and instead kept her at home to live with them and her older brother. As schools were not required to educate students with disabilities prior to the 1975 passage of the Education for All Handicapped Children Act (now Individuals with Disabilities Education Act), the public school her brother attended would not admit her. Her parents became active in their local chapter of the National Association for Retarded Children (now simply the ARC). As doctors had labeled Susannah *trainable,* she was allowed to attend a special day care run by the ARC while her mother attended parenting classes, but she had no other formal educational or recreational activities. After 5 years on the waiting list, at age 11 she enrolled in one of the few private schools for students with disabilities. As a teenager, she participated in special day camps and in a church group for children with intellectual disabilities.

Susannah graduated from her private school at age 18 and began attending a newly developed sheltered workshop for adults with intellectual disabilities. She spent her days sorting buttons and was paid pennies an hour. Although the stated purpose of the sheltered workshop was to train people for future jobs, no one from her enclave had ever left for a paying job. She continued living at home and working at the sheltered workshop, socializing with other people with intellectual disabilities. In particular, she remained lifelong friends with a woman from her private school, Sarah, who lived in an apartment with three other adults with intellectual disabilities less than six blocks from Susannah's house and attended the same church. A local charity took people with intellectual disabilities on "nature adventures," which Susannah and Sarah attended regularly. Aside from her family, church, and close neighbors, Susannah had relatively little interaction with people without disabilities who were not paid staff members or volunteers.

When Susannah was 33, a new social service program opened that provided supported employment opportunities to people with intellectual disabilities. With the help of a job coach, Susannah got her first paid employment position as a cleaner of an office building. She worked at several other positions before her placement counselor secured her dream job, as an aid at a garden center, where she makes slightly over minimum wage. Susannah has now worked at the garden center for 8 years, mostly helping in the greenhouse. She is friends with some of the other workers at the garden center and particularly enjoys eating her lunch in the workroom with the other workers and attending the quarterly staff parties.

In the past few years, Susannah and her family have experienced a number of changes. Susannah's father died unexpectedly last year, and her mother is in rapidly declining health, with a terminal disease expected to take her life within the year. Although Susannah is not yet 50, her mother and her doctor have noticed that she is showing signs of early aging, including fairly severe arthritis in her hands and knees. Susannah has also been much less cheerful in the past year; she has been refusing to do some basic tasks at work and has been acting out for the first time in her life. Her most notable behavior is her complete refusal to acknowledge her mother and coworkers at times.

Susannah's parents never expected Susannah to outlive them and have done no planning for Susannah's future if both of them should pass away before her. Susannah's older brother, who lives out of state and has two grown daughters, is concerned with how his mother can continue to care for Susannah and is contemplating moving Susannah to his home.

Susannah's brother contacted Susannah's county social worker and an advocate from the ARC to discuss the current situation. Based on the advocate's suggestion, her brother took her to a doctor who had some experience working with people with developmental disabilities. Her previous doctor had no such training and had treated her simply for her arthritis. The new doctor recommended that she have a complete geriatric medical screening and used the mother as a key informant for her cognitive functioning. Based on the doctor's assessment, Susannah was diagnosed with very early stages of dementia; he prescribed her a new antidementia drug. Perhaps more important, the doctor also discovered a severe hearing loss. Susannah was fitted for a hearing aid, which resulted in an immediate positive change in her behavior at work. Apparently Susannah was not ignoring requests from her coworkers or others, but rather simply did not hear their requests.

Next, based on the recommendation of the social worker, Susannah's brother attended a person-centered later-life planning session at a local agency near his home. At this training, he learned about financial and residential planning, as well as the effectiveness of a person-centered approach to later-life planning. After this meeting, he suggested to the social worker that they conduct a later-life planning session for Susannah. Based on Susannah's and her mother's suggestions, 12 people participated in a personal future planning meeting for Susannah, run by a specialist from the agency. These included Susannah, her mother, her older brother, one of her two nieces, the county social worker, her supported work job coach, the minister of her church, her boss and a coworker from the garden center, her lifelong friend from school, the director of the nature adventure charity, and her next-door neighbor. At this meeting, Susannah and her circle of support brainstormed and discussed possibilities for Susannah's later years. It became clear that Susannah did not wish to move out of the state and would be happy as long as she could be near Sarah and work at the garden center. Sarah said that one of her roommates might be moving out, and Susannah indicated a desire to live with Sarah. Her brother has always assumed that Susannah would simply move in with him, and it had never occurred to him that she would not want to. The planning specialist explained to him that research has shown that later-life satisfaction improves for people with disabilities if they are involved in making decisions for their future.

After this enlightening meeting, the social worker helped Susannah, her brother, and her mother to develop a later-life plan for Susannah. The social worker began working to get Susannah eligible for state funding so that she might be eligible for a waiver slot in Sarah's residence, though they would be lucky if the timing was perfect for this arrangement. All were concerned about how the change in location would impact Susannah, particularly as she had lived in one house her entire life.

Susannah's mother's health was rapidly declining, so they made the decision that her brother would immediately assume partial guardianship for Susannah, covering financial and health matters. In addition, they decided that it made financial sense for the mother to leave her estate to the brother to avoid future eligibility problems for state support for Susannah. They also helped Susannah develop a living will. They placed all of this information in a letter of intent as well as in appropriate legal documents.

As Susannah indicated that she wanted to remain working at the garden center instead of retiring, the social worker arranged for her to decrease the hours she was working from 27 to 15 per week. The plan was to maintain contact with the job coach and further reduce hours if necessary. Furthermore, the director of the nature adventure charity mentioned during the planning meeting that it was likely that he could get a volunteer to take her individually into a nature setting on a regular basis in the future.

This process, which was initiated in a crisis mode, ended positively for all involved. Susannah received medical interventions from a trained medical professional and participated in life planning for her residential living, finances, and retirement.

EVIDENCE-BASED POLICY RECOMMENDATIONS

- Increase supports for community-based residential options for older people with disabilities, including requiring states to fully implement their *Olmstead* plans.
- Increase support for consumer-directed options for older people with disabilities and their families for residential and other supportive services.
- Increase formal cross-system collaboration and cooperation between the aging and disability sectors to address residential and support services for older people with disabilities.
- Increase access to community agency programs and services for older people with disabilities.

FUTURE RESEARCH DIRECTIONS

As older people with developmental disabilities are a relatively new group, there is currently a paucity of information on effective supports and services to help them live quality lives in their later years. Thus, there is a very limited evidence-based practice foundation for such services or interventions. Almost all areas of possible support for people with disability need further research, ranging from assessment of age-related health conditions to end-of-life care. Areas of particular concern include research relating to supports that allow individuals to age in place and evidence relating to consumer control for this population.

There also is a need for more rigorous research in this area that would produce highly rigorous results without harming individuals with disabilities. There has been very little randomization in research related to people with developmental disabilities. Oliver et al. (2002) note some of the difficulties in building an evidence base for developing best practice guidelines for working with people with developmental disabilities. Some key ethical issues they noted when trying to conduct a randomized study can be generalized for completing any research with people with intellectual disabilities. These include ethical concerns with randomization, such as informed consent concerns, as well as methodological considerations relating to such issues as necessary length of intervention periods and the minimal changes that occur in these populations compared to others.

Another future direction in research is to include older people with disabilities more explicitly in the process of creating evidence for practice. A key notion within the disability movement is the philosophy *Nothing about us without us.* For many years, professionals and academics have been involved in determining not only the services people with disabilities would receive, but also the key issues and problems that needed further investigation. There is a trend within some disability communities, particularly in the United Kingdom, toward consumer-controlled research, in which the consumers of social services would be fully or partially in charge of the research process, from raising research questions to conducting and analyzing the research (Beresford, 2002). Although the extent of consumer involvement can vary, those researching and testing interventions in the area of disability services should be including people with disabilities in the research process in a meaningful way that does not tokenize their participation.

FEDERAL DISABILITY LAWS AFFECTING OLDER PEOPLE

1963: Mental Retardation Facilities and Community Mental Health Centers Construction Act (PL 88-164)

Authorizes federal funds for the construction of research centers, university-affiliated training programs, and community service facilities for people of all ages with intellectual disabilities.

1965: Social Security Act Amendments of 1965 (PL 89-97)

Title XVIII establishes Medicare, which authorizes health insurance benefits for eligible older people and people with disabilities. Title XIX establishes Medicaid, which provides grants-in-aid to states to provide medical assistance programs for low-income people of all ages.

1968: Architectural Barriers Act of 1968 (PL 90-480)

Requires facilities and buildings designed, constructed, remodeled, or financed by the federal government to be accessible to people of all ages with disabilities.

1971: Amendments to Title XIX of the Social Security Act (PL 92-223)

Amends the Medicaid section of the Social Security Act to authorize states to use Medicaid funds to provide active treatment and other services to people of all ages with intellectual disabilities residing in certified intermediate care facilities (ICF-MRs).

1972: Social Security Amendments of 1972 (PL 92-603)

Establishes Title XVI, the Supplemental Security Income (SSI) program, which authorizes cash benefits to eligible older people and people with disabilities.

1973: Section 504 of The Rehabilitation Act of 1973 (the Rehab Act; PL 93-112)

Prohibits discrimination on the basis of disability against qualified persons with disabilities by any program or activity receiving federal funds.

1975: The Developmental Disabilities Assistance and Bill of Rights Act (PL 94103)

Establishes federal funding to developmental disabilities councils, protection and advocacy agencies, and university-affiliated programs; establishes a bill of rights for persons with deveopmental disabilities.

1980: The Civil Rights of Institutionalized Persons Act (CRIPA; PL 96-247)

42 U.S.C. § 1997 *et seq.*

Gives U.S. attorney general authority to investigate institutional conditions run by or on behalf of state and local government institutions (including institutions for people with developmental disabilities) and to file lawsuits to remedy a pattern or practice of unlawful conditions.

1981: Omnibus Budget Reconciliation Act (PL 97-35)

Authorizes the Department of Health and Human Services to grant Home and Community Based Waivers (HCBS Waivers) to allow states to provide community-based services to individuals who would otherwise require care in an institutional setting.

1987: Omnibus Reconciliation Act of 1987, Section II (Nursing Home Reform Act) 100-203

Requires states to complete a Pre-Admission Screening and Resident Review (PASARR) to ensure that people with intellectual or developmental disabilities, or people with mental illness are not placed in nursing homes when they do not require skilled nursing care.

1988: The Fair Housing Act Amendments of 1988 (PL 100-430)

Adds people with disabilities as a group protected from discrimination in housing, allows that people with disabilities can adapt their housing to meet their accessibility needs, and includes accessibility requirements for specific new multifamily dwellings.

1988: Technology-Related Assistance for Individuals with Disabilities Act Amendments (the "Tech Act"; PL 100-407)

Provides grants to states to develop a statewide service delivery system to provide assistive technology to people of all ages with disabilities.

1990: Americans with Disabilities Act of 1990 (ADA; PL 101-336)

Prohibits discrimination on the basis of disability to individuals with disabilities of all ages in employment, state and local government, public accommodations, commercial facilities, transportation, and telecommunications.

2000: Developmental Disabilities Assistance and Bill of Rights Act (DD Act; PL 106-402)

42 U.S.C. 15001 *et seq.*

Adds the Family Support Act to the DD Act, which provides support for families with a disabled family member regardless of age, including aging parents of adults with disabilities. Also provides support to direct support professionals assisting individuals of all ages with disabilities.

REFERENCES

Abery, B., & McBride, M. (1998). Look and understand before you leap. *Impact, 11,* 2–3.

Adler, M. C., & Hendershot, G. E. (2000). Federal disability surveys in the United States: Lessons and challenges. *Proceedings of the Survey Research Methods Section, American Statistical Association.* Available from http://www.amstat.org/Sections/Srms/Proceedings/papers/2000_014.pdf.

American Association of Retired Persons. (2003). *Beyond 50: A Report to the Nation on Independent Living and Disability.* Washington, DC: Author.

Americans with Disabilities Act of 1990, 42 U.S.C.A. (1990).

Ball, S., Holland, A., Huppert, F., Treppner, P., Watson, P., & Hon, J. (2004). The modified CAMDEX informant interview is a valid and reliable tool for use in the diagnosis of dementia in adults with Down's syndrome. *Journal of Intellectual Disability Research, 48*(6), 611–620.

Barber, J., Cooper, B., & Owen, L. (1994). The short-term effects of relocation on the intellectually disabled. *Research in Social Work Practice, 4,* 248–258.

Batavia, A. (1998). Prospects for a National Personal Assistance Services Program: Enhancing Choice for People with Disabilities. *American Rehabilitation, 24*(4), 2–8.

Bayer, A. H., & Harper, L. (2000). *Fixing to stay: A national survey of housing and home modification issues.* Washington, DC: American Association of Retired Persons. Retrieved January 31, 2007, from http://www.drcog.org/documents/Fixing%20to%20Stay_A%20National%20Study.pdf.

Beatty, P., Richmond, G., Tepper, S., & DeJong, G. (1998). Personal assistance for people with physical disabilities: Consumer-direction and satisfaction with services. *Archives of Physical Medicine and Rehabilitation, 79,* 674–677.

Benjamin, A. E., Matthias, R., & Franke, T. M. (2000). Comparing consumer-directed and agency models for providing supportive services at home. *Health Services Research, 35*(1), 351–366.

Beresford, P. (2002). User involvement in research and evaluation: Liberation of regulation. *Social Policy and Society, 1*(2), 95–105.

Bond, G. R. (2004). Supported employment: Evidence for an evidence-based practice. *Psychiatric Rehabilitation Journal, 27*(4), 345–359.

Bond, G. R., Becker, D. R., Drake, R. E., Rapp, C. A., Meisler, N., Lehman, A. F., et al. (2001). Implementing supported employment as an evidence-based practice. *Psychiatric Services, 52,* 313–322.

Braddock, D. (1999). Aging and developmental disabilities: Demographic and policy issues affecting American families. *Mental Retardation, 37*(2), 155–161.

Braunschweig, C., Gomez, S., Sheean, P., Tomey, K., Rimmer, J., & Heller, T. (2004). Nutritional status and risk factors for chronic disease in urban-dwelling adults with Down syndrome. *American Journal on Mental Retardation, 109*(2), 186–193.

Brisenden, S. (1986). Independent living and the medical model of disability. *Disability, Handicap, and Society, 1*(2), 173–178.

Carlsen, W., Galliuzzi, K., Forman, L., & Cavalieri, T. (1994). Comprehensive geriatric assessment: Applications for community residing, elderly people with mental retardation/developmental disabilities. *Mental Retardation, 32* 334–340.

Carter, G., & Jancar, J. (1983). Mortality in the mentally handicapped: A fifty year survey at State Park Group Hospitals (1930–1980). *Journal of Mental Deficiency Research, 27,* 143–156.

Crowther, R. E., Marshall, M., Bond, G. R., & Huxley, P. (2001). Helping people with severe mental illness to obtain work: Systematic review. *British Medical Journal, 322,* 204–208.

Davis, S. (1997). *A national status report of waiting lists of people with mental retardation for community services.* Arlington, TX: The Arc.

Davis, S., & Berkobien, R. (1994). *Meeting the needs and challenges of at-risk, two-generation, elderly families.* Silver Spring, MD: The Arc.

Deb, S., & Braganza, J. (1999). Comparison of rating scales for the diagnosis of dementia in adults with Down syndrome. *Journal of Intellectual Disability Research, 43,* 400–407.

Developmental Disabilities and Bill of Rights Act of 2000, 42 U.S.C.A. (2000).

Dinani, S., & Carpenter, S. (1990). Down syndrome and thyroid disorder. *Journal of Mental Deficiency Research, 34,* 187–193.

Doka, K., & Lavin, C. (2003). The paradox of aging with developmental disabilities: Increasing needs, declining resources. *Aging International, 28*(2), 135–155.

Donnelly, M., McGilloway, S., Mays, N., Perry, S., Knapp, M., Kavanagh, S., et al. (1994). *Opening new doors: An evaluation of community care for people discharged from psychiatric and mental handicap hospitals.* London: HMSO.

Doty, P. (2000). The federal role in the move toward consumer direction. *Generations, 24*(3), 10–15.

Doty, P., Kasper, J., & Litvak S. (1996). Consumer directed models of personal care: Lessons from Medicaid. *Milbank Quarterly, 74*(3), 377–409.

Ettinger, W. H., Jr., Fried, L. P., Harris, T., Shemanski, L., Schulz, R., & Robbins, J. (1994). Self-reported causes of physical disability in older people: The Cardiovascular Health Study. *Journal of the American Geriatrics Society, 42,* 1035–1044.

Eustis, N. N., & Fischer, L. R. (1992). Common needs, different solutions? Younger and older homecare clients. *Generations, 16*(1), 17–23.

Evenhuis, H. (1996). Further evaluation of the Dementia Questionnaire for Persons with Mental Retardation. *Journal of Intellectual Disabilities Research, 40*(4), 369–373.

Evenhuis, H., Henderson, C., Beange, H., Lennox, N., & Chicoine, B. (2000). *Healthy aging—Adults with intellectual disabilities: Physical health issues.* Geneva, Switzerland: World Health Organization.

Factor, A. R. (2004, April 15). *The NFCSP as a resource for families of individuals with developmental disabilities.* Presentation at the ASA/NCoA Joint Conference, San Francisco.

Fujiura, G. T. (1998). The demography of family households. *American Journal on Mental Retardation, 103,* 225–235.

Fujiura, G., Roccoforte, J., & Braddock, D. (1994). Costs of family care for adults with mental retardation and related developmental disabilities. *American Journal on Mental Retardation, 99,* 250–261.

Glickman, L. L., Brandt, K. J., & Caro, F. G. (1994). *Self-direction in home care for older people.* Boston: University of Massachusetts, Gerontology Institute and Center.

Hammel, J., Lai, J., & Heller, T. (2002). The impact of assistive technology and environmental interventions on function and living situation status with people who are ageing with developmental disabilities. *Disability and Rehabilitation, 24*(1/3), 93–105.

Harrington, C., & Kitchener, M. (2003). *Medicaid long-term care: Changes, innovations, and cost containment.* San Francisco: University of California, San Francisco. Retrieved January 27, 2007, from http://www.ncsl.org/programs/health/harrington.

Hawkins, B. A. (1993). Leisure participation and life satisfaction of older adults with mental retardation and Down syndrome. In E. Sutton, A. R. Factor, B. A. Hawkins, T. Heller, & G. B. Seltzer (Eds.), *Older adults with developmental disabilities: Optimizing choice and change* (pp. 141–156). Baltimore: Brookes.

Hayden, M., & Heller, T. (1997). Support, problem-solving/coping ability, and personal burden of younger and older caregivers with mental retardation. *Mental Retardation, 35,* 364–372.

Heller, T. (1988). Transitions: Coming in and out of community residence. In M. Janicki, M. Krauss, & M. Seltzer (Eds.), *Community residences for persons with developmental disabilities: Here to stay* (pp. 149–158). Baltimore: Paul H. Brookes.

Heller, T. (1999). Emerging models. In S. S. Herr & G. Weber (Eds.), *Aging, rights and quality of life: Prospects for older people with developmental disabilities* (pp. 149–166). Baltimore: Paul H. Brookes.

Heller, T., Caldwell, J., & Factor, A. (2000). *Supporting adults with intellectual and developmental disabilities and their families in future planning and advocacy.* Chicago: Rehabilitation Research and Training Center on Aging with Developmental Disabilities, University of Illinois at Chicago.

Heller, T., Caldwell, J., & Factor, A. (2003). *Supporting adults with intellectual and developmental disabilities and their families in future planning and advocacy.* Chicago: Rehabilitation Research and Training Center on Aging and Developmental Disabilities, University of Illinois at Chicago.

Heller, T., & Factor, A. (1991). Permanency planning for adults with mental retardation living with family members. *American Journal on Mental Retardation, 96*(2), 163–176.

Heller, T., Factor, A., & Hahn, J. (1999). Residential transitions from nursing homes for adults with cerebral palsy. *Disability and Rehabilitation, 21*(5), 277–283.

Heller, T., Hsieh, K., & Rimmer, J. (2002). Barriers and supports for exercise participation among adults with Down syndrome. *Journal of Gerontological Social Work, 38*(1/2), 161–178.

Heller, T., Hsieh, K., & Rimmer, J. (2004). Attitudinal and psychological outcomes of a fitness and health education program on adults with Down syndrome. *American Journal on Mental Retardation, 109*(2), 175–185.

Heller, T., Janicki, M., Hammel, J., & Factor, A. (2002). Promoting healthy aging, family support and age-friendly communities for persons aging with developmental disabilities. *Report of the 2001 Invitational Research Symposium on Aging with Developmental Disabilities.* Chicago: University of Illinois, Department of Disability and Human Development, Rehabilitation Research and Training Center on Aging with Developmental Disabilities.

Heller, T., Miller, A., Ksieh, K., & Sterns, H. (2000). Later-life planning: Promoting knowledge of options and choice-making. *Mental Retardation, 85*(5), 395–406.

Herr, S. S., & Weber, G. (1999). Prospects for ensuring rights, quality supports and a good old age. In S. S. Herr & G. Weber (Eds.), *Aging, rights and quality of life: Prospects for older people with developmental disabilities* (pp. 343–370). Baltimore: Paul H. Brookes.

Holland, A., Hon, J., Huppert, A., & Stevens, F. (2000). Incidence and course of dementia in people with Down syndrome: Findings from a population-based study. *Journal of Intellectual Disability Research, 44*(2), 138–146.

International Communications Research. (1997, December 3–16). *AARP long-term care insert: Tabulation report.* Washington, DC: American Association of Retired Persons.

Janicki, M. (1992). Lifelong disability and aging. In L. Rowitz (Ed.), *Mental retardation in the year 2000* (pp. 115–127). New York: Springer-Verlag.

Janicki, M., & Dalton, J. (2000). Prevalence of dementia and impact on intellectual disability services. *Mental Retardation, 38*(3), 276–288.

Janicki, M., Dalton, A., Henderson, C., & Davidson, P. (1999). Mortality and morbidity among older adults with intellectual disability: Health services considerations. *Disability and Rehabilitation, 21*, 284–294.

Janicki, M., Heller, T., Seltzer, M. M., & Hogg, J. (1996). Practice guidelines for the clinical assessment and care management of Alzheimer's disease and other dementias among adults with intellectual disabilities. *Journal of Intellectual Disability Research, 40*, 374–382.

Janicki, M., McCallion, P., & Dalton, A. (2002). Dementia-related care decision-making in group homes for persons with intellectual disabilities. *Journal of Gerontological Social Work, 38*(1/2), 179–195.

Kaufman, A., Adams, J., & Campbell, V. (1991). Permanency planning by older parents who care for adult children with mental retardation. *Mental Retardation, 5*, 293–300.

Larson, S., & Lakin, C. (1989). Deinstitutionalization of persons with mental retardation: The impact on daily living skills. *Policy research brief: A summary of research on policy issues affecting persons with developmental disabilities: Vol. 1.* Minneapolis: University of Minnesota, Research and Training Center on Community Living.

Leonard, H., & Wen, X. (2002). The epidemiology of mental retardation: Challenges and opportunities in the new millennium. *Mental Retardation and Developmental Disabilities Research Reviews, 8*, 117–134.

Lightfoot, E., Hewitt, A., & Sauer, J. (2004). Organizational change and restructuring to provide consumer directed supports. In S. Larson & A. Hewitt (Eds.), *Effective recruitment, retention and training: Strategies for human services organizations.* Baltimore: Paul H. Brookes.

Lightfoot, E., & Lum, Y. (in press). The role of the ADA on employment for older workers with disabilities. *Journal of Social Services Research.*

Litzinger, M., Duvall, B., & Little, P. (1993). Movement of individuals with complex epilepsy from an institution to the community: Seizure control and functional outcomes. *American Journal on Mental Retardation, 98* 52–57.

Ludlow, B. (1999). Life after loss: Legal, ethical and practical issues. In S. S. Herr & G. Weber (Eds.), *Aging, rights and quality of life* (pp. 189–221). Baltimore: Paul H. Brookes.

Lum, Y., & Lightfoot, E. (2003). The impact of health on retirement saving among older workers. *Social Work Research, 27*(1), 31–44.

Magana, S. (1999). Puerto Rican families caring for an adult with mental retardation: Role of familism. *American Journal on Mental Retardation, 104*(5), 466–482.

Mahon, M., & Goatcher, S. (1999). Later-life planning for older adults with mental retardation: A field experiment. *Mental Retardation, 37*(5), 371–382.

Mahon, M., & Mactavish, J. (2000). A sense of belonging: Older adults' perspectives on social integration. In M. Janicki & E. Ansello (Eds.), *Community supports for aging adults with lifelong disabilities* (pp. 41–53). Baltimore: Paul H. Brookes.

Mahoney, K. J., Simone, K., & Simon-Rusinowitz, L. (Fall 2000). Early lessons from the Cash and Counseling Demonstration and Evaluation. *Generations, 24*(1), 41–46.

Mahoney, K., Simon-Rusinowitz, L. Desmond, S., Shoop, D., Squillace, M., & Fay, R. (1998). Determining consumers' preferences for a cash option: New York telephone survey findings. *American Rehabilitation, 24*(4), 1–19.

McNeil, J. (2001). Americans with disabilities 1997. *Current Population Reports: U.S. Census Bureau.*

Messinger-Rapport, B., & Rapport, D. (1997). Primary care for the developmentally disabled adult. *Journal of General Internal Medicine, 12*(10), 629–636.

Muentz, M., & Frese, F., III. (2001). Getting ready for recovery: Reconciling mandatory treatment with the recovery vision. *Psychiatric Rehabilitation Journal, 25*(1), 35–42.

Nadash, P. (1998). Independent Choices. *American Rehabilitation, 24*(3), 15–21.

National Association of Social Workers. (1996). *NASW code of ethics.* Washington, DC: Author.

National Center for Health Statistics. (1993). *Chartbook on health data on older Americans: United States, 1992* (Series 3, No 29). Washington, DC: Author.

National Council on Disability. (2005). *The Social Security Administration's efforts to promote employment for people with disabilities: New solutions for old problems.* Washington, DC: Author.

Oliver, P., Piachaud, J., Done, J., Reagan, A., Cooray, S., & Tyrer, P. (2002). Difficulties in conducting a randomized controlled trial of health service interventions in intellectual disability: Implications for evidence-based practice. *Journal of Intellectual Disabiltiy Research, 46*(4), 340–345.

Olmstead et al. v. L. C. et al., 527 U.S. 581 (1999).

Podgorski, C., Kessler, K., Cacia, B., Peterson, D., & Henderson, C. (2004). Physical activity intervention for older adults with intellectual disability: Report on a pilot project. *Mental Retardation, 42*(4), 272–283.

President's Committee on Intellectual Disabilities. (2003). *Why was the term intellectual disabilities substituted for mental retardation?* Retrieved March 1, 2006 from http://faq.acf.hhs.gov.

Program in Aging and Developmental Disabilities. (2006). *Strong Center for Developmental Disabilities, Program in Aging and Developmental Disabilities.* Retrieved March 12, 2006 from http://www.urmc.edu/gchas/div/scdd/padd/conferen.htm.

Prouty, R., & Lakin, K. C. (Eds.). (1998, May). *Residential services for persons with developmental disabilities: Status and trends through 1997.* Minneapolis: University of Minnesota, Research and Training Center on Community Living, Institute on Community Integration.

Puri, B., Ho, K., & Singh, I. (2001). Age of seizure onset in adults with Down syndrome. *International Journal of Clinical Practice, 55,* 442–444.

Rehabilitation Engineering Research Center on Technology for Successful Aging. (1999). *Executive summary.* Gainesville: Rehabilitation Engineering Research Center on Technology for Successful Aging, University of Florida.

Reilly, K. O., & Conliffe, C. (2002). Facilitating future planning for ageing adults with intellectual disabilities using a planning tool that incorporates quality of life domains. *Journal of Gerontological Social Work, 37,* 105–119.

Rimmer, H., Braddock, D., & Marks, B. (1995). Health characteristics and behaviors of adults with mental retardation in three living arrangements. *Research in Developmental Disabilities, 16,* 489–499.

Rimmer, H., Heller, T., Wang, E., & Valerio, I. (2004). Improvements in physical fitness in adults with Down syndrome. *Mental Retardation, 36,* 175–181.

Rubenstein, L., Robbins, K., Josephson, B., Schulman, B., & Osterweil, D. (1990). The value of assessing falls in an elderly population: A randomized clinical trial. *Annals of Internal Medicine, 113,* 308–316.

Scherer, M. J., Coombs, F. K., & Hansen, N. K. (2003). Policy issues in evaluating and se-lecting assistive technology and other resources for persons with disabilities. In F. E. Menz & D. F. Thomas (Eds.), *Bridging gaps: Refining the disability research agenda for reha-bilitation and the social sciences—Conference Proceedings* (pp. 165–186). Menomonie: Uni-versity of Wisconsin, Stout; Stout Vocational Rehabilitation Institute, Research and Training Centers.

Seltzer, M. M. (2004). Introduction to the special issue on aging. *American Journal on Men-tal Retardation, 109*(2), 81–82.

Seltzer, G. B., & Luchterhand, C. (1994). Health and well-being of older persons with de-velopmental disabilities: a clinical review. In M. M. Seltzer, M. W. Krauss, & M. P. Jan-icki (Eds.), *Life course perspectives on adulthood and old age* (pp. 109–142). Washington, DC: American Association on Mental Retardation.

Shapiro, J. (1993). *No Pity: People with Disabilities Forging a New Civil Rights Movement.* New York: Random House.

Shultz, J., Aman, M., Kelbley, T., Wallace, C., Burt, D., Primeaux-Hart, S., et al. (2004). Evaluation of screening tools for dementia in older adults with mental retardation. *American Journal on Mental Retardation, 109*(2), 98–110.

Smith, G. (1997). Aging families of adults with mental retardation: Patterns and corre-lates of service use, need, and knowledge. *American Journal on Mental Retardation, 102,* 13–26.

Smith, G. C., Fullmer, E. M., & Tobin, S. S. (1994). Living outside the system: An explo-ration of older families who do not use day programs. In M. M. Seltzer, M. W. Krauss, & M. P. Janicki (Eds.), *Life course perspectives on adulthood and old age* (pp. 19–38). Wash-ington, DC: American Association on Mental Retardation.

Smith, G., Majeski, R., & McClenny, B. (1996). Psychoeducational support groups for aging parents: Development and preliminary outcomes. *Mental Retardation, 34,* 172–181.

Stancliffe, R., & Lakin, C. (2004). *Costs and outcomes of community services for persons with intellectual and developmental disabilities.* Minneapolis: Research and Training Center on Community Living, Institute on Community Integration, University of Minnesota.

Strydom, A., & Hassiotis, A. (2003). Diagnostic instruments for dementia in older people with intellectual disability in clinical practice. *Aging and Mental Health, 7*(6), 431–437.

Sushila, R., Mammen, P., Russell, P., & Sudhakar, S. (2005). Emerging trends in accepting the term intellectual disability in the world disability literature. *Journal of Intellectual Disabilities, 9*(3), 187–192.

Sutton, E., Sterns, A., & Schwartz-Park, L. (1993). Realities of retirement and preretire-ment planning. In E. Sutton, A. Factor, B. Hawkins, T. Heller, & G. Geltzer (Eds.), *Older adults with developmental disabilities: Optimizing choice and change* (pp. 95–106). Bal-timore: Paul H. Brookes.

Twamley, E. W., Jeste, D. V., & Lehman, A. F. (2003). Vocational rehabilitation in schizo-phrenia and other psychotic disorders: A literature review and meta-analysis of ran-domized controlled trials. *Journal of Nervous and Mental Diseases, 191,* 515–523.

U.S. Census, Current Population Reports, Special Studies. (1996). *P23-190 65+ in the United States.* Washington, DC: U.S. Government Printing Office.

Van Allen, M., Fung, J., & Jurenka, S. (1999). Health care concerns and guidelines for adults with Down syndrome. *American Journal of Medical Genetics, 89,* 100–110.

Verbrugge, L. M., & Jette, A. M. (1994). The disablement process. *Social Science and Medi-cine, 38*(1), 1–14.

Walsh, K., Kasner, T., & Criscione, T. (1997). Characteristics of hospitalizations for people with developmental disabilities: Utilization, costs, and impact of care coordination. *American Journal on Mental Retardation, 100,* 505–520.

Warren, D. (1998, May). *The health care needs of the aging person with mental retardation.* Paper presented at the 122nd annual meeting of the American Association of Mental Retardation, Washington, DC.

Wolf, D., Hunt, K., & Knickman, J. (2005). Perspectives on the recent decline in disability at older ages. *Milbank Quarterly, 83*(3), 365–395.

Wolfensberger, W. (1971). *The principle of normalization in human services.* Toronto, Ontario, Canada: National Institute on Mental Retardation (now the Roeher Institute).

World Health Organization. (2002). *Toward a common language for functioning, disability and health: ICF.* Geneva, Switzerland: Author.

Young, L., Ashman, A., Sigafoos, J., & Grevell, P. (2001). Closure of the Challinor Centre II: an extended report on 95 individuals after 12 months of community living. *Journal of Intellectual and Developmental Disability, 26,* 51–66.

Zigman, W., Schupf, N., Devenny, D., Miezejeski, C., Ryan, R., & Urv, T. (2004). Incidence and prevalence of dementia in elderly adults with mental retardation without Down syndrome. *American Journal on Mental Retardation, 109*(2), 126–141.

CHAPTER 9

Sleep Disturbances

MARY ANN LEITZ

ACK OF SLEEP and poor quality sleep have major negative effects on all individuals, but especially the elderly. The rate of sleep disorders is much higher for the elderly and escalates in intensity and frequency due to deterioration of physical and psychiatric status that occurs with normal aging. Sleep problems cause health problems, mood disturbances, decreased energy, emotional instability, and inability to concentrate and negatively impact personal relationships. A relationship between illness and sleep disturbances has been established; individuals who do not receive adequate sleep have higher rates of illness and immunity to ward off communicable illnesses drops (Leitz, 2005; Martin, Shochat, & Ancoli-Israel, 2000).

Sleep disturbances are one of the most frequent complaints reported to physicians by adults. Surveys of physicians find that approximately 10 million Americans annually identify sleep disturbances as the main reason they visit their doctors. Sleep disturbances are the most frequent complaint of the elderly to their physicians, and physicians write most prescriptions for sleep medication for the elderly (Hauri & Linde, 1996; Morgan, 1987; Roth, 1993). Patients report overall decreased number of hours of sleep, decreased levels of satisfaction with the quality of sleep, problems falling and staying asleep, more frequent awakenings during the night, earlier rising, and more need for daytime naps. Overall they report a decrease in level of satisfaction with their sleep quality (Martin et al., 2000).

Sleep disturbances thus are very common. According to a 1993 Harris poll, as many as half of all adults felt sleep deprived (Hauri & Linde, 1996). Ito et al. (2000) studied the rate of sleep disturbances in 518 (255 men and 263 women) 65-year-olds. Findings indicated that 50% of the sample reported sleep disturbances. The most frequent problem reported was falling asleep. Researchers also found a relationship between depression, poor health, and sleep disturbances: The greater the number of sleep problems, the more depressed and ill subjects felt. Subjects specifically reported shorter sleep periods, increased awakenings, easy arousal, daytime fatigue, and feeling the need for a daytime nap (Roth, 1993).

Studies have indicated that sleep problems of even short duration have a negative impact on functioning. A study of adults living in Los Angeles (Chokroverty, 2000) found that as many as 33% of subjects reported having some type of sleep disturbance that resulted in feelings of fatigue and sleepiness during the day. In a sample of college students ($N = 1,414$), Ban and Lee (2001) found approximately 40% reported problems sleeping, with measurable loss of productivity, difficulty concentrating, increased number of accidents, increase in mood disturbances, and an inability to complete assigned academic projects. These findings are supported by Heuer and Klien (2003), who studied volunteers who were sleep deprived for only one night. Findings indicated that subjects exhibited decreased learning capacity and inability to complete assignments the next day.

NORMAL SLEEP

Falling asleep is a process that involves complicated, intricate interactions between neurological and chemical processes. Gradually and slowly, the conscious mind is isolated from the external environment, and motor functions and alertness to surroundings are decreased (Dement & Vaughan, 1999; Hauri & Linde, 1996).

Sleep needs vary among individuals, but a range of 4 to 8 hours of sleep a night is considered necessary for normal functioning (Dement & Vaughan, 1999; Hauri & Linde, 1996; Van Dongen, Maislin, Mullington, & Dinges, 2003). However, sleep is easily disturbed by many different physical and emotional problems. The older the individual, the more likely he or she is to have the type of problems that directly impact sleep. Approximately 50% of individuals 60 years old report chronic sleep problems, and 100% of those 90 and older experience sleep disturbances. The quality of sleep also deteriorates with age. The elderly are more likely to report frequent nighttime awakenings and describe themselves as light sleepers who are easily awakened (Martin et al., 2000).

The elderly experience the same sleep disorders as young adults but at higher rates. They experience more obstructive sleep apnea, restless leg syndrome, and periodic limb movement disorders. Sleep for the elderly is further complicated by other conditions frequently found in this age group, including chronic pain, frequent urination, arthritis, inactivity, Alzheimer's disease, and Parkinson's disease (Asplund, 2004; Dement & Vaughan, 1999; Foley, Ancoli-Israel, Britz, & Walsh, 2004). They also experience an increase in psychological and environmental stresses that may interfere with sleep.

Anxiety and depression are common problems for the elderly. Many experience major losses, including the death of a spouse and elderly family members, loss of home and independence, and other major lifestyle changes, such as financial problems. With longer life expectancies, the elderly are faced with supporting themselves financially for many years after retirement. Many retire between the ages of 65 and 72 but live for another 25 to 30 years. Although many elderly persons remain active and healthy, the older they are the more likely they are to have health problems. This can challenge their independence and cause severe financial strain due to the necessity of supporting themselves and also paying for medical care (Barbar et al., 2000; Dement & Vaughan, 1999; Loiselle, Means, & Edinger, 2005; Piccone & Barth, 1983). As a result of these financial, physical, emotional, and social problems, the elderly frequently experience a lower standard of living, which results in depression and anxiety.

STAGES OF SLEEP

Sleep is composed of several stages, and we cycle through the different stages several times during the night. Sleep is also composed of core sleep and optimal sleep. Core sleep occurs in the first part of the night and is necessary for normal functioning and body and brain recovery and healing from the stressors of daily life. Optimal sleep occurs later in the night and is required to feel rested and energetic. The amount of optimal sleep determines the quality of sleep. There are two main stages of sleep: nonrapid eye movement (NREM) sleep and rapid eye movement (REM) sleep; NREM is further separated into Stages I, II, III, IV.

1. *Stage I NREM:* Stage I comprises only 8% of the total night's sleep. There is a gradual decrease of the level of consciousness and awareness of external stimuli. Heart rate, respiratory rate, and blood pressure also decrease. Sleep during Stage I is very light. Individuals sleep are only partially asleep and are easily awakened by even slight stimulation. If awakened during this stage, individuals may not even know they had been asleep. The elderly exhibit longer and more frequent Stage I sleep and therefore are more easily aroused. As a result, they experience poor quality of sleep. They spend less time in the deeper stages of sleep and as a result do not feel well rested or benefit from the natural healing that occurs while in deep sleep (Chokroverty, 2000; Morgan, 1987).

2. *Stages II, III, and IV NREM:* Combined, these stages comprise approximately 42% of sleep during the night. As individuals cycle through these stages, they fall into ever deepening sleep, until finally, in Stage IV, sleep is so deep that it is difficult to arouse individuals. Core sleep occurs in Stages III and IV, which are the deepest stages of sleep (Hauri & Linde, 1996). Heart rate, respiration rate, and blood pressure are at their lowest during these stages. This allows the cardiovascular system to rest, which helps prevent cardiovascular diseases. The elderly spend less time in these deeper stages, which results in their bodily functions being unable to slow to the same level as younger adults so they do not experience the same healing benefits of sleep (Chokroverty, 2000; Morgan, 1987).

3. *REM:* Rapid eye movement sleep accounts for approximately 50% of all sleep. Dreaming occurs during this stage. Although our bodies are paralyzed, eye movement under the closed lids can be seen. The actual function of dreams has been debated for decades, but it is clear that they are very important for normal functioning. Individuals who are deprived of dreams report feeling increased fatigue, irritability, and anxiety. Lack of dreaming is commonly caused by illness or medication and results in increased feelings of irritability, emotional instability, and feelings of being unable to cope with everyday demands. When individuals who were deprived of dreams begin to dream again, the brain appears to make up for lost REM periods. It has been reported that when dreams do resume, they are much longer, more bizarre, and more kinetic (Hauri & Linde, 1996). A study in which a group of subjects were deprived of REM sleep for four consecutive nights

showed that subjects were easily angered, frequently confused, and emotionally labile. When they were allowed to sleep normally, including REM sleep, subjects experienced longer and more frequent dream periods. They also reported that their dreams were extremely vivid, sometimes colorful, and bizarre (Dement & Vaughan, 1999). REM sleep is easily disrupted by illness, medication, chronic conditions, and sleep disturbances (Dement & Vaughan, 1999). The length of REM sleep has been found to naturally decrease with age so that the elderly experience fewer and shorter REM periods. The older the individual, the more disrupted the REM sleep. The natural aging process results in decreased REM periods even if the individual is in good health. Many health problems associated with aging and medications to treat these illnesses decrease REM sleep even further (Dement & Vaughan, 1999; Morgan, 1987).

Among the elderly overall, the quality and length of sleep is decreased due to the changing pattern of sleep, with longer periods in the lighter stages and shorter periods in the deeper stages of sleep.

CIRCADIAN RHYTHMS

One of the most valuable discoveries in sleep research was the realization that our bodies function on a 24-hour biological clock, or circadian rhythm, that is regulated by chemical substances that establish sleep-wake cycles (Chokroverty, 2000). Normal circadian rhythm results in being awake in the day and sleepy in the night. Sleep-wake cycles are controlled by both internal influences (circadian rhythms) and external influences (environmental). Circadian rhythms are controlled by hormone levels in the brain that are affected by exposure to light and dark. Melatonin is the main sleep hormone that is secreted by the hypothalamus, which causes and controls sleep. It is released in the dark and inhibited in bright light. Therefore, levels of melatonin are at their highest during the night when sleeping in dark rooms and lowest in the daylight. Melatonin acts on the brain and the body to cause feelings of being sleepy, decreases body temperature, decreases blood flow to the brain, increases relaxation, and induces sleep. The elderly experience a reduction in the production of melatonin, resulting in disrupted sleep (Chokroverty, 2000; Dement & Vaughan, 1999; Dunlap, 1998; Green & Menaker, 2003; Pandi-Perumal, Zisapel, Srinivasan, & Cardinali, 2005; Van Someren, 2000).

Sleep debt is another factor of sleep-wake cycles. Energy used to complete daily activities results in greater levels of fatigue. The more we do during the day, the more tired we feel in the evening. This energy depletion creates a sleep debt. Sleep debt is the amount of sleep the body needs to be rested. The greater the sleep debt, the more sleep is needed (Dement & Vaughan, 1999). As the day progresses, fatigue increases until individuals feel increasingly tired. Eventually, individuals become so tired that they begin to focus on their feelings of fatigue and experience a strong desire to go to sleep (Van Dongen et al., 2003).

Both the level of melatonin and the amount of sleep debt are reduced in the elderly. Changes in the aging brain cause decreases in the amount of melatonin produced. Additionally, melatonin is produced only in the dark. Many elderly sleep with some type of light on in the room to avoid falls should they get out of bed during the night. This reduces the amount of melatonin produced by the brain. Napping negatively affects both melatonin production and sleep debt. Many elderly feel the need to nap in the day. Daytime sleep disrupts sleep-wake cycles and is not as restful as nighttime sleep. Melatonin is not produced during daylight napping. Napping also reduces sleep debt, so individuals will not feel tired at night and will not feel the need to sleep. Circadian rhythms are disrupted, so individuals will feel sleepy in the day and awake at night (Loiselle et al., 2005; Van Someren, 2000).

SLEEP DISTURBANCES IN THE ELDERLY

Sleep disturbances can occur at any age but are more likely to occur in the elderly. Psychological and physiological changes that are part of the natural aging process negatively impact sleep both directly and indirectly. Direct influences are caused by degeneration of the nervous system and physiological processes that affect sleep-wake cycles. Indirect causes of sleep disturbances in the elderly are the result of illnesses and physical conditions. The most common of these are arthritis, diabetes, increased urination, and dementia. The elderly report spending more time in bed but less time asleep, with resultant daytime sleepiness and fatigue. Feelings of daytime fatigue can encourage the elderly to take naps, which decreases sleep debt, which further interferes with night sleeping. The elderly are 25% more likely to nap than other adult age groups, with an average of 30 minutes spent napping each day (Martin et al., 2000).

However, sleep disturbances in the elderly are more commonly caused by specific conditions related to aging, including sleep-disordered breathing, periodic limb movement, circadian rhythm changes, medical illness and/or medications, and Alzheimer's disease and dementia. Treatments that specifically target these conditions and good sleep hygiene practices help to resolve or at least decrease sleep problems (Martin et al., 2000).

TYPES OF SLEEP DISTURBANCES

The most common sleep disturbances in the elderly are disorders that prevent the onset of sleep or cause frequent awakenings. These include insomnia, circadian rhythm sleep disorders, restless leg syndrome, periodic limb movement disorders, sleep apnea, and neurological, physical, and psychiatric conditions.

INSOMNIA

Insomnia is the inability to either fall or stay asleep. Insomnia sufferers may be unable to fall asleep, but then may stay asleep the rest of the night. Others may fall asleep easily but do not stay asleep or experience early-morning risings. These individuals also have difficulty getting up in the morning and do not feel rested after sleep (Piccone & Barth, 1983). There are many causes of insomnia, but for the elderly the cause is usually poor sleep hygiene, stress, medication, acute illnesses, inactivity, depression, anxiety, and poor diet (Brostrom & Johansson, 2005; Chokroverty, 2000). Insomnia can be acute, short term, or chronic and can be learned. A cycle can develop where frustration and anxiety prevent sleep, and being unable to fall asleep creates more frustration and anxiety. Many insomnia sufferers even avoid going to bed when sleepy because they fear experiencing the frustration of being unable to fall asleep. The elderly are frequently caught in this frustrating cycle. As many as 40% of all elderly report experiencing chronic insomnia. Complaints of insomnia increase with age, and the natural aging process can be the primary cause of insomnia. Insomnia can also be secondary to several conditions related to the natural aging process and is a common side effect of chronic pain, neurological conditions, depression, illnesses, and medications and medical treatments. Daytime napping can cause nighttime insomnia due to decreased sleep debt (Chokroverty, 2000; Martin et al., 2000).

POOR SLEEP HYGIENE

Poor sleep hygiene is related to lifestyle and environmental factors that disrupt and prevent sleep. Poor sleep hygiene found in the elderly includes poor diet, use of alcohol, drugs, and tobacco, lack of exercise, napping, and bedroom environment. Sleep hygiene that is conducive to sleep is especially difficult for those living in assisted living facilities or with family and for individuals who may not be able to financially afford a comfortable bedroom (Chokroverty, 2000; Dement & Vaughan, 1999; Loiselle et al., 2005).

RESTLESS LEG SYNDROME

Restless leg syndrome is a sensorimotor disorder. This condition results in an overwhelming desire and need to move the legs. Restless leg syndrome occurs when lying in bed or after sitting for long periods. Young adults may have this condition, but the severity increases as they age. The elderly can develop this condition due to degenerative processes of aging. Approximately 10% of all adults suffer from restless leg syndrome, and it occurs equally in men and women. It tends to run in families and is chronic and progressive. As individuals are resting they feel a strong urge to move their legs, and leg movements are voluntary. Individuals are awake and choose to move their legs to get relief (Chokroverty, 2000). This condition is exacerbated by anxiety, depression, illness, aging, sedentary lifestyles, and physical illnesses. Common medical conditions that can cause restless leg syndrome include diabetes and diabetic peripheral neuropathy, anemia, renal failure, liver problems, and medications (Chokroverty, 1994; Loiselle et al., 2005). The elderly are susceptible to all of these conditions (Chokroverty, 2000).

PERIODIC LIMB MOVEMENT DISORDERS

Unlike restless leg syndrome, periodic limb movements are involuntary and occur while asleep. This disorder causes brief severe contraction of the limbs, usually the legs, and is characterized by myoclonus (contract-release) movements that can occur every 30 seconds. Movements are unconscious but can awaken sleeping individuals. Restless leg syndrome and periodic limb movement disorders are related. Approximately 80% of those with periodic limb movement also have restless leg syndrome. Periodic limb movement disorders occur during Stage II NREM sleep and can occur alone or in combination with other disorders. When the elderly do cycle into the deeper stages of sleep, limb movements can awaken them. Severity and frequency vary (Chokroverty, 2000). The likelihood of this condition increases with age and is associated with neurological degeneration and physical illnesses (Martin et al., 2000). Causes and exacerbation of periodic limb movement disorders are related to conditions common to the elderly, most frequently venous insufficiency in lower limbs, hypertension, and osteoarthritis (Chokroverty, 1994; Loiselle et al., 2005).

SLEEP APNEA

The rate of sleep apnea in the elderly is estimated to be as high as 62% (Lugaresi, 1993). Sleep apnea is the "absence of respiration" (Hauri & Linde, 1996, p. 201). While sleeping, breathing stops for a few seconds. This is caused by the collapse of the trachea, which prevents the passage of air, which stops breathing (Hauri & Linde, 1996). Muscles relax and become flaccid during sleep. The muscles in the trachea can become so flaccid that the trachea actually collapses and breathing stops. Individuals begin to choke and awaken, muscles contract, rigidity in the trachea is restored, and breathing resumes. This cycle can occur many times during the night. Symptoms include loud snoring, choking while asleep, cessation of breathing, frequent awakenings, frequent nighttime urination, daytime sleepiness, forgetfulness, morning headache, insomnia, night sweating, and gastrointestinal reflux, which causes coughing and aspiration (Chokroverty, 2000; Hauri & Linde, 1996; Piccone & Barth, 1983). Precipitating factors include nasotracheal abnormalities, overbite, enlarged tongue and tonsils, tissue that blocks the airway, obesity, alcohol use, medications, medical conditions, menopause, old age, large neck size, and genetics (Chokroverty, 2000). Sleep apnea can have very serious effects. It causes insomnia, daytime sleepiness, impaired concentration, fatigue, high blood pressure, increased stroke risk, decreased concentration, cognitive problems, attention deficits, and higher risk for myocardial infarction and other cardiac problems (Chokroverty, 2000; Piccone & Barth, 1983). The degenerative process of aging results in anatomical and physiological changes in the lungs. The airway becomes smaller due to changes in supportive tissues. Additionally, the elderly have smaller diameter bronchi, resulting in decreased air passage. The lungs do not expand and contract as effectively as when young, and individuals experience increased difficulty breathing (Avidan, 2005). Sleep apnea is more serious in individuals who have underlying physical conditions such as cardiac disorders, cerebrovascular problems, and metabolic disorders, all of which are more common in the elderly (Lugaresi, 1993).

CIRCADIAN RHYTHM DISORDERS

Circadian rhythm sleep disorders are caused by disruption of the sleep-wake cycle. Any lifestyle, psychological, or physical condition can disrupt this cycle. For young adults, disruptions of normal sleep-wake cycles are most commonly caused by jet lag and shift work. For the elderly, the most common causes are illnesses, hospitalizations, physical discomfort, and daytime napping. Many complain that they are not sleepy at night but are very sleepy at inappropriate times. The elderly experience physical, social, and environmental changes and are more susceptible to temporary changes in schedules and living conditions that can disrupt normal sleep-wake cycles. Chronic disruption of normal cycles will result in random sleep periods that further upset the cycle. Individuals are sleepy during the day and early evenings, but not sleepy at bedtime (Billiard, 1993).

NEUROLOGICAL AND PSYCHIATRIC CONDITIONS

The elderly have high rates of depression, adjustment disorders, and anxiety. Old age is a time of major life changes. Family members and friends have died, and many feel lonely. Living situations can change drastically. Individuals may have to leave the home in which they lived for many years and move to an assisted living situation or a smaller, more manageable home. They may have to live with family members because they are not able to care for themselves properly or cannot financially afford to do so. Retirement can be traumatic. Retirees who have spent their entire adult lives working suddenly have no reason to get up in the mornings. Many may have been forced into retirement and suffer overwhelming feelings of loss, decreased stimulation, loss of income and status, and feelings of betrayal and rejection. Other conditions are social isolation, boredom, and inactivity. Depression caused by both physical and social changes experienced by the elderly is common. One of the primary symptoms of depression is disrupted sleep with insomnia, frequent awakenings, and reduced quality of sleep (Ito et al., 2000).

Alzheimer's disease and dementia can also cause sleep disturbances in the elderly due to neurological deterioration. Dementia can be caused by other conditions, but 70% of all dementias are caused by Alzheimer's disease, a progressive neurological condition that gradually destroys the brain. As the disease progresses and destroys more of the brain, sleep patterns and circadian rhythms are disturbed. Confusion, agitation, and aggression are common symptoms of middle-stage Alzheimer's. Alzheimer's and dementia are characterized by quiet, restful days and extreme agitation, restlessness, and delirium during the night (Hauri & Linde, 1996; Morley, 1993).

Sleep disturbances in the elderly are more resistant to treatment than those in younger adults; some can be so resistant that they are never resolved. However, the elderly are not without options. There are strategies that can be used to fight these frustrating and debilitating conditions.

UNIVERSAL MEASURES OF PREVENTION FOR SLEEP DISTURBANCES

Sleep disturbances in the elderly may not be avoidable. However, there are strategies that may help manage these problems.

SLEEP ASSESSMENTS

It is very helpful for the elderly, or their caregivers, to complete detailed sleep assessments. Sleep assessments and diaries should be as detailed as possible. Individuals should write down all daily activities, food eaten, physical conditions, medical treatments and medications taken, and a detailed description of their moods and feelings for each day. For example, they should write down the type of food they ate, the way the food was prepared, and the amount eaten (Chokroverty, 2000; Dement & Vaughn, 1999). A careful assessment provides a clear picture of the individual's day, which is used to identify and analyze any problem areas. In addition, a detailed sleep diary or sleep log should be maintained for an entire 24-hour period, including awake periods. Sleep logs should record hours of sleep, quality of sleep, number of nighttime awakenings, feelings on awakening, when one feels tired and when one feels rested, and periods of insufficient sleep. These two records can be combined and used to provide a clear illustration of an individual's day and can also be used to evaluate the improvement or deterioration of conditions and treatments that affect sleep (Chokroverty, 2000; Dement & Vaughan, 1999).

SLEEP HYGIENE

Developing good sleep hygiene is very effective in aiding sleep for all adults, but especially for the elderly. Sleep for the elderly can be elusive and easily disrupted. Good sleep hygiene can help induce sleep, increase relaxation, and help the elderly fall asleep. There are several strategies that can be used to improve sleep hygiene. For the elderly these include improvement or maintenance of health status by maintaining a healthy diet, compliance with their medical regimen, physical exercise approved by their physician, reduction of stress, continued social interactions, and mental stimulation (Chokroverty, 2000; Hauri & Linde, 1996; Piccone & Barth, 1983). Additionally, the elderly should avoid napping unless they are ill because it reduces sleep debt and can disrupt circadian rhythms (Dement & Vaughan, 1999; Piccone & Barth, 1983). Short rest periods may be needed due to physical problems or to recover from exertion and exercise. However, rest periods should not be longer than necessary and sleep should be avoided (Martin et al., 2000). Bedrooms should be pleasant, uncluttered, neat, and clean. At night the room should be dark to enhance production of melatonin and quiet to reduce external stimulation and prevent arousal. The temperature in the room should be comfortable. Usually it is more conducive to sleep to have the room slightly cooler than in the day (Piccone & Barth, 1983). It is important to have good supportive and comfortable mattresses and pillows. It is especially important for the elderly to have a mattress that supports their body without causing pressure points that can lead to bed ulcers and skin breakdowns. It is important that the elderly maintain a sleep ritual. A sleep ritual is a set routine that individuals follow every night before they go to bed. It signals the body and brain that they are preparing for sleep (Chokroverty, 2000; Piccone & Barth, 1983). The elderly should engage in quiet time before they go to bed, such as watching television, reading, or listening to music; this helps the brain and body to relax and prepare for sleep. Any stimulating activities or conversations should be avoided during this period (Hauri & Linde, 1996). It is even more important for the elderly to have stimulating days with regular social contact to minimize isolation, depression, and anxiety. Active lives also increase sleep debt and reduce the tendency to nap.

SELECTIVE MEASURES FOR THE PREVENTION OF SLEEP DISTURBANCES

Universal measures are generally effective in preventing sleep disturbances, but older individuals may need to use more specific and aggressive preventive measures. Most elderly develop many of the conditions that are identified risk factors for sleep disturbances. Neurological conditions such as restless leg syndrome and periodic limb movements that are present in young adults increase in intensity and frequency with age. Therefore, strategies should be more focused and aggressive.

INSOMNIA

The easiest technique to prevent insomnia is to develop good sleep hygiene. If the elderly are unable to follow these steps themselves they should enlist someone to help ensure that their environment is conducive to sleep (Dement & Vaughan, 1999). The elderly benefit from stress reduction techniques such as gentle exercises and stretches, deep breathing, meditation, warm baths, and massage, which may also reduce pain and stiffness from conditions such as arthritis. It is especially important for the elderly to treat depression, which is a very common cause of insomnia. They should obtain any needed psychiatric treatment, maintain good social contacts, adequate exercise, and diet, and continue as many enjoyable activities as possible (Dement & Vaughan, 1999; Ito et al., 2000).

SLEEP APNEA

Sleep apnea is very common in the elderly. They can use the same techniques that are used by younger adults, which include maintaining normal weight, treating sinus, throat, and respiratory problems, and avoiding tobacco, alcohol, and drugs (Hauri & Linde, 1996). Surgical treatments to remove excess tissue and restructure the throat should be performed only if absolutely necessary. Surgery and anesthesia always carry risks, and these risks are greatly increased for the elderly (Chokroverty, 2000; Dement & Vaughan, 1999). Elderly persons have obtained encouraging results by using nasal continuous positive airway pressure (CPAP). This method is a very effective and conservative treatment for sleep apnea. A small mask is worn over the nose while sleeping; a machine connected to the mask forces air into the throat while sleeping. This prevents the trachea from becoming flaccid and collapsing. However, careful evaluation and assessment for the appropriateness of CPAP must be conducted by a physician. The CPAP is not a cure and must be used properly every night, which necessitates training. Users must understand the equipment, know how and why it is used, and be willing to cooperate with treatments (Martin et al., 2000). Less drastic methods involve oral appliances that push the jaw forward, holding the airway open. These devices do reduce snoring and sleep apnea but are not as effective as the CPAP method. Oral devices must also be prescribed by either a physician or a dentist and must be properly fitted, which requires several office visits and can be very costly. These devices must also be used nightly. Weight loss, reduction in alcohol intake, and avoiding tranquilizers and narcotics are also effective in reducing sleep apnea (Martin et al., 2000).

RESTLESS LEG SYNDROME AND PERIODIC LIMB DISORDERS

Individuals who have these disorders in old age probably had them in milder forms when they were younger. Although these conditions cannot be avoided, their intensity and frequency can be reduced. Effective strategies include regular exercise, gentle stretching before bedtime, and walking during the day. The physical status of the elderly may necessitate that they take several short, slow walks during the day instead of one long walk. Short, slow walks are effective in minimizing restless leg syndrome and periodic limb disorders. However, any exercise must be approved by their physician. Other strategies that help are massage, warm baths, and heat/ice compresses (Hauri & Linde, 1996). New medications have been shown to be effective in reducing periodic limb movements and restless leg syndrome. These medications actually reduce the number of leg kicks and movements during the night. Sedatives and hypnotics have been used in the past; however, these medications do not actually reduce the movements, but make arousal more difficult so the individuals do not awaken. As with all medications, careful management and prescribing must be used with the elderly. Medications must be taken correctly and may need supervision to prevent improper use, accidental overdose, and interactions with other medications. A careful medical assessment must be made by the physician to determine the appropriateness of the medication and to supervise medication use, side effects, and treatment outcomes (Martin et al., 2000).

MEDICAL, NEUROLOGICAL, AND PSYCHIATRIC CONDITIONS

To prevent sleep disturbances secondary to other conditions it is necessary to treat the underlying condition. A thorough assessment by a physician is required to determine any precursors or conditions that may be present. Because sleep disturbances are secondary symptoms, treating the primary condition will resolve or reduce sleep problems (Chokroverty, 2000; Hauri & Linde, 1996; Martin et al., 2000). Medications and treatments to treat either the underlying conditions or the secondary insomnia must be prescribed and carefully monitored by physicians. Medications can improve sleep, but they can have serious side effects and drug interactions. Medication ordered for the elderly to treat both the underlying conditions and secondary sleep disturbances should be prescribed in the smallest possible doses of the mildest medication. Additionally, care should be taken that the elderly are not taking duplicate medications to treat the same conditions or medications that will interact with medications for other conditions. The elderly do not always take their medication reliably as prescribed by their physician. Often they are confused about what they are taking and for what reasons. They may ignore drug reactions or interactions, not tell their doctor, or even increase the medication, thinking they feel ill because they are not taking enough. It is helpful for the elderly to write down their medications, doses, and frequency as a convenient tool. Nonmedical approaches may also be considered for the elderly, including those listed earlier (Morgan, 1987).

CIRCADIAN RHYTHM DISTURBANCES

Circadian rhythms that regulate sleep-wake cycles are themselves regulated by exposure to light. Circadian rhythm disturbances can be treated in a safe and conservative manner by using light therapy. Light therapy involves a timed and regulated exposure to light, either natural sunlight or sunlamp. Exposure to light in the morning advances the sleep cycle so that individuals become sleepy earlier in the evenings. This is helpful when individuals do not feel sleepy until late in the night. Conversely, light therapy used in the early evening will delay circadian rhythms, which delays sleepiness. This is useful for those individuals who become sleepy too early in the evening. A problem for even healthy and active elderly persons is that they usually have less exposure to sunlight in their normal days. They tend to stay inside for longer periods of time, and physical or psychiatric conditions and treatments can prevent individuals from spending time outdoors. Care should be taken when light therapy is used by the elderly. If the elderly are confused or forgetful, or otherwise unreliable, they should be supervised during light therapy to avoid dangerous and painful burns. Time spent in sunlight must also be monitored to avoid burns and skin cancers (Billiard, 1993).

PRACTICE AND POLICY IMPLICATIONS

Sleep disturbances in the elderly can be devastating to their health and overall physical, social, and psychological functioning. Professionals must become knowledgeable about specific sleep disturbances and how they affect the elderly. Additionally, the sensitive and fragile health status of the elderly must be understood and accommodated. Appropriate measures must be recommended and referrals to a gerontologist must be made when necessary.

Even healthy older adults are more susceptible to the complications and negative effects of sleep problems. Working directly with the elderly and their caregivers in helping them understand and manage sleep problems can be very effective in resolving this devastating problem. While it may be necessary to refer individuals to specialists in the field of gerontology, clinicians can teach the elderly about sleep disturbances and encourage them to maintain a lifestyle that can minimize these problems. All treatments should be coordinated and integrated into a treatment plan that addresses all of the problems and conditions associated with sleep problems, and the treatment plan should be incorporated into individuals' everyday lives. Professionals who work with the elderly must also monitor treatments and medications to avoid dangerous complications and interactions. Even if clinicians do not work in gerontology or sleep disturbances, they must educate themselves so that their clients receive the highest level of care.

It may be necessary for the elderly to be evaluated by a sleep center for a definitive diagnosis. Sophisticated and sensitive diagnosis identifies specific problems and determines severity and intensity and suggests appropriate treatments. However, this type of assessment is very expensive and can be upsetting for elderly who are depressed, anxious, and emotionally labile. With changes in insurance and third-party payments, sleep studies and treatments may be unaffordable for many elderly, especially if their only medical coverage is Medicare. Professionals must support their patients through this process and must frequently become advocates to obtain needed services. Careful detailed records must be kept that describe the type of sleep disturbances and the effects they have on the overall functioning and health of the elderly. This information can be used to identify needs and craft effective and appropriate treatment approaches specifically designed for the elderly.

FUTURE DIRECTIONS

Even after decades of sleep research, there is much to discover about sleep. However, many discoveries have led to improvement, control, and even prevention of sleep disorders. As the field of gerontology continues to improve services and treatments for the elderly, help for sleep disorders will also be discovered. Knowledge of how normal aging interacts with physical and psychiatric conditions in the elderly will aid in the development of effective and safe measures that specifically target sleep disorders in this age group. It is documented that sleep disturbances increase with age and sleep problems are frequently secondary problems related to illness and normal aging. This makes sleep disturbances in the elderly difficult and complicated to both prevent and treat. The devastating health and psychological risk of sleep disorders and the precarious health status of the elderly make the prevention of sleep disorders a priority.

CONCLUSION

As this chapter illustrates, the elderly have many of the same sleep disturbances as younger adults, but their age changes the focus and type of recommended treatments. They also experience conditions specific to their age group. The elderly have many changes in their physical and emotional status which can cause or exacerbate sleep problems. Treating sleep disturbances in this age group is complicated and delicate and requires careful assessment and treatment. Sleep disturbances can be devastating to the fragile health status and social functioning of this population and can rob the elderly of the opportunity to experience satisfying and enjoyable lives.

REFERENCES

Asplund, R. (2004). Nocturia, nocturnal polyuria, and sleep quality in the elderly. *Journal of Psychosomatic Research, 56*(5), 517–525.

Avidan, A. Y. (2005). Sleep disordered breathing in the geriatric patient population. In M. P. Mattson (Ed.), *Advances in cell aging and gerontology: Vol. 17. Sleep and aging.* San Diego, CA: Elsevier.

Ban, D. J., & Lee, T. J. (2001). Sleep duration, subjective sleep disturbances and associated factors among university students in Korea. *Journal of Korean Medical Science, 16,* 475–480.

Barbar, S. J., Enright, P. L., Boyle, P., Foley, D., Sharp, D. S., Petrovitch, H., et al. (2000). Sleep disturbances and their correlates in elderly Japanese-American males residing in Hawaii. *Journal of Gerontology: Series A, Biological Science and Medical Science, 55*(7), 406–411.

Billiard, M. (1993). Circadian rhythm modification in aging. In J. L. Albarede, J. E. Morley, R. Roth, & B. J. Vellas (Eds.), *Sleep disorders and insomnia in the elderly.* New York: Springer.

Brostrom, A., & Johansson, P. (2005). Sleep disturbances in patients with chronic heart failure and their holistic consequences: What different care actions can be implemented? *European Journal of Cardiovascular Nursing, 4*(3), 183–197.

Chokroverty, S. (2000). *Clinical companion to sleep disorders medicine* (2nd ed.). Boston: Butterworth-Heinemann.

Dement, W. C., & Vaughan, C. (1999). *The promise of sleep: A pioneer in sleep medicine explores the vital connection between health, happiness, and a good night's sleep.* New York: Dell.

Dunlap, J. (1998). An end in the beginning. *Science, 26*(2), 1548–1549.

Foley, D., Ancoli-Israel, S., Britz, P., & Walsh, J. (2004). Sleep disturbances and chronic disease in older adults: Results of the 2003 National Sleep Foundation Sleep in American Survey. *Journal of Psychosomatic Research, 56*(5), 497–502.

Green, C. B., & Menaker, M. (2003). Clocks on the brain. *Science, 301,* 319–320.

Hauri, H., & Linde, S. (1996). *No more sleepless nights* (2nd ed.). New York: Wiley.

Heuer, H., & Klien, W. (2003). One night of total sleep deprivation impairs implicit learning in the serial reaction task, but not the behavioral expression of knowledge. *Neuropsychology, 17*(3), 507–516.

Ito, Y., Tamakoshi, A., Yamaki, K., Wakai, K., Kawanura, T., Takagi, K., et al. (2000). Sleep disturbances and its correlates among elderly Japanese. *Archives of Gerontology and Geriatrics, 30*(2), 85–100.

Leitz, M. A. (2005). Sleep disturbances. In C. N. Dulmus & L. A Rapp-Paglicci (Eds.), *Handbook of preventive interventions for adults* (pp. 280–299). Hoboken, NJ: Wiley.

Loiselle, M. M., Means, M. K., & Edinger, J. D. (2005). Sleep disturbances in aging. In M. P. Mattson (Ed.), *Advances in cell aging and gerontology: Sleep and aging* (pp. 33–59). San Diego, CA: Elsevier.

Lugaresi, S. E. (1993). Sleep apnea syndrome controversy. In J. L. Albarede, J. E. Morley, T. Roth, & B. J. Vellas (Eds.), *Sleep disorders and insomnia in the elderly* (pp. 17–22). New York: Springer.

Martin, J., Shochat, T., & Ancoli-Israel, S. (2000). Assessment and treatment of sleep disturbances in older adults. *Clinical Psychology Review, 20*(6), 783–805.

Morgan, K. (1987). *Sleep and aging: A research-based guide to sleep in later life.* Baltimore: Johns Hopkins University Press.

Morley, J. (1993). Nocturnal agitation. In J. L. Albarede, J. E. Morley, R. Roth, & B. J. Vellas (Eds.), *Sleep Disorders and Insomnia in the Elderly* (pp. 109–126). Paris, New York, & Tokyo: Serdi Publisher, Springer Publisher & Nankodo Publisher.

Pandi-Perumal, S. R., Zisapel, N., Srinivasan, V., & Cardinali, D. P. (2005). Melatonin and sleep in aging population. *Experimental Gerontology, 40*(12), 911–925.

Piccone, P. M., & Barth, R. P. (1983). Sleep: An expanding field of practice and research. *Social Work, 24,* 228–233.

Roth, T. (1993). Sleep in the elderly: A clinical challenge. In J. L. Albarede, J. E. Morley, T. Roth, & B. J. Vellas (Eds.), *Sleep disorders and insomnia in the elderly.* New York: Springer.

Van Dongen, H. P. A., Maislin, G., Mullington, J. M., & Dinges, D. R. (2003). The cumulative cost of additional wakefulness: Dose-response effects on neurobehavioral functions and sleep physiology from chronic sleep restriction and total sleep deprivation. *Sleep, 26*(2), 117–126.

Van Someren, E. J. W. (2000). Circadian and sleep disturbances in the elderly. *Experimental Gerontology, 35*(9/10), 1229–1234.

CHAPTER 10

Sexuality and Intimacy

LINDA J. BROCK and GLEN JENNINGS

S EXUALITY IN THE human is more than biology and reproduction. Whether or not sexuality is expressed with the genitals, with or without partners, it is central to human identity and is essential to wholeness in the life experience. Sexuality includes gender identity and gender roles, attractions and desires, and sexual behaviors. Yet it also is reflected in sensuality, body image, and sense of attractiveness. How a person dresses and moves is an expression of her or his sexuality. Sexuality can be experienced alone through such actions as bathing, grooming, and application of cosmetics, as well as through genital self-pleasuring. Sexuality with a partner can be expressed through touching, talking, eye contact, flirting, kissing, holding hands, sharing erotic poetry, dancing, hugging, cuddling, acts of care and kindness, and the giving of gifts, as well as through genital contact. Sexuality includes, perhaps most important, the unique experience of intimacy and love, the creation of a profound connection with another human while being acutely aware of one's own sense of wholeness as a separate person.

Each individual's sexuality is constantly shaped by personal experiences and societal messages that become attitudes and beliefs, in turn influencing sexual behavior. Much of sexuality is socially constructed, influenced by culture, time, place, relationships, and the human need to create meaning, individually and as a group. Sexuality and the sexual scripts through which individuals act out their sexuality (Gagnon, 1977; Mahay, Laumann, & Michaels, 2001) emerge from the confluence of biology, psychology, sociology, ethnicity and culture, religion and spirituality. Each individual brings these and other elements to bear in differing combinations and varying ways across his or her life course. Such a broad and deep definition of sexuality applies to the very end of life and is the assumption behind this chapter.

Older persons, individuals in later life age 60 and older, constitute a category spanning more than 40 years, based on life spans that can and do reach 100 years. It is essential to keep in mind the many differences of this group: birth cohort, life experiences, ethnicity, socioeconomic level, sexual orientation, health status, relationship status, and educational level, to name a few (Gott, 2003). Some older persons are frail, dependent nursing home residents; others are active community members, working at the peak of their careers. Some live alone after the loss of a mate; some enjoy stable, committed relationships; and others engage in frequent dating with a variety of partners. Some live in exclusive retirement communities, traveling and enjoying sports and other leisure activities. Some live on the edge financially, staying with adult children or other relatives. Older persons may have university degrees or have dropped out of high school; may have chronic illnesses, physical or mental disabilities, or be in excellent health. Older persons may have immigrated, bringing values and meanings from a different land or, although born here, be a part of the hundreds of different cultures that make up American society. Older persons are heterosexual, bisexual, gay, lesbian, transgendered, and intersexed. Generalizing about sexuality and older persons should be undertaken with great caution.

The study of sexuality and older persons is a largely unexplored and still developing field (Gott & Hinchliff, 2003). For example, the well-known study of sexual behavior conducted by Laumann, Gagnon, Michael, and Michaels (1994) interviewed only participants 18 to 59 years of age, excluding older adults entirely. Differences in definitions of both sexuality and older persons, as well as a variety of often unaddressed confounding variables such as those mentioned earlier, make comparison of the available studies difficult. Much of the available research also tends to privilege (hetero) sexual intercourse as a measure of sexual activity and legal marriage as a measure of relationship, overlooking other behaviors and relationship arrangements. Many studies take a problem-centered approach to sexuality during later life that misses the opportunity to report positive information about the sexual lives of people 60 and over. In addition, much available research focuses more on biological and health-related issues than on a psychosocial and systemic relational perspective. In this chapter, a strength-based, positive approach open to the richness of diversity both in individuals and relationships is used as a lens through which to view the sexuality and intimacy of older persons.

WHAT WE THINK WE KNOW

Despite the lack of a broad and deep body of empirical data, most societies have developed beliefs and attitudes about older persons and sexuality. Common assumptions exist across many of the world's societies that older persons do not, cannot, or should not engage in sex (Global Study of Sexual Attitudes and Behaviors, 2002). The widespread assumption of a sexless old age (Kellett, 2000) is familiar to those who work with the elderly. Older persons themselves across past decades have also been well acquainted with the idea that their expression of sexuality is not acceptable. Some have internalized this traditional taboo; many others may have disagreed but been unwilling to resist it openly (Brock & Jennings, 1999). The stereotype of the sexless older person continues to influence public policy as well as research agendas (Gott & Hinchliff, 2003).

The limited information available on the sexuality of older persons indicates changes in, rather than cessation of, sexual activity and sexual desire in later life (Brecher, 1984; Budd, 1999; DeLamater & Sill, 2005; Dunn & Cutler, 2000). Psychological and social influences on sexuality are especially neglected in research. When these influences are taken into account, the availability of a partner, health issues, and sexual attitudes held by an individual become key variables explaining the sexual lives of older persons (DeLamater & Sills, 2005; Gott & Hinchliff, 2003; Shaw, 1994).

TRENDS

In the decades since the publication of the Kinsey reports (Kinsey, Pomeroy, & Martin, 1948; Kinsey, Pomeroy, Martin, & Gebhard, 1953), sexuality has been discussed more openly in the print and broadcast media, and recently on the Internet. The widely held social construction of a sexless old age has begun to be replaced by a new concept of aging well—an assumption that all older persons "*should* be physically healthy and sexually active" (Gross & Blundo, 2005, p. 87). Will this "emerging myth" (Gott & Hinchliff, 2003, p. 1627) ultimately prove as controlling of older persons as its opposite has been? Will one stereotype be replaced by another?

The older persons who participated in past sexuality research were born prior to the end of World War II. They came of age before the Sexual Revolution of the 1960s and in the absence of reliable information about sexuality.

The first of the 76 million baby boomers, born between January 1, 1946, and December 31, 1964, began turning 60 in 2006. These individuals "constitute the largest number of persons ever born in a single generation from 1905 until the end of the twentieth century in the United States" (Maples & Abney, 2006, p. 3). As this large birth cohort of Americans becomes older persons, they bring with them changing sexual beliefs, attitudes, and life experiences. The baby boomers are a diverse group, despite the tendency of mass media to present them as homogeneous. The experiences of the oldest and the youngest of the generation are vastly different. This generation has experienced an unprecedented rate of marital dissolution and the growing acceptance of gay and lesbian relationships (Burgess, 2004). They have seen the development and marketing of oral contraceptives and the discovery and spread of the human immunodeficiency virus (HIV). They have had access to more information on human sexuality than any prior group. Even though their sexual attitudes and beliefs were socially constructed in this milieu, research assessing their basic factual sex knowledge has found most to be woefully lacking (Reinisch & Beasley, 1990). How will the life experiences of this cohort influence their construction of sexuality? How will they understand relationships and intimacy? What similarities and differences will be found between them and the men and women who preceded them?

Mass media have focused for 60 years on the baby boomers' impact on American society as they moved across the life span. The media have catered to the assumed needs and wants of these 76 million individuals through each stage of their lives. Shifts in the content of popular media can be observed as the supposed needs of the now older boomers are being addressed, despite little actual knowledge of the enormous variety of sexual interests, desires, behaviors, attitudes, or beliefs of this huge audience. These men and women are healthier, more affluent, and better educated than any generation before them (Maples & Abney, 2006). They are accustomed to being focused on as a driving force in society. In light of the fact that this generation has experienced profound political power, it is likely that they will be far less willing to accept the notion that their sexual expression is invalid (Richard, 2002).

In recent decades the number of couples of all ages cohabiting without marriage has dramatically increased, as has society's acceptance of these living arrangements (Strong, DeVault, Sayad, & Yarber, 2005). Although some older individuals will continue to sanction sexual expression only within marriage, more will be sexually involved with partners to whom they are not married, and whom they do not intend to marry, for a variety of reasons. Same-sex couples, who may have been hiding their relationships for years, are living together all across the country. Many of these couples, denied legal marriage in most of the United States are only now openly acknowledging the true importance of their partners. Increasing societal acceptance of same-sex relationships, particularly among the young, will likely help couples of all ages to more freely express their sexuality.

Another ongoing societal process is the medicalization of sexuality. Sexuality, particularly in older persons, has been increasingly seen as a health or medical issue (Tiefer, 2004). Massive publicity on erectile dysfunction medications, such as Viagra, Cialis, and Levitra, has further medicalized the discourse on sexuality in later life (Gross & Blundo, 2005). Pharmaceuticals will continue to play an increasing role in the sexuality of older persons because these oral therapies are easy to use and private, making them attractive to a generation accustomed to rapid medical advances and simple solutions available from their primary care physician. These medications can have a dramatic effect on sexual functioning for some and will likely continue to be prescribed for and experimented with by people of all ages. Continued research on oral pharmaceuticals promises physiological enhancement of the sexual lives of individuals and couples, including older persons. Yet what influences all these processes will have on the social construction of sexuality and intimate relationships for this group of older persons of the twenty-first century is still conjecture.

SEXUAL FUNCTIONING IN LATER LIFE

The human body develops and changes throughout the life cycle. Developmental sexual changes occur in older females and males, and these changes need not prevent the continued expression and enjoyment of sexuality, although some adaptation may be necessary for most. In women, menopause, which marks the end of the menstrual cycle and of fertility and a decline in the production of the hormone estrogen, results in a slowing of the arousal response, thinning of the vaginal walls, and decrease in vaginal lubrication (Sanders, 1999; Sharpe, 2004). However, when women continue to engage in behaviors that arouse them sexually, whether alone or with partners, the vaginal sexual changes tend to be minimized for many (Bachmann & Nevadansky, 2000), and the sense of sexual satisfaction may remain the same (Sharpe, 2004). Testosterone levels in women usually decline with age, but what level of this hormone is required for the continuation of sexual function and desire in any individual is not known (Kingsberg, 2002).

Among the typical physical sexual changes for males associated with aging are a slowing down of the erection response, especially to indirect stimulation; less firm erections; a decrease in the force of ejaculation and in the quantity of semen released; a lengthening of the time needed to experience orgasm; and a longer refractory period, the time it takes for a male to again experience orgasm. Males have no inevitable "male menopause" or "andropause" comparable to the female menopause, no decline in testosterone that can be shown to be caused directly by advancing age, although the majority of older men experience a decline (Sanders, 1999). As with females, the minimum level of testosterone needed to sustain sexual interest and function is not known. Men often remain fertile until the end of life (Sharpe, 2004).

The physical changes in the body and its sexual processes do not occur without context, however. What meaning do older persons place on these changes? In a society that focuses on youth as the standard for strength and beauty, many people in later life are influenced to develop a negative body image as they age. Males often tend to focus negatively on changes in their sexual functioning, particularly erection, and women to have concerns about their sexual attractiveness (Stimson, Wase, & Stimson, 1981). Older adults may fail to appreciate the possible advantages of the more leisurely approach to lovemaking that is available to the older individual or couple. Appreciation for the person within the body may receive more emphasis when one lives in an older body. The typical view of sexuality as erection focused invites men to negatively appraise their sexual performance when changes in erectile functioning occur. In time, their fears of being unable to engage in intercourse in the same way as before may prompt some men to avoid all sexual activities. Women may see erection changes as a sign that they are no longer attractive, an idea that seems to them to be confirmed when their male partner avoids sexual contact. Instead, both could benefit from framing the change as an opportunity to expand their repertoire of sexual behaviors to include more than just the genitals, continuing to provide pleasure for themselves and their partners (Deacon, Minichiello, & Plummer, 1995). Aging, in itself, does not cause sexual dysfunction (Sharpe, 2004).

SEXUAL DESIRE

The literature on sexual desire in older adults is mixed in its findings. Varying definitions of sexual desire across studies present a challenge in comparing one piece of research with another. Some studies have not operationally defined desire. Others have assumed that frequency of sexual intercourse is a measure of sexual desire, ignoring desire that may go unfulfilled because of health problems, negative attitudes, or lack of a partner. Gott and Hinchliff (2003, p. 1626) note that in many studies it seems that the researchers assumed that "if older people are not sexually active sex is not important to them."

DeLamater and Sill (2005, p. 139), noting that no universally accepted definition of desire exists in the literature, defined sexual desire for their research "in terms of cognitive events (sexual thoughts, sexual fantasies)" that motivate sexual experience. Using data from the 1999 AARP/Modern Maturity Sexuality Survey of persons 45 and older, they examined the association between sexual desire and several biopsychosocial factors. They reported a decrease in sexual desire associated with aging in both males and females, but not until age 75 or older did half or more of the participants report a low level of desire. The effects of the participants' attitudes toward sexuality were more predictive of sexual desire than any other factor measured. Significant predictors of continuing desire were rating sex as important to oneself and to one's relationship and, especially for women, being in a relationship.

Little research has asked older persons directly about their sexual behaviors, attitudes, or what sexuality means to them. Qualitative research is especially suited to exploring such questions because it allows the participants to speak for themselves. Gott and Hinchliff's (2003) study of 21 men and 23 women in the United Kingdom ages 50 to 92 explored, with both quantitative and qualitative methods, how important sex was to the participants. They found that all those who had a sexual partner placed some importance on sex. Those who reported sex as unimportant said that if they had a partner or had better health, sex would be important to them. Those in their 70s and 80s rated sex as less important than did the younger participants, but barriers to sex, such as health problems of the participant or the partner, or not having a partner, rather than age itself, were the attributions presented. Sex was reported as more pleasurable and of more importance compared with the past for a minority of these elderly participants.

INTIMACY AND SEXUAL POTENTIAL

Most people, including most professionals working with the elderly, think of sexual desire as a hunger for sexual behavior, usually defined as (hetero) sexual intercourse, followed by satiation after orgasm. Although the desire-as-hunger model, often called sex drive and associated with hormone levels, presents a part of the picture of sexuality, it overlooks the psychosocial aspects of the salience of the partner and the relationship. A relational model prioritizes desire for the partner, desire during sex, rather than simply desire for sexual activity itself. The hunger model suggests that desire comes out of emptiness, an emotionally immature stance that pushes people to attempt to fill or complete themselves by fusing with another. Schnarch (1991, 1997, 2002) encourages the definition of sexual desire as desire for the partner or desire *during* partnered sexual activity of any kind. This relational approach to desire leads to a more emotionally mature stance for each of the partners, an understanding of self as filled with love *for* the other rather than as empty and needing to be filled *by* the other. Desire in the emotionally mature person comes out of fullness, wholeness, a faith in oneself as powerfully loving and lovable, as complete and desirable, in and of oneself.

In an intensely erotic and intimate sexual experience, there is a powerful sense of self and *separateness* combined with a profound awareness of deep desire for and *connectedness* with the beloved partner—a paradox. Sexual expression from this perspective leads to self-validated intimacy rather than other-validated intimacy, a more emotionally mature position. Self-validated individuals are confident of their worth even without confirmation by a partner, whereas the other-validated need constant reassurance from others. Schnarch (1991) suggests that reaching this position, reaching one's sexual potential, rarely happens before middle or late life.

How might sexual potential be defined? Is human sexual expression only about successful movement through a sexual response cycle that ends with an orgasm? Is the pleasure of an erect penis, a lubricated vagina, increased heartbeat and respiration, or muscle tension the only purpose? If one has experienced orgasm, with another or alone, has one experienced the essence of sexuality, of sexual fulfillment, of sexual potential? What lies beyond orgasm? Is it possible to experience profoundly intense eroticism and intimacy, a passionate, transcendent sexual experience, without orgasm (Schnarch, 1991)?

Couples can be divided into three groups: the sexually dysfunctional, the sexually functional, and the "blessed few" (Schnarch, 1991, p. 71). Dysfunctional sex is characterized by overfocusing on the genital sexual response cycle and the sex drive model by an overanxious couple. Sex is seen as work. It lacks fun, playfulness, passion, and intimacy. Either partner may feel a "need" for sex rather than a desire for the partner, or may feel no interest in sexual behavior at all, which he or she experiences as inadequacy and the partner experiences as rejection. The couple may feel no real human connection during sexual activity, resulting in low levels of excitement or fears of inadequate "performance." These couples are usually not well developed emotionally. They lack a healthy balance between separateness and togetherness in relationships and have difficulty distinguishing between their thinking and feeling (Bowen, 1978; Kerr & Bowen, 1988). They may be emotionally fused or emotionally cut off from each other. They may be either excessively rational or emotionally reactive about their difficulties.

Biological factors such as low levels of hormones, illness, disability, or interference from medications may also influence sexual interaction. Yet for humans, the most important part of sexual experience is the meanings they place on it (Schnarch, 1991, 1997, 2002).

Most individuals and most couples in committed relationships and marriages experience functional sex most of the time. They want to have sex, they experience excitement and orgasm, and they define sex genitally. Over time, boredom and a lack of freshness or sense of novelty are common problems in couples who are not growing and accepting life's changes. Their "need" for sex still comes out of emptiness or partial emptiness. Each partner is focused on the desire for the sexual act and the release from tension. Many couples settle for functional sex rather than struggle with the hard work of filling their own emptiness by developing more self-confidence and emotional maturity. It takes well-developed humans who take responsibility for their own experience of sexuality to create passion, to spark eroticism. As the older partners in a long-term sexual relationship become more and more important to each other, they come to realize that, if the relationship continues, one partner will likely have to bury the other and suffer the intense pain that comes from the loss of a beloved partner. Out of lack of faith in their ability to handle such pain, many couples hold back from loving too completely, too well. Few couples use the sacredness of marriage and committed relationships to grow themselves up, to increase their tolerance for such anxiety (Schnarch, 1991, 1997).

Some couples experience sex as a transcendent spiritual encounter or connection with self, partner, and their God or the universe (Ogden, 1999, 2002; Schnarch, 1991; Shaw, 1994). A model of sexuality based on spirituality is very different from the traditional model of sexuality. It includes the physical and the psychological as well as the meanings that each of these has for the individual. It combines thinking and meaning making with intense feeling and ecstatic emotions. It involves having developed enough emotional maturity to be able to let go of the need to self-protect and to allow the self to be vulnerable. These couples are able to experience giving, receiving, and taking in the sexual encounter as indistinguishable from each other. These blessed few define passion as something far greater than the usual definition of simple physical desire or lust. They feel a passion for the partner, for life, for the universe or God. This passion involves mind- and brain-directed sex rather than genital- and hormone-driven sex. Sexuality based on an individual's spirituality is more about the meanings attached to sex than about the actual physical behaviors involved (Ogden, 2002). Few couples consistently experience the intense passion and eroticism of spirituality-based sex—many may never have such experiences. Those who do have transcendent sexual experiences typically are older couples in committed long-term relation-ships (Ogden, 2002; Schnarch, 1997; Shaw, 1994).

Shaw (1994, p. 134) conducted interviews with 65 men and women ranging in age from 50 to 92, asking, "To what do you attribute your present sexual growth and maturity?" The individuals and couples selected were people who, by their self-report, "seemed to be living life as fully and gloriously as their health per-mitted whether alone or with a partner" (p. 134). One description of personal sex-uality from this diverse group was the following from a 72-year-old: "I now experience my fingers as increasingly sensitive instruments of exploration, as radar alert digitals that can know the nibbling, grasping, undulating response of her flowing excitement" (p. 136).

A retired couple noted:

> We have been together for 43 years. The physical aspect of our marriage gets better each year, I think because we can tell each other the truth in every situation that af-fects our relationship. It isn't always pleasant but it's always lively. (p. 136)

Clearly, these older people conceptualize their sexuality relationally, as does this participant, who described her relationship with herself:

> At age 60+ I am a woman convinced that masturbation is the ongoing love affair I can have throughout my lifetime. My relationship with myself is the only constant I can count on. Husbands and lovers may come and go, but I am always here for my-self. (p. 137)

Older persons who experience sexuality in this manner are likely in the minority, yet their experience is as much a part of sexuality and aging as is the experience of those who might be placed in the sexually dysfunctional or functional cate-gories. Knowing that such transcendent experiences exist may prompt more cou-ples and individuals to move toward fulfilling their sexual potential.

ACKNOWLEDGING THE SEXUALITY OF OLDER PERSONS IN PRACTICE

Gerontology professionals and all who work with older persons are faced with the same myths about sexuality that the elderly themselves encounter. They also face the same lack of empirical information about the day-to-day sexual lives of older people. Reared in a society that has denied that older adults are or can be sexual—or more recently, almost seems to be insisting that they must be sexual—both service providers and their clients often struggle to understand the meaning of sexuality in later life. As the population ages, more programs are being devel-oped to raise the awareness of professionals (Lacy, 2002). Basic sex education re-garding what is known about elder sexuality is needed for those who serve older adults. In addition, training in developing greater comfort with sexuality in later life, in all of its many aspects, and improved skills in communicating about sexu-ality have been called for (Bonner, 1997).

BECOMING COMFORTABLE WITH THE SEXUALITY OF OLDER PERSONS

Gerontology professionals are often influenced by society's distaste for sexual expression in the elderly (Blackwell & Hunt, 1980; Hillman, 2000; Hillman &

Stricker, 1994; Nay, 1992). The discomfort service providers may experience when encountering sexuality in older persons creates barriers that can limit the free expression of sexuality and intimacy in their older clients. Education about sexuality in later life can be extremely useful to those who work with older persons, yet knowledge alone may not be enough to change negative attitudes and to create comfort. Learning the facts and dispelling the myths—myths that often lie out of awareness yet exert a powerful influence on attitudes and behaviors toward elderly sexuality—can greatly increase familiarity and comfort for professionals and staff when this learning is coupled with practice.

Why is it that so many physicians and nurses do not initiate conversations about sexuality with their older patients, waiting instead for the patients to bring up the topic themselves, or not even noticing that it has not been brought up? Why do many caregivers in nursing homes continue to be embarrassed, frightened, or amused by the sexual expressions of the residents? Why is it that some social workers carefully assess all their clients' needs except their sexuality needs? Why are administrators often embarrassed when callers ask what provisions their institutions make for the privacy of their residents to engage in sexual activity alone or with others? Despite their best intentions, many who work with the elderly still find themselves struggling with many complex thoughts and emotions that interfere with their ability to be most effective with those they serve. Language, both verbal and nonverbal, can either facilitate or close down open communication about sexuality and intimacy. When discussion is limited, the result is a client who has missed an opportunity to gain knowledge that can improve her or his sexual life (Brock & Jennings, 1999).

How can physicians, nurses, therapists, counselors, social workers, caregivers, and other service providers increase their comfort level? A good place to begin is with an honest self-assessment of one's personal attitudes and beliefs about sexuality in the elderly.

Personal Self-Assessment   The following questions constitute a useful self-assessment:

- Can I actually picture a couple in their 80s enjoying passionate, vibrant sex?
- Am I just a bit resentful when I realize that some older couples have a better sex life than I do?
- Am I comfortable with the idea of a woman or a man in late life masturbating to orgasm, self-pleasuring?
- How comfortable am I with the thought of an older couple giving and receiving oral sex? Can I imagine them experiencing passionate deep kissing?
- Do I assume that all the older people I work with are heterosexual unless I'm told otherwise?
- Can I picture an older male couple or female couple enjoying their lovemaking?
- How do I feel about an older widow or widower having sex with a variety of dating partners and not wanting to marry any of them?
- How easy is it for me to assess for sexually transmitted infections and HIV/AIDS when interviewing an older patient?
- How easily do I initiate a discussion of the sexuality and intimacy needs of my older clients?
- Do I feel secretly relieved when the topic of sex is not mentioned and reassure myself that I am protecting the older adult's privacy?

- How do I react when a "sexual situation" presents itself in my work with the elderly?
- What does my silence, changing of the subject, not taking the hint, laughing, or looking embarrassed communicate to my clients?

Once the gerontology professional knows the areas where personal growth is needed, action can begin. Some service providers may wish to take a formal sexuality education course with an experiential component designed to provide practice in developing greater comfort with issues of sexuality in later life. Others may decide to engage in their own personal growth program, tailored to the needs they have become aware of through self-assessment (Brock & Jennings, 1999). Those responsible for supervising the work of others serving older persons may implement training programs (Bonner, 1997; Hammond & Bonney, 1985; Walker & Harington, 2002).

Approaches to Increase Comfort and Skills   To become better at comfortably picturing the sexual expression of older persons and accepting it as valid and healthy, viewing videos depicting the elderly as sexually active can be very helpful. For example, *Moonstruck* (Palmer & Jewison, 1998) includes a romantic, late-night bedroom scene involving a couple in their 70s, followed by the playful, sexy morning after as they work in their delicatessen. *Wrestling Ernest Hemingway* (T. Black, Wizan, & Haines, 1993) features the very different ways that two older men, one divorced many times and the other never married, experience and express their sexuality. *Finnegan Begin Again* (Frost & Silver, 1984) portrays the intimate story of a man involved in May-December and then December-May relationships. A group of older friends, all now widowed, is depicted in *The Cemetery Club* (Brown & Duke, 1993), as each one experiences her sexuality in her own unique way. *Grumpy Old Men* (Berman & Petrie, 1993) combines laughter and tears in telling the story of three generations of men in two families. These are only a few examples of many movies that feature older adult sexuality. Additionally, sexuality education videos are available, such as *The Couples Guide to Great Sex over 40: Volume I* (Carson & Wiley, 1995), which interviews a couple in their 60s and features them enjoying their sensuality and sexuality, sharing a bubble bath with candlelight, soft music, and wine.

Reading about the sexual lives of the elderly is also useful. *Love, Sex, and Aging* (Brecher, 1984) reports, in their own words, the diverse responses to a nationwide survey of 50- to 93-year-olds and features such quotations as the following from an 82-year-old widow: "To be able to successfully masturbate in the later years . . . gives one a continued feeling of being a person . . . still a woman, still a man. . . . It keeps a necessary spark burning which says, 'I'm yet alive—all of me!'" (p. 241).

Reading chapter 14 in *Constructing the Sexual Crucible* (Schnarch, 1991), which includes the sexually explicit transcripts of the sex therapy sessions of a couple in their 60s seeking help for the husband's erectile dysfunction, can promote knowledge about resolving sexual difficulties as well as increasing comfort with sexual expression in later life. Such reading can help service providers gain a clearer picture of the variation in sexuality in late life.

Sometimes reluctance to talk openly with older persons stems from experiences with one's own parents as being unable to talk comfortably about sex and a respectful desire not to offend or embarrass an older person. One 37-year-old woman interviewed about the sexual discussions in her home as she grew up with her mother reported, "The information I got from her, more in an unspoken way, was, this was something you didn't really talk about. Bad, kind of" (Brock & Jennings, 1993, p. 63). Another woman, age 34, noted that when, as a teen, she initiated a conversation about sex with her mother,

> she would be embarrassed. You know—like say nothing or say, "I don't know." So you just don't put your parents usually in a position where you make them uncomfortable, out of respect—well, respect. You just think, "Well, this embarrasses her, so I'll just go ask someone else." (Brock & Jennings, p. 63)

Yet the elderly often want open communication about sexuality with their health care providers (Aizenberg, Weizman, & Barak, 2002). They hold back out of concern that they will be labeled a "dirty old man" or be patronized as "cute" for wanting a sexual life at their age. If they are single or widowed, they may worry about being labeled immoral for wanting to express their sexuality with partners or wanting to pleasure themselves. Many older adults will wait for the service provider to open the topic or may talk around the issue or make sexual jokes, looking for permission to say more. When the professional is able to pick up on these hints from the client or comfortably initiate a sexual discussion, the older person is often relieved and then able to gain the information and reassurance needed (Brock & Jennings, 1999).

When service providers have concluded from their self-assessment that they may be, at times, annoyed that "older folks do it better" (Cross, 1993, p. 9), they might comfort themselves with the knowledge that older couples are reaping the benefits of a lifetime of physical and emotional experience, often filled with a joy and emotional maturity that allows them to be more relaxed and at ease when making love. Recognizing the need to better understand one's own sexuality as an important part of being effective in working with older persons is a sign of maturity in the professional (Hammond & Bonney, 1985; Katzman & Katzman, 1985). Gerontology professionals can explore the unresolved sexuality issues in their own lives that may lead to discomfort in their work. Through reading books such as *Passionate Marriage* (Schnarch, 1997), which addresses personal growth in committed relationships, and through seeking sex therapy, relationship counseling, or other avenues to resolve their own sexuality issues, professionals can promote the development of their emotional maturity, whatever their age (Brock & Jennings, 1999).

Those whose self-assessment indicates a need to become more comfortable when discussing sexually transmitted infections and HIV/AIDS with the elderly need to know that in the decade ending in 2003, the total number of HIV/AIDS cases in adults 50 and over had risen from 16,288 to 90,513 ("Late Life Sex Ed," 2003). The number of older women with HIV/AIDS had grown faster than that of older men, and most women's cases involved heterosexual contact (Levy, 2001). Older women experiencing vaginal dryness may have more tears and abrasions, putting them at greater risk of infection. When physicians and other health care providers assume their older patients are not engaging in any sexual behaviors, they miss the chance to educate and to properly diagnose HIV and other sexually transmitted infections ("Late Life Sex Ed," 2003). Older individuals can and do engage in unsafe sex, whether knowingly or not, and need accurate information and encouragement to protect themselves.

If one's personal assessment points to discomfort or lack of knowledge about sexual orientation variation, many resources are available, including the following books: *Gay and Gray: The Older Homosexual Man* (Berger, 1995), *Couple Therapy with Gay Men* (Greenan & Tunnell, 2003), *Lesbians over 60 Speak for Themselves* (Kehoe, 1989), and *The Lesbian Family Life Cycle* (Slater, 1995).

Quam (1993) discussed a variety of sexual and relationship concerns that may affect older lesbian and gay individuals. For example, many fear that their partners will be turned away by professionals as outsiders rather than being accepted as spouses, or that their families of choice may not be treated with the same respect as families of origin or families of procreation. Deevy (1990) provided some excellent suggestions for discussing these clients' sexuality needs. Asking open-ended questions such as "Who is most important to you?" rather than "Are you married, widowed, or divorced?" (p. 37) is one of the many examples offered to open space for older persons to be themselves if they wish to come out. Gerontology professionals can reassure older gay and lesbian individuals who may have spent a lifetime hiding their sexual orientation from a disapproving society that they and their relationships are valued and respected. Altman (1999) noted that homosexually oriented individuals may be isolated and invisible to service providers, who seem not to realize that gay and lesbian people grow old too. Ward, Vass, Aggarwal, Garfield, and Cybyk (2005) found that the homosexual population in care settings is not acknowledged, rendered invisible by heterosexist assumptions, or disapproved of or ridiculed. Yet on a positive note, research has shown that for many the process of building a gay or lesbian identity in a rejecting society has helped in developing coping mechanisms that are useful in resisting the stigma of aging (Altman, 1999; Sharpe, 2004).

Another way for service providers to become more comfortable and knowledgeable about gay, lesbian, bisexual, and transgendered sexuality is to attend a meeting of Parents, Families and Friends of Lesbians and Gays (P-FLAG). Most large cities have a chapter where visitors are welcome. The national organization maintains an extensive website at www.pflag.org containing much useful information.

Often, learning more about some basic approaches used in communicating about sexuality can greatly improve a professional's effectiveness in working with older persons. For those interested in improving their ability to communicate about elder sexuality, one area to focus on is the client's level of sexual language (Brock & Jennings, 1999). People vary in the vocabulary they use when discussing sexuality. At least five levels of language may be used: scientific language (vulva, coitus, ejaculate, fellatio, cunnilingus), common discourse (womb, breasts, having sex, oral sex), euphemisms (down there, marital relations, come, thing, it), street talk (fuck, screw, jack off, knockers, going down on, pussy), and childhood (wee wee, weenie, boobies). Matching the client's level of language and careful questioning by the service provider can ensure that each fully understands what the other intends to communicate and can ensure greater comfort for all. When the professional is shocked or repulsed by street talk or amused at the use of childhood language, clients may refuse to talk further. These may be the only terms that some older adults know, so it is the responsibility of the professional to offer acceptance and comfort with their ways of talking. Over time, it may be possible to help clients develop a more varied and appropriate approach to discussing sexuality (Brock & Jennings, 1999).

In opening discussions of sexual topics, it is useful to begin with the least sensitive topic and to be as open, comfortable, and matter-of-fact as possible. The older person should be seen as the guide in whether comfort is being maintained in the conversation. Third-person phrasing is useful, for example, "Many older adults find that pleasuring themselves is a behavior they enjoy," rather than second-person phrasing such as "It's okay for you to pleasure yourself." The phrase "many older adults" allows the patient a sense of choice, whereas the use of "you" is more directive and personal. Third-person phrasing provides some conversational distance and will likely increase comfort (Brock & Jennings, 1999).

Gerontology professionals wanting to increase their comfort in sexuality discussions with older persons can gain valuable practice by interviewing one of their parents or another older relative. Approaching her or him as a consultant who can assist with development of this professional skill, the service provider can begin with a question such as "What are your thoughts about sexuality and older persons?" or "What can you tell me about how you learned about sexuality growing up?" Very general topics or topics focused in the past are often a good place to begin. While listening to the older relative, one can monitor the comfort level of self and other by noticing muscle tension, breathing, tone of voice, and pace in speaking. The body mirrors the level of comfort. As one releases tension, a corresponding sense of ease usually becomes apparent in the interviewee as well. Although many may hesitate at the idea of discussing sexuality with a parent or other older relative, families are a rich resource when it comes to increasing comfort levels. When professionals become comfortable with those of greatest importance to them and can see them as sexual people, they will likely be highly effective in working with older clients (Brock & Jennings, 1999).

HELPING OLDER PERSONS WITH SEXUAL DIFFICULTIES

An older person may present for treatment of a sexual difficulty to her or his physician, who will conduct a comprehensive physical examination, blood analysis, and interview concerning the onset and course of the problem, as well as a sexual and relationship history. Often, older persons seek the help of a marriage and family therapist, couple or relationship counselor, psychologist, social worker, or sex therapist first, without seeing a physician. In that case, the older client should be referred for a comprehensive exam before beginning therapy or counseling, just as a younger client should be.

Once physical health issues have been attended to or ruled out by the physician, assessment and treatment can begin with the individual or couple. It is important that therapists and clients alike think in terms of "people experiencing sexual difficulties" rather than "sexually dysfunctional people"; the former opens up a much more positive and hopeful frame for addressing the difficulties from a base of client strengths and resilience (Donahey & Miller, 2001).

Biological, sociocultural, and psychological factors all impact male and female sexuality and sexual function, either enhancing sexual expression or promoting sexual difficulties (Greenberg, Bruess, & Haffner, 2004). All of these elements, in turn, are affected by the quality of the relationship and the context in which the sexual expression takes place. Life is a process of continual change and moment-to-moment happenings. From a phenomenological perspective, it is clear that the meanings each individual and couple chooses to place on these changes determine much of how the changes will impact them (Aanstoos, 2001).

Donahey and Miller (2001, p. 212) write, "Research on the common factors suggests that successful 'sex therapy' is more about therapy with people who happen to be experiencing sexual difficulties than about the application of a unique therapeutic modality or treatment technique (e.g., squeeze technique, sensate focus)" (p. 212). Therapeutic techniques and approaches are many and varied, derived from dozens of theoretical foundations. Among the choices of models and approaches are the Permission, Limited Information, Specific Suggestions, and Intensive Therapy (PLISSIT) model (Annon, 1976), the Masters and Johnson (1970) model, the Kaplan (1974) model, other behavioral models (Leiblum & Rosen, 2000; LoPiccolo & LoPiccolo, 1978), the McCarthy model (McCarthy & McCarthy, 2003), Barbach's (1991) program, and the Crucible Approach (Schnarch, 1991, 1997, 2002). The choice of approach should take into account the context of the clients, for example, starting with suggestions for new sexual positions (a behavioral technique) for those whose arthritis pain is limiting sexual interactions. In other cases, basic sexuality education may be needed. As with any therapy for any type of problem, issues of gender, ethnicity and culture, religion and spirituality, sexual orientation, illness and health, and many other factors are a part of the context of the work.

Older persons and couples experience the same difficulties as the young, but the most common of these difficulties for older men is erectile difficulty and decreased sexual desire and for older women is difficulty with vaginal lubrication and decreased sexual desire. Even these specific types of problems are best seen in context rather than as isolated issues. Changes associated with aging certainly contribute to these sexual difficulties (LoPiccolo, 1991); however, whether a suggestion of a vaginal lubricant or a trial of an erection-enhancing drug is effective will lie partly in the meanings the individual and couple place on the issue and in the quality of the couple relationship. The majority of sexual difficulties involving decreased sexual desire may be more about the relationship than about the need for hormone therapy, although testosterone therapy is indicated in some cases. Many cases of these difficulties that involve only biological factors are easily resolved by physicians. The majority of cases involve a complex web of contextual sociocultural, psychological, and relational factors (Greenberg et al., 2004). These may include negative sexual attitudes, fears of sexual inadequacy, the sexual double standard and other narrow conceptions of masculinity and femininity, rigid religious restrictions on sexuality, unrealistic expectations created by mass media, narrow sexual scripts, habituation to routinized sexual interactions, guilt, grief, depression, and myriad relationship issues such as resentments, conflict, jealousy, affairs, and abuse.

An in-depth discussion of sexual couple therapy with older adults is beyond the scope of this chapter. Many excellent research-based works are available, among them *Rekindling Sexual Desire: A Step-by-Step Program to Help Low-Sex and No-Sex Marriages* (McCarthy & McCarthy, 2003), *The Handbook of Sexuality in Close Relationships* (Harvey, Wenzel, & Sprecher, 2004), *New Directions in Sex Therapy: Innovations and Alternatives* (Kleinplatz, 2001), *Quickies: The Handbook of Brief Sex Therapy* (Green & Flemons, 2004), *Handbook of Clinical Sexuality for Mental Health Professionals* (Levine, Risen, & Althof, 2003), *Constructing the Sexual Crucible: An Integration of Sexual and Marital Therapy* (Schnarch, 1991), and *Resurrecting Sex: Resolving Sexual Problems and Rejuvenating Your Relationship* (Schnarch, 2002). These books contain much useful material for the mental health professional whose work with older adults includes helping them improve their sexual lives.

Case Studies

The following case studies illustrate the aliveness, sensuality, and sexuality present in the lives of older persons. As with the young, the variation in the sexuality of older adults is noteworthy.

Louis and Judy

Louis was an 84-year-old retired electrician who worked in his own small business until age 82, when he had a mild stroke. The stroke signaled to Louis that he should retire; he had trained a younger man as his assistant for 17 years and had always discussed selling the business to him.

Retirement was a big adjustment for Louis. He had always enjoyed his work and found great satisfaction in pleasing his customers. He had always bragged about the importance of everyone being a "productive citizen" and a proud taxpayer. He had been a significant citizen in his rural community and had been active in its social life with his wife, Helen, for many years. Much of what had always filled Louis with pride was now taken from him.

Louis and Helen had an enjoyable social and sex life for 50-some years, until Helen had a massive heart attack and died. It was shortly after Helen's death that Louis experienced the mild stroke and was told by his physician that he should retire and slow down.

Louis was lost without his identity of electrician and community activist, and without his beloved Helen. Their two children, a son and a daughter, had moved from the area during their young adult years and had established their families and careers in neighboring states. The son lived 6 hours away and the daughter lived 9 hours away.

As Louis's health deteriorated, depression seemed to consume his life, and he occasionally thought about suicide. Finally, at his doctor's insistence and with encouragement from his son and daughter, Louis agreed to go to the local nursing home and give it a try for a few months—-but certainly no longer. At the nursing home, Louis's depression increased and he became more negative as he observed many of his former customers and friends struggling in poor health, some using wheelchairs or walkers, and some having to be fed. Louis gave the staff a bad time and often spent long hours sitting on the patio in deep depression. He was adamant with his doctor and the nursing staff that he would not take *any* antidepressant and did not want them to mention it again.

During the 4th month of Louis's trial with the nursing home, an 82-year-old woman, Judy, moved into the independent living section of the facility. Judy was a retired schoolteacher who had lost her mate 9 years before. She was lonely and decided that living in a group setting was her best option for this chapter of her life. As a young woman, Judy had dated and been sexual with men, although she had always found both men and women sexually attractive. Her last committed relationship had been with a female coworker, Joanne, 10 years her senior.

Judy was an only child from a small extended family. Both of her parents had been killed in an auto accident when she was 43 years old. Judy had thought about marriage at times, but never met the man she thought was Mr. Right. Her few distant relatives had openly welcomed her relationship with Joanne and seemed interested in her life fulfillment and happiness. After Joanne's death, Judy said life would go forward for her. She had lived alone for 9 years and was in good health when she joined the center.

Judy seemed to take an interest in Louis. She occasionally asked if she could join him for meals and if she could just sit with him on the patio and enjoy the colorful sunsets. At first, Louis was rather rude to her. He appeared almost to take satisfaction in his depression and was not very talkative. Judy sat quietly and gently began conversations when Louis seemed able to tolerate the engagement. Over time, Louis seemed to open up to Judy's attempts to engage him in conversations. After a while he began to seek her out for company at meal times and to ask her to join him in watching the sunset or an early full moon come up in the East. Then one Friday morning after breakfast, Louis asked Judy if she would be willing to accompany him on the bus that the nursing home provided to visit the local senior center for the Friday night dance and social time. Judy accepted, and both found that they had a pleasant time. Each especially enjoyed the closeness of holding one another and slow dancing.

They grew closer rather quickly. Louis seemed to abandon his complaints about being in the nursing home, became more pleasant with others, especially with the staff, and expressed less grief over the loss of his work identity. He talked less and less about the loss of his beloved Helen. His depression lifted a great deal and he found himself inviting Judy to join him in activities such as walks around the grounds, walks to a nearby duck pond at the local community college, and on field trips the facility provided.

Some of the staff at the facility began to make fun of Louis and Judy, calling them "the old geezer lovers." Two of the more mature members of the staff discussed with management the need for training about the importance of sexuality and intimacy in later life. They gently educated the staff about the advantages to all, clients and staff, when the residents' needs for touching and contact comfort, sensuality, sexuality, and relationships were treated with respect and dignity.

Although neither Louis nor Judy had engaged in intercourse for a number of years, they discovered that they both greatly enjoyed touching each other, kissing, and giving each other hand, facial, arm, and foot massages. Louis seemed to rediscover his sensuality, lost during his grieving, and got great pleasure and joy from kissing and touching and from joking and sharing time with Judy. Once Louis wandered into Judy's room and found her with a book. He asked what she was reading. She replied, "Some of my favorite poetry!" Louis asked her to read it to him. He found that he deeply enjoyed spending time with Judy and having her read poetry aloud to him. Judy, too, greatly enjoyed their "poetry and love talk time" together, and it became a regular part of their days. The staff noted that Louis's depression lifted and he spent more time joking and socializing with the other residents and the staff.

Louis's daughter and son were accepting of their father's behavior and his new relationship and enjoyed seeing him happier. They repeatedly told Judy how much they appreciated what she meant to their father. They brought her small gifts or flowers when they came to visit. The nursing home staff enjoyed seeing Louis, Judy, and one of Louis's children going out for dinner on the rare visits and special occasions. The children felt good knowing that their father had someone close by that loved, appreciated, and cared about him. They also enjoyed knowing that he again had someone to love, as they remembered him as a very loving husband to their mother and a caring father. They knew he had much love to give and would be happier doing so.

Although some would not count Judy and Louis as a sexually active couple, the companionship, social events, poetry reading, touching, kissing, holding hands, going on walks, and watching the sun go down and the moon come up became very sensual and sexually fulfilling for both and provided much satisfaction as they approached the end of life.

George and Florence

This case is based on the second author's private practice in marital and family therapy with an emphasis in sex therapy. The couple was referred by Florence's gynecologist when she shared with him how upset her husband was about not having erections. George (age 71) and Florence (age 68) related in their first session how upset George was about his inability to have and maintain erections. Florence said she enjoys sex, but that George's erections are not that important to her, as they can have fun without his erections. George appeared to be much older than his years, was overweight and in poor physical shape, yet he told of continuing to work full time as a maintenance engineer for a small church-related college. He reported having congestive heart failure, an enlarged heart, and an irregular heartbeat and taking medication for his high blood pressure. He said he had tried injections for erections, without success, and taking Viagra, approved by his cardiologist and primary care physician. With Viagra he said he has occasional minimal erections, but cannot maintain them long enough for intercourse to occur.

Florence described herself as fat and in poor physical shape. She works full time in billing and supplies for a local tech company. She reported taking medications for blood pressure and acid reflux and a "water pill." Although Florence was not especially disappointed at the loss of George's erections, which she accepted as "just how things are," she was annoyed that he seemed lately to be continually requesting sexual activity, kissing and hugging her "constantly."

George said that erections are very important to him as that is "the measure of a man." During the first session they both talked about the rich and glorious sex life they have had since marrying as virgins shortly after graduating from high school. Although neither had had other sexual partners, perhaps leading some to assume that their sexual repertoire was limited, that was not the case. Florence talked about George being good at oral sex because he has a "stout and durable tongue" that pleases her. Each spoke of the many things they have tried over the years. They both laughed as they talked about their rich sexual lives and some of the "kinky" sexual experiences they have tried, especially after their children left home. They have always been open to self-pleasuring and manually stimulating each other. They reported that it has been great!

Despite George's rich sexual life, in many ways his definitions of sexuality, sensuality, and masculinity remained limited. His sense of "having sex" remained focused on his having erections. He was not aware of the difference in cerebral erections and tactile erections, so a discussion was initiated by the therapist about how cerebral erections, which occur rather automatically from a variety of nonphysical triggers, may cease to occur for most males anywhere between 35 and 70 years of age. Tactile erections can still occur, but as men age, it may take more, and often unique, physical stimulation for erections to develop. It was evident that this was new information for George and Florence.

Attention was given during the following sessions to the couple's sexual socialization and the sexual scripts that both of the partners had internalized about sex, intimacy, sexuality, men and women, and masculinity and femininity. Much time in the sessions was spent sorting out George's concerns about erections. Was it erections that he most wanted? Or was it ejaculation? Or was it orgasms that concerned him most? It was new information to George that it is possible, although much less common, for men to experience any one of the three without the others, and that they can occur in different combinations.

When the couple was asked in a session to stand up and hug each other for as long as possible, it was evident that George needed more "togetherness" than Florence. Florence became a bit uncomfortable and tried to break the hug three times before achieving success on the fourth attempt. During the hugging George kept kissing and nibbling on Florence's ear and neck. Later George talked about how he likes to cuddle much more than Florence does.

Much of the therapy focused on expanding George's sexual scripts about what it means to be a man. He was encouraged to spend more time with his adult children and to open up his communication with his children and grandchildren, to help more in various ways around the house, to engage in more "feminine" nurturing activities, and to observe men in nontraditional activities. Florence worked on becoming more comfortable with togetherness in different forms, such as more touching, more hugging, more kissing, more cuddling, and more shared household work. She gradually began to initiate sexual interactions more often with George and enjoyed their closeness more.

Both Florence and George benefited from information about typical sexual changes that occur with aging. Some of this information distracted George from focusing too much on erections and encouraged him to get some of his own togetherness needs satisfied in ways other than intercourse. The couple had engaged in giving and receiving oral sex on many occasions, yet Florence was amazed at what she experienced when she first gave George oral sex while his penis was flaccid. She was surprised at how much sensual pleasure she felt. This experience reflects one example of their limited sexual scripts: "Fellatio can occur only if a man has an erection." George was asked to observe more carefully the differing sensations while being stimulated in the flaccid state and the erect state. He reported that he actually felt greater stimulation in the flaccid state. He learned to enjoy more of his sensuality and sexuality without the necessity of an erection.

As George explored and expanded his sexual scripts to include more ways of touching and being intimate, he opened up his ideas about masculinity and became more satisfied with his sexual life and less dependent on erections. As time passed, even though George was able to achieve and maintain an erection only on rare occasions, he became more satisfied with life as an older man. The modifications to his sexual scripts seemed to free him to consider himself still a "real man," now defined more broadly.

Although George and Florence had enjoyed vital sexuality for over 40 years of their marriage, they lacked adequate physiological sexual information and were embedded in narrow and restrictive sexual scripts. One challenge in working with older persons is helping them to expand and modify their sexual scripts regarding what it means to be masculine or feminine. What does it mean to be sexual? What is sensuality? What are some new ways of loving? How do you love yourself and your partner differently as you age? These scripts are influenced by family of origin, religious upbringing, sexual experiences, and much more. Many older persons have made major changes in their sexual scripts throughout their lives on their own, especially at retirement time, when many individuals take stock of the years past and look forward to the time remaining. Others are stuck and need help in making these shifts in meaning for their sexual lives.

SOCIAL POLICY AND SEXUALITY IN LATER LIFE

Information on sexuality is a pressing need among older persons (Sharpe, 2004). Sexual enrichment education for older persons, including information about sexual anatomy, physiology, sexual pleasure, intimacy and companionship, and the changes that may be a part of the aging process could greatly enhance the lives of older adults (Deacon et al., 1995; Richard, 2001; White & Catania, 1982). Many of today's older women and men may have negative attitudes toward self-pleasuring and open discussion of sexuality and intimacy issues and may lack adequate knowledge of HIV/AIDS and other sexually transmitted infections (Blank, 2000; Levy, 2001/2002). They may have grown up with limited definitions of sexual pleasuring in which sexual intercourse was considered the only appropriate behavior. The need for older persons to expand their conceptualization of acceptable sexual behaviors can be addressed through sexual enhancement education (Badgwell, 1982; Cogen & Steinman, 1990; Hawton, Goth, & Day, 1994; Levine, 1998). Specific programs and approaches are needed to promote positive attitudes among older persons, such as a senior sexuality workshop offered as a part of the Northwest Wellness Conference for Seniors held in Seattle (Richard, 2001). Such programs could be made available to adults in late life through local senior community centers so that all, regardless of income, could access them.

The elderly themselves are not the only ones who need information about sexuality. Education on sexuality and intimacy in late life ought to be a part of the training for all human service providers who work in the gerontology field. Sexual myths, taboos, and attitudes need to be addressed, and basic respect for the importance of sexuality and intimacy in the lives of older persons must be conveyed. Nay (1992, p. 314) spoke of the value of sexuality for older men and women eloquently: "Sex in late life is associated with pleasure, release from tension, communication, mutual tenderness, passion, affirmation of one's body and its functioning, a sense of identity, and security when the outside world threatens people with hazards and losses." Integrating this information into all aspects of caring for older persons could greatly enhance their well-being.

Variation in the sexuality needs of older persons must also be addressed. Not all older men and women are heterosexual. Sexual orientation differences must be acknowledged and respected by those who work with older adults. Ward et al. (2005) have called for information for caregivers on sexual orientation and how to handle the anxiety and discomfort that many feel in dealing with the issue. The older gay and lesbian population has the same needs for sexual expression and sharing of intimacy as heterosexual individuals.

Policy changes in older persons' communal living arrangements, assisted living centers, and nursing homes allowing greater privacy for residents to engage in sexual activity could foster freedom for intimacy and healthy sexual expression to flourish. The current lack of privacy in nursing facilities may lead to inappropriate sexual expression by some individuals (Ward et al., 2005).

Limited economic resources often prevent older persons from having opportunities for greater sexual fulfillment. With many retired women existing on incomes of $7,000 yearly and many couples having joint incomes of $25,000 or less, their opportunities for engagement with others are limited (Bach, 2002). Adequate economic resources could permit freedom from worry about maintaining minimal living standards and facilitate the enjoyment of sexuality and intimacy (DeLamater & Sill, 2005). Programs that help older persons to achieve a higher income level could have a positive influence on every aspect of their lives.

As important as the medical aspects of aging are, taking a strictly physical health perspective in addressing elderly adults' needs may lead to limiting or overlooking the salience of emotional and relational influences on the overall quality of life. Too often, established health policies and procedures prevent or make it difficult for older persons to express their sexuality and achieve greater intimacy (Rossi, 1994). There is a need for medical personnel to speak more openly with older persons about the influence of their medications on their feelings, especially on their expression of intimacy and sexuality (Crenshaw & Goldberg, 1996; Finger, Lund, & Slagle, 1997). Too often group data are presented about the impact of prescription drugs on sexuality, ignoring individual variation. Although the data may suggest that a particular drug has little impact on sexuality, it may be very limiting for a specific individual's sexuality. As important as intimacy is at all stages of life, more attention must be focused on how specific drugs may be impacting the individual's sexual life.

FUTURE RESEARCH DIRECTIONS

With the increasing numbers of older persons around the world, more and better research that examines many different aspects of sexuality in later life is needed. Much of the limited research available has taken a quantitative approach and often has not been rigorous enough in terms of sampling, research methodology, and statistical analysis (Wiederman, 2004). More quantitative and qualitative research with both broad and focused sampling is needed. The following are some suggestions for research that would provide better data for enhancing older people's sexual lives.

Research is limited on older women and men in their 80s and 90s who are leading rich sexual lives (Shaw, 1994), especially those who are doing so in spite of serious health problems. Qualitative research is particularly suited for such studies. A few of the participants in Gott and Hinchliff's (2003) well-designed study using qualitative and quantitative data reported sex as very important to them in later life as compared to unimportant earlier in their lives. A follow-up study on these older persons might be most useful.

More research that looks at how sexual attitudes and sexual knowledge influence older people's sexual behavior and sexual satisfaction is needed. Sexual attitudes and sexual knowledge impact one's individual sexual behavior and sexuality in relationships, yet little is known about how these affect each other. More research is needed that looks at the level of sexual knowledge and the sexual attitudes of the current generation entering the ranks of older persons. Interestingly, one study found more similarity in the sexual attitudes of teen females and those of their grandmothers than between the teens and their own mothers (S. Black, 1988).

Hormones play a role in older people's sexuality, yet there is little dependable information on the influence of hormone levels on older women's and older men's sexuality (Sharpe, 2004). Confounding variables, limited sample sizes, and other methodological issues complicate such research (Wiederman, 2004). How is it that a decline in one person's hormone level has no effect on his or her sexual desire or satisfaction, while in another the same decline has a dramatic effect?

Research exploring how early sexual experiences influence sexuality over the life course is limited. Much could be learned by exploring how such events, positive and negative, may impact sexual attitudes and sexual behavior during the final decades of the life span.

Limited research on aging and sexuality within and across ethnic groups exists (Mahay et al., 2001). Each ethnic group contains subcultures and variations in acculturation to the majority group, as well as variations in education and socioeconomic level. Surely there are differences in ideologies, meanings, definitions, beliefs, attitudes, and behaviors within these subcultures that also vary with age. These differences and similarities, if illuminated, could foster an understanding of human diversity leading to sexual respect, dignity, and freedom for all.

More research connecting the use of pharmaceuticals and their impact on sexual attitudes, desire, and functioning would be useful. Little is known about the impact of pharmaceuticals on the sexual lives of older persons.

There is great need for both quantitative and qualitative research that explores exactly what older persons are doing sexually, using the broadest possible definitions of sexual behavior. Too often research is genitally focused. What is missed with this limited definition? The richness of qualitative research would do much to foster sexual freedom and inform gerontology service providers and society at large about the variability of sexuality in the lives of older persons (Hillman, 2000).

How do individual personal characteristics, relationship factors, life contexts, and cultural settings influence sexual desire and sexual pleasure? How does overall quality of life and enjoyment in other areas of life impact one's sexuality in later life? How does life context enhance or hinder the expression of one's sexuality? Is there a difference in the sexual life of older couples who are retired compared to that of older couples still working full time? How different is the sexual life of older couples who are rearing grandchildren versus those free of such responsibilities? There is a need for research that examines how life contexts impact sexual desire and sexual pleasures.

Little is known about how religious and spiritual beliefs impact the older couple's sexuality. Couples of mixed religious backgrounds may or may not express their sexuality in different ways than couples with the same religious background. Does level of religious devotion have an influence? For example, do devout older Catholic couples express their sexuality in the same ways as the less devout? The spiritual setting is extremely challenging to sort out as spirituality is multidimensional and can lead to many different combinations of independent variables (Ogden, 2002). Yet this kind of research could be very helpful in assisting older couples with their sexuality issues.

Research into what constitutes a rich sexual life for the older person would help to define what constitutes sexual dysfunction in older women and older men. It would be of great benefit to sex therapists as they attempt to help older individuals and couples.

Research that takes a functional approach would greatly assist us in understanding the sexuality of older persons. A functional approach would examine how the older person's sexuality promotes life satisfaction, or causes problems for one or both partners. Much of the current research examines how one's sexuality compares to that of others. Statistical norms do not explain the qualitative aspects of people's sexuality. Opportunities should not become obligations.

Much of the research has been limited by sampling techniques, research design, and limitations imposed by questionnaires. Large segments of the older population have been excluded from sampling. Many sexuality studies have had extremely small samples, limiting the ability to generalize to larger populations of older adults. Often the design of studies has been too narrow, using closed questionnaires with few or no opportunities for the participants' input. For the research professional, much remains to be done in the largely unexplored field of sexuality in late life.

CONCLUSION

Gerontology service providers will be working with an ever-increasing older population, predicted to double in size to 72 million people in the next 25 years (U.S. Census Bureau, 2006). Because sexuality and intimacy are essential elements in the lives of all humans, they must be addressed in the lives of all older persons. All who care for older persons are challenged to become more knowledgeable about and more comfortable with sexuality and intimacy in the final decades of life.

REFERENCES

Aanstoos, C. M. (2001). Phenomenology of sexuality. In P. J. Kleinplatz (Ed.), *New directions in sex therapy: Innovations and alternatives* (pp. 69–90). New York: Brunner/Routledge.

Aizenberg, D., Weizman, A., & Barak, Y. (2002). Attitudes toward sexuality among nursing home residents. *Sexuality and Disability, 20,* 185–189.

Altman, C. (1999). Gay and lesbian seniors: Unique challenges of coming out in later life. *SIECUS Report, 27*(3), 14–17.

Annon, J. S. (1976). *The behavioral treatment of sexual problems: Brief therapy.* New York: Harper & Row.

Bach, D. (2002). *Smart couples finish rich.* New York: Broadway.

Bachmann, G., & Nevadansky, N. (2000). Diagnosis and treatment of atrophic vaginitis. *American Family Physician, 61,* 3090–3096.

Badgwell, N. (1982). *Sexual enrichment program effectiveness with normal couples.* Unpublished doctoral dissertation, Texas Woman's University, Denton.

Barbach, L. (1991). *For yourself: The fulfillment of female sexuality.* New York: New American Library.

Berger, R. M. (1995). *Gay and gray: The older homosexual man* (2nd ed.). New York: Haworth.

Berman, R. C. (Producer), & Petrie, D. (Director). (1993). *Grumpy old men* [Videotape]. United States: Warner Home Video.

Black, S. (1988). *Across three generations: A study of religiosity and sexual attitudes.* Unpublished master's thesis, Texas Woman's University, Denton.

Black, T., & Wizan, J. (Producers), & Haines, R. (Director). (1993). *Wrestling Ernest Hemingway* [Videotape]. United States: Warner Home Video.

Blackwell, D. L., & Hunt, S. S. (1980). Sexuality and aging: Staff attitudes toward sexual expression among nursing home residents. *Journal of Minority Aging, 5,* 273–277.

Blank, J. (2000). *Good vibrations: The new complete guide to vibrators.* San Francisco: Down There Press.

Bonner, G. (1997). Helping health care professionals on issues of intimacy and sexuality among the aging. *SIECUS Report, 25*(5), 4–7.

Bowen, M. (1978). *Family therapy in clinical practice.* New York: Aronson.

Brecher, E. M. (1984). *Love, sex, and aging: A Consumers Union report.* Boston: Little, Brown.

Brock, L. J., & Jennings, G. (1993). Sexuality education: What daughters in their 30s wish their mothers had told them. *Family Relations, 42*, 61–65.

Brock, L. J., & Jennings, G. (1999). Getting comfortable with senior sexuality. *Southwest Journal on Aging, 15*(1), 15–21.

Brown, D. (Producer), & Duke, B. (Director). (1993). *The cemetery club* [Videotape]. United States: Touchstone Home Video.

Budd, K. (1999, September/October). The facts of life. *Modern Maturity,* 86–87.

Burgess, E. O. (2004). Sexuality in midlife and later life couples. In J. H. Harvey, A. Wenzel, & S. Sprecher (Eds.), *The handbook of sexuality in close relationships* (pp. 437–454). Mahwah, NJ: Erlbaum.

Carson, C., & Wiley, D. (1995). *The couples guide to great sex over 40: Vol. I* [Videotape]. (Available from Sinclair Institute, P. O. Box 8865, Chapel Hill, NC 27515)

Cogen, R., & Steinman, W. (1990). Sexual function and practice in elderly men of lower socioeconomic status. *Journal of Family Practice, 32,* 162–166.

Crenshaw, T. L., & Goldberg, J. P. (1996). *Sexual pharmacology: Drugs that affect sexual functioning.* New York: Norton.

Cross, R. J. (1993). What doctors and others need to know: Six facts on human sexuality and aging. *SIECUS Report, 21*(5), 7–9.

Deacon, S., Minichiello, V., & Plummer, D. (1995). Sexuality and older people: Revisiting the assumptions. *Educational Gerontology, 21,* 497–513.

Deevy, S. (1990). Older lesbian women: An invisible minority. *Journal of Gerontological Nursing, 16*(5), 35–39.

DeLamater, J., & Sill, M. (2005). Sexual desire in later life. *Journal of Sex Research, 42,* 138–149.

Donahey, K. M., & Miller, S. D. (2001). "What works" in sex therapy: A common factors perspective. In P. J. Kleinplatz (Ed.), *New directions in sex therapy: Innovations and alternatives* (pp. 210–233). New York: Brunner/Routledge.

Dunn, M. E., & Cutler, N. (2000). Sexual issues in older adults. *AIDS Patient Care and STDs, 14,* 67–69.

Finger, W., Lund, M., & Slagle, M. (1997). Medications that may contribute to sexual disorders. *Journal of Family Practice, 44,* 33–43.

Frost, G. (Producer), & Silver, J. M. (Director). (1984). *Finnegan Begin Again* [Videotape]. United States: HBO Premier Films.

Gagnon, J. (1977). *Human sexualities.* New York: Scott, Foresman.

Global Study of Sexual Attitudes and Behaviors. (2002). *Global Study of Sexual Attitudes and Behaviors.* Retrieved February 18, 2006, from http://www.pfizerglobalstudy.com/study-results.arp.

Gott, M. (2003). Review essay. *Sexualities, Evolution and Gender, 5,* 41–44.

Gott, M., & Hinchliff, S. (2003). How important is sex in later life? The views of older people. *Social Science and Medicine, 56,* 1617–1628.

Green, S., & Flemmons, D. (2004). *Quickies: The handbook of brief sex therapy.* New York: Norton.

Greenan, D. E., & Tunnell, G. (2003). *Couple therapy with gay men.* New York: Guilford Press.

Greenberg, J. S., Bruess, C. E., & Haffner, D. W. (2004). *Exploring the dimensions of human sexuality* (2nd ed.). Boston: Jones & Bartlett.

Gross, G., & Blundo, R. (2005). Viagra: Medical technology constructing aging masculinity. *Journal of Sociology and Social Welfare, 32*, 85–97.

Hammond, D. B., & Bonney, W. C. (1985). Results of sex education for support persons working with the elderly. *Journal of Sex Education and Therapy, 11*(2), 42–45.

Harvey, J. H., Wenzel, A., & Sprecher, S. (Eds.). (2004). *The handbook of sexuality in close relationships.* Mahwah, NJ: Erlbaum.

Hawton, K., Goth, D., & Day, A. (1994). Sexual function in a community sample of middle-aged women with partners: Effects of age, marital, socioeconomic, psychiatric, gynecological, and menopausal factors. *Archives of Sexual Behavior, 23*, 375–395.

Hillman, J. L. (2000). *Clinical perspectives on elderly sexuality.* New York: Kluwer Academic/Plenum Press.

Hillman, J. L., & Stricker, G. (1994). A linkage of knowledge and attitudes toward elderly sexuality: Not necessarily a uniform relationship. *Gerontologist, 34*, 256–260.

Kaplan, H. (1974). *The new sex therapy: Active treatment of sexual dysfunction.* New York: Brunner/Mazel.

Katzman, E. M., & Katzman, L. S. (1985). Outcomes of sexuality course in nursing education. *Journal of Sex Education and Therapy, 12*(2), 33–36.

Kehoe, M. (1989). *Lesbians over 60 speak for themselves.* New York: Harrington Pore Press.

Kellett, J. (2000). Older adult sexuality. In L. Szuchman & F. Muscarella (Eds.), *Psychological perspectives on human sexuality* (pp. 355–384). New York: Wiley.

Kerr, M., & Bowen, M. (1988). *Family evaluation: An approach based on Bowen theory.* New York: Guilford Press.

Kingsberg, S. A. (2002). The impact of aging on sexual functioning in women and their partners. *Archives of Sexual Behavior, 31*, 431–437.

Kinsey, A., Pomeroy, W., & Martin, C. (1948). *Sexual behavior in the human male.* Philadelphia: Saunders.

Kinsey, A., Pomeroy, W., Martin, C., & Gebhard, P. (1953). *Sexual behavior in the human female.* Philadelphia: Saunders.

Kleinplatz, P. J. (Ed.). (2001). *New directions in sex therapy: Innovations and alternatives.* New York: Brunner/Routledge.

Lacy, K. K. (2002). Mature sexuality: Patient realities and provider challenges. *SIECUS Report, 30*(2), 22–29.

Late life sex ed: AIDS prevention. (2003). *Contemporary Sexuality, 37*(8), 8.

Laumann, E., Gagnon, J., Michael, R., & Michaels, S. (1994). *The social organization of sexuality.* Chicago: University of Chicago Press.

Leiblum, S. R., & Rosen, R. C. (2000). *Principles and practice of sex therapy* (3rd ed.). New York: Guilford Press.

Levine, S. B. (1998). *Sexuality in midlife.* New York: Plenum Press.

Levine, S. B., Risen, C. B., & Althof, S. E. (Eds.). (2003). *Handbook of clinical sexuality for mental health professionals.* New York: Brunner-Routledge.

Levy, J. A. (2001/2002). HIV and AIDS in people over 50. *SIECUS Report, 30*(2), 10–15.

LoPiccolo, J. (1991). Counseling and therapy for sexual problems in the elderly. *Clinics in Geriatric Medicine, 7*, 161–179.

LoPiccolo, J., & LoPiccolo, L. (Eds.). (1978). *Handbook of sex therapy.* New York: Plenum Press.

Mahay, J., Laumann, E. O., & Michaels, S. (2001). Race, gender, and class in sexual scripts. In E. O. Laumann & R. T. Michael (Eds.), *Sex, love, and health in America* (pp. 197–238). Chicago: University of Chicago Press.

Maples, M. F., & Abney, P. C. (2006). Baby boomers mature and gerontological counseling comes of age. *Journal of Counseling and Development, 84*, 3–9.

Masters, W. H., & Johnson, V. E. (1970). *Human sexual inadequacy.* Boston: Little, Brown.

McCarthy, B., & McCarthy, E. (2003). *Rekindling desire: A step-by-step program to help low-sex and no-sex marriages.* New York: Brunner/Routledge.

Nay, R. (1992). Sexuality and aged women in nursing homes. *Geriatric Nursing, 13,* 312–314.

Ogden, G. (1999). *Women who love sex.* Cambridge, MA: Womanspirit Press.

Ogden, G. (2002). Integrating sexuality and spirituality: A group therapy approach to women's sexual dilemmas. In P. J. Kleinplatz (Ed.), *New directions in sex therapy: Innovations and alternatives* (pp. 322–346). Philadelphia: Brunner-Routledge.

Palmer, P., & Jewison, N. (Producers), & Jewison, N. (Director). (1988). *Moonstruck* [Videotape]. United States: MGM/UA Home Video.

Quam, J. K. (1993). Gay and lesbian aging. *SIECUS Report, 21*(5), 10–12.

Reinisch, J., & Beasley, R. (1990). *Kinsey Institute's new report on sex.* New York: St. Martin's Press.

Richard, D. (2001). With age comes wisdom—With wisdom, new lessons. *Contemporary Sexuality, 35*(1), 4–5, 10.

Richard, D. (2002). Senior sexuality. *Contemporary Sexuality, 36,* 1–6.

Rossi, A. (Ed.). (1994). *Sexuality across the life course.* Chicago: University of Chicago Press.

Sanders, S. A. (1999). Midlife sexuality: The need to integrate biological, psychological and social perspectives. *SIECUS Report, 27*(3), 3–7.

Schnarch, D. (1991). *Constructing the sexual crucible: An integration of sexual and marital therapy.* New York: Norton.

Schnarch, D. (1997). *Passionate marriage: Love, sex, and intimacy in emotionally committed relationships.* New York: Norton.

Schnarch, D. (2002). *Resurrecting sex: Resolving sexual problems and rejuvenating your relationship.* New York: HarperCollins.

Sharpe, T. H. (2004). Introduction to sexuality in late life. *Family Journal, 12,* 199–205.

Shaw, J. (1994). Aging and sexual potential. *Journal of Sex Education and Counseling, 20,* 134–139.

Slater, S. (1995). *The lesbian family life cycle.* New York: Simon & Schuster.

Stimson, A., Wase, J., & Stimson, J. (1981). Sexuality and self-esteem among the aged. *Research in Aging, 3,* 228–239.

Strong, B., DeVault, C., Sayad, B. W., & Yarber, W. L. (2005). *Human sexuality in contemporary America* (5th ed.). New York: McGraw-Hill.

Tiefer, L. (2004). *Sex is not a natural act, and other essays* (2nd ed.). Boulder, CO: Westview Press.

U.S. Census Bureau. (2006). *Dramatic changes in U.S. aging highlighted in new census, NIH report.* Retrieved March 21, 2006, from http://www.census.gov/Press-Release/www/releases/archives/aging_population/006544.html.

Walker, B. L., & Harington, D. (2002). Effects of staff training on staff knowledge and attitudes about sexuality. *Educational Gerontology, 28,* 639–654.

Ward, R., Vass, A. A., Aggarwal, N., Garfield, C., & Cybyk, B. (2005). A kiss is still a kiss? The construction of sexuality in dementia care. *Dementia, 4*(1), 49–72.

White, C. B., & Catania, J. A. (1982). Psychoeducational intervention for sexuality with the aged, family members of the aged, and people who work with the aged. *International Journal of Aging and Human Development, 15,* 121–138.

Wiederman, M. W. (2004). Methodological issues in studying sexuality in close relationships. In J. H. Harvey, A. Wenzel, & S. Sprecher (Eds.), *Handbook of sexuality in close relationships* (pp. 31–56). Mahwah, NJ: Erlbaum.

CHAPTER 11

Depression

LESLIE HASCHE and NANCY MORROW-HOWELL

EPRESSION IS WIDELY recognized as having deleterious effects on a person's quality of life (Spitzer et al., 1995), as being a leading worldwide cause of disability (C. J. Murray & Lopez, 1996), and as being one of the costliest conditions to society in terms of health care dollars (Thorpe, Florence, & Joski, 2004). Furthermore, clinically significant depression (i.e., major depression, dysthymia, and minor depression) in older adults is associated with several negative outcomes, such as increased disability (Penninx et al., 1998), decreased quality of life, and shortened life span (Penninx et al., 2001). Older adults with depression exhibit poorer outcomes on other medical conditions, such as diabetes and heart disease, due to how depression decreases a person's ability to adhere to medication regimens, to diet recommendations, and to other recommended health behaviors (Katon, 1996). Specifically, depression increases risk of overall mortality, even when controlling for other health conditions, lifestyle factors, and demographics (Adamson, Price, Breeze, Bulpitt, & Fletcher, 2005; Unützer, Patrick, Marmon, Simon, & Katon, 2002), and depression is a leading risk factor for suicide in late life (Lebowitz et al., 1997). With this knowledge, depression should be seen as a public health concern for the nation's older adults and their families.

Therefore, evidence-based depression treatments are a pressing gerontological concern not only as a mental health need, but also due to the overlapping impact of depression on quality of life, disability, health outcomes, and mortality. Unfortunately, depression is often undetected and inadequately treated, especially in older adults (Charney et al., 2003), where depression is sometimes misperceived as a part of normal aging. Depression in late life is often narrowly attributed to the other developmental life events that coincide with old age, such as loss of social support, retirement, and medical illness. However, as this review of the literature shows, other biological, psychological, and social factors are associated with depression, and these factors go above and beyond the normal process of aging.

With the knowledge that depression leads to multiple negative outcomes for older adults, and that depression is not an acceptable or normal part of the aging process, it is necessary to learn how to detect and adequately intervene with depressed older adults. Effective depression interventions are available and supported by evidence—so now the challenge is to connect the knowledge and resources with the older adults in need. This chapter reviews the current knowledge of how and why older adults are experiencing depression, presents evidence-based interventions for depression that stretch across the continuum of services, and provides specific recommendations for treatment guidelines, policy initiatives, and research agendas.

DEFINING CLINICALLY SIGNIFICANT DEPRESSION

Over the past 2 decades, a wealth of literature has expanded our understanding of how older adults experience depression. The definition of late-life depression has several variations depending on clinical purpose and on specificity in subtype (Blazer, 2003). It is further complicated due to the lack of a clear test to determine if someone is depressed. The determination of a depression diagnosis does not come from blood work or an X-ray, like other medical diagnoses. To determine diagnosis, it is necessary to consider specific symptom profiles, duration of symptoms, and the standard nomenclature for mental disorders.

Depression is classified as an affective disorder and often subcategorized as major depression, Dysthymic Disorder, and subthreshold depression, which is also known as subsyndromal or minor depression. These overarching classifications can be specified (a) by precipitating events or causes such as bereavement or vascular depression, (b) by symptom profile such as psychotic depression and melancholic depression, and (c) by course, which includes late-onset versus early-onset depression. Early onset refers to an older adult who has experienced a depressive episode at a previous time in the life course; late onset refers to an older adult who is experiencing his or her first episode of depression (Devanand et al., 2002). Overall, major depression, dysthymia, and subthreshold depression have established measurements that have been the basis for most of the literature, research studies, treatment guidelines, and practice reimbursement; therefore, these categories are the predominant forms of classifying depression. The subtypes are used to provide more specific descriptions of the symptoms, causes, and appropriate treatment options.

Major Depressive Disorder

Major Depressive Disorder constitutes a formal diagnosis in the fourth edition of the *Diagnostic and Statistical Manual of Mental Disorders* (*DSM-IV*; American Psychiatric Association, 1994). It has no age specifications and includes a combination of symptoms that persist for almost every day, most of the day, for at least 2 weeks. A person must exhibit one or both of the two cardinal symptoms. The first symptom is experiencing a low mood or dysphoria, which can also be referred to as sad, blue, gloomy, or depressed. The second cardinal symptom is anhedonia, which is defined as a loss of interest in activities that the older adult typically would have found pleasurable. Activities are broadly defined to include work, interpersonal relationships, hobbies, sexual activity, and other individualized definitions of "activities of interest." The person must also exhibit four or more of the following symptoms: feelings of worthlessness or inappropriate guilt, diminished ability to concentrate or make decisions, fatigue, psychomotor agitation or retardation, difficulty sleeping or sleeping too much, significant increase or decrease in appetite or weight, and recurrent thoughts of death or suicidal ideations. In assessing for these symptoms it is often recommended to ask about "change in behavior" to distinguish between perpetual difficulties and episodic difficulties that are due to the depression (Blazer, 1993).

Dysthymia

Dysthymic Disorder is also defined by the *DSM-IV* and has a similar symptom list. Dysthymia is distinct from major depression; it is less severe as individuals are not required to meet the criterion of four symptoms. However, dysthymia is persistent, lasting 2 years or longer. The symptom profile of dysthymia often includes more long-standing difficulties with self-esteem or hopelessness. It can also include poor appetite or overeating, difficulties with low energy or fatigue, and poor concentration. The other diagnostic criteria for both major depression and dysthymia is that the symptoms must interfere significantly with the person's functioning and must not be caused by another comorbid condition or substance use. Both dysthymia and major depression can also be further specified by the course of the illness (i.e., partial remission, full remission, chronic, single episode).

Subthreshold Depression

The third type, subthreshold depression, may be identified according to the *DSM-IV* appendix on minor depression or according to several different depression scales. The main description is that it consists of three to four *DSM-IV* symptoms for depression, but not enough to meet diagnostic criteria; thus the person is experiencing a less severe version of depression. This category has generated a wealth of research by gerontologists who assert that even though subthreshold depression in older adults does not meet *DSM-IV* criteria, it does have similar negative outcomes and responds similarly to depression treatments (Chopra et al., 2005; Hybels, Blazer, & Pieper, 2001). Even though the literature supports the use of this definition, it has rarely been applied to treatment settings because most insurance providers do not provide coverage for the care of subthreshold depression.

Overall, these definitions are adequate in describing what is known as "clinically significant depression"; however, they fail to sufficiently describe the etiology of the depression. Furthermore, important sociological criticisms of the diagnostic criteria exist. The first concern is with the social construction of specific disorders, in that what is considered a disorder is subjective and defined by time, context, and culture (Aneshensal & Phelan, 1999). A second criticism, coming primarily from gerontologists, is that due to the diagnostic criteria's strong influences on the service delivery system, the system is biased against older adults because older adults more often fall into the category of subthreshold depression. A leading argument is that older adults vary in their symptoms in comparison to younger adults, thus they do not fit the *DSM-IV* criteria for major depression or dysthymia (Chopra et al., 2005). Older adults with depression may report more somatic complaints, such as problems with fatigue, insomnia, weight loss, and withdrawal, instead of clearly describing problems with low mood (Lyness et al., 1996; McAvay, Raue, Brown, & Bruce, 2005). This masking of sadness with complaints of aches, pains, and other physical symptoms may lead to decreased detection of the depression (Kirmayer, Robbins, Dworkind, & Yaffe, 1993).

This variance in symptom presentation is confounded by the fact that several of the depressive symptoms can be symptoms of other medical conditions or even assumed to be the natural process of aging. Examples include changes in sleeping patterns, changes in appetite, fatigue, changes in concentration, and even thoughts of death. With the variation in symptoms and the overlapping of symptoms with comorbid conditions, the nomenclature for depression diagnoses can fail to account for the broad range of symptom presentation by older adults (Areán & Ayalon, 2005).

Evidence-based geriatric psychiatry guidelines recommend that when comorbid medical or substance abuse conditions are present, differential diagnosis is needed, as is individualized treatment, to address both the issues of depression and the co-occurring disorders (Shanmugham, Karp, Drayer, Reynolds, & Alexopoulos, 2005). In fact, on discharge from inpatient psychiatry care for depression, Morrow-Howell, Proctor, Rubin, and Thompson (2000) have documented that older adults present with multiple aftercare needs across medical, psychiatric, and psychosocial realms. In a study of depressed elderly patients discharged home from acute psychiatric care, medical comorbidity was associated with greater functional impairment and increased medical and psychiatric service needs (Proctor et al., 2003). Disease-specific differences are reported to occur in the rates of remission for depressed geriatric patients receiving usual care, but when patients were provided a depression care manager and algorithm-based care, the association between medical comorbidity and treatment outcomes was insignificant (Bogner et al., 2005). Therefore, as will be discussed later in screening for depression, a practitioner working with older adults needs to be alert to the variety of symptom profiles, the availability of specific screens for older adults, and the need for clinical exploration of the overlapping symptoms related to other conditions.

EPIDEMIOLOGY OF DEPRESSION AND SUICIDE

Depression is a primary concern for older adults because it is one of the most common mental health problems affecting later life. Approximately 8% to 16% of community-dwelling older adults experience clinically significant depression (Beekman, Copeland, & Prince, 1999; Blazer, Burchett, Service, & George, 1991), and rates of major depression range from 1% to 4% (Beekman et al., 1995). Another reason to review the epidemiology of late-life depression is that prevalence rates vary by subpopulations of older adults. For example, older adults hospitalized for medical and surgical services have rates of major depression of 10% to 12%, and 23% for significant depressive symptoms (Koenig, Meador, Cohen, & Blazer, 1988). For older adults who visit a primary care provider, rates of major depression are estimated to be between 5% and 10% (Schulberg et al., 1998). Other settings that have increased comorbid medical and functional impairments have even higher rates of depression. Among older adults receiving public community long-term care services, 26% experience clinically significant depression and 6% meet criteria for current major depression (Morrow-Howell et al., 2005). In long-term care institutions the estimated rate of major depression is 12% and the rate for clinically significant depression is 35% (Parmelee, Katz, & Lawton, 1989).

Another subpopulation has high rates of depression that is not linked to medical and physical issues, but to life circumstances. Caregivers range in age, but almost half of all caregivers are above the age of 50, and older adults are more likely to provide long-term care (i.e., over 10 years of care) than other age groups (National Alliance for Caregivers & American Association of Retired Persons, 2004). Caregiving responsibilities are associated with higher levels of depression, with reported rates up to 31% of caregivers with clinically significant depression (Dew et al., 2004; Toseland, McCallion, Smith, & Banks, 2004). Spousal caregivers had higher rates of depression than other familial caregivers (Schulz, O'Brien, Bookwala, & Fleissner, 1995). The caregiver subpopulation breaks away from the other subpopulations, which are based on medical settings rather than role. This group provides insight into the variety of social and psychological risk factors that are associated with late-life depression, along with the known biological risk factors. Risk factors include female sex, lack of social support, disability, previous depression, and negative life events, such as death of a spouse (Cole, 2005; Schoevers et al., 2000).

As mentioned earlier, one reason to be concerned with the rates of depression in older adults is because depression is a leading indicator of suicide risk. According to the Centers for Disease Control (2006), 5,393 Americans over age 65 committed suicide in 2001. Risk of suicide increases with age, and older adults have the highest rate of suicide of any age group. Along with increasing age, male sex, and Caucasian ethnicity, other risk factors for late-life suicide include depressive symptoms, perceived poor health status, unmarried status, and lack of social support (Turvey et al., 2002). Unlike in younger age groups, a prior suicide attempt is not as indicative of risk because older adults have a ratio of attempts to completed suicides of approximately 4:1; whereas, estimates for the U.S. population as a whole range between 8:1 and 20:1 (Pearson & Brown, 2000). Given the rates of depression and suicide in older adults, it is alarming to learn about the unmet needs of this population in detection and treatment.

With the available knowledge of the prevalence of depression and suicide in older adults, it is disconcerting that most late-life depression remains undetected and is inadequately treated. It has been widely reported that only about half of the population meeting diagnostic criteria receive any sort of treatment from either the specialty mental health sector, primary care setting, or other human services (Reiger et al., 1993). This trend in unmet mental health care needs persists with older adults, who are much less likely to seek specialty mental health care. Only 14% of depressed older adults receives antidepressant treatment and 50% never complete mental health referrals (Callahan, Hui, Nienaber, & Musick, 1994).

The primary care setting is the predominant provider for mental health care to older adults, and there is still persistent disparity in the recognition and treatment of late-life depression in this setting. Older adults are less likely than young or middle-aged adults to perceive a need for mental health care, obtain specialty mental health care, or even to receive referrals from primary care physicians for mental health specialty care (Klap, Tschantz Unroe, & Unützer, 2003). For those older adults who do receive depression treatment in the primary care setting, the rates of detection and receiving adequate treatment are below average for primary care patients (Katon, Von Korff, Lin, Bush, & Ormel, 1992; Simon, 2002;

Simon et al., 1995). In general, older adults are less likely to be screened for alcohol, drug, and mental disorders, including depression, than young and middle-aged adults in the primary care setting (Edlund, Unützer, & Wells, 2004). Approximately 58% of older adults who commit suicide saw their primary care physician in the prior month (Luoma, Martin, & Pearson, 2002).

Some of the factors proposed to contribute to the inadequate detection of late-life depression include stigma and competing demands. The surgeon general's report on mental health identified how problems of stigma contribute to the avoidance of discussing depression in the patient-provider interaction (U.S. Department of Health and Human Services, 1999). Stigma is hypothesized to specifically influence provider behavior toward late-life depression (Schwenk, 2002). The competing demands on the primary care provider to address other, multiple physical problems may also overshadow the detection of depression in the time-limited provider encounters (Klinkman, 1997). Fortunately, several interventions and research initiatives are demonstrating methods for improving the detection and care provided in primary care settings for older adults by addressing the issue of stigma, competing demands, and fiscal and time constraints. These multifaceted interventions are reviewed later; first we must clarify the current state of knowledge on the causes of depression so that we have a theoretical basis for the recommended treatment approaches.

ETIOLOGY

The three dominant theories for explaining the causes of depression are biological, cognitive, and behavioral. Rather than having a single cause, there appears to be a variety of genetic, neuropathological, and psychosocial factors that may work separately or together to cause depression (Drevets & Todd, 1997). Each of these theories contributes to the general understanding of depression, to prominent treatment models, and to the specific recommendations to address late-life depression.

BIOLOGICAL THEORY

Literature increasingly recognizes that depression in late life is associated with brain abnormalities and may be related to genetic susceptibility (Blazer, 2003). For example, depression may be related to the production, supply, or level of activity of specific neurotransmitters. Medical illnesses, head injuries, heredity, and medications may all impact the regular functioning of neurotransmitters. Researchers have identified specific neurotransmitters related to depression, such as monoamine neurotransmitters that act as mood regulators and peptide neurotransmitters that act on pain reduction and pleasure (Blazer, 2003). Serotonin activity, which also is a brain chemical impacting mood, has been demonstrated to significantly differ for depressed elderly patients compared to elderly controls or older adults with Alzheimer's disease (Nemeroff et al., 1988).

Two other factors have strengthened the possibility of biological causation. First, empirical findings support that some medical illnesses directly cause a major depressive episode. Farber and Black (1997) describe illnesses that cause "secondary depression," such as Parkinson's disease, stroke, dementing disorders, cardiovascular disease, and multiple sclerosis. Such illnesses have direct physiological effects on the brain, so it is not surprising that damage to the brain could cause mood disturbances. Second, widespread evidence demonstrates the effectiveness of pharmacological treatments for depression (Charney et al., 2003). Understanding how the antidepressants affect neurotransmitter functioning leads to theories of how brain functions are related to moderating mood. Finally, most biological theories are based on associations; therefore, the issue of causality is not fully determined. Depression in late life does not occur solely to those who are sick nor to all of those who are sick with a specific illness. Therefore, other factors should be identified to understand who out of the healthy people or people with medical conditions is more susceptible to depression.

COGNITIVE THEORY

Complementing the biological theories, two psychologically based theories have remained prominent in the literature discussion. Aaron Beck developed cognitive theory to explain how negative distortions in the thought process cause depression (Beck, Rush, Shaw, & Emery, 1979). Examples of negative distortions are unrealistic expectations, overgeneralizations, overreactions, and personalization. For example, the same negative life event may occur to two people, yet only one person develops depression. According to Beck, it is this person's negative thought reactions to the event that cause the depression, whereas the other person's undistorted thought process protects him or her from experiencing depression. This internal interpretation of the event explains the causes of depression (Thase & Beck, 1993). Research findings have supported this theory: Older adults with major depression perceived greater negative impact of life events than older adults with dysthymia or older adults in a healthy control group (Devenand, Kim, Kaykina, Paykin, & Sackeim, 2002).

BEHAVIOR THEORY

The other prominent psychological theory explaining depression in older adults draws from the behavioral response of learned helplessness, where initiating any action in a perpetually stressful environment leads to expecting only minimal change in outcomes (Blazer, 2003). The total number of negative life events and daily hassles has been associated with late-life depression through a meta-analysis (Kraaij, Arensman, & Spinhoven, 2002). The behavior concept of positive reinforcement has also been applied to older adult depression. Lewinsohn and MacPhillamy (1974) used empirical findings to demonstrate that depressed people engage in fewer behaviors than do nondepressed people. In particular, depressed people engage in less pleasant (positively reinforcing) behaviors, which results in a feedback loop of declines in mood and decreases in pleasant behaviors. Complicating this theory is that a person's change in activity level is rarely seen as the sole cause of depression, yet change in activity level is a symptom of depression, which confounds the question of causality even more.

SOCIAL THEORIES

Limited evidence-based literature articulates social causes of depression, yet a few initial findings are important to consider. Broadening the scope beyond the individual biological and psychological factors, it is necessary to consider a prominent sociological perspective on aging and recent exploratory qualitative research. The life course perspective depicts how individual age-defined path-ways interact with social roles and obligations (i.e., work and family) and with life transitions, social conditions, and future options (Elder, 1994). Therefore, when understanding the experience of late-life depression, the history of a per-son's development and expected transitions through social institutions and or-ganizations is considered through detailing the cohort-specific influences, contextual factors, and maturity processes of each individual (Knight, 2004). By using this perspective, Mirowsky and Ross (1992) reported increasing levels of depression for older adults in comparison to other age groups through their life course analysis. They report that even though both young and old may be more likely to be unemployed, have lower incomes, and be unmarried than those in middle adulthood, these statuses (i.e., for older adults, retirement, widowhood, etc.) have different meanings in the two groups, which leads to more feelings of powerlessness, and subsequently more depression for older adults.

Recent qualitative research regarding depressed older adults' beliefs about causes of depression further highlights a social model of depression. This cross-cultural comparison demonstrated that culture is associated with varying be-liefs on the causes of depression. In particular, Lawrence and colleagues (2006, p. 23) conclude that a majority of their participants considered depression "an illness arising from the adverse personal and social circumstances that can ac-crue in old age" and that "an acceptance of the social and aging precipitants of depressees was not incompatible with the concept of depression as an illness." The participants listed causes such as aging and loss of independence; bereave-ment; loneliness; relationship changes; biological factors; personality, social, and financial causes; and past experiences. This review of the etiology of depression in late life argues for a biopsychosocial approach that incorporates the knowl-edge base of multiple disciplines to best guide the development and implementa-tion of evidence-based treatments.

PROGNOSIS

Overall, depression has long been considered to be the most treatable psychiatric disorder affecting older adults (Blazer, 1993; Gellis, 2006). Treatment by antide-pressants and by psychotherapy have been well supported in the literature as de-creasing the duration and severity of depression in this age group (Baldwin et al., 2003; Blazer, 2003; Mackin & Areán, 2005; Shanmugham et al., 2005). In fact, it can be expected that effective treatments will positively impact the depression out-come after just 6 to 12 weeks for the majority of patients (Schulberg, Katon, Simon, & Rush, 1999). With the basic premise that depression is amenable to treatment, depression is often divided into three prognostic categories: single ep-isode, recurrent, and chronic (Blazer, 1993). In single-episodic depression, a per-son experiences only one episode of major depression that may have a natural course of less than 1 year. If not presenting high-risk symptoms (such as suicidal-ity) and if provided adequate treatment in primary care, persons with a single ep-isode of depression may be sufficiently cared for in an outpatient primary care setting and not require specialty mental health care (Schulberg et al., 1999).

The second prognostic category describes persons with recurrent depression. Here the depression follows an episodic pattern, and a person experiences at least two episodes of depression that are separated by at least one remission in symptoms. A remission could last for decades, or could just be 1 year without significant depressive symptoms. Often the course runs through a full episode of major depression, partial remission, and eventual remission. Mitchell and Subramaniam's (2005) systematic review of the prognosis of late-life depression documented that older adults experience remission rates similar to that of middle-aged adults, yet may be at higher risk for relapse. Their recommendation to provide long-term treatment for maintenance and prevention of relapse matches the suggestions of several other groups (Segal, Pearson, & Thase, 2003; Shanmugham et al., 2005). For recurrent depression, treatment may be offered in a collaborative approach, with the primary care physician providing maintenance care and seeking specialty mental health consultation or referral for the reoccurrence of a major depressive episode (Alexopoulos et al., 2005).

The third category describes persons who experience a more chronic duration of depression that does not appear to have episodic breaks in symptoms. This form of depression describes people who persistently report symptoms sufficient for major depression diagnostic criteria for 2 or more years (American Psychiatric Association, 1994). A single episode of depression that does not receive adequate depression treatment may fit this category, but so too would long-duration depressive episodes that do not respond to adequate treatment. This unremitting depression is sometimes referred to as "treatment-resistant" depression and often requires specialty mental health care to manage the symptoms and multiple treatment needs. Some factors associated with increased chronicity of depression are perceived impaired social support, increased medical comorbidity, and impaired physical functioning (Hayes et al., 1997).

As mentioned earlier, some of the dangers of not treating depression are increased risk of suicide and mortality, increased physical disability, and increased risk for complications of other medical conditions. Late-life depression not only impacts the individual's quality of life, but also leads to increased social costs through the association with general health care dollars and loss of productivity (Katon, Lin, Russo, & Unützer, 2003; Wells, 1997). As it is clear that the prognosis of clinically significant depression can be positively impacted by effective interventions, it is therefore necessary to clearly understand how these evidence-based interventions can be implemented in a variety of aging, social, and health care settings.

EVIDENCE-BASED INTERVENTIONS

SCREENING

Using standardized questionnaires in a systematic manner to increase detection of depression is the basic premise of screening protocols. The screens may be self-administered, in written or computerized formats, or administered by staff or clinicians to older adults. The screens result in a score that indicates probable depression and then flag the case for further evaluation by either the primary care physician or other clinicians. Yet screening is a debatable solution because screening alone does not equate to positive health outcomes (Palmer & Coyne, 2003). One study demonstrated that just handing the completed screener to the primary care physician may not ensure that the screening occurs or that the information is utilized in treatment planning (Dobscha, Gerrity, & Ward, 2001). In fact, the U.S. Preventive Services Task Force (2002) concluded that there is currently insufficient evidence to recommend for or against routine use of standardized questionnaires to screen for depression in primary care patients, and that if screening is implemented, the settings must ensure that procedures conducive to accurate diagnosis, effective treatment, and careful follow-up are also implemented (Pignone et al., 2002).

The failed attempts to improve the adequacy of depression treatment by solely promoting the use of screening highlighted the need for sustainable, multifaceted supports to the structure and organization of care (Gilbody, Whitty, Grimshaw, & Thomas, 2003). Even though screening alone has not been associated with improved depression rates of treatment and detection, screening is still a pivotal component of evidence-based care. Clear evaluation of how the numerous depression screeners are appropriately or inappropriately used across settings and service populations remains important.

The literature demonstrates that numerous screening options are available for detecting depression. These scales vary in length, administration style, scoring complexity, and underlying assumptions. Some of these scales were designed for specific use in medical settings; others were designed specifically for older adults. When selecting a screen for use, practitioners should compare the possible depression screeners on four domains, as described by Corcoran (1991): (1) sample characteristics, (2) reliability, (3) validity, and (4) practicality.

In the first domain, sample characteristics, the focus was on identifying measures that were validated for older adult populations or specific clinic populations (e.g., primary care settings), diversity in populations, and languages available. Examples of depression screens tested on older adults are listed in Table 11.1. The second domain for consideration in selecting a screening instrument is the methodological concern for reliability—the ability of the measure to yield the same value of a construct over time, situation, or other influences of error (Kerlinger, 1986). Likewise, the third domain is the validity of the screening instrument—the accuracy of the measure. Often, validity is measured by two factors: specificity and sensitivity. Sensitivity refers to the instrument's ability to correctly identify participants with depression (i.e., true positives). Specificity is the ability to correctly identify those who do not have depression (true negatives; Robison, Gruman, Gaztambide, & Blank, 2002). In clinical practice, the focus has been on ensuring high sensitivity because clinicians do not want to risk unrecognized depression. However, low specificity also becomes a concern for resource allocation because referring false-positive clients for full mental health evaluation leads to resources being spent unnecessarily. This is especially problematic in settings were competing demands and limited resources already confine the reach of mental health service use (Nease, Klinkman, & Volk, 2002).

The sources provided for each screening instrument in Table 11.1 describe the respective evidence for the validity and reliability of each measure identified for use with older adults. Both Mulrow et al. (1995) and Williams, Pignone, Ramirez, and Perez Stellato (2002) concluded that multiple instruments with reasonable operating characteristics are available for depression screening. Williams et al. concluded that because operating characteristics among the instruments are equivalent, selecting a depression screener should depend on factors of feasibility, administration, and scoring ease.

Table 11.1

Overview of Select Depression Screens for Older Adults

Instrument	Source	Sample Settings[a]	Number of items	Scope	Item Response	Time Frame	Score Range	Usual Cutoff Point	Literacy Level[b]
Beck Depression Inventory (BDI)	Steer, Cavalieri, Leonard, & Beck (1999)	Older adults in academic and VA	21, 13, 7	Depression-specific, includes somatic symptoms	Four statements of symptom severity per item	Today	0–63	10–19 mild, 20–29 moderate, 30+ severe	Easy
Center for Epidemiologic Studies Depression Screen (CES-D)	Radloff & Teri (1986)	Older adults in academic and community	20, 10	Depression-specific	Four frequency ratings: "less than 1 day" to "most to all" (5–7 days)	Past week	0–60	16+	Easy
Duke Anxiety and Depression Scale (DADS)	Parkerson & Broadhead (1997)	Primary care	7, 10	Anxiety and depression	Three frequency ratings: "yes, somewhat, no" for three items; "none, some, a lot" for four items	Past week	0–100	31+	Average
Geriatric Depression Scale (GDS)	Arthur et al. (1999)	Functionally impaired older adults in community	30, 15	Depression-specific, omits most somatic symptoms	Yes or no	Past week	0–30	11+	Easy
General Health Questionnaire (GHQ)	Bashir, Blizard, Jenkins, & Mann (1996)	Primary care	30, 28, 12	Psychiatric illness	Four frequency ratings: "not at all" to "much more than usual"	Past few weeks	0–28	4+	Easy
Hospital Anxiety Depression Scale (HADS)	Hermann (1997)	Primary care and hospital	14	Depression and anxiety	Four statements of symptom severity per item	Past week	0–21	11+	Difficult

(continued)

279

Table 11.1 *Continued*

Instrument	Source	Sample Settings[a]	Number of items	Scope	Item Response	Time Frame	Score Range	Usual Cutoff Point	Literacy Level[b]
Hopkins Symptom Checklist (HSCL)	Nettelbladt, Hansson, Stefansson, Borgquist, & Nordstrom (1993)	Older adults in primary care	25, 13	Multiple versions and components	Four frequency ratings: "not at all" to "much more than usual"	Past week	25–100	43+	Average
Inventory for Depression (ID)	Rush (1999)	Older adults in VA	15	Depression-specific	Two items, yes or no; Three items of normal, overt, or covert symptoms	Recently	0–15	10+	Easy
Medical Outcomes Study Depression Scale (MOS-D)	Nagel, Lynch, & Tamburrino (1998)	Primary care	8	Depression-specific	Frequency ratings: "less than 1 day" to "most or all" (5–7 days)	Past week	0–1	0.06+	Average
Primary Care Evaluation of Mental Disorders (PRIME-MD)	Spitzer et al. (1994)	Primary care adults and older adults	2	Multiple components with depression	Yes or no	Past month	0–2	1+	Average
Patient Health Questionnaire (PHQ-9)	Kroenke, Spitzer, & Williams (2001)	Primary care adults and older adults	9	Multiple components with depression	Four frequency ratings: "not at all" to "nearly every day"	Past 2 weeks	0–27	0–4 none, 5–9 mild, 10–14 moderate, 15–19 major, 20–27 severe	Average

(continued)

Instrument	Source	Setting	No. of items	Type	Response format	Time frame	Score range	Cutoff	Literacy level[b]
Symptom Driven Diagnostic System—Primary Care (SDDS-PC)	Broadhead et al. (1995)	Primary care	5	Multiple components with depression	Yes or no	Past month	0–5	2+	Easy
Zung Self-Assessment Depression Scale (SDS)	Zung (1965)	Primary care	20	Depression-specific	Four frequency ratings: "little of the time" to "most of the time"	Recently	25–100	50–59 mild, 60–69 moderate, 70+ severe	Easy
SELFCARE	Bird, MacDonald, Mann, & Philpot (1987)	Older adults in community	12	Depression-specific	Four to nine frequency ratings that vary by question	Varying times	0–12	6+	Average
Single-question	Williams et al. (1999)	Academic primary care	1	Depression-specific	Yes or no	Past year	0–1	1	Easy

[a] VA = Veterans Affairs.
[b] Literacy level: Easy = Third- to fifth-grade reading level; Average = Sixth- to ninth-grade reading level; Difficult = Ninth-grade reading level or higher.

Adapted from "Identifying Depression in Primary Care: A Literature Synthesis of Case-Finding Instruments," by J. W. Williams, M. Pignone, G. Ramirez, and C. Perez Stellato, 2002, *General Hospital Psychiatry, 24,* pp. 225–237; and *Assessment of Depression in Older Adults,* by E. L. Woodhead and S. Stoner, paper presented at the Gerontological Society of America, Orlando, FL, November 2005. Adapted with permission.

Other issues of practicality are the instrument's length, the time it takes to complete, whether or not it requires someone to administer it, its social acceptability and utility, its purpose, and its method of scoring (Corcoran, 1991). Some depression screens, such as the Primary Care Evaluation of Mental Disorders (PRIME-MD) 2-item screener (Löwe, Kroenke, & Grafe, 2005), conclude only whether or not the older adult may be experiencing probable depression. Such measures tend to be short and easy to administer but are limited in the information they provide. A longer scale, such as the 15-item Geriatric Depression Scale, may require more time for administration and scoring, but it has an added informative value because it provides a measure of the depression severity (Arthur, Jagger, Lindesay, Graham, & Clarke, 1999). The Patient Health Questionnaire 9 (PHQ-9) not only provides a measure of severity, but also provides information on *DSM-IV* symptoms of depression, including a question about suicide risk (Kroenke, Spitzer, & Williams, 2001). Therefore, choosing between these two instruments depends on specific purpose and needs. Areán and Ayalon (2005) use similar criteria—psychometric quality, ease of administration, and clinical characteristics—in reviewing depression screening tools; they conclude that for older primary care patients, the PHQ-9 or Center for Epidemiological Studies Depression Scalre-Revised (CES-D-R) may be most appropriate due to ease of administration, uniformity and universality for use with various age groups, and ability to effectively detect depression.

In summary, when selecting a depression screen to implement it is necessary to plan for the follow-up procedures for initiating depression treatment and how one will monitor the effectiveness of the care provided. Here are several questions to consider when reviewing the evidence for which screener to use:

- Do the testing samples for the depression screen represent the target population?
- Is the literature on the depression screen up to date?
- Does the literature provide information on reliability and validity of the screen?
- Is the sensitivity (true positives) and specificity (true negatives) for the screen acceptable for the resources and needs of the target setting?
- Is the depression screen of appropriate length and social acceptability?
- Does the depression screen provide information about severity?
- Is the depression screen feasible to administer, score, and incorporate into routine practice?
- Is the depression screen available in the languages needed by the target population?
- Does the depression screen detail specific symptoms of concern (e.g., suicidality)?

The following recommendations are provided to improve the likelihood that the depression screen will not only be practical for transfer to new settings, but also will have beneficial impact on the depression care provided to older adults:

- Ensure that older adults have extended time, space, and assistance when needed to complete self-administered forms.

- Use process evaluation to verify the consumer friendliness, cultural competency, and provider satisfaction of the measure with each new population.
- Monitor response rate through the percentage of participants completing it, the rate of the screener outcome's being incorporated into the treatment plan (e.g., through diagnosis, referral, or other relevant interventions), and the impact on participant outcomes on depression severity, quality of life, and disability days.

PHARMACOTHERAPY

The use of medications to effectively treat depression is not unique to older adults; however, because older adults take more drugs than younger adults in general and because the number of drugs taken tends to increase with age, the issue of pharmacotherapy to treat late-life depression does require a specific knowledge base in geriatrics (American Medical Association [AMA], 2002). Survey data suggest that older adults take an average of three prescription and nonprescription drugs daily (Hanlon, Schmader, Ruby, & Weinberger, 2001). Further complicating the use of pharmacotherapy to treat late-life depression is the knowledge that taking a greater number of drugs is associated with an increased risk for adverse drug reactions (AMA, 2002), which puts older adults at disproportionate risk. Not only are drug-drug interactions a concern, but so too are drug-disease interactions that may put older adults at risk (McLeod, Huang, Tanblyn, & Gayton, 1997). Also, pharmacokinetic changes that coincide with aging may alter the absorption, distribution, hepatic metabolism, and renal excretion processes that influence the impact of any one prescription medication (AMA, 2002). Therefore, it is necessary to review evidence-based pharmacotherapy interventions for depression that are specific to the needs and characteristics of older adults.

General guidelines for geriatric pharmacotherapy focus on the principles of efficacy, safety, appropriateness of drug and dose (i.e., "Start low and go slow"), the complexity of the treatment regimen, cost, and patient compliance (AMA, 2002). Table 11.2 lists appropriate drug recommendations for older adults with depression. Although guidelines identify selective serotonin reuptake inhibitors (SSRIs) as the first-line treatment of choice due to their receiving the highest ratings for efficacy and tolerability, even though evidence-based reviews report that tricyclic antidepressants (TCAs) had similar tolerability (Alexopoulos et al., 2001; Baldwin et al., 2003; Colenda et al., 2003; Raj, 2004; Segal, Pearson, & Thase, 2003; Shanmugham et al., 2005). The expert guidelines provide the caveat that the consequences of the TCAs' side effects are more serious than those of SSRIs (Shanmugham et al., 2005). In deciding which SSRI should be used, it is important to note that not only do the pharmacokinetic profiles of the SSRIs vary, but also that each SSRI is associated with its own specific risks for side effects and drug-drug interactions (Trivedi, 2003). Thus, choice of which antidepressant to prescribe should be guided by each individual patient's potential for drug interactions, simplicity of dosing, and side effect profile (Baldwin et al., 2003; Shanmugham et al., 2005). It is also important to note inappropriate prescribing practices that may lead to depression in certain disease groups or that identify specific considerations for not prescribing antidepressants due to the risks to the older patients,

Table 11.2

Guidelines for Common Antidepressants to Treat Late-Life Depression

Antidepressant Medication (Generic Name)	Dose (mg)*		Comments
	Range	Usual	
SSRIs			
Fluoxetine HCl (Prozac)	10–60	20	Has a long half-life.
Sertraline HCl (Zoloft)	25–150	75	Potential for diarrhea; do not give with pimozide (Orap).
Paroxetine HCl (Paxil) Paroxetine HCl, controlled-release (Paxil CR)	10–40	20	Side effects may include dry mouth, constipation, weakness/ fatigue, nausea, weight gain.
Citralopram hydrobromide (Celexa)	10–40	20	Activating, morning dosing. Relatively few drug interactions. Side effects may include dry mouth.
Escitalopram oxalate (Lexapro)	10–20	10	Activating, morning dosing. Few drug interactions.
TCAs			
Nortriptyline HCl (Aventyl, Pamelor)	10–125	50	Anticholinergic effects, weight gain, weakness/fatigue.
Desipramine	75–200	100–200	Tachycardia, insomnia/agitation.
Others			
Bupropion HCl (Wellbutrin)	100–300	150	Potential for weight loss. Also marketed as Zyban for use as smoking deterrent.
Venlafaxine extended-release (Effexor XR)	37.5–225	112.5	Potential nausea, agitation/insomnia; 1% to 3% risk of elevated blood pressure.
Mirtazapine (Remeron)	7.5–45	22.5	Potential sedation, weight gain.

*Start at lower end of range and adjust dose upward every 2 to 3 weeks, depending on response.

Adapted from "Depression in the Elderly: Tailoring Medical Therapy to Their Special Needs," by A. Raj, 2004, *Postgrad Medicine Special Report, 115,* retrieved March 20, 2006, from http://www.postgradmed.com/issues/2004 /06_04/raj.htm; and "Pharmacological Treatment of Depression in Older Primary Care Patients: The PROSPECT Algorithm," by B. H. Mulsant et al., 2001, *International Journal of Geriatric Psychiatry, 16,* pp. 585–592. Adapted with permission.

as is described in Table 11.3. McLeod et al. (1997) provide alternative pharmacological therapy recommendations in these recognized inappropriate practices.

Evidence-based pharmacotherapy for the treatment of depression not only incorporates knowing which medications to use at what levels, but also a structured treatment algorithm that describes how and when a physician should change the treatment strategies of patients who experience partial or no response to the first course of antidepressant treatment. Critical decision points are specified to ensure that proper and timely evaluation of the patient's response is addressed. If the patient has not reached remission, second- or third-line treatment options include a provider's choice of augmentation with a second medication, combination of two medications, or an antidepressant plus psychotherapy, and switching to a

Table 11.3
Identification of Contraindicated Medications for Late Life Depression

Risk to Patient	Alternative Therapy
Medications that May Cause Depression	
• Prescription of reserpine to treat hypertension	Another antihypertensive drug.
• Beta-blockers to treat hypertension	Monitor for possible depression and pursue treatment as needed.
• Many anticancer drugs	Monitor for possible depression and pursue treatment as needed.
• Interferon alfa medication	Monitor for possible depression and pursue treatment as needed.
Medical Conditions That May Cause Depression	
• Hypothyroidism	Check TSH level on diagnosis of depression.
Inappropriate Prescription of Antidepressants	
• TCA antidepressant for patients with a history of glaucoma, benign prostatic hyperplasia, or heart block	Use SSRI antidepressant.
• SSRI for patients already receiving an monamine oxidase (MAO) inhibitor to treat depression	Avoid combing, ensure a wash-out period of at least 7 days if switching an MAO inhibitor to an SSRI.
• TCA to treat depression for patients with a history of postural hypotension	Use SSRI, with monitoring of blood pressure.
• TCA with active metabolites (e.g., imipramine or amitriptyline) to treat depression	Use TCA without active metabolites or SSRI.
• Prescription of methylphenidate to treat depression	Use SSRI or short half-life TCA without active metabolites.

Adapted from "Defining Inappropriate Practices in Prescribing for Elderly People: A National Consensus Panel," by P. J. McLeod, A. R. Huang, R. M. Tamblyn, and D.C. Gayton, 1997, *Canadian Medication Association Journal, 156*(3), pp. 385–391; and "Depression in the Elderly: Tailoring Medical Therapy to Their Special Needs," by A. Raj, 2004, *Postgrad Medicine Special Report, 115*, retrieved March 20, 2006, from http://www.postgradmed .com/issues/2004/06_04/raj.htm. Adapted with permission.

different medication (Trivedi, 2003). Examples of treatment algorithms for depression in general include the Texas Medication Algorithm Project and the Sequenced Treatment Alternatives to Relieve Depression. Large multisite randomized clinical trials of depression interventions for older adults have also developed their own treatment algorithms, such as the Improving Mood and Promoting Access and Collaborative Treatment (IMPACT; Unützer, Katon, et al., 2002) and the Prevention of Suicide in Primary Care Elderly Collaborative Trial (PROSPECT; Bruce et al., 2004).

With the majority of older adults being responsible for taking their own medications, achieving optimal compliance involves the provider's medication selection; routine assessment of the outcome, including information about medication use from the patient and family or other caretaker; and increasing the patient's health literacy. Unintentional noncompliance may be due to cognitive problems with memory or confusion and impaired physical functioning (AMA, 2002). Strategies to increase compliance include the following:

- Improving communication between physician and patient
- Utilizing written instructions along with verbal instructions
- Timing the medication administration to match the patient's daily schedule
- Using mechanical aids to assist in reminding or organizing drugs
- Specifying in prescriptions that medications should not be dispensed in safety-cap containers (AMA, 2002)

Addressing compliance is an issue not only for the patient and the prescribing physician; it is recommended that family members, caregivers, and even social service providers receive training in medication management and education about adverse drug reactions.

PSYCHOTHERAPY

Several evidence-based therapeutic interventions for depression are available. However, because late-life depression is complicated by an increase in the number of comorbid medical conditions, changing developmental stages, transitioning life events, and changing roles of older adults, and because older adults' principal service use is through primary care physicians (Areán et al., 2003; Blazer, 2003; Oxman, Dietrich, & Schulberg, 2003), the intervention's effectiveness must be tested specifically with this age group. Fortunately, several models of effective individual and group therapeutic interventions are recommended for work with depressed older adults (Scogin, Welsh, Hanson, Stump, & Coates, 2005). As mentioned earlier, these interventions are primarily based on the psychological theories of what causes depression in late life. Furthermore, psychotherapy has been indicated to be a highly effective alternative or addition to pharmacotherapy in treating late-life depression (Mackin & Areán, 2005). Several variations of psychotherapy have been used with depressed older adults; the literature provides specific evidence for four specific approaches: (1) behavior therapy, (2) cognitive therapy, (3) problem-solving therapy, and (4) interpersonal therapy.

Behavior Therapy   Behavioral therapy approaches attempt to increase participation in pleasant activities so that mood will rise (Lewinsohn, Biglan, & Zeiss, 1976). By using baseline measurements, behavior contracts, monitoring, and evaluation of results, this therapy has also become structured. These intervention tasks promote the client's ability to recognize and alter the impact of events on his or her mood by increasing involvement in pleasant events. There is even a list of over 250 activities, called the Pleasant Event Schedule, to help the older adult generate ideas (Lewinsohn & Libet, 1972). The effectiveness of behavior therapy alone (Lewinsohn et al., 1976; L. W. Thompson, Gallagher, & Steinmetz Breckenridge, 1987) and in conjunction with other therapies (Ciechanowski et al., 2004) is supported in the literature. A practitioner can obtain skills in behavioral therapy through coursework or continuing education programs.

Cognitive-Behavioral Therapy   Cognitive theory has been used as a brief therapy based on manualized steps to identify and alter negative thought processes that can lead to depression. Sometimes referred to as cognitive-behavioral therapy (CBT), it has an educational component of teaching clients about cognitive distortions, about skills to evaluate their thought processes, and then about how to correct the negative distortions—which may then lead to an elevated mood (Beck et al., 1979). This therapy has been specifically modified for use in treating late-life depression (Laidlaw, Thompson, Dick-Siskin, & Gallagher-Thompson, 2003).

Cognitive-behavioral therapy has the largest evidence base for the treatment of depression in older adults (Areán & Ayalon, 2005; Scogin et al., 2005). Alone, CBT has been found to be a beneficial treatment for late-life depression (Campbell, 1992; Floyd, Scogin, McKendree-Smith, Floyd, & Rokke, 2004). Areán, Gum, and colleagues (2005) have also reported the effectiveness of CBT combined with case management in decreasing depression for low-income older adults. Empirical studies regarding depression interventions for older adults have supported the comparable effectiveness of CBT with other psychotherapies (i.e., interpersonal therapy, psychodynamic therapy; Gallagher-Thompson & Steffen, 1994; L. W. Thompson et al., 1987). A combination of CBT and medication was more effective than CBT alone or medication alone (L. W. Thompson, Coon, & Gallagher-Thompson, 2001). Several versions of manualized cognitive therapy are available for both individual and group treatment. More recently, Simon, Ludman, Tutty, Operskalski, and Von Korff (2004) reported results from a randomized controlled trial that participation rates are high for a telephone psychotherapy program using cognitive therapy; this intervention resulted in lower depression severity of the adult participants. Specialized training to conduct cognitive therapy is available in professional schools and through continuing education events.

One criticism of CBT is that the exact mechanisms that make it effective are unclear: It could be the therapeutic relationship, the metacognition development of being able to step back prior to responding, or that CBT results in attitude changes (Blazer, 2003). Another criticism is that CBT is as effective as other psychotherapies, not more effective, as reported earlier. Therefore, other forms of therapy can cause the same result of decreased depression; it is not clear, due to spurious factors that result in similar outcomes of decreased depression, that cognitions cause depression.

Problem-Solving Therapy for Primary Care This therapy, known by the acronym PST-PC, incorporates components of both cognitive and behavioral theories into a specific approach for the primary care setting (Catalan et al., 1991). It uses a partnership model and focuses on using clients' strengths to improve on real-world problems that matter to the client (e.g., loneliness, need to clean house, need to schedule appointments). Repeated difficulties with these problems lead to thoughts and feelings of hopelessness and helplessness. This therapy addresses negative thought distortions by initially providing education on how problems are a normal and predictable part of living, that depression is a sign that a problem is present, that the older adult has some degree of control over the problem, and that effective solutions exist (Areán, Hegel, & Reynolds, 2001).

A session usually lasts about 30 minutes, with four to eight sessions total. Depressed older adults are instructed to use seven steps to solve problems: (1) clarifying and defining the problem, (2) setting a realistic goal, (3) generating multiple solutions through brainstorming, (4) evaluating and comparing the solutions using pro and con lists, (5) selecting a feasible solution, (6) implementing the solution through an action plan, and (7) evaluating the outcome. Additionally, PST-PC incorporates behavior activation by planning weekly pleasant activity schedules and monitoring the older adult's activity level. Treatment has included a step-down approach, using group therapy to conduct maintenance sessions with older adults in partial remission of depression.

Problem-solving therapy for primary care has empirical support for use in primary care clinics (Mynors-Wallis, 2003; Unützer, Katon, et al., 2002), senior service agencies (Ciechanowski et al., 2004), and other community settings (Alexopoulos, Raue, & Areán, 2003). This therapeutic approach has also increased the positive treatment outcomes of minority patients (Areán, Ayalon, et al., 2005). It is a highly structured, manualized therapy program that can be conducted by non-mental health clinicians; however, research has shown that mental health practitioners are more likely to maintain treatment fidelity to the PST-PC model (Hegel et al., 2002).

Interpersonal Therapy   Klerman, Weissman, Rounsaville, and Chevron (1984) developed interpersonal psychotherapy (IPT) as a time-limited, outpatient treatment for depression that addresses difficulties with current interpersonal relationships through active discussions. These difficulties are categorized into four conflict areas: grief, interpersonal conflict with specific people, role transitions, and interpersonal deficits that interfere when interacting with people in general. The therapeutic process is divided into three phases. First, one to three sessions focus on conducting an assessment of not only the depression but also the client's social functioning and close relationships and patterns and expectations of interacting in relationships. Second, over the course of the next 8 to 12 weeks, specific strategies to address the interpersonal problem area are enacted. Third, the last four sessions involve increasing the client's renewed sense of independence and competence and preparing for termination (Feijo de Mello, Mari, Bacaltchuk, Verdeli, & Neugebauer, 2005).

Interpersonal psychotherapy has been adapted to work specifically with depressed older adults in primary care (IPT-PC; Bruce et al., 2004). The same four conflict areas guide the treatment; however, Areán and colleagues (2001) have identified that the main areas of conflict are grief and role transition. The adaptation also follows the three phases of treatment, but alterations include increased participation of family members and conducting sessions via the telephone. Results of testing IPT-PC specifically are not currently available. Used in conjuncture with medications in a collaborative care approach IPT-PC does not appear to adversely affect treatment outcomes (Bruce et al., 2004).

Even though IPT in general has supporting evidence for treatment of depression in adults of all ages (Feijo de Mello et al., 2005), few studies report specifically on the effectiveness of IPT with depressed older adults. Reynolds and colleagues (1999) did present evidence that IPT is most effective when combined with pharmacotherapy and is particularly helpful to patients with chronic depression, which supports previous evidence of IPT for late-life depression (Sloane, Staples, & Schneider, 1985). However, monthly maintenance IPT sessions were not as effective as maintenance pharmacotherapy in preventing recurrent depression (Reynolds et al., 2006). Miller and colleagues (2001) also reported initial findings that IPT was beneficial for depressed elders with cognitive impairment.

In summary, several forms of evidence-based psychotherapy are available for intervening with depressed older adults (Scogin et al., 2005). Psychotherapy is recommended as a stand-alone treatment for mild depression or as an addition to providing pharmacological therapy for major depression (Shanmugham et al., 2005). In their recent review of treatment options for late-life depression in primary care, Areán and Ayalon (2005) found that there is not sufficient research evidence to conclusively state which therapeutic approach is best. Again, paying attention to the specific setting and administrative needs and to the client's characteristics should guide treatment selection. Otherwise, selection of the psychotherapeutic approach should take into consideration the assessment of client needs, client treatment preferences, and the practitioner's skills and competency for any specific therapeutic approach.

ELECTROCONVULSIVE THERAPY

For some older adults with depression electroconvulsive therapy (ECT) has demonstrated effectiveness in alleviating depression when other treatments have failed or when a rapid response is needed due to the severity and immediate risks of untreated depression. Electroconvulsive therapy requires a medical doctor to administer an electrical induction of seizures to the brain in a series of 6 to 12 treatment sessions on an inpatient or outpatient basis (U.S. Department of Health and Human Services, 1999). Often treatments are initiated while a patient is hospitalized to monitor for effect and then may be continued on an outpatient basis under the supervision of a psychiatrist. Because depression seems to be prevalent among people in old age and the use of prescription medication may be less effective and safe for this particular population, ECT serves as an important alternative. It appears to be effective for short-term outcomes and safe (Tew et al., 1999; van der Wurff, Stek, Hoogendijk, & Beekman, 2003). In fact, older adults constitute more than half of patients with depression who receive ECT (Tew et al., 1999).

As mentioned, the use of medication to treat depression may exacerbate problems among older adults due to a tendency for slower response and medical comorbidities (U.S. Department of Health and Human Services, 1999). Furthermore, older adults presenting with depression may have more immediate needs due to the fact that their illness may be accompanied by serious health concerns such as dehydration, disability, malnutrition, and immobility (Anderson, 2001; Tew et al., 1999; U.S. Department of Health and Human Services, 1999). As stated by Tew et al., "The degree of impairment associated with severe geriatric depression [warrants] rapid intervention" (p. 1868), which ECT may be better able to provide than medication. Reasons for selecting ECT as a first-line treatment for older adults with severe depression include the following: (a) ECT can promote a faster response than pharmacotherapy, (b) drug interactions are infrequent, and (c) early intervention is beneficial to treatment response (Tew et al., 1999).

The effectiveness of ECT in acute treatment of depressed older adults is supported by systematic reviews, naturalistic follow-up studies, and retrospective studies (van der Wurff et al., 2003). Tew et al. (1999) offered support of the previous statement with findings illustrating the effectiveness of ECT among multiple populations, including the oldest old (75+) despite their cognitive impairments and large physical illness burdens. A study by Rao and Lyketsos (2000) also found ECT to be effective among depressed older adults with dementia; 40% of the sample responded positively to ECT treatment. Examining the efficacy of ECT among older adults in 14 studies, van der Wurff et al. (2003, p. 897) found, "The immediate outcome figures are superior for ECT in all studies, varying from 48% complete recovery to 92% improvement on ECT."

Immediate results are promising, but the long-term results are much more tentative. Benbow (1987) cautions that ECT-treated patients suffered from increased readmission rates, with 36% of the patients having a readmission within 6 months. These results may imply that although ECT seems to elicit a positive acute response to depression in older age, caution should be used when attempting to predict long-term recovery. A study undertaken by Tew et al. (1999) points to this issue as an area in need of further study.

Common side effects for all recipients of ECT include confusion, temporary memory impairment, head and muscle aches, and nausea (Anderson, 2001; U.S. Department of Health and Human Services, 1999). In extreme instances, ECT has been known to lead to death; Kelly and Zisselman (2000) reported 2 to 4 deaths per 100,000 ECT treatments. Despite the possibility of side effects, ECT appears to be a relatively safe treatment option for older adults. Tew et al. (1999) found the oldest old (75+) to be just as tolerant of the treatment as those in the lower age ranges. Van der Wurff et al. (2003) reported a small number of serious events, but the majority of side effects tend to be mild and/or short-lived. The surgeon general concluded that "there are no absolute medical contraindications to ECT" (U.S. Department of Health and Human Services, 1999, p. 355). Some heart conditions may require doctors to exercise caution (U.S. Department of Health and Human Services, 1999); however, the regularly occurring cardiovascular complications are of the less severe and shorter-lasting kind (van der Wurff et al., 2003). Thus, ECT, when administered over a limited time period under controlled conditions, is considered safe. Evidence supports its short-term effectiveness as a treatment for severe depression in late life.

DISEASE MANAGEMENT PROGRAMS AND COLLABORATIVE CARE

Due to the knowledge that a large portion of depressed older adults do not receive many of the evidence-based depression treatments just described or specialty mental health services (Charney et al., 2003), a new focus has been on integrating evidence-based depression treatment into non-mental health settings. In particular, disease management programs were adapted to improve depression treatment for younger and older adults. The theory for the disease management programs was derived from the evidence-based model for treating chronic illness: the chronic care model (Bodenheimer, Wagner, & Grumbach, 2002). By assessing how provider-patient interactions are enhanced or hindered by community resources, policies, and organization of the health care system (e.g., self-management support, delivery system design, decision support, and clinical information systems), this model synthesizes system and practice changes associated with better outcomes in chronic illness (Austin, Wagner, Hindmarsh, & Davis, 2000; Bodenheimer, Wagner, & Grumbach, 2002). These disease management programs incorporated evidence-based guidelines, patient self-management, systematic screening, routine follow-up care, interdisciplinary teams, and, in some studies, a designated staff member (i.e., depression care manager) to manage the patients' depression treatment and interactions with service providers (Austin et al., 2000; Oxman et al., 2003). Systematic reviews have supported the effectiveness of disease management programs for treating depression in adults (Badamgarav et al., 2003; Neumeyer-Gromen, Lampert, Stark, & Kallischnigg, 2004).

In late-life depression treatment, these disease management programs have also become known as collaborative care models. Several randomized controlled trials of various collaborative care components have demonstrated the usefulness of providing accessible and effective treatment in a variety of settings, such as in primary care settings (Boult et al., 2001; Bruce et al., 2004; Oslin et al., 2003; Unutzer et al., 2001), hospitals (Oslin et al., 2004; Shah, Odutoye, & De, 2001), community senior services settings and public housing (Ciechanowski et al., 2004; Rabins et al., 2000), and home health care (Blanchard, Watereus, & Mann, 1999). Furthermore, several of these studies demonstrated positive outcomes associated with collaborative care treatment, decreased depression severity and symptomatology (Boult et al., 2001; Bruce et al., 2004; Ciechanowski et al., 2004; Rabins et al., 2000; Unutzer, Katon, et al., 2002), and decreased functional impairment (Boult et al., 2001; Ciechanowski et al., 2004; Unutzer, Katon, et al., 2002).

In general, these studies vary in the different collaborative components included, but they typically involved a nurse or social worker acting as a dedicated depression care manager with psychiatric clinical supervision, a stepped-care algorithm, and a systematic tracking system to assess depression severity. As this is a multifaceted approach that incorporates several evidence-based intervention components, what constitutes required features is still being debated. In particular, the depression care manager has been highlighted as a key element for future research to clarify the practicality and fiscal feasibility of transferring this intervention to practice settings (Oxman et al., 2003).

To further exemplify the strengths of collaborative care, it is helpful to discuss one prominent study. Unützer, Katon, et al. (2002) report on a multisite study based in primary care called IMPACT. The IMPACT study used a specific collaborative care model to integrate evidence-based depression treatments into primary care clinics. This collaborative care model used a depression care manager to:

- Conduct systematic assessments using standardized depression screens.
- Educate older adults about depression and prompt behavior activation.
- Provide brief psychotherapy using PST-PC.
- Facilitate consultation with primary care physicians and psychiatrists to promote evidence-based medication management.
- Ensure follow-up to track depression outcomes, which would inform patient's progression through the stepped-care treatment algorithm.

Several articles regarding IMPACT's results report significant findings on the following outcomes: long-term decrease in depression severity and improved functioning (Katon et al., 2002), improved arthritis outcomes and pain management (Lin et al., 2003), improved diabetes management (Williams et al., 2004), decreased medical expenditures (Simon et al., 2001), and decreased racial and ethnic disparities in treatment outcomes (Areán, Gum, et al., 2005).

In conclusion, disease management programs (i.e., collaborative care) are effective in treating late-life depression in a variety of settings when using a depression care manager to coordinate the multiple evidence-based practice interventions, including screening, pharmacotherapy, psychotherapy, and referral to specialty mental health care as needed.

Suicide Prevention

Several recent articles have detailed recommendations for suicide prevention specifically for older adults, and they all highlight the importance of adequate depression detection and treatment for this population (Heisel & Duberstein, 2005; Pearson & Brown, 2000; Schulberg et al., 2004). Following the evidence-based practices for depression treatment just described (psychotherapy, pharmacotherapy, and ECT), this section details evidence-based interventions that go above and beyond depression treatment to promote suicide prevention. In particular, several suicide prevention efforts have targeted increasing the knowledge and skills of primary care physicians and other practitioners to detect and address suicide risk among their general client population ("National Strategy for Suicide Prevention: Goals and Objectives for Action," Public Health Service, 2001).

Even though systematic or standardized screening has not been recommended for suicide prevention in primary care settings, training primary care physicians to conduct suicide assessments and follow management algorithms has been supported (Schulberg et al., 2004). For example, the Respect Engineering Systems for Primary Care Treatment of Depression treatment trial used an item from a standardized depression screener to trigger a systematic inquiry about the patient's suicide risk and specified proper management plans for implementation (Bartels et al., 2004). The PROSPECT trial, mentioned earlier, demonstrated that a collaborative care approach with a treatment algorithm incorporating pharmacotherapy and/or interpersonal therapy resulted in decreased suicidal ideation and depression for older primary care patients when compared to usual primary care practice (Bruce et al., 2004).

Assessment of suicidal thoughts should include attention to known unmodifiable risk factors (i.e., age and sex); the clinical presentation of mental disorders, substance abuse, and pain; and direct questions about the severity of the older adult's suicidal ideations and plans and the feasibility of the plans. For older adults, an opening for the clinician to pursue this line of questioning would be through more general end-of-life discussions (Schulberg et al., 2004).

Another avenue of suicide prevention is to ensure that crisis intervention services are trained to address the specific risks and needs of older adults. However, few studies address the effectiveness of crisis interventions, such as crisis hotlines, or older adults' use of these services (Pearson & Brown, 2000). McIntosh (1995) did provide a review of telephone outreach programs that demonstrated some promise in reducing psychological distress and suicidal ideation. Overall, multiple evidence-based treatment components are useful for addressing both depression and suicide risk. Using treatment algorithms and collaborative care approaches, such as PROSPECT, can increase not only the use of efficacious pharmacological and psychotherapeutic interventions, but also improve access to treatment for older adults who are at risk for suicide.

Case Studies

To illustrate the use of the evidence-based practices in treating late-life depression, two case studies are presented next. First is a description of an elderly woman who has had long-standing major depression. Her case study exemplifies the multiple domains of causes and treatment needs related to managing her chronic depression. The second case study provides an overview of an implementation study of the IMPACT collaborative care model in a community-based practice setting, thus highlighting the bench-to-trench process of integrating evidence-based depression treatment. All identifying information has been altered to protect the confidentiality of the individuals.

Mrs. J

As an 84-year-old widowed woman living on her own in the community, Mrs. J prides herself on her independence and persistence. As a participant in a study on depression in community long-term care, Mrs. J was excited to contribute her knowledge and preferences to help inform future depression treatments for older adults. Mrs. J openly described how she has experienced depression since her 20s, when a series of traumatic events led to a "breakdown." Since that time, she has experienced a cycle of depressive episodes that has included at least one remission lasting over a decade. However, because Mrs. J has aged with a combination of changes in roles, increased physical health problems that have made it more difficult for her to leave her home, and financial difficulties, she reports a more chronic duration of her depressive symptoms. Medical comorbidities of arthritis and diabetes affect not only her health and functioning, but also her ability to "get out" like she used to. Thus, she describes how her isolation leads to escalating depression due to boredom and loneliness. Mrs. J, who has previously received extensive education on depression through prior specialty mental health care, including hospitalizations, and her own self-learning through reading, clearly identifies her current symptoms of low mood, loss of interest, fatigue, trouble sleeping, overeating, and persistent thoughts of hopelessness. Though adamant about not thinking about suicide, she does admit increased passive thoughts of her eventual death.

To address her depression, Mrs. J works with a psychiatrist to obtain pharmacotherapy; however, she acknowledges not maintaining regular appointments due to her difficulties with transportation. She does report that she adheres closely to the medications prescribed and has a home health nurse who assists in setting up her pill box. She has previously worked with both a cognitive-behavioral therapist and an interpersonal therapist, but due to her current physical limitations and low finances, she reports not receiving any therapy at this time. When asked about her therapeutic experiences, she described how the specific techniques to increase her coping skills were helpful, but what she really cared for was having someone take the time to listen to her problems. The other current support Mrs. J receives is from a home health care agency that provides in-home assistance 3 times a week for personal care and chore-worker tasks, which Mrs. J describes as invaluable to maintaining her independent household and as a way to get social contact during the week.

With her chronic depression and medical comorbidities, Mrs. J's case demonstrates how evidence-based practices could be integrated for someone who is already actively receiving treatment to further alleviate and monitor her depression. For example, introducing a systematic screening of her depression severity may be necessary to help inform the effectiveness of the current pharmacotherapy regimen, along with helping her to identify that change does occur in the level of her depression. Evidence-based psychotherapy such as problem-solving therapy may be conducted in-home or over the telephone to help her address some of her problems of boredom and isolation. Also, having someone collaborating with Mrs. J to increase her behavior activation through scheduling feasible pleasant activities may further break up her monotony. Finally, by integrating collaborative care into her treatment, Mrs. J may experience a more streamlined system of care for not only her depression but also her arthritis and diabetes. Collaborative care would also introduce a care manager to do proactive tracking of depression, assist with coordinating the multiple professionals involved, and ensure that active treatment is pursued until the depression is alleviated through a stepped-care algorithm.

The Delta "Collaborative Care" Project

The second case study overviews not a specific older adult's experience with obtaining evidence-based depression treatment, but how a system that is overly burdened by depression is attempting to incorporate collaborative care to promote the use of evidence-based treatments for its clients. In a pilot project in a small region of a midwestern state's public community long-term care agency, steps to incorporate the key elements of the IMPACT model are currently under way. The clients were at increased risk for depression due to the characteristics of the client population, which has eligibility requirements of below poverty-level income and high functional impairment. This agency first recognized the burden of depression through a clinical epidemiologic study that reported that 1 in 4 of their new clients experienced depression (Morrow-Howell et al., 2005).

Through guidance and support from the IMPACT investigators, this agency collaborated with local researchers on adapting collaborative care for their agency. Agency stakeholders, researchers, and the depression care managers attended training sessions conducted by the original IMPACT investigators and followed the IMPACT training manuals. Agency caseworkers then referred their clients with depression to the depression care manager to receive a full assessment, which included a standardized screen for depression, the PHQ-9. Under the supervision of a local mental health specialist, the depression care manager established a treatment plan that included either pharmacotherapy or brief problem-solving therapy. Treatment choice was guided by the client's preference, previous effective use of each modality, and the acuity of the depression. Through in-home visits by the depression care manager, all clients received psychoeducation by watching an educational video on depression and discussion, behavior activation in weekly pleasant activities, and systematic tracking of outcomes by completing the PHQ-9 on a regular basis. The depression care manager used a stepped-care algorithm and consultation with the client's primary care physician and the consulting specialty mental health clinician to adjust treatment as needed. Although early in its implementation, this study has already shown promise as a means of offering evidence-based interventions to vulnerable, home-bound older adults with depression.

EVIDENCE-BASED POLICY RECOMMENDATIONS

Currently, older Americans can obtain coverage for mental health diagnosis and treatment from Medicare, Medicaid, and private insurance. In general, insurance coverage for mental health care is less than coverage for physical health care, and often coverage is exhausted in the face of ongoing mental health needs (Unützer, Schoenbaum, Druss, & Katon, 2006). In 1996, Congress passed the Mental Health Parity Act, which required that most plans offer similar limits on mental and physical health coverage; 30 states have laws requiring comparable coverage for mental and physical health (Smyer & Shea, 2003). Yet these laws have not resulted in meaningful changes (Frank, Goldman, & McGuire, 2001).

Almost all Americans over the age of 65 have Medicare Part A, which will pay for up to 190 days of psychiatric inpatient days during a person's lifetime (there is no lifetime limit on psychiatric stays in general hospitals). Partial hospitalization is also covered, with no day limits, but there is a 20% copayment. Postacute care in skilled nursing facilities is covered, but this coverage is for rehabilitative, not long-term, care (Cano & Hennessy, 1997). Medicare Part B pays for outpatient mental health care provided by physicians, psychiatrists, clinical psychologists, clinical social workers, and other mental health specialists. If these providers serve an older patient who is hospitalized, 80% of allowed charges are covered. However, in the outpatient setting, 50% of allowed charges are covered (Rosenbach & Ammering, 1997). The new Medicare Part D now covers the cost of psychotropic drugs. It is not yet clear how different formularies available to older adults will affect their use of psychotropic medications.

Although lack of parity in the Medicare program has long been recognized, it is less widely acknowledged that current policy fails to support the adaptation of evidence-based practice models. Policy initiatives that are currently being advocated by geriatric mental health experts are based on evidence that collaborative care models (e.g., IMPACT) are effective and adaptable to care settings that reach a large number of older adults (e.g., primary care clinics and public housing). Research on effective depression intervention programs points to two key ingredients: (1) systematic case management by a trained clinical staff to facilitate case identification, assessment, education, coordination of a treatment plan, monitoring, and follow-up; and (2) consultation between the care manager, primary care provider, and consulting psychiatrist (Unützer et al., 2006). Yet these key components are not currently covered by Medicare. That is, many of the case management and consultation functions, including any contact made over the telephone, are not covered. Further, regulations prevent a primary care visit and a mental health visit at a single clinic on the same day, limiting the coordination of care required in effective treatment programs. Thus, revisions of Medicare policies are necessary to advance the integration of evidence-based practice.

Medicaid varies by state, but by federal law, state programs must cover inpatient and outpatient services, physician services, and skilled nursing home services for the mental health needs of older adults. Only the poorest of older adults qualify, and low reimbursement rates discourage providers from serving this population (Smyer & Shea, 2003). The Balanced Budget Act of 1997 permitted states to further reduce outpatient payments (L. Murray & Eppig, 2002). In the past decade, strained state budgets have led to mental health service provision for only the most severely mentally ill older adults (National Alliance for the Mentally Ill

[NAMI], 2006). Indeed, mental health advocates argue that Medicaid coverage extends only to low-income older adults with severe and persistent mental illness and fails to address the large public health issue of more common diagnoses of depression and anxiety (Unützer et al., 2006).

Advocates argue that financial incentives need to be offered by public and private insurers to encourage providers to employ evidence-based practices. Further, there is concern that "carve-out" programs, which separate mental health care from mainstream medical services, contribute to fragmented and uncoordinated care (Unützer et al., 2006). In fact, Aetna Insurance Company has terminated a contract with a carve-out company and is initiating a three-prong approach to depression: training of primary care physicians and office staff to screen for depression, a care management system, and access to mental health specialists (Moran, 2006).

FUTURE DIRECTIONS

Future directions in depression care are currently being shaped by three major forces: the President's New Freedom Commission on Mental Health, the National Alliance for the Mentally Ill, and the 2005 White House Conference on Aging.

In 2002, President Bush appointed a committee to conduct a comprehensive study of the mental health service delivery system and advise him on strategies to improve care (Hogan, 2006). The President's New Freedom Commission on Mental Health (U. S. Department of Health and Human Services, 2004) identified barriers to care, including those discussed in this chapter: fragmentation of the service system, out-of-date Medicare policies, stigma due to mental illness and advanced age, mismatch between services covered and those preferred, and lack of adequate preventive interventions and programs that aid in early identification. The report clearly indicated that state-of-the-art treatments, based on decades of scientific efforts, are not being transferred into community settings. One of the goals set by the report is to move outreach, assessment, and early intervention into low-stigma settings, settings where clients are in touch with helping professionals who can identify mental health needs and link them to mental health providers. Although the report was not directed to older adults with mental disorder, the calls for elimination of disparities in provision of health and mental health services and for culturally competent and consumer-directed services certainly apply.

Following up on the President's New Freedom Commission's finding that the service system was in poor condition, NAMI (2006) conducted a survey and grading of the mental health care system in each state. The survey determined that the national mental health service system is failing; with the country getting no better than a D on the report card. All but five states received a C or below. The survey gathered information from staff at the State Mental Health Authority, from consumers, and from public records about 10 elements: comprehensive services and support; integrated system; sufficient funding; consumer- and family-driven systems; safe and respectful treatment environments; accessible information for consumers and families; access to acute care and long-term care treatment; cultural competence; health promotion and mortality reduction; and mental health workforce. In the face of the poor performance of the states on these 10 elements,

NAMI made recommendations, including tying funding to performance and outcomes; investing in evidence-based and emerging best practices; improving data collection, reporting, and transparency of information; involving consumers and families in all aspects of the system; and eliminating discrimination. Several state innovations were recognized (NAMI, 2006), including local municipalities taking the lead to address mental health needs through tax and bond proposals; regulations to reduce use of seclusion and restraints; partnerships between mental health agencies and universities to promote implementation of evidence-based practices; and efforts to ensure appropriate linguistic skills of the mental health workforce.

The delegates of the 2005 White House Conference voted mental health into the top 10 concerns for policy development over the next decade (White House Conference on Aging [WHCOA] Policy Committee, 2006). Resolution number 8 was "to improve recognition, assessment, and treatment of mental illness and depression among older Americans." For almost 2 years before the conference, the WHCOA Policy Committee collected public input to guide the delegates' discussion, and there was much content put forth on mental health. For example, the National Coalition for Mental Health and Aging stated that its overall objective was to get WHCOA to address mental health with the same urgency as physical health, as recommended by the President's New Freedom Commission Report (National Coalition for Mental Health and Aging, 2005). The National Coalition's testimony to the WHCOA Policy Committee emphasized the expected increase in need and demand by aging baby boomers and the fact that currently almost two thirds of older adults with mental disorder do not get needed services. The coalition also presented a set of resolutions: Assure access to affordable and comprehensive range of services (outreach, home- and community-based services, prevention, intervention, acute care, long-term care); assure age-appropriate, culturally competent, and consumer-driven services; amend statutes to guarantee parity in coverage and reimbursement for mental health, physical health, and substance abuse; eliminate exclusions based on preexisting conditions; ensure Medicare clients have access to the full range of medicines; improve and effectively coordinate benefits at all government levels for dual eligibles; and promote, coordinate, and finance the movement of evidence-based and emerging practices from research to service.

The delegates endorsed the need to focus national attention on mental health in our aging society. The final report from WHCOA has not yet been given to the president or the public, so it is not clear what implementation strategies will be suggested or how much momentum WHCOA will actually create.

There is much similarity in the messages coming from the President's New Freedom Commission, NAMI's state report, and the 2005 WHCOA. Clearly, progress on the issues raised in these forums depends on bridging the gap between research knowledge and practice and policies related to mental health treatment. Practitioners have questioned the usefulness and sustainability of current research knowledge. Future directions in research need to increase the ecological validity of studies so that real-world clients in real-world situations participate in studies whose findings translate to practice settings. For example, the majority of current research findings are based on studies that omit patients with comorbidities in order to control the confounding variables in determining treatment effectiveness.

Researchers need to use "patients included for their medical comorbidity rather than excluded because of it" (Schwenk, 2002, p. 162).

Research also needs to focus on the usefulness and sustainability of empirically supported treatment knowledge to the practice setting. For example, several collaborative care studies on colocating specialty mental health providers or depression care specialists in non-mental health service settings have demonstrated effectiveness, but have failed to sustain interventions beyond their grant funding due to lack of resources to support the collaboration (Lin et al., 1997; Oishi et al., 2003). Research initiatives must consider the real-world decision factors of resource availability in order to have an impact on the actual delivery of depression treatment to older adults.

Much of the research on mental health in later life has focused on depression, yet anxiety is as common as, if not more common than, depression, and other mental disorders threaten the quality of late life. Researchers should extend the demonstration and evaluation of treatment models to disorders beyond depression.

It is clear that effective treatments exist for depression in later life. It is also clear that older clients do not receive these treatments and that providers fail to achieve outcomes that would be expected with these evidence-based practices. Evidence-based guidelines are available, yet efforts to ensure the use of these guidelines generally have failed (C. Thompson et al., 2000). There is critical need for research to illuminate strategies that get effective treatments to older adults, by changing behaviors of older consumers, families, and primary care and specialty care providers and by changing policies and systems of care that facilitate the use of evidence-based interventions.

REFERENCES

Adamson, J. A., Price, G. M., Breeze, E., Bulpitt, C. J., & Fletcher, A. E. (2005). Are older people dying of depression? Findings from the Medical Research Council Trial of the Assessment and Management of Older People in the Community. *Journal of the American Geriatric Society, 53,* 1128–1132.

Alexopoulos, G. S., Katz, I. R., Bruce, M. L., Heo, M., Ten Have, T., Raue, P., et al. (2005). Remission in depressed geriatric primary care patients: A report from the PROSPECT study. *American Journal of Psychiatry, 162,* 718–724.

Alexopoulos, G. S., Katz, I. R., Reynolds, C. F., Carpenter, D., Docherty, J. P., & Ross, R. W. (2001). Pharmacotherapy of depression in older patients: A summary of the expert consensus guidelines. *Journal of Psychiatry Practice, 7*(6), 361–376.

Alexopoulos, G. S., Raue, P., & Areán, P. (2003). Problem-solving therapy versus supportive therapy in geriatric major depression with executive dysfunction. *American Journal of Geriatric Psychiatry, 11*(1), 46–52.

American Medical Association. (2002). Featured report: *Improving the Quality of Geriatric Pharmacotherapy* (A-02). Retrieved January 17, 2006, from http://www.ama-assn.org /ama/pub/category/print/13592.html.

American Psychiatric Association. (1994). *Diagnostic and statistical manual of mental disorders* (4th ed.). Washington, DC: Author.

Anderson, S. M. (2001). *Electroconvulsive therapy in depressed older adults.* Retrieved March 31, 2006, from http://www.stenmorten.com/ect/ect_older_adults.pdf.

Aneshensal, C. S., & Phelan, J. C. (1999). *Handbook of sociology of mental health.* New York: Kluwer Academic.

Areán, P. A., & Ayalon, L. (2005). Assessment and treatment of depressed older adults in primary care. *Clinical Psychology: Science and Practice, 12*(3), 321–335.

Areán, P. A., Ayalon, L., Hunkeler, E., Lin, E., Tang, L., Harpole, L., et al. (2005). Improving depression care for older minority patients treated in primary care: Results from the IMPACT study. *Medical Care, 43,* 381–390.

Areán, P. A., Cook, B. L., Gallagher-Thompson, D., Hegel, M. T., Schulberg, H. C., & Schulz, R. (2003). Guidelines for conducting geropsychotherapy research. *American Journal of Geriatric Psychiatry, 11,* 9–16.

Areán, P. A., Gum, A., McCulloch, C. E., Bostrom, A., Gallagher-Thompson, D., & Thompson, L. (2005). Treatment of depression in low-income older adults. *Psychology and Aging, 20,* 601–609.

Areán, P. A., Hegel, M. T., & Reynolds, C. F. (2001). Treating depression in older medical patients with psychotherapy. *Journal of Clinical Geropsychology, 7*(2), 93–104.

Arthur, A., Jagger, C., Lindesay, J., Graham, C., & Clarke, M. (1999). Using an annual over-75 health check to screen for depression: Validation of the short Geriatric Depression Scale (GDS-15) within general practice. *International Journal of Geriatric Psychiatry, 14,* 431–439.

Austin, B., Wagner, E., Hindmarsh, M., & Davis, C. (2000). Elements of effective chronic care: A model for optimizing outcomes for the chronically ill. *Epilepsy and Behavior, 1,* S15—S20.

Badamgarav, E., Weingarten, S. R., Henning, J. M., Knight, K., Hasselblad, V., Gano, A., et al. (2003). Effectiveness of disease management programs in depression: A systematic review. *American Journal of Psychiatry, 160,* 2080–2090.

Baldwin, R. C., Anderson, D., Black, S., Evans, S., Jones, R., Wilson, K., et al. (2003). Guideline for the management of late-life depression in primary care. *International Journal of Geriatric Psychiatry, 18,* 829–838.

Bartels, S. J., Coakley, E. H., Zubritsky, C., Ware, J. H., Miles, K. M., Areán, P. A., et al. (2004). Improving access to geriatric mental health services: A randomized trial comparing treatment engagement with integrated versus enhanced referral care for depression, anxiety, and at-risk alcohol use. *American Journal of Psychiatry, 161,* 1455–1462.

Bashir, K., Blizard, R., Jenkins, R., & Mann, A. (1996). Validation of the 12-item general health questionnaire in British general practice. *Primary Care Psychiatry, 2*(4), 245–248.

Beck, A. T., Rush, A. J., Shaw, B. F., & Emery, G. (1979). *Cognitive therapy of depression.* New York: Guilford Press.

Beekman, A., Copeland, J., & Prince, M. (1999). Review of community prevalence of depression in later life. *British Journal of Psychiatry, 174,* 307–311.

Beekman, A., Deeg, D., Van Tilberg, T., Smit, J., Jooijer, C., & Van Tilberg, W. (1995). Major and minor depression in later life: A study of prevalence and risk factors. *Journal of Affective Disorders, 36,* 65–75.

Benbow, S. M. (1987). The use of electroconvulsive therapy in old age. *International Journal of Geriatric Psychiatry, 2,* 25–30.

Bird, A. S., MacDonald, A. J., Mann, A. H., & Philpot, M. P. (1987). Preliminary experience with the SELFCARE(D): A self-rating depression questionnaire for use in elderly, non-institutionalized subjects. *International Journal of Geriatric Psychiatry, 2,* 31–38.

Blanchard, M. R., Watereus, A., & Mann, A. H. (1999). Can a brief intervention have a longer-term benefit? The case of the research nurse and depressed older people in the community. *International Journal of Geriatric Psychiatry, 14,* 733–738.

Blazer, D. G. (1993). *Depression in late life* (2nd ed.). St. Louis, MO: Mosby.

Blazer, D. G. (2003). Depression in late life: Review and commentary. *Journal of Gerontology: Medical Sciences, 58A*(3), 249–265.

Blazer, D., Burchett, B., Service, C., & George, L. K. (1991). The association of age and depression among the elderly: An epidemiologic exploration. *Journal of Gerontology: Medical Sciences, 46*(6), 210–215.

Bodenheimer, T., Wagner, E. H., & Grumbach, K. (2002). Improving primary care for patients with chronic illness. *Journal of the American Medical Association, 288*(14), 1775–1779.

Bogner, H. R., Cary, M. S., Bruce, M. L., Reynolds, C. F., Mulsant, B., Ten Have, T., et al. (2005). The role of medical comorbidity in outcome of major depression in primary care: The PROSPECT study. *American Journal of Geriatric Psychiatry, 13*, 861–868.

Boult, C., Boult, L. B., Morishita, L., Dowd, B., Kane, R. L., & Urdangarin, C. F. (2001). A randomized clinical trial of outpatient geriatric evaluation and management. *Journal of the American Geriatric Society, 49*(4), 351–359.

Broadhead, W. E., Leon, A. C., Weissman, M. M., Barrett, J. E., Blacklow, R. S., Gilbert, T. T., et al. (1995). Development and validation of the SDSS-PC screen for multiple mental disorders in primary care. *Archives of Family Medicine, 4*, 211–219.

Bruce, M. L., Ten Have, T. R., Reynolds, C. F., Katz, I. I., Schulberg, H. C., Mulsant, B. H., et al. (2004). Reducing suicidal ideation and depressive symptoms in depressed older primary care patients: A randomized controlled trial. *Journal of the American Medical Association, 291*, 1081–1091.

Callahan, C. M., Hui, S. L., Nienaber, C. A., & Musick, B. S. (1994). Longitudinal study of depression and health services use among elderly primary care patients. *Journal of the American Geriatric Society, 42*, 833–838.

Campbell, J. M. (1992). Treating depression in well older adults: Use of diaries in cognitive therapy. *Issues in Mental Health Nursing, 13*, 19–29.

Cano, C., & Hennessy, K. D. (1997). Medicare Part A utilization and expenditures for psychiatric services: 1995. *Health Care Financing Review, 18*(3), 177–194.

Catalan, J., Gath, D. H., Anastasiades, P., Bond, S. A., Day, A., & Hall, L. (1991). Evaluation of a brief psychological treatment for emotional disorders in primary care. *Psychological Medicine, 21*, 1013–1018.

Centers for Disease Control and Prevention, National Center for Injury Prevention and Control. (2006). *Suicide fact sheet.* Retrieved February 16, 2006, from http://www.cdc.gov/ncipc/factsheets/suifacts.htm.

Charney, D. S., Reynolds, C. F., Lewis, L., Lebowitz, B. D., Sunderland, T., Alexopoulos, G. S., et al. (2003). Depression and bipolar support alliance consensus statement on the unmet needs in diagnosis and treatment of mood disorders in late life. *Archives of General Psychiatry, 60*, 664–672.

Chopra, M. P., Zubritsky, C., Knott, K., Ten Have, T., Hadley, T., Coyne, J. C., et al. (2005). Importance of subsyndromal symptoms of depression in elderly patients. *American Journal of Geriatric Psychiatry, 13*, 597–606.

Ciechanowski, P., Wagner, E., Schmaling, K., Schwartz, S., Williams, B., Diehr, P., et al. (2004). Community-integrated home-based depression treatment in older adults: A randomized controlled trial. *Journal of the American Medical Association, 291*(13), 1569–1577.

Cole, M. G. (2005). Evidence-based review of risk factors for geriatric depression and brief preventive interventions. *Psychiatric Clinics of North America, 28*, 785–803.

Colenda, C. C., Wagenaar, D. B., Mickus, M. M., Steven, C., Tanielian, T., & Pincus, H. A. (2003). Comparing clinical practice with guideline recommendations for the treatment of depression in geriatric patients: Findings from the APA Practice Research Network. *American Journal of Geriatric Psychiatry, 11*(4), 448–457.

Corcoran, K. J. (1991). Selecting a measuring instrument. In R. M. Grinnell Jr. (Ed.), *Social work research and evaluation* (3rd ed., pp. 135–155). Itasca, IL: Peacock.

Devanand, D. P., Adorno, E., Cheng, J., Burt, T., Pelton, G. H., Roose, S. P., et al. (2002). Late onset dysthymic disorder and major depression differ from early onset dysthymic disorder and major depression in elderly outpatients. *Journal of Affective Disorders, 78,* 259–267.

Devenand, D., Kim, M., Kaykina, N., & Sackeim, H. (2002). Adverse life events in elderly patients with major depression or dysthymia and in healthy control subjects. *American Journal of Geriatric Psychiatry, 10,* 265–274.

Dew, M. A., Myaskovsky, L., Dimartini, A. F., Switzer, G. E., Schulberg, H. C., & Kormos, R. L. (2004). Onset, timing, and risk for depression and anxiety in family caregivers to heart transplant recipients. *Psychological Medicine, 34,* 1065–1082.

Dobscha, S. K., Gerrity, M. S., & Ward, M. F. (2001). Effectiveness of an intervention to improve primary care provider recognition of depression. *Effective Clinical Practice, 4*(4), 163–171.

Drevets, W. C., & Todd, R. D. (1997). Depression, mania, and related disorders. In S. Guze (Ed.), *Adult psychiatry* (pp. 99–142). St. Louis, MO: Mosby.

Edlund, M. J., Unützer, J., & Wells, K. B. (2004). Clinical screening and treatment of alcohol, drug, and mental problems in primary care: Results from health care for communities. *Medical Care, 42,* 1158–1166.

Elder, G. H. (1994). Time, human agency, and social change: Perspectives on the life course. *Social Psychology Quarterly, 57*(1), 4–15.

Farber, N. B., & Black, K. J. (1997). Psychiatry disorders associated with general medical conditions. In S. Guze (Ed.), *Adult psychiatry* (pp. 407–426). St. Louis, MO: Mosby.

Feijo de Mello, M., Mari, J., Bacaltchuk, J., Verdeli, H., & Neugebauer, R. (2005). A systematic review of research findings on the efficacy of interpersonal therapy for depressive disorders. *European Archives of Psychiatry in Clinical Neuroscience, 255,* 75–82.

Floyd, M., Scogin, F., McKendree-Smith, N. L., Floyd, D. L., & Rokke, P. D. (2004). Cognitive therapy for depression: A comparison of individual psychotherapy and bibliotherapy for depressed older adults. *Behavior Modification, 28,* 297–318.

Frank, R., Goldman, H., & McGuire, T. (2001). Will parity in coverage result in better mental health care? *New England Journal of Medicine, 345,* 1701–1704.

Gallagher-Thompson, D. E., & Steffen, A. M. (1994). Comparative effects of cognitive-behavioral and brief psychodynamic psychotherapies for depressed family caregivers. *Journal of Consulting and Clinical Psychology, 62,* 543–549.

Gellis, Z. (2006). Older adults with mental and emotional problems. In B. Berkman (Ed.), *Handbook of social work in health and aging* (pp. 213–216). New York: Oxford University Press.

Gilbody, S., Whitty, P., Grimshaw, J., & Thomas, R. (2003). Educational and organizational interventions to improve the management of depression in primary care: A systematic review. *Journal of the American Medical Association, 289*(23), 3145–3151.

Hanlon, J. T., Schmader, K. E., Ruby, C. M., & Weinberger, M. (2001). Suboptimal prescribing in older inpatients and outpatients. *Journal of the American Geriatric Society, 49,* 200–209.

Hayes, J. C., Krishnan, K. R., George, L. K., Pieper, C. F., Flint, E. P., & Blazer, D. G. (1997). Psychosocial and physical correlates of chronic depression. *Psychiatry Research, 72,* 149–159.

Hegel, M. T., Imming, J., Cyr-Provost, M., Noel, P. H., Areán, P. A., & Unützer, J. (2002). Role of behavioral health professionals in collaborative stepped care treatment model for depression in primary care: Project IMPACT. *Families, Systems and Health, 20*(3), 265–277.

Heisel, M. J., & Duberstein, P. R. (2005). Suicide prevention in older adults. *Clinical Psychology: Science and Practice, 12*(3), 242–259.

Hermann, C. (1997). International experiences with the Hospital Anxiety and Depression Scale: A review of validation data and clinical results. *Journal of Psychosomatic Research, 42*(1), 17–41.

Hogan, M. (2006). The President's New Freedom Commission: Recommendations to transform mental health care in America. *Psychiatric Services, 54,* 1467–1474.

Hybels, C. F., Blazer, D. G., & Pieper, C. F. (2001). Toward a threshold for subthreshold depression: Analysis of correlates of depression severity of symptoms using data from an elderly community sample. *Gerontologist, 41*(3), 357–365.

Katon, W. (1996). The impact of major depression on chronic medical illness. *General Hospital Psychiatry, 18,* 215–219.

Katon, W. J., Lin, E., Russo, J., & Unützer, J. (2003). Increased medical costs of a population-based sample of depressed elderly patients. *Archives of General Psychiatry, 60,* 897–903.

Katon, W., Russo, J., Von Korff, M., Lin, E., Simon, G., Bush, T., et al. (2002). Long-term effects of a collaborative care intervention in persistently depressed primary care patients. *Journal of General Internal Medicine, 17*(10), 741–748.

Katon, W., Von Korff, M., Lin, E., Bush, T., & Ormel, J. (1992). Adequacy and duration of antidepressant treatment in primary care. *Medical Care, 30,* 67–76.

Kelly, K. G., & Zisselman, M. (2000). Update on electroconvulsive therapy (ECT) in older adults. *Journal of the American Geriatrics Society, 48,* 560–566.

Kerlinger, F. (1986). *Foundations of behavioral research* (3rd ed). New York: Holt, Rinehart and Winston.

Kirmayer, L. J., Robbins, J. M., Dworkind, M., & Yafe, M. J. (1993). Somatization and the recognition of depression and anxiety in primary care. *American Journal of Psychiatry, 150,* 734–741.

Klap, R., Tschantz Unroe, K., & Unützer, J. (2003). Caring for mental illness in the United States: A focus on older adults. *American Journal of Geriatric Psychiatry, 11,* 517–524.

Klerman, G. L., Weissman, M. M., Rounsaville, B. J., & Chevron, E. S. (1984). *Interpersonal psychotherapy of depression.* New York: Basic Books.

Klinkman, M. S. (1997). Competing demands in psychosocial care: A model for the identification and treatment of depressive disorders in primary care. *General Hospital Psychiatry, 19,* 98–111.

Knight, B. (2004). *Psychotherapy with older adults.* Newbury Park, CA: Sage.

Koenig, H., Meador, K., Cohen, H., & Blazer, D. G. (1988). Depression in elderly hospitalized patients with medical illness. *Archives of Internal Medicine, 148,* 1929–1936.

Kraaij, V., Arensman, E., & Spinhoven, P. (2002). Negative life events and depression in elderly persons: A meta-analysis. *Journal of Gerontological Psychology, and Social Sciences, 57B,* 87–94.

Kroenke, K., Spitzer, R. L., & Williams, J. B. (2001). The PHQ-9: Validity of a brief depression severity measure. *Journal of General Internal Medicine, 16,* 606–613.

Laidlaw, K., Thompson, L. W., Dick-Siskin, L., & Gallagher-Thompson, D. (2003). *Cognitive behavior therapy with older people*. Hoboken, NJ: Wiley.

Lawrence, V., Murray, J., Banerjee, S., Turner, S., Sangha, K., Byng, R., et al. (2006). Concepts and causation of depression: A cross-cultural study of the beliefs of older adults. *Gerontologist, 46*(1), 23–32.

Lebowitz, B. D., Pearson, J. L., Schneider, L. S., Reynolds, C. F., Alexopoulos, G. S., Bruce, M. L., et al. (1997). Diagnosis and treatment of depression in late life. *Journal of the American Medical Association, 278*, 1186–1190.

Lewinsohn, P. M., Biglan, A., & Zeiss, A. M. (1976). Behavioral treatment of depression. In P. O. Davidson (Ed.), *Behavioral management of anxiety, depression and pain* (pp. 91–146). New York: Brunner/Mazel.

Lewinsohn, P. M., & Libet, L. (1972). Pleasant events, activity schedules and depression. *Journal of Abnormal Psychology, 97*, 251–264.

Lewinsohn, P. M., & MacPhillamy, D. (1974). The relationship between age and engagement in pleasant activities. *Journals of Gerontology, 29*, 290–294.

Lin, E. H., Katon, W. J., Simon, G. E., Von Korff, M., Bush, T. M., Rutter, C. M., et al. (1997). Achieving guidelines for the treatment of depression in primary care: Is physician education enough? *Medical Care, 35*(8), 831–842.

Lin, E. H., Katon, W., Von Korff, M., Tang, L., Williams, J., Kroenke, K., et al. (2003). Effect of improving depression care on pain and functional outcomes among older adults with arthritis: A randomized controlled trial. *Journal of the American Medical Association, 290*(18), 2428–2434.

Löwe, B., Kroenke, K., & Grafe, K. (2005). Detecting and monitoring depression with a two-item questionnaire (PHQ-2). *Journal of Psychosomatic Research, 58*, 163–171.

Luoma, J. B., Martin, C. E., & Pearson, J. L. (2002). Contact with mental health and primary care providers before suicide: A review of the evidence. *American Journal of Psychiatry, 159*, 909–916.

Lyness, J. M., Bruce, M. L., Koenig, H. G., Parmelee, P. A., Schultz, R., Lawton, M. P., et al. (1996). Depression and medical illness in late life: Report of a symposium. *Journal of the American Geriatric Society, 44*, 198–203.

Mackin, R. S., & Areán, P. A. (2005). Evidence-based psychotherapeutic interventions for geriatric depression. *Psychiatric Clinics of North America, 28*, 805–820.

McAvay, G. J., Raue, P. J., Brown, E. L., & Bruce, M. L. (2005). Symptoms of depression in older home-care patients: Patient and informant reports. *Psychology and Aging, 20*(3), 507–518.

McIntosh, J. I. (1995). Suicide prevention in the elderly (age 65–99). *Suicide and Life Threatening Behavior, 25*, 180–192.

McLeod, P. J., Huang, A. R., Tamblyn, R. M., & Gayton, D. C. (1997). Defining inappropriate practices in prescribing for elderly people: A national consensus panel. *Canadian Medication Association Journal, 156*(3), 385–391.

Miller, M. D., Cornes, C., Rank, E., Ehrenpreis, L., Silberman, R., Schlernitzauer, M. A., et al. (2001). Interpersonal psychotherapy for late-life depression: Past, present, and future. *Journal of Psychotherapy Practice and Research, 10*(4), 231–238.

Mirowsky, J., & Ross, C. J. (1992). Age and depression. *Journal of Health and Social Behavior, 33*, 187–205.

Mitchell, A. J., & Subramaniam, H. (2005). Prognosis of depression in old age compared to middle age: A systematic review of comparative studies. *American Journal of Psychiatry, 162*(9), 1588–1601.

Moran, M. (2006). Professional news: Aetna to pay for depression screening by primary care physicians. *Psychiatric News, 41*(2), 5.

Morrow-Howell, N. L., Proctor, E. K., Choi, S., Lawerence, L., Brooks, A., Hasche, L., et al. (2005). *Depression in community long-term care: Implications for intervention development.* Manuscript submitted for publication.

Morrow-Howell, N. L., Proctor, E. K., Rubin, E. H., & Thompson, S. (2000). Service needs of depressed older adults following acute psychiatric care. *Aging and Mental Health, 4,* 330–338.

Mulrow, C. D., Williams, J. W., Gerety, M. B., Ramirez, G., Montiel, O. M., & Kerber, C. (1995). Case-finding instruments for depression in primary care settings. *Annals of Internal Medicine, 122*(12), 913–921.

Mulsant, B. H., Alexopoulos, G. S., Reynolds, C. F., Katz, I. R., Abrams, R., Oslin, D., et al. (2001). Pharmacological treatment of depression in older primary care patients: The PROSPECT algorithm. *International Journal of Geriatric Psychiatry, 16,* 585–592.

Murray, C. J., & Lopez, A. D. (1996). *Global burden of disease: A comprehensive assessment of mortality and disability, injuries, and risk factors in 1990 and projected to 2020.* Cambridge, MA: Harvard University Press.

Murray, L., & Eppig, F. (2002). Insurance trends for the Medicare population. *Health Care Financing Review, 23,* 9–15.

Mynors-Wallis, L. (2003). Problem-solving treatment: Evidence for effectiveness and feasibility in primary care. *International Journal of Psychiatry in Medicine, 26*(3), 249–262.

Nagel, R., Lynch, D., & Tamburrino, M. (1998). Validity of the medical outcomes study depression screener in family practice training centers and community settings. *Family Medicine, 30*(5), 362–365.

National Alliance for Caregiving & American Association of Retired Persons. (2004). *Caregiving in the United States* (Funded by Met Life Foundation). Retrieved November 16, 2004, from http://www.caregiving.org/04finalreport.pdf.

National Alliance for the Mentally Ill. (2006). *Grading the states: A report on America's health care system for serious mental illness.* Arlington, VA: Author.

National Coalition for Mental Health and Aging. (2005). *National Coalition on Mental Health and Aging WHCOA listening session, January 24, 2005.* Retrieved March 30, 2006, from http://www.whcoa.gov/about/policy/meetings/meetings.asp#LS.

Nease, D. E., Klinkman, M. S., & Volk, R. J. (2002). Improved detection of depression in primary care through severity evaluation. *Journal of Family Practice, 51*(12), 1065–1070.

Nemeroff, C., Knight, D., Krishnan, K., Slotkin, T., Bisette, G., & Blazer, D. (1988). Marked reduction in the number of platelet titrated imipramine binding sites in geriatric depression. *American Journal of Geriatric Psychiatry, 45,* 919–923.

Nettelbladt, P., Hansson, L., Stefansson, C. G., Borgquist, L., & Nordstrom, G. (1993). Test characteristics of the Hopkins Symptom Check List-25 (HSCL-25) in Sweden, using the Present State Examination (PSE-9) as a caseness criterion. *Social Psychiatry and Psychiatric Epidemiology, 28*(3), 130–133.

Neumeyer-Gromen, A., Lampert, T., Stark, K., & Kallischnigg, G. (2004). Disease management programs for depression: A systematic review and meta-analysis of randomized controlled trials. *Medical Care, 42*(12), 1211–1221.

Oishi, S. M., Shoai, R., Katon, W., Callahan, C., Unützer, J., & the IMPACT Investigators. (2003). Impacting late life depression: Integrating a depression intervention into primary care. *Psychiatric Quarterly, 74*(1), 75–89.

Oslin, D. W., Sayers, S., Ross, J., Kane, V., Ten Have, T., Conigliaro, J., et al. (2003). Disease management for depression and at-risk drinking via telephone in an older population of veterans. *Psychosomatic Medicine, 65*(6), 931–937.

Oslin, D. W., Thompson, R., Kallan, M. J., Ten Have, T., Blow, F. C., Bastani, R., et al. (2004). Treatment effects from UPBEAT: A randomized trial of care management for behavioral health problems in hospitalized elderly patients. *Journal of Geriatric Psychiatry and Neurology, 17*(2), 99–106.

Oxman, T. E., Dietrich, A. J., & Schulberg, H. C. (2003). The depression care manager and mental health specialist as collaborators within primary care. *American Journal of Geriatric Psychiatry, 11*(5), 507–516.

Palmer, S. C., & Coyne, J. C. (2003). Screening for depression in medical care: Pitfalls, alternatives and revised priorities. *Journal of Psychosomatic Research, 54*, 279–287.

Parkerson, G. R., & Broadhead, W. E. (1997). Screening for anxiety and depression in primary care with the Duke Anxiety-Depression Scale. *Family Medicine, 29*(3), 177–181.

Parmelee, P., Katz, I., & Lawton, M. (1989). Depression among institutionalized aged: Assessment and prevalence estimation. *Journal of Gerontology: Medical Science, 44M*, 22–29.

Pearson, J. L., & Brown, G. K. (2000). Suicide prevention in late life: Directions for science and practice. *Clinical Psychology Review, 20*(6), 685–705.

Penninx, B. W., Geerlings, S., Deeg, D. J., VanEijk, J., Van Tilling, W., & Beekman, A. (2001). Minor depression and major depression and the risk of death in older persons. *Archives of General Psychiatry, 56*, 889–895.

Penninx, B. W., Guralink, J. M., Ferrucci, L., Simonsick, E. L., Deeg, D. J., & Wallace, R. B. (1998). Depressive symptoms and physical decline in community-dwelling older persons. *Journal of the American Medical Association, 279*(29), 1720–1726.

Pignone, M. P., Gaynes, B. N., Rushoton, J. L., Mills Burchell, C., Orleans, T., Mulrow, C. D., et al. (2002). Screening for depression in adults: A summary of the evidence for the U.S. Preventive Services Task Force. *Annals of Internal Medicine, 136*(10), 765–776.

Proctor, E. K., Morrow-Howell, N. L., Doré, P., Wentz, J., Rubin, E. H., Thompson, S., et al. (2003). Comorbid medical conditions among depressed elderly patients discharged home after acute psychiatric care. *American Journal of Geriatric Psychiatry, 11*(3), 329–338.

Public Health Service. (2001). *National strategy for suicide prevention: goals and objectives for action.* Rockville, MD: U.S. Department of Health and Human Services.

Rabins, P. V., Black, B. S., Roca, R., German, P., McGuire, M., Robbins, B., et al. (2000). Effectiveness of a nurse-based outreach program for identifying and treating psychiatric illness in the elderly. *Journal of the American Medical Association, 283*(21), 2802–2809.

Radloff, L. S., & Teri, L. (1986). Use of the Center for Epidemiological Studies Depression Scale for older adults. *Clinical Gerontologist, 5*, 119–136.

Raj, A. (2004). Depression in the elderly: Tailoring medical therapy to their special needs. *Postgrad Medicine Special Report, 115.* Retrieved March 20, 2006, from http://www.postgradmed.com/issues/2004/06_04/raj.htm.

Rao, V., & Lyketsos, C. G. (2000). The benefits of ECT for patients with primary dementia who also suffer from depression. *International Journal of Geriatric Psychiatry, 15*, 729–735.

Reiger, D. A., Narrow, W. E., Rae, D. S., Mandersheid, R. W., Locke, B. Z., & Goodwin, F. K. (1993). The de facto U.S. mental and addictive disorders service system: Epidemiological Catchment Area prospective 1-year prevalence rates of disorders and services. *Mental and Addictive Disorders Services, 50*, 85–94.

Reynolds, C. F., Dew, M. A., Pollock, B. G., Mulsant, B. H., Frank, E., Miller, M. D., et al. (2006). Maintenance treatment of major depression in old age. *New England Journal of Medicine, 354*, 1130–1138.

Reynolds, C. F., Frank, E., Perel, J. M., Imber, S. D., Cornes, C., Miller, M. D., et al. (1999). Nortriptyline and interpersonal psychotherapy as maintenance therapies for recurrent major depression: A randomized controlled trial in patients older than 59 years. *Journal of the American Medical Association, 281,* 39–45.

Robison, J., Gruman, C., Gaztambide, S., & Blank, K. (2002). Screening for depression in middle-aged and older Puerto Rican primary care patients. *Journal of Gerontology: Medical Sciences, 57A*(5), 308–314.

Rosenbach, M. L., & Ammering, C. J. (1997). Trends in Medicare Part B mental health utilization and expenditures: 1987–1992. *Health Care Financing Review, 18*(3), 19–43.

Rush, J. A. (1996). The Inventory of Depressive Symptomatology (IDS): Psychometric properties. *Psychological Medicine, 26,* 477–486.

Schoevers, R. A., Beekman, A. T. F., Deeg, D. J. H., Geerlings, M. I., Jonker, C., & Van Tilberg, W. (2000). Risk factors for depression in later life: Results of a prospective community based study (AMSTEL). *Journal of Affective Disorders, 59,* 127–137.

Schulberg, H. C., Hyg, M. S., Bruce, M. L., Lee, P. W., Williams, J. W., & Dietrich, A. J. (2004). Preventing suicide in primary care patients: The primary care physician's role. *General Hospital Psychiatry, 26,* 337–345.

Schulberg, H. C., Katon, W. J., Simon, G. E., & Rush, A. J. (1999). Best clinical practice: Guidelines for managing major depression in primary medical care. *Journal of Clinical Psychiatry, 60*(7), 19–26.

Schulberg, H., Mulsant, B., Schulz, R., Rollman, B., Houck, P., & Reynolds, C. (1998). Characteristics and course of major depression in older primary care patients. *International Journal of Psychiatric Medicine, 28,* 421–436.

Schulz, R., O'Brien, A. T., Bookwala, J., & Fleissner, K. (1995). Psychiatric and physical morbidity effects of Alzheimer's disease caregiving: Prevalence, correlates, and causes. *Gerontologist, 5,* 771–791.

Schwenk, T. L. (2002). Diagnosis of late life depression: The view from primary care. *Biological Psychiatry, 52,* 157–163.

Scogin, F., Welsh, D., Hanson, A., Stump, J., & Coates, A. (2005). Evidence-based psychotherapies for depression in older adults. *Clinical Psychology: Science and Practice, 12,* 222–237.

Segal, Z. V., Pearson, J. L., & Thase, M. E. (2003). Challenges in preventing relapse in major depression: Report of a National Institute of Mental Health workshop on state of the science of relapse prevention in major depression. *Journal of Affective Disorders, 77*(2), 97–108.

Shah, A., Odutoye, K., & De, T. (2001). Depression in acutely medically ill elderly inpatients: A pilot study of early identification and intervention by formal psychogeriatric consultation. *Journal of Affective Disorders, 62*(3), 233–240.

Shanmugham, B., Karp, J., Drayer, R., Reynolds, C. F., & Alexopoulos, G. (2005). Evidence-based pharmacologic interventions for geriatric depression. *Psychiatric Clinics of North America, 28,* 821–835.

Simon, G. E. (2002). Evidence review: Efficacy and effectiveness of antidepressant treatment in primary care. *General Hospital Psychiatry, 24,* 213–224.

Simon, G. E., Lin, E. H., Katon, W., Saunders, K., Von Korff, M., Walker, E., et al. (1995). Outcomes of "inadequate" antidepressant treatment. *Journal of General Internal Medicine, 10,* 663–670.

Simon, G. E., Ludman, E. J., Tutty, S., Operskalski, B., & Von Korff, M. (2004). Telephone psychotherapy and telephone care management for primary care patients starting antidepressant treatment: A randomized controlled trial. *Journal of the American Medical Association, 292*(8), 935–942.

Simon, G. E., Manning, W. G., Katzelnick, D. J., Pearson, S. D., Henk, H. J., & Helstad, C. S. (2001). Cost-effectiveness of systematic depression treatment for high utilizers of general medical care. *Archives of General Psychiatry, 58*(2), 181–187.

Sloane, R. B., Staples, F. R., & Schneider, L. S. (1985). Interpersonal therapy versus nortiptyline for depression in the elderly. In G. D. Burrows, T. R. Norman, & L. Dennerstein (Eds.), *Clinical and pharmacological studies in psychiatric disorders* (pp. 344–346). London: John Libbey.

Smyer, M., & Shea, D. (2003). Mental health financing. In L. Vitt (Ed.), *Encyclopedia of retirement and finance* (pp. 544–553). Westport, CT: Greenwood Press.

Spitzer, R. L., Kroenke, K., Linzer, M., Hahn, S. R., Williams, J. B., deGruy, F. V., et al. (1995). Health-related quality of life in primary care patients with mental disorders: Results from the PRIME-MD 1000 study. *Journal of the American Medical Association, 274*(19), 1511–1517.

Spitzer, R. L., Williams, J. B., Kroenke, K., Linzer, M., deGruy, F. V., Hahn, S. R., et al. (1994). Utility of a new procedure for diagnosing mental disorders in primary care: The PRIME-MD 1000 Study. *Journal of the American Medical Association, 272*(22), 1749–1756.

Steer, R. A., Cavalieri, T. A., Leonard, D. M., & Beck, A. T. (1999). Use of the Beck Depression Inventory for Primary Care to screen for major depression disorders. *General Hospital Psychiatry, 21*(2), 106–111.

Tew, J. D., Mulsant, B. H., Haskett, R. F., Prudic, J., Thase, M. E., Crowe, R. R., et al. (1999). Acute efficacy of ECT in the treatment of major depression in the old-old. *American Journal of Psychiatry, 156*(12), 1865–1870.

Thase, M. E., & Beck, A. T. (1993). Overview of cognitive therapy. In J. Wright (Ed.), *Cognitive therapy with inpatients: Developing a cognitive milieu* (pp. 3–34). New York: Guilford Press.

Thompson, C., Kinmonth, A. L., Stevens, L., Pevele, R. C., Stevens, A., Ostler, K. J., et al. (2000). Effects of clinical-practice guideline and practice-based education on detection and outcomes of depression in primary care. *Lancet, 355*, 185–191.

Thompson, L. W., Coon, D., & Gallagher-Thompson, D. (2001). Comparison of desipramine and cognitive/behavioral therapy in the treatment of elderly outpatients with mild-to-moderate depression. *American Journal of Geriatric Psychiatry, 9*, 225–240.

Thompson, L. W., Gallagher, D., & Steinmetz Breckenridge, J. (1987). Comparative effectiveness of psychotherapies for depressed elders. *Journal of Consulting and Clinical Psychology, 55*(3), 385–390.

Thorpe, K. E., Florence, C. S., & Joski, P. (2004). Which medical conditions account for the rise in health care spending? *Health Affairs, W4*, 437–445.

Toseland, R. W., McCallion, P., Smith, T., & Banks, S. (2004). Supporting caregivers of frail older adults in an HMO setting. *American Journal of Orthopsychiatry, 74*(3), 349–364.

Trivedi, M. H. (2003). Using treatment algorithms to bring patients to remission. *Journal of Clinical Psychiatry, 64*(2), 8–13.

Turvey, C. L., Conwell, Y., Jones, M. P., Phillips, C., Simonsick, E., Pearson, J. L., et al. (2002). Risk factors for late-life suicide: A prospective community-based study. *American Journal of Geriatric Psychiatry, 10*(4), 398–406.

U.S. Department of Health and Human Services. (1999). *Mental health: A report of the surgeon general*. Rockville, MD: Author.

U. S. Department of Health and Human Services. (2004). *New freedom commission on mental health: Achieving the promise*. Rockville, MD: Author.

U.S. Preventive Services Task Force. (2002). Screening for depression: Recommendations and rationale. *Annals of Internal Medicine, 136*(10), 760–764.

Unützer, J., Katon, W., Callahan, C. M., Williams, J. W., Hunkeler, E., Harpole, L., et al. (2002). Collaborative care management of late life depression in the primary care setting: A randomized controlled trial. *Journal of the American Medical Association, 288*(22), 2836–2845.

Unützer, J., Patrick, D. L., Marmon, T., Simon, G. E., & Katon, W. J. (2002). Depressive symptoms and mortality in a prospective study of 2,558 older adults. *American Journal of Geriatric Psychiatry, 10*(5), 521–530.

Unützer, J., Schoenbaum, M., Druss, B., & Katon, W. (2006). Transforming mental health care at the interface with general medicine. *Psychiatric Services, 57*, 37–47.

Van der Wurff, F. B., Stek, M. L., Hoogendijk, W. J. G., & Beekman, A. T. F. (2003). The efficacy and safety of ECT in depressed older adults: A literature review. *International Journal of Geriatric Psychiatry, 18*, 894–904.

Wells, K. B. (1997). Caring for depression in primary care: Defining and illustrating the policy context. *Journal of Clinical Psychiatry, 58*(1), 24–27.

White House Conference on Aging Policy Committee. (2006). *Preliminary report to the governors*. Retrieved March 30, 2006, from http://www.whcoa.gov/about/resolutions.

Williams, J. W., Katon, W., Lin, E. H., Noel, P. H., Worchel, J., Cornell, J., et al. (2004). The effectiveness of depression care management on diabetes-related outcomes in older patients. *Annals of Internal Medicine, 140*(2), 1015–1024.

Williams, J. W., Mulrow, C. D., Kroenke, K., Dhanda, R., Badgett, R. G., Omori, D., et al. (1999). Case-finding for depression in primary care: A randomized trial. *American Journal of Medicine, 106*, 36–43.

Williams, J. W., Pignone, M., Ramirez, G., & Perez Stellato, C. (2002). Identifying depression in primary care: A literature synthesis of case-finding instruments. *General Hospital Psychiatry, 24*, 225–237.

Woodhead, E. L., & Stoner, S. (2005, November). *Assessment of depression in older adults*. Paper presented at the Gerontological Society of America, Orlando, FL.

Zung, W. W. (1965). A self-rating depression scale. *Archives of General Psychiatry, 12*(1), 63–70.

CHAPTER 12

Substance Abuse

NOELL L. ROWAN and ANNA C. FAUL

T HE POPULATION OF the United States is aging, as evidenced by the increase in the older adult population from 3.1 million in 1900 to 35 million in 2000. The U.S. Census Bureau (He, Sengupta, Velkoff, & DeBarros, 2005) projects that a substantial increase in the number of older people (age 65 and older) will occur between 2010 and 2030. It is estimated that the older population will grow from 35 million in 2000 to 72 million in 2030—nearly 20% of the total U.S. population. The median age in the United States in 2000 was 35.3, 12.4 years older than in 1900, with a projected median age in 2030 of 39 years (He et al., 2005). It is predicted that the number of adults over 65 will grow by an average of 2.8% annually between 2010 and 2030 (Blow, 2000; Center for Substance Abuse Treatment [CSAT], 1998).

Alcohol and drug abuse and misuse among older adults are one of the fastest growing public health problems in the United States. The current aging population has more liberal attitudes toward substance use than older adults from a generation or two ago, resulting in expectations that the drug abuse problem will increase in the years to come (Shibusawa, 2006). Evidence is starting to grow showing that this new generation of older adults will have high levels of substance-related health problems. The use of alcohol, combined with the inappropriate use of medications, is nationally reported as the leading problem for admission of older adults to substance abuse treatment facilities (Ray, 2002).

Despite the fact that alcohol and drug misuse affects as many as 17% of older adults, the problem does not receive enough prominence in the literature, probably due to substance use being more common among younger adults (ages 18 to 49) than among older adults (50 and older; Blow, 2000; CSAT, 1998; Shibusawa, 2006). In this chapter, the incidence and prevalence of substance abuse among the elderly is discussed, as well as evidence-based approaches to assessment and intervention.

TRENDS AND INCIDENCE

Substance abuse among the elderly includes not only alcohol and illicit drug use, but also prescription and over-the-counter drug abuse. The separation between alcohol use and drug use is becoming blurred, mainly due to the inappropriate use of prescription and over-the-counter medications (Ray, 2002). More and more older adults are now also using illicit drugs, casting doubt on the "maturing-out theory," which claims that people age out of illicit drug use or die prematurely from abuse (Shibusawa, 2006).

The following sections address alcohol abuse, misuse of prescription and over-the-counter medications, and illicit drug abuse. In an effort to clarify the trends and incidents associated with alcohol and other drugs, each is discussed separately.

ALCOHOL ABUSE

Many older people associate alcohol use with socialization and use alcohol in moderation. However, there are a growing number of older adults who use alcohol as a way to cope with some life events and to help them relax (Hooyman & Kiyak, 2002).

The overall prevalence of drinking is relatively low among people 65 and older (National Center for Health Statistics [NCHS], 2000). In 2000, about 50% of the population ages 18 to 44 were regular consumers of alcohol, compared with 46% of adults ages 45 to 64 and 29% of older adults (He et al., 2005).

Despite the lower prevalence of alcohol consumption by older adults, alcohol abuse and misuse is the major substance abuse problem in this population. In each year from 1995 to 2002, alcohol was the most frequently reported primary substance of abuse among those admitted to a treatment facility (The DASIS Report, 2005). It is estimated that 4% to 20% of community-dwelling older adults abuse alcohol (Shibusawa, 2006). These percentages translate to an estimated 2.5 million older adults with problems related to alcohol (Blow, 2000; CSAT, 1998). In health care settings, 6% to 11% of older adults exhibit symptoms of alcoholism; in psychiatric settings, 20% of older adults exhibit similar symptoms; and in emergency rooms, 14% (Shibusawa, 2006). Rates for alcohol-related hospitalizations among older adults are similar to those for heart attacks. Forty-nine percent of older nursing home residents show signs of alcoholism, some of whom may be using nursing homes for short-term rehabilitation (Blow, 2000; CSAT, 1998).

The National Institute of Alcohol Abuse and Alcoholism recommends that older adults drink no more than one alcoholic drink per day because of age-related physical changes. The central nervous system, liver, and kidneys become less tolerant of alcohol with age because of the physiological changes taking place due to the aging process. Despite this recommendation, studies have shown that 20% of residents in retirement communities have two or more drinks per day (Gurnack, 1997; Hooyman & Kiyak, 2002; Shibusawa, 2006).

In 2000, 40.7% of White men over 65 were current regular alcohol users (at least 12 drinks in a week), with lower percentages reported by Hispanic men (35.6%) and African American men (23.7%; NCHS, 2000). Despite the elevated regular usage of alcohol by White men, African American and Hispanic older men demonstrate the highest prevalence of alcohol dependence (Shibusawa, 2006). Overall, alcohol abuse is 4 times more common in older men than women.

Despite these alarming figures, they still represent an underestimation of the true problem. It is difficult to obtain accurate statistics on the prevalence of alcoholism in older adults, due mainly to the stigma associated with this condition among older adults, nonspecific symptoms for older adults, and inadequate screening methods specific for older adults (He et al., 2005; Hooyman & Kiyak, 2002).

MISUSE AND ABUSE OF PRESCRIPTION AND OVER-THE-COUNTER MEDICATION

Adults over 65 consume more prescribed and over-the-counter medications than any other age group in the United States (Blow, 2000; CSAT, 1998). Older adults spend $15 billion a year on prescription drugs, four times the amount spent by younger populations. Prescriptions filled by older adults represent approximately 30% of prescription expenditures (Hooyman & Kiyak, 2002). An average older patient takes 5.3 prescription medicines per day. Over-the-counter medications commonly used by older adults are pain relievers, sleeping aids, cold remedies, antacids, laxatives, and vitamins (Shibusawa, 2006). A large amount of prescriptions for older adults are for psychoactive, mood-changing drugs that have the potential for misuse, abuse, or dependency (Blow, 2000; CSAT, 1998).

The literature distinguishes between misuse and abuse of prescription and over-the-counter medication. Misuse refers to the inappropriate use of medications that can be caused by difficulties with reading and following prescription labels, keeping track of medications, and taking inappropriate dosages. Vision and hearing loss can increase the misuse of prescription and over-the-counter medications among older adults. Physicians can also cause misuse by inappropriate prescribing of medications. Problems with drugs generally fall into the misuse category and are unintentional (Blow, 2000; CSAT, 1998; Shibusawa, 2006).

Abuse, on the other hand, refers to the use of medication in a way that is nontherapeutic and not for its intended purposes. A typical form of abuse occurs when older adults use prescription or over-the-counter medications as a form of self-medication. Unintentional misuse can progress into abuse if an older adult continues to use a medication nontherapeutically for the desirable effects it provides (Blow, 2000; CSAT, 1998; Shibusawa, 2006).

The most commonly prescribed psychoactive medications for older adults (with potential for abuse) are benzodiazepines, antidepressants, and opiate/opioid analgesics. Benzodiazepines, which are prescribed for conditions such as insomnia, anxiety, and chronic pain, are prescribed widely among older adults. Studies report that 17% to 23% of drugs prescribed to older adults in North America are benzodiazepines (Blow, 2000; CSAT, 1998; Shibusawa, 2006). The drug-taking patterns of psychoactive prescription drug users can be described on a continuum that ranges from appropriate use for medical or psychiatric indications through misuse to persistent abuse and dependence (Blow, 2000; CSAT, 1998; Shibusawa, 2006). Older women are more likely than men to receive psychoactive drugs, and drug dependence is more common among older women than men (Shibusawa, 2006).

ILLICIT DRUG ABUSE AND DEPENDENCE

According to the 2000 National Household Survey on Drug Abuse, 568,000 adults age 55 or older (1% of all older adults in the United States), reported using illicit drugs in 2000 (Substance Abuse and Mental Health Administration, 2001). The Epidemiologic Catchment Area Study indicates a lifetime prevalence of illegal drug use of 1.6% of persons over 65 (Patterson & Jeste, 1999). Data gathered through surveys of homeless individuals and drug arrest data indicate that illicit drug use in the elderly population is not very common (Atkinson, Ganzini, & Bernstein, 1992).

The general belief is that most older adults who use or are dependent on illegal drugs start using these drugs early on in their lives (Blow, Oslin, & Barry, 2002). The popular maturing-out theory suggests that people age out of illicit drug use or die prematurely from abuse. However, methadone treatment and needle exchange programs have added to the longevity of heroin and injection drug users. Also, the number of older adults who start using crack cocaine for the first time after age 50 is slowly on the increase (Shibusawa, 2006).

The National Survey on Drug Abuse provides one of the few nationwide longitudinal studies that allow examination of drug use trends over time in specific age cohorts. In 1979, overall, 27% of younger baby boomers (born between 1946 and 1964), ages 21 to 33—almost 14 million people—reported using any illicit drug during the past month. The prevalence rate has remained stable but higher than for age-matched cohorts from previous generations. These data suggest that some baby boomers have continued to use illicit drugs as they age. Marijuana is the most commonly used illicit drug by older adults, at a rate of 1.1% (National Survey on Drug Use and Health, 2005). Due to large numbers of baby boomers, it can be expected that larger numbers of current drug users will reach age 65 and have a potential impact on treatment programs and other resources (Patterson & Jeste, 1999).

ETIOLOGY AND PROGNOSIS

At all ages, women drink less than men (Fingerhood, 2000). It is therefore understandable that older men are much more likely than older women to have alcohol-related problems, mainly due to a longer history of problem drinking than women (Blow, 2000). Older women are less likely to drink and less likely to drink heavily, although they are more likely than men to start drinking heavily later in life (Menninger, 2002). Gomberg (1995) found that men reported a mean age at onset of 27.0 years, whereas women reported 46.2 years.

A specific distinction must be made between chronic alcoholics or early-onset drinkers and situational alcoholics or late-onset drinkers. About two thirds of elderly individuals with alcoholism problems are early-onset drinkers (Benshoff & Harrawood, 2003). Throughout their lives, they have turned to alcohol to cope with a range of psychosocial or medical problems. Drinking has become an overlearned, maladaptive coping response. Psychiatric comorbidity is common among this group, particularly major affective disorders and thought disorders. Alcohol-related physical complications like cirrhosis are common for chronic alcoholics (Blow, 2000; Hanson & Gutheil, 2004). More men than women are classified into the early-onset drinking group.

Late-onset drinkers or situational alcoholics are more likely to have begun or to have increased drinking in response to a negative life situation or event such as retirement, divorce, death of a spouse, decline in status in the community, or health setbacks (Benshoff & Harrawood, 2003; McInnis-Dittrich, 2005). About one third of older adults with drinking problems are late-onset abusers, with more women identified in this category (Hanson & Gutheil, 2004; McInnis-Dittrich, 2005). Alcohol abuse is more prevalent among older adults who have been separated or divorced and among men who have been widowed. Varied disorders may be triggered in older men when their wife dies: depression, development of alcohol problems, and suicide (National Institute on Alcohol Abuse and Alcoholism, 1988). Other losses of family members may also trigger alcohol abuse. When older adults retire, they may lose significant income as well as job-related social support systems and the structure of self-esteem that work provides. Other losses include diminished mobility, impaired sensory capabilities, and declining health due to chronic illnesses. All of these losses may trigger isolation and alcohol abuse. Some researchers suggest that increased amounts of free time and lessening of role responsibilities may serve as an etiological factor for why women start drinking later in their lives (Blow, 2000). Moving to a retirement community may also trigger overdrinking, when the social activities provide more opportunities to drink (Abrams, 2002).

Drinking patterns in late-onset abusers have created fewer cumulative negative stressors on family and friends. They may also lead to fewer physical and mental health problems and stronger societal connections; late-onset abusers are less likely to have ever been in an alcohol treatment program. This group therefore has a better prognosis for recovery because they have not suffered the physically and psychologically devastating effects of long-term alcohol and drug problems (Benshoff & Harrawood, 2003).

A strong relationship exists between developing a substance use disorder earlier in life and experiencing a recurrence in later life. Some recovering alcoholics with long periods of sobriety undergo a recurrence of alcoholic drinking as a result of major losses or an excess of free time. A previous drinking problem is the strongest indicator of a problem in later life. Genetic factors are also important in alcohol-related behaviors. Studies provide strong evidence that drinking behaviors are greatly influenced by genetics throughout the life span (Blow, 2000).

A variety of factors influence the use and potential for misuse of psychoactive prescription drugs and over-the-counter medications by older adults. Old age, poor physical health, and female sex are most consistently correlated with psychoactive prescription drug use in the literature (Blow, 2000). The Epidemiological Catchment Area (ECA) study reports that benzodiazepine use was predicted by being elderly, White, female, less educated, and separated or divorced, by having experienced a greater number of negative life events, and by having a psychiatric diagnosis (Patterson & Jeste, 1999).

Among older women, use of psychoactive drugs is correlated with late-life divorce, widowhood, less education, poorer health, and more depression and anxiety. Older women are nearly twice as likely as older men to develop a diagnosable anxiety disorder. Bereavement often precipitates anxiety. Anxiety is also common after a severe traumatic event (Blow, 2000).

Many mature women use prescription and over-the-counter medications appropriately. Unfortunately, there are some older women who dangerously overuse the drugs or mix them with alcohol. This inappropriate use can lead to chronic abuse or addiction; mixing sedating psychoactive drugs with alcohol usually accelerates the development of a dependence on the drug because the alcohol magnifies the drug's effect (Abrams, 2002).

A variety of health care system-related factors place older adult users of psychoactive prescription drugs at risk for misuse, abuse, or dependence. Potentially dangerous prescribing practices include ordering medications without a clear diagnosis, prescribing them without medical monitoring for too long a period of time, selecting drugs with a high risk for side effects in older adults at the doses given, ordering drugs without checking whether they interact adversely with other medications the older adult is taking, and failure to provide instructions for patients regarding how and when to take medications and what side effects to expect (Blow, 2000).

The medical consequences of acute alcohol intoxication are more severe in the elderly than in other age groups. Due to the human aging process, physiological changes occur in the older adult that account for the development of problems secondary to alcohol use even when the older adult did not increase the amount of alcohol intake over the years. One of the major problems for older adults is the decreased absorption rate in the gastrointestinal system, occurring as a result of decreased blood flow to that system. Drugs and alcohol therefore remain in the body longer and at higher rates of concentration. Reduced hepatic blood flow and decreased enzyme efficiency diminish the liver's functional capacity to metabolize drugs and alcohol. Older adults therefore keep an increased amount of drugs in their body for longer periods of time. The mortality rate for cirrhotic liver disease in older adults is about twice the mortality rate for the general population (Benshoff & Harrawood, 2003; Menninger, 2002).

Aging decreases the proportion of body water and increases the proportion of body fat. Therefore, the concentration of alcohol and the sensitivity to alcohol is increased because alcohol is a water-soluble substance. Concentration of lipid soluble drugs, particularly benzodiazepines, increases and prolongs their effects. For many older adults, the decrease in body mass is so significant that the typical adult dose of a medication, particularly a sedative-hypnotic medication, may be far too high (Benshoff & Harrawood, 2003).

Many medications used by the elderly have the potential for inducing tolerance, withdrawal syndromes, and harmful medical consequences such as cognitive changes, renal disease, and liver disease. Illness and mortality rates associated with misusing prescription and nonprescription medications are on the increase (Blow et al., 2002; Fingerhood, 2000).

The consequences of substance abuse are numerous and tend to mimic other problems that are common among older adults. Vague symptoms such as irritability, stomach upset, weight loss, malnutrition, depression, and insomnia may be the first signs of a problem. Later, evidence of liver, kidney, and heart disease, osteoporosis, incontinence, and pancreatitis may become evident. Problems associated with the misuse of benzodiazepines overlap with those of alcohol abuse and may include drowsiness, sedation, confusion, memory loss, falls, and other types of accidents. When used in combination, the adverse effects of alcohol and benzodiazepines may be severe (Finfgeld-Connett, 2004).

The most common causes of death in older substance abusers are cirrhosis of the liver; cancers of the mouth, esophagus, pharynx, lung, and liver; breast cancer in women; and trauma. Gastrointestinal and liver diseases are the main complications of alcohol use among older adults. Esophagitis, ulcer disease, and gastritis are all more common in the older drinker; aspirin and other nonsteroidal anti-inflammatory drugs commonly taken by older people add to the risk of these alcohol-related problems. Alcohol may lead to malabsorption of vitamins and cause chronic diarrhea. Alcohol is also the second leading cause of acute pancreatitis in older people, after gallstone disease, and is the cause of chronic pancreatitis in many cases. The complications associated with alcohol use in older adults are no different than in younger people. However, the complications may be more severe and occur at lower levels of alcohol consumption than in younger people (Fingerhood, 2000).

Despite the severe effects of substance abuse in older adults, several barriers exist that make proper identification of substance abusers difficult. Problem use of alcohol and other drugs in older adults does not necessarily meet the criteria for substance abuse or dependence as defined by the *Diagnostic and Statistical Manual of Mental Disorders*, fourth edition (*DSM-IV-TR*; American Psychiatric Association, 2000). The criteria for problematic abuse or dependence do provide for common communication among service providers in terms of an operational definition and subsequent treatment. However, these criteria (see Table 12.1) may present challenges when applying them to older adults.

The criterion of tolerance for substance dependence may not apply to older adults with alcoholism due to the high sensitivity and higher blood levels at lower consumption amounts. Because older persons are more sensitive to the effects of alcohol and other medications, their consumption of lower quantities of alcohol may not meet the criterion of spending a great deal of time in activities related to substance use. Menninger (2002) reports that the criteria for physiological dependence with withdrawal may not be detected in older people with late-onset alcoholism. However, cognitive dysfunction may interfere with older persons' ability to monitor their drinking.

Another concern with the *DSM-IV-TR* criteria for substance abuse and dependence in older adults is the criterion of failure to fulfill major role obligations at work, as this may have changed with retirement or isolation from regular social interaction. These concerns, along with denial of chemical abuse and dependence, make screening, assessment, and diagnosis challenging with older adult clients.

Menninger (2002) identified several barriers to being able to identify alcohol and other drug misuse in older adults. As illustrated in Table 12.2, these barriers make it easier to see why older adults have been underidentified and underdiagnosed.

EVIDENCE-BASED INTERVENTIONS

Screening and Assessment

Before health professionals can intervene, it is important to know the common signs and symptoms of substance abuse in older adults and to effectively screen for any problems with alcohol or other drugs. A careful and thorough history must be compiled to include a history of first chemical use, regular using patterns, heavy using patterns (including a question about frequency and amount as well as any related consequences with all chemicals such as tobacco, alcohol, anxiolytics, hypnotics, and prescribed, borrowed, over-the-counter, and street drugs). This history should also include the current patterns of use of chemicals, attitudes toward aging and drinking alcohol and using other drugs, and a nutritional and current diet status.

Table 12.1

DSM-IV-TR Criteria for Substance Abuse and Dependence

Abuse

A. A maladaptive pattern of substance use, leading to clinically significant impairment or distress, as manifested by one (or more) of the following, occurring within a 12-month period:

 (1) recurrent substance use resulting in a failure to fulfill major role obligations at work, school, or home (e.g., repeated absences or poor work performance related to substance use; substance-related absences, suspensions, or expulsions from school; neglect of children or household)

 (2) recurrent substance use in situations in which it is physically hazardous (e.g., driving an automobile or operating a machine when impaired by substance use)

 (3) recurrent substance-related legal problems (e.g., arrests for substance-related disorderly conduct)

 (4) continued substance use despite having persistent or recurrent social or interpersonal problems caused or exacerbated by the effects of the substance (e.g., arguments with spouse about consequences of intoxication, physical fights)

B. The symptoms have never met the criteria for Substance Dependence for this class of substance.

Dependence

A. A maladaptive pattern of substance use, leading to clinically significant impairment or distress, as manifested by three (or more) of the following, occurring at any time in the same 12-month period:

 (1) tolerance, as defined by either of the following:
   (a) a need for markedly increased amounts of the substance to achieve intoxication or desired effect;
   (b) markedly diminished effect with continued use of the same amount of the substance.

 (2) withdrawal, as manifested by either of the following:
   (a) the characteristic withdrawal syndrome for the substance;
   (b) the same (or closely related) substance is taken to relieve or avoid withdrawal symptoms.

 (3) the substance is often taken in larger amounts or over a longer period than was intended.

 (4) there is a persistent desire or unsuccessful efforts to cut down or control substance use.

 (5) a great deal of time is spent in activities necessary to obtain the substance (e.g., visiting multiple doctors or driving long distances), use the substance (e.g., chain-smoking), or recover from its effects.

 (6) important social, occupational, or recreational activities are given up or reduced because of substance use.

 (7) the substance use is continued despite knowledge of having a persistent or recurrent physical or psychological problem that is likely to have been caused or exacerbated by the substance (e.g., current cocaine use despite recognition of cocaine-induced depression, or continued drinking despite recognition that an ulcer was made worse by alcohol consumption).

Source: Diagnostic and Statistical Manual of Mental Disorders, fourth edition, text revision (pp. 110–111, 114–115), by the American Psychiatric Association, 2000, Washington, DC: Author.

Table 12.2
Barriers to Identifying Alcohol and Other Drug Misuse in Older Adults

Barrier	Example
Beliefs about aging held by health care providers and family members	Physicians or family members may not pay attention to drinking or using patterns if they think those patterns are a reaction to the stressors of aging.
Pessimism about prognosis in older people who drink alcohol or misuse other drugs	Health care providers or family members may not be aware of treatment resources for elderly alcoholics or drug addicts and the chances of recovery.
Denial of addiction to alcohol or other drugs	Shame about alcohol or other drug use is common among older people, and some may believe alcoholism and other drug addiction is a moral weakness.
Fewer social warning signs in older people	There are fewer alcohol-or drug-related legal or occupational problems.
Concurrent medical conditions skew the clinical picture in older people	Symptoms are disguised when other illnesses such as anemia, peripheral neuropathy, or altered cognition are present.
Addiction may happen unknowingly	Some over-the-counter medications contain significant amounts of alcohol.

Some common signs and symptoms of problematic use of alcohol and other drugs in the older population are indicated in the literature. For example, Blow et al. (2002) described the guidelines for older adults and use of alcohol. It is recommended by the National Institute on Alcohol Abuse and Alcoholism (Dufour & Fuller, 1995) and the CSAT's Treatment Improvement Protocol (TIP; 1998) on older adults to limit consumption to no more than one standard drink (one 12-ounce beer, 5-ounce glass of wine, or 1.5 ounces [one shot] of liquor) per day or seven drinks per week. Further, it is advised that a person 65 or older should not consume more than two standard drinks on any one occasion.

Blow et al. (2002) and Fingerhood (2000) presented signs and symptoms of potential substance misuse and abuse in older adults. The list includes anxiety, increased tolerance to alcohol or medications, blackouts, dizziness, legal difficulties, depression, mood swings, memory loss, loss of motivation, disorientation, new difficulties with activities of daily living, new challenges in decision making, diminished hygiene, drug-seeking behavior, doctor shopping, falls, bruises, burns, family or marital problems, idiopathic seizures, financial problems, sleep disturbance, headaches, social isolation, incontinence, and poor nutrition. A decreased tolerance has also been noted in older adults due to the increased chemical sensitivity in this population. For instance, elderly persons can consume alcohol less frequently and per occasion drink a decreased amount and still experience the same effect as do young alcoholics (Thibault & Maly, 1993).

Accurate recognition of problematic behaviors and illness must include a clear definition of target symptoms and behavior, the principle that change in the symptoms or behavior leads to an improved quality of life, and a description that the problems are not rare (Gurnack, Atkinson, & Osgood, 2002). Identification of at-risk substance use and problematic behaviors and illness through careful screening and assessment techniques is crucial to providing quality services.

Although the interview with a practitioner remains the clinician's greatest asset, standardized screening tools provide a rapid, sensitive, inexpensive, and more objective perspective in the screening for problematic use to assist in focusing suitable treatment options (Gurnack et al., 2002). There are several screening tools being used by practitioners: CAGE, Michigan Alcohol Screening Test-Geriatric Version (MAST-G), Short Form Michigan Alcohol Screening Test-Geriatric Version (SMAST-G), Alcohol Use Disorders Identification Test (AUDIT), and Alcohol Related Problems Survey (ARPS).

The CAGE (Ewing, 1984; Mayfield, McLeod, & Hall, 1974) is the most widely used alcohol-problem screening tool. It is very brief, with only four items, and is easily administered in a nonthreatening manner in an interview. The four items pertain to wanting to **C**ut down, feeling **A**nnoyed that people criticize one's drinking, feeling **G**uilty about others criticizing one's drinking, and having an **E**ye-opener drink in the morning to get rid of a hangover or to get motivated. Two positive responses indicate that further assessment is needed to determine an abusive, dependent, or otherwise problematic use of alcohol (Buellens & Aertgeerts, 2004). The typical clinical cutoff score is two positive responses; however, some authors suggest lowering the cutoff to one positive response when screening the elderly (Buellens & Aertgeerts, 2004; Conigliaro, Kraemer, & McNeil, 2000). Buchsbaum, Buchanan, Welsh, Centor, and Schnoll (1992) reported that a cutoff of one positive answer on the CAGE yielded a sensitivity of 86% and a specificity of 78% in distinguishing problematic alcohol behaviors in the elderly.

The SMAST-G is the short form of the Michigan Alcoholism Screening Test— Geriatric Version (MAST-G). This test was developed as a screen for alcohol problems in the elderly; it consists of 10 items (SMAST-G) and 24 items (MAST-G; Blow, 1998; Blow et al., 1992; Moore, 1972). More than five positive answers indicates an alcohol problem. The test has a sensitivity of 91% to 93% and a specificity of 65% to 84% when compared with *DSM* criteria (Blow et al., 1992; Joseph, Ganzin, & Atkinson, 1995; Morton, Jones, & Manganaro, 1996).

The Alcohol Use Disorders Identification Test (AUDIT) is a 10-item instrument developed to screen for alcohol use disorders and focuses on consumption (Babor, de la Fuenta, Saunders, & Grant, 1992). Morton and colleagues (1996) found that when using a cutoff score of 8, the AUDIT appeared useful but less sensitive than the CAGE. The AUDIT demonstrated a sensitivity of 33% and a specificity of 91%.

The Alcohol Related Problems Survey (ARPS) is a 10-item self-administered reliable and valid instrument developed specifically for older adults (Fink, Elliott, Tsai, & Beck, 2005; Fink et al., 2002; Moore, Hays, Reuben, & Beck, 2000). This survey focuses on early detection of alcohol-related problems and is recommended for use in primary care settings. There is also a computerized version called the CARPS that has been used in a study by Fink et al. (2005) to demonstrate that older primary care patients can effectively decrease alcohol consumption and other drinking risks when given personalized information about how their drinking affects their health.

These screening tools have shown some success in assisting with intervention for alcohol problems in the elderly, but it is still important to consider that they are only self-report measures and that urine drug screens and a comprehensive interview by a qualified professional are crucial for a more detailed and substantive clinical assessment. Urine drug screens continue to be useful as both a screening mechanism and as a confirmation of self-report. The majority of drugs of abuse remain detectable in a urine drug screen for 4 or more days, and there is an option of increasing the reliability of the drug screen through ordering a chain of custody (Barry, Oslin, & Blow, 2001).

Research literature has urged that substance abuse treatment services for older persons should begin with screening in the primary care provider's (PCP) setting due to the frequency of visits made to the PCP (6 to 8 times) per year (Emlet, Hawks, & Callahan, 2001; Fink et al., 2005; Gunter & Arndt, 2004; Saleh & Szebenyi, 2005). It is possible that if screening and referral to appropriate substance abuse treatment were to occur as standard practice in PCP offices, urgent visits to emergency rooms might decline.

Saleh and Szebenyi (2005) studied data from 11 states from the Healthcare Cost and Utilization Project State Inpatient Databases ($N = 2,309,872$) in relation to resource use of elderly with alcohol-related diagnoses. This research revealed the necessity for proper linkages between hospital emergency rooms and substance abuse treatment facilities equipped to provide medical detoxification services for older clients to decrease the added resource burden acquired by alcohol-related emergency room admissions.

Emlet et al. (2001) explained that social workers acting on behalf of their older clients have an obligation to educate family members or caregivers and other health care providers about problematic alcohol and other drug use among the elderly. Due to the issues unique to older adults (i.e., historical and cultural factors that lead to their feeling disgraced), older adults may find it increasingly difficult to identify their drinking or using other drugs as problematic. The complexity of identification of problem alcohol or drug use among the elderly may be further complicated by chronic medical conditions (Blow, 1998). It is also recommended that feedback from the screening instruments be given to the client immediately to maximize treatment intervention opportunities.

The U.S. Department of Health and Human Services, Substance Abuse and Mental Health Services Administration, CAST (1998) TIP Series 26 recommends a specific way to communicate the screening and assessment results to elderly clients. The first point is to provide a description of how the alcohol or prescription drug abuse affects the older adult's health or functional status. Second, the assessor should provide concrete information about how substance abuse or dependence is very treatable and explain treatment options in an effort to ultimately maintain independence and improve quality of life. Third, if symptoms appear severe, recommending further assessment to provide more information on how to proceed with treatment is suggested. If symptoms do not appear severe, having a discussion about monitoring progress over a few weeks and a willingness to make changes is appropriate. Finally, if the situation is dire, with an apparent need for detoxification, admission to an inpatient facility may be the most prudent option.

Once the screening and assessment are completed, the treatment provider can then make a determination about the appropriate level and intensity of care. Decisions about the referral of clients after the screening and assessment process has been completed need to be guided by knowledge of available resources as well as appropriate levels of care that match the clinical symptoms of the particular client. Linking clients with appropriate referrals often begins with referral to the least intensive options.

LEAST INTENSIVE TREATMENT OPTIONS

Least intensive treatment options include brief intervention, intervention, and motivational counseling. The evidence suggests that 10% to 30% of problem drinkers who do not meet criteria for dependence decrease their drinking to moderate levels after a brief intervention by a physician or other clinician (CSAT, 1998). Brief intervention techniques can range from relatively unstructured counseling and feedback to more formal structured therapy that relies on concepts and applications from motivational psychology (Miller & Rollnick, 1991). If the client does not respond to brief intervention techniques, intervention and motivation counseling are other options that can be explored.

Intervention occurs under the guidance of a skilled counselor with many significant members of the substance abusing client's life in an effort to be direct about their concerns and experiences with the drinking and drug behavior (Johnson, 1973). This process is designed to break down the delusion of denial that is pervasive in alcohol and other drug dependence.

Motivational counseling involves an acknowledgment of differences in readiness for change and offers an alternative approach for meeting people where they are (Miller & Rollnick, 1991). The skilled counselor listens respectfully to the client and accepts the older adult's viewpoint as a starting point toward change and intervention. This type of intervention can serve as a prelude to other therapeutic interventions.

Gunter and Arndt (2004) suggest that if the patient is an at-risk drinker or drug user, brief education can be effective in lessening the level of alcohol or other drug intake. For late-onset substance abusers who are not in need of detoxification, motivational interviewing techniques may be sufficient to bring about change. Among late-onset substance abusers (not in need of detoxification) there may be a reactive pattern of relatively short duration to a situational stressor.

Older people who are experiencing difficulties related to drinking alcohol but do not meet the criteria for alcohol dependence may be best served with brief intervention (Fingerhood, 2000). Fleming, Barry, Manwell, Johnson, and London (1997); Fleming et al. (2002); and Wilk, Jensen, and Havighurst (1997) reported that brief intervention can decrease drinking to a moderate level in up to one third of individuals. The process of providing brief intervention includes identification of the problem, a discussion of consequences, and a determined plan of care. This intervention is designed to take place over 2 to 3 sessions approximately 15 minutes each in a nonconfrontational and supportive style (Fingerhood, 2000).

OUTPATIENT AND INPATIENT TREATMENT OPTIONS

Specialized outpatient programs vary tremendously in the intensity of care. Partial hospitalization programs require attending 5-day, day-long treatments within a hospital but returning home in the evenings. Intensive outpatient programs involve approximately 2 to 3 hours of treatment each day, sometimes 3 to 5 days a week. Traditional outpatient treatment involves weekly sessions in a low-intensity environment.

Elderly clients who do meet the criteria for dependence need more structured intervention; however, strategies of brief intervention may be effective in creating a treatment plan. Structured intervention for clients with substance dependence includes detoxification and subsequent rehabilitation.

It is crucial to consider the age-related differences in the detoxification needs in treatment for alcohol withdrawal. For instance, older alcoholics commonly will have a delayed onset of withdrawal symptoms, with symptoms beginning several days after the last drink of alcohol was consumed. Kraemer, Conigliaro, and Saitz (1999) found that confusion is often the first recognizable symptom of withdrawal, instead of tremors, which are more readily detected in younger alcoholics. These researchers also suggest that severity and duration of withdrawal increases with age. With the delayed withdrawal symptoms, the family interview becomes increasingly important for collateral information.

An inpatient treatment facility is the best option for an older person who meets criteria for substance dependence, lacks social support, struggles with major medical illness, failed at attempted outpatient tapering or detoxification, and has an increased potential for morbidity with withdrawal. Coexisting medical problems increase the morbidity of substance withdrawal, which can justify the need for medical monitoring while under detoxification (Fingerhood, 2000). In the elderly, it becomes increasingly important to monitor for adverse effects from pharmacological intervention during detoxification of withdrawal symptoms, as benzodiazepines used in this process can create difficulties in gait, cognition, and incontinence (Fingerhood, 2000).

When making referrals to an inpatient treatment facility, it is good ethical practice to inquire about specific interventions that the facility utilizes to meet the needs of the elderly. Social workers and other professionals have the opportunity to advocate for older clients to obtain adequate services for them.

As previously mentioned, selecting appropriate treatment services usually includes looking into the least intensive treatment options, such as brief intervention, intervention, and motivational counseling. These strategies may be more appropriate as a part of pretreatment while moving clients into more specialized treatment by assisting to overcome resistance and ambivalence about changing their use of chemicals. The treatment planning process should include age-specific treatment recommendations that fit the needs of each client.

AGE-SPECIFIC TREATMENT

The literature suggests that treatment outcomes are improved when elderly clients receive age-specific treatment (Benshoff & Harrawood, 2003; Blow, 1998; Fingerhood, 2000; McInnis-Dittrich, 2005; Norton, 1998). Blow (1998) emphasized that there are few treatment outcome studies for this population reported in the literature, which is attributed to the challenges in follow-up after completion of treatment and the complexity of researching elderly substance abusers.

In one notable exception, Lemke and Moos (2002) compared groups of younger and middle-aged (55 and older) patients in inpatient alcohol treatment programs ($n = 432$ in each age group). The sample included alcoholic patients in inpatient substance abuse treatment programs in 12 Veterans Administration medical centers from varied regions in the United States. Findings suggest that when older clients were integrated with younger clients, the treatment outcomes were comparable and positive. Older clients appeared to have been well integrated in mixed-age programs, were more likely to have a longer length of stay, and expressed high levels of satisfaction. Moreover, the older clients in this study experienced significant positive change on nearly all measures of behavior and attitudes toward treatment. Lemke and Moos (2002) noted the possibility that their study participants may have been selected for the treatment program using criteria that made the different age groups more similar and easier to treat within a mixed-age context. These researchers made it clear that their data could not address the question of whether the older clients might have shown better outcomes if they had been in programs that were specifically tailored to their needs. However, the findings do suggest that there were no gross age inequities in the mixed-age treatment programs and that there were similarities in treatment interventions across the age range.

Another notable exception is a study of 137 male veterans with alcohol problems who were randomly assigned after detoxification to age-specific treatment or standard mixed-age treatment (Kashner, Rodell, Ogden, Guggenheim, & Karson, 1992). Treatment outcomes at 6 months and 1 year demonstrated that age-specific program clients were 2.9 times more likely at 6 months and 2.1 times more likely at 1 year to report abstinence when compared with mixed-age group clients.

The results of these studies show that the question of whether older adults actually achieve better treatment outcomes in age-specific treatment has not received adequate study. However, treatment programs should cultivate a culture of respect for older clients to reduce the stigma of addiction and the stigma of aging.

Norton (1998) recommended that psychoeducational, peer support, family, and cognitive-behavioral interventions tailored to meet the needs of elderly clients make for efficacious approaches. Benshoff and Harrawood (2003) and McInnis-Dittrich (2005) suggest that intervention with older clients calls for a slower pace in combination with a supportive, nonconfrontational style in individual and group settings composed of same-age peers. Elderly clients can do well in 12-step support groups as an adjunct to 12-step facilitated and other types of professional intervention. Professionals referring clients to 12-step groups need to be well informed about the strengths and shortcomings of these groups, such as Alcoholics Anonymous and Narcotics Anonymous, to effectively connect older clients with these groups.

EVIDENCE-BASED PRACTICE GUIDELINES

The Consensus Panel (CSAT, 1998) advises that treatment programs for older adults focus on more than just the substance abuse problems, due to the complexity of the aging process and associated conditions. Individual psychological and health-related issues tend to become more complicated with age (CSAT, 1998). These challenges call for flexibility when setting goals and determining appropriate plans of care. For example, interruptions in treatment for substance abuse may occur due to necessary hospitalizations due to illnesses. Also, adjustments to substance abuse treatment related to fatigue or various physical limitations may be needed.

GENDER ISSUES

Gender issues may also play an important role in treating older clients for substance abuse. The Consensus Panel (CSAT, 1998) observed many older women deferring to men in treatment groups; they were also less likely to become leaders or to build self-confidence. A seasoned therapist could assist in turning these gender roles around to enhance the therapeutic group relationships.

Satre and Arean (2005) found that older women were more likely to decrease their problematic drinking when it was associated with a serious health condition. These results may assist practitioners with interventions for older women specific to identifying factors related to health that may be a catalyst for drinking cessation.

In a study by Brennan, Kagay, Geppert, and Moos (2000), findings showed that many women constitute elderly Medicare inpatients with substance use disorders ($N = 22,768$; 37% were women). These researchers reported that these patients often had prior substance-related hospitalizations, coexisting psychiatric conditions, accidents involving poisoning, adverse drug reactions, and falls. This study purports that elderly women may benefit from treatment that focuses on their psychiatric disorders and accidental risks as well as their substance abuse.

Personal issues related to substance abuse may be difficult for group members to discuss in the presence of members of the opposite sex. Older adults may have an increased need for privacy, which may provide barriers to self-disclosure (CSAT, 1998). The Consensus Panel recommends that in these situations, separate gender-specific groups be made available.

TREATMENT APPROACHES

As previously described, brief interventions in the form of educational sessions and motivational counseling have shown positive results in the research literature to date (Bartels et al., 2002; CSAT, 1998; Hanson & Gutheil, 2004). In addition to these less intensive therapeutic approaches, the Consensus Panel (CSAT, 1998) recommends several treatment approaches that have been effective with older substance-abusing clients. These approaches include cognitive-behavioral, group-based, individual-based, medical and psychiatric care, family therapy, case management services, and specialized treatment for issues with prescription drug abuse. Each of these approaches are described next.

Cognitive-behavioral approaches, specifically behavior modification, self-management techniques, and cognitive-behavioral therapies, are recommended to assist with eliminating or decreasing substance abuse (CSAT, 1998; Morin et al., 2004). These techniques can be applied to individual and group sessions to identify and make changes to self-defeating thought patterns and beliefs. The cognitive-behavioral approaches establish a method for focusing on specific problems that affect substance-abusing behavior. By exploring thoughts and feelings, triggers to abusing substances, and the positive and negative consequences associated with substance abuse, an improvement in insight, awareness, thinking, and behavior can occur.

Group-based approaches are also recommended as particularly beneficial to substance-abusing clients. Because social isolation is a pervasive problem among older adults who abuse substances, involvement in group therapy can provide a healing experience. Group approaches may take many forms (e.g., educational, socialization, therapy, support), depending on the needs of the clients. Group experiences can provide an opportunity to share with and gain acceptance from group members and alleviate issues with excessive guilt and shame. Groups can focus on specific aging issues and incorporate new coping skills. The literature suggests that older adults bond into groups at a more rapid pace than do younger adults (CSAT, 1998; Finkel, 1990).

Individual therapy has been shown to be helpful to older adults with substance abuse, especially in the beginning stages (CSAT, 1998). Therapists who approach the sessions in a nonthreatening, supportive way and with genuine respect for confidentiality can create a successful therapeutic relationship. A clear explanation of confidentiality is paramount to the building of trust and rapport. Private sessions with older adults can assist in clarifying issues to bring forward in a group therapy setting as well as to process complicated issues that they may be too embarrassed to discuss outside of an individual session.

As was previously described, the attention to medical issues, especially for the older adult population, is critical to the successful treatment of substance abuse. Stabilization of medical and psychiatric problems should be primary for the elderly in order for optimal participation in substance abuse treatment and subsequent recovery (CSAT, 1998). Of course, addressing the medical and mental health needs of older clients will need to be concurrent with substance abuse treatment once stabilized. Sometimes linking an older alcoholic or other drug addict to a health care provider can make a profound difference, as many are without adequate medical services.

Involvement of family or significant others in substance abuse treatment for older adults is recommended by the Consensus Panel (CSAT, 1998) after detailed information is obtained about the family and the interplay of dynamics. A proper treatment plan can be designed, which may include family therapy intervention if the treatment providers deem that it would be helpful in the client's situation. Sensitivity and extensive skill are called for in eliciting family information, especially with an older population, along with the particular skills required to provide substance abuse treatment.

Case management services may be vital for substance-abusing elderly clients. Case management involves coordinating various social, health, and welfare services in an effort to provide supportive service to an older adult's treatment and subsequent recovery (CSAT, 1998). Referral to myriad services and providing multiple linkages to community outreach programs that the older adult may have not been aware of prior to treatment may make a significant difference in the quality of life of these clients.

Specialized treatment for older adults struggling with prescription drug abuse is imperative due to the many difficulties that stem from unintentional misuse. It is paramount that treatment providers grasp the dangers of how practitioners' prescribing behavior contributes to the prescription drug abuse problems in order to effectively advocate for and empower elderly clients and properly address the issues with uninformed health care providers (CSAT, 1998).

Educating older adults and their family members about medication compliance strategies can be accomplished through using materials already published and in community settings such as home health care agencies and state and local offices of aging. Brief educational sessions devoted to increasing awareness can make positive contributions in the overall health of older adults. Thorough assessment with an exploration of underlying issues is recommended, as well as open discussions about issues related to prescription drug abuse with the client, the substance abuse treatment provider, and the health care provider (CSAT, 1998).

Case Study and Evidence-Based Practice Application

Raymond R is a 74-year-old Caucasian male who lives with his wife of 49 years in a single-family residence. He is a retired school teacher who earned a master's degree in education and is Methodist. Raymond was a participant in a program designed to provide evidence-based services to community-dwelling older adults (age 65 and older) in medically underserved areas to ensure access to quality geriatric assessment and self-management intervention services. This program was funded by Health Resources and Services Administration as a research study to improve health outcomes of older adults in medically underserved areas. The overarching goal of the program was to improve the health of older adults by providing as many resources as possible so that they could remain in their own homes as long as possible. The program provided an in-home assessment and a self-management plan of care by a social worker and a physical therapist. Recommendations were provided to Raymond in an effort to improve his health. Brief interventions in the form of telehealth with supportive health-related phone calls were delivered at random to clients in the experimental group. Other clients (in the control group) were given the plan of care with individualized recommendations and were to manage the plan of care on their own until a follow-up in-home assessment at 12 weeks.

Raymond voluntarily enrolled into the program by responding to an ad in the community newspaper. He was provided with a full explanation of the program and signed informed consent and HIPAA forms in order for treatment services to be provided. The social worker and physical therapist provided an evidence-based assessment, which involved administering multiple instruments representing both disciplines over a 2-session period.

The assessment instruments used by both disciplines included multiple questionnaires determined by the evidence-based search to be best practice for assessing well to mildly impaired community-dwelling older adults. Instruments used in the assessment process included but were not limited to questionnaires pertaining to health history, current health status, medications, nutrition, health care providers, coping styles, fatigue and pain level estimates, confidence about doing things, personal and home hygiene, resources used to manage health, the CAGE screening tool (Ewing, 1984; Mayfield, McLeod, & Hall, 1974), Geriatric Depression Scale (5/15; Weeks, McGann, Michaels, & Penninx, 2003), Lubben's (1988) Family Network Scale, the Mini-Cog (Tuokko, Hadjistavropoulos, Miller, & Beattie, 1992), the Functional Reach Test (Duncan, Weiner, Chandler, & Studenski, 1990), the Sit to Stand Test (Jones, Rikli, & Beam, 1999), and the Timed Get Up and Go Test (Podsiadlo & Richardson, 1991).

Raymond's score on the CAGE was a 3 out of 4, which indicates problematic use of alcohol with a potential for alcohol abuse or dependence. He answered yes to feeling he ought to cut down on his drinking, that his wife annoyed him by criticizing his drinking, and feeling bad or guilty about his drinking. He described drinking only one "cocktail" per day.

He did not indicate any issues with nutrition; scored a 1 out of 5 on the Geriatric Depression Scale, which indicates no signs of depression; and scored a 33 out of 60 on the Lubben Family Network Scale, in which he reported having relatives that he felt at ease with to discuss personal matters. He identified only one close friend. On the Mini-Cog, he scored a 3 out of 3 on the recall and a 3 out of 4 on the Clock Drawing Test, which indicated no signs of dementia, allowing him to remain in the program. However, a 3 on the Clock Drawing Test does demonstrate some concern with cognitive status and warrants further evaluation. He showed concern with dealing with pain and fatigue, as they interfere with activities at times. There were no concerns with home or personal hygiene. In reference to health resources, he reported attending regular fitness programs and focusing on activities to help manage health concerns. Past medical history includes a head injury. Medications include Ritalin and Hydrocodone. He reports taking Ritalin to stay awake and not taking Hydrocodone because of unwanted side effects. He also reports taking epidural injections for stenosis. In the Physical Therapist's Systems Review, he was not impaired in cardiovascular and integumentary systems. He was slightly overweight according to the Body Mass Index. His upper-body strength was determined to be normal. On the functional reach test, his average score was 7 inches, which placed him in moderate risk for falls. On the Sit to Stand Test, he scored a 7 in 30 seconds, which indicated weakness in lower extremities. On the TUG or Get Up and Go Test, he took 11.5 seconds; this means he was slightly impaired and indicated a decrease in agility, strength, and balance. He also became short of breath for the Get Up and Go and Sit to Stand tests.

Raymond's primary care physician was given a summary of the assessment results and recommendations from the team working with him. After conducting a thorough health history and evidence-based assessment, the team determined that Raymond needed further evaluation for alcohol abuse or dependence. There was also concern for continued assessment about his cognitive status, given the failed Clock Drawing Test. He was provided with appropriate referral sources to obtain these services. The social worker was careful to present these recommendations with tact and sensitivity. He was referred to a local alcohol and drug counseling center that would accept his insurance provider. The team also recommended an exercise program for improvement of strength and cardiovascular endurance. A recommendation was made to perform low back and abdominal exercises for spinal stenosis.

Raymond's response to the recommendation by the social worker and physical therapist was very positive, and he agreed to follow their recommendations. He was to be reassessed in 12 weeks. Unfortunately, after 1 month of his involvement with the plan of care, he had to have spinal surgery. Due to the requirements of the research program that clients have no major surgeries in the prior 6 months, he had to then be dropped from the program.

Raymond's case provides a real-world example of an evidence-based interdisciplinary assessment utilizing the CAGE to explore problematic alcohol use as well as a brief intervention. The social work team member engaged Raymond with rapport building and administered the CAGE in a nonthreatening, supportive manner. Raymond was forthcoming about feeling he needed to cut down on his drinking, that he was annoyed at times by his wife's concerns, and that he felt guilty about his drinking. The social worker engaged Raymond in a brief intervention by discussing the CAGE results, which were indicative of a need for further evaluation and probable subsequent substance abuse treatment. The social worker informed Raymond about the health risks associated with his drinking and in combination with Ritalin and Hydrocodone. The social worker provided handouts so that he could read further about these health risks. He was given a referral for further evaluation with a local alcohol and other drug treatment center. Raymond signed the plan of care and verbally agreed to these recommendations as well as other previously mentioned recommendations.

The advantages that the social worker had in this case was that Raymond voluntarily sought involvement in the research and service program, and he was interested in improving his health. Therefore, the skilled social worker and physical therapist tailored their recommendations for the plan of care to his sincere concern to improve his overall health. These types of brief, structured interventions are used to ameliorate the substance abuse problem and perhaps interrupt the trajectory of a more serious problem with alcohol dependence (DiClemente, Bellino, & Neavins, 1999; Heather, 1995; O'Hare, 2005; U.S. Department of Health and Human Services, 1997, 2000). Though brief, these interventions can be sufficient in assisting the modification of substance use to forestall more serious problems.

EVIDENCE-BASED POLICY RECOMMENDATIONS

Implications for policy can be derived from the research literature to date. The authors are currently working on the aforementioned Geriatric Evaluation and Self-Management Services Project, which has begun to produce improved outcomes in terms of health indicators and cost-benefit analysis. Receiving interdisciplinary in-home assessments from social workers and physical therapists, older adults are screened for alcohol abuse or dependence problems and a variety of other health-related risk factors and can be given brief interventions to assist in decreasing future substance abuse and other related health problems. These types of projects need to be recognized by policy makers as interventions that can and will make a significant contribution to the quality of life of the elderly as well as to decrease the need for acute hospitalizations and other health-related costs.

Abrams (2002) discussed the vital need for increased education about and awareness of substance abuse in the elderly to inform policy. She recommends that policy be developed to improve prevention and detection of substance abuse among older adults. The argument that school-age children have a greater need for substance abuse prevention programs does not hold weight when the statistics about the potential impact of the baby boom generation are considered. More specifically, future cohorts of the elderly, who did not experience Prohibition and who were involved in the Vietnam War and the drug culture of the 1960s, may have more significant drug and alcohol issues than the current generation of the elderly (Gurnack et al., 2002). Abrams (2002) also argued that it is only through prevention, detection, and treatment of abuse that the substance abuser may escape permanent physical and mental damage.

These points emphasize the importance of competency training for care providers of the elderly to be able to identify those at risk and those who indicate a problem with chemical abuse or dependence. Once proper training is obtained, various disciplines of elder care providers can perform their unique roles in a concerted successful effort to prevent, detect, and treat substance abuse among the older population. Furthermore, it is crucial to develop a vocabulary to facilitate a dialogue about the substance abuse problem in older adults to move beyond thinking of the elderly person as a "drunk" or a "drug addict" and instead as a person who has a disease that is very treatable.

There is also the important point about addressing the cost of substance abuse treatment that needs to be considered in policy decisions. Cornelius (2002) urges policy makers to find ways to pay for the provision of substance abuse services as well as supporting treatment designs that reflect the diversity of the clients involved.

In a data analysis of the National Household Survey on Drug Abuse in 1994 (*N* = 10,158) and 1998 (*N* = 12,892), Oggins (2003) found that in alcohol or other drug using samples of mixed-age groups, most paid for treatment out of pocket even despite reported increases in employer-paid insurance. The results of this study emphasize that often the insured population is not well informed about the details of their health insurance, specifically for alcohol or other drug treatment; many do not realize that they have coverage and end up paying more than they have to. The findings also recommend an expansion of no-cost treatment, with funds extracted from increased taxation on liquor, cigarettes, tobacco settlements, and savings in incarceration costs due to nonviolent offenders being sent to treatment.

With ongoing changes to the provisions of treatment services from inpatient to outpatient and shifts in reimbursement structures, coverage of effective treatment is of increasing concern. These changes in treatment provisions put much emphasis on the need for ongoing research.

FUTURE DIRECTIONS FOR RESEARCH

Substance abuse among the elderly is a growing concern that threatens to pose serious consequences for older adults and health providers. Efforts in the future need to be focused on outcome studies for addiction treatment, such as Project MATCH (Project MATCH Research Group, 1997), wherein individually delivered treatments are evaluated for their effectiveness. Controlled trials of various models of treatment addressing topics such as prescription drug dependence in the elderly are very much needed (Finlayson, 1998). In addition, exploration of how the Minnesota model, 12-step facilitation, motivational interviewing, cognitive-behavioral therapy, and other treatment models may need to be restructured in an effort to meet the needs of the elderly substance abuser is also needed.

The Consensus Panel (CSAT, 1998) reported that future research with older adults needs to address alcohol and other drug consumption in terms of varying patterns of use along the life course, gender and ethnic differences, health care cost comparisons between those maintaining abstinence and those who reduce consumption, early and late onset of alcohol and drug problems, and the development of valid screening instruments for illicit and prescription drug use. Other recommended areas for research with older adults are treatment (e.g., prevention and early intervention techniques, use of technology, efficacy of age-specific treatment, older subgroups, and risk factors), biomedical (e.g., medication interactions, medical consequences of moderate to heavy consumption of alcohol or illicit drugs), and behavioral and psychological (e.g., relationship between demographics and alcohol and drug abuse, reasons for changing drinking patterns, stress and coping in relation to substance abuse), as well as special issues (e.g., homelessness, elder abuse and neglect, underrepresentation of older adults in treatment facilities; CSAT, 1998).

Conducting rigorous research studies in the field of aging and substance abuse needs to be a high priority. This type of evidence can provide vital knowledge to inform health care providers, policy makers, older adults, and families in an effort to improve our response to the ever increasing aging population. An absence of these types of investigations and related education will create enormous costs to one of the most vulnerable and rapidly growing groups in society.

REFERENCES

Abrams, S. (2002). Inebriated elders: The problem of substance abuse among the elderly. *Elder Law Journal, 9*(2), 229–255.

American Psychiatric Association. (2000). *Diagnostic and statistical manual of mental disorders* (4th ed., text rev.). Washington, DC: Author.

Atkinson, R. M., Ganzini, L., & Bernstein, M. J. (1992). Alcohol and substance-use disorders in the elderly. In J. E. Birren, R. B. Sloane, & G. D. Cohen (Eds.), *Handbook of mental health and aging* (2nd ed., pp. 515–555). San Diego, CA: Academic Press.

Babor, T. F., de la Fuenta, J. R., Saunders, J., & Grant, M. (1992). *AUDIT: The Alcohol Use Disorders Identification Test—Guidelines for its use in primary health care.* Geneva, Switzerland: World Health Organization.

Barry, K. L., Oslin, D. W., & Blow, F. C. (2001). *Alcohol problems in older adults: Prevention and management.* New York: Springer.

Bartels, S. J., Dums, A. R., Oxman, T. E., Schneider, L. S., Arean, P. A., Alexopoulos, G. S., et al. (2002). Evidence-based practices in geriatric mental health care. *Psychiatric Services (53)*11, 1419–1423.

Benshoff, J. J., & Harrawood, L. K. (2003). Substance abuse and the elderly: Unique issues and concerns. *Journal of Rehabilitation, 69*(2), 43–48.

Blow, F. C. (1998). The spectrum of alcohol interventions for older adults. In E. S. Gomberg, A. M. Hegedus, & R. A. Zucker (Eds.), *Alcohol problems and aging* (pp. 373–396). Bethesda, MD: U.S. Department of Health and Human Services.

Blow, F. C. (2000). Substance abuse among older adults: An invisible epidemic. In F. C. Blow (Ed., Consensus Panel Chair), *Substance abuse among older adults* (DHHS Publication No. SMA 98-3179, Treatment Improvement Protocol Series 26). Rockville, MD: Substance Abuse and Mental Health Services Administration, Office of Applied Studies. Retrieved February 25, 2006, from http://www.health.org /govpubs/BKD250.

Blow, F. C., Blower, K. J., Schulenberg, J. E., Demo-Dananberg, L. M., Young, J. P., & Beresford, T. P. (1992). The Michigan Alcoholism Screening Test—Geriatric Version (MAST-G): A new elderly-specific screening instrument. *Alcoholism: Clinical and Experimental Research, 16,* 372.

Blow, F. C., Oslin, D. W., & Barry, K. L. (2002). Misuse and abuse of alcohol, illicit drugs, and psychoactive medication among older people. *Generations,* 50–54.

Brennan, P. L., Kagay, C. R., Geppert, J. J., & Moos, R. H. (2000). Elderly Medicare inpatients with substance use disorders: Characteristics and predictors of hospital readmissions over a 4-year interval. *Journal of Studies on Alcohol,* 891–895.

Buchsbaum, D. G., Buchanan, R., Welsh, J., Centor, R., & Schnoll, S. (1992). Screening for drinking disorders in the elderly using the CAGE questionnaire. *Journal of the American Geriatric Society, 40,* 662–665.

Buellens, J., & Aertgeerts, B. (2004). Screening for alcohol abuse and dependence in older people using *DSM* criteria: A review. *Aging and Mental Health, 8*(1), 76–82.

Center for Substance Abuse Treatment. (1998). *Substance abuse among older adults* (Treatment Improvement Protocol Series, No. 26, CSAT Publication No. SMA 98-3179). Rockville, MD: U.S. Department of Health and Human Services, Public Health Service, and Substance Abuse and Mental Health Services Administration.

Conigliaro, J., Kraemer, K., & McNeil, M. (2000). Alcohol screening instruments for elderly populations. *Journal of Geriatric Psychiatry and Neurology, 13*(3), 106–114.

Cornelius, L. J. (2002). Defining substance abusers using a prism: What you see is what you get. *Health and Social Work, 27*(3), 234–237.

The DASIS Report. (2005). *Older adults in substance abuse treatment: Update.* Retrieved February 25, 2006, from http://www.oas.samhsa.gov/dasis.htm.

DiClemente, C. C., Bellino, L. E., & Neavins, T. M. (1999). Motivation for change and alcoholism treatment. *Alcohol Research and Health, 23,* 86–92.

Dufour, M., & Fuller, R. K. (1995). Alcohol in the elderly. *Annual Review of Medicine, 46,* 123–132.

Duncan, P. W., Weiner, K. D., Chandler, J., & Studenski, S. (1990). Functional reach: A new clinical measure of balance. *Journal of Gerontology, 45*(6), 192–197.

Emlet, C. A., Hawks, H., & Callahan, J. (2001). Alcohol use and abuse in a population of community dwelling, frail older adults. *Journal of Gerontological Social Work, 35*(4), 21–33.

Ewing, J. A. (1984). Detecting alcoholism: The CAGE questionnaire. *Journal of the American Medical Association, 252,* 1905–1907.

Finfgeld-Connett, D. L. (2004). Treatment of substance misuse in older women using a brief intervention model. *Journal of Gerontological Nursing, 30*–37.

Fingerhood, M. (2000). Substance abuse in older people. *Journal of the American Geriatric Society, 48,* 985–995.

Fink, A., Elliott, M., Tsai, M., & Beck, J. (2005). An evaluation of an intervention to assist primary care physicians in screening and educating older patients who use alcohol. *Journal of the American Geriatrics Society, 53*(11), 1937–1943.

Fink, A., Tsai, M., Hays, R. D., Moore, A. A., Morton, S. C., Spritzer, K., et al. (2002). Comparing the Alcohol-Related Problems Survey (ARPS) to traditional alcohol screening instruments in elderly outpatients. *Archives of Gerontology and Geriatrics, 34,* 55–78.

Finkel, S. L. (1990). Group psychotherapy with older people. *Hospital and Community Psychiatry, 41,* 1189–1191.

Finlayson, R. E. (1998). Prescription drug dependence in the elderly: The clinical pathway to recovery. *Journal of Mental Health and Aging, 4*(2), 233–249.

Fleming, M. F., Barry, K. L., Manwell, L. B., Johnson, K., & London, R. (1997). Brief physician advice for problem alcohol drinkers: A randomized control trial in community-based primary care practices. *Journal of the American Medical Association, 277,* 1039–1045.

Fleming, M. F., Mundt, M. P., French, M. T., Manwell, L. B., Stauffacher, E. A., & Barry, K. L. (2002). Brief physician advice for alcohol problems: A randomized community based trial. *Journal of Family Practice, 48,* 378–384.

Gomberg, E. S. L. (1995). Older women and alcohol use and abuse. In M. Galanter (Ed.), *Recent developments in alcoholism: (12). Alcoholism and women* (pp. 61–79). New York: Plenum Press.

Gunter, T. D., & Arndt, S. (2004, March/April). Maximizing treatment of substance abuse in the elderly. *Behavioral Health Management,* 38–43.

Gurnack, A. M. (1997). *Older adults' misuse of alcohol, medicines, and other drugs.* New York: Springer.

Gurnack, A. M., Atkinson, R., & Osgood, N. J. (2002). *Treating alcohol and drug abuse in the elderly.* New York: Springer.

Hanson, M., & Gutheil, I. A. (2004). Motivational strategies with alcohol-involved older adults: Implications for social work practice. *Social Work, 49*(3), 364–372.

He, W., Sengupta, M., Velkoff, V. A., & DeBarros, K. A. (2005). *U.S. Census Bureau current population reports: 65+ in the United States* (pp. 23–209). Washington, DC: U.S. Government Printing Office.

Heather, N. (1995). Brief intervention strategies. In R. K. Hester & W. R. Miller (Eds.), *Handbook of alcoholism treatment approaches: Effective alternatives* (2nd ed., pp. 105–122). Boston: Allyn & Bacon.

Hooyman, N. R., & Kiyak, H. A. (2002). *Social gerontology: A multidisciplinary perspective.* Boston: Allyn & Bacon.

Johnson, V. E. (1973). *I'll quit tomorrow.* New York: Harper & Row.

Jones, C. J., Rikli, R. E., & Beam, W. C. (1999). A 30-s chair-stand test as a measure of lower body strength in community-residing older adults. *Research Quarterly for Exercise and Sport, 70*, 113–119.

Joseph, C. I., Ganzin, L., & Atkinson, R. M. (1995). Screening for alcohol use disorders in the nursing home. *Journal of the American Geriatrics Society, 43*, 368–373.

Kashner, T. M., Rodell, D. E., Ogden, S. R., Guggenheim, F. G., & Karson, C. N. (1992). Outcomes and costs of two VA inpatient programs for older alcoholic patients. *Hospital and Community Psychiatry, 43*, 985–989.

Kraemer, W. L., Conigliaro, J., & Saitz, R. (1999). Managing alcohol withdrawal in the elderly. *Drugs and Aging, 14*, 405–425.

Lemke, S., & Moos, R. H. (2002). Prognosis of older patients in mixed-age alcoholism treatment programs. *Journal of Substance Abuse Treatment, 22*(1), 33–43.

Lubben, J. E. (1988). Assessing social networks among elderly populations. *Journal of Family Community Health, 11*, 45–52.

Mayfield, D. G., McLeod, G., & Hall, P. (1974). The CAGE questionnaire: Validation of a new alcoholism screening instrument. *American Journal of Psychiatry, 131*, 1121–1123.

McInnis-Dittrich, K. (2005). *Social work with elders: A biopsychosocial approach to assessment and intervention.* Boston: Allyn & Bacon.

Menninger, J. A. (2002). Assessment and treatment of alcoholism and substance-related disorders in the elderly. *Bulletin of the Menninger Clinic, 66*(2), 166–183.

Miller, W. R., & Rollnick, S. (1991). *Motivational interviewing.* New York: Guilford Press.

Moore, A. A., Hays, R. D., Reuben, D. B., & Beck, J. C. (2000). Using a criterion standard to validate the Alcohol-Related Problems Survey (ARPS): A screening measure to identify harmful and hazardous drinking in older persons. *Aging: Clinical and Experimental Research, 12*, 221–227.

Moore, R. A. (1972). The diagnosis of alcoholism in a psychiatric hospital: A trial of the Michigan Alcoholism Screening Test (MAST). *American Journal of Psychiatry, 128*(12), 1565–1569.

Morin, C. M., Bastien, C., Guay, B., Radouco-Thomas, M., Leblanc, J., & Vallieres, A. (2004). Randomized clinical trial of supervised tapering and cognitive behavior therapy to facilitate benzodiazepine discontinuation in older adults with chronic insomnia. *American Journal of Psychiatry, 161*, 332–342.

Morton, J. L., Jones, T. V., & Manganaro, M. A. (1996). Performance of alcoholism screening questionnaires in elderly veterans. *American Journal of Medicine, 101*, 153–159.

National Center for Health Statistics. (2000). *National Health Interview Survey, selected years.* Retrieved February 26, 2005, from http://www.cdc.gov/nchs/nhis.htm.

National Institute on Alcohol Abuse and Alcoholism. (1988). Alcohol and aging. *Alcohol Alert, 2,* 1–5.

National Survey on Drug Use and Health. (2005). Retrieved February 25, 2006, from www.oas.samhsa.gov/2k5/olderadults/olderadults.cfm.

Norton, E. D. (1998). Counseling substance abusing older adults. *Educational Gerontology, 24,* 373–390.

Oggins, J. (2003). Changes in health insurance and payment for substance use treatment. *American Journal of Drug and Alcohol Abuse, 29*(1), 55–74.

O'Hare, T. (2005). *Evidence-based practices for social workers: An interdisciplinary approach.* Chicago: Lyceum Books.

Patterson, T. L., & Jeste, D. V. (1999). The potential impact of the baby-boom generation on substance abuse among elderly persons. *Mental Health and Aging, 50*(9), 1184–1188.

Podsiadlo, D., & Richardson, S. (1991). The timed "Up and Go": A test of basic functional mobility for frail elderly persons. *Journal of the American Geriatric Society, 39,* 142–148.

Project MATCH Research Group. (1997). Matching alcoholism treatment to clients' heterogeneity: Project MATCH posttreatment drinking outcomes. *Journal of Studies on Alcohol, 58,* 7–29.

Ray, W. A. (2002). Psychotropic drugs and injuries among the elderly: A review. *Journal of Clinical Psychopharmacology, 12,* 386–396.

Saleh, S. S., & Szebenyi, S. E. (2005). Resource use of elderly emergency department patients with alcohol-related diagnoses. *Journal of Substance Abuse Treatment, 29,* 313–319.

Satre, D. D., & Arean, P. A. (2005). Effects of gender, ethnicity, and medical illness on drinking cessation in older primary care patients. *Journal of Aging and Health, 17*(1), 70–84.

Shibusawa, T. (2006). Older adults with substance/alcohol abuse problems. In B. Berkman (Ed.), *Handbook of social work in health and aging* (pp. 141–148). New York: Oxford University Press.

Substance Abuse and Mental Health Administration. (2001). *Expanded National Household Survey.* Retrieved February 26, 2005, from www.samhsa.gov/hhsurvey.

Thibault, J. M., & Maly, R. C. (1993). Recognition and treatment of substance abuse in the elderly. *Primary Care, 20,* 155–165.

Tuokko, H., Hadjistavropoulos, T., Miller, J. A., Beattie, B. L. (1992). The Clock Test: A sensitive measure to differentiate normal elderly from those with Alzheimer disease. *Journal of the American Geriatric Society, 40,* 579–584.

U.S. Department of Health and Human Services. (1997). *Ninth special report to Congress on alcohol and health.* Washington, DC: U.S. Government Printing Office.

U.S. Department of Health and Human Services. (2000). *10th special report to Congress on alcohol and health.* Washington, DC: U.S. Government Printing Office.

Weeks, S. K., McGann, P. E., Michaels, T. K., & Penninx, B. W. (2003). Comparing various short-form geriatric depression scales leads to the GDS-5/15. *Journal of Nursing Scholarship, 35*(2), 133–137.

Wilk, A. I., Jensen, N. M., & Havighurst, T. C. (1997). Meta-analysis of randomized clinical trials addressing brief interventions in heavy alcohol drinkers. *Journal of General Internal Medicine, 12,* 274–283.

CHAPTER 13

Alzheimer's Disease

MASAHIRO SHIGETA and AKIRA HOMMA

OVERVIEW OF ALZHEIMER'S DISEASE

HISTORY AND PROFILE OF ALZHEIMER'S DISEASE

Alois Alzheimer (1864–1915), a psychiatrist and neuropathologist, reported the case of a 51-year-old woman (Auguste D) with dementia that started with delusions of jealousy. As memory impairment progressed rapidly, she lost her way when she went out and she became unable to read and write. Sometimes she hid her belongings, and her husband could not understand such behavior. She died 4.5 years after the clinical onset. In the postmortem study of her brain, Alzheimer reported deposits of "peculiar substances" (plaques) distributed widely in the brain and "dense bundles" (neurofibrillary tangles) within the nerve cells. There were subsequent reports of several patients with similar features. Emil Kraepelin (1913) named the disease "Alzheimer's disease" in the eighth edition of his textbook, *Psychiatrie.*

Alzheimer's disease (AD) is the most common neuropsychiatric disorder. Patients with AD show progressive deterioration of memory and other cognitive functions such as thinking, decision making, attention, reasoning, and calculation, and finally loss of mental and physical functions. Diagnostically important symptoms of AD include aphasia, apraxia, agnosia, and disturbances in executive function. Aphasia in AD is characterized by forgetting correct wording and the inability to follow conversations. Apraxia is generally defined as loss of the ability to carry out purposeful movements in the absence of motor disorders such as palsy, ataxia, and involuntary movement. Agnosia is generally defined as loss of the power to recognize the importance of external stimuli: auditory, visual, olfactory, gustatory, and tactile. Executive function involves the cognitive processes used to complete complex tasks. Patients with impairment of executive function cannot perform the series of procedures involved in a task.

Not only cognitive symptoms but also behavioral and psychological symptoms are common in patients with AD. These symptoms are brought together as behavioral and psychological symptoms of dementia (BPSD). The BPSD are defined as the symptoms of disturbed perception, thought content, and mood and behavior that frequently manifest in patients with dementia. Some BPSD are assessed at an interview of the patient or a relative; others are assessed by observing the patient's behavior. The former symptoms include anxiety, depressed mood, hallucinations and delusions; the latter symptoms: aggression, screaming, restlessness, agitation, wandering, culturally inappropriate behaviors, sexual disinhibition, hoarding, cursing, and shadowing. The BPSD are more or less stressful for caregivers, and their management is a critical issue in the daily lives of the caregivers and their families.

Two forms of AD are clinically recognized in terms of age at onset: early onset and late onset. Early-onset AD is relatively rare, and its symptoms begin to appear before age 65. Late-onset AD is the most common form and appears after age 65. It is known that there is a familial AD, which is a rare form, accounting for fewer than 5% of all AD cases.

PREVALENCE AND INCIDENCE OF ALZHEIMER'S DISEASE

Prevalence is defined as the percentage of the number of cases of a disease in a statistical population at a specified time. Jorm, Korten, and Henderson (1987) statistically analyzed the data from studies of the prevalence of dementia between 1945 and 1985. Variations in prevalence reflected differences in methodology, such as screening design and diagnostic criteria, as well as in study site characteristics (institutionalization and life expectancy; Katzman & Kawas, 1994). However, the relationship between prevalence and age was consistent across the studies, with prevalence doubling every 5.1 years (Jorm et al., 1987). This exponential rise in prevalence was observed especially in the 65- to 85-year age range.

There are highly accurate diagnostic criteria for AD in the clinical setting, such as the criteria specified by the National Institute of Neurological and Communicative Diseases and Stroke/Alzheimer's Disease and Related Disorders Association (NINCDS-ADRDA; McKhann et al., 1984). However, in field surveys, differentiation of AD is sometimes difficult, because coexisting factors, such as cerebrovascular factors, make the diagnosis ambiguous. Differential diagnosis among AD with cerebrovascular disease, AD with vascular dementia, and vascular dementia is often unsatisfactory (Katzman & Kawas, 1994).

National differences in the relative prevalence of AD and vascular dementia were reported from a meta-analysis (Jorm et al., 1987). Vascular dementia was more common in Russian studies, AD in Western European countries, and no significant difference was observed in American studies. The national differences might be caused not only by the diagnostic procedures but also by the age structure of the population. With the rapid increase in the old-old population in Japan, recent surveys there have reported that AD is now more common than vascular dementia (Meguro et al., 2002; Nakamura et al., 2003; Shigeta, 2004).

The incidence is a number equal to the fraction of the population that contracts a particular disease during a given period of time. It thus refers to the annual diagnosis rate or the number of new cases of AD diagnosed each year. It reflects differences in the time of the investigation and regional differences more sensitively than prevalence. However, incidence studies have not been performed as frequently as prevalence studies because of the need for repeated surveys for the former. Several incidence surveys have been conducted in Mannheim, Germany (Bickel & Cooper, 1994), southwestern France (Letenneur,

Commenges, Dartigues, & Barberger-Gateau, 1994), Cambridge, England (Brayne et al., 1995), Rotterdam, Netherlands (Ott, Breteler, van Harskamp, Stijnen, & Hofman, 1998), southern Taiwan (Liu et al., 1998), and Odense, Denmark (Andersen et al., 1999). The incidence of all dementias ranged from 1.07 to 2.95, according to these surveys. Many incidence data were distributed between 1% and 2%. On the other hand, the incidence of AD showed wider variation: The lowest value was 0.54 (southern Taiwan), and the highest was 2.7 (Cambridge). For epidemiological studies of dementia, the differential diagnoses (causes of dementia) include not only AD, cerebrovascular dementia, and other types of dementia, but also "unknown" or "uncertain" types of dementia. The frequency or ratio of such unknown or uncertain types also varied among the surveys, and could influence the frequency or ratio of AD. The incidence is also affected by the screening method and the diagnostic procedures for the dementia subtypes.

The cost of the management of patients with AD includes the physician's visits, laboratory testing, medications, nursing services, home care, day care, and more. Alzheimer's disease has thus become one of the most serious health economic issues as well as a public health problem in advanced countries because of the growing number of elderly people who are affected by AD.

CAUSES AND RISK FACTORS OF ALZHEIMER'S DISEASE

Alzheimer's disease is now considered to be caused by a combination of genetic and environmental factors. Familial AD of early-onset type is linked to at least three genes: encoding the amyloid precursor protein (APP) on chromosome 21, and genes for presenilin 1 and 2 on chromosomes 14 and 1, respectively. Presenilin mutations are more frequent than APP mutations. However, altogether these mutations account for only approximately 0.1% of all patients with AD, and the cause of almost all sporadic cases of AD remains unknown.

Studies have been conducted to ascertain whether certain chemicals or other toxins in the environment play a role in causing AD. Environmental factors that have been proposed include aluminum, zinc, toxins in contaminated food, and viruses. However, to date there is little solid evidence of their involvement, even though the possibility cannot be excluded. Other hypotheses about the causes of AD include oxidation damage, estrogen deficiency, and inflammation. These possibilities are under investigation.

Apolipoprotein E4 Gene   Apolipoprotein E4 (ApoE4, chromosome 19) is a genetic risk factor for late-onset AD (Strittmatter et al., 1993; Wisniewski, Golabek, Matsubara, Ghiso, & Frangione, 1993). People who have ApoE4 are at higher risk of developing AD and are likely to develop AD earlier in life. However, it is not a consistent cause: Some people with ApoE4 do not get AD, and some without ApoE4 get AD. The development of late-onset AD is considered to be influenced by more than one gene.

Age   A number of factors that increase a person's risk of developing AD have been studied. One of the strongest risk factors for AD is age. The risk of AD increases after age 65 and rises exponentially after age 75. While 1% of the population has

AD at age 65, approximately half of the population over 85 years old has it. On the other hand, the relationship between age and prevalence is complex for subjects younger than 65 or older than 85. The prevalence in those age groups is also influenced by other factors, in addition to age.

Family History   Another strong risk factor is family history, especially for early-onset cases (Chandra, Philipose, Bell, Lazaroff, & Schoenberg, 1987; Heston, Mastri, Anderson, & White, 1981). Case-control studies of AD were reanalyzed to examine the association of AD with family history (van Duijn et al., 1991). The relative risk of AD for those with at least one first-degree relative with dementia was 3.5. When focusing on the age at onset of AD, the relative risk decreased with increasing onset age. However, even among patients with onset of disease after 80 years, there were still significantly more subjects with one or more first-degree relatives with dementia compared to the controls. The relative risk of AD was significantly lower in patients who had one first-degree relative with dementia compared to those who had two or more affected relatives.

Down Syndrome   Neuropathological changes that are observed in the brain of patients with Down syndrome are similar to those in AD. More than half of Down syndrome patients develop AD. A family history of Down syndrome is also a risk factor for AD (Amaducci et al., 1986; Hofman et al., 1991). The presence and number of first-degree relatives with Down syndrome are strongly related to the development of AD.

Head Trauma   The relationship between head trauma and AD has been studied, because AD-like neuropathological changes in the brain were observed in the brains of punch-drunk syndrome patients. Exposure to head trauma with loss of consciousness may be associated with the development of AD. Stronger associations were observed in cases without a positive family history of dementia and in men (Mortimer et al., 1991).

Depressive State   One of the psychological risk factors considered in a collaborative analysis of case-control studies was depression as medical history, especially for presenile and senile persons (Jorm et al., 1991). While depressive symptoms may be part of the symptoms of the preclinical stages of AD, depressive episodes that occurred even more than 10 years before the onset of AD were associated with the development of AD (Kokmen, Chandra, & Schoenberg, 1988).

Sex   Women are more likely to get AD than men, but the reason is not known. There is an argument that women are at higher risk of AD because they live longer than men. However, this tendency was observed in each age stage (Lopez Pousa, Llinas Regla, Vilalta Franch, & Lozano Fernandez de Pinedo, 1995). Moreover, women get AD more easily even when the factor of life expectancy is excluded statistically (Cummings, Vinters, Cole, & Khachaturian, 1998).

Education Level   Several surveys reported that a lower education level was associated with the development of AD. Because the results of cognitive test batteries are influenced by education level, different cut-off points were used for different education levels and confirmed this association (Zhang et al., 1990). This association can be understood as follows. When one receives a longer education and achieves higher cognitive functions, dementia symptoms do not appear until the pathologic changes in the brain become more severe. It can be assumed that a longer education has a preventive effect against the clinical appearance of AD.

Lifestyles Previous studies suggested that lifestyles that include mental and physical activity and an active social network have a protective effect against dementia (Fratiglioni, Paillard-Borg, & Winblad, 2004), even though the evidence is not strong enough to support preventive and therapeutic strategies. To investigate the association between physical activity at midlife and the subsequent development of dementia and AD, approximately 21-year follow-up data were presented. Leisure-time physical activity at midlife at least twice a week was associated with a reduced risk of dementia and AD (Rovio et al., 2005). Moreover, a 6.2-year follow-up study of 1,740 persons older than 65 without cognitive impairment were completed to determine whether regular exercise is associated with a reduced risk for dementia and AD. The study found that the incidence rate of dementia for participants who exercised 3 or more times per week was significantly lower than that of participants who exercised fewer than 3 times a week (Larson et al., 2006). The effect of social networks on the risk of cognitive impairment was estimated in a longitudinal, epidemiological, clinicopathological study. Eighty-nine elderly people without dementia underwent annual clinical evaluations. Social network data were obtained by structured interview, and brain autopsy was done at the time of death. Although cognitive function was inversely related to disease pathology in the brain, social network size modified the association between pathology and cognitive function. Even at more severe levels of disease pathology, cognitive function remained higher for participants with larger network sizes (Bennett, Schneider, Tang, Arnold, & Wilson, 2006). The hypothesis that an active and socially integrated lifestyle protects against dementia and AD indicates the possibilities of the development of interventions for prevention and treatment of AD.

Miscellaneous Other possible positive and negative risk factors for AD are a medical history of hypothyroidism, mother's age at birth, and smoking. These factors need to be further studied and discussed.

Prognosis and Mortality

Prognosis There are possible prognostic models using the rate of progression in cognitive decline, dependence in activities of daily living (ADL), institutionalization, and survival as parameters. A 4.5-year prospective study was performed using "total dependence in activities of daily living," "incontinence," and "institutionalization at follow-up" as end points. The results suggested that the initial degree of severity rather than the variation in the rate of progression correlates most closely with the prognosis in the early to intermediate stages of AD (Drachman, O'Donnell, Lew, & Swearer, 1990). The relationship between disease severity and prognosis should be taken into account before discussing the differences in the rates of disease progression. When using "survival" as the prognostic parameter for the population 75 years and older, older age, male sex, low education, comorbidity, and functional disability were associated with shorter survival (Aguero-Torres, Fratiglioni, Guo, Viitanen, & Winblad, 1998).

A population-based prospective study of persons 55 years and older was conducted, and high age and low cognitive performance were the strongest predictors of institutionalization and death (Ruitenberg et al., 2001). The relationship between the presence of psychotic symptoms and dependence in both basic and instrumental ADL were investigated in patients with AD who were referred to a memory clinic. Dependence in ADL was associated with psychotic symptoms as well as cognitive decline and depression, but the possible causal relationship between psychotic symptoms and dependence in ADL needs to be further investigated (Tran, Bedard, Molloy, Dubois, & Lever, 2003). On the other hand, the annual rates of change in the cognitive and functional scales have been calculated in AD patients and investigated in relation to the clinical predictors (Swanwick, Coen, Coakley, & Lawlor, 1998). Although age and duration of symptoms at entry were not predictive of the rate of decline partly because of the large variability in the progression rate, male sex was associated with a faster decline in cognition.

Risk Factors of Mortality   The number of remaining years of life and the risk factors for mortality of demented patients are the most important factors in terms of social and economic issues. Larger numbers of older adults will require more social services and care, with an attendant increase in medical costs.

Estimates of the median survival from the clinical onset of dementia vary from 5 to 9.3 years. However, previous studies may have underestimated the deleterious effects of dementia because patients with rapidly progressing dementia died before commencement of the studies (length bias). Recently, the median survival from the onset of dementia symptoms, with adjustment for length bias, was estimated in the Canadian Study of Health and Aging (Wolfson et al., 2001). From a random sample of 10,263 subjects 65 years and older, 821 subjects with dementia, including 648 patients with AD, were followed up for 5 years. The estimated median survival was 3.3 years after the adjustment for the length bias, even though the mean age at sampling was 83.8 years (Kawas & Brookmeyer, 2001). In the Personnes Agees Quid prospective population-based cohort study in France, 2,923 elderly were followed up for 8 years, and 281 persons were diagnosed as having incident dementia. The median survival time of the demented patients was 4.5 years (Helmer, Joly, Letenneur, Commenges, & Dartigues, 2001). These studies thus showed shorter survival than in the earlier studies.

A number of surveys were recently conducted to study the survival and risk factors associated with dementia. An 8-year follow-up study showed that deaths from cerebrovascular diseases and respiratory disease were more frequent in patients with dementia than in persons without dementia (Helmer et al., 2001). With regard to late-stage AD, a 5-year follow-up study in a long-term care facility showed that better physical health and the presence of delusions were associated with longer survival (Carlson et al., 2001). For early-onset AD, a 5-year follow-up study of 46- to 64-year-old persons showed that male sex, earlier onset, concurrent physical illness at the time of diagnosis, and a low score on the Mini-Mental State Examination increased the likelihood of death (Ueki, Shinjo, Shimode, Nakajima, & Morita, 2001).

There is a sex difference in mortality of patients with dementia. Men with AD have an increased risk of mortality relative to women. A 2-year follow-up study of AD patients age 65 found that the most important predictors of the age at death in men were the severity of dementia and occurrence of delirium (Lapane et al., 2001). In women, the age at death was associated with dependence in physical functioning, pressure ulcers, aphasia, depression, and malnutrition. The presence of comorbid conditions, including cerebrovascular diseases, Parkinson's disease, and pulmonary disease, were associated with accelerated age at death, and the association was more evident in women than men.

MILD COGNITIVE IMPAIRMENT

There are people who are not demented but show mild memory loss or mild decline of other cognitive functions exceeding what would be expected for their age and educational level. Studies have suggested that people with cognitive decline consisting mainly of memory loss are at higher risk of dementia. There is a transitional condition between normal aging and dementia. That condition has been discussed as age-associated memory impairment, age-associated cognitive decline, mild cognitive disorder, age-related cognitive decline, mild neurocognitive disorder, and cognitive impairment with no dementia. More recently, attention has been paid to what is thought to be a transitional state to dementia, referred to as mild cognitive impairment (MCI; Petersen et al., 1999). This is the clinical state of individuals who are memory impaired but are otherwise functioning well and do not meet the clinical criteria for dementia. The clinical criteria for MCI are shown in Table 13.1. Recent recommendations for MCI criteria include the following points: (a) The person is neither normal nor demented; (b) there is evidence of cognitive deterioration shown by either objectively measured decline over time or subjective report of decline by self or informant in conjunction with objective cognitive deficits; and (c) activities of daily living are preserved and complex instrumental functions are either intact or minimally impaired (Winblad et al., 2004).

Table 13.1
Criteria of Mild Cognitive Impairment (MCI)

Memory complaint, preferably corroborated by an informant
Objective memory impairment
Normal general cognitive function
Intact activities of daily living
Not demented

Source: "Mild Cognitive Impairment: Clinical Characterization and Outcome," by R. C. Petersen et al., 1999, *Archives of Neurology, 56*, pp. 303–308. Reprinted with permission.

Not all people with MCI develop dementia, but many do. Epidemiological studies addressed the conversion rate of MCI to dementia. Longitudinal studies published between 1991 and 2001 were reviewed and summarized, and the annual conversion rate from MCI to dementia in the studies was found to vary from 2% to 31% (Bruscoli & Lovestone, 2004). A meta-analysis of all 1,616 subjects gave a calculated mean annual conversion rate of 10.24% (95% CI: 6.9% to 11.9%). The variation in the conversion rate may be explained by the following factors. The mean age of the cohort ranged from 61.2 to 80.9, although the incidence of AD and dementia in the elderly increases with age regardless of the presence or absence of MCI. The follow-up period could have influenced the conversion rate; it ranged from a minimum of 1.5 years to a maximum of 10 years. Some studies were conducted in clinical settings, and others in community settings. The mean annual conversion rate was higher in clinic attenders and lower in community-dwelling volunteers. Moreover, the most critical issue underlying the variation among the studies was the criteria used to diagnose MCI. Further discussion of the standard criteria for MCI is needed.

AN EVIDENCE-BASED ASSESSMENT OF ALZHEIMER'S DISEASE

DIAGNOSTIC CRITERIA

The concept of dementia was described in the 10th revision of the *International Statistical Classification of Diseases and Related Health Problems* (ICD-10; World Health Organization, 2003) and the *Diagnostic and Statistical Manual of Mental Disorders*, third edition, revised (*DSM-III-R*; American Psychiatric Association, 1987), which were recommended by the Quality Standards Subcommittee of the American Academy of Neurology (Knopman et al., 2001). Both these diagnostic criteria stipulate that dementia should be caused by a brain disease, should be chronic and progressive, and necessarily affects higher cognitive functions. Also, differentiation from other conditions such as delirium and depression is necessary.

Several sets of diagnostic criteria and scores have been developed for differentiation of the dementia subtypes, including AD. The NINCDS-ADRDA criteria were introduced in 1984 (McKhann et al., 1984) and confirmed the availability of valid operationalized criteria for AD. These criteria have been used more widely than others in research as well as in clinical settings and are recommended by the Quality Standards Subcommittee of the American Academy of Neurology (Knopman et al., 2001). In the criteria, three degrees of certainty are described: probable AD, possible AD, and definite AD. The clinical diagnosis of AD is based on a profile of symptoms, characteristic history, and the absence of other causes of dementia. The following elements should be confirmed after the establishment of the presence of dementia. It is specified that deficits are required not only in memory but also in other cognitive functions, such as language ability, constructional ability, thinking, or executive function. Such deficits should show gradual onset, with progressive decline over a period of years. To secure the certainty of the diagnosis, an upper age limit of 90 is set in the criteria because it is sometimes difficult to determine the significance of cognitive impairment in such very old people, even if for practical reasons the diagnosis of AD is the mode for patients 90 and older in the clinical setting. Differential diagnosis should be done by confirmation of the absence of other causes on the basis of the medical history, examination, and investigation. When another significant brain disease is present besides AD, such as cerebrovascular disease, diagnostic difficulties arise. It is important to note that the presence of concurrent disorders, which may contribute to the dementia, does not necessarily preclude a diagnosis of AD. An advantage of these criteria is that they require clinical evaluation, cognitive assessment, and routine blood screening, but not novel or extensive techniques. The NINCDS-ADRDA criteria have been repeatedly evaluated in a number of studies and have shown high interrater reliability (Farrer et al., 1994; Kukull et al., 1990; see Table 13.2).

Table 13.2
Criteria for Clinical Diagnosis of Alzheimer's Disease

I. The criteria for the clinical diagnosis of PROBABLE Alzheimer's disease include:
- Dementia established by clinical examination and documented by the Mini-Mental Test; Blessed Dementia Scale, or some similar examination, and confirmed by neuropsychological tests;
- Deficits in two or more areas of cognition;
- Progressive worsening of memory and other cognitive functions;
- No disturbance of consciousness;
- Onset between ages 40 and 90, most often after age 65; and
- Absence of systemic disorders or other brain diseases that in and of themselves could account for the progressive deficits in memory and cognition.

II. Other clinical features consistent with the diagnosis of PROBABLE Alzheimer's disease, after exclusion of causes of dementia other than Alzheimer's disease, include:
- Progressive deterioration of specific cognitive functions such as language (aphasia), motor skills (apraxia), and perception (agnosia);
- Impaired activities of daily living and altered patterns of behavior;
- Family history of similar disorders, particularly if confirmed neuropathologically;
- Laboratory results of:
  Normal lumbar puncture as evaluated by standard techniques;
  Normal pattern or non-specific changes in EEG, such as increased slow-wave activity;
  Evidence of cerebral atrophy on CT with progression documented by serial observation.

III. Other clinical features consistent with the diagnosis of PROBABLE Alzheimer's disease, after exclusion of causes of dementia other than Alzheimer's disease, include:
- Plateaus in the course of progression of the illness;
- Associated symptoms of depression, insomnia, incontinence, delusions, illusions, hallucinations, catastrophic verbal, emotional, or physical outbursts, sexual disorders, and weight loss;
- Other neurological abnormalities in some patients, especially with more advanced disease and including motor signs such as increased muscle tone, myoclonus, or gait disorder;
- Seizures in advanced disease;
- CT normal for age.

(continued)

Table 13.2 *Continued*

IV. Features that make the diagnosis of PROBABLE Alzheimer's disease uncertain or unlikely include:
  - Sudden, apoplectic onset;
  - Focal neurological findings such as hemiparesis, sensory loss, visual field deficits, and incoordination early in the course of the illness;
  - Seizures or gait disturbances at the onset or very early in the course of the illness.

V. Clinical diagnosis of possible Alzheimer's disease:
  - May be made on the basis of the dementia syndrome, in the absence of other neurological, psychiatric, or systemic disorders sufficient to cause dementia, and in the presence of variations in the onset, in the presentation, or in the clinical course;
  - May be made in the presence of a second systemic or brain disorder sufficient to produce dementia, which is not considered to be the cause of dementia;
  - Should be used in research studies when single gradually progressive severe cognitive deficit is identified in the absence of other identifiable cause.

VI. Criteria for diagnosis of definite Alzheimer's disease are:
  - The clinical criteria for probable Alzheimer's disease and histopathological evidence obtained from a biopsy or autopsy.

VII. Classification of Alzheimer's disease for research purposes should specify features that may differentiate subtypes of the disorder, such as:
  - Familial occurrence;
  - Onset before age of 65;
  - Presence of trisomy-21.

Source: "Clinical Diagnosis of Alzheimer's Disease: Report of the NINCDS-ADRDA Work Group under the Auspices of Department of Health and Human Services Task Force on Alzheimer's Disease," by G. McKhann et al., 1984, *Neurology, 34*, pp. 939–944. Reprinted with permission.

INTERVIEW SCHEDULE

PSYCHOGERIATRIC ASSESSMENT SCALES

The Psychogeriatric Assessment Scales (PAS; Jorm et al., 1995) provides an assessment of the clinical changes seen in both dementia and depression. It is a set of scales covering the clinical domains of dementia and depression as defined by the *ICD-10* (World Health Organization, 2003) and *DSM-III-R* (American Psychiatric Association, 1994). It should be applied by a trained lay interviewer or clinician after familiarization with the manual, and usually takes 10 minutes for each subject. The scales are based on the items in the Canberra Interview of the Elderly (Mackinnon et al., 1993), which is a standardized diagnostic interview administered by lay interviewers that involves both examination of the subject and interview of an informant. The purpose of the PAS is to describe a brief yet comprehensive profile of a subject's mental state using a straightforward interview which can be quickly administered by lay interviewers after training. It is intended for use in clinical settings as well as for research purposes. When the PAS was developed, various factors were analyzed using three samples—two clinical samples and one population sample—to derive a set of independent dimensions underlying the clinical domains of dementia and depression, and then latent trait analysis was applied to select a subset of items having the most appropriate psychometric properties relative to each other. Five factors emerged from the principal component analysis of each item in the scales: cognitive decline, cognitive impairment, behavior change, stroke, and depression. The internal consistency of the PAS ranged from .58 to .86, and the test-retest correlation was between .47 and .66; its validity was proven against other mood and cognitive scales.

GERIATRIC MENTAL STATE SCHEDULE

The Geriatric Mental State Schedule (GMSS; Copeland et al., 1976; Gurland et al., 1976) is a standardized, semistructured interview schedule for measuring a wide range of psychopathology in elderly people in both institutionalized and communal settings. It is based on the Present State Examination (PSE; Luria & McHugh, 1977; Wing, Nixon, von Cranach, & Strauss, 1977) and the Psychiatric Status Schedule (PSS; Spitzer, Endicott, Fleiss, & Cohen, 1970). Many of the items of the GMSS were adopted from the eighth edition of the PSE, with additional items taken from the PSS. The GMSS consists of a number of detailed questions concerning the patient's psychopathology and behavior in the prior month; it allows classification of the patient by symptom profile and can depict changes in that profile over time. There is extensive literature on the GMSS. Many different factors have been derived from the results (see Table 13.3). There is also a computerized algorithm of proven reliability and validity, the Automated Geriatric Examination for Computer Assisted Taxonomy (AGECAT; Copeland, Dewey, & Griffiths-Jones, 1986; Copeland, Dewey, Wood, et al., 1986).

Table 13.3
Factors Derived from the Geriatric Mental State Schedule (GMSS)

 1. Depression
 2. Anxiety
 3. Impaired memory
 4. Retarded speech
 5. Hypomania
 6. Somatic concerns
 7. Observed belligerence
 8. Reported belligerence
 9. Obsessions
10. Drug alcohol dependence
11. Cortical dysfunction
12. Disorientation
13. Lack of insight
14. Depersonalization-derealization
15. Paranoid delusion
16. Subjective experience of disordered thought
17. Visual hallucination
18. Auditory hallucination
19. Abnormal motor movements
20. Nonsocial speech
21. Incomprehensibility

Source: "A Semi-Structured Clinical Interview for the Assessment of Diagnosis and Mental State in the Elderly—The Geriatric Mental State Schedule: Pt. I. Development and Reliability," by J. R. Copeland et al., 1976, *Psychological Medicine, 6*, pp. 439–449. Reprinted with permission.

GLOBAL ASSESSMENT

FUNCTIONAL ASSESSMENT STAGING

Evaluation of the functional performance and activities of daily living skills is an essential aspect of the assessment of dementia patients. Functional Assessment Staging (FAST; Reisberg, 1988; Sclan & Reisberg, 1992) was developed on the basis of empirical and systematic examination of the functional decline occurring in patients with AD. By classifying the progress of AD in terms of functional stages, the FAST helps health professionals and caregivers meet the needs of AD patients. It permits specific evaluation of the changes in function throughout the entire course of AD. The FAST is shown in Table 13.4.

The FAST divides the disease process of AD into seven major stages of functional abilities and losses, with a total of 16 successive stages and substages: Stage 1: no cognitive decline; Stage 2 (Forgetfulness): very mild cognitive decline; Stage 3 (Early Confusional): mild cognitive decline, earliest clear-cut deficits; Stage 4 (Late

Table 13.4
Functional Assessment Staging (FAST)

Stage 1: No cognitive decline.
  No subjective complaints of memory deficit. No memory deficit evident on clinical interviews.

Stage 2 (Forgetfulness): Very mild cognitive decline.
  Subjective complaints of memory deficit, most frequently in the following area:
    Forgetting where one has placed familiar objects;
    Forgetting names one formerly knew well.
  No objective evidence of memory deficit on clinical interview. No objective deficits in employment or social situations. Appropriate concern regarding symptoms.

Stage 3 (Early Confusional): Mild cognitive decline. Earliest clear-cut deficits.
  Manifestations in more than one of the following areas:
    Patient may have gotten lost when traveling to an unfamiliar location;
    Co-workers become aware of patient's relatively low performance;
    Word and name finding deficit becomes evident to intimates;
    Patient may read a passage of a book and retain relatively little material;
    Patient may demonstrate decreased facility in remembering names on introduction to new people;
    Patient may have lost or misplaced an object of value;
    Concentration deficit may be evident on clinical testing.
  Objective evidence of memory deficit obtained only with an intensive interview. Denial begins to become manifest in patients. Mild to moderate anxiety accompanies symptoms.

Stage 4 (Late Confusional): Moderate cognitive decline. Clear-cut deficit on careful clinical interview.
  Deficit manifest in following areas:
    Decreased knowledge of current and recent events;
    May exhibit some deficit in memory of one's personal history;
    Concentration deficit elicited on serial subtractions;
    Decreased ability to travel, handle finances, etc.

Table 13.4 *Continued*

Frequently no deficit in the following areas:

Orientation to time and person;

Recognition of familiar persons and faces;

Ability to travel to familiar locations.

Inability to perform complex tasks. Denial is dominant defense mechanism. Flattening of affect and withdrawal from challenging situations occur.

Stage 5 (Early Dementia): Moderately severe cognitive decline. Patient can no longer survive without some assistance. Patients are unable during interview to recall a major relevant aspect of their current lives, e.g., an address or telephone number of many years, the names of close family members (such as grandchildren), the name of the high school or college from which they graduated. Frequently some disorientation to time (date, day of week, season, etc.) or to place. An educated person may have difficulty counting back from 40 by 4s or from 20 by 2s. Persons at this stage retain knowledge of many major facts regarding themselves and others. They invariably know their own names and generally know their spouse's and children's names. They require no assistance with toileting and eating, but may have some difficulty choosing the proper clothing to wear.

Stage 6 (Middle Dementia): Severe cognitive decline. May occasionally forget the name of the spouse on whom they are entirely dependent for survival. Will be largely unaware of all recent events and experiences in their lives. They retain some knowledge of their past lives but this is very sketchy. Generally unaware of their surroundings, the year, the season, etc. May have difficulty counting from 10, both backward and sometimes forward. Will require some assistance with activities of daily living, e.g., may become incontinent, will require travel assistance but occasionally will display ability to recall familiar locations. Diurnal rhythm frequently disturbed. Almost always recall their own names. Frequently continue to be able to distinguish familiar from unfamiliar persons in their environment.

Personality and emotional changes occur. These are quite variable and include:

Delusional behavior, e.g., patients may accuse their spouse of being an impostor, may talk to imaginary figures in the environment, or to their own reflection in the mirror;

Obsessive symptoms, e.g., person may continually repeat simple cleaning activities;

Anxiety agitation, and even previously nonexistent violent behavior may occur;

Cognitive abulla, i.e., loss of willpower because an individual cannot carry a thought long enough to determine a purposeful course of action.

Stage 7 (Late Dementia): Very severe cognitive decline. All verbal abilities are lost. Frequently there is no speech at all—only grunting. Incontinent of urine, requires assistance toileting and feeding. Loss of basic psychomotor skills, e.g., ability to walk, sit and head control. The brain appears to no longer be able to tell the body what to do. Generalized and cortical neurologic signs and symptoms are frequently present.

Source: "Functional Assessment Staging (FAST)," by B. Reisberg, 1988, *Psychopharmacology Bulletin, 24,* pp. 653–659. Reprinted with permission.

Table 13.5

Clinical Dementia Rating (CDR)

Cognitive-Function Category	Impairment Level and CDR Score (0, 0.5, 1, 2, 3)				
	None 0	Questionable 0.5	Mild 1	Moderate 2	Severe 3
Memory	No memory loss or slight inconsistent forgetfulness	Consistent slight forgetfulness; partial recollection of events; "benign" forgetfulness	Moderate memory loss; more marked for recent events; defect interferes with everyday activities	Severe memory loss; only highly learned material retained; new material rapidly lost	Severe memory loss; only fragments remain
Orientation	Fully oriented	Fully oriented except for slight difficulty with time relationships	Moderate difficulty with time relationships; oriented for place at examination; may have geographic disorientation elsewhere	Severe difficulty with time relationships; usually disoriented to time, often to place	Oriented to person only
Judgment and problem solving	Solves everyday problems and handles business and financial affairs well; judgment good in relation to past performance	Slight impairment in solving problems, similarities, and differences	Moderate difficulty in handling problems, similarities, and differences; social judgment usually maintained	Severely impaired in handling problems, similarities, and differences; social judgment usually impaired	Unable to make judgments or solve problems
Community affairs	Independent function at usual level in job, shopping, volunteer, and social groups	Slight impairment in these activities	Unable to function independently at these activities although may still be engaged in some; appears normal to casual inspection	No pretense of independent function outside home; Appears well enough to be taken to functions outside a family home	No pretense of independent function outside home; Appears too ill to be taken to functions outside a family home
Home and hobbies	Life at home, hobbies, and intellectual interests well maintained	Life at home, hobbies, and intellectual interests slightly impaired	Mild but definite impairment of function at home; more difficult chores abandoned; more complicated hobbies and interests abandoned	Only simple chores preserved; very restricted interests, poorly maintained	No significant function in home
Personal care	Fully capable of self-care		Needs prompting	Requires assistance in dressing, hygiene, keeping of personal effects	Requires much help with personal care; frequent incontinence

Source: "A New Clinical Scale for the Staging of Dementia," by C. P. Hughes, L. Berg, W. L. Danziger, L. A. Coben, and R. L. Martin, 1982, *British Journal of Psychiatry, 140,* pp. 566–572. Reprinted with permission.

Confusional): moderate cognitive decline, clear-cut deficit on careful clinical interview; Stage 5 (Early Dementia): moderately severe cognitive decline; Stage 6 (Middle Dementia): Severe cognitive decline; Stage 7 (Late Dementia): very severe cognitive decline. Reliability of the FAST has been demonstrated with intraclass correlations of above .85. Concurrent validity has been assessed against the Global Deterioration Scale and a number of neuropsychological tests (Reisberg, Sclan, Franssen, Kluger, & Ferris, 1994). The sensitivity of the FAST to the entire course of AD, even in its most severe stages, may be indicative of the potential value of this instrument for further investigation of the temporal longitudinal course of AD.

CLINICAL DEMENTIA RATING

The Clinical Dementia Rating (CDR; Hughes, Berg, Danziger, Coben, & Martin, 1982) scale is the most widely used in clinical practice as well as research to assess the severity of disease progression. The CDR is helpful as a guide in the clinical management of AD as well as other dementias. A trained physician, nurse, psychologist, or other health professional administers the CDR to both the patient and a reliable informant or collateral source such as a family member as a semistructured interview. The CDR is shown in Table 13.5.

Impairment levels are determined for six cognitive function categories: (1) Memory, (2) Orientation, (3) Judgment, (4) Community Affairs, (5) Home and Hobbies, and (6) Personal Care. A 5-point scale is used to rate the function in each category: 0 = Normal (no significant problem); 0.5 = Questionable impairment (more than just normal aging); 1 = Mild impairment (mildly impaired relative to peers); 2 = Moderate impairment; 3 = Severe impairment. The scores for each category are then analyzed using scoring rules to determine an overall CDR score. The CDR table provides descriptive anchors that guide the rater in making appropriate ratings based on interview data and clinical judgment. Subjects who receive a score of 1 or greater show clear signs of dementia. The reliability of the CDR has been further established (Berg et al., 1992). Longitudinal data are available on its use (Berg et al., 1988; Galasko et al., 1995), and it has been validated against neuropathological information (Morris, McKeel, Fulling, Torack, & Berg, 1988; Morris et al., 1991).

COGNITIVE ASSESSMENT

MINI-MENTAL STATE EXAMINATION

The Mini-Mental State Examination (MMSE; Folstein, Folstein, & McHugh, 1975; Folstein, Robins, & Helzer, 1983) is a quantitative measure of cognitive status in adults. It is a brief questionnaire and can be used to screen for cognitive impairment, to estimate the severity of cognitive impairment at a given point in time, to follow the course of cognitive changes in an individual over time, and to document an individual's response to treatment. The MMSE has shown validity and reliability in psychiatric, neurologic, geriatric, and other medical populations. It has also been used as a research tool to screen for cognitive disorders in epidemiological studies and to follow cognitive changes in clinical trials. It is presented in Table 13.6.

Table 13.6
The Mini-Mental State Exam (MMSE)

Patient _____   Examiner _____

Date _____

Maximum
Score

Orientation

5   ( )   What is the (year) (season) (date) (day) (month)?

5   ( )   Where are we (state) (country) (town) (hospital) (floor)?

Registration

3   ( )   Name 3 objects: 1 second to say each. Then ask the patient all 3 after you have said them. Give 1 point for each correct answer. Then repeat them until he/she learns all 3. Count trials and record.

Trials _____

Attention and Calculation

5   ( )   Serial 7s. 1 point for each correct answer. Stop after 5 answers. Alternatively spell "world" backward.

Recall

3   ( )   Ask for the 3 objects repeated above. Give 1 point for each correct answer.

Language

2   ( )   Name a pencil and watch.

1   ( )   Repeat the following "No ifs, ands, or buts"

3   ( )   Follow a 3-stage command:

"Take a paper in your hand, fold it in half, and put it on the floor."

1   ( )   Read and obey the following: CLOSE YOUR EYES

1   ( )   Write a sentence.

1   ( )   Copy the design shown.

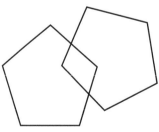

_____ Total Score

Source: "Mini-Mental State: A Practical Method for Grading the State of Patients for the Clinician," by M. F. Folstein, S. E. Folstein, and P. R. McHugh, 1975, *Journal of Psychiatric Research, 12,* pp. 189–198. Reprinted with permission.

Although the MMSE has limited specificity with respect to individual clinical syndromes, it represents a brief, standardized method for grading cognitive mental status. It assesses orientation, attention, immediate and short-term recall, language, and the ability to follow simple verbal and written commands. Furthermore, it provides a total score that places the individual on a scale of cognitive function. Details of extensive subsequent validity and reliability studies are described by Tombaugh and McIntyre (1992). Loewenstein and colleagues (2000) tested the utility of an additional delayed recall of the 3 items as a screening test for mild cognitive impairment. Extended delayed recall of the 3 items was at 5-minute intervals. Sensitivity of 83.3% and specificity of 90% was achieved in differentiating cases with mild cognitive impairment from individuals with normal cognition.

THE 7-MINUTE SCREEN

To recognize AD, which tends to be missed in primary care, the 7-Minute Screen (Solomon & Pendlebury, 1998) was developed as a brief neurocognitive screening battery. It covers multiple cognitive domains of orientation, memory, visuospatial function, and verbal fluency and takes approximately 7 to 11 minutes, including scoring. It can be rapidly administered by allied health professionals without authentic training. No clinical judgment is needed. The portion assessing the orientation is the Benton Temporal Orientation Test, which assesses the ability to identify the month, date, year, day, and time of day (Benton, 1983). The portion assessing the memory is an abbreviated version of the Enhanced Cued Recall Test, which uses 16 items presented pictorially (Grober, Buschke, Crystal, Bang, & Dresner, 1988). The subject is instructed to encode the items and recall them with cues, and then recall again without cues. When the subject cannot recall any additional items, the examiner provides appropriate cues for the remaining items. The score for this portion is the total number of items remembered in both the uncued and cued recall. The portion assessing the visuospatial function is a clock-drawing test with a simple scoring system (Freedman et al., 1994). The examiner says to the subject, "I want you to draw a clock with all the numbers on it. Make it large." The subject is then asked to draw the clock hands set at 20 minutes before 4 o'clock. A score is determined using the scoring system. The portion that focuses on expressive language is a test of verbal fluency (Monsch et al., 1992; Risen, 1980). The examiner asks the subject to name as many members of the category "animals" as possible during a 1-minute period. The score is the total number of items named. It was reported that the 7-Minute Screen gave more accurate results than the MMSE for patients with mild or very mild AD.

INFORMANT QUESTIONNAIRE ON COGNITIVE DECLINE IN THE ELDERLY

The Informant Questionnaire on Cognitive Decline in the Elderly (IQCODE; Jorm & Jacomb, 1989) is a questionnaire administered to an informant about changes in the subject's cognitive function in everyday life (see Table 13.7). It evaluates cognitive decline independent of premorbid ability. There are long and short versions of the IQCODE.

Table 13.7

Items from Informant Questionnaire on Cognitive Decline in the Elderly (IQCODE)

---

1. Remembering things about family and friends, e.g., occupations, birthdays, addresses
2. Remembering things that have happened recently
3. Recalling conversations a few days later
4. Remembering his/her address and telephone number
5. Remembering what day and month it is
6. Remembering where things are usually kept
7. Remembering where to find things that have been put in a different place from usual
8. Knowing how to work familiar machines around the house
9. Learning to use a new gadget or machine around the house
10. Learning new things in general
11. Following a story in a book or on TV
12. Making decisions on everyday matters
13. Handling money for shopping
14. Handling financial matters, e.g., the pension, dealing with the bank
15. Handling other every day arithmetic problems, for example, knowing how much food to buy, knowing how long between visits from family or friends
16. Using his/her intelligence to understand what's going on and to reason things through

---

Source: "The Informant Questionnarie on Cognitive Decline in the Elderly (IQCODE): Socio-Demographic Correlates, Reliability, Validity and Some Norms," by A. F. Jorm and P. A. Jacomb, 1989, *Psychological Medicine, 19*(4), pp. 1015–1022. Reprinted with permission.

The examiner asks the informant to recall what the subject was like 10 years ago and to compare that with what the subject is like now. The examiner then asks the informant to indicate whether each of the situations shown in the table of the IQCODE has improved, stayed the same, or gotten worse during the past 10 years. The short version of the IQCODE includes 16 situations. The judgment is chosen from five evaluations: "Much improved," "A bit improved," "Not much change," "A bit worse," and "Much worse." It is important to compare the subject's present performance with 10 years ago. For instance, if 10 years ago the subject always forgot where he or she had left things, and he or she still does, then this would be considered "Not much change." The internal consistency of the IQCODE was .93; the validity, measured against MMSE, showed a correlation of .78. Further studies have shown that the IQCODE is as good as the MMSE in the diagnosis of dementia (Jorm et al., 1991, 1996). A 16-item version has been found to perform as well as the long version (Jorm, 1994). Validity has been affirmed by showing that subjects rated as having moderate or severe decline were found to have greater change on the cognitive tests (Jorm et al., 1996).

Severe Impairment Battery

The cognitive function of very impaired patients cannot be measured with standard neuropsychological tests. To assess these severely demented patients, the Severe Impaired Battery (SIB; Panisset, Roudier, Saxton, & Boller, 1994; Schmitt et al., 1997) was developed. The SIB takes into account the specific behavioral and cognitive deficits associated with severe dementia. It takes approximately 20 minutes to administer. It is composed of very simple one-step commands that are presented in conjunction with gesture cues. The six major subscales are Attention, Orientation,

Language, Memory, Visuospatial Ability, and Construction. There are also brief evaluations of praxis and the patient's ability to respond appropriately when his or her name is called. In addition, there is an assessment of social interaction skills abstracted from the Communicative Activities in Daily Living Scale (Holland, 1980).

FUNCTIONAL ASSESSMENT

ALZHEIMER'S DISEASE COOPERATIVE STUDY—ACTIVITIES OF DAILY LIVING

The Alzheimer's Disease Cooperative Study—Activities of Daily Living (ADCS-ADL; Galasko, Schmitt, Thomas, Jin, & Bennett, 2005) inventory consists of a comprehensive battery of activities of daily living questions used to assess the functional capabilities of patients. Although ADL includes a wide range of activities, ADL scores should have broad applicability and reflect the severity of ADL impairment. A set of informant-based items describing the performance of ADL was developed to identify which ADL domains are useful for assessment of patients in clinical research on AD. A total of 45 ADL items selected on the basis of a literature review and clinical experience were tested. They were then narrowed to 27 items that were widely applicable, showed good test-retest reliability between repeated estimations, and correlated with the severity of dementia. The modified ADCS-ADL inventory was thus established (Galasko et al., 1997). Each ADL item is rated from the highest level of independent performance to complete loss. The investigator applies the inventory by interviewing a caregiver who is familiar with the behavior of the patient.

Patients with AD who have reached a stage of moderate to severe dementia are still capable of performing a limited range of ADL. From a large pool of ADL data in a cohort, 19 items were chosen in consideration of their applicability, reliability, good scaling, concordant validity, and sensitivity in detecting changes in performance over a period of months. The subset of items, including ratings of the patient's ability to eat, dress, bathe, telephone, travel, shop, and perform other household chores, has been validated for the assessment of patients with moderate to severe dementia. This is the modified ADCS-ADL—severe inventory (Galasko et al., 2005), which has a scoring range of 0 to 54, with the lower scores indicating greater functional impairment.

DISABILITY ASSESSMENT FOR DEMENTIA

The Disability Assessment for Dementia (DAD; Gelinas, Gauthier, McIntyre, & Gauthier, 1999) is an assessment tool for functional disability, designed to meet the specific needs of community-dwelling elderly patients who have AD. Functional disability is measured with the DAD by evaluating the basic, instrumental, and leisure activities of daily life. The basic ADL are related to self-care and include dressing, hygiene, continence, and eating. The instrumental ADL are related to maintenance in a specific environment and include meal preparation, telephoning, housework, taking care of finances and correspondence, going on an outing, taking medication, and the ability to stay safely at home. The leisure activities go beyond self-maintenance and are for the purpose of recreation. To understand the cognitive dimensions of disabilities in ADL, the activities have been subdivided into initiation, planning and organization, and effective performance.

BEHAVIORAL ASSESSMENT

BEHAVIOR PATHOLOGY IN ALZHEIMER'S DISEASE RATING SCALE

Before development of the Behavior Pathology in Alzheimer's Disease (BEHAVE-AD; Reisberg, Auer, & Monteiro, 1996) rating scale, several scales, including the Symptoms of Psychosis in Alzheimer's Disease (Reisberg & Ferris, 1985), were available for measuring behavioral disturbances and psychiatric disorders in patients with AD. However, such scales generally mixed cognitive disturbances with behavioral symptoms or included functional impairment. The BEHAVE-AD scale was developed to measure behavioral disturbances related to dementia separately from the cognitive and functional disturbances. Separate assessment of each symptomatic domain is particularly important because behavioral disturbances of dementia might be amenable to treatment.

The items of BEHAVE-AD are shown in Table 13.8. The rating scale consists of seven categories, including 25 items of behavioral disturbances. Each symptom is

Table 13.8
Symptoms of Behavioral Pathology in Alzheimer's
Disease (BEHAVE-AD) Rating Scale

Category	Example
Paranoid and delusional ideation	"People are stealing things" delusion "One's house is not one's house" delusion "Spouse (or other caregiver) is an imposter" delusion Delusion of abandonment (e.g., to an institution) Delusion of infidelity Other suspiciousness or paranoia Other delusions
Hallucinations	Visual Auditory Olfactory Haptic Other
Activity disturbances	Wandering Purposeless activity Inappropriate activity
Aggressiveness	Verbal outbursts Physical threats and violence Agitation
Diurnal rhythm disturbances	Day-night disturbances
Affective disturbances	Tearfulness Depressed mood
Anxieties and phobias	Anxiety about upcoming events Other anxieties Fear of being left alone Other phobias

Source: "Behavioral Pathology in Alzheimer's Disease (BEHAVE-AD) Rating Scale," by B. Reisberg, S. R. Auer, and I. M. Monteiro, 1996, International Psychogeriatrics, 8(Suppl. 3), pp. 301–308. Reprinted with permission.

scored on a 4-point scale of severity: 0 = Not present; 1 = Present; 2 = Present, generally with an emotional component; and 3 = Present, generally with an emotional and physical component. The rating scale also contains a 4-point global assessment of the overall magnitude of the behavioral symptoms in terms of disturbance to the caregiver or danger to the patient. Sclan and colleagues (1996) determined interrater reliability of the scale transculturally, including patients from France. Interrater reliability was excellent, with agreement coefficients ranging from .65 to .91. Patterson and colleagues (1990) reported very good reliability rating (kappa value = .62 to 1.00 on 20 of the 25 items, with percentage agreement of between 82% and 100%).

COHEN-MANSFIELD AGITATION INVENTORY

Agitation can be operationally defined as inappropriate verbal, vocal, or motor activity that is not judged by an observer to result directly from the needs or confusion of the agitated individual (Cohen-Mansfield & Billig, 1986). Agitation is not a diagnostic term but a term describing a group of symptoms. Agitated behavior is socially inappropriate and may be manifested in three ways: abusive or aggressive behavior toward self or others; appropriate behavior performed with inappropriate frequency, such as repeatedly asking questions; and inappropriate behavior according to the social standards for a given situation, such as taking off one's clothes in the activity room of a nursing home (Cohen-Mansfield, Marx, & Rosenthal, 1989).

The purpose of the Cohen-Mansfield Agitation Inventory (CMAI; Cohen-Mansfield, 1996) is to assess the frequency of manifestation of agitated behavior in elderly persons. The CMAI was developed for use in nursing homes. Although originally developed for research purposes, it has recently also been used for clinical purposes. It has thus been used by family caregivers, social workers, activity directors of senior day care centers, and other clinical staff members, as well as researchers. The items of the CMAI are presented in Table 13.9. The CMAI

Table 13.9
Cohen-Mansfield Agitation Inventory (CMAI)

1. Pace, aimless wandering
2. Inappropriate dress or disrobing
3. Spitting (including at meals)
4. Cursing or verbal aggression
5. Constant unwarranted request for attention or help
6. Repetitive sentences or questions
7. Hitting (including self)
8. Kicking
9. Grabbing onto people
10. Pushing
11. Throwing things
12. Strange noises (weird laughter or crying)
13. Screaming
14. Biting

Source: "Conceptualization of Agitation: Results Based on the Cohen-Mansfield Agitation Inventory and the Agitation Behavior Mapping Instrument," by J. Cohen-Mansfield, 1996, *International Psychogeriatrics*, *8*(Suppl. 3), pp. 309–315. Reprinted with permission.

consists of 29 items, each rated on a 7-point scale of frequency: 1 = Never; 2 = Less than once a week; 3 = Once or twice a week; 4 = Several times a week; 5 = Once or twice a day; 6 = Several times a day; 7 = Several times an hour. The CMAI questions pertain to the prior 2 weeks.

CURRENT STATUS AND FUTURE OUTLOOK FOR DRUG TREATMENT: A MECHANISM-BASED APPROACH

CHOLINESTERASE INHIBITORS FOR SYMPTOMATIC TREATMENT

It is possible to prescribe any of four cholinesterase inhibitors (ChEls), that is, tacrin, donepezil, rivastigmine, and galantamine, as well as the N-methyl-D-asparate antagonist, memantine, to treat AD. The efficacy and safety of these drugs have already been established. They are used for so-called symptomatic treatment, and the purpose of administering these drugs is to delay progression of the symptoms associated with AD. Many institutes and pharmaceutical companies are vigorously pursuing development of immunotherapy using vaccines and other drugs as disease modifiers as well as basic therapeutic drugs such as secretase, but none of the potential products has reached the stage of clinical application.

Recently, there have been reports describing the efficacy of ChEls. Assessments of the efficacies of donepezil, rivastigmine, galantamine, and memantine were published by the AD2000 Collaborative Study Group (Courtney et al., 2004) and by Kaduszkiewicz, Zimmermann, Beck-Bornholdt, and van den Bussche (2005). Here, we would like to discuss the efficacy of ChEls, focusing mainly on the findings of these two studies cited. With respect to the future outlook for AD drugs, we summarize and briefly comment on the results of studies that used ChEls to treat mild cognitive impairment.

Current Status of Cholinesterase Inhibitors for Treating Alzheimer's Disease A meta-analysis of the efficacy of three ChEI drugs (donepezil, galantamine, and rivastigmine) was performed based on 121 original articles and 34 review papers, which were selected from 2,285 reports on AD published between 1992 and 2002 (Ritchie, Ames, Clayton, & Lai, 2004). The results of 10 donepezil, six galantamine, and five revastigmine studies were compared using regression analysis in terms of the dose-dependence effect and the dropout rate. All three drugs were confirmed to be superior to the placebo with respect to the results of cognitive test batteries. However, whereas donepezil and rivastigmine exhibited a greater effect at high doses, a significant dose-dependent effect was not observed for galantamine. For the global clinical assessment, the treated groups were superior to the placebo, but a definite correlation between the dose and effect was not observed for donepezil and galantamine. For the dropout rates, there were not significant differences among the three drugs, other than the high dose of donepezil. In other words, even though the mechanisms of action of the three drugs are somewhat different—the Acetyleholinesterase (AChE) inhibitory action of donepezil is more potent than its Y Butirilcolinesterasa (BuCE) inhibitory action, the potentiating action of galantamine on nicotine receptors is potent, and rivastigmine has both AChE and BuChE inhibitory actions—there were no substantial differences in the clinical usefulness of the drugs when evaluating them using the cognitive test batteries and the global clinical assessment. More recently, the review of 26 randomized controlled trials confirmed that the results for ChEIs were similar to the results just cited (Takeda et al., 2006). The authors of the review attempted to draw conclusions concerning the effects on quality of life and to compare the drugs, but they were unable to come to any conclusions due to the limited number of reports. Adverse drug effects due to ChEIs were reviewed in the report of Kaduszkiewicz and colleagues (2005). The incidence of adverse drug effects with each of the three drugs increased as the administered dose was increased, but it is difficult to compare the three drugs because little was reported about the dose or time of onset of the adverse effects. It may be possible to state that the typical nongastrointestinal adverse effects of the drugs were insomnia for donepezil and dizziness for galantamine and rivastigmine.

Kaduszkiewicz and colleagues (2005) reviewed 22 randomized, double-blind, placebo-controlled studies conducted on ChEIs between 1989 and 2004. The reports were selected based on specific criteria. The criteria in their analysis included methodological parameters: the inclusion and exclusion criteria for the subjects; the method of randomization; methods and criteria for stratification, blinding, outcome measures, and method of analysis; significant level; power of the tests; whether or not both groups that participated in the study received the same treatment; aspects relating to the results such as baseline data, adverse drug effects, intention-to-treat analysis, number of subjects included in the analysis, outcome of assessment end points, and conformity of the results; and overall interpretation of the research, such as whether the name of the sponsor was clearly stated, the study methods, and clinical significance. In their review, Kaduszkiewicz and colleagues did not examine the characteristics of the clinical efficacy among ChEIs, but rather determined the efficacy of ChEIs overall from the point of view of the study design. They concluded, as in past evidence-based reviews, that the efficacy of ChEIs was confirmed in several clinical trials. On the other hand, the efficacy measured using the assessment scales used in the clinical trials was modest, and they pointed out that there were many methodological deficiencies in the studies themselves. Furthermore, they pointed out that it was impossible to conclude whether donepezil was effective or not based on the results in the AD2000 study because the study period was not established beforehand and because the results for the 5 mg and 10 mg groups were not shown separately. Kaduszkiewicz and colleagues stated that although the three ChEIs were effective, their overall efficacy in the treatment of AD was not really that high. However, we believe this was not an appropriate statement, because they did not consider such aspects as the health insurance systems of the different countries or the degree of recognition of AD by family physicians. Finally, it should be emphasized that consistent results were obtained in the studies that used the three ChEIs.

N-methyl-D-asparate Antagonist   Memantine is the only agent other than the cholinesterase inhibitors that has been approved for treatment of AD. It is a moderate-affinity, noncompetitive N-methyl-D-aspartate receptor antagonist and currently the only agent approved for moderately severe to severe AD in Europe and for moderate to severe AD in the United States. Consistent reduction of the deterioration rate on global, cognitive, functional, and behavioral measurements was shown in the memantine treatment group compared to the usual care group in a recent clinical trial (Bullock, 2006). In the meta-analysis of clinical trials for memantine treatment, improvements versus the placebo were seen in individual activities of daily living and behavior, particularly agitation and cognitive function (McShane, Areosa Sastre, & Minakaran, 2006). Efficacy of memantine was demonstrated in patients with newly diagnosed AD, patients previously or currently receiving ChEIs, and both institutionalized and community-dwelling AD patients. Increased dependency and institutionalization are significant cost drivers in AD. Memantine is able to reduce dependency and caregiver time required. This effect is important from the point of view that AD progression, caregiver burden, and health care costs are interrelated.

FUTURE OUTLOOK FOR ALZHEIMER'S DISEASE DRUGS: EXTRAPOLATION FROM TRIALS OF PATIENTS WITH MILD COGNITIVE IMPAIRMENT

It has been shown that several subtypes of mild cognitive impairment exist, and there is still a lack of consensus on whether or not to consider MCI to be a precursor state of AD. However, there is general agreement that MCI is a risk factor for the onset of dementia. Not everyone who has MCI will develop AD, and some patients who do not have MCI will develop AD (Knopman et al., 2003; Snowdon, 2003). Recently, several studies have been conducted on subjects with amnestic MCI, which is believed to exhibit the most typical clinical picture, course, and outcome among the various subtypes of MCI. It is known that neuropathological changes exist prior to the onset of clinical symptoms of AD. Thus, if we assume that MCI is an precursor state of AD as demonstrated by existing neuropathological changes (Kordower et al., 2001; Mitchell et al., 2002; Mufson et al., 2002) or images, or neuropsychological test results (Arnaiz & Almkvist, 2003), then it is indeed appropriate to conduct a treatment trial of MCI, whose objective is to delay, even if only slightly, the onset of the clinical symptoms of AD. Although satisfactory results have not been obtained, we have reviewed the results reported thus far and here attempt to discuss them. The need for a disease modifier such as ChEI will increase in the future. Important information may be obtained from discussion about a study design of ChEIs. The ChEI studies conducted thus far are summarized in Table 13.2.

As is clear in Table 13.2, there were no study results that successfully achieved the initial objective, although the efficacy of a ChEI as symptomatic therapy was confirmed for donepezil when the study period was 6 months and in a study whose objective was 3-year secondary prevention. It can be seen that very similar selection criteria were used for the subjects of the studies in Table 13.2. However, if we consider that there was a large range in the conversion rate to AD, that is, from 4.5% and 6.4% per year for rofecoxib to 16% for donepezil + vitamin E, it is possible that the subjects selected were extremely heterogeneous. Visser, Scheltens, and Verhey (2005) retrospectively examined the accuracy of the diagnostic criteria used in MCI studies and pointed out that there were large discrepancies in the definitions of cognitive impairment. Rubinsztein and Easton (1999) performed a meta-analysis of the frequency of apoE4 in 42 reports and found it to be 32% in patients at least 65 years old with sporadic AD and 41% in those less than 65. Taking this into consideration, the criteria for cognitive impairment in donepezil + vitamin E studies were strict. The subjects were selected using those criteria with a high predictive value and they showed high conversion rates. This resulted in the selection of subjects with relatively high degrees of impairment compared to other studies because of the high percentage of apoE4.

Even with respect to the diagnostic criteria for AD, there have been several reports dealing with the interrater reliability in multicenter studies, as well as clinical neuropathological reports. If we consider that the results of MCI were not satisfactory and there is no consensus concerning the clinical diagnostic criteria for MCI, it may be necessary to add some types of biological markers as criteria for MCI. Visser and colleagues (2002) used the Preclinical AD Scale (PAS), which combines age, MMSE score, degree of functional impairment, neuropsychological test results, medial temporal lobe atrophy, and apoE subtype; they reported that it has high levels of detection and specificity for the precursor state of AD. Although the PAS is an important tool for MCI detection, further studies are urgently needed.

The primary end points (outcome measures) for treatment of MCI also need to be considered. The primary outcome measures used in these MCI studies were revised or modified versions of conventional test batteries and scales such as Alzheimer's Disease Assessment Scale (ADAS) and Clinician Interview Based Impression of Change (CIBIC), which are initially designed according to Food and Drug Administration guidelines for AD. With respect to ADAS, much knowledge has been obtained regarding the changes in cognitive impairment over time, and it is known that the rate of change is related to the baseline severity (Mohs, 1996). Such information for the change in cognitive function would be very useful for distinguishing between changes in MCI and changes due to normal aging, because there is almost no knowledge or information like this for healthy individuals (Graham, Cully, Snow, Massman, & Doody, 2004).

Clinical trials conducted to date on ChEIs in the treatment of MCI have studied amnestic MCI; this is understandable, as it makes the control group homogeneous, but it is doubtful whether that aim was adequately achieved in light of the differences in the rate of conversion to AD (see Table 13.10). This means that conclusions concerning the effects of ChEIs on the progression of MCI cannot be drawn on the basis of past results. Recently, Hashimoto and colleagues (2005) used MRI and showed that atrophy of the hippocampus was delayed in a group of subjects treated with donepezil compared with a nontreatment group. The results of their study are in agreement with those of a longitudinal study (Gron, Brandenburg, Wunderlich, & Riepe, 2006), that used a neuropsychological test to examine hippocampal function in MCI before and after galantamine administration. If we assume that donepezil has an effect not only on the symptoms of AD but also on the pathogenesis of the disease, then it is possible to rationalize therapy and studies on MCI using ChEIs, including donepezil.

Table 13.10

Clinical Trials of Subjects with Mild Cognitive Impairment (MCI)

	Donepezil + Vitamin E	Donepezil	Rivastigmine	Galantamine 1	Galantamine 2	Rofecoxib	Piracetam
Affiliation (year at trial)	69 sites, United States and Canada (1999)	Multicenter, United States	69 centers, 14 countries (1999)	Multicenter in 8 European countries, United States, and Canada (2001)	Multicenter in 4 European countries, United States, Canada, Argentina, and Australia (2001)	Multicenter	69 sites in 16 European countries (2000)
Design	RCT, PCDB, 3 groups	RCT, PCDB, Parallel design	RCT, PCDB, Parallel design	RCT, PCDB, Parallel design	RCT, PCDB, Parallel design	RCT, PCDB, Parallel design	RCT, PCDB, 3 groups
Dosage/day	Vitamine E, donepezil: 10mg	10 mg/day	3–12 mg/day	16 or 24 mg/day flexible dose	16 or 24 mg/day flexible dose	25 mg/day	4,800 mg/day, 9,600 mg/day
Trial period	3 years	24 weeks	3 years + 1 year extension	24 months	24 months	2–3 years + 1 year extension	12 months
Subject selection	Amnestic MCI, HDRS < 13, CDR 0.5	Amnestic MCI, CDR 0.5, MMSE > 25	Amnestic MCI, CDR 0.5, HDRS < 13	Amnestic MCI, CDR 0.5	Amnestic MCI, CDR 0.5	Amnestic MCI, CDR 0.5, MMSE > 23, BDRS < 4, HDRS < 13	Amnestic MCI, CDR 0.5, HDRS < 18, etc.
Subjects	769	269	1,018	995	1,062	1,457	675
Age (years)	55–90 (mean: 72.9)	Mean 73	Mean 70.5	>50	>50	≥65	50–89 (mean: 68)
ApoE e4	58% donepezil 55% vitamin E 53% placebo	Not available	41% (49% of all subjects were clarified)	26.4% galantamine 29.5% placebo	24.4% galantamine 23.5% placebo	35% rofecoxib 36% placebo	43% (60% of the subjects were clarified)

358

Primary measure	Time to clinical diagnosis of AD	Delayed recall test, ADAS-cog, CGIC-MCI	Time to clinical diagnosis of AD, Change on cognitive function	Incident dementia, CDR-SB	Incident dementia, CDR-SB	Incident AD	Symptom change, CBCS
Conversion rate	16%/year	Not available	19.4%/3–4 years	13% galantamine, 18% placebo/2 years	17% galantamine and 21% placebo/2 years	6.4% rofecoxib 4.5% placebo	Not available
Drop-out rate	12%/ year	20%	43%	Not available	Not available	45% rofecoxib 45% placebo	27% 4,800mg 21% 9,600mg 24% placebo
Adverse events	Not available	88% donepezil 73% placebo	96% rivastigmine 93% placebo	90% galantamine 86% placebo	90% galantamine 86% placebo	90% rofecoxib 92% placebo	72% 4,800mg 68% 9,600mg 76% placebo
Results	Significant effects for conversion rate and cognitive function in the first 18 months. Significant effects for 36 months in the subjects with ApoE4.	Significant effects for ADAS-cog, Immediate and delayed recall tests and digit symbol backward, and patient global assessment were significant for all subjects.	No significant results for primary measures.	No effects on conversion rate and ADAS-cog, positive effects on CDR-SB and attention, atrophy rate on brain volume.	No effects on conversion rate, ADAS-cog or CDR-SB. Positive effects on attention.	No significant improvements for primary and secondary measures.	No significant difference for primary and secondary measures.

Note: ADAS-cog = Alzheimer's Disease Assessment Scale, Cognitive subscale; BDRS = Blessed Dementia Rating Scale; CBCS = Cognitive Battery Composite Score; CDR = Clinical Dementia Rating Scale—Sum of Boxes; CGIC = Clinical Global Impression of Change Scale; HDRS = Hamilton Depression Rating Scale; PCDB = placebo-controled double blind study; RCT = Randomized control study.

Source: "Clinical Trials in Mild Cognitive Impairment: Lessons for the Future," by Jelic V., M. Kivipelto, and B. Winblad, 2006, *Journal of Neurology, Neurosurgery, and Psychiatry, 77,* pp. 429–438. Reprinted with permission.

We have attempted to summarize the efficacies of three ChEIs that are presently being used around the world, as well as introduce and comment on interesting reports that have appeared recently. We have also summarized the results of recent studies that used ChEIs to treat MCI and discussed future directions.

REFERENCES

Aguero-Torres, H., Fratiglioni, L., Guo, Z., Viitanen, M., & Winblad, B. (1998). Prognostic factors in very old demented adults: A 7-year follow-up from a population-based survey in Stockholm. *Journal of the American Geriatrics Society, 46,* 444–452.

Amaducci, L. A., Fratiglioni, L., Rocca, W. A., Fieschi, C., Livrea, P., Pedone, D. et al. (1986). Risk factors for clinically diagnosed Alzheimer's disease: A case-control study of an Italian population. *Neurology, 36,* 922–931.

American Psychiatric Association. (1987). *Diagnostic and statistical manual of mental disorders* (3rd ed., rev.). Washington, DC: Author.

American Psychiatric Association. (1994). *Diagnostic and statistical manual of mental disorders* (4th ed.). Washington, DC: Author.

Andersen, K., Nielsen, H., Lolk, A., Andersen, J., Becker, I., & Kragh-Sorensen, P. (1999). Incidence of very mild to severe dementia and Alzheimer's disease in Denmark: The Odense Study. *Neurology, 52,* 85–90.

Arnaiz, E., & Almkvist, O. (2003). Neuropsychological features of mild cognitive impairment and preclinical Alzheimer's disease. *Acta Neurologica Scandinavica Supplementum, 179,* 34–41.

Bennett, D. A., Schneider, J. A., Tang, Y., Arnold, S. E., & Wilson, R. S. (2006). The effect of social networks on the relation between Alzheimer's disease pathology and level of cognitive function in old people: A longitudinal cohort study. *Lancet Neurology, 5,* 406–412.

Benton, A. L. (1983). *Contributions to neuropsychological assessment.* New York: Oxford University Press.

Berg, L., Miller, J. P., Baty, J., Rubin, E. H., Morris, J. C., & Figiel, G. (1992). Mild senile dementia of the Alzheimer type 4: Evaluation of intervention. *Annals of Neurology, 31,* 242–249.

Berg, L., Miller, J. R., Storandt, M., Duchek, J., Morris, J. C., Rubin, E. H., et al. (1988). Mild senile dementia of the Alzheimer type 2: Longitudinal assessment. *Annals of Neurology, 23,* 477–484.

Bickel, H., & Cooper, B. (1994). Incidence and relative risk of dementia in an urban elderly population: Findings of a prospective field study. *Psychological Medicine, 24,* 179–192.

Brayne, C., Gill, C., Huppert F.A., Barkley, C., Gehlhaari, E., Girling, D. M., et al. (1995). Incidence of clinically diagnosed subtypes of dementia in an elderly population: Cambridge Project for Later Life. *British Journal of Psychiatry, 167,* 255–262.

Bruscoli, M., & Lovestone, S. (2004). Is MCI really just early dementia? A systematic review of conversion studies. *International Psychogeriatrics, 16,* 129–140.

Bullock, R. (2006). Efficacy and safety of memantine in moderate-to-severe Alzheimer disease: The evidence to date. *Alzheimer Disease and Associated Disorders, 20,* 23–29.

Carlson, M. C., Brandt, J., Steele, C., Baker, A., Stern, Y., & Lyketsos, C. G. (2001). Predictor index of mortality in dementia patients upon entry into long-term care. *Journals of Gerontology Series, A., Biological Sciences and Medical Sciences, 56,* M567–M570.

Chandra, V., Philipose, V., Bell, P. A., Lazaroff, A., & Schoenberg, B. S. (1987). Case-control study of late onset "probable Alzheimer's disease." *Neurology, 37,* 1295–1300.

Cohen-Mansfield, J. (1996). Conceptualization of agitation: Results based on the Cohen-Mansfield Agitation Inventory and the Agitation Behavior Mapping Instrument. *International Psychogeriatrics, 8*(Suppl. 3), 309–315.

Cohen-Mansfield, J., & Billig, N. (1986). Agitated behaviors in the elderly, I: A conceptual review. *Journal of the American Geriatrics Society, 34*, 711–721.

Cohen-Mansfield, J., Marx, M. S., & Rosenthal, A. S. (1989). A description of agitation in a nursing home. *Journal of Gerontology, 44*, M77–M84.

Copeland, J. R., Dewey, M. E., & Griffiths-Jones, H. M. (1986). A computerized psychiatric diagnostic system and case nomenclature for elderly subjects: GMS and AGECAT. *Psychological Medicine, 16*, 89–99.

Copeland, J. R., Dewey, M. E., Wood, N., Searle, R., Davidson, I. A., & McWilliam, C. (1986). Range of mental illness among the elderly in the community: Prevalence in Liverpool using the GMS-AGECAT package. *British Journal of Psychiatry, 16*, 815–823.

Copeland, J. R.,Kelleher, M. J., Kellett, J. M., Gourlay, A. J., Gurland, B. J., Fleiss, J. L., et al. (1976). A semi-structured clinical interview for the assessment of diagnosis and mental state in the elderly: The Geriatric Mental State Schedule—I. Development and reliability. *Psychological Medicine, 6*, 439–449.

Courtney, C., Farrell, D., Gray R., Hills, R., Lynch, L., Sellwood, E., et al. (2004). Long-term donepezil treatment in 565 patients with Alzheimer's disease (AD2000): Randomised double-blind trial. *Lancet, 363*, 2105–2115.

Cummings, J. L., Vinters, H. V., Cole, G. M., & Khachaturian, Z. S. (1998). Alzheimer's disease: Etiologies, pathophysiology, cognitive reserve, and treatment opportunities. *Neurology, 51*, S2–S17.

Drachman, D. A., O'Donnell, B. F., Lew, R. A., & Swearer, J. M. (1990). The prognosis in Alzheimer's disease: "How far" rather than "how fast" best predicts the course. *Archives of Neurology, 47*, 851–856.

Farrer, L. A., Cupples, A., Blackburn, D. K., Kiely, S., Averbaeh, J. H., Growdon, L., et al. (1994). Interrater agreement for diagnosis of Alzheimer's disease: The MIRAGE study. *Neurology, 44*, 652–656.

Folstein, M. F., Folstein, S. E., & McHugh, P. R. (1975). Mini-mental state: A practical method for grading the state of patients for the clinician. *Journal of Psychiatric Research, 12*, 189–198.

Folstein, M. F., Robins, L. N., & Helzer, J. E. (1983). The Mini-Mental State Examination. *Archives of General Psychiatry, 40*, 812.

Fratiglioni, L., Paillard-Borg, S., & Winblad, B. (2004). An active and socially integrated lifestyle in late life might protect against dementia. *Lancet Neurology, 3*, 343–353.

Freedman, M., Leach, L., Kaplan, E., Winocur, G., Shulman, K. I., & Delis, D. (1994). *Clock drawing: A neuropsychological analysis.* New York: Oxford University Press.

Galasko, D., Bennett, D., Sano, M., Ernesto, C. Thomas, R., Grundman, M., et al. (1997). An inventory to assess activities of daily living for clinical trials in Alzheimer's disease (The Alzheimer's Disease Cooperative Study). *Alzheimer Disease and Associated Disorders, 11*(Suppl. 2), S33–S39.

Galasko, D., Edland, S. D., Morris, J. C., Clark, C., Mohs, R., & Koss, E. (1995). The Consortium to Establish a Registry for Alzheimer's Disease (CERAD): Pt. XI. Clinical milestones in patients with Alzheimer's disease followed over 3 years. *Neurology, 45*, 1451–1455.

Galasko, D., Schmitt, F., Thomas, R., Jin, S., & Bennett, D. (2005). Detailed assessment of activities of daily living in moderate to severe Alzheimer's disease. *Journal of the International Neuropsychological Society, 11*, 446–453.

Gelinas, I., Gauthier, L., McIntyre, M., & Gauthier, S. (1999). Development of a functional measure for persons with Alzheimer's Disease: The Disability Assessment for Dementia. *American Journal of Occupational Therapy, 53*(5), 471–481.

Graham, D. P., Cully, J. A., Snow, A. L., Massman, P., & Doody, R. (2004). The Alzheimer's Disease Assessment Scale—Cognitive subscale: Normative data for older adult controls. *Alzheimer Disease and Associated Disorders, 18*, 236–240.

Grober, E., Buschke, H., Crystal, H., Bang, S., & Dresner, R. (1988). Screening for dementia by memory testing. *Neurology, 38*, 900–903.

Gron, G., Brandenburg, I., Wunderlich, A. P., & Riepe, M. W. (2006). Inhibition of hippocampal function in mild cognitive impairment: Targeting the cholinergic hypothesis. *Neurobiology of Aging, 27*, 78–87.

Gurland, B. J., Fleiss, J. L., Goldberg, K., Sharpe, L., Copeland, J. R., Kelleher, M. J., et al. (1976). A semi-structured clinical interview for the assessment of diagnosis and mental state in the elderly: The Geriatric Mental State Schedule—II. A factor analysis. *Psychological Medicine, 6*, 451–459.

Hashimoto, M., Kazui, H., Matsumoto, K., Nakano, Y., Yasuda, M., & Mori, E. (2005). Does donepezil treatment slow the progression of hippocampal atrophy in patients with Alzheimer's disease? *American Journal of Psychiatry, 162*, 676–682.

Helmer, C., Joly, P., Letenneur, L., Commenges, D., & Dartigues, J. F. (2001). Mortality with dementia: Results from a French prospective community-based cohort. *American Journal of Epidemiology, 154*, 642–648.

Heston, L. L., Mastri, A. R., Anderson, V. E., & White, J. (1981). Dementia of the Alzheimer type: Clinical genetics, natural history, and associated conditions. *Archives of General Psychiatry, 38*, 1085–1090.

Hofman, A., Rocca, W. A., Brayne, B., Breteler M. M. B., Clarke, M., Cooper, B., et al. (1991). The prevalence of dementia in Europe: A collaborative Study of 1980–1990 findings. *International Journal of Epidemiology, 20*, 736–748.

Holland, A. (1980). *Communicative activities in daily living: Manual.* Baltimore: University Park Press.

Hughes, C. P., Berg, L., Danziger, W. L., Coben, L. A., & Martin, R. L. (1982). A new clinical scale for the staging of dementia. *British Journal of Psychiatry, 140*, 566–572.

Jelic V., Kivipelto, M., & Winblad B. (2006). Clinical trials in mild cognitive impairment: Lessons for the future. *Journal of Neurology, Neurosurgery, and Psychiatry, 77*, 429–438.

Jorm, A. F. (1994). A short form of the Informant Questionnaire on Cognitive Decline in the Elderly (IQCODE): Development and cross-validation. *Psychological Medicine, 24*, 145–153.

Jorm, A. F., Christensen, H., Henderson, A. S., Jacomb, P. A., Korten, A. E., & Mackinnon, A. (1996). Informant ratings of cognitive decline of elderly people: Relationship to longitudinal change on cognitive tests. *Age and Aging, 25*, 125–129.

Jorm, A. F., & Jacomb, P. A. (1989). The Informant Questionnarie on Cognitive Decline in the Elderly (IQCODE): Socio-demographic correlates, reliability, validity and some norms. *Psychological Medicine, 19*(4), 1015–1022.

Jorm, A. F., Korten, A. E., & Henderson, A. S. (1987). The prevalence of dementia: A quantitative integration of the literature. *Acta Psychiatrica Scandinavica, 76*, 465–479.

Jorm, A. F., Mackinnon, A. J., Christensen, H., Henderson, A. S., Jacomb, P. A., & Korten, A. E. (1997). The Psychogeriatric Assessment Scales (PAS): Further data on psychometric properties and validity from a longitudinal study of the elderly. *International Journal of Geriatric Psychiatry, 12*, 93–100.

Jorm, A. F., Mackinnon, A. J., Hendersen, A. S., Scott, L. R., Christensen, H., Korten, A. E., et al. (1995). The Psychogeriatric Assessment Scales: A multi-dimensional alternative to categorical diagnoses of dementia and depression in the elderly. *Psychological Medicine, 25*, 447–460.

Jorm, A. F., Scott, R., Cullen, J. S., & Mackinnon, A. J. (1991). Performance of the Informant Questionnaire on Cognitive Decline in the Elderly (IQCODE) as a screening test for dementia. *Psychological Medicine, 21*, 785–790.

Jorm, A. F., van Duijn, C. M., Chandra, V., Fratiglioni, L., Graves, A. B., Heyman, A. et al. (1991). Psychiatric history and related exposures as risk factors for Alzheimer's disease: A collaborative re-analysis of case-control studies (EURODEM Risk Factors Research Group). *International Journal of Epidemiology, 20* (Suppl. 2), S43–S47.

Kaduszkiewicz, H., Zimmermann, T., Beck-Bornholdt, H. P., & van den Bussche, H. (2005). Cholinesterase inhibitors for patients with Alzheimer's disease: Systematic review of randomised clinical trials. *BMJ: British Medical Journal/British Medical Association, 331*, 321–327.

Katzman, R., & Kawas, C. H. (1994). The epidemiology of dementia and Alzheimer disease. In R. D. Terry, R. Katzman, & K. L. Bick (Eds.), *Alzheimer disease* (pp. 105–122). New York: Raven Press.

Kawas, C. H., & Brookmeyer, R. (2001). Aging and the public health effects of dementia. *New England Journal of Medicine, 344*, 1160–1161.

Knopman, D. S., DeKosky, S. T., Cummings, J. L., Chui, H., Corey-Bloom, J., Relkin, N., et al. (2001). Practice parameter: Diagnosis of dementia (an evidence-based review) (Report of the Quality Standards Subcommittee of the American Academy of Neurology). *Neurology, 56*, 1143–1153.

Knopman, D. S., Parisi, J. E., Salvaiali, A., Floriach-Robert, M., Boeve, B. F., Ivnik, R. J., et al. (2003). Neuropathology of cognitively normal elderly. *Journal of Neuropathology and Experimental Neurology, 62*, 1087–1095.

Kokmen, E., Chandra, V., & Schoenberg, B. S. (1988). Trends in incidence of dementing illness in Rochester, Minnesota, in three quinquennial periods, 1960–1974. *Neurology, 38*, 975–980.

Kordower, J. H., Chu, Y., Stebbins, G. T., DeKosky, S. T., Cochran, E. J., Bennett, D. A., et al. (2001). Loss and atrophy of layer II entorhinal cortex neurons in elderly people with mild cognitive impairment. *Annals of Neurology, 49*, 202–213.

Kraepelin, E. (1913), *Psychiatrie*. Bristol, England: Bristol Thoemmes Press.

Kukull, W. A., Larson, E. B., Reifler, B. V., Lampe, T. H., Yerby, M. S., & Hughes, J. P. (1990). The validity of 3 clinical diagnostic criteria for Alzheimer's disease. *Neurology, 40*, 1364–1369.

Lapane, K. L., Gambassi, G., Landi, F., Sgadari, A., Mor, V., & Bernabei, R. (2001). Gender differences in predictors of mortality in nursing home residents with AD. *Neurology, 56*, 650–654.

Larson, E. B., Wang, L., Bowen, J. D., McCormick, W. C., Teri, L., Crane, P., et al. (2006). Exercise is associated with reduced risk for incident dementia among persons 65 years of age and older. *Annals of Internal Medicine, 144*, 73–81.

Letenneur, L., Commenges, D., Dartigues, J. F., & Barberger-Gateau, P. (1994). Incidence of dementia and Alzheimer's disease in elderly community residents of south-western France. *International Journal of Epidemiology, 23*, 1256–1261.

Liu, C. K., Lai, C. L., Tai, C. T., Lin, R. T., Yen, Y. Y., & Howng, S. L. (1998). Incidence and subtypes of dementia in southern Taiwan: Impact of socio-demographic factors. *Neurology, 50*, 1572–1579.

Loewenstein, D. A., Barker, W. W., Harwood, D. G., Luis, S., Acevedo, A., Rodriguez, J., et al. (2000). Utility of a modified Mini-Mental State Examination with extended delayed recall in screening for mild cognitive impairment and dementia among community dwelling elders. *International Journal of Geriatric Psychiatry, 15*, 434–440.

Lopez Pousa, S., Llinas Regla, J., Vilalta Franch, J., & Lozano Fernandez de Pinedo, L. (1995). The prevalence of dementia in Girona. *Neurologia, 10,* 189–193.

Luria, R. E., & McHugh, P. R. (1977). Reliability and clinical utility of the "Wing" Present State Examination. *Archives of General Psychiatry, 224,* 866–871.

Mackinnon, A., Christensen, H., Cullen, J. S., Doyle, C. J., Henderson, A. S., Jorm, A. F., et al. (1993). The Canberra Interview for the Elderly: Assessment of its validity in the diagnosis of dementia and depression. *Acta Psychiatrica Scandinavica, 87,* 146–151.

McKhann, G., Drachman, D., Folstein, M., Katzman, R., Price, D., & Stadlan, E. M. (1984). Clinical diagnosis of Alzheimer's disease: Report of the NINCDS-ADRDA Work Group under the auspices of Department of Health and Human Services Task Force on Alzheimer's Disease. *Neurology, 34,* 939–944.

McShane, R., Areosa Sastre, A., & Minakaran, N. (2006). *Memantine for dementia* [Computer file]. Available from Cochrane Database of Systematic Reviews, 2, CD003154.

Meguro, K., Ishii, H., Yamaguchi, S., Shimada, M., Sato, M., Hashimoto, R., et al. (2002). Prevalence of dementia and dementing diseases in Japan: The Tajiri project. *Archives of Neurology, 59,* 1109–1114.

Mitchell, T. W.,Mufson, E. J., Schneider, J. A., Cochran, E. J., Nissanov, J., Han, L., et al. (2002). Parahippocampal tau pathology in healthy aging, mild cognitive impairment, and early Alzheimer's disease. *Annals of Neurology, 51,* 182–189.

Mohs, R. C. (1996). The Alzheimer's Disease Assessment Scale. *International Psychogeriatrics, 8,* 195–203.

Monsch, A. U., Bondi, M. W., Butters, N., Salmon, D. P., Katzman, R., & Thal, L. J. (1992). Comparisons of verbal fluency tasks in the detection of dementia of the Alzheimer type. *Archives of Neurology, 49,* 1253–1258.

Morris, J. C., McKeel, D. W. J., Fulling, K., Torack, R. M., & Berg, L. (1988). Validation of clinical diagnostic criteria for Alzheimer's disease. *Annals of Neurology, 24,* 17–22.

Morris, J. C., McKeel, D. W., Storandt, M., Rubin, E. H., Price, J. L., Grant E. A. et al. (1991). Very mild Alzheimer's disease: Informant-based clinical, psychometric, and pathologic distinction from normal aging. *Neurology, 41,* 469–478.

Mortimer, J. A., van Duijn, C. M., Fratiglioni, L., Graves, A. B., Heyman, A., Jorm, A. F., et al. (1991). Head trauma as a risk factor for Alzheimer's disease: A collaborative reanalysis of case-control studies (EURODEM Risk Factors Research Group). *International Journal of Epidemiology, 20*(Suppl. 2), S28–S35.

Mufson, E. J., Ma, S. Y., Dills, J., Cochran, E. J., Leurgans, S., Wuu, J., et al. (2002). Loss of basal forebrain P75(NTR) immunoreactivity in subjects with mild cognitive impairment and Alzheimer's disease. *Journal of Comparative Neurology, 443,* 136–153.

Nakamura, S., Shigeta, M., Iwamoto, M., Tsuno, N., Ninna, R., Homma, A., et al. (2003). Prevalence and predominance of Alzheimer type dementia in rural Japan. *Psychogeriatrics, 3,* 97–103.

Ott, A., Breteler, M. M., van Harskamp, F., Stijnen, T., & Hofman, A. (1998). Incidence and risk of dementia: The Rotterdam Study. *American Journal of Epidemiology, 147,* 574–580.

Panisset, M., Roudier, M., Saxton, J., & Boller, F. (1994). Severe impairment battery: A neuropsychological test for severely demented patients. *Archives of Neurology, 51,* 41–45.

Patterson, M. B., Schnell, A. H., Martin, R. J., Mendez, M. F., Smyth, K. A., & Whitehouse, P. J. (1990). Assessment of behavioral and affective symptoms in Alzheimer's disease. *Journal of Geriatric Psychiatry and Neurology, 3,* 21–30.

Petersen, R. C., Smith, G. E., Waring, S. C., Ivnik, R. J., Tangalos, E. G., & Kokmen, E. (1999). Mild cognitive impairment: Clinical characterization and outcome. *Archives of Neurology, 56,* 303–308.

Reisberg, B. (1988). Functional assessment staging (FAST). *Psychopharmacology Bulletin, 24,* 653–659.

Reisberg, B., Auer, S. R., & Monteiro, I. M. (1996). Behavioral pathology in Alzheimer's disease (BEHAVE-AD) rating scale. *International Psychogeriatrics, 8*(Suppl. 3), 301–308.

Reisberg, B., & Ferris, S. H. (1985). A clinical rating scale for symptoms of psychosis in Alzheimer's disease. *Psychopharmacology Bulletin, 21,* 101–104.

Reisberg, B., Sclan, S. G., Franssen, E., Kluger, A., & Ferris, S. (1994). Dementia staging in chronic care populations. *Alzheimer Disease and Associated Disorders, 8,* S188–S205.

Risen, W. (1980). Verbal fluency in aging and dementia. *Journal of Clinical Neuropsychology, 2,* 135–146.

Ritchie, C. W., Ames, D., Clayton, T., & Lai, R. (2004). Metaanalysis of randomized trials of the efficacy and safety of donepezil, galantamine, and rivastigmine for the treatment of Alzheimer disease. *American Journal of Geriatric Psychiatry, 12,* 358–369.

Rovio, S., Kareholt, I., Helkala, E. L., Viitanen, M., Winblad, B., Tuomilento, J., et al. (2005). Leisure-time physical activity at midlife and the risk of dementia and Alzheimer's disease. *Lancet Neurology, 4,* 705–711.

Rubinsztein, D. C., & Easton, D. F. (1999). Apolipoprotein E genetic variation and Alzheimer's disease: A meta-analysis. *Dementia and Geriatric Cognitive Disorders, 10,* 199–209.

Ruitenberg, A., Kalmijn, S., de Ridder, M. A. J., Redekop, W. K., van Harskamp, A., Hofman, A., et al. (2001). Prognosis of Alzheimer's disease: The Rotterdam Study. *Neuroepidemiology, 20,* 188–195.

Schmitt, F. A., Ashford, C., Ernesto, J., Saxton, L. S., Schneider, C. M., Clark, S., et al. (1997). The Severe Impairment Battery: Concurrent validity and the assessment of longitudinal change in Alzheimer's disease (The Alzheimer's Disease Cooperative Study). *Alzheimer Disease and Associated Disorders, 11,* 51–56.

Sclan, S. G., & Reisberg, B. (1992). Functional assessment staging (FAST) in Alzheimer's disease: Reliability, validity, and ordinality. *International Psychogeriatrics, 4*(Suppl. 1), 55–69.

Sclan, S. G., Saillon, A., Franssen, E., Hugonot-Diener, L., Saillon, A., & Reisberg, B. (1996). The Behavior Pathology in Alzheimer's Disease Rating Scale (Behave-AD): Reliability and analysis of symptom category scores. *International Journal of Geriatric Psychiatry, 11,* 819–830.

Shigeta, M. (2004). Epidemiology: Rapid increase in Alzheimer's disease prevalence in Japan. *Psychogeriatrics, 4,* 117–119.

Snowdon, D. A. (2003). Healthy aging and dementia: Findings from the Nun Study. *Annals of Internal Medicine, 139,* 450–454.

Solomon, P. R., & Pendlebury, W. W. (1998). Recognition of Alzheimer's Disease: the 7-Minute Screen. *Family Medicine, 30*(4), 265–271.

Spitzer, R. L., Endicott, J., Fleiss, J. L., & Cohen, J. (1970). The psychiatric status schedule: A technique for evaluating psychopathology and impairment in role functioning. *Archives of General Psychiatry, 23,* 41–55.

Strittmatter, W. J., Saunders, A. M., Schmechel, D., Pericak-Vance, M., Enghild, J., Salvesen, G. S., & Roses, A. D. (1993). Apolipoprotein E: High-avidity binding to beta-amyloid and increased frequency of type 4 allele in late-onset familial Alzheimer disease. *Proceedings of the National Academy of Sciences, USA, 90,* 1977–1981.

Swanwick, G. R., Coen, R. F., Coakley, D., & Lawlor, B. A. (1998). Assessment of progression and prognosis in "possible" and "probable" Alzheimer's disease. *International Journal of Geriatric Psychiatry, 13,* 331–335.

Takeda, A., Clegg, A., Kirby, J., Picot, E., Payne, C., & Green, C. (2006). A systematic review of the clinical effectiveness of donepezil, rivastigmine and galantamine on cognition, quality of life and adverse events in Alzheimer's disease. *International Journal of Geriatric Psychiatry, 21,* 17–28.

Tombaugh, T. N., & McIntyre, N. J. (1992). The Mini-Mental State Examination: A comprehensive review. *Journal of the American Geriatrics Society, 40,* 922–935.

Tran, M., Bedard, M., Molloy, D. W., Dubois, S., & Lever, J. A. (2003). Associations between psychotic symptoms and dependence in activities of daily living among older adults with Alzheimer's disease. *International Psychogeriatrics, 15,* 171–179.

Ueki, A., Shinjo, H., Shimode, H., Nakajima, T., & Morita, Y. (2001). Factors associated with mortality in patients with early-onset Alzheimer's disease: A 5-year longitudinal study. *International Journal of Geriatric Psychiatry, 16,* 810–815.

van Duijn, C. M., Clayton, D., Chandra, V., Fratiglioni, L., Graves, A. B., Heyman, A., et al. (1991). Familial aggregation of Alzheimer's disease and related disorders: A collaborative re-analysis of case-control studies (EURODEM Risk Factors Research Group). *International Journal of Epidemiology, 20,* S13–S20.

Visser, P. J., Scheltens, P., & Verhey, F. R. (2005). Do MCI criteria in drug trials accurately identify subjects with predementia Alzheimer's disease? *Journal of Neurology, Neurosurgery, and Psychiatry, 76,* 1348–1354.

Visser, P. J., Verhey, F. R. J., Schelteng, P., Cruts, M., Ponds, R. W., & van Broeckhover, C. L. (2002). Diagnostic accuracy of the Preclinical AD Scale (PAS) in cognitively mildly impaired subjects. *Journal of Neurology, 249,* 312–319.

Winblad, B., Palmer, K., Kivipelto, M., Jelic, V., Fratiglioni, L., Wahlund, L. O., et al. (2004). Mild cognitive impairment: Beyond controversies, towards a consensus: Report of the International Working Group on Mild Cognitive Impairment. *Journal of Internal Medicine, 256,* 240–246.

Wing, J., Nixon, J., von Cranach, M., & Strauss, A. (1977). Further developments of the "present state examination" and CATEGO system. *Archiv fur Psychiatrie und Nervenkrankheiten, 224,* 151–160.

Wisniewski, T., Golabek, A., Matsubara, E., Ghiso, J., & Frangione, B. (1993). Apolipoprotein E: Binding to soluble Alzheimer's beta-amyloid. *Biochemical and Biophysical Research Communications, 90,* 359–365.

Wolfson, C., Wolfson, D. B., Asgharian, M., M'Lan, C. E., Ostbye, T., Rockwood, K., et al. (2001). A reevaluation of the duration of survival after the onset of dementia. *New England Journal of Medicine, 344,* 1111–1116.

World Health Organization. (2003). *International statistical classification of diseases and related health problems* (ICD-10, 2nd ed.). Geneva, Switzerland: Author.

Zhang, M. Y., Qu, G. Y., Katzman, R., Lu, E., Wang, Z. Y., Cha, G. J., et al. (1990). The prevalence of dementia and Alzheimer's disease in Shanghai, China: Impact of age, gender, and education. *Annals of Neurology, 27,* 428–437.

CHAPTER 14

Grief and Bereavement

ROBERT O. HANSSON, BERT HAYSLIP JR., and MARGARET S. STROEBE

THE NATURE OF GRIEF

It is often the case that grief and bereavement accompany the aging process via the increasing likelihood of the deaths of friends, parents, a spouse, and ultimately oneself. Irrespective of the veracity of this presumed association, its uncritical acceptance may have the unfortunate consequence of desensitizing others to the impact of the loss of valued relationships on older adults (Kastenbaum, 1978). It is for this reason that understanding the role that grief and adjustment to bereavement play in the lives of older persons is so critically important.

Irrespective of age, the experience of grief is best understood to include two components: an emotional reaction to losing a close attachment relationship and a need to cope with "secondary stressors" resulting from the death, for example, disrupted finances, threats to family security, or having to assume new responsibilities for family and household maintenance (M. S. Stroebe & Schut, 1999). As most grieving persons can attest, this reflects the distinction between the private and the public experience of the loss of a loved one, which in many respects do not parallel one another.

Understandably, then, the symptomatology of grief can be complex. It involves a broad mix of potentially disruptive emotions (e.g., depression, anxiety, loneliness, and guilt), physiologic-somatic symptoms, disrupted functions (e.g., disturbances in sleeping patterns and cognitive functioning, changes in self-regulation, immune functioning), a diminished capacity to cope, increased vulnerability to illness and disease, and increased mortality rates (Shuchter & Zisook, 1993; W. Stroebe & Stroebe, 1987). In this respect, the distinction between what would be characterized as "normal" grieving and "pathological" grieving hinges on the extent to which the loss of a valued relationship interferes with the older person's everyday functioning, work performance, relationships with others, emotional and cognitive status, and health. Consider the following case example of pathological grief.

Case Study

Debra, a 62-year-old female, learned that her 37-year-old adult son had been killed by a bus while biking. She had not seen him in some years, and theirs had been a characteristically conflicted and distant relationship, about which she felt quite guilty; she indicated that she felt she had somehow "failed" him as a mother. Debra reacted to her son's death dramatically: Shortly after his funeral, she began to have difficulty in her work as a computer programmer, missing work more often than not, withdrawing from friends and coworkers, and making more mistakes than normal. Moreover, she had a great deal of difficulty talking about her son's death and her relationship to him. Within a month of his death, she quit her job and stayed at home, spending a great deal of time by herself, not eating well, and having difficulties functioning on a daily basis. Eventually, and at the urging of her husband, she sought professional help and developed an interest in gardening. Ultimately, after 2 years, she returned to work. At present, she seems to have put his death into perspective and is moving on with life.

Especially among older adults, despite the fact that for such persons the experience of loss becomes increasingly normative in nature, individual grief reactions may vary in their intensity and duration. Most bereaved persons, however, are eventually able to adapt, returning to preloss baseline with respect to such indicators as depression and physical symptoms. Some, however, experience a more complicated grief experience, perhaps in response to the traumatic circumstances of the death (Prigerson & Jacobs, 2001), the implications of concurrent life stressors, or individual vulnerabilities.

It will not go unnoticed by gerontologists or geriatricians that this symptom picture overlaps considerably with the experience of older persons generally as they attempt to deal with normative, age-related life transitions or with life stressors characteristic of old age. Concerns thus arise with respect to distinguishing between the consequences of bereavement and the consequences of aging-related problems more generally; any needed interventions would likely parallel, in part, those provided in response to other, serious life stressors.

Table 14.1 provides some perspective on the experience of loss throughout the life span. It summarizes current patterns of death rates by age for the United States. It is clear from this table that old age is a time in which bereavements may become more frequent; older adults may thus face an accumulation of grief experiences, compounding the consequences for emotional and practical coping and

Table 14.1
Death Rates by Age (All Causes): United States 2000

Age (Years)	Deaths per 100,000
All ages	854
55–64	992
65–74	2,399
75–84	5,666
85 and older	15,524

Source: Health, United States, 2003 (Special Excerpt: Trend Tables on 65 and Older Population), by the U.S. Department of Health and Human Services, 2003, Washington, DC: Centers for Disease Control and Prevention, National Center for Health Statistics.

for the stability of support networks. Conjugal bereavements, in particular, rise in incidence with age; among community living elders, 20% of those age 65 to 74, 39% of those age 75 to 84, and 63% of those age 85+ have become widowed (Federal Interagency Forum on Aging-Related Statistics, 2004). In addition to the death of one's spouse, the deaths of siblings and lifelong friends can have especially heavy impact.

The causes of death also change with old age. In early life, they are more likely to involve traumatic circumstances such as accidents, homicide, suicide, cancers, and acute illnesses. In mid- and late life, however, the emphasis tends to shift toward chronic illness such as heart disease, respiratory and vascular diseases, and influenza or pneumonia (U.S. Department of Health and Human Services, 2002). This pattern of changing causes of death across the life span suggests at least two important implications for the experience of bereavement. First, bereavements of older persons less frequently involve a traumatic death. Second, conjugal bereavements among older persons are more likely to have previously involved the burden of a prolonged care-giving experience, a circumstance that will have elicited coping and adaptation efforts prior to the death itself.

RESEARCH ON AGING AND BEREAVEMENT

Early empirical research on bereavement treated age as one of many potential risk variables for poor outcome. These studies were cross-sectional and often found younger bereaved persons to have experienced greater distress from the death (Archer, 1999; Parkes, 2001; C. Sanders, 1989). Post hoc explanations of such data were readily available (e.g., that the death of an older spouse is less unexpected), and researchers moved on to other issues (Hansson & Stroebe, in press).

The early research, then, was not formulated from a gerontological perspective:

- It did not recognize that age, per se, is an imperfect predictor of mental or physical status, of vulnerability to stressful life events, or of competence to adapt.
- It did not recognize the potential variability within older populations with respect to their vulnerability to the consequences of loss, the likely nature and course of their grief reaction, their coping resources and resiliency.
- It did not reflect an appreciation of the nature of late-life development.
- It did not consider the various contexts of aging as they might interface with the contexts of the death of a loved one (Hansson & Stroebe, in press).

In addition, much of the early research suffered a variety of methodological shortcomings:

- Most studies were cross-sectional, precluding consideration of long-term outcomes or of generational influences.
- Prebereavement baseline assessments were typically unavailable.
- Cause of death was often not considered.
- Men, ethnic populations, institutionalized elderly, and nonconjugal bereavements (e.g., by siblings or grandparents) were often undersampled.
- Appropriate control groups of nonbereaving younger and older persons were often not included.

- Little consideration was given to issues of the validity of assessment among older populations.
- Assessed outcomes were often limited to snapshots of current physical and mental health status, precluding examination of important dynamics such as coping and the emergence of social support, examination of the differential trajectories over time of the various classes of outcome variables, or mortality patterns.
- The possibility that relationships between age and any aspect of the bereavement reaction might be nonlinear (e.g., that middle-aged persons would be more or less affected than either younger or older persons) was typically not considered (Hansson & Stroebe, in press).

Subsequently, researchers began to explore aging and bereavement from more complex, gerontological perspectives. The important epidemiological studies are now longitudinal in nature and guided by a richer base of life span developmental theory. The focus is now on more complex questions, such as the following:

- How might the configuration of bereavement symptoms change or become more complex in old age?
- Might the nature of bereavement symptoms reflect a greater physical component in late life?
- What might be the implications of residual, unresolved symptomatology for subsequent processes of disablement in late life?
- Might research from the area of aging and emotion explain earlier findings of lower intensity grief among older persons?
- To what extent might the contexts of aging in general (e.g., reduced economic status, smaller social networks) operate as risk or protective factors in the bereavements of older persons?
- Might an increased incidence of bereavements in late life result in a cumulative bereavement effect?
- How does the bereavement experience vary across older persons, and what are the sources of such variability (e.g., person, social, and cultural factors)?
- How might adaptations to previous losses (successful or unsuccessful) affect vulnerability?
- What forms of intervention may be appropriate for older bereaved persons; how might standard interventions need to be adapted for older persons; and how should we think about goals for (and evaluation of) intervention?

OUTCOME STUDIES ON AGING AND BEREAVEMENT

HETEROGENEITY OF THE BEREAVEMENT RESPONSE

An important and pervasive finding in contemporary outcome studies of older bereaved persons concerns the *heterogeneity* of their reactions, consistent with the fact that between-person variability is greater among older persons than among younger and middle-aged persons (Nelson & Dannefer, 1992). Each older person enters a bereavement experience with a unique mix of mental and physical abilities, coping resources, and adaptive reserves. It is thus consistent that researchers have found older persons to have diverse reactions to the loss of a loved one. In one longitudinal study of elderly widowed persons, Lund, Caserta, and Dimond

(1993) found that some respondents experienced severe distress, as might be expected. Others, however, appeared able to meet this challenge, to learn the skills needed to cope, and to find a way to adjust to the loss. In addition, these researchers found considerable within-respondent variability of experience. That is, an older widowed person might cope well in some areas of her life but do poorly in others.

Bonanno, Wortman, and Nesse (2004) illustrated the issue of diversity of response from a different perspective. They found it possible to classify a sample of elderly widowed persons into five distinct bereavement patterns with respect to experienced depression. One group (termed "resilient") experienced relatively little preloss depression, and their depressive symptoms remained low for 18 months after the death. A "common grief pattern" group saw a loss-related spike in depressive symptoms, but these declined over the 18 months postloss. A "chronic grief" pattern involved a postloss increase in depression, which then remained high for the 18 months. A "depressed-improved" pattern involved persons with high predeath depression, which then declined over the 18 months. A "chronic depressed" pattern involved high preloss symptoms that remained high during all follow-up assessments.

RESILIENCE IN THE RESPONSE TO BEREAVEMENT

Another important finding is that many older bereaved adults exhibit considerable resilience. Lund, Caserta, and Dimond (1989, 1993) reported that over 80% of their conjugally bereaved elderly respondents were successfully coping with the consequences of their loss, were managing their health and their relationships with some success, and felt reasonable life satisfaction. Many respondents reported that this was an adaptive process and that they had successfully learned new skills needed for their changed lives. A study by Fry (1998) echoed these findings; most of her elderly bereaved respondents reported that they had experienced some success in adapting to the death and its emotional and practical consequences, resulting in increased feelings of personal control and autonomy. In this respect, a great deal of recent attention has been devoted to the study of resilience among older men (see, e.g., Carr, 2006; Moore & Stratton, 2002; Wolff & Wortman, 2006), underscoring the importance of identifying those older individuals who are able to assimilate the loss of a spouse, child, friend, parent, or grandchild into their identities as individuals, parents, husbands/wives, or adult children.

CONTEXTUAL ISSUES IN LATE-LIFE BEREAVEMENT

A number of contextual parameters influence the experience of bereavement in old age. Losing a spouse of many years can be especially disorganizing for older persons, as it disrupts lifelong social roles, affects income, support systems, and social opportunities, and may signal increasing dependency on support systems that may not fill one's needs (Lopata, 1993, 1996). In addition, elderly bereaved persons are more likely to be women and to live alone. They are unlikely to remarry, and because many are childless, they have diminished access to needed support (O'Bryant & Hansson, 1994). Simply because of their age, they are likely to have experienced a greater number of deaths of their loved ones. And in the case of the death of a younger family member, their grief may not be viewed with as much concern as that of younger grieving family members. The elderly may be viewed instead as a "secondary griever," their symptoms may be misattributed to age, and their grief "disenfranchised" (Moss & Moss, 1989). As we explore later in this chapter, because of their advanced age, they will more likely experience the death of a child or grandchild, with potentially devastating consequences (Fry, 1997; Hayslip & White, in press; Moss & Moss, 1994).

Consequences of Bereavement among Older Adults

A number of longitudinal studies of older bereaved persons have now appeared. These studies vary in their focus and duration. It would appear, however, that older adults experience a mix of physical, emotional, cognitive, and social consequences similar to those found among younger bereaved. The course of the grief reaction also appears similar to that of younger persons. Acknowledging individual variations, the pattern reflects an elevation of symptoms in the first months postloss, and then gradually diminishing symptoms as the individual finds some success in adaptation.

This pattern was nicely illustrated in a study of recently widowed elderly persons and matched controls (Gallagher-Thompson, Futterman, Farberow, Thompson, & Peterson, 1993; Thompson, Gallagher-Thompson, Futterman, Gilewski, & Peterson, 1991). Respondents in this study were assessed over a period of 30 months postloss with respect to indicators of depression, grief-specific distress, mental health symptoms, and mortality risk. In the first 2 months postloss, the bereaved experienced increased levels of general and grief-specific psychological distress and physical illness. By 12 months postloss, the bereaved group no longer differed significantly from controls on measures of psychopathology, depression, or physical complaints. Scores on emotional symptoms more specific to grief, however, continued to be higher among the bereaved throughout the course of the 30-month study.

Researchers have also provided insights regarding the consequences of bereavement for interpersonal functioning among older persons. Lopata's (1996) studies of elderly American widows, for example, identified loneliness as a common and highly distressing consequence. The loss of a long-time spouse often signifies the loss of one's core emotional ties, shared experiences and worldviews, patterns of behavior, and validation of self as someone to be unconditionally loved. Lopata's respondents reported not only emotional loneliness (for a specific person), but also a broader social loneliness. Such findings have been widely replicated, for example, in studies by Lund et al. (1993) and van Baarsen, van Duijn, Smit, Snijders, and Knipscheer (2001–2002).

Longitudinal studies have also provided considerable insight into the physical health consequences of bereavement for older persons. Here, however, we provide the reader of such research with a cautionary note: Many of these studies failed to consider the importance of prebereavement health status (Murrell, Himmelfarb, & Phifer, 1988). This presents a serious problem for the interpretation of health findings in bereavement research because so many adults age 65 and older suffer from a chronic and progressive disease process, such as arthritis, diabetes, cancer, stroke, hypertension, heart disease, vision loss, and physical disability (Federal Interagency Forum on Aging-Related Statistics, 2004). Such conditions are known in the health literature to render one more vulnerable to subsequent physiological events, but might also be considered a "coping deficit," with implications for one's potential to cope and adapt to subsequent illness or life stress. In this context, it is instructive that a longitudinal study of older bereaved persons by Murrell et al. (1988) found that bereavement contributed little unique variance to health status after controlling for predeath health status. This issue, then, suggests one important way that the bereavement experience of older persons differs from that of most younger persons. But the effect may be twofold; older bereaved persons will likely have been in poorer health, reflecting age-related factors, but they may also have been experiencing elevated health symptoms owing to the stress of caregiving for the spouse who died.

Bereavement in late life also appears to influence normal functioning important to survival. One example is nutrition. Rosenbloom and Whittington (1993) found that elderly widows (compared to matched married controls) reported elevated loneliness and poorer appetite at mealtimes. They were more likely to consume unhealthy snacks, had generally lower overall nutrition, were less likely to take nutritional supplements, and experienced more unintended weight loss. Scores on a measure of grief resolution significantly predicted meal quality and enjoyment and weight loss.

A broader array of physical disruptions can undermine stability and adaptive coping on the part of elderly bereaved persons. Disruptions of sleep and social (and circadian) rhythm stability also appear important. L. F. Brown et al. (1996) found bereavement-related depression to predict increased problems with sleep and rhythm patterns and in adjusting to the loss. It is consistent, then, that widowhood is a significant predictor of first entry to a nursing home (Wolinsky & Johnson, 1992).

The experience of pain may similarly be affected. Bradbeer, Helme, Yong, Kendig, and Gibson (2003) found that widowed elderly adults were 3 times more likely to indicate significant (severe and activity-limiting) pain, compared to non-widowed controls. In a path analysis, they demonstrated that the relationship between widowed status and experienced pain was mediated by bereavement-related mood status (widowhood alone accounted for only 1% of the variance in experienced pain, but a path model reflecting widowhood $\rightarrow$ mood disturbance $\rightarrow$ pain accounted for 17% of the variance in pain).

Finally, studies have also examined the potential for excess mortality among older bereaved persons. Two general patterns seem to emerge from these analyses. Older bereaved persons appear somewhat less at risk for death due to the stress of bereavement than younger persons (M. S. Stroebe & Stroebe, 1993). It also appears that causes of death among the bereaved who are very old reflect the causes in the broader very old population in general, suggesting that after accounting for age-related physical decline, little variance remains to be accounted for by the stress of bereavement (Bowling, 1994).

Many of the longitudinal bereavement studies on older persons have used depression as a core indicator of adjustment. It is worth noting, however, that reliance on depression in research can be problematic among older populations. One reason is the issue of medical comorbidity (Blazer, 2003). That is, patients with chronic pain, heart disease, stroke, or diabetes typically report elevated depression regardless of marital status. On the other hand, depression can also exacerbate medical problems (e.g., heart disease, weight loss, and osteoporosis), and it is associated with increased use of medical services (Blazer, 2003). Another reason is the difficulty inherent in interpreting depression scores among the elderly (Gatz & Fiske, 2003). Depressive symptoms among the elderly may differ from those seen in younger populations; confusion may arise in attributing certain symptoms either to depression or to physical disorders; cognitive decline may undermine reliability of assessment protocols; and persons with major depression are less likely to live into very old age (Gatz & Fiske, 2003). That said, in these studies bereavement has been a consistent predictor of depression (Harwood, 2001; Parkes, 1997; Rosenzweig, Prigerson, Miller, & Reynolds, 1997). It is also a concern that among older persons, untreated depression is an important risk factor for suicide (Szanto et al., 2002). Widowed men (age 60 and over) are at particular risk; they are 3 times more likely than married men to commit suicide (Li, 1995).

ISSUES OF CONTEXT AND TRANSITION IN LATE-LIFE BEREAVEMENT

Bereavement does not occur in a vacuum. Contextual factors can increase or decrease risk with respect to adaptation. In this section, we describe a number of these factors.

Transitions from Caregiving

Causes of death in old age generally involve chronic conditions or disease process. Bereavements have the potential to become more complex because they involve a transition from a stressful period of caregiving. For some elderly bereaved persons, dealing with both caregiver stress and subsequent bereavement may result in an accumulation of stress that may compound any negative consequences. For many others, however, coping with one's care-giving responsibilities may enhance coping skills and sense of personal mastery. Consistent with this reasoning, Wells and Kendig (1997) found that older widowed persons who had previously been spouse caregivers experienced less depression than either married-current caregivers or widows who had not previously engaged in caregiving. Wolff and Wortman (2006) note that among resilient widows and widowers, the death of a spouse represents the end of a chronic stressor rather the beginning of a series of difficult bereavement-related adjustments.

The burden of caregiving can be extensive, however, and can have lasting consequences for some older persons. This was illustrated in a study by Robinson-Whelen, Tata, and MacCallum (2001) that compared depressive symptoms among elderly caregivers over a 3-year period postbereavement to matched control groups of continuing caregivers and noncaregivers. At prebereavement assessment, both caregiver groups were experiencing more depression than noncaregiving controls, and this pattern continued to be observed out to 3 years postloss. Similarly, at prebereavement assessment, perceived stress was highest among the caregiver-bereaved group. Over the period of the study, perceived stress among the caregiver-bereaved eventually dropped to levels reported by continuing caregivers, but for both caregiver groups remained higher than among controls for the remainder of the study.

Schulz et al. (2001) examined these relationships more directly. Their study classified older, recently widowed persons on the basis of the extent to which their caregiving involved strain (reflecting their patient's health, disability, or need for assistance with activities of daily living prior to the death), and on the basis of rated caregiver strain. The caregiver-strained group was found to experience higher depressive symptoms at prebereavement assessment and throughout the study. Caregiver-strained respondents at predeath assessment also reported more risky health behaviors (e.g., forgetting medications and doctor's appointments). After the death, however, problematic health behavior diminished to the level of the nonstrained group, perhaps reflecting a relief from the demanding responsibilities of caregiving and the infusion of assistance from family.

A number of specific issues arise in the context of the transition from caregiving to bereavement. As in the broader care-giving burden literature, there is evidence of diminished personal control and social isolation, in addition to emotional distress (Ferrario, Cardillo, Vicario, Balzarini, & Zotti, 2004). Caregiving for some kinds of patients (e.g., terminal cancer patients) can also involve traumatic exposure, witnessing a loved one in extreme pain who may become dehydrated, unable to eat, and confused and may choke or vomit. Such experiences are particularly common among spouse caregivers and appear to have an effect on subsequent depression and adjustment above and beyond the effects of caregiver burden (Prigerson et al., 2003).

The transition from care-giving bereavement also appears particularly difficult when the patient is cognitively impaired. As we discuss further later in the chapter, caregiving for Alzheimer's patients, for example, demands more time, often requiring the caregiver to withdraw from other social and employment responsibilities. The disease is chronic and unpredictable, further increasing stress. It eventually involves not only the provision of complete personal care, but also a deep sadness and degree of uncertainty, each of which is associated with caregiver outcomes (Marwit & Meuser, 2002).

CONCURRENT STRESSORS

Old age is a time when stressful life events tend to cluster. A bereavement may be accompanied by problems with health, economic disruption, and mandated change of residence (and having to leave old friends). But small events (e.g., family conflicts, pain, things in the house not working) can also accumulate and contribute significant distress over and above the effects of larger events such as bereavement (Murdoch, Guarnaccia, Hayslip, & McKibbin, 1998).

COPING RESOURCES

As at any age, older adults vary with respect to the personal and social coping resources on which they can draw in dealing with a bereavement. A study by Gass (1987) found that such resources (e.g., social support, religious beliefs, prior health, and financial security) can influence an older person's appraisal of threats associated with the death and appear to enhance both physical and psychological outcomes. In this context, it is a concern that the percentage of surviving spouses living in poverty rises significantly in the 1st year after the loss of a spouse (Hungerford, 2001), especially among women (Zick & Smith, 1991).

Women are more vulnerable to economic risk in widowhood (Lopata, 1993; Wortman, Silver, & Kessler, 1993). Those in the oldest cohorts are more likely to be dependent on a spouse for income, insurance, and pension coverage (Blieszner, 1993). It is a concern, then, that women (especially) who experience economic insecurity in widowhood experience increased depression (Van Grootheest, Beekman, Van Gronou, & Deeg, 1999). Fortunately, many who fall below the poverty line after bereavement recover a degree of economic security within a few years as they begin to receive benefits, find work, or are assisted by family (Bound, Duncan, Laren, & Olenick, 1991).

Broader forms of social and family support for older bereaved persons have been the focus of much research. Social support in general has been widely found to be related to positive physical and mental health outcomes. It provides practical support, but also an emotional component of felt closeness and acceptance, and enhances feelings of self-efficacy (Antonucci, Langfahl, & Akiyama, 2004; Charles & Mavandadi, 2004; Lopata, 1993, 1996). Under conditions of such emotional support, healthy persons tend to experience fewer symptoms and a more effective immune system. Persons who are already at increased health risk because of age or chronic illness experience higher levels of function and survival (Charles & Mavandadi, 2004).

Older adults are likely to be more dependent on family support networks, and families typically rise to the occasion to provide support. But in late life, support needs become more complicated and more medical in nature. At this time, the family network itself may also be aging, becoming smaller, more frail, more stressed, and less able to provide the kind of support that best matches an older person's needs (Hansson & Carpenter, 1994).

Much research has now been conducted on the role of social support specific to bereavement, but the results have been somewhat of a surprise. Recent reviews of this literature find main effects for support, but no consistent evidence that it buffers or protects against the consequences specific to bereavement. Such findings would be consistent with attachment theories of the grief reaction, in that support appears to help all people with respect to their instrumental, informational, and general emotional needs, while recognizing that a lost attachment figure (and what that person provides) cannot be replaced (W. Stroebe, Stroebe, Abakoumkin, & Schut, 1996; W. Stroebe, Zech, Stroebe, & Abakoumkin, in press).

Sex-related resources also appear relevant in adjustment to late-life bereavements. Reviews of this literature strongly suggest that older bereaved men are at greater risk (W. Stroebe & Schut, 2001), in part because of the nonnormative nature of the death of the wife. They appear, for example, to experience more depression (Lee, Willetts, & Seccombe, 1998; van Grootheest et al., 1999). Such increased risk may reflect a selection artifact, however. For example, healthier widowers are more likely to remarry, so are less likely to be classified as widowed when included in studies. Similarly, because men live a shorter life, they would likely be younger (and in an earlier, more intense phase of their bereavement) when assessed. On the other hand, older widowed men are likely to have less competent health and nutritional habits, relative to women, and appear less likely to have the social skill mix needed to access and maintain important social support networks (Lee, DeMaris, Bavin, & Sullivan, 2001).

An emerging consensus among researchers suggests two general types of coping, *loss-oriented* and *restoration-oriented*, that may be required in a bereavement. These are most prominently captured in the dual process model (DPM) of coping with bereavement (M. S. Stroebe & Schut, 1999, 2001). Loss-oriented coping challenges reflect the emotional distress of losing a beloved attachment figure. Their focus is on the lost relationship, emotional bonds to the deceased, yearning, painful memories, coming to terms with irrevocable separation, and finding a way to work through grief-related feelings of anxiety, depression, and uncertainty. Restoration-oriented coping challenges, on the other hand, involve dealing with secondary stressors associated with the loss. These can involve a need to make major life adjustments or to deal with the practical consequences of the death, such as economic disruption, need to assume new responsibilities, or to learn new practical coping skills having to do with employment, household and family management, or coming to terms with a world in which the deceased is no longer present. The DPM proposes that over time bereaved individuals will feel a need to oscillate between attending to loss- and restoration-oriented coping demands, and that such oscillation can serve as an emotion-regulation mechanism, allowing occasional respite from emotional process and responding as needed to practical matters that emerge.

LATE-LIFE DEVELOPMENTAL PROCESSES AND BEREAVEMENT

DEVELOPMENTAL PROCESSES AND COPING WITH LATE-LIFE BEREAVEMENT

A number of developmental processes pertaining to *physical health, emotion,* and *cognition* would be expected to influence coping with bereavement in late life. We summarize some of these in this section.

PHYSICAL HEALTH STATUS

Diminished health associated with old age would be expected to compound the problem of adapting to a significant life stressor such as bereavement. The symptomatology of bereavement includes a strong physiological component, which would be expected to exacerbate preexisting chronic conditions or disease process. And the deterioration of the body's protective and regulatory systems affects one's adaptive reserves and homeostatic capacity, increasing risk during any emerging health crisis. Diminished energy can render some active coping strategies infeasible. Sensory loss may lead to increased dependency simply for activities of daily living and survival. Furthermore, any unresolved, residual physical symptoms resulting from the bereavement might be expected to play an important role in future disablement among older persons (Aldwin & Gilmer, 1999; Hansson & Stroebe, in press; Jette, 1996).

EMOTIONAL PROCESSES

Research by Lawton, Kleban, Rajagopal, and Dean (1992) suggested a "dampening" of emotional experience among older adults generally. This involves a general narrowing of the "intensity, frequency, duration, or quality" of their emotional responses (p. 338). Lawton and colleagues found that older persons reported focusing greater effort (and having more success) on managing their emotions. Respondents also reported more stability in their positive moods, attempts to arrange their lives so as to encounter fewer intense (positive or negative) emotions, and a diminished likelihood of experiencing the physical sensations usually associated with intense emotional experience.

There is evidence also that older persons become more effective at emotion regulation more generally. They tend to report fewer negative emotional experiences and greater efforts to enhance positive emotions (Birditt & Fingerman, 2003; Charles, Mather, & Carstensen, 2003; Gross et al., 1997). They also appear to focus on enhancement of the balance of positive to negative emotions in their relationships with their spouse (Carstensen, Gottman, & Levenson, 1995) and in their interactions with their children (Pasupathi, Henry, & Carstensen, 2002). During an emotional episode they are more likely to experience more differentiated and complex emotions, for example, acknowledging the co-occurrence of a greater number of distinct emotions and of a mix of positive and negative emotions (Carstensen, Pasupathi, Mayr, & Nesselroade, 2000; Ong & Bergeman, 2004). If aging is thus associated with a maturation and dampening of emotional experience, with greater expertise in emotion regulation, and with efforts to manage relationships with an eye to maintaining a positive emotional balance, older persons would be expected to more easily adapt to stressful life events, even to bereavements. The greater emotional heterogeneity and specificity with age (Charles, 2005; Kunzmann & Gruhn, 2005), however, argues against overgeneralizations regarding one's emotional response to death in later life; individual differences in reactivity and specificity in responding to death is a function of the nature of one's relationship to the deceased as well as the cause of death.

It is important to point out that the successful management and monitoring of one's emotions may be critical in developing and maintaining social support networks. In acknowledging and expressing negative emotions (anger, sadness, depression) to a degree, one may invite efforts by family, friends, and neighbors to provide needed emotional and instrumental support, contributing to one's quality of life and sense of well-being (Krause, 2006). Moreover, decreases in negative affect and increases in positive affect, in concert with increased emotional control in later life (George, 2006), are likely to make one more attractive as a griever, discouraging the disenfranchised grief (Doka, 1989, 2002) that might otherwise characterize the loss of a spouse in later life, especially among women, for whom economic hardship is greater (Utz, 2006).

Interestingly, although existing support networks may be greater and the death of a husband (or, for that matter, a parent) may be seen as normative in nature, this very sense of the normativeness of loss in later life may come at the cost of providing opportunities for emotional expression and venting of strong emotions and past regrets or, alternatively, the desire to move on with one's life. In this respect, Williams-Conway, Hayslip, and Tandy (1991) found that while health care professionals attributed more distress and difficulty in adjusting to their husband's deaths to widows than the latter reported, such persons significantly underestimated the extent and depth of widows' yearning for their husbands and feelings of isolation. Interestingly, although Sable (1991) found that older women eventually came to terms with the death of their husbands, many (78%) said that they simply learned to live without them but that emotionally they would never get over the loss.

COGNITIVE PROCESSES

Cognitive competence would also seem relevant to the ability to cope with both loss-oriented and restoration-oriented challenges. For example, studies have found that many older adults are able to maintain into late life those abilities associated with crystallized intelligence (verbal meaning) as well as everyday problem solving (Hayslip & Sterns, 1979; Horn & Hofer, 1992; Marsiske & Margrett, 2006; Schaie, 1994). The maintenance of such skills are largely tied to the accumulation of experience as well as opportunities for the everyday use of one's skills. In light of the relative familiarity of the experience of loss in later life, reliance on previous coping strategies that have proven useful in the past can indeed be adaptive in coping with the loss-oriented and restoration-oriented aspects of late-life loss. Such changes therefore suggest a continued ability to deal with loss-oriented challenges in bereavement (e.g., finding meaning in the death, resolving relationship issues). On the other hand, to the extent that restoration-oriented coping (e.g., with finances, housing, employment) may require numeric or abstract reasoning abilities, it may be a concern that such abilities are more sensitive to the aging process. Under such circumstances, formal assistance in coping or, at the minimum, meaningful and timely social support may be important.

More broadly, the cognitive literature suggests important adaptive possibilities in late life, some of which seem relevant to coping or adaptation with bereavement. For example, some older persons would be expected to have developed in their cognitive abilities in such a way as to suggest postformal thought (Sinnott, 1996). This would be expected to reflect a greater complexity in thinking about problems, increased appreciation for the contextual variables that shape problems and potential solutions, and an increased sensitivity to multiple perspectives and for how understanding of a problem may change with time and experience. Similarly, many older adults may have benefited from their considerable life experience, acquiring factual and procedural expertise and perspective with respect to managing life's problems (Baltes, Smith, & Staudinger, 1992). Maturation and developing wisdom about life matters would be expected to enhance both loss- and restoration-oriented coping and adaptation.

The development of age-appropriate coping strategies and skills would also be expected to enhance adaptation to late-life bereavement. Older adults are observed to continue actively coping, but goals for coping and strategies appear to change in response to life stressors that are becoming chronic and less controllable (Aldwin, 1991; Lazarus, 1996). At least three models of coping in old age are of interest in this connection. First, there is often a shift in emphasis from problem-focused to emotion-focused coping (Aldwin, 1991). Second, a shift from assimilative to more accommodative coping has been noted (Brandstadter & Renner, 1990). Accommodative coping recognizes a need in old age to understand one's realistic limits, revise or lower coping standards, and find new ways to satisfy needs and to accommodate to changing circumstances. In this respect, accommodative coping represents the use of what Schultz and Heckhausen (1996) have termed *secondary control:* altering one's view of the world or oneself rather than attempt to directly alter the course of events or change the external environment. Finally, Baltes and Baltes (1990) proposed three coping strategies in their model of selective optimization and compensation. This model acknowledges that it is adaptive in late life to recognize that it will be difficult to continue to maintain competence in all domains of one's life and that it will be important to make some choices regarding those life goals and abilities that are most important to continue to pursue (selection). Having made these choices, it is possible to focus (and intensify) remaining efforts and energies on those selected goals and abilities (optimization). At some point, however, most older adults are likely to experience the loss of a valued ability through irreversible age-related change. At such times it will be important to find alternative strategies or resources with which to compensate for those losses (compensation). Considerable research now confirms the adaptive value of such shifts in coping in late life, as evidenced by maintenance of one's sense of mastery, well-being, and life satisfaction in the face of age-related loss (e.g., Freund & Baltes, 2002; Rothermund & Brandtstädter, 2003).

THE INTERFACE OF BEREAVEMENT WITH OTHER LATE-LIFE EVENTS AND TRANSITIONS

The previous discussion of the contextual influences on late-life bereavement warrants some discussion of other late-life transitions, some of which are normative and some of which are not, and their relationship to grief and bereavement. In this respect, we briefly discuss the grandparent role, grandparents raising grandchildren, retirement, and relocation from one's home to a nursing home or assisted living facility.

GRANDPARENTING

It is has observed that later life can be understood in the context of gains and losses (Baltes, 1997), wherein the proportion of gains and losses experienced changes with increased age. With regard to grandparenting, it is reasonable to assume that for many older adults, the acquisition of the grandparent role is viewed positively, especially given the fact that grandparents actively and accurately anticipate the nature of their role as such in advance of the birth of their grandchild (Somary & Stricker, 1998). Yet grandparents, especially if they are actively involved in the lives of their grandchildren and contingent on the meaning they assign to the grandparent role, may be asked to become more involved in child care. Involvement in their grandchild's life may reflect a productive and fulfilling manifestation of a "companionate" style (Cherlin & Furstenberg, 1986); however, responding to the *expectation* that one will necessarily share child care responsibilities (i.e., a surrogate parent style) can potentially interfere with one's sense of privacy in the context of marriage and lifestyle choices (e.g., being able to travel). Such consequences have not been the subject of empirical research; nevertheless, they are losses with which some grandparents may cope.

More important, some grandparents may grieve over the loss of contact with their grandchildren. As the adult child helps to mediate the degree of contact between grandparents and grandchildren (Uhlenberg & Hammill, 1998), disagreements between adult children and their parents about child-rearing issues can undermine opportunities for and the quality of relationships with grandchildren. In this respect, "token" grandparents report feeling emotionally isolated from their grandchildren (Kornhaber, 1996).

Another manifestation of the grief that grandparents feel is when they lose contact with their grandchildren because of the divorce of their adult child, or through family disagreements, or because of geographical separation. Drew and Smith (2002) reported that such grandparents experienced intense grief, lowered quality of life, and poorer emotional and physical health; the effects of a family feud had the most impact, followed by divorce, and then geographic separation. In the context of divorce, Edrenberg and Smith (2003) found that relationships with grandchildren were most satisfying when visits with both a daughter and a grandchild were maintained, even when contact with the latter was frequent. In this respect, being prevented from having contact with grandchildren via relationships with adult children-in-law has profound negative emotional consequences for grandparents, as also is the case when an adult child dies or when the adult child remarries after divorce (Kruk, 1995). In the event of divorce, less physical and emotional contact with grandchildren is associated with poorer physical health and emotional well-being (Drew & Smith, 1999). Some states have enacted laws to guarantee grandparents' visitation rights in the event of divorce (Falk & Falk, 2002). Complementarily, when grandparents divorce, they report feeling less close to their grandchildren, less likely to play a friend role, and more conflicts with grandchildren, though such effects are moderated by the quality of the relationship with the adult child (King, 2003).

In the event of a grandchild's death, grandparents are often seen as "forgotten grievers" (Ponzetti & Johnson, 1991) to the extent that attention is focused on the impact of the child's death on the parents (see Reed, 2003). It is often presumed that grandparents have had more experience with death, and so will need less support and education in their adjustment to their grandchild's death. The scientific literature is just emerging as it relates to grandparents' emotional needs when a grandchild dies, but it has been observed that their grief is likely to be twofold: They grieve for their adult child as well as for themselves (Reed, 2003). Family customs and rituals may not meet a grandparent's needs, and grandparents are put in the delicate position of attempting to support their adult child as well as meet their own needs for support from others. In many respects, such grandparents' grief is indeed disenfranchised (Doka, 1989, 2002).

A related issue pertains to the grief grandparents face when raising a grandchild. As the circumstances that make such caregiving more likely are negative and often socially stigmatizing (i.e., the death or divorce of an adult child, incarceration, parental abuse, or abandonment of the child; see Hayslip & Kaminski, 2005), the gravity of these grandparents' needs for social support and understanding will likely not be appreciated or understood by others (Miltenberger, Hayslip, Harris, & Kaminski, 2003–2004). The loss or interruption of future plans, a lessening of one's privacy, the loss of income or good health, as well as the loss of the formerly defined relationship with a grandchild that one must now care for, represent factors that are often perceived as irreversible and, indeed, quite personal by custodial grandparents. As stated by Baird (2003, p. 64), a custodial grandparent, "There are constant reminders of losses incurred: the retirement of a friend, watching a neighbor's grandchild come and go, lack of personal time with a spouse, lost contact with another friend."

The grief of grandparents raising grandchildren who are either HIV positive or whose parents have died from HIV disease is overwhelming (Joslin, 2002; Winston, 2003). Not only are such grandparents stigmatized, but they suffer from a lack of emotional and tangible support from others, when it is highly likely that their HIV-positive grandchild will also die. Such grandparents, who are often African American and whose grief is often disenfranchised, sometimes experience an overwhelming sense of loss and depression and manifest behaviors and thoughts characteristic of pathological grief (see earlier discussion). Some studies (e.g., Winston, 2003) suggest that it is the grandparents' own sense of a spiritual relationship with God as well as their sense of familism (see Joslin, 2002; Poindexter & Linsk, 1998) that enables them to cope with the profound sense of isolation, feeling different, and hopelessness that often accompanies caring for an HIV-inflected child.

RETIREMENT AND RELOCATION

Although there is little published research on grief among older persons as it relates to retirement and relocation, each transition clearly implies a separation from something that one has imbued with a great deal of emotional and psychosocial importance. In the case of retirement, the loss of one's identity as a productive member of society and as a provider for one's family, as well as the loss of relationships with friends and coworkers, are issues confronting most individuals who retire from the workforce (see Adams & Beehr, 2003).

Although preretirement planning may mitigate the adjustments that are otherwise present when persons retire, or in some cases when retirements are unplanned (i.e., when persons must retire due to ill health or if they are part of a movement to downsize), specific discussions of the role of grief in adjusting to or preparing for retirement are notably absent in the literature. Likewise, although changes in well-being are typically identified as a primary consequence of retirement planning or adjustment to the retirement role, the role of grief in this process has gone unexplored. In this respect, Blazer (2002), in the context of interpersonal therapy for late-life depression, recommends consciously connecting depression to the life transition (e.g., retirement) as well as helping the older person reframe the life transition in more positive terms. The role of grief in helping or hurting the development of a postretirement identity as well as a factor in determining adjustment to retirement certainly requires more attention than it has garnered thus far.

NURSING HOME PLACEMENT AND GRIEF

Nursing homes (and assisted living facilities) rarely provide resources for families to deal with the grief they are experiencing in having to make the decision to institutionalize a family member, or to help older persons come to terms with the necessary abandonment of the house in which they may have spent most of their adult lives, raised their children, and enjoyed their relationship together. Although professional resources are rare, Silin (2001) does provide guidelines for families in dealing with the grief that accompanies making health care decisions in the nursing home context. Casarett, Hirschman, and Henry (2001) note that as patients approach death, their needs for hospice care in the context of the nursing home increase, though such needs are different from those of community-based hospice patients. Their shorter, more rapid death trajectory may make it difficult to meet not only their needs for pain control, but also the family's needs for end-of-life care.

Keay (2002) notes that many staff are not trained in providing end-of-life care to patients and families. Staff also experience grief and may need advocates in taking an active role in planning and decision making, in addition to transferring the older patient to a hospital in a timely manner, when death seems imminent.

Nursing home staff need to be better trained in listening and communication skills in meeting the family's needs.

In contrast to the attention paid to the family, we know little about the sense of loss older persons themselves experience when they must give up personal possessions or part with friends and neighbors in order to move into a nursing home (see Quadagno, 2002), or when a husband and wife are separated from one another after having been institutionalized. As relocation effects are substantial in their impact on both mortality and mental health via a breakdown in social support networks and enforced isolation (see George, 2006), it is likely that grief, which accompanies the perceived irreplaceable loss of one's health and independence with admission to a long-term care facility, accounts for at least some impact on health and mortality among older persons relocating to nursing homes.

ALZHEIMER'S DISEASE

Perhaps more relevant to institutional care is grief associated with the reasons one is likely to need such care in the first place. In this respect, Alzheimer's disease (AD), regarded as a terminal illness by the Alzheimer's Association, is associated with a series of adjustments by both the older person and his or her family and friends to the loss of the ability to care for oneself and cognitive and physical/health-related changes that are progressive in nature (Welsh-Bohmer & Warren, 2006); it is often preceded by a prolonged period of mild cognitive impairment (Peterson, 2003). For Alzheimer's patients and their families and caregivers, grief is characterized by progressive degrees of reactions to loss as the patient's condition worsens. Caregivers must cope with what has been termed *ambiguous loss* (Boss, 1999): Their loved one is physically present and still living, and yet in other ways has died. In this respect, the grief that family members feel is both ambiguous and anticipatory (see Meuser & Marwit, 2001) in nature. Marwit and Meuser (2002) note the paucity of research on the grief that AD caregivers experience, and identify diversity in grief reactions as the dominant characteristic of AD caregiver grief. Such grief is influenced by (a) the caregiver's relationship to the patient (spouse, child); (b) caregiver sex; (c) the domain relevant to loss (e.g., loss of the relationship per se, communicative difficulties); (d) whether home care or nursing home care was provided; (e) whether anger, sadness, depression, or guilt were reported as the dominant emotion; and (f) whether social support and anticipatory grief were experienced prior to death. All of these factors influenced postdeath adjustment (Meuser & Marwit, 2001).

Perhaps what differentiates the grief associated with AD is that persons eventually no longer resemble—physically, emotionally, cognitively, or interpersonally—the person they were prior to diagnosis. Indeed, many spouses grieve long before death occurs, describing this process as an "endless funeral" (T. Brown & Kleist, 1999). Alzheimer's patients may not recognize family members, recall important events bonding them to spouse or children, or remember who they themselves are. Being repeatedly exposed to such changes in a loved one brings about what caregivers label "chronic sorrow" (Mayer, 2001).

In coping with the progressive loss of the person they once knew, caregivers and family must give up previously established ways of relating to and communicating with the family member afflicted with AD, deal with a loss of intimacy, and yet be aware of the impact of grief on what is now a redefined relationship with a demented family member; it is for this reason that AD has been likened to the "long goodbye" by the Alzheimer's Association. Key to understanding such grief reactions is the necessity for both Alzheimer's victims and their families to reconstruct who they are and their relationships to others (Robinson, Clare, & Evans, 2005). Such reframing is associated with better postdeath adjustment among caregivers (Boerner, Schultz, & Horowitz, 2004). Moreover, such benefits are greater if both caregivers and AD patients, to the extent possible, actively participate in efforts to learn about the disease and allow for the expression of sadness, regret, anger, or guilt, all of which are common components of the response to loss (see S. Sanders & Sharp, 2004). To the extent that Alzheimer's patients may ultimately require hospice care, attending to the emotional and psychosocial adjustments associated with dying are completely congruent with hospice philosophy, which involves treating the patient and family as a unit, emphasizing quality of life, and continued attention to issues of grief both before and after the patient dies (Hayslip & Hansson, in press).

IMPLICATIONS FOR SERVICES, SUPPORT, AND COUNSELING INTERVENTIONS

Most bereaved persons (including the elderly bereaved) do not experience a traumatic or unduly complicated grief experience. Many, however, will experience a devastating degree of emotional and physical distress, requiring adaptation. As we have noted, some suffer prolonged health outcomes, for example, in cases where the bereavement exacerbates preexisting conditions or disease process, with the potential to contribute to the disablement process. In later life, a conjugal bereavement may also disrupt one's economic security and social support network and for some period of time may increase isolation, loneliness, and the capacity to live independently. There are, therefore, implied consequences and costs to society, as some older bereaved persons begin to require more support, more specialized (perhaps medical) care, and possibly some form of housing support (Hansson & Stroebe, 2003).

Recent reviews of the bereavement treatment literature have now concluded that interventions aimed at reducing grief and related symptoms are *not universally* helpful (Jordan & Neimeyer, 2003; Schut, Stroebe, van den Bout, & Terheggen, 2001). For example, Schut et al. reviewed the efficacy studies in three categories of intervention. The first of these involved *primary preventive interventions*, in which all persons who had experienced a death received some form of intervention (e.g., crisis counseling, telephone outreach, inclusion in self-help or therapy groups). The second category involved *secondary preventive interventions*, directed toward bereaved individuals considered to be at high risk because they have insufficient social support or had experienced a traumatic death, had lost a child, or were experiencing other stressors concurrent to the bereavement. Secondary interventions included counseling, practical or emotional support, and mutual help groups. The third category, termed *tertiary preventive intervention*, focused on individuals experiencing a complicated or morbid grief or diagnosed with a bereavement-related psychopathology, and involved a variety of guided mourning techniques, flooding, desensitization, religious-oriented therapy, behavior therapy, and dynamic therapy.

An overall conclusion from the review by Schut and colleagues (2001) was that the potential utility of interventions to reduce grief-related symptoms appears to depend on the severity of one's grief experience. Formal interventions were usually not helpful when provided to bereaved persons who had not indicated a need or who did not exhibit any compelling risk factors (i.e., the primary preventive intervention studies), and sometimes were actually associated with increased symptoms. Similarly, interventions appeared useful only for some bereaved persons selected on the basis of known risk factors (the secondary preventive intervention studies). Only among bereaved persons already exhibiting a complicated grief or an especially serious bereavement-related outcome (e.g., depressive disorder) did therapeutic intervention appear consistently useful (the tertiary preventive interventions).

A variety of explanations have been proposed for this pattern of efficacy findings. For example, in uncomplicated bereavements (the most frequent category), coping and adaptation are naturally occurring processes; bereaved controls in these studies tend to experience a reduction in symptoms over the period of the study. In the primary and secondary preventive intervention studies, bereaved respondents tend not to be self-referred, but rather are recruited into the research. It is thus difficult to interpret degree of motivation or need for the intervention. Finally, delays incurred postdeath in the process of recruiting bereaved respondents for primary and secondary intervention studies mean that these interventions will likely occur later in the course of one's bereavement, after symptoms have already begun to recede in response to any coping or adaptation efforts (Jordan & Neimeyer, 2003; Schut et al., 2001).

GOALS FOR INTERVENTION WITH OLDER BEREAVED PERSONS

Our sense from the research is that in most cases, interventions with older bereaved persons will not need to focus primarily on reduction of grief symptoms. Interventions will be less likely, therefore, to involve formal therapy protocols. Consistent with recent thinking about geropsychotherapy generally, interventions should probably focus instead on more flexible goals for adaptation, life satisfaction, and social functioning (Arean et al., 2003). From this perspective, goals would emphasize the management of symptoms and the rehabilitation of functioning, rather than reductions in grief (Hansson & Stroebe, 2003). An emphasis would be placed on protecting the older bereaved person's existing strengths and resources and preventing any disabling consequences of the bereavement (APA Working Group on the Older Adult, 1998; Jette, 1996; Schulz & Martire, 1998). An additional theme from the intervention research with older adults is a need to consider a wider range of potential targets for intervention. The bereavement intervention literature we have cited, for example, tends to focus on the bereaved individual as the target of intervention, and then measures degree of resolved grief (Jordan & Neimeyer, 2003; Schut et al., 2001). In addition, we advocate greater attention to the variability in grief reactions across persons, relationships types, death trajectories, and environmental contexts.

It is important for the care community to identify for treatment those older bereaved persons who are at higher risk because of dispositional or contextual vulnerabilities or a difficult psychiatric history or who may have experienced a traumatic loss (Jordan & Neimeyer, 2003). But for most, a more productive effort would likely focus on enhancing naturally occurring personal and social processes important to adaptation. We described earlier (in terms of the DPM) that a mix of loss-oriented and restoration-oriented coping demands will need to be faced. These will range from having to find meaning in and acceptance of the death, to dealing with secondary stressors involving finances, household management, and changing roles and responsibilities.

Intervention might then best focus on encouraging and enhancing the bereaved individual's family, friends, and community in their efforts to provide companionship and emotional and instrumental support (Raphael, Middleton, Martinek, & Misso, 1993). These natural, supportive networks play an important role in providing a safe and comforting environment for the bereaved individual's adaptation. Among the elderly, however, this can sometimes be problematic. Many older persons, in addition to the stress of the bereavement, will be at increased risk because of chronic health conditions, disability, or cognitive limitations, requiring a more rigorous assessment of their needs and their ability to function and adapt to their new circumstances (Hansson & Stroebe, 2003). To the extent that their grief is ambiguous or disenfranchised, we emphasize the identification of such older persons as being at risk for pathological grief reactions and stress the importance of timely and continued interventions involving education, psychotherapy, and social support, to include attention to physical health and cognitive skills both before and after the death of a loved one.

CONCLUSION

Seven themes from our discussion deserve emphasis. *First,* bereavement is a natural phenomenon, not a medical problem. Most older persons experience it as emotionally and perhaps physically distressing, but they eventually find a way to adapt. The experience tends to make demands for emotional adjustments, but also demands to deal with secondary stressors that have more practical implications for one's life.

Second, among older persons, contextual variables have enormous influence on the nature and course of bereavement. For example, causes of death change, with implications for degree of related trauma, issues of economic security, and efficacy of family support networks. There is a likelihood that conjugal bereavements will involve transitions from extended periods of caregiving.

Third, among older adults (as in the young), the bereavement experience reveals much individual variability and much resiliency in coping with loss.

Fourth, in old age the stress of bereavement interacts with other late-life events and transitions (e.g., adjustments to custodial grandparenting, retirement, relocation, Alzheimer's disease, hospice, nursing home environments). In this respect, the losses of such life transitions are often more difficult to deal with than would appear at first blush and may go unrecognized as important influences on the health and well-being of older persons and their families.

Fifth, we have proposed elsewhere (Hansson & Stroebe, in press) that at some point the emphasis might usefully be shifted from the effects of aging on bereavement to a consideration of the effects of late-life bereavement on the aging process. In particular, we have suggested that unresolved, residual physical symptoms of bereavement among frail older persons need to be examined with respect to their implications for the process of disablement.

Sixth, bereavement intervention research thus far has concluded that formal psychotherapeutic interventions to reduce grief symptoms are not universally efficacious. They are unlikely to be useful when targeted at bereaved persons not identified to be at special risk or who have not self-selected into therapy. They are only occasionally useful for persons selected on the basis of risk factors. But they are quite useful among bereaved persons who already exhibit complicated bereavements or related psychopathology. The existing intervention research is not large enough to date to systematically consider these conclusions with respect to varying age groups, but our sense is that there is little reason to expect age-related differences in these patterns.

Seventh, the intervention research suggests two age-related themes. (1) Many psychotherapy interventions can be effective with older individuals who exhibit complicated psychological symptoms. This has been amply discussed by Knight (2004), who dispels several myths about aging and grief (e.g., that grief necessarily implies "working through" a death, that grief is accompanied by depression), and who emphasizes the specificity of the grief response in older persons. (2) Grief interventions should be targeted more broadly, to include attempts to strengthen and stabilize family and community support networks, in addition to the focus on reducing psychological and physical symptoms of individuals. In this respect, there are indeed positive aspects of grieving, wherein relationships that were formerly lost can be redefined and rediscovered, new roles and directions in life can be pursued, and not only individuals but also families and communities can grow having coped with the loss of a valued teacher, mentor, parent, spouse, citizen, or community activist.

REFERENCES

Adams, G., & Beehr, T. (2003). *Retirement: Reasons, processes, and results.* New York: Springer.

Aldwin, C. M. (1991). Does age affect the stress and coping process? Implications of age differences in perceived control. *Journal of Gerontology: Psychological Sciences, 46,* P174–P180.

Aldwin, C. M., & Gilmer, D. F. (1999). Immunity, disease processes, and optimal aging. In J. C. Cavanaugh & S. K. Whitbourne (Eds.), *Gerontology: An interdisciplinary perspective* (pp. 123–154). New York: Oxford University Press.

Antonucci, T. C., Langfahl, E. S., & Akiyama, H. (2004). Relationships as outcomes and contexts. In F. R. Lang & K. L. Fingerman (Eds.), *Growing together: Personal relationships across the lifespan* (pp. 24–44). Cambridge, England: Cambridge University Press.

APA Working Group on the Older Adult. (1998). What practitioners should know about working with older adults. *Professional Psychology: Research and Practice, 29,* 413–427.

Archer, J. (1999). *The nature of grief: The evolution and psychology of reactions to loss.* London: Routledge.

Arean, P. A., Cook, B. L., Gallagher-Thompson, D., Hegel, M. T., Schulberg, H. C., & Schulz, R. (2003). Guidelines for conducting geropsychotherapy research. *American Journal of Geriatric Psychiatry, 11,* 9–16.

Baird, A. (2003). Through my eyes: Service needs of grandparents who raise their grandchildren from the perspective of a custodial grandmother. In B. Hayslip & J. Patrick (Eds.), *Working with custodial grandparents* (pp. 59–65). New York: Springer.

Baltes, P. B. (1997). On the incomplete architecture of human ontogeny. *American Psychologist, 51,* 702–714.

Baltes, P. B., & Baltes, M. (1990). Psychological perspectives on successful aging: The model of selective optimization with compensation. In P. B. Baltes & M. Baltes (Eds.), *Successful aging: Perspectives from the behavioral sciences* (pp. 1–34). Cambridge, England: Cambridge University Press.

Baltes, P. B., Smith, J., & Staudinger, U. M. (1992). Wisdom and successful aging. In T. B. Sonderegger (Ed.), *Nebraska Symposium on Motivation* (pp. 123–167). Lincoln: University of Nebraska Press.

Birditt, K. S., & Fingerman, K. L. (2003). Age and gender differences in adults' descriptions of emotional reactions to interpersonal problems. *Journal of Gerontology: Psychological Sciences, 58B*, P237–P245.

Blazer, D. (2002). *Depression in late life* (3rd ed.). New York: Springer.

Blazer, D. G. (2003). Depression in late life: Review and commentary. *Journal of Gerontology: Medical Sciences, 58A*(3), 249–265.

Blieszner, R. (1993). A socialist-feminist perspective on widowhood. *Journal of Aging Studies, 7*, 171–182.

Boerner, K., Schultz, K., & Horowitz, A. (2004). Positive aspects of caregiving and adaptation to bereavement. *Psychology and Aging, 19*, 668–675.

Bonanno, G. A., Wortman, C. B., & Nesse, R. M. (2004). Prospective patterns of resilience and maladjustment during widowhood. *Psychology and Aging, 19*, 260–271.

Boss, P. (1999). *Ambiguous loss: Learning to live with unresolved grief.* Cambridge, MA: Harvard University Press.

Bound, J., Duncan, G. J., Laren, D. S., & Olenick, L. (1991). Poverty dynamics in widowhood. *Journal of Gerontology: Social Sciences, 46*(3), S115–S124.

Bowling, A. (1994). Mortality after bereavement: An analysis of mortality rates and associations with mortality 13 years after bereavement. *International Journal of Geriatric Psychiatry, 9*, 445–459.

Bradbeer, M., Helme, R. D., Yong, H. H., Kendig, H. L., & Gibson, S. J. (2003). Widowhood and other demographic associations of pain in independent older people. *Clinical Journal of Pain, 19*, 247–254.

Brandstadter, J., & Renner, G. (1990). Tenacious goal pursuit and flexible goal adjustment: Explication and age-related analysis of assimilative and accommodative strategies of coping. *Psychology and Aging, 5*, 58–67.

Brown, L. F., Reynolds, C. F., III, Monk, T. H., Prigerson, H. G., Dew, M. A., Houck, P. R., et al. (1996). Social rhythm stability following late-life spousal bereavement: Associations with depression and sleep impairment. *Psychiatry Research, 62*, 161–169.

Brown, T., & Kleist, D. (1999). Alzheimer's disease and the family: Current research. *Family Journal: Counseling and Therapy for Couples and Families, 1*, 54–57.

Carr, D. (2006). Methodological issues in studying late life bereavement. In D. Carr, R. Nesse, & C. Wortman (Eds.), *Spousal bereavement in late life* (pp. 19–48). New York: Springer.

Carstensen, L. L., Gottman, J. M., & Levenson, R. W. (1995). Emotional behavior in long-term marriage. *Psychology and Aging, 10*, 140–149.

Carstensen, L. L., Pasupathi, M., Mayr, U., & Nesselroade, J. R. (2000). Emotional experience in everyday life across the adult life span. *Journal of Personality and Social Psychology, 79*, 644–655.

Casarett, D. J., Hirschman, K., & Henry, R. (2001). Does hospice have a role in nursing home care at the end of life? *Journal of the American Geriatrics Society, 49*, 1493–1498.

Charles, S. T. (2005). Viewing injustice: Greater emotional heterogeneity with age. *Psychology and Aging, 20*, 159–164.

Charles, S. T., Mather, M., & Carstensen, L. L. (2003). Aging and emotional memory: The forgettable nature of negative images for older adults. *Journal of Experimental Psychology: General, 132,* 310–324.

Charles, S. T., & Mavandadi, S. (2004). Social support and physical health across the life span: Socioemotional influences. In F. R. Lang & K. L. Fingerman (Eds.), *Growing together: Personal relationships across the lifespan* (pp. 240–267). Cambridge, England: Cambridge University Press.

Cherlin, A., & Furstenberg, F. (1986). *The new American grandparent.* New York: Basic Books.

Doka, K. (1989). *Disenfranchised grief: Recognizing hidden sorrow.* Lexington, MA: Lexington.

Doka, K. (2002). *Disenfranchised grief: New directions, challenges, and strategies for practice.* Champaign, IL: Research Press.

Drew, L., & Smith, P. (1999). The impact of parental separation/divorce on grandparent-grandchild relationships. *International Journal of Aging and Human Development, 48,* 191–216.

Drew, L., & Smith, P. (2002). Implications for grandparents when they lose contact with their grandchildren: Divorce, family feud, and geographical separation. *Journal of Mental Health and Aging, 8,* 95–119.

Edrenberg, M., & Smith, P. (2003). Grandmother-grandchild contacts before and after an adult daughter's divorce. *Journal of Divorce and Remarriage, 39,* 27–43.

Falk, U., & Falk, G. (2002). *Grandparents: A new look at the supporting generation.* Amherst, NY: Prometheus.

Federal Interagency Forum on Aging-Related Statistics. (2004). *Older Americans 2004: Key indicators of well-being.* Washington, DC: U.S. Government Printing Office.

Ferrario, S. R., Cardillo, V., Vicario, F., Balzarini, E., & Zotti, A. M. (2004). Advanced cancer at home: Caregiving and bereavement. *Palliative Medicine, 18,* 129–136.

Freund, A. M., & Baltes, P. B. (2002). Life-management strategies of selection, optimization, and compensation: Measurement by self-report and construct validity. *Journal of Personality and Social Psychology, 82,* 642–662.

Fry, P. S. (1997). Grandparents' reactions to the death of a grandchild: An exploratory factor analytic study. *Omega, 35,* 119–140.

Fry, P. S. (1998). Spousal loss in late life: A 1-year follow-up of perceived changes in life meaning and psychosocial functioning following bereavement. *Journal of Personal and Interpersonal Loss, 3,* 369–391.

Gallagher-Thompson, D., Futterman, A., Farberow, N., Thompson, L. W., & Peterson, J. (1993). The impact of spousal bereavement on older widows and widowers. In M. S. Stroebe, W. Stroebe, & R. O. Hansson (Eds.), *Handbook of bereavement: Theory, research, and intervention* (pp. 227–239). Cambridge, England: Cambridge University Press.

Gass, K. A. (1987). The health of conjugally bereaved older widows: The role of appraisal, coping and resources. *Research in Nursing and Health, 10,* 39–47.

Gatz, M., & Fiske, A. (2003). Aging women and depression. *Professional Psychology: Research and Practice, 34,* 3–9.

George, L. (2006). Quality of life. In R. Binstock & L. George (Eds.), *Handbook of aging and the social sciences* (6th ed., pp. 321–338). San Antonio, TX: Academic Press.

Gross, J. J., Carstensen, L. L., Pasupathi, M., Tsai, J., Skorpen, C. G., & Hsu, A. Y. C. (1997). Emotion and aging: Experience, expression, and control. *Psychology and Aging, 12,* 590–599.

Hansson, R. O., & Carpenter, B. N. (1994). *Relationships in old age: Coping with the challenge of transition.* New York: Guilford Press.

Hansson, R. O., & Stroebe, M. S. (2003). Grief, older adulthood. In T. P. Gullotta & M. Bloom (Eds.), *Encyclopedia of primary prevention and health promotion* (pp. 515–521). New York: Kluwer Academic/Plenum Press.

Hansson, R. O., & Stroebe, M. S. (in press). *Bereavement in late life: Development, coping and adaptation.* Washington, DC: American Psychological Association.

Harwood, D. (2001). Grief in old age. *Reviews in Clinical Gerontology, 11,* 167–175.

Hayslip, B., & Hansson, R. O. (in press). Hospice. In J. E. Birren (Ed.), *Encyclopedia of gerontology.* Oxford: Elsevier.

Hayslip, B., & Kaminski, P. (2005). Grandparents raising their grandchildren: A review of the literature and implications for practice. *Gerontologist, 45,* 262–269.

Hayslip, B., & Sterns, H. (1979). Age differences in relationships between fluid and crystallized intelligences and problem solving. *Journal of Gerontology, 34,* 404–414.

Hayslip, B., & White, D. (in press). Grandparents as grievers. In M. S. Stroebe, R. O. Hansson, W. Stroebe, & H. Schut (Eds.), *Handbook of bereavement research* (3rd ed.). Washington, DC: American Psychological Association.

Horn, J. L., & Hofer, S. (1992). Major abilities and development during the adult period. In R. Sternberg & C. Berg (Eds.), *Intellectual development* (pp. 44–99). New York: Cambridge University Press.

Hungerford, T. L. (2001). The economic consequences of widowhood on elderly women in the United States and Germany. *Gerontologist, 41,* 103–110.

Jette, A. M. (1996). Disability trends and transitions. In R. H. Binstock & L. K. George (Eds.), *Handbook of aging and the social sciences* (pp. 94–116). San Diego, CA: Academic Press.

Jordan, J. R., & Neimeyer, R. A. (2003). Does grief counseling work? *Death Studies, 27,* 765–786.

Joslin, D. (2002). *Invisible caregivers: Older adults raising children in the wake of HIV/AIDS.* New York: Columbia University Press.

Kastenbaum, R. (1978). Death, dying, and bereavement in old age: New developments and their possible implications for psychosocial care. *Aged Care and Services Review, 1,* 1–10.

Keay, T. (2002). Issues of loss and grief in long-term care facilities. In K. Doka (Ed.), *Living with loss in later life* (pp. 18–31). Washington, DC: National Hospice Foundation.

King, V. (2003). The legacy of a grandparent's divorce: Consequences for grandparents and grandchildren. *Journal of Marriage and the Family, 65,* 170–183.

Knight, B. (2004). *Psychotherapy with older adults.* Thousand Oaks, CA: Sage.

Kornhaber, A. (1996). *Contemporary grandparenting.* Thousand Oaks, CA: Sage.

Krause, N. (2006). Social relationships in later life. In R. Binstock & L. George (Eds.), *Handbook of aging and the social sciences* (6th ed., pp. 182–201). San Antonio, TX: Academic Press.

Kruk, E. (1995). Grandparent-grandchild contact loss: Findings from a study of "grandparents' rights" members. *Canadian Journal of Aging, 14,* 737–754.

Kunzmann, U., & Gruhn, D. (2005). Age differences in emotional reactivity: The sample case of sadness. *Psychology and Aging, 20,* 47–59.

Lawton, M. P., Kleban, M. H., Rajagopal, D., & Dean, J. (1992). Dimensions of affective experience in three age groups. *Psychology and Aging, 7,* 171–184.

Lazarus, R. S. (1996). The role of coping in the emotions and how coping changes over the life course. In C. Magai & S. H. McFadden (Eds.), *Handbook of emotion, adult development, and aging* (pp. 289–306). San Diego, CA: Academic Press.

Lee, G. R., DeMaris, A., Bavin, S., & Sullivan, R. (2001). Gender differences in the depressive effect of widowhood in later life. *Journal of Gerontology: Social Sciences, 56B,* S56–S61.

Lee, G. R., Willetts, M. C., & Seccombe, K. (1998). Widowhood and depression. *Research on Aging, 20,* 611–630.

Li, G. (1995). The interaction effect of bereavement and sex on the risk of suicide in the elderly: An historical cohort study. *Social Science and Medicine, 40,* 825–828.

Lopata, H. Z. (1993). The support systems of American urban widows. In M. S. Stroebe, W. Stroebe, & R. O. Hansson (Eds.), *Handbook of bereavement: Theory, research, and intervention* (pp. 381–396). Cambridge, England: Cambridge University Press.

Lopata, H. Z. (1996). *Current widowhood: Myths and realities.* Thousand Oaks, CA: Sage.

Lund, D. A., Caserta, M. S., & Dimond, M. F. (1989). Impact of spousal bereavement on the subjective well-being of older adults. In D. A. Lund (Ed.), *Older bereaved spouses: Research with practical implications* (pp. 3–15). New York: Taylor & Francis/Hemisphere.

Lund, D. A., Caserta, M. S., & Dimond, M. F. (1993). The course of spousal bereavement in later life. In M. S. Stroebe, W. Stroebe, & R. O. Hansson (Eds.), *Handbook of bereavement: Theory, research, and intervention* (pp. 240–254). Cambridge, England: Cambridge University Press.

Marsiske, M., & Margrett, J. (2006). Everyday problem solving and decision-making. In J. E. Birren & K. W. Schaie (Eds.), *Handbook of the psychology of aging* (6th ed., pp. 315–342). San Antonio, TX: Academic Press.

Marwit, S. J., & Meuser, T. M. (2002). Development and initial validation of an inventory to assess grief in caregivers of persons with Alzheimer's disease. *Gerontologist, 42,* 751–765.

Mayer, M. (2001). Chronic sorrow in caregiving spouses of patients with Alzheimer's disease. *Journal of Aging and Identity, 6,* 49–60.

Meuser, T. M., & Marwit, S. J. (2001). A comprehensive stage-sensitive model of grief in dementia caregiving. *Gerontologist, 41,* 658–670.

Miltenberger, P., Hayslip, B., Harris, B., & Kaminski, P. (2003–2004). Perceptions of the losses experienced by custodial grandmothers. *Omega, 48,* 245–262.

Moore, A., & Stratton, D. (2002). *Resilient widowers: Older men speak for themselves.* New York: Springer.

Moss, M. S., & Moss, S. Z. (1989). Death of the very old. In K. J. Doka (Ed.), *Disenfranchised grief: Recognizing hidden sorrow* (pp. 213–227). Lexington, MA: Lexington Books.

Moss, M. S., & Moss, S. Z. (1994). Death and bereavement. In R. Blieszner & V. H. Bedford (Eds.), *Aging and the family: Theory and research* (pp. 422–439). Westport, CT: Praeger.

Murdock, M. E., Guarnaccia, C. A., Hayslip, B., Jr., & McKibbin, C. L. (1998). The contribution of small life events to the psychological distress of married and widowed older women. *Journal of Women and Aging, 10,* 3–22.

Murrell, S. A., Himmelfarb, S., & Phifer, J. F. (1988). Effects of bereavement/loss and pre-event status on subsequent physical health in older adults. *International Journal of Aging and Human Development, 27,* 89–107.

Nelson, E., & Dannefer, D. (1992). Aged heterogeneity: Fact or fiction? The fate of diversity in gerontological research. *Gerontologist, 32,* 17–23.

O'Bryant, S. L., & Hansson, R. O. (1994). Widowhood. In R. Blieszner & V. H. Bedford (Eds.), *Aging and the family: Theory and research* (pp. 440–458). Westport, CT: Praeger.

Ong, A. D., & Bergeman, C. S. (2004). The complexity of emotions in later life. *Journal of Gerontology: Psychological Sciences, 59B,* P117–P122.

Parkes, C. M. (1997). Bereavement and mental health in the elderly. *Reviews in Clinical Gerontology, 7,* 47–53.

Parkes, C. M. (2001). *Bereavement: Studies of grief in adult life* (3rd ed.). New York: Routledge/Taylor & Francis.

Pasupathi, M., Henry, R. M., & Carstensen, L. L. (2002). Age and ethnicity differences in storytelling to young children: Emotionality, relationality, and socialization. *Psychology and Aging, 17,* 610–621.

Peterson, R. (2003). *Mild cognitive impairment.* Oxford: Oxford University Press.

Poindexter, C., & Linsk, N. (1998, September/October). The sources of social support in a sample of HIV infected older minority caregivers. *Families in Society,* 491–503.

Ponzetti, J., & Johnson, M. (1991). The forgotten grievers: Grandparents' reactions to the death of grandchildren. *Death Studies, 15,* 157–163.

Prigerson, H. G., Cherlin, E., Chen, J. H., Kasl, S. V., Hurzeler, R., & Bradley, E. H. (2003). The Stressful Caregiving Adult Reactions to Experiences of Dying (SCARED) scale. *American Journal of Geriatric Psychiatry, 11,* 309–319.

Prigerson, H., & Jacobs, S. (2001). Traumatic grief as a distinct disorder: A rationale, consensus criteria, and a preliminary empirical test. In M. Stroebe, R. O. Hansson, W. Stroebe, & H. Schut (Eds.), *Handbook of bereavement research: Consequences, coping, and care* (pp. 613–645). Washington, DC: American Psychological Association.

Quadagno, J. (2002). *Aging and the life course: An introduction to social gerontology* (2nd ed.). Boston: McGraw-Hill.

Raphael, B., Middleton, W., Martinek, N., & Misso, V. (1993). Counseling and therapy of the bereaved. In M. S. Stroebe, W. Stroebe, & R. O. Hansson (Eds.), *Handbook of bereavement: Theory, research, and intervention* (pp. 427–453). Cambridge, England: Cambridge University Press.

Reed, M. (2003). *Grandparents cry twice: Help for bereaved grandparents.* Amityville, NY: Baywood.

Robinson, L., Clare, L., & Evans, K. (2005). Making sense of dementia and adjusting to loss: Psychological reactions to a diagnosis of dementia in couples. *Journal of Aging and Mental Health, 9,* 337–347.

Robinson-Whelen, S., Tata, Y., & MacCallum, R. (2001). Long-term caregiving: What happens when it ends? *Journal of Abnormal Psychology, 110,* 573–584.

Rosenbloom, C. A., & Whittington, F. J. (1993). The effects of bereavement on eating behaviors and nutrient intakes in elderly widowed persons. *Journal of Gerontology: Social Sciences, 48,* S223–S229.

Rosenzweig, A., Prigerson, H., Miller, M. D., & Reynolds, C. F., III. (1997). Bereavement and late-life depression: Grief and its complications in the elderly. *Annual Review of Medicine, 48,* 421–428.

Rothermund, K., & Brandtstadter, J. (2003). Coping with deficits and losses in later life: From compensatory action to accommodation. *Psychology and Aging, 18,* 896–905.

Sable, P. (1991). Attachment, loss of spouse, and grief in elderly adults. *Omega, 23,* 129–142.

Sanders, C. (1989). *Grief: The mourning after.* New York: Wiley.

Sanders, S., & Sharp, A. (2004). Utilization of a psychoeducational group approach for addressing issues of grief and loss in caregivers of individuals with Alzheimer's disease. *Journal of Social Work in Long Term Care, 3,* 71–89.

Schaie, K. W. (1994). The course of adult intellectual development. *American Psychologist, 49,* 304–313.

Shuchter, S., & Zisook, S. (1993). The course of normal grief. In M. Stroebe, W. Stroebe, & R. O. Hansson (Eds.), *Handbook of bereavement: Consequences, coping, and care* (pp. 23–43). New York: Cambridge University Press.

Schulz, R., Beach, S. R., Lind, B., Martire, L. M., Zdaniuk, B., Hirsch, C., et al. (2001). Involvement in caregiving and adjustment to death of a spouse. *Journal of the American Medical Association, 285,* 3123–3129.

Schulz, R., & Heckhausen, J. (1996). A life span model of successful aging. *American Psychologist, 51,* 702–714.

Schulz, R., & Martire, L. M. (1998). Intervention research with older adults: Introduction, overview, and future directions. *Annual Review of Gerontology and Geriatrics, 18,* 1–16.

Schut, H., Stroebe, M., van den Bout, J., & Terheggen, M. (2001). The efficacy of bereavement interventions: Who benefits? In M. S. Stroebe, R. O. Hansson, W. Stroebe, & H. Schut (Eds.), *Handbook of bereavement research: Consequences, coping and care* (pp. 705–737). Washington, DC: American Psychological Association.

Silin, P. S. (2001). *Nursing homes: The family's journey.* Johns Hopkins University Press: Baltimore, MD.

Sinnott, J. (1996). The developmental approach: Post formal thought as adaptive intelligence. In F. Blanchard-Fields & T. M. Hess (Eds.), *Perspectives on cognitive change in adulthood and aging* (pp. 358–383). New York: McGraw-Hill.

Somary, K., & Stricker, G. (1998). Becoming a grandparent: A longitudinal study of expectations and experiences as a function of sex and lineage. *Gerontologist, 38,* 53–61.

Stroebe, M. S., & Schut, H. A. W. (1999). The dual process model of coping with bereavement: Rationale and description. *Death Studies, 23,* 197–224.

Stroebe, M. S., & Schut, H. (2001). Meaning making in the dual process model. In R. Neimeyer (Ed.), *Meaning reconstruction and the experience of loss* (pp. 55–73). Washington, DC: American Psychological Association.

Stroebe, M. S., & Stroebe, W. (1993). The mortality of bereavement: A review. In M. S. Stroebe, W. Stroebe, & R. O. Hansson (Eds.), *Handbook of bereavement: Theory, research, and intervention* (pp. 175–195). Cambridge, England: Cambridge University Press.

Stroebe, W., & Schut, H. A. W. (2001). Risk factors in bereavement outcome: A methodological and empirical review. In M. S. Stroebe, R. O. Hansson, W. Stroebe, & H. Schut (Eds.), *Handbook of bereavement research: Consequences, coping and care* (pp. 349–371). Washington, DC: American Psychological Association.

Stroebe, W., & Stroebe, M. S. (1987). *Bereavement and health: The psychological and physical consequences of partner loss.* Cambridge, England: Cambridge University Press.

Stroebe, W., Stroebe, M., Abakoumkin, G., & Schut, H. (1996). Social and emotional loneliness: A comparison of attachment and stress theory explanations. *Journal of Personality and Social Psychology, 70,* 1241–1249.

Stroebe, W., Zech, E., Stroebe, M., & Abakoumkin, G. (in press). Does social support help in bereavement? *Journal of Social and Clinical Psychology.*

Szanto, K., Gildengers, A., Mulsant, B. H., Brown, G., Alexopoulos, G. S., & Reynolds, C. F., III. (2002). Identification of suicidal ideation and prevention of suicidal behavior in the elderly. *Drugs and Aging, 19,* 11–24.

Thompson, L. W., Gallagher-Thompson, D., Futterman, A., Gilewski, M. J., & Peterson, J. (1991). The effects of late-life spousal bereavement over a 30-month interval. *Psychology and Aging, 6,* 434–441.

Uhlenberg, P., & Hammill, B. (1998). Frequency of grandparent contact with grandchild sets: Six factors that make a difference. *Gerontologist, 38,* 276–285.

U.S. Department of Health and Human Services. (2002, September 16). *National vital statistics report* (Vol. 50, No. 16). Hyattsville, MD: Centers for Disease Control and Prevention, National Center for Health Statistics. Available from http://www.cdc.gov/nchs/fastats/pdf/hvsr_16t1.pdf.

U.S. Department of Health and Human Services. (2003). *Health, United States, 2003* (Special excerpt: Trend tables on 65 and older population). Washington, DC: Centers for Disease Control and Prevention, National Center for Health Statistics.

Utz, R. L. (2006). Economic and practical adjustments to late life spousal loss. In D. Carr, R. Nesse, & C. Wortman (Eds.), *Spousal bereavement in late life* (pp. 167–194). New York: Springer.

van Baarsen, B., van Duijn, M. A. J., Smit, J. H., Snijders, T. A. B., & Knipscheer, K. P. M. (2001–2002). Patterns of adjustment to partner loss in old age: The widowhood adaptation longitudinal study. *Omega, 44,* 5–36.

van Grootheest, D. S., Beekman, A. T. F., Van Groenou, M. I. B., & Deeg, D. J. H. (1999). Sex differences in depression after widowhood: Do men suffer more? *Social Psychiatry and Psychiatric Epidemiology, 34,* 391–398.

Wells, Y. D., & Kendig, H. L. (1997). Health and well-being of spouse caregivers and the widowed. *Gerontologist, 37,* 666–674.

Welsh-Bohmer, K. A., & Warren, L. H. (2006). Neurodegenerative dementias. In D. K. Attix & K. A. Welsh-Bohmer (Eds.), *Geriatric neuropsychology: Assessment and intervention* (pp. 56–88). New York: Guilford Press.

Williams-Conway, S., Hayslip, B., & Tandy, R. (1991). Similarity of perceptions of bereavement experiences between widows and professionals. *Omega, 23,* 35–49.

Winston, C. (2003). African American grandmothers parenting grandchild orphaned by AIDS: Grieving and coping with loss. *Illness, crisis, and loss, 11,* 350–361.

Wolff, K., & Wortman, C. (2006). Psychological consequences of spousal loss among older adults: Understanding the diversity of responses. In D. Carr, R. Nesse, & C. Wortman (Eds.), *Spousal bereavement in late life* (pp. 81–116). New York: Springer.

Wolinsky, F. D., & Johnson, R. J. (1992). Widowhood, health status, and the use of health services by older adults: A cross-sectional and prospective approach. *Journal of Gerontology: Social Sciences, 47,* S8–S16.

Wortman, C. B., Silver, R. C., & Kessler, R. C. (1993). The meaning of loss and adjustment to bereavement. In M. S. Stroebe, W. Stroebe, & R. O. Hansson (Eds.), *Handbook of bereavement: Theory, research, and intervention* (pp. 349–366). Cambridge, England: Cambridge University Press.

Zick, C. D., & Smith, K. R. (1991). Patterns of economic change surrounding the death of a spouse. *Journal of Gerontology: Social Sciences, 46,* S310–S320.

PART IV

EVIDENCE-BASED FAMILY AND COMMUNITY PRACTICE

CHAPTER 15

Parenting Grandchildren

HWA-OK HANNAH PARK and JAN STEVEN GREENBERG

During the decades of the 1970s and 1980s, researchers focused on the significance and meaning of grandparenthood and on the grandparents' level of satisfaction with this role (Cherlin & Furstenberg, 1986; Kornhaber, 1985; Troll, 1983; Wood & Robertson, 1976). This interest in grandparenthood was explained, in part, by increases in the life expectancy of individuals along with improvements in the health of older adults and a rapid growth in the number of single-parent families due to divorce or nonmarital parenthood (Pruchno & Johnson, 1996; Robertson, 1995). Longer life expectancy and improved health and functioning of older adults has both extended the length of the grandparenting role as well as the number of years in which older adults remain actively involved in the life of their grandchildren. Whereas in 1900, most grandchildren never knew their grandparents, by 2000 over 96% of children under the age of 20 had at least one living grandparent (Cherlin & Furstenberg, 1986; Uhlenberg & Kirby, 1998).

During the past decade, the focus has shifted away from the normative role of grandparenthood to the role of grandparents as caregivers to their grandchildren (Fuller-Thomson, Minkler, & Driver, 1997). According to the U.S. Census Bureau, the number of children under 18 living in households headed by a grandparent has grown from 2.2 million (or 3.2% of children in the United States) in 1970 to approximately 4 million (or 5.5% of children) in 1997 (Lugaila, 1998). Although the majority of grandparent-headed households also include at least one of the grandchild's parents, since 1990 the fastest growing type of grandparent-headed household is one in which the grandparents and their grandchildren reside together without the grandchild's parents. By 2000, it has been estimated that approximately 2.4 million grandparents were responsible for most of the basic needs of their grandchildren (Bryson, 2001).

The role of grandparent caregiving has many challenges in common with those faced by elders caring for a frail elderly family member. Both grandparent caregivers and caregivers of elders are faced with multiple care-giving demands that require an output of time and energy at a time in their lives when they may be experiencing diminished capacity due to age-related changes. In addition, the challenges of caregiving are likely to have rippling effects, producing additional strains in the areas of finances and family and social relationships. Finally, although the burdens of care are always present, both groups of caregivers are likely to experience many aspects of the care-giving role as rewarding and providing feelings of intimacy and a sense of meaning and purpose in life (Jendrek, 1993; Kramer, 1997; Minkler & Roe, 1993; Schwartz & Gidron, 2002).

Yet the differences between caring for a grandchild and caring for a frail elderly relative are greater than the similarities. First, the distinctive nature of the grandparent-grandchild relationship gives rise to several unique stressors faced by grandparent caregivers that are not commonly encountered by other care-giving populations. Whereas most caregivers for the elderly are legally empowered to make decisions for the elder, legal custody of a child is not automatically bestowed on grandparent caregivers. Grandparents thus must seek the parents' permission to make decisions for the child. This can be quite stressful if the grandparent and parent have differing views of what is in the best interest of the child. In addition, although all caregivers face housing challenges, grandparent caregivers living in public housing for seniors, which is not uncommon, may fear eviction if their skipped-generation family configuration violates the existing regulations for senior housing. Another challenge faced by grandparent caregivers is dealing with school systems, which are oriented toward younger families. These are but a few examples of the stressors encountered by many grandparent caregivers that are not typically faced by caregivers of frail elders.

Second, whereas most caregivers of older adults will outlive the care recipient, a major burden for grandparent caregivers is worrying about the future wellbeing of their grandchild after the grandparents' death. "What will happen when I'm gone?" is a universal concern. Third, grandparent caregivers may be viewed by others as not being able to care for their grandchildren. Older grandparents may especially feel that they are being closely watched and quite vulnerable to having their grandchild taken away (Janicki, McCallion, Grant-Griffin, & Kolomer, 2000). This is rarely a concern among spousal or filial caregivers of older adults or parents caring for children with disabilities.

Fourth, most caregivers are providing care for a frail elder because of the elder's chronic cognitive, mental, or physical disability, whereas grandparents typically have assumed the care-giving role because of the parents' incapacity. Thus, it is not uncommon for grandparents to not only have care-giving responsibilities for their grandchild but also be providing considerable support and assistance to the grandchild's parent. Finally, whereas the trajectory of an elder's disability is typically one of increasing disability of the care recipient and greater dependence on the caregiver, grandchildren move toward greater independence as they age. As the grandchild moves into adolescence, grandparents have diminishing influence over the grandchild's behavior. Coping with adolescence is in general a stressful time for parents, and may be amplified for grandparents because of the wider cultural gap between the generations. As we discuss in this chapter, these unique challenges faced by grandparents must be considered in developing community-based programs and services to target grandparents caring for their grandchild.

This chapter begins with an overview of the literature on the prevalence of the grandparent care-giving phenomenon and provides a description of the characteristics of this emerging and growing population. Next, we examine the context of grandparent caregiving, reasons for providing primary care to grandchildren, the impact of caregiving on grandparents, and factors associated with the well-being of grandparent caregivers. Economic policy issues related to grandparent caregivers are reviewed and evidence-based interventions for grandparent caregivers and their families are considered. Finally, recommendations for practice, policy, and future research are discussed.

A PROFILE OF GRANDPARENT CAREGIVERS IN THE UNITED STATES

PREVALENCE

As shown in Figure 15.1, in 2000 5.3% (approximately 3.8 million) children under the age of 18 lived in a household headed by grandparents, and of these, 1.4 million lived in a grandparent-headed household with neither parent being

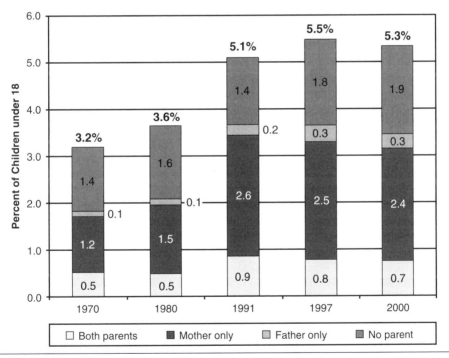

Figure 15.1   Grandchildren in Grandparents' Home, by Presence of Parents. *Sources: Table CH-7: Grandchildren Living in the Home of Their Grandparents: 1970 to Present,* by the U.S. Bureau of the Census, 2004, retrieved May 10, 2006, from www.census.gov /population/socdemo/hh-fam/tabCH-7.pdf. Data from 1970 and 1980 censuses and 1991, 1997, and 2000, Current Population Surveys as reported in *America's Families and Living Arrangements: 2000* (U.S. Census Bureau, Current Population Reports, Series P20-537), by J. Fields and L. Casper, 2001, Washington, DC: U.S. Government Printing Office, and earlier reports.

present, a family structure we refer to as the "skipped generation." Between 1970 and 1991, substantial increases occurred in the number of children living with a single parent in a grandparent's home. In 1970, approximately 817,000 or 1.2% of children lived with their mother in their grandparent's home. By 1991, this increased to 1,674,000 or 2.6% of children. As shown in Figure 15.1, there also was a considerable increase between 1991 and 1997 in the number of grandchildren living with their grandparents only. In 1991, 1.4% of children (937,000) lived with their grandparents only; by 1997 the number grew to 1.8% (1,309,000). The number of these skipped-generation households (no parent present) continued to increase in 2000, although other family structures involving grandparents remained stable or showed a slight decline.

As can be seen in Table 15.1, the likelihood of a child living with his or her grandparents is strongly influenced by race. In 2001, African American children were more than twice as likely as White children to be living with their grandparents. For both African American and White children, there has been a dramatic drop in the number of children living in a two-parent household along with their grandparent. The number of White children who live with a single parent and a grandparent increased by 55% between 1940 and 2001. In contrast, there has been a 155% increase during the same period in the number of African American children living with a single parent and grandparent. The proportion of White children living with a grandparent only (an indicator that the grandparent is the sole caregiver of the grandchild) has been relatively stable since 1970. Although the proportion of African American children living in this type of family declined between 1960 and 1980, this trend has reversed itself in recent years and grew approximately 6% between 1980 and 2001.

Table 15.1
Percent of Children under 18 with Grandparent in Home by Number of Parents in Home and Race: 1940–2001

Year	Total			Two Parents			One Parent			No Parent		
	White	Black	Racial Diff. (W–B)	White	Black	Racial Diff. (W–B)	White	Black	Racial Diff. (W–B)	White	Black	Racial Diff. (W–B)
1940	10.3	16.0	−5.7	7.2	5.3	1.9	1.8	3.1	−1.3	1.3	7.6	−6.3
1950	10.6	18.5	−7.9	7.7	6.9	0.8	1.8	4.0	−2.2	1.1	7.6	−6.5
1960	6.8	15.8	−9.0	4.7	5.2	−0.5	1.4	4.4	−3.0	0.7	6.2	−5.5
1970	5.4	13.0	−7.6	3.0	3.5	−0.5	1.2	4.6	−3.4	0.9	4.9	−4.0
1980	4.8	12.2	−7.4	2.3	1.7	0.6	1.5	5.7	−4.2	1.0	4.8	−3.8
1991	5.3	14.9	−9.6	2.1	1.1	1.0	2.3	8.4	−6.1	0.9	5.4	−4.5
2001	6.8	14.8	−8.0	2.7	1.6	1.1	2.8	7.9	−5.1	1.2	5.1	−3.9

Sources: America's Children: Resources from Family, Government, and the Economy, by D. J. Hernandez and D. E. Meyer, 1993, New York: Russell Sage Foundation; "Grandparenthood over Time: Historical and Demographic Trends" (pp. 23–39), by P. Uhlenberg and J. B. Kirby, in M. E. Szinovacz (Ed.), *Handbook on Grandparenthood*, 1998, Westport, CT: Greenwood Press; *The Diverse Living Arrangements of Children: Summer 1991* (Current Population Reports, Household Economic Studies, P70-38) by the U.S. Bureau of the Census, 1994, Washington, DC: U.S. Government Printing Office, retrieved May 10, 2006, from http://www.census.gov /population/socdemo/child/p70-38.pdf; and *Table C2: Household Relationship and Living Arrangements of Children under 18 Years*, by the U.S. Bureau of the Census, 2001b, retrieved May 10, 2006, from http://www .census.gov/population/www/socdemo/hh-fam/p20-537_00.html. Reprinted with permission.

Demographic Characteristics of Grandparent-Headed Families

Bryson and Casper (1999), using data from the 1997 Current Population Survey (CPS), report that 51% of grandparent-headed families are maintained by both grandparents, 43% by grandmothers with no spouse present, and only 6% by grandfathers alone, regardless of the presence of a parent. Among these families, substantial differences emerge between grandmothers living in skipped-generation families (no parent present) and other grandparent-headed family structures (i.e., grandmothers living with a grandchild and the grandchild's parent; grandmothers living with their spouse, a grandchild, and the grandchild's parent; and grandfather-headed families). As shown in Table 15.2, single grandmother caregivers in skipped-generation families were more likely than other grandparent heads of household to be Black, poor, and in poor or fair health and less likely to have graduated from high school and be employed.

U.S. Census Bureau data do not allow one to determine how families headed by grandparent caregivers differ from other families headed by grandparents who do not live with grandchildren because the Census Bureau does not ask respondents whether they are grandparents. Grandparent families are identifiable only if the respondent has grandchildren in the household. To investigate how grandparents caring for grandchildren differ from the general population of grandparents without these care-giving responsibilities, Fuller-Thomson et al. (1997) investigated the characteristics of grandparents who had assumed primary responsibilities for their grandchildren for at least 6 months ("custodial grandparents," as the authors referred to them), using data from the 1992–1994 National Survey of Families and Households (NSFH). They found that more than 1 in 10 grandparents (10.9% of 3,477 grandparents in the study) in the United States cared for a grandchild for at least 6 months at some point in their lives. Among the final sample of 173 custodial grandparents interviewed, 77% were women and the majority (62%) were non-Hispanic White; 27% were Black, 54% were married, and 43% had less than a high school education. The mean age of the custodial grandparents in 1993 was 59.4 years. They had mean incomes of $31,643 and 23% reported living in poverty. When compared to grandparents with no primary responsibilities for a grandchildren's care, custodial grandparents were more likely to be younger, Black, women, and living in poverty. These grandparent caregivers were less likely to have completed high school and less likely to be currently married.

In summary, a common profile of grandparent caregivers is emerging. First, grandmothers are more likely to be caring for grandchildren than are grandfathers. As has been noted, women are far more likely to provide the vast majority of family care over their life course (Neal, Chapman, Ingersoll-Dayton, & Emlen, 1993) than men, who tend to assume a supportive and secondary role (Goldberg-Glen & Sands, 2000). Thus, it is not surprising that the CPS data indicate that 62% of grandparents who maintained families for their grandchildren in 1997 were grandmothers (Bryson & Casper, 1999).

Second, many care-giving grandparents are younger than age 65, with many still in their midlife (aged 45 to 55), which casts doubt on the "frail, dependent grandparents" image. Many care-giving grandparents are still actively providing care for their older parents and working part or full time (Jendrek, 2003).

Third, although the phenomenon of grandparent caregiving appears to have become more common across racial groups, children living in grandparent-headed households are disproportionately represented by minority groups. In

Table 15.2

Characteristics of Grandparents Who Coreside with Grandchildren
in Grandparent-Maintained Families: 1997

| | | Grandparent-Maintained Families | | | | |
| | | Skipped-Generational Household (No Parent) | | Three-Generational Household (At Least One Parent) | | |
Characteristics	Total	Grand-mother Only	Both Grand-parents	Grand-mother Only	Both Grand-parents	Grand-father Only*
Grandmothers, total (number)	2,292	340	412	702	838	(X)
Percent distribution of grandmothers	100.0	100.0	100.0	100.0	100.0	(X)
Age						
Under 45	19.4	6.9	14.8	24.2	22.9	(X)
45–54	36.0	34.1	35.2	30.1	42.0	(X)
55–64	29.5	36.9	36.4	25.4	26.5	(X)
65 and older	15.1	22.2	13.6	20.3	8.6	(X)
Race and Ethnicity						
Caucasian	48.0	27.9	62.8	38.6	56.7	(X)
African American	31.0	53.5	18.8	45.4	16.0	(X)
Hispanic	16.4	15.8	15.3	12.5	20.5	(X)
Other	4.5	2.8	3.2	3.5	6.8	(X)
Education						
< High school graduate	35.5	45.9	41.0	36.6	27.7	(X)
High school graduate	40.2	30.4	39.3	38.5	45.9	(X)
Some college	24.3	23.7	19.7	25.0	26.4	(X)
Marital Status						
Married, spouse present	56.1	0.9	100.0	4.8	100.0	(X)
Divorced, separated	22.9	50.3	na	50.4	na	(X)
Widowed	15.4	36.1	na	32.9	na	(X)
Never married	5.5	12.7	na	11.9	na	(X)
Work Experience in 1996						
Did not work	43.6	61.8	46.3	38.2	39.3	(X)
Worked part-time	19.6	16.8	21.5	16.3	22.5	(X)
Worked full-time	36.9	21.4	32.2	45.6	38.3	(X)
Mean Income						
Total household	$43,783	$19,750	$41,709	$35,334	$61,632	(X)
Grandmother's	$14,063	$13,402	$11,028	$16,906	$13,440	(X)
Poverty Status						
Poor	23.0	57.2	14.4	26.9	10.0	(X)
Not poor	77.0	42.8	85.6	73.1	90.0	(X)
General State of Health						
Fair or poor	33.6	51.0	28.9	36.4	26.5	(X)
Good	31.2	27.9	32.4	26.4	36.0	(X)
Very good	21.9	12.0	27.2	22.9	22.6	(X)
Excellent	13.3	9.1	11.6	14.3	14.9	(X)

(continued)

Table 15.2 *(Continued)*

Characteristics	Total	Grandparent-Maintained Families				
		Skipped-Generational Household (No Parent)		Three-Generational Household (At Least One Parent)		Grand-father Only*
		Grand-mother Only	Both Grand-parents	Grand-mother Only	Both Grand-parents	
Grandfathers, total (number)	1,402	(X)	412	(X)	838	152
Percent distribution of grandfathers	100.0	(X)	100.0	(X)	100.0	100.0
Age						
Under 45	14.9	(X)	11.0	(X)	16.9	13.8
45 to 54	32.0	(X)	23.7	(X)	38.4	19.3
55 to 64	32.6	(X)	38.8	(X)	29.9	31.0
65 and older	20.5	(X)	26.5	(X)	14.8	35.9
Race and Ethnicity						
Caucasian	60.3	(X)	63.6	(X)	59.0	58.1
African American	18.3	(X)	19.5	(X)	16.2	26.0
Hispanic	17.3	(X)	14.6	(X)	19.2	14.1
Other	4.2	(X)	2.2	(X)	5.6	1.7
Education						
< High school graduate	37.1	(X)	40.6	(X)	35.3	37.7
High school graduate	37.1	(X)	36.1	(X)	37.6	36.6
Some college	25.8	(X)	23.3	(X)	27.1	25.6
Marital Status						
Married, spouse present	90.1	(X)	100.0	(X)	100.0	8.6
Divorced, separated	6.1	(X)	(X)	(X)	(X)	56.0
Widowed	3.2	(X)	(X)	(X)	(X)	29.0
Never married	0.7	(X)	(X)	(X)	(X)	6.4
Work Experience in 1996						
Did not work	27.9	(X)	30.6	(X)	22.7	49.3
Worked part-time	17.5	(X)	19.9	(X)	17.4	12.0
Worked full-time	54.5	(X)	49.5	(X)	59.9	38.7
Mean Income						
Total household	$53,811	(X)	$41,709	(X)	$61,632	$43,476
Grandmother's	$27,259	(X)	$24,852	(X)	$29,296	$22,561
Poverty Status						
Poor	12.4	(X)	14.4	(X)	10.0	19.9
Not poor	87.6	(X)	85.6	(X)	90.0	80.1
General State of Health						
Fair or poor	28.7	(X)	32.7	(X)	24.6	40.0
Good	33.9	(X)	31.1	(X)	35.6	31.9
Very good	22.0	(X)	21.5	(X)	24.4	10.1
Excellent	15.4	(X)	14.7	(X)	15.3	18.0

Note: Numbers in thousands, Percent distribution of characteristics. (X) = Not applicable.

* Grandfather-maintained families may or may not include a parent of the children. The investigators combined skipped- with three-generation families headed by grandfathers in their report due to the small sample size, as compared to the size of other types of grandparent-headed families.

Adapted from *Coresident Grandparents and Grandchildren: U.S. Bureau of the Census, Current Population Reports, P23–198.* by K. R. Bryson, and L. Casper, (1999), retrieved May 9, 2006, from http://www.census.gov

2000, 12.1% of all African American children under 18 years of age were living with grandparents, compared to 6.1% of Hispanic and 3.4% of Caucasian children (U.S. Bureau of the Census, 2001b). With regard to the lifetime prevalence of grandparent primary caregiving, a U.S. national study using the NSFH suggests that about 30% of African American grandmothers and 14% of African American grandfathers had assumed primary responsibility for a grandchild for at least 6 months (Szinovacz, 1998), compared with 11% of the total number of 3,477 grandparents in the study who did so (Fuller-Thomson et al., 1997).

Finally, one of the most striking findings is the disproportionately high level of poverty among grandparent caregivers. In the 1997 CPS data, 57% of single grandmother caregivers in the skipped-generation families lived in poverty (Casper & Bryson, 1998), and 58% of the 479 self-identified grandparent primary caregivers in an American Association of Retired Persons' study reported living on a fixed income (Woodworth, 1996). Thus, the prototypical grandparent caring for a grandchild is an African American single woman in midlife who is living in poverty.

CONTEXT OF GRANDPARENT CAREGIVING

REASONS FOR PROVIDING PRIMARY CARE TO GRANDCHILDREN

The available evidence suggests that grandparents do not seek out the role of co-parent or caregiver to their grandchildren, but are thrust into the role because of problems in the lives of their adult children (Goodman & Silverstein, 2002; Jendrek, 1993; Pruchno & McKenney, 2000). These problems include parental substance abuse (Burton, 1992; Goodman & Silverstein, 2002; Joslin & Brouard, 1995; Kelley, 1993; Minkler & Roe, 1993; Pruchno & McKenney, 2000), child abuse, neglect, or abandonment (Dubowitz & Feigelman, 1993; Jendrek, 1994), incarceration (Dressel & Barnhill, 1994; Woodworth, 1996), divorce (Cherlin & Furstenberg, 1986), AIDS (Burnette, 1997; Joslin & Brouard, 1995), teenage parenthood (Goodman & Silverstein, 2002; Pruchno & McKenney, 2000), and parental death (Jendrek, 1994). Other researchers note that the legal mandates and related changes in child welfare reimbursement policies and practices, which have significantly increased placement with relatives, help explain part of the increase in grandparent care (Bell & Garner, 1996; Harden, Clark, & Maguire, 1997).

However, the reasons grandparents assume primary care-giving responsibilities for their grandchildren are very complex and interrelated. For example, a biological parent's dependency on alcohol or drugs may result in child abuse or neglect. Financial difficulties resulting from parental unemployment were also found to be common reasons for grandparents assuming primary care of grandchildren (Burnette, 1997; Minkler, Berrick, & Needell, 1999; Woodworth, 1996). Thus, the reasons for assuming a care-giving role for a grandchild are tied in fundamental ways to one another. Although conceptually one can distinguish among the reasons, in the real lives of these families they are so closely interrelated that efforts to distinguish the primary from the secondary reasons for taking on the role are often quite arbitrary.

IMPACT OF CAREGIVING ON GRANDPARENTS

Research examining the psychological well-being of grandparent primary caregivers has documented the elevated psychological distress among this population. Recent research has identified these older caregivers as "hidden patients"

(Roe, Minkler, Saunders, & Thomson, 1996), particularly if they live in poor communities or have insufficient economic resources (Joslin & Harrison, 1998). Grandparent primary caretakers have generally been found to have elevated levels of psychological distress, in particular depressive symptoms, compared to grandparents who provide supplemental care to grandchildren (Bowers & Myers, 1999; Musil, 2000), filial or spousal caregivers (Strawbridge, Wallhagen, Shema, & Kaplan, 1997), age-matched peers who are not caregivers (Minkler, Fuller-Thomson, Miller, & Driver, 1997), a normative sample of parents (Kelley, 1993), or members of the general population (Janicki et al., 2000; Kelley, Whitley, Sipe, & Yorker, 2000).

In one of the more rigorously designed longitudinal studies of caregivers, spanning 20 years, Strawbridge and his colleagues (1997) compared three groups of caregivers (filial caregivers, spousal caregivers, and grandparent caregivers) to noncaregivers. They found that, in 1974, filial and spousal caregivers did not differ from noncaregivers, but grandparent caregivers had poorer health than noncaregivers and more stressful life events (e.g., serious illness, financial problems, marital problems) than the other two groups. Analysis of the second wave of data collected 20 years later revealed that the depressive symptoms of all three groups were greater than that of noncaregivers. Also, grandparents reported poorer mental and physical health and more activity limitations than the other two groups. The authors concluded that filial and spousal caregiving constitute a new burden in an otherwise "normal" life, whereas caring for grandchildren represents "yet another aspect of a difficult life course" (p. 505).

In addition, grandparent caregiving affects not only mental health but also physical health. Grandmother caregivers experienced poorer physical health and a greater number of physical limitations than grandmothers who were not caregivers (Caputo, 2001) and biological mothers with low incomes (Bachman & Chase-Landsdale, 2005). Single grandmother caregivers rated their health as being poorer compared to married grandmother caregivers or married women living with a spouse (Solomon & Marx, 1999). High rates of insomnia as well as hypertension, back and stomach problems, and the frequent presence of multiple chronic health problems have been reported in both national and smaller-scale studies of grandparents raising grandchildren (Dowdell, 1995; Kelley, 1993; Roe et al., 1996). When the caregivers were great-grandmothers or had several grandchildren, they experienced a greater decline in health over the previous year. Great-grandparents or those caring for several grandchildren might lack the energy and vitality necessary to attend to the range of problems that resulted in their rearing their grandchildren. However, these grandparents were likely to minimize their health problems so that they might be up to the task of caring for their grandchildren (Pinson-Millburn, Fabian, Schlossberg, & Pyle, 1996).

Although most research has focused on declines in physical and mental health of grandparent caregivers, there is a growing attention to the effect of caregiving on the grandparent's social network. Increased social isolation has been widely recognized as a consequence of caregiving generally, and more specifically among grandparents caring for grandchildren. A study of urban African American grandparents by Burton and deVries (1992) found that the caregivers often felt socially isolated. Those caring for grandchildren in skipped-generation households as a result of parental AIDS or substance abuse experienced feelings of alienation (Joslin & Harrison, 1998). Social alienation was also experienced by many younger, formerly working grandmothers who had to quit their jobs and leave behind valued work-based social ties to care for their grandchildren abandoned by crack-cocaine-addicted parents (Minkler & Roe, 1993). Thus, available research indicates that although grandparent caregivers may experience rewards from the care-giving role, there are measurable costs in terms of poorer health, increased levels of depressive symptoms, and growing social isolation.

FACTORS AFFECTING THE PHYSICAL AND MENTAL HEALTH OF CAREGIVERS

Although grandparent caregivers overall experience heightened levels of physical and psychological distress and increased social isolation, there is considerable individual heterogeneity. For some grandparents caregiving takes a significant toll on their well-being; others are able to maintain their physical and mental health. In an effort to understand this heterogeneity, researchers have begun to identify the effect of different challenges on the well-being of grandparent caregivers and the social and psychological resources that might mitigate these effects.

Given that grandparents' primary caregiving often occurs in response to a crisis, the difficulties experienced by the children (e.g., an intensification of behavioral or emotional problems) add to the care-giving challenges associated with assuming a primary care-giving role (Burnette, 2000; Hayslip, Shore, Henderson, & Lambert, 1998; Janicki et al., 2000). Consistent with the general literature on caregiving, grandparent primary caregivers face a greater risk of depression when caring for grandchildren with behavioral or emotional problems (Burnette, 2000; Hayslip et al., 1998). Higher levels of distress with the parenting role was found when grandparents report their grandchildren had a greater number of problems (e.g., resisted authority, difficulty learning, and hyperactivity), as compared to grandparents who perceived their grandchildren as having fewer difficulties (Emick & Hayslip, 1999). In a longitudinal study, grandparents caring for grandchildren with behavior problems reported higher levels of parental stress than those caring for grandchildren without such problems (Hayslip, Emick, Henderson, & Elias, 2002).

One potential source of stress is the day-to-day demands of caregiving, which can range from meeting the daily care needs of small children to helping with school work and providing transportation to and after school events. Although intuitively one would assume that grandparents who provide the greatest amount of care would have the poorest outcomes, the available evidence is inconclusive. In comparing the psychological distress among 101 grandmothers with grandchildren age 14 years or younger, Bowers and Myers (1999) found that, at the bivariate level, full-time caregivers reported higher levels of care-giving burden and parenting stress than part-time caregivers, but the group difference in parenting stress disappeared in the multivariate context. In a national study of 867 grandmothers who maintained households for their grandchildren, grandmothers in skipped-generation households were more likely than those in three-generation households to report higher levels of care-giving burden, whereas the two groups were not different in satisfaction with the care-giving role, positive affect, and negative affect (Pruchno & McKenney, 2000).

Yet Musil and Ahmad (2002) reported that grandmothers providing supplemental caregiving were more likely to experience depressive symptoms than primary caregivers when their age, education, employment, and marital status were controlled. Using the two waves of the NSFH (1987–1988 and 1992–1994), Szino-vacz, DeViney, and Atkinson (1999) reported that grandmothers who became the sole caregiver of their grandchildren between Time 1 and Time 2 were more likely to be depressed than those who between Time 1 and Time 2 became caregivers but shared it with the child's parents living in the household. However, they found higher levels of depressive symptoms among the grandmothers who continuously coresided with grandchildren and the parent at both waves than among grandparents who continuously lived with the grandchildren alone. Thus, the relationship between the amount of care provided and the well-being of the grandparent caregivers is complex and depends on the outcome of interest, whether the grandparent is the sole caregiver or shares caregiving with the child's parent, and whether or not the grandparent has recently transitioned into the role.

A common source of stress for some grandparents is ongoing conflict and tension in the relationship with the child's parent (Goodman & Silverstein, 2002). The literature on kinship care suggests that parents whose children are cared for by relatives do not simply disappear. Difficulties in the interactions with a grandchild's parent who is ill, incarcerated, or addicted were found to be one of the main sources of long-term stress for grandparent primary caregivers (Barnhill, 1996; Burton, 1992; Minkler, Roe, & Price, 1992). In in-depth interviews with 38 grandparent primary caregivers, Weber and Waldrop (2000) found that the adult children's chronic problems (e.g., having been in and out of drug rehabilitation) generate ongoing tension and conflict among all the family members. They also found that the adult children's criminal activities and unexpected life patterns created fear for the safety of the grandparents and grandchildren. A qualitative study of 10 grandparent primary caregivers found that given the difficult relationships with their troubled adult children, the grandparent caregivers often expressed feelings of personal loss (e.g., loss of their freedom, loss of their child, loss of their peer group) and feelings of guilt and disappointment about the inability or failure of their own child to parent (Morrow-Kondos, Weber, Cooper, & Hesser, 1997).

Many grandparents caring for grandchildren do not have legal authority for the grandchildren (i.e., legal custody, guardianship, or adoption). As a result, common parental tasks such as enrolling the grandchildren in school, day care, and sports activities can be difficult and frustrating, as can obtaining routine medical and dental care. Some grandparents may not be financially able to assume the considerable legal fees to obtain legal custody, and others may not wish to prove in court that their child is an incompetent parent (Flint & Perez-Porter, 1997; Morrow-Kondos et al., 1997).

Finally, financial problems are the most frequently cited source of stress for grandparent caregivers. The other stressors faced by care-giving grandparents are often compounded by significant economic difficulties, particularly among low-income grandparents (Woodworth, 1996). As noted earlier, the households headed by single grandmother caregivers have substantively higher poverty rates than other grandparent-headed family units. It is noteworthy that older grandparent caregivers who retired or who were not working at the time they assumed care-giving responsibilities often suffer from the financial burdens of increased educational, medical, dental, housing, food, and clothing expenses of caring for grandchildren (Burton, 1992; Creighton, 1991; Emick & Hayslip, 1999). Some of these grandparents reported spending their life savings, overspending an already insufficient Social Security check, or relying on welfare programs (Gibson, 1999; Mullen, 1996). For working grandparents, the assumption of care-giving responsibilities may mean quitting a job, reducing work hours, making other job-related sacrifices, or paying the substantial costs for day care and babysitters, which may place their own future economic well-being at risk (Rodgers & Jones, 1999; Sands & Goldberg-Glen, 1998). Although it is clear that grandparent caregivers experience financial strain, it is unclear whether their financial difficulties result from taking over the care-giving responsibility or from chronic financial problems prior to assuming care. Szinovacz et al. (1999) examined the change in family income prior to and after caring for grandchildren and reported that having grandchildren in the household was not associated with the change in family income.

Researchers have consistently found a significant relationship between financial strain and psychological distress among grandparent primary caregivers. Joslin (2000) documented that high psychological distress, measured by the Brief Symptoms Inventory, was found among low-income grandparent primary caregivers of grandchildren orphaned by HIV/AIDS. Data from the 1997 and 1999 National Survey of America's Families documented the importance of poverty status in predicting depressive symptoms of 1,363 grandmother primary caregivers (Park, 2004). Elevated depressive symptoms were found among those who were extremely poor (i.e., below 50% of the federal poverty line [FPL]) and poor (i.e., between 50% and 100% of the FPL) when compared to those who were nonpoor (i.e., above 200% of the FPL). Rodgers-Farmer (1999) assessed the economic strains endured by 82 care-giving grandmothers by a single item asking about their perception of income sufficiency, and found that those grandmothers who perceived that their income was insufficient were more likely to be depressed than the grandmothers who perceived that their income was sufficient. However, poverty status was not significant in predicting depression among 74 Latino grandparent primary caregivers (Burnette, 1999a, 1999b, 2000). This may suggest that the effect of financial strain on psychological distress is moderated by ethnicity.

Among the resources that help mitigate the effects of care-giving demands on caregiver well-being, many researchers have reported on the beneficial effects of informal support in meeting the needs of family caregivers (Burnette, 1999b; Kramer & Lambert, 1999; Li, Seltzer, & Greenberg, 1997; Pruchno, Patrick, & Burant, 1997). However, only a few researchers have examined the role of social support with respect to grandparent caregivers. Utilizing data from the 1997 Study of Intergenerational Linkages II, a national sample consisting of 2,000 individuals age 18 and older, Giarrusso, Silverstein, and Feng (2000) tested the potential of confidants to moderate the effect of stress on the self-esteem of 162 grandparents. They found that the number of people the grandparent caregivers perceived as confidants moderated the effect of care-giving stress on the grandparent's self-esteem. More specifically, the grandparent caregivers who had more individuals in whom they could confide were better protected from the negative psychological effects of stress (i.e., lower self-esteem) when compared with grandparents who had fewer confidants. However, Landry-Meyer, Gerard, and Guzell (2005) did not find evidence of the buffering effect of social support on caregiver stress among 133 grandparent caregivers; however, they did find a positive, direct effect of informal and formal social support on stress outcomes. Similarly, in a study of 41 grandparent primary caregivers conducted by Kelley (1993), social isolation and the restriction of roles were significant predictors of psychological distress measured by the General Severity Index.

There is well-established evidence that social activity and participation is associated with better physical health, lower mortality, and increased psychological well-being among older adults (Jackson & Antonucci, 1992; Utz, Carr, Nesse, & Wortman, 2002). Again, however, there is limited information available about the potential effects of social participation on the psychological well-being of grandparent caregivers. Minkler et al. (1997) found that whether or not a care-giving grandparent socialized at least once a week was not significantly associated with level of depressive symptoms. In contrast, Szinovacz et al. (1999) found a small effect of social contacts (measured by church attendance or participation in social church events) on depressive symptoms among grandmother primary caregivers. Specifically, grandmother primary caregivers who participated in social events at church reported lower levels of depressive symptoms than those who did not. Park's (2004) study revealed that weekly attendance at religious services was directly associated with lower levels of depressive symptoms. These two studies point to the role of religion or spirituality as a resource to grandparents coping with the challenges of raising grandchildren.

In addition, Park's (2004) study found evidence of a buffering effect of volunteer activities. Care demands were significantly associated with higher levels of depressive symptoms only for grandmothers with lower levels of volunteer activities. The social companionship obtained through volunteer activities may decrease the grandmother caregivers' depression by meeting their needs for affiliation or by helping to divert their thoughts away from worrying about the problems they face (e.g., caring for grandchildren with disabilities). Moreover, a greater number of roles and multiple identities occupied by grandmother caregivers may provide a sense of purpose in life or be a source of self-esteem, which may enhance their psychological health. However, it is worth noting that for certain caregivers, multiple roles may be an additional stressor, depending on the nature of the role. Grandparent caregivers with full-time jobs reported having less energy to devote to child care (Hayslip et al., 1998). They may not only have work and grandparent care-giving responsibilities, but also be caring for aging parents or their own children. With this caveat, the general pattern of research findings suggests that grandmother primary caregivers directly benefit from a large network of friends and social participation in church and community activities.

With respect to demographic factors, Minkler et al. (1997) found that increased psychological distress was associated with being female, poorer health, and younger age. The relationship of sex and health to psychological distress is consistent with the more general literature on the relationship of sex and health to depressive symptoms. However, the relationship of grandparent's age to psychological distress is less expected, as one would assume that age-related changes would interact with the demands of caring for young children in taking a toll on grandparent well-being. It remains unclear whether in studying grandparent caregiving, age may be a proxy for another variable (e.g., caring for grandchildren of adolescent parents) that might shed light on this unexpected relationship between caregiver age and well-being.

Race and ethnicity are additional factors that condition the context in which an individual grandparent caregiver responds to stress (Dilworth-Anderson, Burton, & Johnson, 1993; Seltzer & Greenberg, 1999). Grandparents in racial and ethnic minority groups are more likely to assume and to be accustomed to a parenting role for their grandchildren, given historical and cultural differences in role expectations. Compared to Caucasian grandmothers, African American grandmothers have historically served as family keepers in response to family crisis and disruptions due to slavery, the parents' migration to look for better economic opportunity, and single parenthood (Burton & Dilworth-Anderson, 1991; Dilworth-Anderson et al., 1993; Jimenez, 2002). With a strong emphasis on familism, Hispanic grandmothers are more likely to live in intergenerational households and to be called on to play a primary care-giving role for grandchildren (C. B. Cox, Brooks, & Valcarcel, 2000; Goodman & Silverstein, 2002).

Recent studies that compared African American and Caucasian grandmother primary caregivers found that the two groups of grandmothers were similar to each other in age, reasons for caregiving, grandchildren's characteristics, and impact on the grandmothers' work life, but found differences in marital status, work status, income, and burden between the groups (Pruchno, 1999; Pruchno & McKenney, 2002). Specifically, African American grandmother caregivers were more likely to be employed outside the home and to have received support services such as Aid to Families with Dependent Children, Food Stamps, and Medicaid than White care-giving grandmothers. Nevertheless, Caucasian grandmothers were more likely than African Americans to feel tired, isolated, and trapped in their role (Pruchno, 1999; Pruchno & McKenney, 2002). Likewise, Musil and Ahmad (2002) found that White grandmother caregivers were more likely than their non-White counterparts to be depressed.

However, other researchers found no difference in depressive symptoms among care-giving grandparents by race and ethnicity (Szinovacz et al., 1999), and still others found elevated rates of distress in African American caregivers. A recent study using data from the 1999 NSAF found that in skipped-generation families, African American grandmothers were more likely than Caucasian grandmothers to report feelings of psychological distress (Mills, Gomez-Smith, & De Leon, 2005). However, Goodman and Silverstein (2002) found that African American grandmothers in three-generation households had poorer mental health than their counterparts in skipped-generation households, whereas the levels of psychological health were not different between those in skipped- and those in three-generation households in the Caucasian or Latino grandmother groups. Burnette (1999a) reported in her study of 74 Latino grandparents that about half of the grandparents had symptoms of mild depression based on the Geriatric Depression Scale.

Additional characteristics associated with grandmothers' stress are educational attainment and marital status. There is evidence of higher levels of depressive symptoms in care-giving grandmothers who have lower levels of education and who are unmarried (Caputo, 2001; Kolomer, McCallion, & Janicki, 2002; Musil & Ahmad, 2002). Elevated psychological distress among more poorly educated grandmother caregivers may occur because those with less education have a more limited ability to access the necessary help and information to care for a grandchild.

Grandmother caregivers who are married or have a partner may report less stress because married individuals have greater financial resources as well as benefit from the emotional support of a spouse. However, Pruchno and McKenney (2000) found higher levels of care-giving burden among grandmother caregivers who were married in skipped-generation households, possibly because the spouse might be disabled, which would place an additional burden on the caregiver.

Although increasing attention in the literature has been given to work-family conflict among caregivers (e.g., Jenkins, 1997; Marks, 1998; Moen, Robinson, & Fields, 1994), little research is available on the relationship between employment and caregiving in the grandparent caregiver population. One exception is a study by Sands and Goldberg-Glen (1998), which examined the effect of employment status on the psychological health of a convenient sample of 123 full-time care-giving grandmothers. The researchers found that 38% of the grandmothers were employed at the time of the interview, although 67% reported that they were employed prior to the onset of care-giving responsibility. Results from the multivariate analysis revealed that employed grandmother caregivers were more likely to have better mental health than those who were unemployed. This finding is consistent with the larger literature suggesting that employed women caregivers are more likely to report higher self-esteem and life satisfaction than those who are unemployed (Moen et al., 1994).

Several conclusions can be reached from this review of the literature about the factors affecting the physical and mental health of caregivers and the psychosocial resources that buffer stress among grandparent caregivers. First, grandparent caregivers face a greater risk of distress when they are caring for children with elevated levels of behavioral or emotional problems. Second, grandparent caregiving takes it greatest toll on women, in poor health, with fewer years of education, and who take on the care-giving role at a younger age. Third, consistent with the larger care-giving literature, informal social support and employment play a protective role in maintaining the health of grandparent caregivers. Whether the protective function of work is due to the increased financial resources that employed grandparents have at their disposable or due to the beneficial effects of multiple roles is unknown but is an important area for future research.

Further, this discussion of the context of caregiving is by necessity an oversimplification of a very complex process. It is often difficult to disentangle factors that increase the risk that one will assume the role of caring for grandchildren from the outcomes of taking on the care-giving role. For example, some coresident grandparents began caring for grandchildren because of parental financial problems (Woodworth, 1996). These grandparents then suffer further financial problems due to the cost of caring for grandchildren (Casper & Bryson, 1998; Pinson-Millburn et al., 1996), which may amplify psychological distress that was present prior to taking on the grandparent role. Hence, preexisting circumstances that may require grandparents to take on the care-giving role may in turn intensify when the care-giving role is assumed and result in an elevated level of distress that was already present, albeit at a lower level, prior to assuming the care-giving role.

FEDERAL AND STATE POLICIES THAT AFFECT GRANDPARENT CAREGIVERS

Grandparent primary caregivers are affected by federal and state policies within two main realms: public income assistance and child welfare. Major sources of financial support for grandparent primary caregivers are cash assistance grants through the welfare system's income assistance program (i.e., Aid to Families with Dependent Children, or, since 1996, Temporary Assistance for Needy Families [TANF]) or foster care payments through the child welfare system. An emerging trend is for states and localities to develop subsidized guardianship and other programs that address the needs of various types of kinship families who are not involved in traditional foster care or TANF program (Leos-Urbel, Bess, & Geen, 2000).

Special rules apply in TANF if the grandparents share the household with a parent (whether the parent is a teen parent or an adult) as well as grandchildren (A. G. Cox & Pebley, 1999). Grandparent caregivers in skipped-generation households may choose either to exclude themselves from the assistance unit (i.e., child-only grant) or to be included as part of the assistance unit (i.e., full grant). Grandparents' income and assets are only counted in determining the grandchildren's eligibility for the grant when grandparents choose to be included. However, if the parent of the grandchildren is present in the grandparent-headed households and is over the age of 18, the child's eligibility criteria for cash assistance are based exclusively on whether that parent is eligible. When the parents themselves are minor children (i.e., under the age of 18), the TANF regulations require the teenage parents to live with their parents (in this case, the grandparent of the newborn) or legal guardian and to be in school or employed as a condition of the assistance (Minkler et al., 1999). In this case, the grandparents' financial resources are not considered to determine the eligibility of the teen parents and grandchildren. It is possible that grandparents who are employed might need to leave their jobs to provide care to the grandchildren. If these grandparents currently receive cash welfare while raising their other children, then becoming the de facto caregiver of the teenage parents' children could make it more difficult for the grandparents to meet the work requirements and possibly cause them to lose the full grant.

Three provisions of the 1996 welfare reform law that are critical for grandparent primary caregivers are work requirements, time limits, and varying levels of cash assistance from individual states. The welfare reform legislation considerably altered the financing and structure of cash aid and other social welfare programs.

Although the federal government imposes some conditions, such as work requirements and time limits, states may now design their own welfare programs. As a result, the effects of the Personal Responsibility and Work Opportunity Reconciliation Act on grandparent primary caregivers vary from state to state.

State sanction policies might affect grandparent primary caregivers who fails to comply with work requirements and do not have good-cause exemptions. Sanctions take the form of reducing or eliminating benefits for the family. Formerly, if an adult fails to meet work requirements, the family grant was reduced by that adult's portion. Under TANF rules, the full amount of the family grant could potentially be sanctioned in some states. Therefore, nonexempted grandparent primary caregivers living in states with full-benefit sanctions must consider whether their failure to comply with work requirements may result in the loss of cash assistance. Even in those states with partial benefit sanctions, grandparent caregivers must evaluate whether receiving child-only grant without work requirements would be more beneficial for their families than receiving full grant with the potential sanction (Mullen & Einhorn, 2000).

In the ongoing debate about welfare reform, concerns have been expressed about the potential unintended consequences of the work exemption. It is possible that grandparents who are exempted from all the requirements might be pressured to take in grandchildren if the grandchildren's parents exhaust their time limits or lose substantial amounts of their benefits due to noncompliance with work requirements (Minkler et al., 1999). Moreover, concern has been raised that parents might leave their children with relatives (who might be grandparents) to avoid the new welfare requirements in order to preserve assistance in the form of child-only grants (Boots & Geen, 1999). However, there is little empirical evidence supporting these concerns.

The maximum TANF benefit varies dramatically from state to state (American Association of Retired Persons, 1998). For instance, in January 2000, the monthly child-only benefits for one grandchild living in the continental United States ranged from a high of $503 in Vermont to a low of $68 in Texas, with a median rate of $221 (U.S. House of Representatives, Committee on Ways and Means, 2000). Although some qualified grandparent primary caregivers may seek public assistance, the level of benefits is often insufficient to allow them to reach the official poverty threshold (Mullen, 2000).

The other source of federally supported payments that can assist grandparent primary caregivers is the foster care program under Title IV-E of the Social Security Act (Karp, 1996). A major difference between foster care and TANF is that children in foster care are in the state's legal custody and not the caregiver's custody. In addition, foster care imposes stringent requirements, including ongoing supervision and oversight from the child welfare agency. The rules and regulations regarding eligibility for foster care payments also vary considerably among states. A grandparent caregiver might be eligible for foster care payments in one state, whereas in another state a grandparent in the same circumstances might qualify only for welfare payments (Boots & Geen, 1999).

Some states provide permanency options to kinship caregivers, the majority of whom are grandparents, for children if the child welfare authorities determine that reunification with the parent is not feasible. These options also provide financial support to kinship caregivers, including adoption assistance and subsidized guardianship (Farrell, Fishman, Laud, & Allen, 2000; Leos-Urbel, Bess, & Geen, 2000). Adoption assistance offers adoptive parents a monthly subsidy, which may not exceed the foster care payment. Subsidized guardianship programs provide monthly payments, which are less than or equal to the state foster care payment, to relatives who become the legal guardians of children in their care.

In summary, due to the lack of uniform regulations from the federal government for state kinship care policies, states have greater flexibility in serving kinship caregiver families. This brings about substantial variability in financial assistance options for grandparent primary caregivers within and across states.

EVIDENCE-BASED INTERVENTIONS FOR GRANDPARENT CAREGIVERS AND THEIR FAMILIES

Grandparents caring for grandchildren have a wide range of needs. Based on a random survey of 6,307 Ohio households, of which 10% consisted of a grandparent providing care to a grandchild, Landry-Meyer (1999) identified six basic needs for this group of caregivers: health care services for the grandchild, health care services for the grandparent, recreational and social activities, accessible and affordable child care, consistent and equitable access to programs and services, and the ability to exercise parental authority and help with permanency planning. Others speak to the need for guidance in managing a child's behavior problems, information and education about services and supports available to grandchildren, and respite care (Hayslip & Patrick, 2003). Chenoweth (2000) has developed a model for effective grandparent education and recommends that four content areas be covered: self-care, guidance, communication, and advocacy. Although a growing number of interventions are being developed to help grandparent caregivers meet their needs for information, support, and services, there exist only a very small number of well-designed studies that address the efficacy of psychosocial interventions to assist grandparents who are caring for a grandchild. Consequently, our discussion includes a number of program for which only anecdotal data exist regarding their effectiveness. We include these programs because they appear quite promising and warrant a more rigorous evaluation to determine their effectiveness.

Programs for grandparent caregivers can be distinguished by whether they target more narrowly behavioral change in the individual grandparent or whether they take a more systemic approach and focus more broadly on the grandchild as well as the grandparent. Among the interventions targeting the individual grandparent, Bratton, Ray, and Moffit (1998) used filial/family play therapy to teach grandparents parenting skills and help them more effectively support their grandchildren. Hayslip (2003) developed a parent skills/psychosocial skills training program specifically designed for grandparents caring for grandchildren. The training program consists of six sessions, ranging between $1\frac{1}{2}$ to 2 hours. The 1st week covers parenting skills, including discipline techniques that foster positive self-work and modeling desirable behavior. The next four sessions teach grandparents how to cope with expressions of grief, depression, and anger in the grandchild, talking to the grandchild about sex and drugs, and helping the grandparent understand and deal with school-related problems. The last session teaches grandparents self-care skills and covers information on legal and financial issues. Grandparent caregivers who received the training reported greater parenting self-efficacy and improved quality of relationship with their grandchild (Hayslip, 2003). However, the magnitude of these effects was modest, and the intervention had no effect on more general measures of well-being such as life satisfaction and depression.

Burnette (1998) conducted an exploratory, small-scale ($N = 11$) evaluation of an 8-week school-based group intervention for grandparents based on a stress and coping model. Each session consisted of a supportive and an educational component. The supportive component included discussions of stigma and feelings of social isolation and concerns about the future care of grandchildren. The educational component addressed resources and services to grandparents raising grandchildren, developing coping strategies, and parent skills training. Grandparents who participated in the intervention reported lower levels of depression over the 8-week period. Grandparents also were less likely to use "distancing" as a coping strategy and were more likely to use problem-focused coping strategies and to seek social support.

Another group of programs and interventions for grandparent caregivers takes a more holistic and multifaceted approach, providing an array of services and supports to grandparent caregivers and their grandchildren. McCallion, Janicki, Grant-Griffin, and Kolomer (2000) developed educational support group services for grandparent caregivers of children with developmental disabilities, which was supplemented by case management services to the grandchild. The support group ran a minimum of six sessions, typically held every 2 weeks, with between 8 to 10 grandparents. To facilitate attendance, in-home or on-site respite for grandchildren and assistance with transportation was provided. The education and support group covered a wide range of topics, including coping with problem behaviors, custody and guardianship issues, negotiating with the school and other systems of care, dealing with the parents of the grandchild, and taking care of oneself (for a complete description, see Kolomer, McCallion, & Overeynder, 2003). In addition to the support group, case managers assisted grandparents with such tasks as helping with entitlement programs; obtaining emergency funds for shelter, housing, and daily expenses; negotiating services through the disability networks; and completing paperwork for guardianship. McCallion, Janicki, and Kolomer (2004) found that grandparents in the educational and support group reported reduced levels of depression and experienced a greater sense of empowerment and mastery over their care-giving situations than grandparents in the wait-list control group.

A program developed by Dannison and Smith (2003) used a systems and community approach involving grandparents, grandchildren, and school personnel. Separate support groups were held for grandparents and grandchildren. The support groups met weekly for 8 consecutive weeks. The grandparent group consisted of 8 to 10 participants; the groups for grandchildren were kept small to enable all children an opportunity to participate. The grandchild group focused on activities to address the child's self-esteem, the development of social skills, and the recognition and appropriate expression of feelings. The grandparent group taught principles of effective parenting and parent education and allowed grandparents an opportunity to share their stories. In addition, school personnel participated in three half-day educational in-service meetings, with the goal of educating school personnel about the needs of grandparent caregivers and identifying opportunities to modify the curriculum and school environment to better meet the needs of grandparent-headed households. Preliminary evidence indicated that this systems intervention resulted in improved social skills and self-confidence in the grandchildren and gains in social support among the grandparents (Dannison & Smith, 2003).

Project GUIDE (Grandparents United: Intergenerational Development Education) is a multifaceted program that provides individual assessment, educational and support groups, case management services, advocacy, and cultural, social, and recreational activities for both grandparents and grandchildren. Grandparents and grandchildren meet weekly for 2 hours. The curriculum for grandparents, which is delivered over a 52-week period, includes sessions on parenting, stress management and reduction, health and nutrition, and conflict resolution. In a descriptive evaluation of the program, Jones and Kennedy (1996) reported that the program helped reduce social isolation, enhanced parenting skills, assisted families in meeting their basic human needs, and improved the self-esteem of children.

Project Healthy Grandparents is another multifaceted program organized around a strengths-based interdisciplinary case management approach to preventing child neglect. Services are specifically targeted to reduce child neglect and provide grandparents with the skills necessary to prevent neglect and improve social support. All participants received services for a period of 1 year. The services included case management, advocacy, legal information, physical health assessment, support groups, and parenting education. Anecdotal evidence suggests that the strengths-based case management model produced gains in self-confidence and a greater sense of empowerment (Whitely, White, Kelley, & Yourke, 1999).

Finally, Grant, Gordon, and Cohen (1997) reported on a grandparent program that took advantage of an existing partnership between a local hospital and school to provide medical and psychosocial services to improve the functioning of both grandparents and grandchildren. By delivering the program within a pediatric school health program, the staff was able to engage grandparents by focusing early meetings on health education concerns. This helped to minimize resistance to participation in the program and to keep people engaged as the content of the group meetings with grandparents changed to address more personal issues.

In summary, there is a burgeoning of psychosocial interventions to help grandparents cope with the demands of parenting a young child in later life, but unfortunately the rigorous evaluation of these programs has not kept pace with their development. For the most part, the current program evaluations are based on relatively small and highly selected samples. In addition, except for the evaluations by Hayslip (2003) and McCallion et al. (2004), all of the studies have used a one-group pre/posttest or posttest-only design, leading to many threats to internal validity. Much of the evidence to support the efficacy of these interventions is anecdotal and based on nonstandardized measures with unknown reliability and validity. Finally, none of the interventions has been replicated in independent studies. Therefore, the evidence base for the efficacy of psychosocial grandparent caregiver programs is quite weak and their implementation in clinical practice should be done with caution.

RECOMMENDATIONS FOR PRACTICE AND POLICY

This review of psychosocial treatment programs suggests core program features that provide guidelines for the development and implementation of interventions for grandparent caregivers in clinical practice. Social support and education serve as the building blocks for effective psychosocial treatments for grandparent caregivers. Social support in the form of group meetings and sharing of personal stories helps grandparents decrease their sense of isolation and realize that they are not alone. This approach has proven very successful for other care-giving groups. The educational component should be a major component of any intervention as grandparents have great and varied needs for information on parenting skills, managing behavior problems, community resources, health care, and custody laws as well as help with financial and future planning. A psychoeducation program is best delivered by an interdisciplinary team because of the complex multiple financial, legal, and health care problems faced by grandparent caregivers. In addition to the core features of support and education, case management services are typically an integral part of programs as grandparents often need assistance securing basic services and health care for their grandchildren.

Practitioners should tailor psychosocial treatment to meet the unique needs of different types of grandparenting situations. Single grandmother caregivers in skipped-generation families with limited financial resources may need more assistance to alleviate their economic hardships, whereas grandmother caregivers in three-generation families may need help learning communication and problem-solving skills for reducing conflict with the child's parents over parenting practices (Harrison, Richman, & Vittimberga, 2000). For grandparents in their 70s and 80s, their primary concern may be planning for their grandchild's future care after the grandparents' death. Therefore, although grandparent caregivers have many similar needs and share many common concerns, we must not lose sight of the fact that there still exists considerable heterogeneity in need requiring individualized treatments to best meet these diverse needs.

In addition, programs and services should be easily accessible without publicly stigmatizing the grandparent as having a problem. Grandmothers may be reluctant to seek services at mental health agencies (Shore & Hayslip, 1994) or apply for public income assistance (Scarcella, Ehrle, & Geen, 2003) because of stigma. Given the higher rates of attendance at religious services among older adults and the high value grandparents place on the education of their grandchildren, programs should be offered in churches or schools to facilitate participation of grandparents who may be most in need of assistance (Park, 2004; Rogers & Henkin, 2000).

Research on grandparent caregivers also has important implications for social policy and formal economic support systems. Given the higher poverty rates among families headed by grandparent caregivers, especially single grandmother caregivers, and the detrimental effects of poverty on mental health, there is a need to reformulate economic policies that place grandparents at a disadvantage. Grandparent caregivers often receive inconsistent and inequitable treatment based on their status as a relative. The various state plans managing TANF funds are also contributing to this unfair treatment of grandparents. The inequity in financial assistance for grandparent-headed families becomes even larger when comparing the receipt of services provided to kinship caregivers and nonrelative foster care parents. Kinship care providers typically do not receive the same level of compensation as nonrelative foster care parents (Kelley et al., 2000). Policy makers can assist grandparent primary caregivers with low incomes by easing the licensing procedures for the more generous and less stigmatizing payments available to foster care parents or by providing alternative financial support programs (e.g., subsidized guardianship) that do not require grandparents to yield the custody of their grandchildren to the state (Bell & Garner, 1996).

Finally, many grandparents are still in the labor force and may be required to meet work requirements to receive welfare benefits. Many employed grandparent caregivers are concerned with the availability and cost of child care and day care services for their grandchildren (Gibson, 1999). The provision of school-age care could decrease the anxiety of grandparent caregivers. Child care must be accessible and include transportation, which is a major concern of grandparent caregivers, particularly of those living in poverty (Burton, 1992; Gibson, 1999).

RECOMMENDATIONS FOR FUTURE RESEARCH

To build our evidence base, two types of research studies are needed. First, replication studies of existing programs are needed to more rigorously evaluate their effectiveness across different samples of grandparent caregivers. Second, there is a need to compare different interventions to determine which is most effective in assisting grandparent caregivers.

Theoretically grounded longitudinal research on grandparent caregivers, particularly regarding the impact of policy changes (e.g., welfare reform) on those living in poverty, is greatly needed. Researchers can take advantage of the natural variation among states in economic support programs for grandparent caregivers to design quasi-experimental studies to examine the impact of different levels of financial assistance on grandparent caregivers and their families. In designing studies that evaluate the impact of welfare reform on grandparent-headed families, specific time points for comparison need to be carefully selected because some states might have administered a pilot program or a waiver project before the official implementation of welfare reform. To ensure that changes in policy occur as intended, an evaluation needs to be accompanied with ongoing monitoring of the implementation of new welfare policies or programs for kinship caregivers.

Another important question that should be considered in assessing policy change impact is about the appropriate time lags across which the effects occur. When this is not known, or when data collection intervals are mismatched to the actual causal time lags, the interpretation of welfare reform effects on grandparent-headed families could be equivocal or misleading. Unfortunately, there exists no rule of thumb to determine a proper time interval between data collection points to examine change (Rogosa, 1979). Whether a 1-year interval is too short or too long depends on the nature of the policy change under investigation. Researchers can make good decisions about the timing of observations only if they have a sound theory guiding the relevant processes (Baltes & Nesselroade, 1979).

To advance our knowledge about factors contributing to the well-being of grandparent caregivers and their grandchildren, longitudinal research is needed to examine the bidirectional nature of effects between grandparents and grandchildren. To date, most of the research has looked at how the effects of grandchildren (i.e., behavior problems) affect the well-being of grandparents. It is equally important to investigate how the levels of grandparenting stress influence parenting behaviors and, ultimately, the well-being of grandchildren. The increased psychological distress observed in grandparent caregivers is a major concern because increased parenting distress is linked to dysfunctional parent-child interactions and poor child outcomes (Kelley et al., 2000). Longitudinal studies would allow us to begin to sort out the nature of bidirectional influences between grandparent caregivers and their grandchildren.

We have a great deal to learn about the influence of sex and ethnicity in shaping the grandparent care-giving experience. Although grandmothers are disproportionately represented among grandparent caregivers (Bryson & Casper, 1999), it should be acknowledged that there are also grandfathers who assume primary care-giving responsibilities for their grandchildren. Research is needed on whether caregiving takes a differential toll on the well-being of grandmother and grandfather caregivers of grandchildren. Similarly, only a few studies have examined variation in the grandparent care-giving experience across different ethnic groups. Research on the role of culture in shaping the grandparent care-giving experience is necessary to guide the development of culturally sensitive psychosocial interventions.

Finally, research is needed on the benefits associated with grandparent care-giving (Jendrek, 1993, 2003). Following trends in the broader care-giving literature (see Kramer, 1997), research on grandparent caregiving has focused more on the burdens of care; yet it is important to examine both positive and negative outcomes that are distinguishable from one another to gain a more comprehensive understanding of the psychological well-being of grandparent caregivers (Pruchno & McKenney, 2002).

CONCLUSION

In recent years there has been growing awareness among both researchers and the public of the increasing number of grandparents who provide care on a consistent basis for their grandchildren. These older persons face numerous challenges that may negatively affect their physical, psychological, emotional, social, and financial well-being. Research reviewed in this chapter suggests that grandparent caregivers and their families could benefit from community-based services designed to respond to various needs of grandparent-headed families. Parenting skills education, accessible and affordable child care, support groups, case management services, and financial assistance are a few suggested services.

To advance our understanding of grandparent caregiving, we need more rigorous methodological studies based on larger, more representative samples that have sufficient variation to examine how the grandparent experience is moderated by family household composition, sex, ethnicity, and the timing of the role in the grandparent's life course. Identifying protective factors associated with ameliorating the stress of grandparent caregiving is essential to develop programs and social policies that strengthen the capacity of grandparents to care for their grandchildren without placing an undue burden on grandparents and in a way that maximizes the well-being of our children.

REFERENCES

American Association of Retired Persons. (1998). *Welfare reform and grandparents*. Retrieved January 22, 2000, from http://www.aarp.org/getans/grandparents.html.

Bachman, H. J., & Chase-Landsdale, P. L. (2005). Custodial grandmothers' physical, mental, and economic well-being: Comparisons of primary caregivers from low-income neighborhoods. *Family Relations, 54,* 475–487.

Baltes, P. B., & Nesselroade, J. R. (1979). History and rationale of longitudinal research. In J. R. Nesselroade & P. B. Baltes (Eds.), *Longitudinal research in the study of behavior and development* (pp. 1–39). New York: Academic Press.

Barnhill, S. (1996). Three generations at risk: Imprisoned women, their children, and grandmother caregivers. *Generations, 21,* 39–40.

Bell, W., & Garner, J. (1996). Kincare. *Journal of Gerontological Social Work, 25*(1/2), 11–20.

Boots, S. W., & Geen, R. (1999). *Family care or foster care? How state policies affect kinship caregivers* (Series A, No. A-34). Washington, DC: Urban Institute.

Bowers, B. F., & Myers, B. J. (1999). Grandmothers providing care for grandchildren: Consequences of various levels of caregiving. *Family Relations, 48,* 303–311.

Bratton, S., Ray, D., & Moffit, K. (1998). Filial/family play therapy: An intervention for custodial grandparents and their grandchildren. *Educational Gerontology, 24,* 391–406.

Bryson, K. R. (2001). *New Census Bureau data on grandparents raising grandchildren.* Unpublished manuscript.

Bryson, K. R., & Casper, L. (1999). *Coresident grandparents and grandchildren* (Current Population Reports, P23-198). Washington, DC: U.S. Bureau of the Census. Retrieved May 9, 2006, from http://www.census.gov/prod/99pubs/p23–198.pdf.

Burnette, D. (1997). Grandmother caregivers in inner-city Latino families: A descriptive profile and informal social supports. *Journal of Multicultural Social Work, 5,* 121–137.

Burnette, D. (1998). Grandparents rearing grandchildren: A school-based small group intervention. *Research in Social Work Practice, 8,* 10–27.

Burnette, D. (1999a). Physical and emotional well-being of custodial grandparents in Latino families. *American Journal of Orthopsychiatry, 69,* 305–318.

Burnette, D. (1999b). Social relationships of Latino grandparent caregivers: A role theory perspective. *Gerontologist, 39,* 49–59.

Burnette, D. (2000). Latino grandparents rearing grandchildren with special needs: Effects on depressive symptomatology. *Journal of Gerontological Social Work, 33*(3), 1–16.

Burton, L. M. (1992). Black grandparents rearing children of drug-addicted parents: Stressors, outcomes, and social service needs. *Gerontologist, 32,* 744–751.

Burton, L. M., & deVries, C. (1992). Challenges and rewards: African American grandparents as surrogate parents. *Generations, 17*(3), 51–54.

Burton, L. M., & Dilworth-Anderson, P. (1991). The intergenerational family roles of aged Black Americans. *Marriage and Family Review, 16,* 311–330.

Caputo, R. K. (2001). Grandparents and coresident grandchildren in a youth cohort. *Journal of Family Issues, 22,* 541–556.

Casper, L. M., & Bryson, K. R. (1998). *Co-resident grandparents and their grandchildren: Grandparent maintained families* (Working Paper No. 26). Washington, DC: U.S. Bureau of the Census, Population Division. Retrieved May 10, 2006, from http://www.census.gov/population/www/documentation/twps0026/twps0026.html.

Chenoweth, L. (2000). Grandparent education. In B. Hayslip Jr. & R. Goldberg-Glen (Eds.), *Grandparents raising grandchildren: Theoretical, empirical, and clinical perspectives* (pp. 307–326). New York: Springer.

Cherlin, A. J., & Furstenberg, F. F., Jr. (1986). *The new American grandparent: A place in the family, a life apart.* New York: Basic Books.

Cox, A. G., & Pebley, A. R. (1999). *Grandparent care and welfare: Assessing the impact of public policy on split and three generation families* (Labor and Population Program, Working Paper Series 99-08). Washington, DC: RAND.

Cox, C. B., Brooks, L. R., & Valcarcel, C. (2000). Culture and caregiving: A study of Latino grandparents. In C. B. Cox (Ed.), *To grandmother's house we go and stay: Perspectives on custodial grandparents* (pp. 218–232). New York: Springer.

Creighton, L. (1991, December 16). Silent saviors. *U.S. News and World Report,* 81–89.

Dannison, L. L., & Smith, A. B. (2003). Custodial grandparents community support program: Lessons learned. *Children and Schools, 25,* 87–95.

Dilworth-Anderson, P., Burton, L., & Johnson, N. (1993). Reframing theories for understanding race, ethnicity, and families. In P. G. Boss, W. J. Doherty, R. LaRossa, W. R. Schumm, & S. K. Steinmetz (Eds.), *Sourcebook of family theories and methods: A contextual approach* (pp. 627–646). New York: Plenum Press.

Dowdell, E. (1995). Caregiver burden: Grandmothers raising their high risk grandchildren. *Journal of Psychosocial Nursing Mental Health Services, 33*(3), 27–30.

Dressel, P. L., & Barnhill, S. K. (1994). Reframing gerontological thought and practices: The case of grandmothers with daughters in prison. *Gerontologist, 34,* 685–691.

Dubowitz, H., & Feigelman, S. (1993). A profile of kinship care. *Child Welfare, 72,* 153–169.

Emick, M. A., & Hayslip, B. (1999). Custodial grandparenting: Stresses, coping skills, and relationships with grandchildren. *International Journal of Aging and Human Development, 48,* 35–61.

Farrell, M., Fishman, M., Laud, S., & Allen, V. (2000). *Understanding the AFDC/TANF child-only caseload: Policies, composition, and characteristics in three states* (The Lewin Group). Retrieved May 10, 2006, from http://aspe.hhs.gov/hsp/child-only-caseload00/index.htm.

Fields, J., & Casper, L. (2001). *America's families and living arrangements: 2000* (U.S. Census Bureau, Current Population Reports, Series P20-537). Washington, DC: U.S. Government Printing Office.

Flint, M. M., & Perez-Porter, M. (1997). Grandparent caregivers: Legal and economic issues. *Journal of Gerontological Social Work, 28*(1/2), 63–76.

Fuller-Thomson, E., Minkler, M., & Driver, D. (1997). A profile of grandparents raising grandchildren in the United States. *Gerontologist, 37,* 406–411.

Giarrusso, R., Silverstein, M., & Feng, D. (2000). Psychological costs and benefits of raising grandchildren: Evidence from a national survey of grandparents. In C. B. Cox (Ed.), *To grandmother's house we go and stay: Perspectives on custodial grandparents* (pp. 71–90). New York: Springer.

Gibson, P. A. (1999). African American grandmothers: New mothers again. *Affilia, 14,* 329–343.

Goldberg-Glen, R. S., & Sands, R. G. (2000). Primary and secondary caregiving grandparents: How different are they? In B. Hayslip Jr. & R. Goldberg-Glen (Eds.), *Grandparents raising grandchildren: Theoretical, empirical, and clinical perspectives* (pp. 161–180). New York: Springer.

Goodman, C., & Silverstein, M. (2002). Grandmothers raising grandchildren: Family structure and well-being in culturally diverse families. *Gerontologist, 42,* 676–689.

Grant, R., Gordon, S., & Cohen, S. (1997). An innovative school-based intergenerational model to serve grandparent caregivers. *Journal of Gerontological Social Work, 28*(1/2), 47–61.

Harden, A. W., Clark, R., & Maguire, K. (1997). *Formal and informal kinship care* (Report for the Office of the Assistant Secretary for Planning and Evaluation, Task Order HHS-100-95-0021). Washington, DC: U.S. Department of Health and Human Services. Retrieved May 10, 2006, from http://aspe.hhs.gov/hsp/cyp/xskincar.htm.

Harrison, K. A., Richman, G. S., & Vittimberga, G. L. (2000). Parental stress in grandparents versus parents raising children with behavior problems. *Journal of Family Issues, 21,* 262–270.

Hayslip, B., Jr. (2003). The impact of a psychosocial intervention on parental efficacy, grandchild relationship quality, and well-being among grandparents raising grandchildren. In B. Hayslip & J. H. Patrick (Eds.), *Working with custodial grandparents* (pp. 163–176). Springer: New York.

Hayslip, B., Jr., Emick, M. A., Henderson, C. E., & Elias, K. (2002). Temporal variations in the experience of custodial grandparenting: A short-term longitudinal study. *Journal of Applied Gerontology, 21,* 139–156.

Hayslip, B., Jr., & Patrick, J. H. (Eds.). (2003). *Working with custodial grandparents.* Springer: New York.

Hayslip, B., Jr., Shore, R., Henderson, C., & Lambert, P. (1998). Custodial grandparenting and the impact of grandchildren with problems on role satisfaction and role meaning. *Journal of Gerontology: Social Sciences, 53,* S164–S173.

Hernandez, D. J., & Meyer, D. E. (1993). *America's children: Resources from family, government, and the economy.* New York: Russell Sage Foundation.

Jackson, J. S., & Antonucci, T. C. (1992). Social support processes in health and effective functioning of the elderly. In M. L. Wykle, E. Kahana, & J. Kowal (Eds.), *Stress and health among the elderly* (pp. 72–95). New York: Springer.

Janicki, M. P., McCallion, P., Grant-Griffin, L., & Kolomer, S. R. (2000). Grandparent caregiver I: Characteristics of the grandparents and the children with disabilities for whom they care. *Journal of Gerontological Social Work, 33*(3), 35–55.

Jendrek, M. P. (1993). Grandparents who parent their grandchildren: Effects on lifestyle. *Journal of Marriage and the Family, 55,* 609–621.

Jendrek, M. P. (1994). Policy concerns of White grandparents who provide regular care to their grandchildren. *Journal of Gerontological Social Work, 23*(1/2), 175–200.

Jendrek, M. P. (2003). Grandparents: Family supporters, custodial caregivers, and dolls. *Gerontologist, 43,* 771–773.

Jenkins, C. L. (1997). Women, work, and caregiving: How do these roles affect women's well-being? *Journal of Women and Aging, 9*(3), 27–45.

Jimenez, J. (2002). The history of grandmothers in the African-American community. *Social Service Review, 76,* 523–551.

Jones, L., & Kennedy, J. (1996). Grandparents United: Intergenerational developmental education. *Child Welfare, 75,* 636–650.

Joslin, D. (2000). Emotional well-being among grandparents raising children affected and orphaned by HIV disease. In B. Hayslip Jr. & R. Goldberg-Glen (Eds.), *Grandparents raising grandchildren: Theoretical, empirical, and clinical perspectives* (pp. 87–105). New York: Springer.

Joslin, D., & Brouard, A. (1995). The prevalence of grandmothers as primary caregivers in a poor pediatric population. *Journal of Community Health, 20,* 383–401.

Joslin, D., & Harrison, R. (1998). "The hidden patient": Older relatives raising children orphaned by AIDS. *Journal of the American Medical Women's Association, 53*(2), 65–71.

Karp, N. (1996). Legal problems of grandparents and other kinship caregivers. *Generations, 21,* 57–60.

Kelley, S. J. (1993). Caregiver stress in grandparents raising grandchildren. *IMAGE: Journal of Nursing Scholarship, 25,* 331–337.

Kelley, S. J., Whitley, D., Sipe, T. A., & Yorker, B. C. (2000). Psychological distress in grandmother kinship care providers: The role of resources, social support, and physical health. *Child Abuse and Neglect, 24,* 311–321.

Kolomer, S. R., McCallion, P., & Janicki, M. P. (2002). African-American grandmother carers of children with disabilities: Predictors of depressive symptoms. *Journal of Gerontological Social Work, 37*(3/4), 45–62.

Kolomer, S. R., McCallion, P., & Overeynder, J. (2003). Why support groups help: Successful interventions for grandparent caregivers of children with developmental disabilities. In B. Hayslip & J. H. Patrick (Eds.), *Working with custodial grandparents* (pp. 111–125). New York: Springer.

Kornhaber, A. (1985). Grandparenthood and the "New Social Contract." In V. L. Bengtson & J. F. Robertson (Eds.), *Grandparenthood* (pp. 159–172). Beverly Hills, CA: Sage.

Kramer, B. J. (1997). Gain in the caregiving experience: Where are we? What next? *Gerontologist, 37,* 218–232.

Kramer, B. J., & Lambert, J. D. (1999). Caregiving as a life course transition among older husbands: A prospective study. *Gerontologist, 39,* 658–667.

Landry-Meyer, L. (1999). Research into action: Recommended intervention strategies for grandparent caregivers. *Family Relations, 48,* 381–389.

Landry-Meyer, L., Gerard, J. M., & Guzell, J. R. (2005). Caregiver stress among grandparents raising grandchildren: The functional role of social support. *Marriage and Family Review, 37*(1/2), 171–190.

Leos-Urbel, J., Bess, R., & Geen, R. (2000). *State policies for assessing and supporting kinship foster parents.* Washington, DC: Urban Institute.

Li, L. W., Seltzer, M. M., & Greenberg, J. S. (1997). Social support and depressive symptoms: Differential patterns in wife and daughter caregivers. *Journal of Gerontology: Social Sciences, 52B,* S200–S211.

Lugaila, T. (1998, March). *Marital status and living arrangements* (Update: Current Population Reports, P20-514). Washington, DC: U.S. Bureau of the Census.

Marks, N. F. (1998). Does it hurt to care? Caregiving, work-family conflict, and midlife well-being. *Journal of Marriage and the Family, 60,* 951–966.

McCallion, P., Janicki, M. P., Grant-Griffin, L., & Kolomer, S. R. (2000). Grandparent caregivers II: Service needs and service provision issues. *Journal of Gerontological Social Work, 33,* 57–84.

McCallion, P., Janicki, M. P., & Kolomer, S. R. (2004). Controlled evaluation of support groups for grandparent caregivers of children with developmental disabilities and delays. *American Journal of Mental Retardation, 109,* 352–361.

Mills, T. L., Gomez-Smith, Z., & De Leon, J. M. (2005). Skipped-generation families: Sources of psychological distress among grandmothers of grandchildren who live in homes where neither parent is present. *Marriage and Family Review, 37*(1/2), 191–212.

Minkler, M., Berrick, J. D., & Needell, B. (1999). The impact of welfare reform on California grandparents raising grandchildren: Reflections from the field. *Journal of Aging and Social Policy, 10,* 45–63.

Minkler, M., Fuller-Thomson, E., Miller, D., & Driver, D. (1997). Depression in grandparents raising grandchildren: Results of a national longitudinal study. *Archives of Family Medicine, 6,* 445–452.

Minkler, M., & Roe, K. M. (1993). *Grandmothers as caregivers: Raising children of the crack cocaine epidemic.* Newbury Park, CA: Sage.

Minkler, M., Roe, K. M., & Price, M. (1992). The physical and emotional health of grandmothers raising grandchildren in the crack cocaine epidemic. *Gerontologist, 32,* 752–761.

Moen, P., Robinson, J., & Fields, V. (1994). Women's work and caregiving roles: A life course approach. *Journal of Gerontology: Social Sciences, 49*(4), S176–S186.

Morrow-Kondos, D., Weber, J. A., Cooper, K., & Hesser, J. L. (1997). Becoming parents again: Grandparents raising grandchildren. *Journal of Gerontological Social Work, 28*(1/2), 35–46.

Mullen, F. (1996). Public benefits: Grandparents, grandchildren, and welfare reform. *Generation, 21,* 61–64.

Mullen, F. (2000). Grandparents and welfare reform. In C. B. Cox (Ed.), *To grandmother's house we go and stay: Perspectives on custodial grandparents* (pp. 113–131). New York: Springer.

Mullen, F., & Einhorn, M. (2000). *The effect of state TANF choices on grandparent-headed households.* Washington, DC: American Association of Retired Persons, Public Policy Institute. Retrieved May 10, 2006, from http://www.aarp.org/research/family/grandparenting/aresearch-import-548-2000-18.html.

Musil, C. M. (2000). Health of grandmothers as caregivers: A 10-month follow-up. *Journal of Women and Aging, 12,* 129–145.

Musil, C. M., & Ahmad, M. (2002). Health of grandmothers: A comparison by caregiver status. *Journal of Aging and Health, 12,* 96–121.

Neal, M. B., Chapman, N. J., Ingersoll-Dayton, B., & Emlen, A. C. (1993). *Balancing work and caregiving for children, adults, and elders.* Newbury Park, CA: Sage.

Park, H. (2004). Grandmothers as primary caregivers: Poverty, care demands, social participation, and psychological distress. *Dissertation Abstracts International* (UMI No. 3127977).

Pinson-Millburn, N. M., Fabian, E. S., Schlossberg, N. K., & Pyle, M. (1996). Grandparents raising grandchildren. *Journal of Counseling and Development, 74,* 548–554.

Pruchno, R. (1999). Raising grandchildren: The experience of Black and White grandmothers. *Gerontologist, 39,* 209–221.

Pruchno, R., & Johnson, K. (1996). Research on grandparenting: Review of current studies and future needs. *Generations, 20*(1), 65–71.

Pruchno, R., & McKenney, D. (2000). Living with grandchildren: The effects of custodial and coresident households on the mental health of grandmothers. *Journal of Mental Health and Aging, 6,* 269–289.

Pruchno, R., & McKenney, D. (2002). Psychological well-being of Black and White grandmothers raising grandchildren: Examination of a two factor model. *Journal of Gerontology: Psychological Sciences, 57*(5), 444–452.

Pruchno, R. A., Patrick, J. H., & Burant, C. J. (1997). African American and White mothers of adults with chronic disabilities: Caregiving burden and satisfaction. *Family Relations, 46,* 335–346.

Robertson, J. F. (1995). Grandparents in an era of rapid change. In R. Blessed & V. Bedford (Eds.), *Handbook of aging and the family* (pp. 243–260). Westport, CT: Greenwood Press.

Rodgers, A. Y., & Jones, R. L. (1999). Grandmothers who are caregivers: An overlooked population. *Child and Adolescent Social Work Journal, 16,* 455–466.

Rodgers-Farmer, A. Y. (1999). Parenting stress, depression, and parenting in grandmothers raising their grandchildren. *Children and Youth Services Review, 21,* 377–388.

Roe, K. M., Minkler, M., Saunders, F. F., & Thomson, G. E. (1996). Health of grandmothers raising children of the crack cocaine epidemic. *Medical Care, 34,* 1072–1084.

Rogers, A., & Henkin, N. (2000). School-based interventions for children in kinship care. In B. Hayslip Jr. & R. Goldberg-Glen (Eds.), *Grandparents raising grandchildren: Theoretical, empirical, and clinical perspectives* (pp. 221–238). New York: Springer.

Rogosa, D. (1979). Causal models in longitudinal research: Rationale, formulation, and interpretation. In J. R. Nesselroade & P. B. Baltes (Eds.), *Longitudinal research in the study of behavior and development* (pp. 263–302). New York: Academic Press.

Sands, R. G., & Goldberg-Glen, R. S. (1998). The impact of employment and serious illness on grandmothers who are raising their grandchildren. *Journal of Women and Aging, 10*(3), 41–58.

Scarcella, C. A., Ehrle, J., & Geen, R. (2003). *Identifying and addressing the needs of children in grandparent care* (Series B, No. B-55). Washington, DC: Urban Institute.

Schwartz, C., & Gidron, R. (2002). Parents of mentally ill adult children living at home: Rewards of caregiving. *Health and Social Work, 27,* 145–154.

Seltzer, M. M., & Greenberg, J. S. (1999). The caregiving context: The intersection of social and individual influences in the experience of family caregiving. In C. D. Ryff & V. W. Marshall (Eds.), *The self and society in aging processes* (pp. 362–397). New York: Springer.

Shore, R. J., & Hayslip, B., Jr. (1994). Custodial grandparenting: Implication for children's development. In A. E. Gottfried & A. W. Gottfried (Eds.), *Redefining families: Implications for children's development* (pp. 171–218). New York: Plenum Press.

Solomon, J. C., & Marx, J. (1999). Who cares? Grandparent/grandchild households. *Journal of Women and Aging, 11*, 3–25.

Strawbridge, W. J., Wallhagen, M. I., Shema, S. J., & Kaplan, G. A. (1997). New burdens or more of the same? Comparing grandparent, spouse, and adult-child caregivers. *Gerontologist, 37*, 505–510.

Szinovacz, M. E. (1998). Grandparents today: A demographic profile. *Gerontologist, 38*, 37–52.

Szinovacz, M. E., DeViney, S., & Atkinson, M. P. (1999). Effects of surrogate parenting on grandparents' well-being. *Journal of Gerontology: Social Sciences, 54B*, S376–S388.

Troll, L. E. (1983). Grandparents: The family watchdogs. In T. H. Brubaker (Ed.), *Family relationships in later life* (pp. 63–74). Beverly Hills, CA: Sage.

Uhlenberg, P., & Kirby, J. B. (1998). Grandparenthood over time: Historical and demographic trends. In M. E. Szinovacz (Ed.), *Handbook on grandparenthood* (pp. 23–39). Westport, CT: Greenwood Press.

U.S. Bureau of the Census. (1994). *The diverse living arrangements of children: Summer 1991* (Current Population Reports, Household Economic Studies, P70-38). Washington, DC: U.S. Government Printing Office. Retrieved May 10, 2006, from http://www.census.gov/population/socdemo/child/p70-38.pdf.

U.S. Bureau of the Census. (2001a). *Living arrangements of children: 2001* (Current Population Reports, Household Economic Studies, P70-104). Washington, DC: U.S. Government Printing Office.

U.S. Bureau of the Census. (2001b). *Table C2: Household relationship and Living arrangements of children under 18 years.* Retrieved May 10, 2006, from http://www.census.gov/population/www/socdemo/hh-fam/p20-537_00.html.

U.S. Bureau of the Census. (2004). *Table CH-7: Grandchildren living in the home of their grandparents: 1970 to present.* Retrieved May 10, 2006, from www.census.gov/population/socdemo/hh-fam/tabCH-7.pdf.

U.S. House of Representatives, Committee on Ways and Means. (2000). *2000 green book: Background material and data on programs within the jurisdiction of the Committee on Ways and Means* (Ways and Means Committee Print 106–114). Washington, DC: U.S. Government Printing Office.

Utz, R. L., Carr, D., Nesse, R., & Wortman, C. B. (2002). The effect of widowhood on older adults' social participation: An evaluation of activity, disengagement, and continuity theories. *Gerontologist, 42*, 522–533.

Weber, J. A., & Waldrop, D. P. (2000). Grandparents raising grandchildren: Families in transition. *Journal of Gerontological Social Work, 33*(2), 27–46.

Whitley, D. M., White, K. R., Kelley, S. J., & Yourke, B. (1999). Strengths-based case management: The application to grandparents raising grandchildren. *Families in Society, 80*, 110–119.

Wood, V., & Robertson, J. (1976). The significance of grandparenthood. In J. Gubrium (Ed.), *Time, roles, and self in old age* (pp. 278–304). New York: Human Science Press.

Woodworth, R. S. (1996). You're not alone . . . you're one in a million. *Child Welfare, 75*, 619–635.

CHAPTER 16

Family Caregiving

RHONDA J. V. MONTGOMERY, JEANNINE M. ROWE,
and KARL KOSLOSKI

T HE PROVISION OF care for frail and disabled relatives is now widely recognized as a common role in later life for most women and many men. Indeed,
family members provide 80% of long-term care in this country, and it has
been estimated that if reimbursed these services would cost $302 billion per year.
That is the equivalent of 6% of the national cost of health care (Arno, 2006).
Clearly, family caregivers are the core of the long-term care workforce, and their
well-being is intricately linked to the well-being of frail older adults.

Over the past 2 decades, much attention has been given to the negative impacts
of caregiving by both social and health practitioners (Pinquart & Sorensen, 2003,
2005). This concern for family caregivers has prompted the National Institute on
Aging to designate caregiving as one of the top priorities for social and behavioral research and has led to the creation of numerous programs for family caregivers. Whereas in the past, the needs of family caregivers were ignored and
frequently treated as an illegitimate basis for government assistance of any type,
now the Administration on Aging, through the National Family Caregiver Support Program (NFCSP), has legitimized family caregivers as a group deserving
assistance. Since the initial implementation of the NFCSP in 2001, there has been
an explosion of newly developed family support programs at both the state and
local levels. This proliferation of family support services makes careful examination of our current knowledge of caregiving for older adults a timely endeavor. In
particular, it is useful to explore ways in which information gained from research
can be used to guide practice and policy.

If social workers are to effectively serve older adults, it is imperative that they
understand the contributions and needs of family caregivers. In this chapter, we
examine the composition of this largely unpaid workforce, the types of tasks and
responsibilities that they undertake, the impact of this role on caregivers' lives
and well-being, and current knowledge about effective methods for supporting
their efforts.

WHO ARE THE CAREGIVERS?

The general consensus in the literature is that, most often, one family member serves as the primary source of care for an impaired elderly person, although others in the network of family and friends may serve as secondary caregivers. This role of primary caregiver is not uniformly embraced by all potential caregivers, nor is it experienced in the same manner by those who assume the role (Acton & Kang, 2001; Anhensel, Pearlin, Mulan, Zarit, & Whitlach, 1995; Miller & Lawton, 1997; Sorensen, Pinquart, & Duberstein, 2002). There is a hierarchy in the selection of the primary caregiver that is linked to sex, generation, and geography. When available, a spouse provides the majority of care. In the absence of a spouse, a daughter is most likely to assume the role. Daughters are twice as likely as sons to become the primary caregiver (AHRQ Research Report, 2001; Campbell & Martin-Matthews, 2003). The crucial role of sex in the hierarchy of obligation to elderly family members is reflected in the fact that after spouses and daughters, it is daughters-in-law and not sons who are the next lines of resort (Ory, Yee, Tennstedt, & Schulz, 2002). Although the participation of sons as primary caregiver rose by 50% between 1984 and 1994, they still accounted for only 15% of primary caregivers in 1994. In the absence of offspring, more distant family members become responsible. It is also the case that the caregiver role tends to fall to the person with the fewest competing responsibilities, including obligations to spouse, children, and employers (Brody, 1990; Stern, 1996; Stueve & O'Donnell, 1989). Geography also influences the selection of the primary caregiver, in that adult children who live closer to a parent are more apt to assume care-giving responsibilities. However, offspring who live at a distance often provide assistance with financial and legal matters and arrange for the provision of direct care by paid caregivers.

Given the high rates of widowhood among the older population and sharing of care-giving responsibilities by multiple siblings, children greatly outnumber spouses as active caregivers (Spillman & Pezzin, 2000). The prevalence of different types of relatives (e.g., spouse, daughter, daughters-in-law, or son) has also been found to differ by ethnicity and income (Dilworth-Anderson & Gibson, 2002).

Daughters and more distant relatives are more prevalent as caregivers in Hispanic and Black populations than they are in White populations, but this trend is moderated among higher income groups (Laditka & Laditka, 2001). Among Asian groups, sons are more frequently identified as caregivers who assist with instrumental activities of daily living (IADLs), and daughters-in-law are more prevalent as caregivers who provide assistance with household tasks and personal care (Youn, Knight, Jeong, & Benton, 1999).

DIVERSITY OF CARE TASKS

Caregivers not only differ in terms of their relationship to the care receiver, but also in the manner in which they embrace and experience the care-giving role. That is, caregivers differ in what they do, how they do it, and how long they do it. In general, the closeness of the familial relationship is directly linked to the amount, type, and duration of care provided. As a rule, relatives who are more closely related to the care recipient provide greater amounts of care, as measured by the types of assistance provided, the time spent performing care tasks, and the length of time they are willing to persist in the care-giving role. Hence, spouses tend to provide more care than adult children, and adult children tend to provide more care than do siblings, nieces or nephews, or grandchildren (Delgado & Tennstedt, 1997a).

There is also substantial evidence that within groups of caregivers who have the same relationship to the care recipient, care activities differ by sex (Delgado & Tennstedt, 1997b; Matthews, 1995; Montgomery & Kamo, 1989). Among spouses, wives tend to provide more hours of care and accept less help from formal providers (Barusch & Spaid, 1996; Dwyer & Conrad, 1992; Merrill, 1997). There is also some evidence that husbands and wives differ in their style of care. Wives are more apt to be concerned with the emotional well-being of their husband and frequently undertake tasks intended to maintain continuity of a husband's identity. Husbands, in contrast, are more apt to approach caregiving using a managerial style primarily focused on the physical needs of their wife (Pinquart & Sorensen, 2006).

Few differences in helping behaviors have been reported between daughters and sons assisting parents who have minimal need for assistance. There is, however, strong evidence of differences between sons and daughters when they are assisting parents who have significant functional or cognitive impairment. When parents are more severely impaired, daughters provide more hours of care than do sons, perform a broader range of care tasks, and are more apt to provide help that must be performed on a regular basis (Cicirelli, Dwyer, & Coward, 1992; Mittelman, 2003). Although daughters often seek assistance from their own immediate family members, including their husband and children, they tend to receive less assistance from siblings or distant kin than do sons. In part, these differences in care patterns reflect a difference between sons and daughters in the duration of the care-giving role. Fewer sons than daughters are willing or able to continue in the care-giving role when the functional level of their parent declines to a level that requires assistance with activities of daily living (ADLs), such as dressing and bathing. Consequently, as a group, daughters are more apt to be caring for parents with greater needs for assistance, and the care recipient is more likely to be residing with a daughter than with a son (Brody, Litvin, Hoffman, & Kleban, 1995). There has been some speculation that this pattern reflects social norms and taboo (Montgomery & Kamo, 1989), but there is also evidence that these patterns are related to stronger normative ties between mothers and daughters (Dilworth-Anderson & Gibson, 2002).

Much less information is available about siblings and caregivers who are more distantly related to the care recipient, as these groups tend to account for a smaller proportion of caregivers and have not been widely studied. Generally, however, these more distant caregivers tend to provide assistance to persons with fewer needs and do so for much shorter periods than that observed for spouses and adult children. There is some evidence, however, that a small segment of siblings and distant relatives do establish close emotional ties with their elderly relative and assume care-giving roles that more closely mirror those of adult children. Certainly, more research needs to be conducted with this somewhat unique group of caregivers to provide a more complete understanding of their experience.

OUTCOMES OF CAREGIVING

An extensive body of work now exists that documents both positive and negative outcomes of caregiving. The large majority of research that has examined these outcomes has been guided by the stress model, which was most clearly articulated by Pearlin and his colleagues (Pearlin, Mullan, Semple, & Skaff, 1990). The model provides a conceptual framework that identifies four domains that make up the stress process: the background and the context of stress, the stressors, the mediators of stress, and the outcomes or manifestations of stress. The background and the context factors include the demographic and ascribed characteristics of the caregiver, the relationship between the caregiver and the care receiver, and aspects of the social and service delivery environment that frame the context in which care is provided. As individuals become caregivers, they are exposed to primary stressors and secondary stressors. Primary stressors are conditions and characteristics of the care receiver that translate into the care tasks and responsibilities that are assumed by the caregiver. These include the care receiver's cognitive status, problematic behaviors, and the need for assistance with ADLs and IADLs. Primary stressors may impact negatively on the caregiver and lead to secondary role and intrapsychic strains. That is to say, primary stressors may produce secondary strains that translate into a subjective sense of role overload and relational deprivation. These secondary strains on the caregiver include constraints on other aspects of the caregiver's life, including family and occupational role and social and recreational activities, and intrapsychic strains such as loss of self-esteem, loss of self, role captivity, and lowered sense of competence. The outcomes of the care-giving stress process may include caregiver depression, a subjective sense of stress or anxiety, and change in caregiver physical and mental health. These in turn can prompt caregivers to leave the care-giving role. In general, negative impacts of caregiving can be grouped under four general headings: infringement on time and lifestyle, impacts on the caregiver/care receiver relationship, mental health, and physical health.

NEGATIVE CONSEQUENCES OF CAREGIVING

Infringement on Time and Activities   The most immediate impact of providing care is the use of the caregiver's time, which often infringes on the time available for other life activities. Caregivers have reported restrictions on personal time and socialization as a result of caregiving. This restriction on caregivers' activities has, in turn, been identified as a critical cause of depression among caregivers (Yee & Schulz, 2000). In addition, the objective demands of providing care impact other aspects of the caregiver's life and may manifest in perceptions of role conflict and overload (Yates, Tennstedt, & Chang, 1999; Yee & Schulz, 2000). The conflict between caregiving and employment has been of particular interest to researchers (Fredriksen & Scharlach, 1997; Kramer & Kipnis, 1995).

Relationship with Care Recipient   As caregiving continues, the change in the caregiver or progression of the disease inevitably impacts the relationship between the caregiver and the care recipient. For example, as cognitive abilities decline and needs for assistance with basic ADLs increase, the individual with dementia becomes less able to contribute reciprocally to the relationship (Ory et al., 2002). This is critical because it is typically this relational connection or history that prompts relatives or friends to assume the care-giving role in the first place. Eventually, the demented individual becomes unable to even recognize or communicate with the caregiver. It is suggested that caregivers are thus faced with additional demands of grieving for the loss of their relationship while continuing to meet objective demands for care (Meuser & Marwit, 2001).

Physical Health   Negative effects of caregiving on the health of caregivers have also been established (Beach et al., 2005; Bookwala et al., 2000). Declines in immune functions have been measured (Kiecolt-Glaser, Glaser, Gravenstein, Malarkey, & Sheridan, 1996), as well as decreases in the rate of wound healing (Kiecolt-Glaser, Maruchas, Malarkey, Mercado, & Glaser, 1995). Women have been found to be less likely to engage in preventive health behaviors such as time for rest and exercise, when compared to men (Burton, Newsom, Schulz, Hirsch, & German, 1997). In addition, cardiovascular changes such as increases in blood pressure have also been found (Vitaliano et al., 2005). Lack of time to devote to self-care and preventive health behaviors due to caregiving demands may contribute to long-term negative health outcomes for caregivers, in addition to direct effects of objective burden and depression (Vitaliano, Young, & Zhang, 2004).

Mental Health and Psychological Outcomes   Impacts on mental health have been variously conceptualized as caregiver distress, burden, strain, depression, and psychological well-being (Chappell & Reid, 2002). Caregiver stress or strain has been linked to both the functional level of the elder and the activities of the caregiver. In general, the demands of assisting with personal care and dealing with problem behaviors of the care recipient and the need for constant supervision are stressful and lead to psychological distress, changes in social activities, and negative feelings about caregiving (Levesque, Cossette, & Laurin, 1995; McKinlay, Crawford, & Tennstedt, 1995; Montgomery, 1989). Increases in depression and anxiety have been reported by caregivers (Schulz et al., 1997; Schulz, O'Brien, Boodwasa, & Fleissner, 1995), and increased psychotropic drug use by caregivers has also been documented, reflecting the negative psychological effects of caregiving (Sleath, Thorpe, Landerman, Doyle, & Clipp, 2005).

POSITIVE OUTCOMES OF CAREGIVING

Although widespread agreement exists that caregiving has negative consequences for many caregivers, positive outcomes have also been observed, including a sense of mastery, positive affect, and an improvement in the quality of the dyadic relationship between the caregiver and the care recipient (Beach, Schulz, Yee, & Jackson, 2000). There is also growing evidence that feelings of caregiver satisfaction or gratification may be linked to subjective meanings attributed to the caregiver role. In their study of role engulfment or loss of self in the care-giving role, Skaff and Pearlin (1992) report that one of their intriguing findings is the lack of relationship between loss of self and self-gain. That is, some caregivers may feel that they have grown as a result of their experiences, but whatever personal enrichment they might experience does not protect them from suffering a loss of identity.

Braithwaite (2000) found that love and intimacy appraisals were not related to burden, but were associated with improved psychological well-being. Similarly, in a qualitative study conducted with 48 caregivers, Noonan, Tennstedt, and Rebelsky (1996) found that predominant themes of care-giving meaning included gratification and satisfaction, family responsibility and reciprocity, and friendship and company. Kramer (1997) analyzed 29 studies that focused on positive gains; she argues for research that focuses on the positive aspects of caregiving. She suggests that understanding the positive gains may enable professionals to work more effectively with families and may enhance theories of care-giving adaptation and well-being. These findings support the proposition that there are uplifts in the care-giving experience that may prevent the stress of caregiving from dominating all spheres of life.

EXPLAINING DIFFERENTIAL IMPACTS AND OUTCOMES

Perhaps the most perplexing question that persists for practitioners despite extensive research about the impact of caregiving on family members concerns the differential impact of the care-giving experience. For some family members caregiving is a difficult experience that has serious negative consequences. Yet other caregivers that have similar responsibilities are able to cope well and report little impact of the experience on their well-being (Call, Finch, Huck, & Kane, 1999; Levesque et al., 1995; Merrill, 1997; Montgomery & Datwyler, 1990; Pyke & Bengston, 1996).

Studies directed toward understanding variation in the consequences of caregiving have focused on a large number of factors: the health characteristics of the care recipient and of the caregiver (Beach et al., 2000; Kramer & Kipnis, 1995), the level and type of care provided (Beach et al., 2000), the gender relationship of the caregiver to the care recipient (Miller & Cafasso, 1992; Miller, McFall, & Montgomery, 1991; Stephens, Townsend, Martire, & Druley, 2001), race and culture (Dilworth-Anderson, Canty Williams, & Gibson, 2002; Farran, Miller, Kaufman, & Davis, 1997; Janevic & Connell, 2001; Knight & McCallum, 1998; Lawton, Rajagopal, Brody, & Kleban, 1992), the length of caregiving (Donaldson & Burns, 1999; Van den Heuvel, Witte, Schure, Sanderman, & Meyboom-de Jong, 2001), and the availability and use of informal and formal sources of support (Bass & Noelker, 1996; Chappell & Reid, 2002).

Functional Level of the Care Recipient   A small number of studies have reported a statistically significant relationship between caregiver outcomes and elder's level of functioning (Beach et al., 2000, 2005); others have noted the absence of a relationship (George & Gwyther, 1986). Caregiver burden may increase incrementally as an additive effect of the demands on increasing care-giving tasks. However, burden is not necessarily proportional to increase in physical disabilities (Braithwaite, 1996). There is also some evidence that declining cognition and problem behaviors contribute to caregiver burden. Levesque, Ducharme, and Lachance (1999) reported greater stress among individuals caring for a demented relative as opposed to those caring for an elder with physical impairments. Again, however, findings have been inconsistent. For example, Barusch and Spaid (1996) observed less burden for some family members caring for a loved one with dementia than for family members caring for a physically disabled person. It has been speculated that the absence of a direct link between elder's level of functioning and caregiver burden is associated with the sex of the caregiver (Montgomery & Williams, 2001).

Gender and Familial Relationships   The two factors most consistently reported to be associated with higher levels of stress are sex and living arrangement. Generally, women and caregivers who reside with the care recipient experience higher levels of stress (Merrill, 1997; Yee & Schulz, 2000). Women are generally believed to experience more primary stress and secondary role strain, and they experience greater occupational disruption as a result of care-giving responsibilities (Merrill, 1997; Winslow, 1999; Yee & Schulz, 2000). These patterns are frequently explained as a consequence of the more intense care and the greater amount of personal care that women provide. Yet even the pattern of greater stress among women caregivers has not been uniformly supported by past research. A number of studies of spouse caregivers report no differences in caregiver outcomes associated with sex (Barusch & Spaid, 1996; Kramer & Kipnis, 1995).

The inconsistencies in findings related to sex have prompted researchers to consider the association of caregiver outcomes within the familial relationship between the care recipient and the receiver (i.e., spouse versus child). Matire and her colleagues (Matire, Parris-Stephens, & Franks, 1997) explained the higher level of strain that they observed among daughters than among wives or husbands as a consequence of multiple and competing roles. Yet a number of investigators have reported lower levels of burden among adult children than spouses. It has also been suggested that spouses may experience more strain because they provide a greater quantity of care and more intense care than do children (Spillman & Pezzin, 2000). However, evidence of a direct link between care load and caregiver burden and stress remains unsubstantiated. An alternative explanation for the lower levels of burden observed among spouses may center on the isolation that spouses experience. In contrast, caregiving may provide an additional role for daughters that enhances well-being by competing with demands of multiple roles (Doress-Worters, 1994). Farkas and Himes (1997) noted that for many of the daughters included in their study the addition of care-giving responsibilities did not limit their involvement in community activities, but instead these activities may have increased and served as a mediating buffer to stress.

Ethnicity   There is a growing body of research that explores how culture or ethnicity influences the care-giving experience. In a review of the care-giving literature, Dilworth-Anderson and colleagues (2002) found that care-giving experiences and outcomes varied by race, ethnicity, and culture. Their examination of literature that included negative effects of caregiving (depression, burden, role strain, psychological distress, and relationship strain) found that, in general, White caregivers were significantly more depressed and burdened than African American caregivers. Hispanic and White caregivers experienced higher levels of role strain compared to African Americans. Findings also show that in general, African American caregivers were more likely than Whites to cope with difficulties of caregiving with prayer, faith in God, and religion in general. Picot and her colleagues suggests that for many African American caregivers faith and prayer may act as a buffer to care-giving stresses and may be associated with perceptions of rewards (Picot, Debanne, Namazi, & Wykle, 1997). African American caregivers were also found to use more positive reappraisal than White caregivers when dealing with the difficulty of caring for their elder (Farran et al., 1997; Knight & McCallum, 1998; Knight, Silverstein, McCallum, & Fox, 2000). Together, these studies underscore the importance of understanding how social and cultural factors influence both caregiver outcomes and appraisals.

Social Support Consistent with the stress model of Pearlin and his colleagues (Pearlin, Turner, & Semple, 1989), social support and formal resources have been identified as specific buffers to caregiver stress. The mediating effect of these variables has been found to vary depending on the care-giving situation. Overall, formal and informal supports are believed to mitigate the burdens of caregiving. Yet empirical evidence of these relationships has been inconsistent (Sorensen et al., 2002). Studies of intervention aimed at enhancing support interventions to relieve caregiver burden have reported mixed results, ranging from lack of psychological benefit for caregivers (Franks & Parris Stephens, 1996) to modest effects (Bourgeois, Schulz, & Burgio, 1996). Similarly, the importance of a network of caregivers to meet multiple demands of caregiving is disputed by studies that suggest that supplementary caregivers are not always beneficial and may indeed contribute to stress due to caregiver conflict (Penrod, Kane, Kane, & Finch, 1995).

FORMAL SUPPORT SERVICES

Current knowledge about the impact of formal service provision also remains somewhat limited (Gottlieb & Johnson, 2000; Kosloski, Montgomery, & Youngbauer, 2001; Sorensen et al., 2002). With the introduction of the National Family Caregiver Support program and greater interest by the National Institute on Aging in caregiver research, a wide range of support services have been developed by state and local agencies to support family caregivers. Both the goals and the content of these support services vary widely. Home health and chore services are frequently available to the family member with care tasks, and skilled nursing care (e.g., home health care) that may exceed the abilities or capacities of informal providers is available. These services may also be made available with the intent to provide caregivers respite or relief from their responsibilities for short periods of time. Respite is usually offered with the expectation that it will enable caregivers to continue in their role as primary sources of long-term care. In addition to direct care services, many programs offer education, counseling, and support groups to enhance the skills of caregivers and address their psychological needs. Although there is some consistency in the types of services available, there is great variation in the structure and content of programs and in the manner in which they are delivered. Each of the different types of caregiver support services and their variations are described next.

RESPITE SERVICES

Respite care is the most frequently requested service by caregivers of dementia patients (Gallagher-Thompson, 1994; Montgomery, 2005; Montgomery & Rowe, 2003; Wykle, 1994) and the most frequently prescribed by practitioners (Montgomery, 2005; Montgomery & Rowe, 2003). Perhaps the reason for this stems from a prevailing belief that respite will relieve the burden or stresses associated with caregiving and allow family caregivers to continue caring when nursing home placement is imminent.

The term *respite care* refers to a range of services designed to give caregivers time off or away from care-giving responsibilities (Gaugler et al., 2003; Montgomery & Kosloski, 1995; Sorensen et al., 2002). These include informal help provided by family members, as well as formal help provided in the home or in group or institutional settings. Informal respite refers to unpaid assistance with care and is typically performed by family members, relatives, friends, or volunteers. Formal respite refers to care for an individual that is typically performed by an employee of a direct service provider.

Formal respite services can be categorized by the location or setting in which the service is delivered and the level of care that is provided. *Out-of-home* services include nonresidential care delivered in group settings such as adult day centers and residential settings such as homes, nursing homes, and, although rare, hospitals. *In-home* services include companion programs and personal care services offered in a recipient's home. Many respite programs offer multiple levels of assistance or offer services in multiple settings. The most common form of out-of-home respite is provided through adult day centers (ADCs). Historically, ADCs were best able to serve clients who needed minimal assistance, and these centers often did not enroll elders who were incontinent or wandered (Montgomery, 1988, 1996). Today, however, adult day programs are viewed as a realistic way to provide respite to caregivers of individuals suffering from Alzheimer's disease or other forms of dementia (Dziegielewski & Ricks, 2000).

Adult day centers vary widely in their hours of operation and the types of services they provide. At one extreme are programs that operate 5 days a week and are open between 8 and 10 hours a day. These comprehensive programs are most often located in urban areas. At the other extreme are adult day programs that operate only 1 or 2 days per week for 3 to 4 hours. These are often located in local churches or community buildings and are frequently referred to as Brookdale models because they were initially funded by a large grant program of the Brookdale Foundation. Between these extremes are a large number of ADC programs that are open for 5 to 6 hours a day. Some of these programs are restricted to 2 or 3 days a week; others operate daily.

Just as there is variation among ADCs in their hours of operation, there is also great variation in the level of care that is provided within day centers. Broadly defined, ADCs provide therapeutic services, personal assistance, meals, social services, transportation, and personal care services, with the goal of allowing families to relinquish care responsibilities for several hours during the day (Gaugler et al., 2003). Many ADCs also perform a range of health-related services and some forms of skilled nursing care (Montgomery, 1988, 1996). Initially most ADC programs operated as *social models* of care by providing "sitting" services for care recipients outside their homes that included a variety of social activities. The goal was to give the caregiver a break from care-giving responsibilities. Centers that follow the social model often offer a range of social activities, such as games, arts and crafts, and discussion groups, and also provide some interaction or attention from staff. This model of service still prevails, but many ADC programs now operate using a medical model of care in order to qualify for reimbursement though Medicaid waiver programs. These programs are staffed with skilled nurses, therapists, and social workers and offer an array of medical services.

In-home respite services include companion programs, homemaker services, and personal care services delivered in the care recipient's home, most often by home health agencies or homemaker services. Like ADC programs, in-home programs vary widely in terms of the level of care and the amount and duration of service available. Some programs limit their services to short periods of 2 to 4 hours; others provide in-home respite for periods of 24 hours or greater. To a large degree, the availability of services is linked to payment sources. Private-pay clients can usually obtain services in any quantity; however, the hours of services available through publicly funded programs are often capped in terms of the number of hours per day or per month. Some programs offer emergency respite services, but most programs require advance notice (Montgomery, 2002).

It is widely believed by service providers and policy makers that this relief from stress will enable caregivers to continue in the care-giving role longer and will translate into the prevention or delay of nursing home placement (Montgomery & Kosloski, 1994). Although these potential benefits of respite for relieving caregiver stress and reducing the public costs of long-term care have been widely touted, evidence to support these assertions has been somewhat limited. The most consistent finding from studies of respite programs is that clients are satisfied with the services they receive (Baumgarten, Lebel, Laprise, Leclerc, & Quinn, 2002; Dziegielewski & Ricks, 2000; Townsend & Kosloski, 2002; Warren, Kerr, Smith, Godkin, & Schalm, 2003).

With respect to the impact of respite services on stress or burden, the findings have been inconsistent. One meta-analysis of 13 studies concluded that respite interventions have been effective at reducing caregiver burden and depression and improving well-being (Sorensen et al., 2002). Indeed, a small number of studies have successfully documented a link between the use of respite services and improved psychological conditions, including decreased burden and stress and increased well-being among caregivers (Dellasega & Zerbe, 2002; Gaugler et al., 2003; Kosloski & Montgomery, 1995; Levesque et al., 1995). Conversely, Baumgarten and colleagues (2002) found that respite care had no or a mild effect on care-giving outcomes. Similarly, an earlier meta-analysis of 18 articles published between 1980 and 1990 on psychosocial interventions and respite care concluded that respite services had a moderate effect (Knight, Lutzky, & Macofsky-Urban, 1993).

There is also limited evidence to support the notion that when respite is provided in an appropriate manner and used in sufficient quantity, it may reduce institutionalization. Most early studies of respite care provided little evidence to support the prevention or delay of nursing home placement. Later findings from a few large studies are more encouraging. Examining data from a study of 541 caregiver and care receiver dyads, Kosloski and Montgomery (1995) found that respite intervention did delay nursing home placement. More recently, Gaugler and his colleagues (2000) found that caregivers were far less likely to institutionalize their relatives when family members provided overnight help and assisted with ADLs.

EDUCATION

Over the past 2 decades numerous educational programs have been developed to help family caregivers. Education interventions are designed to provide caregivers with critical information that will enhance their abilities to provide care and cope with the associated stresses. Most of these programs are intended to either increase the knowledge or skills of caregivers to provide care or address the psychoemotional needs of caregivers by teaching self-care or coping skills. Skill-focused educational programs include those that teach about specific disease processes, direct care skills, and behavior management.

In addition to providing standardized information about the disease process, disruptive behaviors, and care-giving skills, psychoeducational programs usually include activities that use dialogue among group members to normalize experiences, give mutual support, and increase connections among the group members (Acton & Kang, 2001). These educational formats usually include lectures, group discussions, and written materials and are always led by a trained leader. Support may be part of a psychoeducational group, but it is secondary to the education content (Sorensen et al., 2002). Psychoeducational programs are more apt to focus on issues such as anger, depression, grief, and loss (Coon, Thompson, Steffen, Sorocco, & Gallagher-Thompson, 2003), as well as cognitive reframing (Depp et al., 2003) and coping (Gallagher-Thompson et al., 2000).

Because caregiver educational programs may have very different foci and goals, it is important for social workers to be aware of the content of programs to which they refer caregivers. Education programs not only vary in content, but they can be delivered in several formats. At one extreme are written, visual, and audio materials that are generally made available through one-on-one contact. At the other extreme are structured group programs led by a trained professional that follow a prescribed curriculum (Acton & Kang, 2001). Many educational programs groups also incorporate a support component. For example, through the discussion of a topic about dementia and the disease process, participants begin to share their experiences and strategies for coping with the challenges of caregiving. It is through discussion of the topic that caregivers come to identify with others and form informal support groups. Educational groups have been shown to effectively increase caregiver knowledge and understanding of disease processes (Burgener, Bakas, Murray, Dunahee, & Tossey, 1998) and problem-solving and coping strategies related to the care-giving experience (Acton & Kang, 2001; Harding & Higginson, 2003; Toseland et al., 2001).

Support Groups

The goal of support groups is to allow caregivers time to come together and receive mutual support from other caregivers (Sorensen et al., 2002). Most often, support groups are informal, unstructured, and without specific content. Like educational programs support groups vary widely in their structure, format, and content (Toseland et al., 2001; Van den Heuvel et al., 2002). Caregivers meet in a variety of places: homes of caregivers (Bass, McClendon, Brennan, & McCarthy, 1998), churches, agency buildings, via telephone (Brown et al., 1999), and even via computers (Czaja & Rubert, 2002). The overarching goal of support groups is to provide a forum for caregivers to share their care-giving experiences (Acton & Kang, 2001). The benefits of support groups include the opportunity for caregivers to have their experiences normalized (Brown et al., 1999; Cook & Heller, 1999; O'Connor, 2002) and to receive encouragement and validation for their efforts (Diehl, Mayer, Foerstl, & Kurz, 2003; Quayhagen et al., 2000). Many support groups also have an educational element that can provide caregivers with important information about the progression of disease, the availability of support services, and resources and strategies for coping. In some groups this information may be shared informally among participants; in other groups, speakers or support group leaders provide this type of information (Diehl et al., 2003; Mahoney, Tarlow, Jones, Tennstedt, & Kasten, 2001).

Although the impact of informal support groups has not been widely assessed, it is generally believed that these informal networks help to improve the quality of life for many caregivers, and there is some evidence that support group interventions have positive impacts on caregiver well-being and coping skills (Sorensen et al., 2002).

COUNSELING

Counseling interventions are designed to identify specific individual needs of the caregiver and to facilitate change by working with caregivers to increase their understanding of problematic behaviors and their reactions to the care-giving experience. Counseling sessions are conducted by trained professionals; they differ from educational interventions in that counselors do not provide standardized information to increase the caregivers' skill in caregiving. Rather, counselors focus on helping caregivers to understand and resolve their reactions to the caregiving process (Acton & Kang, 2001). Counseling can be done through group meetings or through individual meetings with family members; the latter are tailored to address the caregiver's individual needs and problems.

CARE MANAGEMENT

In addition to direct care services, most programs that serve families offer assistance through care management services. Care managers assist families by coordinating services and, in many situations, help arrange for the delivery of these services. Often, care management serves as a first point of entry for families who make their way into a system that is complex and often difficult to navigate. The majority of care management is performed by social workers, who provide a range of services: screening, assessment, planning, linking, monitoring, advocacy, and evaluation (Austin & McClelland, 1996). The overarching goal of care management is to link the family with services.

Despite the fact that the primary responsibility of care managers is to serve as the link between caregivers and services, care management has recently become viewed as a discrete service that can sufficiently address the individual needs of caregivers. This assumption is problematic given the needs of many family caregivers for direct services and the limited training and capacity of care managers to provide caregivers with appropriate education or counseling. If the primary goal of care management is to link caregivers to appropriate services, then success with this process will depend on the implementation of an appropriate assessment process.

CAREGIVER ASSESSMENT

With the recognition that family members who provide care to persons with chronic or disabling conditions are themselves at risk comes a mandate for assessing caregivers' needs. If the burdens and health risks that stem from the strains of caregiving are to be adequately addressed it is important for social workers who serve this group to be aware of the types and levels of stress that are being experienced as well as the care environment. Over the past 2 years the value of a systematic assessment of family caregiver needs has gained attention and moved to the public policy agenda (Maslow, Levine, & Reinhard, 2005). A major conclusion stemming from a recent National Censuses Development Conference sponsored by the Family Caregiver Alliance (2006a, 2006b) concerns the current gap between research and practice. Despite considerable consensus that social workers need to understand the role of caregiving and its multiple stressors when developing a care plan for a care recipient, most federal and state programs that offer home- and community-based services do not include a formal assessment process for the caregiver.

A central principle to emerge from the consensus conference is that caregiver assessment should embrace a family-centered perspective, inclusive of the needs and preferences of both the care recipient and the family caregiver. Although the consensus conference contributed to a growing public call for the inclusion of caregiver assessment protocols, the exact nature of this process and of the tools to be used remains a point of discussion. Seven domains were identified in the final consensus report as essential for inclusion in any assessment: (1) the care-giving context, which includes the physical and social environments; (2) caregivers' perceptions of health and functional status of the care recipient; (3) caregiver values and preference; (4) measures of well-being (e.g., self-rated health and depression); (5) consequences of caregiving, including measures of caregiver strain and perceived benefits; (6) caregivers' skills, knowledge, and ability to provide care; and (7) the availability of formal and informal supports (Family Caregiver Alliance, 2006b).

EFFECTIVE TARGETING OF SERVICES

Despite a general belief among service providers that caregiver support services are valuable, provider organizations and social workers continue to wrestle with two issues as they attempt to meet the needs of caregivers. First, a large number of family caregivers who are judged to be in need of support services either do not use them at all or use them too late to benefit from them. Second, results from intervention studies have generally failed to provide clear guidance to practitioners (Pillemer, Suitor, & Wethington, 2003).

INSIGHTS INTO NONUSE OF SERVICES

A small number of studies that have examined patterns of respite use provide some important insights into the reasons that caregivers fail to use services (Cox, 1997; Kosloski & Montgomery, 1994; Kosloski et al., 2001). Nonusers comprise two groups of people. There is one group that is simply unaware of the availability of a service. This group can be reached simply by improvement and expansion of outreach activities. The second group of nonusers consists of persons who do not perceive themselves as needing a specific service (Cox, 1997). A caregiver's perception of need is subjective, and many caregivers make a decision about need based on factors other than the functional level or care needs of the care recipient. Two factors that have been linked to perceived need are high levels of caregiver stress and the absence of an alternative caregiver in an individual's informal network of family and friends (Kosloski et al., 2001). The perception of need can also be influenced by culturally based attitudes and beliefs about personal obligations to provide care. For example, caregivers have reported not using respite due to guilt or the sense of failure that they incur when they abdicate care tasks to others. Others have reported a reluctance to leave the elder with a stranger, believing that a respite program may be too upsetting for the relative (Cox, 1997; Hooyman & Gonyea, 1995; Kosloski et al., 2001). These reasons reflect normative expectations and cultural beliefs about familial responsibility. Several studies have noted a strong sense of filial responsibility among African Americans, Asian Americans, Latinos, and other minority groups that includes the responsibility to engage in direct care (Clark & Huttlinger, 1998; Cox, 1993; Delgado & Tennstedt, 1997b; Henderson & Gutierrez-Mayka, 1992; Ishii-Kuntz, 1997). These beliefs about family responsibility may prevent some caregivers from perceiving themselves to be in need of services (Kosloski, Montgomery, & Karner, 1999).

Variations among ethnic groups in family structures and the availability of alternative caregivers may also contribute to differences in patterns of service use. A number of studies have found that minority groups draw on a wider circle of helpers than do Caucasians (Forester, Young, & Langhorne, 1999; Ishii-Kuntz, 1997; Laditka & Laditka, 2001). Both Latino and African American caregivers obtain help from members of the extended family. Fictive kin serve as a source of informal support for African Americans, who, like the Latino population, tend to rely more on informal services (i.e., family, friends, and volunteers) and are less likely to use formal services, which they often perceive as less accessible. These findings suggest that race and culture play a significant role in how minority groups view the utility of services and consequently their judgment of need for respite services and ultimately their use of services.

In addition to personal beliefs, characteristics of the services or service delivery may influence caregiver's perception of need. A number of studies have noted that nonuse of services is linked to inappropriate targeting of services to caregivers' needs (Horowitz, 1985; Montgomery & Kosloski, 2000) or barriers created by providers in the manner in which services are delivered. The costs for services, lack of transportation, cumbersome assessment process, and eligibility criteria have all been identified as barriers that may influence caregivers' perceptions of need for services (Caserta, 1987; Gwyther & Ballard, 1990; Montgomery, Marquis, Schaefer, & Kosloski, 2002; Montoro-Rodriguez, Kosloski, & Montgomery, 2003).

CHALLENGES TO THE EFFECTIVE TARGETING OF SERVICES

Currently, there is little information available to guide care managers or service providers as they make decisions about the effective allocation and delivery of services (Knight et al., 1993). A large majority of intervention studies have failed to support a statistically significant link between specific caregiver support services and relief of caregiver stress (Acton & Kang, 2001; Pillemer et al., 2003; Sorensen et al., 2002; Yin, Zhou, & Bashford, 2002) or have identified effect sizes that are not clinically significant (Knight et al., 1993; Schulz et al., 2002; Sorensen et al., 2002). The most promising findings regarding the positive impact of support services have emerged from intervention studies that have included multiple and a relatively comprehensive set of support services (Acton & Kang, 2001; Burgio, Solano, Fisher, Stevens, & Gallagher-Thompson, 2003; Mittelman, 2000; Mittelman et al., 1993; Schulz, Gallagher-Thompson, Haley, & Czaja, 2000). Although informative and important, this finding does not provide critical information for targeting specific services in a service package (Bourgeois et al., 1996; Burgio et al., 2003; Pillemer et al., 2003). The need to understand more about which services are most expedient for serving different types of caregivers at different points in their care-giving careers remains a challenge for service providers (Coon, Gallagher-Thompson, & Thompson, 2003; Knight et al., 1993; Sorensen et al., 2002). This challenge has been the focus of several studies conducted by Montgomery and Kosloski (Kosloski, Schaefer, Allwardt, Montgomery, & Karner, 2002; Montgomery, 2002) and has led to the development of the caregiver identity theory, which has important implications for targeting of support services.

CAREGIVER IDENTITY THEORY AND PRACTICE IMPLICATIONS

The caregiver identity theory is an extension of the caregiver marker framework, which was advanced as a tool useful for guiding the design and delivery of support services (Montgomery & Kosloski, 2000, 2001, in press). The caregiver identity theory also builds on research (Sherrell, Buckwalter, & Morhardt, 2001) that indicates that caregivers will not use services that they do not "perceive as needed or useful" (Montgomery & Kosloski, 2001, p. 13). The underlying premise of the model is that caregiving is a dynamic change process. This change process includes changes in care activities, changes in the relationship between the caregiver and the care recipient, and changes in the caregiver's identity.

IDENTITY CHANGE

According to the theory, the care-giving role emerges out of an existing role relationship, usually a familial role such as daughter, wife, or husband. As the needs of the care recipient increase in quantity and intensity over time, the initial familial relationship gives way to a relationship characterized by caregiving and corresponding changes in the caregiver's role and identity in relation to the care recipient. This identity change occurs because the care tasks that are required to maintain the health of the care recipient become inconsistent with the expectations associated with the caregiver's initial familial role. Most often this shift in identity is necessitated by a significant increase in the level of dependency of the care recipient. Other significant changes in the care context might include an increase or decrease in the availability of informal or formal supports or a change in living arrangement.

For most caregivers of persons with chronic conditions or dementia, the change in role identity is a slow and insidious process that occurs in stops and starts. Initially, the care needs of the elder may be relatively small and the corresponding care tasks may represent only minimal extensions of the familial role relationship. For example, a daughter may quite easily and without experiencing stress assist her mother who has some memory impairment with paying bills, shopping, or transportation to appointments. As the disease progresses, the needs of the mother, and resultant demands placed on the daughter, increase. The daughter's activities gradually increase in intensity and become inconsistent with the norms that she has internalized with respect to her role as a daughter. Consequently the daughter begins to assume a "caregiver" identity. Thus, over time, the care-giving activities transform the initial mother-daughter relationship into a *care-giving* relationship.

Montgomery and Kosloski (in press) have identified five phases of the care-giving career that are linked to changes in the care recipient's need for assistance. Figure 16.1 illustrates the phases. Phase I of the career is the period of role onset. This period begins at the point that a caregiver assists the care recipient in a manner that is not usually a part of the caregiver's familial (e.g., daughter or spouse) role. In this first phase of the care process, caregivers are rarely aware of their care-giving role identity. Phase II of the care-giving career begins when the caregiver acknowledges that his or her care activities are beyond the normal scope of the initial familial role. This is the point of self-identification as a caregiver (Montgomery & Kosloski, 2000). During this phase of the career, a caregiver is still maintaining his or her primary familial identity in relation to the care recipient, but acknowledges the presence of the caregiver role. Phase III begins when the care needs of the care recipient increase in quantity and intensity to a level that requires assistance that is substantially beyond the normal boundaries of the initial familial relationship. At this point, the caregiver is often torn between maintaining his or her initial identity as a relative and assuming the role of caregiver as a primary identity in relation to the care recipient. Caregivers who opt to continue with their care-giving tasks through Phase III usually increase the intensity of care they provide over time to such an extent that the caregiver role comes to dominate the dyadic relationship. Eventually, the caregiver considers placing the care recipient in some other setting such as assisted living or a nursing home. At that point in time the caregiver moves into Phase IV. For many spouses, Phase IV can continue for an extended time period in which the caregiver continues to revisit the option of nursing home placement. The final phase of the care-giving career, Phase V, begins when the care recipient is moved to a setting that relieves the caregiver of primary responsibility for care. Most often this phase entails placement in a nursing home, but it could be movement to the home of another family member or movement into an assisted living facility. During this final phase, the caregiver is often able to shift his or her primary identity back to the initial familial role and significantly reduce the salience of the caregiver role (Coe & Neufeld, 1999). The salience of the caregiver role relative to the familial role would be very similar to that experienced in Phase II.

During this change process there are lag periods when there is a misfit between what a caregiver is doing and what the caregiver thinks he or she should be doing given his or her personal identity. The core tenet of the caregiver identity theory is that caregivers will experience distress during those periods when they are engaged in activities that are inconsistent with their views of self. Subsequently, this distress will prompt caregivers to be open to and seek help. These

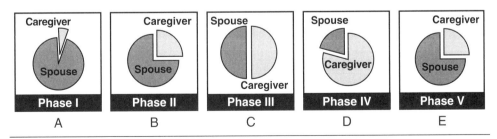

Figure 16.1   Caregiver Identities Mapped to Phases of Care-Giving Career.

points of distress may be viewed as periods in the care-giving process at which a caregiver is "servable." For example, a daughter who began her care-giving career by assisting with shopping and banking matters may now find herself engaging in activities with respect to her parent that she never engaged in previously, such as assisting with meal preparation or bathing. *Simply put, her activities are now discrepant with her previous role identity.* Furthermore, these activities make time demands that limit her other role performances (e.g., time for being a spouse, for being a mother to her own children, for friendship roles). The end result is incongruence between what the daughter is now doing as a caregiver and the way she views herself and her obligations as a daughter. In the context of the caregiver identity model, the personal expectations or rules that individuals use to define "appropriate behavior" for themselves are referred to as "identity standards." It is the incongruence between the care-giving tasks and personal identity standards that causes caregivers' distress. In turn, it is this distress that prompts caregivers to take actions to restore congruence between their care behaviors and their personal expectations. When caregivers experience discrepancy between what they are doing and their personal expectations or rules, they are most apt to accept support services.

Tremendous variation exists in the trajectory of care-giving careers. Movement between phases is not a universal experience for caregivers, nor is it a steady, smooth process. Many caregivers, especially adult children, exit from the care-giving role during Phase II or Phase III and move directly into Phase V. The type and level of impairment that the care recipient exhibits, the relative stability of functioning level, the physical and social environment in which care is provided, and the initial familial relationship between the caregiver and the care recipient all influence the care-giving trajectory. The only uniform aspect of the care-giving process is that caregivers experience significant distress at the points of transition between the phases. To successfully support caregivers at these stress points, it is necessary to identify and deliver those services that reduce the discrepancy between their care activities and their sense of self.

Practice Implications

Several insights emerge from the caregiver identity theory that can help social workers effectively target support to caregivers. First, the theory highlights the fact that specific care tasks, such as managing behavior problems or engaging in personal care tasks, are not inherently stressful. Rather, it is the performance of care tasks that are inconsistent with one's identity that is stressful to a caregiver. With this knowledge that a major source of stress is a discrepancy between *what a caregiver is doing* and *what he or she expects* to be doing, the goal for selecting a support service becomes clear: to reduce stress by reducing the discrepancy. Clearly, no single support service will be uniformly effective, because no single care activity or responsibility is more or less stressful to the full range of caregivers. In short, the theory both explains and underscores the fact that shotgun approaches to offering services tend to be very inefficient strategies for supporting caregivers (Coon, Gallagher-Thompson, et al., 2003). At the same time, the theory provides important guidance for effectively targeting services.

Targeting Supports toward Stress Reduction   Social workers can strategically target support services when they are informed with an understanding that the primary goal of support services should be the reduction of distress that stems from a caregiver's judgment that his or her behaviors are inconsistent with his or her expectations. Essentially, there are three strategies that can be used to help caregivers avoid or alleviate stress. Support services can aid caregivers by helping them to (1) change their behaviors to bring them in line with their identity standard, (2) change their self-appraisal, or (3) change their identity standard. When specific support services such as respite care, education programs, counseling, support groups, or case management are understood to be mechanisms for achieving one or more of these three outcomes, providers will be better able to target services to effectively help caregivers.

Change of Behaviors   The most direct way to create congruence between a caregiver's behavior and his or her identity standard is to change the caregiver's behaviors to make them consistent with an established identity standard. For most caregivers, this means avoiding care tasks that infringe upon an initial familial role (e.g., daughter role), which usually leads to obtaining outside assistance. The introduction of in-home chore services, respite care, and meal programs can all serve this purpose, depending on the needs of the care recipient and the relationship of the caregiver to the care receiver. A daughter who cares for her mother may maintain congruence between her care activities and her internalized norms for performing as a daughter (e.g., her identity standards) by using respite services. Respite care may relieve the daughter from the time demands associated with her care-giving responsibilities and allow her sufficient time for other roles in her life, such as being a spouse, a mother, or an employee. That is, the daughter is able to maintain her initial role identity as daughter by shifting care tasks that are not consistent with this identity to other formal or informal helpers.

Enhance Self-Appraisal   A second avenue for relieving caregiver distress caused by the perception of incongruence between a caregiver's actions and his or her identity standard is to alter the caregiver's self-appraisal in some way. This can be accomplished by helping caregivers to cognitively reframe their situation and thereby counter any negative self-evaluation. For example, a common lament of social workers concerns caregivers' reluctance to use respite services in a timely way. The identity theory offers insights here as well as guidance for practice. Caregivers may not accept respite services because of their belief that the use of such supports is inconsistent with their personal norms or identity standard. That is to say, a wife might not be open to using services because she believes that "a good wife" must provide care herself. In this case, the issue is one of changing the caregiver's self-appraisal by changing her norms to accept that respite use is an appropriate behavior. This can be accomplished by helping her to cognitively reframe her situation and thereby counter any negative self-evaluation. Sometimes this entails countering negative messages that caregivers may receive from the care recipient or other family members (Levesque et al., 1995). Another example of this type of intervention would be a social worker assisting the caregiver to see the adult day center as mutually beneficial to the care recipient and the caregiver. By explaining that adult day services not only give the caregivers a rest that will improve their ability to continue providing care, but also give the care recipient new opportunities for socialization, the social worker could help the caregiver see use of day services as appropriate. This type of cognitive reframing allows caregivers to transform negative feelings into positive appraisals.

Change of Identity Standard   A third means to reduce distress caused by incongruence between identity standards and behavior is to help the caregiver alter his or her identity standards. When discrepancies are small, providers can help caregivers to stretch an identity standard to fit the behavior and thereby allow a positive self-appraisal. A daughter operating primarily in the role of daughter may expand or stretch her identity standard to include such tasks as daily telephone check-up calls, weekly shopping, or even weekly housekeeping for her parent. This extension of her personal norms allows the daughter to appraise her care activities as consistent with the daughter role. She can judge herself to be acting as a "good" daughter within the constraints of her current identity standard. This strategy is consistent with the work of Sherrell and her colleagues (2001, p. 390), who recommend that when working with adult children, counselors should emphasize psychological processes of change that will help "endow the experience of caregiving with new meaning."

When incongruence between behaviors and identity standards leads to significant distress, it may be necessary to encourage caregivers to adopt a new identity that will be accompanied by a new set of rules or identity standards. Through education or counseling caregivers can be taught about the changing needs of the care recipient and encouraged to embrace an identity in relation to the care recipient that places greater emphasis on the caregiver role than on the initial familial role. In the case of the daughter caring for her mother, the daughter may come to define herself primarily as a caregiver. With this shift in identity, the daughter may comfortably discontinue activities associated with other roles (e.g., employee, friend, or club member) that are less salient or less central to her overall role (Coe & Neufeld, 1999). An emotion-focused strategy of acceptance described by Levesque and her colleagues (1995) serves as an example of an intervention that may lead to identity change. Through this educational program caregivers were encouraged to focus on the present reality. By acknowledging the current condition of their loved one, caregivers were helped to begin the process of accepting daily losses and a new identity.

Multiple Support Services as Vehicles to Change   It is important to note that a variety of support services can be used to reduce discrepancy, regardless of which type of change is being attempted (e.g., change in behavior, change in self-appraisal, change in identity standard). For example, one way to relieve a spouse caregiver of care tasks that she deems too excessive may be to teach the caregiver more efficient or effective ways of performing tasks such as grooming or bathing. In this way the care tasks can be reduced to a level that is manageable and more congruent with an existing identity standard. This same change might be accomplished by introducing an in-home respite program that offers personal care services. In short, multiple support services could be used to help caregivers maintain congruence between an existing identity standard and the caregiver's behaviors.

Multiple Benefits of a Single Support Service   Just as it is possible to use a number of different support services to achieve a desired change for a caregiver, it is possible that a single support service can be used to achieve multiple changes. For example, an education program can reduce stress by teaching a caregiver more efficient or effective methods for performing care tasks and in this way directly change the caregiver's behavior. An education program can also help caregivers to make a realistic self-appraisal of their performance. Similarly, a support group can help a caregiver to adjust behavior to fit an existing identity or can serve as a source of positive feedback to reinforce a positive self-appraisal.

FAMILY CAREGIVING IN THE CONTEXT OF PUBLIC POLICY

Any examination of the activities and needs of family caregivers would be incomplete without a discussion of the interface between informal caregiving and public policy. Historically, in all societies, the family has been the primary, and most often sole, source of assistance for dependent elders (Caro, in press). The emergence of public interventions to support family caregivers has taken place in more advanced societies over the past 3 decades. The range and intensity of these services have varied considerably across nations and across states within the United States. The belief that society has the primary or a significant responsibility for elder care has been most fully embraced in the Scandinavian countries, where home care services have been made available as a right for senior citizens (Johansson & Sundstrom, in press; Stuart & Boll Hansen, in press). In the United States, long-term care policies and practices have been built on the premise that the family is, and should be, the primary party responsible for care (Montgomery, 1999). Policy built on this premise persists despite changing demographics and social trends that have limited the number of family members available to provide care. Specifically, family size has decreased and women have entered the workforce in greater numbers.

Summarizing findings from an extensive review of published studies that have examined laws and policy relevant to elder policy, Hill (in press) concludes that in the United States there is a general trend toward increased use of a broader definition of family. This broader definition implies that spouses, the nuclear family, extended kin, stepkin, and sometimes in-laws constitute an ongoing collective, whose members share economic resources and risks over their lives and beyond. However, there is considerable variation among states in the laws that are created and the rules that are enforced with respect to family financial obligations and accountability. Some states facilitate conservation of family resources; others are far more concerned with minimizing public assistance and public costs. More problematic than the variation in the laws concerned with financial obligations is the ambivalence exhibited in public policy with regard to obligations of family members for direct care of dependent elders. Although there are no laws that require family members to provide care, the absence of feasible alternatives in the form of public services or financial resources often forces family members to undertake care tasks that tax their capabilities and exhaust their personal resources. Moreover, the costs of such care are not equally distributed in society, but are more heavily borne by women and low-income and minority groups.

To a large extent, then, the failure of policy makers to create programs to support family caregivers reflects an underlying belief that family members should be responsible for elder care and the belief that the introduction of public support services will cause families to abdicate this obligation. One consequence of this situation is a bias toward institutional care that is built into public policies in most states, due to the fact that Medicaid will cover the costs of support services delivered in institutional settings that are not covered in community-based settings. While most states have obtained waivers to use Medicaid funds to cover home- and community-based services (HCBS), the needs of family members are not treated as a legitimate basis for eligibility for such services. Most HCBS waiver programs treat family members as resources available to provide assistance to dependent elders. Services are not offered for the benefit of family caregivers, nor are the strengths and needs of family members assessed (Family Caregiver Alliance, 2006a, 2006b).

The one exception to this trend is the National Family Caregiver Support Program. Yet the NFCSP is very uneven across states and within states as to the types services made available to family caregivers. As Feinberg and Newman (in press) note, the modest level of funding for the NFCSP has left substantial gaps in caregiver services. These gaps limit the choices of caregivers and prevent them from obtaining services that best meet their needs. Consequently, a significant challenge for social workers who are attempting to meet the needs of family caregivers continues to be the lack of services. Long-term care reform is needed. Such reform would recognize the family as the primary source of care and include legitimate support services. Such recognition by policy makers will require strong advocacy efforts from families, social workers, and provider organizations. Until that time, family caregivers will continue to be the unsung and undersupported heroes of elder care.

REFERENCES

Acton, G. J., & Kang, J. (2001). Interventions to reduce the burden of caregiving for an adult with dementia: A meta-analysis. *Research in Nursing and Health, 24*(5), 349–360.

AHRQ Research Report. (2001). *The characteristics of long-term care users* (AHRQ Publication No. 00-0049). Rockville, MD: Agency for Healthcare Research and Quality.

Anhensel, C., Pearlin, L., Mulan, J., Zarit, S., & Whitlach, C. (1995). *Profiles in caregiving: The unexpected career.* San Diego, CA: Academic Press.

Arno, P. S. (2006, January 25–27). *Economic value of informal caregiving: 2004.* Paper presented at the Care Coordination and the Caregiver Forum, Department of Veteran Affairs, National Institute of Health, Bethesda, MD.

Austin, C. D., & McClelland, R. W. (1996). *Case management practice.* Milwaukee, WI: Families International.

Barusch, A. S., & Spaid, W. M. (1996). Spouse caregivers and the caregiving experience: Does cognitive impairment make a difference? *Journal of Gerontological Social Work, 25*(3/4), 93–106.

Bass, D. M., McClendon, M. J., Brennan, P. F., & McCarthy, C. (1998). The buffering effect of a computer support network on caregiver strain. *Journal of Aging and Health, 10*(1), 20–43.

Bass, D. M., & Noelker, L. S. (1996). The moderating influence of service use on negative caregiving consequences. *Journals of Gerontology: Psychological Sciences and Social Sciences, 51B,* S121.

Baumgarten, M., Lebel, P., Laprise, H., Leclerc, C., & Quinn, C. (2002). Adult day care for the frail elderly: Outcomes, satisfaction, and cost. *Journal of Aging and Health, 14,* 237.

Beach, S. R., Schulz, R., Williamson, G. M., Miller, L. S., Weiner, M. F., & Lance, C. E. (2005). Risk factors for potentially harmful informal caregiver behavior. *Journal of the American Geriatrics Society, 53*(2), 255–261.

Beach, S. R., Schulz, R., Yee, J. L., & Jackson, S. (2000). Negative and positive health effects of caring for a disabled spouse: Longitudinal findings from the caregiver health effects study. *Psychology and Aging, 15*(2), 259–271.

Bookwala, J., Yee, J. L., Schulz, R., Williamson, G. M., Shaffer, D. R., & Parmelee, P. A. (2000). Caregiving and detrimental mental and physical health outcomes. In G. M. Williamson, P. A. Parmelee, & D. R. Shaffer (Eds.), *Physical illness and depression in older adults: A handbook of theory, research, and practice* (pp. 93–131). New York: Kluwer Academic/Plenum Press.

Bourgeois, M. S., Schulz, R., & Burgio, L. (1996). Interventions for caregivers of patients with Alzheimer's disease: A review and analysis of content, process, and outcomes. *International Journal of Aging and Human Development, 43,* 35–92.

Braithwaite, V. (1996). Understanding stress in informal caregiving: Is burden a problem of the individual or of society? *Research on Aging, 18*(2), 139–173.

Braithwaite, V. (2000). Contextual or general stress outcomes: Making choices through caregiving appraisals. *Gerontologist, 40*(6), 706–717.

Brody, E. M. (1990). *Women in the middle: Their parent-child years.* New York: Springer.

Brody, E. M., Litvin, S. J., Hoffman, C., & Kleban, M. H. (1995). Marital status of caregiving daughters and co-residence with dependent parents. *Gerontologist, 35*(1), 75–85.

Brown, R., Pain, K., Berwald, C., Hirschi, P., Delehanty, R., & Miller, H. (1999). Distance education and caregiver support groups: Comparison of traditional and telephone groups. *Journal of Head Trauma Rehabilitation, 14,* 257.

Burgener, S. C., Bakas, T., Murray, C., Dunahee, J., & Tossey, S. (1998). Effective caregiving approaches for patients with Alzheimer's disease. *Geriatric Nursing, 19*(3), 121–126.

Burgio, L. D., Solano, N., Fisher, S. E., Stevens, A., & Gallagher-Thompson, D. (2003). Skill-building: Psychoeducational strategies. In D. W. Coon, D. Gallagher-Thompson, & L. W. Thompson (Eds.), *Innovative interventions to reduce dementia caregiver distress: A clinical guide* (pp. 119–138). New York: Springer.

Burton, L. C., Newsom, J., Schulz, R., Hirsch, C. H., & German, P. S. (1997). Preventative health behaviors among spousal caregivers. *Preventative Medicine, 26,* 162–169.

Call, C. T., Finch, M. A., Huck, S. M., & Kane, R. A. (1999). Caregiver burden from a social exchange perspective: Caring for older people after hospital discharge. *Journal of Marriage and the Family, 61,* 688–699.

Campbell, L. D., & Martin-Matthews, A. (2003). The gendered nature of men's filial care. *Journals of Gerontology: Psychological Sciences and Social Sciences, 58B*(6), S350–S358.

Caro, F. G. (in press). Introduction: Family and aging policy [Special issue]. *Journal of Aging and Social Policy, 18*(3/4).

Caserta, M. S. (1987). Caregivers to dementia patients: The utilization of community services. *Gerontologist, 27*(2), 209–214.

Chappell, N. L., & Reid, R. C. (2002). Burden and well-being among caregivers: Examining the distinction. *Gerontologist, 42*(6), 772–780.

Cicirelli, V. G., Dwyer, J. W., & Coward, R. T. (1992). Siblings as caregivers in middle and old age. In J. W. Dwyer & R. T. Coward (Eds.), *Gender, families, and elder care* (pp. 84–101). Newbury Park, CA: Sage.

Clark, M., & Huttlinger, K. (1998). Elder care among Mexican American families. *Clinical Nursing Research, 7*(1), 64–81.

Coe, M., & Neufeld, A. (1999). Male caregivers' use of formal support. *Western Journal of Nursing Research, 21*(4), 568–588.

Cook, J. A., & Heller, T. (1999). The effect of support group participation on caregiver burden among parents of adult offspring with severe mental illness. *Family Relations, 48,* 405.

Coon, D. W., Gallagher-Thompson, D., & Thompson, L. W. (2003). *Innovative interventions to reduce dementia caregiver distress.* New York: Springer.

Coon, D. W., Thompson, L., Steffen, A., Sorocco, K., & Gallagher-Thompson, D. (2003). Anger and depression management: Psychoeducational skill training interventions for women caregivers of a relative with dementia. *Gerontologist, 43*(5), 678–689.

Cox, C. (1993). Service needs and interests: A comparison of African American and White caregivers seeking Alzheimer's assistance. *Journal of Alzheimer's Care and Related Disorders and Research, 8*(3), 33–40.

Cox, C. (1997). Findings from a statewide program of respite care: A comparison of service users, stoppers, and nonusers. *Gerontologist, 37*(4), 511–517.

Czaja, S. J., & Rubert, M. P. (2002). Telecommunications technology as an aid to family caregivers of persons with dementia. *Psychosomatic Medicine, 64*(3), 469–476.

Delgado, M., & Tennstedt, S. (1997a). Making the case for culturally appropriate community services: Puerto Rican elders and their caregivers. *Health and Social Work, 22,* 246–255.

Delgado, M., & Tennstedt, S. (1997b). Puerto Rican sons as primary caregivers of elderly parents. *Social Work, 18*(2), 125–134.

Dellasega, C., & Zerbe, T. M. (2002). Caregivers of frail rural older adults: Effects of an advanced practice nursing intervention. *Journal of Gerontological Nursing, 28,* 40–49.

Depp, C., Krisztal, E., Cardenas, V., Oportot, M., Mausbach, B., Ambler, C., et al. (2003). Treatment options for improving wellbeing in dementia family caregivers: The case for psychoeducational interventions. *Clinical Psychologist, 7*(1), 21–31.

Diehl, J., Mayer, T., Foerstl, H., & Kurz, A. F. (2003). A support group for caregivers of patients with frontotemporal dementia. *Dementia: The International Journal of Social Research and Practice, 2*(2), 151–161.

Dilworth-Anderson, P., Canty Williams, I., & Gibson, B. E. (2002). Issues of race, ethnicity, and culture in caregiving research: A 20-year review (1980–2000). *Gerontologist, 42*(2), 237–272.

Dilworth-Anderson, P., & Gibson, B. E. (2002). The cultural influence of values, norms, meanings, and perceptions in understanding dementia in ethnic minorities. *Alzheimer Disease and Associated Disorders, 16,* S56-S63.

Donaldson, C., & Burns, A. (1999). Burden of Alzheimer's disease: Helping the patient and caregiver. *Journal of Geriatric Psychiatry and Neurology, 12,* 21–28.

Doress-Worters, P. B. (1994). Adding elder care to women's multiple roles: A critical review of the caregiver stress and multiple roles literature. *Sex Roles: A Journal of Research, 31*(9/10), 597–617.

Dwyer, J. W., & Conrad, R. T. (Eds.). (1992). *Gender and family care of the elderly.* Newbury Park, CA: Sage.

Dziegielewski, S. F., & Ricks, J. L. (2000). Adult day programs for elderly who are mentally impaired and the measurement of caregiver satisfaction. *Activities, Adaptation and Aging, 24*(4), 51–64.

Family Caregiver Alliance. (2006a). *A national consensus development conference: Vol. 1. Caregiver assessment—Principles, guidelines, and strategies for change.* San Francisco: National Center on Caregiving at Family Caregiver Alliance.

Family Caregiver Alliance. (2006b). *A national consensus development conference: Vol. 2. Caregiver assessment: Voices and views.* San Francisco: National Center on Caregiving at Family Caregiver Alliance.

Farkas, J. I., & Himes, C. L. (1997). The influence of caregiving and employment on the voluntary activities of midlife and older women. *Journals of Gerontology: Psychological and Social Sciences, 52B*(4), 180–189.

Farran, C. J., Miller, B. H., Kaufman, J. E., & Davis, L. (1997). Race, finding meaning, and caregiver distress. *Journal of Aging and Health, 9*(3), 316–333.

Feinberg, L. F., & Newman, S. L. (in press). Preliminary experiences of the state in implementing the National Family Caregiver Support Program: A 50-state study. International view on family and aging policy [Special issue]. *Journal of Aging and Social Policy, 18*(3/4).

Forester, A., Young, J., & Langhorne, P. (1999). Systematic review of day hospital care for elderly people: The day hospital group. *British Medical Journal*(318), 837–841.

Franks, M., & Parris Stephens, M. A. (1996). Social support in the context of caregiving husbands' provision of support to wives involved in parent care. *Journals of Gerontology: Psychological and Social Sciences, 51B*(1), P43–P53.

Fredriksen, K., & Scharlach, A. E. (1997). Caregiving and employment: The impact of workplace characteristics on role strain. *Journal of Gerontological Social Work, 28*(4), 3–20.

Gallagher-Thompson, D. (1994). Direct services and interventions for caregivers: A review of extant programs and a look to the future. In M. H. Cantor (Ed.), *Family caregiving: Agenda for the future* (pp. 102–122). San Francisco: American Society on Aging.

Gallagher-Thompson, D., Lovett, S., Rose, J., McKibbin, C., Coon, D., & Futterman, A. (2000). Impact of psychoeducational intervention on distressed family caregivers. *Journal of Clinical Geropsychology, 6*, 91–110.

Gaugler, J. E., Edwards, A. B., Femia, E. E., Zarit, S. H., Stephens, M. A., Townsend, A., et al. (2000). Predictors of institutionalization of cognitively impaired elders: Family help and the timing of placement. *Journals of Gerontology: Psychological Sciences and Social Sciences, 55B*(4), P247–P255.

Gaugler, J. E., Jarrott, S. E., Zarit, S. H., Stephens, M.-A. P., Townsend, A., & Greene, R. (2003). Adult day service use and reductions in caregiving hours: Effects on stress and psychological well-being for dementia caregivers. *International Journal of Geriatric Psychiatry, 18*(1), 55–62.

George, L. K., & Gwyther, L. P. (1986). Caregiver well-being: A multidimensional examination of family caregivers of demented adults. *Gerontologist, 26*(3), 253–259.

Gottlieb, B. H., & Johnson, J. (2000). Respite programs for caregivers of persons with dementia: A review with practice implications. *Aging and Mental Health, 4*(2), 119–129.

Gwyther, L. P., & Ballard, E. L. (1990). *Overcoming barriers to appropriate service use: Effective individualized strategies for Alzheimer's care.* Durham, NC: Duke University Center for Study of Aging.

Harding, R., & Higginson, I. J. (2003). What is the best way to help caregivers in cancer and palliative care? A systematic literature review of interventions and their effectiveness. *Palliative Medicine, 17*, 63.

Henderson, J. N., & Gutierrez-Mayka, M. (1992). Ethnocultural themes in caregiving to Alzheimer's disease patients in Hispanic families. *Clinical Gerontologist, 11*, 59–74.

Hill, G. J. (in press). State policy decisions in the 1990s with implications for the financial well-being of later-life families: International view on family and aging policy [Special issue]. *Journal of Aging and Social Policy, 18*(3/4).

Hooyman, N. R., & Gonyea, J. (1995). Social services and social support. In D. S. Foster (Ed.), *Feminist perspectives on family care: Vol. 6. Policies for gender justice* (pp. 271–272). Thousand Oaks, CA: Sage.

Horowitz, A. (1985). Family caregiving to frail elderly. *Annual Review of Gerontology and Geriatrics, 5*, 194–246.

Ishii-Kuntz, M. (1997). Intergenerational relationships among Chinese, Japanese, and Korean Americans. *Family Relations, 46*, 23–32.

Janevic, M. R., & Connell, C. M. (2001). Racial, ethnic, and cultural differences in the dementia caregiving experience: Recent findings. *Gerontologist, 41*(3), 334–347.

Johansson, J., & Sundstrom, G. (in press). Polices and practices in support of family caregivers: Filial obligations redefined in Sweden. International view on family and aging policy [Special issue]. *Journal of Aging and Social Policy, 18*(3/4).

Kiecolt-Glaser, J., Glaser, R., Gravenstein, S., Malarkey, W., & Sheridan, J. (1996). Chronic stress alters the immune response to influenza virus vaccine in older adults. *Proceedings of the National Academy of Sciences, USA, 93,* 3043–3047.

Kiecolt-Glaser, J., Maruchas, P., Malarkey, W., Mercado, A., & Glaser, R. (1995). Slowing of wound healing by psychological stress. *Lancet, 346*(8984), 1194–1197.

Knight, B. G., Lutzky, S. M., & Macofsky-Urban, F. (1993). A meta-analytic review of interventions for caregiver distress: Recommendations for future research. *Gerontologist, 33*(2), 240–248.

Knight, B. G., & McCallum, T. J. (1998). Heart rate reactivity and depression in African-American and White dementia caregivers: Reporting bias or positive coping? *Aging and Mental Health, 2*(3), 212–221.

Knight, B. G., Silverstein, M., McCallum, T. J., & Fox, L. S. (2000). A sociocultural stress and coping model for mental health outcomes among African American caregivers in southern California. *Journals of Gerontology: Psychological and Social Sciences, 55B*(3), P142–P150.

Kosloski, K., & Montgomery, R. J. V. (1994). Investigating patterns of service use by families providing care for dependent elders. *Journal of Aging and Health, 6,* 17–37.

Kosloski, K., & Montgomery, R. J. V. (1995). The impact of respite use on nursing home placement. *Gerontologist, 35*(1), 67–74.

Kosloski, K., Montgomery, R. J. V., & Karner, T. X. (1999). Differences in the perceived need for assistive services by culturally diverse caregivers of persons with dementia. *Journal of Applied Gerontology, 18*(2), 239–256.

Kosloski, K., Montgomery, R. J. V., & Youngbauer, J. (2001). Utilization of respite services: A comparison of users, seekers, and nonseekers. *Journal of Applied Gerontology, 20*(1), 111–132.

Kosloski, K., Schaefer, J., Allwardt, D., Montgomery, R. J. V., & Karner, T. (2002). The role of cultural factors on clients' attitudes toward caregiving, perceptions of service delivery, and service utilization. *Home Health Care Services Quarterly*(3/4), 65–88.

Kramer, B. J. (1997). Gain in caregiving experience: Where are we? What next? *Gerontologist, 37,* 218–232.

Kramer, B. J., & Kipnis, S. (1995). Eldercare and work-role conflict: Toward an understanding of gender differences in caregiver burden. *Gerontologist, 35*(3), 340–349.

Laditka, J. N., & Laditka, S. B. (2001). Adult children helping older parents: Variations in likelihood and hours by gender, race, and family role. *Research on Aging, 23*(4), 429–456.

Lawton, M. P., Rajagopal, D., Brody, E., & Kleban, M. H. (1992). The dynamics of caregiving for a demented elder among Black and White families. *Journal of Gerontology: Social Sciences, 47,* S156–S164.

Levesque, L., Cossette, S., & Laurin, L. (1995). A multidimensional examination of the psychological and social well-being of caregivers of a demented relative. *Research on Aging, 17*(3), 332–361.

Levesque, L., Ducharme, F., & Lachance, L. (1999). Is there a difference between family caregiving of institutionalized elders with or without dementia? *Western Journal of Nursing Research, 21*(4), 473–497.

Mahoney, D. M., Tarlow, B. J., Jones, R. N., Tennstedt, S., & Kasten, L. (2001). Factors affecting the use of a telephone-based intervention for caregivers of people with Alzheimer's disease. *Journal of Telemedicine and Telecare, 7*(3), 139–148.

Maslow, K., Levine, C., & Reinhard, C. (September, 2005). *Assessment of family caregivers: A public policy perspective.* Paper presented at the Family Caregiver Alliance, San Francisco.

Matire, M., Parris-Stephens, M. A., & Franks, M. M. (1997). Multiple roles of women caregivers: Feelings of mastery and self-esteem as predictors of psychosocial well-being. *Journal of Women and Aging, 9*(1/2), 117–132.

Matthews, S. H. (1995). Gender and the division of filial responsibility between lone sisters and their brothers. *Journals of Gerontology: Psychological and Social Sciences, 50B,* S312–S320.

McKinlay, J. B., Crawford, S. L., & Tennstedt, S. L. (1995). The everyday impacts of providing informal care to dependent elders and their consequences for the care recipients. *Journal of Aging and Health, 7,* 4.

Merrill, D. (1997). *Caring for elderly parents: Juggling work, family, and caregiving in middle and working class families.* Westport, CT: Auburn House.

Meuser, T. M., & Marwit, S. J. (2001). A comprehensive, stage-sensitive model of grief in dementia caregiving. *Gerontologist, 41*(5), 658–670.

Miller, B., & Cafasso, L. (1992). Gender differences in caregiving: Fact or artifact? *Gerontologist, 32,* 498–507.

Miller, B., & Lawton, P. (1997). Introduction: Finding balance in caregiver research. *Gerontologist, 37,* 216–217.

Miller, B., McFall, S., & Montgomery, A. (1991). The impact of elder health, caregiver involvement, and global stress on two dimensions of caregiver burden. *Journal of Gerontology, 46*(1), S9–S19.

Mittelman, M. S. (2000). Effect of support and counseling on caregivers of patients with Alzheimer's disease. *International Psychogeriatrics, 12*(1), 341–346.

Mittelman, M. S. (2003). Community caregiving. *Alzheimer's Care Quarterly, 4*(4), 273–285.

Mittelman, M. S., Ferris, S. H., Steinberg, G., Shulman, E., Mackell, J. A., Ambinder, A., et al. (1993). An intervention that delays institutionalization of Alzheimer's disease patients: Treatment of spouse-caregivers. *Gerontologist, 33*(6), 730–740.

Montgomery, R. J. V. (1988). Respite services for family caregivers. In M. D. Peterson & D. L. White (Eds.), *Health care for the elderly: An information sourcebook* (pp. 382–401). Newbury Park, CA: Sage.

Montgomery, R. J. V. (1989). Investigating caregiver burden. In K. S. Markides & C. L. Cooper (Eds.), *Aging stress and health* (pp. 201–218). New York: Wiley.

Montgomery, R. J. V. (1996). Examining respite care: Promises and limitations. In R. Kane & J. Dobrof Penrod (Eds.), *Family caregiving in a caring society: Policy perceptions* (pp. 29–45). Thousand Oaks, CA: Sage.

Montgomery, R. J. V. (1999). The family role in the context of long-term care. *Journal of Aging and Health, 11*(3), 401–434.

Montgomery, R. J. V. (2002). *A new look at community based respite programs: Utilization, satisfaction, and development.* New York: Haworth Press.

Montgomery, R. J. V. (2005). *Findings from care manager focus groups conducted in Wisconsin, Michigan, Washington, and Florida.* Unpublished manuscript, University of Wisconsin, Milwaukee.

Montgomery, R. J., & Datwyler, M. M. (1990). Women and men in the caregiving role. *Generations: Journal of the American Society on Aging, 14*(3), 34–38.

Montgomery, R. J. V., & Kamo, Y. (1989). Parent care by sons and daughters. In J. A. Mancini (Ed.), *Aging parents and adult children* (pp. 213–230). Lexington, MA: Lexington Books.

Montgomery, R. J. V., & Kosloski, K. (1994). A longitudinal analysis of nursing home placement for dependent elders cared for by spouses versus adult children. *Journal of Gerontology: Social Studies, 49*(2), S62–S74.

Montgomery, R. J. V., & Kosloski, K. (1995). Respite revisited: Re-assessing the impact. In P. R. Katz, R. Kane, & M. D. Mezey (Eds.), *Quality care in geriatric settings.* New York: Springer.

Montgomery, R. J. V., & Kosloski, K. (2000). Family caregiving: Change, continuity, and diversity. In R. Rubinstein & M. Lawton (Eds.), *Alzheimer's disease and related dementias: Strategies in care and research* (pp. 143–171). New York: Springer.

Montgomery, R. J. V., & Kosloski, K. (2001). *Change, continuity, and diversity among caregivers* (Selected Issue Briefs). Milwaukee: University of Wisconsin, NFCSP.

Montgomery, R. J. V., & Kosloski, K. (in press). Pathways to a caregiver identity for older adults. In R. C. Talley & R. J. V. Montgomery (Eds.), *Caregiving across the life span.* New York: Oxford University Press.

Montgomery, R. J. V., Marquis, J., Schaefer, J., & Kosloski, K. D. (2002). Profiles of respite use. In R. J. V. Montgomery (Ed.), *A new look at community-based respite programs* (pp. 33–64). New York: Haworth Press.

Montgomery, R. J. V., & Rowe, J. M. (2003). Care manager focus groups. Savannah and Atlanta, GA.

Montgomery, R. J. V., & Williams, K. N. (2001). Implications of differential impacts of caregiving for future research on Alzheimer care. *Aging and Mental Health, 5*(Suppl. 1), S23–S34.

Montoro-Rodriguez, J., Kosloski, K., & Montgomery, R. J. V. (2003). Evaluating a practice-oriented service model to increase the use of respite services among minorities and rural caregivers. *Gerontologist, 43*(6), 916–924.

Noonan, A. E., Tennstedt, S. L., & Rebelsky, F. G. (1996). Making the best of it: Themes of meaning among informal caregivers to elderly. *Journal of Aging Studies, 10,* 313–327.

O'Connor, D. L. (2002). Toward empowerment: Revisioning family support groups. *Social Work with Groups, 25,* 37.

Ory, M., Yee, J. L., Tennstedt, S. L., & Schulz, R. (2002). The extent and impact of dementia care: Unique challenges experienced by family caregivers. In R. Schulz (Ed.), *Handbook on dementia caregiving.* New York: Springer.

Pearlin, L. I., Mullan, J. T., Semple, S. J., & Skaff, M. M. (1990). Caregiving and the stress process: An overview of concepts and their measures. *Gerontologist, 30*(5), 583–594.

Pearlin, L. I., Turner, H., & Semple, S. (1989). Coping and the mediation of caregiver stress. In E. Light & B. D. Lebowitz (Eds.), *Alzheimer's disease treatment and family stress: Directions for research* (pp. 198–217). Rockville, MD: U.S. Department of Health and Human Services.

Penrod, J. D., Kane, R. A., Kane, R. L., & Finch, M. D. (1995). Who cares? The size, scope, and composition of the caregiver support system. *Gerontologist, 35*(4), 489–498.

Picot, S. J., Debanne, S. M., Namazi, K. H., & Wykle, M. L. (1997). Religiosity and perceived rewards of Black and White caregivers. *The Gerontologist, 37*(1), 89–101.

Pillemer, K., Suitor, J., & Wethington, E. (2003). Integrating theory, basic research, and intervention: Two case studies from caregiving research [Special issue]. *Gerontologist, 43*(1), 19–28.

Pinquart, M., & Sorensen, S. (2003). Associations of stressors and uplifts of caregiving with caregiver burden and depressive mood: A meta-analysis. *Journals of Gerontology: Psychological and Social Sciences, 58B*(2), P112–P128.

Pinquart, M., & Sorensen, S. (2005). Ethnic differences in stressors, resources, and psychological outcomes of family caregiving: A meta-analysis. *Gerontologist, 45*(1), 90–106.

Pinquart, M., & Sorensen, S. (2006). Gender differences in caregiver stressors, social resources, and health: An updated meta-analysis. *Journals of Gerontology: Psychological and Social Sciences, 61B*(1), P33–P45.

Pyke, K. D., & Bengston, V. L. (1996). Caring more or less: Individualistic and collectivist systems of family eldercare. *Journal of Marriage and the Family, 58*(2), 379–393.

Quayhagen, M. P., Quayhagen, M., Corbeil, R. R., Hendrix, R. C., Jackson, J. E., Snyder, L., et al. (2000). Coping with dementia: Evaluation of four non pharmacologic interventions. *International Psychogeriatrics, 12*(2), 249–265.

Schulz, R., Gallagher-Thompson, D., Haley, W. E., & Czaja, S. J. (2000). Understanding the interventions process: A theoretical/conceptual framework for intervention approaches to caregiving. In R. Schulz (Ed.), *Handbook on dementia caregiving: Evidence-based interventions for family caregivers* (pp. 33–60). New York: Springer.

Schulz, R., Newsom, J., Mittlelmark, M., Burton, L., Hirssch, C., & Jackson, S. (1997). Health effects of caregiving: The Caregiver Health Effects Study—An ancillary study of the Cardiovascular Health Study. *Annals of Behavioral Medicine, 19*(2), 110–116.

Schulz, R., O'Brien, A., Boodwasa, J., & Fleissner, K. (1995). Psychiatric and physical morbidity effects of dementia caregiving: Prevalence, correlates, and causes. *Gerontologist, 35*(6), 771–779.

Schulz, R., O'Brien, A., Czaja, S., Ory, M., Norris, R., N., Martire, L. M., et al. (2002). Dementia caregiver intervention research: In search of clinical significance. *Gerontologist, 42*, 589–602.

Sherrell, K., Buckwalter, K. C., & Morhardt, D. (2001). Negotiating family relationships: Dementia care as a midlife developmental task. *Families in Society: The Journal of Contemporary Human Services*, 383–392.

Skaff, M. M., & Pearlin, L. I. (1992). Caregiving: Role engulfment and the loss of self. *Gerontologist, 32*(5), 656A–664A.

Sleath, B., Thorpe, J., Landerman, L. R., Doyle, M., & Clipp, E. (2005). African-American and White caregivers of older adults with dementia: Differences in depressive symptomatology and psychotropic drug use. *Journal of the American Geriatrics Society, 53*(3), 397–404.

Sorensen, S., Pinquart, M., & Duberstein, P. (2002). How effective are interventions with caregivers? An updated meta-analysis. *Gerontologist, 42*(3), 356–372.

Spillman, B. C., & Pezzin, L. E. (2000). Potential and active family caregivers: Changing networks and the "sandwich generation." *Millbank Quarterly, 78*(3), 347–374.

Stephens, M. A. P., Townsend, A. L., Martire, L. M., & Druley, J. A. (2001). Balancing parent care with other roles: Interrole conflict of adult daughter caregivers. *Journals of Gerontology: Psychological Sciences and Social Sciences, 56B*(1), P24–P34.

Stern, S. (1996). Measuring child work and residence adjustments to parents' long-term care needs. *Gerontologist, 36*, 76–87.

Stuart, M., & Boll Hansen, E. (in press). Danish home care policy and the family: Implications for the United States. International view on family and aging policy [Special issue]. *Journal of Aging and Social Policy, 18*(3/4).

Stueve, A., & O'Donnell, L. (1989). Interactions between women and their elderly parents: Constraints of daughters' employment. *Research on Aging, 11*, 331–353.

Toseland, R. W., McCallion, P., Smith, T., Huck, S., Bourgeois, P., & Garstka, T. A. (2001). Health education groups for caregivers in an HMO. *Journal of Clinical Psychology, 57*(4), 551–570.

Townsend, D., & Kosloski, K. (2002). Factors related to client satisfaction with community-based respite services. *Home Health Care Services Quarterly, 21*(3/4), 89–106.

Van den Heuvel, E. T. P., Witte, L. P., Schure, L. M., Sanderman, R., & Meyboom-de Jong, B. (2001). Risk factors for burn-out in caregivers of stroke patients, and possibilities for intervention. *Clinical Rehabilitation, 15*(6), 669–677.

Van den Heuvel, E. T. P., Witte, L. P., Stewart, R. E., Schure, L. M., Sanderman, R., & Meyboom-de Jong, B. (2002). Long-term effects of a group support program and an individual support program for informal caregivers of stroke patients: Which caregivers benefit the most? *Patient Education and Counseling, 47*(4), 291–299.

Vitaliano, P. P., Echeverria, D., Yi, J., Phillips, P. E. M., Young, H., & Siegler, I. C. (2005). Psychophysiological mediators of caregiver stress and differential cognitive decline. *Psychology and Aging, 20*(3), 402–411.

Vitaliano, P. P., Young, H. M., & Zhang, J. (2004). Is caregiving a risk factor for illness? *Current Directions in Psychological Science, 13*(1), 13–16.

Warren, S., Kerr, J. R., Smith, D., Godkin, D., & Schalm, C. (2003). The impact of adult day programs on family caregivers of elderly relatives. *Journal of Community Health Nursing, 20*, 209–221.

Winslow, B. C. P. (1999). Patterns of burden in wives who care for husbands with dementia. *Nursing Clinics of North America, 34*(2), 275–287.

Wykle, M. L. (1994). Physical and mental health of women caregivers of older adults. *Journal of Gerontological Nursing, 20*(3), 48–49.

Yates, M. E., Tennstedt, S., & Chang, B. (1999). Contributors to and mediators of psychological well-being for informal caregivers. *Journals of Gerontology: Psychological and Social Sciences, 54B*(1), 12–22.

Yee, J. L., & Schulz, R. (2000). Gender differences in psychiatric morbidity among family caregivers: A review and analysis. *Gerontologist, 40*, 147–164.

Yin, T., Zhou, Q., & Bashford, C. (2002). Burden on family members: Caring for frail elderly—A meta-analysis of interventions. *Nursing Research, 51*(3), 199–208.

Youn, G., Knight, B. G., Jeong, H.-S., & Benton, D. (1999). Differences in familism values and caregiving outcomes among Korean, Korean American, and White American dementia caregivers. *Psychology and Aging, 14*(3), 355–364.

CHAPTER 17

Community- and Facility-Based Care

GRETCHEN E. ALKEMA, KATHLEEN H. WILBER,
and SUSAN M. ENGUIDANOS

THIS CHAPTER FOCUSES on a range of programs and services developed for older adults who need chronic care services. Types of support available include both community-based and facility-based care. These services are designed to offer therapeutic, compensatory, and palliative care for older adults with multiple chronic health conditions and functional limitations.

Our goal in this chapter is twofold: (1) to provide a general conceptual overview of the need for chronic care and its historical interface with community-based and facility-based services, and (2) to review what is known about several specific types of community- and facility-based services. We focus on services that link medical and social care such as skilled nursing facilities, assisted living facilities, adult day services, and hospice. We begin the chapter by presenting the core values that we believe affect a broad variety of chronic care services, and then develop categories of services according to their settings and purpose. We discuss the prevalence of major chronic care conditions and the etiology of chronic care. We then present research findings on some of the prominent types of services within the chronic care continuum. We conclude by applying evidence-based practices to a case study and discuss practice implications and policy recommendations.

It is important to clarify from the outset that these are challenging goals. For most chronic care services, there is no national policy or regulations, which means that there is a great deal of state and local variation. In addition, chronic care service delivery networks are developing rapidly, changing and evolving to meet emerging needs within shifting fiscal and policy constraints. Robyn Stone (2000, p. 2), a prominent gerontologist, notes that the broad area of long-term care is increasingly complex and "not easy to define [because] the boundaries among primary, acute, and long-term care have blurred." We agree.

WHAT IS CHRONIC CARE?

Chronic care is an umbrella term that includes acute, subacute, postacute, and primary facility-based care, in-home care, and community-based services. As the range of services available for older adults with chronic conditions has increased, the term *chronic care* has evolved to describe any combination of medical (acute, primary, postacute, ambulatory) and social services. Although this type of support traditionally has been called long-term care, the terminology is changing for several reasons. Originally, long-term care referred to nursing home care. During the past several decades, a variety of programs and services were developed to support older adults in community settings and in their own homes, often called home-and community-based services (HCBS). Chronic care typically involves multiple organizations interacting in a loose network rather than in a tight bureaucratic structure. In addition to services, chronic care is often defined by the population served, including individuals who are functionally impaired and/or who have medically complex chronic conditions. Terminology to describe those receiving services varies. For example, those who receive care in facilities are called *residents*, those served in day care are called *participants*, care managers usually refer to their *clients*, and those receiving hospice are *patients*.

Characteristics of chronic care services include the following:

- Are supportive and concerned with maintaining or improving functioning over an extended period of time, usually 90 days or more
- Encompass social and environmental needs, and are therefore broader than the acute care medical model
- Are often low-tech, high-touch, hands-on services
- Affect multiple aspects of life over an extended period of time
- Are provided on a formal or informal (family and friends) basis
- Are difficult to define due to variability within services and blurred boundaries across services
- Include a wide range of health services, health-related support services, and housing
- Involve a broad range of help with daily activities that chronically disabled individuals need for a prolonged period of time (Stone, 2000)

About 60% of those who use chronic care services are older adults. Although on any given day only about 4% of those age 65 and over are in facility-based care (i.e., nursing homes), about 14% of older adults require functional assistance of some type. Consumers of chronic care services also include children and adults under the age of 65 with developmental disabilities, severe chronic mental disorders, HIV/AIDS, or disabling physical disabilities. Trends such as population aging, technological advances, the restructuring of health care services toward less hospital-based care, managed care, and alternative delivery systems are transforming the field of chronic care service delivery. These trends result in increased demand for services and expanded efforts to identify and apply effective innovations in multiple settings.

Figure 17.1 illustrates the categories and types of services that may be included under the rubric of chronic care. The continuum of chronic care services for older adults includes a wide range of medically and socially focused services (Alkema, Shannon, & Wilber, 2003; Dychtwald & Zitter, 1991). These services are

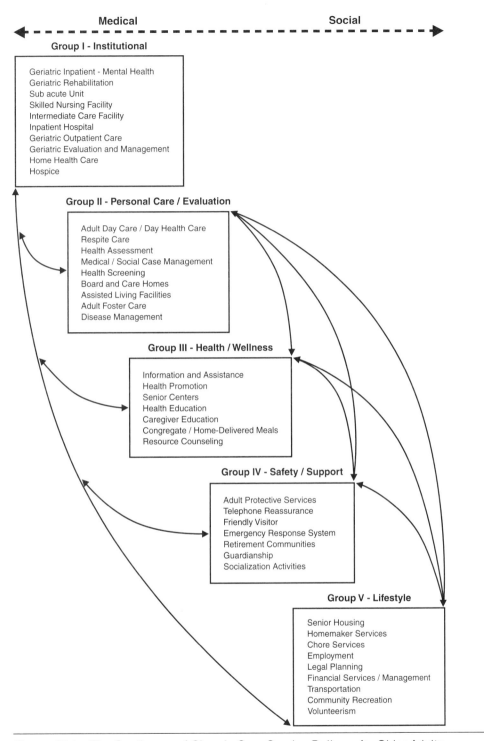

Figure 17.1 The Continuum of Chronic Care Service Delivery for Older Adults. Adapted from "Using Interagency Collaboration to Serve Older Adults with Chronic Care Needs: The Care Advocate Program," by G. E. Alkema, G. R. Shannon, and K. H. Wilber, 2003, *Family and Community Health, 26*(3), 221–229. Adapted with permission.

provided in private homes, community settings, and a variety of 24-hour facilities. Starting at the highest level of intensity, services extend from institutional-level care, such as hospitals and nursing facilities, down to lifestyle services, which include legal and financial advice, transportation, and recreation services. Intensity and dosage of an intervention varies significantly within each specific service type based on what is appropriate for the consumer's needs (Weissert, Chernew, & Hirth, 2003). The arrows represent links between service groups, signifying that consumers and providers may access any level of care needed as all groups are connected to each other, and they can access a direct link back to institutional-level care when appropriate. As policy makers and practitioners work toward creating a true chronic care model integrating medical and social care, they must account for myriad service options available and unique configurations of these services together to address the multiple and often unpredictable needs of older adults with chronic conditions.

CORE VALUES GUIDING SERVICE DELIVERY TO OLDER ADULTS

One of the major challenges in serving older and dependent adults is to provide the appropriate level of support while safeguarding basic rights of autonomy and self-determination. A fundamental approach to keep the important goal of safety from incorrectly trumping individual freedom is to operationalize these values in programs available for older adults (Wilber, 2000; Wilber & Alkema, 2006). These core values include (a) striving to offer the least restrictive appropriate alternative; (b) facilitating the older person's ability to live wherever he or she is most comfortable, often called "aging in place"; (c) centering decisions to the greatest extent possible around client preferences and expressed needs through programs that offer consumer choice and direction; (d) drawing from the repertoire of available interventions to develop an individualized plan of treatment; (e) supporting informal caregivers; and (f) clinically integrating medical, social, and housing services. Ideally these values are operationalized in the context of self-determination and person-environment fit, offering providers appropriate tools to balance respect for the client's personal freedom with legitimate concerns about personal safety.

The *least restrictive appropriate alternative* is a term that originated with a court case, *Lake v. Cameron* (1966), in which the District of Columbia Court of Appeals ruled that less restrictive alternatives must be sought before an individual may be held in an institution. Since then, this ruling solidified the values that consumers should be served with as few constraints placed on them as possible, and their rights and liberties should be recognized and respected. This trend is evident in state efforts to implement the *Olmstead* decision, also based on a court ruling. *Olmstead v. L.C.* was decided by the U.S. Supreme Court in 1999. Based on the federal Americans with Disabilities Act (ADA), the Court found that the ADA prohibits states from unnecessarily institutionalizing individuals with disabilities due to the state's failure to serve them in the most integrated setting appropriate to their needs and preferences. Although states must respond by making reasonable accommodations for community care options, states are not required to fundamentally alter their existing programs (Rosenbaum, 2000). For a comprehensive update on state planning to meet the *Olmstead* decision, see Fox-Grage, Folkemer, and Lewis (2004).

Aging in place (Callahan, 1993), which we broaden to encompass *aging wherever the older adult wants to live*, recognizes that individuals should not be forced to relocate to different settings due to needing higher levels of care. Rather, to the extent possible, services should be designed so that consumers can use them in the setting of their choice, typically their home, and should be flexible enough to address changing needs. Aging in place includes home modifications to make the living environment manageable and safe (Pynoos, Nishita, & Perelman, 2003), and incorporating personal care or other compensatory services into the home environment. Another example of residential-based services that support this mission is a movement toward cohousing and intentional communities (Thomas, 2004). Day services, such as adult day care (discussed later in this chapter), may also help with aging in place when there is adequate transportation to facilitate access and when services support independent living.

Consumer-centered and consumer-directed care suggest that, to the extent feasible, the recipient of services makes decisions about care rather than the provider dictating the approach. To support informed decisions, providers need to listen to recipients' concerns and questions, inform them of available choices, and discuss the consequences of using available options (Curry & Wetle, 2001; Kaufman & Becker, 1996). Recent studies of consumer-directed services in the United States suggest two general models of implementing consumer-directed support when providing personal care (Benjamin, 2001). The first model provides full decision-making power to consumers, who are responsible for hiring, firing, and managing care providers, and finances the service provision through a fiscal intermediary. The second model, exemplified in the Cash and Counseling Program, provides a fixed monthly allowance in a spending account that participants can spend toward disability-related goods and services (B. Phillips & Schneider, 2002). Cash comes with support from professional case management counseling and fiscal management to assist consumers with the hiring, firing, and supervising of care through a local contracted agency. By balancing consumer choice with professional support, this model can be adapted to consumers of varying functioning levels. Additionally, literature on the philosophy of consumer direction acknowledges that older adults desire professional support to help with identifying and assisting with service needs, but maintains that the consumer is responsible for decisions about when, if, and how he or she wants to use services (Coleman, 2001; R. A. Kane, 2001; Squillace & Firman, 2002).

Support for family caregiving challenges the long-held myth that families relinquish the care of their older adult relatives to nonfamily providers. In reality, among older adults not residing in 24-hour care facilities, unpaid informal caregivers provide about 80% of the care (Doty, Stone, Jackson, & Drabek, 2001; Wiener, Illston, & Hanley, 1994). Given the high demands of caring for a frail older person, high stress, burnout, and caregiver burden may become problems (Zarit, Reever, & Bach-Peterson, 1980). Formal services that value, support, and complement informal care, including counseling, support groups, and respite services, offer useful means to ensure continuity and service effectiveness.

Individualized treatment plans are an important component of chronic care services given that a one-size-fits-all approach will not meet the varied needs of diverse older adults. Given that community- and facility-based services have the potential to affect every aspect of an individual's life, treatment planning should be personalized and targeted to both the needs and preferences of the older adult. Individualized treatment planning begins with a thorough assessment process, including assessment of the older adult's needs and preferences and the informal and professional care systems that provide assistance (Moxley, 1989). Based on this assessment, treatment plans are developed in context of the older adult's service preferences, availability and geographic proximity of those services, and eligibility requirements. Treatment plans serve as guiding strategies to implementing needed services and should be dynamic and responsive to the individual's changing needs.

Finally, given that chronic care services tend to be highly fragmented, the array of specialized services needed by each person must be woven together into a *clinically integrated* service package for each consumer. Chronic care is a complex endeavor, involving a variety of health and social services offered in different settings by a variety of different professionals and paraprofessionals. Its complexity includes different terminology, administration, financing, and reimbursement. The fragmentation of health and social care delivery systems, described by the Institute of Medicine (2001, p. 4) as a "nightmare to navigate," makes it difficult for those with chronic conditions to gain access to services and coordinate them across the different types of care needed. Clinical integration of services seeks to overcome the fragmentation that results from multiple programs and providers engaging in the older person's care. When it is necessary to weave together services from numerous providers, the goal of clinical integration is to provide services that consumers perceive to be seamless. Specific means for clinical integration include case management, multidisciplinary teams, coordination of services offered by different organizations, and service integration within a single organization. Regardless of the approach, it is important that the fragmented delivery system does not negatively affect the older adult's ability to access and use care (see Box 17.1).

Box 17.1

Chronic care services are also distinct in that they include therapeutic, compensatory, and palliative approaches. Whereas acute health care focuses more on therapeutic treatment, the long-term care component of chronic care traditionally focuses on compensatory and palliative care (R. A. Kane, Kane, & Ladd, 1998). Although therapeutic care has been the focus in health care, the increasing need for chronic care services requires attention from compensatory and palliative care.

Therapeutic treatment emphasizes:

- Getting better
- Treatment
- Improved functioning
- Reduced decline

Compensatory care focuses on:

- Adapting to disability
- Compensating for areas of impairment
- Consumer focus and control

Palliative care focuses on:

- Increasing daily comfort
- Controlling pain
- Supporting clients and their caregivers at any stage of a serious illness

TRENDS AND INCIDENCE

Chronic conditions are highly prevalent in the United States, affecting over 125 million people, or about 40% of the population (Anderson & Horvath, 2002; Wu & Green, 2000). By 2020, this number is expected to increase to 157 million people (Wu & Green, 2000). The five most common chronic health conditions are hypertension (26%), mental conditions (22%), respiratory diseases (18%), arthritis (13%), and heart disease (12%). One of these—heart disease—and four others (cancers, strokes, chronic obstructive pulmonary disease, and diabetes) are responsible for two-thirds of all deaths in the United States (Centers for Disease Control and Prevention, 2002). Nearly half of those diagnosed with a chronic condition (one-fifth of the U.S. population) cope with more than one such condition (Wu & Green, 2000).

In addition to diagnoses, another way to define who needs chronic care services is by identifying people who have functional impairment. Feldman and Kane (2003) note that defining functioning as "activities of daily living" (ADLs) is a key concept for long-term care research and provides the backbone of long-term care practice. Katz, Ford, Moscovitz, Jackson, and Jaffe (1963) defined ADLs as bathing, dressing, toileting, transferring, continence control, and eating. A few years later, Lawton and Brody (1969) added a related category which they called instrumental activities of daily living (IADLs). Whereas ADLs focus on personal care, IADLs address a person's ability to manage the environment: managing money, using the telephone, grocery shopping, personal shopping, using transportation, housekeeping, and managing medications. In 2003, 35% of Americans age 65 and above reported having at least one ADL or IADL limitation caused by a chronic condition (National Center for Health Statistics, 2005). Ten percent of those age 75 and above reported an ADL limitation, and 18% reported an IADL limitation due to a chronic condition (National Center for Health Statistics, 2005). Twenty-five percent of those with a chronic condition experience at least one activity limitation, and those with multiple chronic conditions are significantly more likely to have activity limitations. For example, 67% of patients with five or more chronic conditions have activity limitations (Anderson & Horvath, 2002). The consequences of having multiple chronic conditions include greater risk for disability, greater need for caregiver support, greater use of health care services, and mortality (Anderson & Horvath, 2002).

Although chronic conditions affect people across the demographic spectrum, women are more likely than men to have a chronic condition (Wu & Green, 2000). The majority of people with chronic conditions are under 65, but those over 65 are more likely to have multiple chronic conditions (Anderson & Horvath, 2002; Wu & Green, 2000). Considering the aging of the population and increasing life expectancy estimates over the next 40 years (Campbell, 1996; Lee, Miller, & Edwards, 2003; O'Hara-Devereaux, Falcon, Li, & Kristensen, 1999), the projected impact of chronic conditions on individuals, caregivers, and the U.S. health care system is substantial. About 70% of health care dollars in the United States are spent on chronic illnesses (Hoffman, Rice, & Sung, 1996).

In addition to affecting physical and functional health, chronic conditions also may affect the mental health and coping abilities of older adults (Germain & Gitterman, 1996), especially if the condition has associated pain. Pain is related to impaired physical function (Scudds & Robertson, 2000; Williamson & Schulz, 1992), physical disability (Scudds & Robertson, 1998), and increased depression (Magni, 1991; Parmelee, Thuras, Katz, & Lawton, 1995) among older adults.

Physical functioning level, number of health conditions, and previous episodes of depression have been consistently associated with depression across studies (Copeland, Chen, & Dewey, 1999; Roberts, Kaplan, Shema, & Strawbridge, 1998). Equally important, depressive symptoms have been linked with increased disability, impaired functioning, increased morbidity and mortality, and decreased quality of life (Herrmann, Black, Lawrence, Szekely, & Szalai, 1998; Lesperance, Frasure-Smith, & Talajic, 1996; Penninx, Leveille, Ferrucci, van Eijk, & Guralnik, 1999; Schoevers et al., 2000; Wells & Sherbourne, 1999). In a large prospective cohort study of older adults in the United States, depressed individuals had a greater decline in physical functioning and performance over a 4-year period than nondepressed participants (Penninx et al., 1998). As a result of these factors, people with multiple chronic conditions often experience reduced quality of life.

IMPACT OF CHRONIC CONDITIONS ON CAREGIVERS

One key component of supporting those with chronic conditions is that they require ongoing care, most often provided by caregivers and health care professionals (Anderson & Horvath, 2002). The Kaiser Family Foundation (2002) estimated that there are approximately 45 million adult caregivers; the vast majority are middle-aged married women, one-third of whom reported having a serious medical condition of their own. About 20% of caregivers stated that their physical health has suffered due to care-giving activities (Kaiser Family Foundation, 2002; Metropolitan Life Insurance Company, 1999). Informal caregivers provide extensive support services: direct personal care (bathing, grooming, etc.), medication assistance, instrumental activities (shopping, meal preparation, etc.), transportation, and care coordination with health service professionals (Kaiser Family Foundation, 2002; Kutner, 2001; Metropolitan Life Insurance Company, 1999). For those with chronic conditions who received assistance with care coordination, over 50% reported that their informal caregivers provide that service (Harris Interactive Inc., 2000).

The economic value of informal caregiving in 2000, based on what services would cost in the private sector, was estimated to be $257 billion (Arno, 2002; Arno, Levine, & Memmott, 1999). Transitions through and out of the labor force indicate another significant cost of caregiving. Informal caregivers who were engaged in paid work reported a high incidence of formal adjustments to their work schedules, including use of paid time off, decreased hours, leaves of absence, transitions from full- to part-time work, and early retirements (Metropolitan Life Insurance Company, 1999). Sixteen percent of those who retired at age 62 did so because of a family member's poor health, and 33% of Californians who retired between ages 45 and 70 did so for personal health reasons (Yelin & Trupin, 1999). The economic costs are realized in the form of out-of-pocket expenses, decreased paychecks, and decreased allotments to retirement savings such as Social Security and defined contribution plans (Coleman & Pandya, 2002; Kaiser Family Foundation, 2002; Metropolitan Life Insurance Company, 1999).

The need to receive ongoing care often generates concerns for people with chronic conditions, including the ability to afford care, fear of losing independence, and worries about becoming a burden to caregivers (Harris Interactive Inc., 2000). Although informal caregivers may provide care for a close family member, many seek some form of professional or paraprofessional guidance about care-giving (Kutner, 2001). Several studies have documented the negative psychological impact on caregivers as a result of the high stress they experience when caring for a loved one (O'Connor, Pollitt, Roth, Brook, & Reiss, 1990; Schulz, O'Brien, Bookwala, & Fleissner, 1995). Among caregivers of people with Alzheimer's and other chronic diseases, there is a positive correlation between the intensity of the caregiver's psychological morbidity and the length of time providing care (Gonzalez-Salvador, Arango, Lyketsos, & Calcedo Barba, 1999). Recent studies have also found that caregivers of loved ones with Alzheimer's disease may suffer from depression due not only to the severity of the symptoms of their infirmed family member, but also due to a lack of available resources (Gonzalez-Salvador et al., 1999; Vitaliano, Russo, Young, & Maiuro, 1991).

Access to Chronic Care Services

It is well known that about 15% of the population lacks basic health insurance coverage, but most people are not aware that traditional health insurance generally does not cover chronic care services such as custodial care in a facility, HCBS, and respite for caregivers. Traditional health care is financed through employer-based funding mechanisms, yet most working individuals do not need or demand long-term care insurance coverage. Traditional health care service delivery employs a medical model that covers two major areas: hospital and physician care, also called acute and primary care. Based on this model, about 90% of Americans lack long-term care insurance coverage to pay for chronic care services. Although most people believe that they are unlikely to need these services, the data suggest otherwise. For example, in 2001, 12 million people in the United States needed some form of chronic care services, and more than half were age 65 and above (Stone, 2000). One study found that 43% of those 65 and above would spend some time in a nursing facility in their lifetime, and more than half would remain for at least 1 year (Kemper & Murtaugh, 1991).

ETIOLOGY AND PROGNOSIS OF FACILITY- AND COMMUNITY-BASED CARE MODELS

In this section we discuss the etiology of several types of facility- and community-based care models that serve older adults with chronic conditions. We discuss the future of these types of care models given the scope of population aging that the United States will experience over the next 50 years.

Facility-Based Care Models

Nursing Homes   The origins of modern chronic care began with the early institutions for the poor: the county home or "poor home" (Singh, 2005). Because these "homes" often served to warehouse people who lacked financial or care-giving resources, they carried the stigma of a service of last resort. Unlike modern-day facilities, they lacked a medical component of care. This type of care expanded during the Depression as homeowners supplemented their income by taking in older adult boarders. The Social Security Act that passed in 1935 included old age assistance, which provided funding and expanded the number of nursing homes.

Nursing homes were used when hospital or medical care failed to provide cura-tive measures for chronic conditions (Abramovice, 1988; Starr, 1984).

In 1960, a shortage of hospital beds increased discharges to less costly nursing homes. Five years later, financial incentives for nursing facilities were part of the passage of two of Lyndon Johnson's Great Society programs: Medicare (for adults age 65 and above) and Medicaid (for low-income people of all ages). New nursing homes were designed according to hospital regulations for services and physical plants. Although Medicaid was not developed to provide custodial care for older adults, funding available through the Medicaid program led to a boom in the nursing home industry (Abramovice, 1988).

With the extensive growth, however, came new problems. Nursing home scan-dals hit the papers in San Diego with tales of neglect and woefully inadequate care. In addition to newspaper articles, a book was published in 1975 called *Tender Loving Greed: How the Incredibly Lucrative Nursing Home "Industry" Is Exploiting America's Old People and Defrauding Us All* (Mendelson, 1975). These exposés resulted in out-rage and created a national backlash against the industry. The 1971 White House Conference on Aging encouraged the development of home- and community-based services as alternatives to nursing home care. One of the most dramatic changes was the industry's transformation from charity and religious-based organizations to 75% proprietary ownership. In addition to increasing involvement from the pro-prietary private sector, small "mom and pop" homes were bought up by corpora-tions, and several large nursing home chains emerged (Abramovice, 1988).

The nursing home scandals led to a two-pronged effort to improve care for older and dependent adults: the development of alternatives to nursing homes and regulatory efforts to improve care in facilities (Miller & Weissert, 2000; Mol-lica, 2003; Weissert, Cready, & Pawelak, 1988). Alternatives included a number of HCBS such as adult day care, personal care, and care management (discussed later). The Nursing Home Reform Act was passed in 1987 to provide fundamen-tal reform to nursing home operations based on review of standards developed by the Institute of Medicine (1986). Sometimes referred to as OBRA '87 because it was part of the congressional Omnibus Budget Reconciliation Act, it included improvements in quality assurance measurement based on resident assessments and care planning. This legislation focused on "residents' rights" and called for reduction in and a rationale for use of restraints (physical and chemical). The Resident Assessment Instrument was developed and implemented to standard-ize the evaluation and care planning for nursing home residents. This assess-ment included the Minimum Data Set, which provides a standardized tool for assessing residents' functional capacity and care needs and is assessed at admis-sion and then quarterly.

Despite progress from OBRA '87 reforms, scandals again made news in the 1990s with a scathing article in *Time* accusing nursing homes of poor care and outright neglect (Carlson, 1995). In response the Senate Aging Committee asked the General Accounting Office (GAO; 1998) to investigate. The GAO report found that nearly one third of California nursing homes surveyed had serious or poten-tially life-threatening care problems; licensing enforcement was not catching many of these problems in the survey process; and when problems were recog-nized, sufficient state- and federal-level enforcement did not exist. Recommenda-tions focused on increasing the federal role of nursing home regulations and enforcement in homes that persisted in providing substandard care.

During this time, a grassroots response to the problems in nursing home settings was evolving under the rubric of "culture change" in all types of facility-based care. Culture change involves a major shift in thinking about how care should be provided, focusing on a philosophy that is more consumer-directed, individualized, supportive, and homelike. The overall goal of culture change is to direct the focus of facility-based care as places where elders can live and grow rather than decline and die (Thomas, 1996, 2004). Some of the more prominent leaders in this effort are the Eden Alternative, the Wellspring Movement, and the Pioneer Network. Traditionally, a quality-of-life perspective for nursing home residents has been subjugated by the primacy of quality of care for three reasons: (1) greater objectivity in measuring quality of care, (2) focus from the disability community to move people out of nursing homes rather than to improve quality of life inside, and (3) lack of definitive measurement of quality of life from the nursing home reform champions (R. A. Kane, 2003).

In addition to increased regulations, federal funding structures began to change for a variety of facility-based providers starting in the 1980s. Hospital reimbursement changed from billing for services after the fact to the prospective payment for diagnostic related groups. This change contributed to the increased discharging of patients with greater health care needs to skilled nursing facilities that received Medicare reimbursement for postacute care. Skilled nursing facilities began expanding their scope of service to include rehabilitation, ventilator patients, dementia care units, and hospice. Hospitals responded to this change by opening their own nursing home wings or "distinct parts," which directly competed with community nursing homes for Medicare-funded rehabilitation patients. In tandem, Medicare payments to nursing facilities and home health organizations increased dramatically and at a much higher rate then other Medicare-funded services. In response, Congress passed legislation in the Balanced Budget Act of 1997 to subsequently fund nursing facilities through a prospective payment system, as they had done with hospitals and physicians previously. All of these changes shifted the financing of Medicare services from fee-for-service arrangements to fixed payments in hopes of controlling costs through a reimbursement system based on patient acuity and staff time required to address the patient's needs.

Other Facility-Based Settings   As nursing homes evolved to meet changing demands, other residential approaches emerged, evolved, and expanded, including assisted living facilities, board and care homes, supportive housing communities, and continuing care retirement communities. Assisted living facilities (ALF) are recognized as a key component of long-term care (Stefanacci & Podrazik, 2005). Building on Zimmerman et al. (2005), ALF provide room, board, 24-hour staffing, and assistance with one or more activities of daily living in 24-hour state-licensed care facilities, excluding licensed health facilities and nursing facilities. Similar to nursing homes, assisted living facilities include housing; however, they differ in that their focus is primarily on hospitality services rather then skilled nursing care or rehabilitation. Some assisted living facilities provide IADL support such as medication management and personal care support for ADLs. These services are often part of a cafeteria plan, where residents can select the special support they need and pay additional monthly premiums accordingly. Although some states do not use the term "assisted living," we use it generically here to include housing and service combinations such as residential care, board and care, and adult family homes.

During the 1990s, ALF were the most rapidly growing type of senior housing (Hawes, Phillips, Rose, Holan, & Sherman, 2003), accounting for 80% of new senior housing projects in the United States (Zimmerman et al., 2005). Data from 1998 reported 11,459 ALF with 611,300 beds and 521,500 residents; the average facility had 53 beds (Hawes et al., 2003). In 2002, one third of all ALF beds (34%) were in three states: Florida, California, and Pennsylvania (Mollica, 2002). Some ALF specialize in supporting residents with dementia care, often called special care units (described later). Prior to the 1960s, older adults with dementia needing extended care were institutionalized in state psychiatric hospitals. This auspice evaporated throughout the 1960s and 1970s when most state psychiatric facilities were closed. As a result, many residents with dementia were "transinstitutionalized" by being relocated to nursing facilities for institutional care (Gerdner & Buckwalter, 1996). Problems arose in nursing homes because people with dementia often have very different care needs from those of the average resident. For example, many nursing facility residents are not ambulatory and cannot perform ADLs, such as feeding and toileting, without physical assistance. The resident with dementia, however, may be ambulatory and may be able to physically execute ADLs, but requires supervision to complete these necessary tasks. Problems managing the care of residents with dementia caused many facilities to inappropriately employ physical and chemical restraints to manage the behavioral manifestations of the dementing illness.

Board and care homes vary regionally. In some states, they are small, privately owned homes that provide housing and supportive care for 4 to 10 residents, whereas in others they may be large facilities indistinguishable from ALF. Licensing for this facility design is also variable. For example, ALF and board and care homes in California are licensed under the category "residential care facilities for the elderly" through the Department of Social Services. In contrast, nursing homes are licensed by the state Department of Health Services, suggesting the philosophical difference in residential models.

A higher cost model that merges both health and social services within the confines of a housing environment for older adults is the continuing care retirement community (CCRC). Also known as "three-tiered communities," CCRCs provide retirement housing, assisted living, and skilled nursing care all on one campus, usually for a negotiated entry fee and monthly premiums. Many also include special care units as a facility wing or separate location to care for people with dementia. These fees vary by community, depending on the type of housing and services they offer. Other CCRCs operate on a rental basis, by which consumers make monthly payments but have no initial entrance fee.

Special Care Units   Launched in the 1970s to manage the unique care needs of people with dementia, special care units (SCU) may be inside existing nursing homes or ALF, or they may be freestanding assisted living-style facilities that serve only people with dementia. Special features offered by SCU are any combination of the following (Gerdner & Beck, 2001; Gerdner & Buckwalter, 1996; Gold, 1991; Ohta & Ohta, 1988):

- Mission and vision statement specific to dementia care
- Separate physical space, if facility has a non-cognitively impaired population

- Aesthetically pleasing, homelike atmosphere
- Secured doorways with an emergency release
- Access to secured outdoor pathways
- Higher staff-to-resident ratio than standard care facilities
- Staff trained in disease progression, communication skills, and behavior management
- Activities tailored to needs of residents with dementia
- Flexible schedules for residents
- Opportunities for greater family involvement in care planning and interventions
- Support groups for both family members and direct care staff

Special care units developed in the chronic care residential spectrum through five main facility styles. Although SCU are not specifically regulated, they must meet the licensing requirements for the auspice where they are housed. The first arrangement is the SCU located inside an existing assisted living facility. Based on a social care model, this type offers a secured wing or floor that provides some specialized support and tailored activities in a separate area. Residents have less autonomy and choice than the general facility population, but must be high-functioning enough to engage in a daily routine similar to other residents. The second type is the assisted living facility designated entirely for people with dementia. This facility often has a secured perimeter and caters only to the needs of people with dementia and their families through a completely dedicated care environment. A third option is an SCU located within a standard nursing home as a designated, secured wing. This design benefits from the support of a skilled unit, with the separateness of the SCU to isolate residents with severe behavior symptoms. State health care licensing agencies regulate these SCU as part of the larger nursing home without any special criteria. The fourth type is a combined campus exclusively for people with dementia providing both assisted living and skilled nursing care. Higher functioning residents can commence at the assisted living level, and then move to the nursing facility area as the disease progresses. This facility must adhere to both assisted living and health care regulations for each qualified area. The fifth option is a variation of the combined campus, where an SCU is located within a CCRC. Although it is the most expensive selection, one benefit of this arrangement is that the well spouse can live near the SCU resident in the same community setting.

Residents and families have two options to pay for SCU: private pay or Medicaid reimbursement. The availability of each funding option depends on the consumer resources, facility auspices, and any Medicaid waivers (described later) operating in a particular state. Most SCU require private payment due to the lack of Medicaid waiver support for ALF. In fact, the average SCU resident is female, Caucasian, and widowed and pays privately for her care (Sloane & Mathew, 1991; Sloane, Zimmerman, & Ory, 2001). Costs of an assisted living-based SCU range from $1,450 to $6,800 per month (Metropolitan Life Insurance Company, 2002a). For SCU operating in a nursing home, payment may come from either funding source. The average private pay rate for standard nursing home care nationwide ranges from $4,350 to $5,110 per month (Metropolitan Life Insurance Company, 2002b). This figure does not account for any additional costs associated with SCU, which escalates the cost of this model (U.S. Congress, Office of Technology Assessment, 1992). Residents may use Medicaid reimbursement to pay for care as long as they meet both financial and functional qualifications. However, people with dementia requiring only 24-hour supervision for serious wandering or aggressive behavior may not be eligible for nursing home admission based on the individual state's level-of-care criteria (O'Keefe, 1999). This no-win situation abandons both potential consumers and their caregivers in the chasm of quality long-term care (Institute of Medicine, 2001).

Community-Based Models

Over the past 3 decades, a number of publicly funded community-based care options have emerged, with two goals: (1) to help maintain high-risk older adults in their home, and (2) to reduce the funding bias toward costly and restrictive facility-based care options. To use government funds to pay for alternatives to facility-based care, states must apply for a waiver that allows them to use Medicaid dollars for nonmedical services. Waivers in general grant an exception to nationwide Medicaid reimbursement requirements, often allowing providers to receive payment for offering nonmedical services or services for a specialized priority population (for a description of Medicaid regulations, see www.cms.hhs.gov). Many state-based care management-centered home- and community-based services were developed through Medicaid waivers. Community-based services that are not funded through Medicaid waivers are most often paid for by state general funds or consumers themselves. Two reasons for this financing structure are (1) Medicaid was developed as a health care program for low-income people, hence the funding was geared to traditional health services; and (2) there was a concern about the "woodwork effect." This term is used to convey the notion that if highly desirable services are funded by public dollars, people will "come out of the woodwork" to take advantage of them.

We examine the effectiveness of some of these alternatives to keep people out of facilities in the section on evidence-based interventions. To set the stage, we describe the etiology and prognosis of three types of community-based services: case management, adult day care, and hospice.

Case Management   Case management is provided by an individual or a team, and organizes, coordinates, and sustains a network of formal and informal supports and activities designed to optimize the functioning and well-being of people with multiple and often complex health and social care needs (Moxley, 1989; Raiff & Shore, 1993). Case management is the critical service within the continuum of long-term care that clinically integrates a variety of services, and is often described as the glue that holds varied services together. Also called care management, case management has been adopted as standard practice of many health care providers and organizations. Although multiple types of professionals in multiple settings can provide case management, for this chapter we discuss case management provided by nurse and social work professionals in the community.

Case management began as a natural extension of nursing and social work practice in the nineteenth century. Several champions facilitated its development, including Dorothea Dix, who worked to improve the lives of those in mental institutions (North Carolina Department of Health and Human Services, 2006), Jane Addams (1912), who created the Settlement House concept, and Mary Richmond, who stressed coordination and consumer direction in social case work (National Association of Social Workers, 1992). Although it continued to evolve throughout the twentieth century, case management emerged as a distinct concept in the 1960s to address the "complex, fragmented, duplicative, uncoordinated, and inaccessible" systems that existed as a result of funding programs through strict categorical channels (Raiff & Shore, 1993, p. 3). In the 1970s, case management became associated with discharge planning from state psychiatric hospitals through de-institutionalization as a method to assist clients with reentry into the community. Similarly, case management in chronic care focused on helping individuals access community-based programs and overcome bureaucracy through the Allied Services Act of 1972 (Quinn, 1993). Three key indicators that facilitated the expansion of case management in chronic care were the independent living movement of the 1970s, increased numbers of chronically ill older adults without sufficient caregiver support, and the search for alternatives to facility-based care, as described earlier.

Starting in the early 1980s, there were two major national demonstrations that used case management as a core service delivery component: the Program of All Inclusive Care for the Elderly (PACE) and the Social Health Maintenance Organization (S/HMO). Although they approached the challenge somewhat differently, the overall goal of these programs was to link Medicare-funded managed care with chronic care services such as adult day care and in-home personal care using case management. State models of case management through waiver programs also developed, such as the Multipurpose Senior Services Programs in California and the Wisconsin Family Care Program. These types of programs use assessment, care planning, evaluation, and linkages with medical and community resources to support older adults who need therapeutic or compensatory support beyond the health care system (Alkema et al., 2003; Anderson & Horvath, 2002; Borrayo, Salmon, Polivka, & Dunlop, 2002). Additionally, several demonstration projects have used social case management both inside (Dunn, Sohl-Kreiger, & Marx, 2001; Enguidanos et al., 2003; Netting & Williams, 1999; Newcomer, Harrington, & Kane, 2002) and outside (Boult, Rassen, Rassen, Moore, & Robinson, 2000; Wilber, Allen, Shannon, & Alongi, 2003) the medical system to link chronically ill patients to community-based services. These linkages improves access to vital community services, such as transportation and home-delivered meals, which greatly impact the access and appropriate use of medical care services (Leutz, Greenlick, DellaPenna, & Thomas, 2003). However, linkages to community-based care are necessary but not sufficient to improve the continuity of care, and must be connected with feedback loops to the client, caregivers, and all service providers involved in a true biopsychosocial framework (Leutz, Greenlick, & Nonnenkamp, 2003).

Adult Day Care   Adult day care (ADC) is a generic term that encompasses a range of community-based services developed to support functionally dependent adults and their caregivers. Key characteristics across different ADC types and models are that they offer community-based health, therapeutic, and social services in a group setting to adults with functional or cognitive impairment at risk of being placed in a nursing home. Goals of ADC include restoring or maintaining participants' optimal functioning and capacity for self-care and delaying or preventing inappropriate institutionalization.

Beginning as a rehabilitation service over half a century ago, ADCs' early development was influenced by the British geriatric day hospital model. In the United States, interest in ADC began to grow in the 1960s and 1970s with the search for effective alternatives to institutionalization (Gaugler, Zarit, Townsend, Stephens, & Green, 2003). Although there is no federal oversight, national standards and certification are provided by the Rehabilitation Accreditation Commission in association with the National Adult Day Services Association (http://www.nadsa.org/accreditation/accreditation-doc.doc).

Adult day care programs serve adults with physical or cognitive impairment and their caregivers. The case mix varies widely, with some programs serving populations with a variety of conditions and some targeted specifically toward individuals with dementia. Studies indicate that there are approximately 3,500 to 4,000 ADC programs in the United States serving about 160,000 adults. About three-quarters of these programs are provided by not-for-profit organizations. About two-thirds are freestanding facilities not associated with a larger organization (Tedesco, 2001). Most ADC programs are open 5 days a week during normal business hours. A small number offer extended weekend or evening service. Although participants may attend for 1 or 2 days a week, there is some evidence that those who use the service regularly—several times a week over a sustained period of time—have improved outcomes (Zarit, Stephens, Townsend, Greene, & Femia, 2003). Adult day care typically includes a standardized assessment of the participant's needs, preferences, and resources and the development of an individualized care plan identifying the type of support and services to be provided.

As with many chronic care programs, there are no federal ADC standards or oversight. As a result, states offer a variety of types of ADC services with different licensure categories and regulations. Although the majority of states license only one or two types of ADC, the terminology, licensing categories, staffing requirements, and regulations vary greatly across states. Examples of terminology are adult day care facilities, adult social day care, Alzheimer's day care, adult day care centers, adult day health care, and medical adult day care centers. Although according to a recent survey, about 53% of ADCs offer a combination of health and social services (Henry, Cox, Reifler, & Asbury, 2000), where there is more than one type of day care the distinction is often between those that offer health and skilled nursing services and those that do not. For example, ADC services can range from basic social and recreational opportunities to intensive health and rehabilitation services such as supervision of and hands-on assistance with the following: ADLs; medication administration; physical, occupational, and speech therapies; skilled nursing and health assessment; and intermittent monitoring of health status. Social work services are an important component in both models (see Box 17.2).

Hospice   Hospice is designed to provide care for individuals in their last 6 months of life and is covered by Medicare (and by Medicaid in 47 states). Unlike traditional medical services, the goal of hospice is enabling older adults with terminal illnesses to receive palliative pain management rather than curative care. Hospice care is largely provided in the home by a multidisciplinary team that may include a physician, nurse, social worker, home health aide, homemaker, and volunteers. However, it is also available in a hospice facility, hospital, or nursing home. Care encompasses psychological, emotional, and spiritual support as well as addressing medical needs. The terminally ill patient and family are considered the unit of care, with counseling and respite services available to the family. In addition, hospice staff are on call for terminally ill patients and their family 24 hours a day,

---

Box 17.2

Adult day health care services include the following:

- Multidisciplinary team of health professionals who:

  —Conduct a comprehensive assessment of each potential participant.
  —Determine and plan the Adult day health care services needed to meet the individual's health and social needs.

- Medical services.
- Nursing services.
- Physical, occupational, and speech therapy.
- Psychiatric and psychological services.
- Social services.
- Planned recreational and social activities.
- Hot meals and nutritional counseling.
- Transportation to and from the center.

---

7 days a week to provide support and medical care when needed (National Hospice and Palliative Care Organization, 2005).

Hospice care in the United States began as a grassroots effort in the 1970s in response to the high cost of dying and the need to improve quality of care for those at the end of life. Interest in hospice continued through the 1970s and led to Health Care Financing Administration sponsorship of a hospice demonstration project. Evidence from this project supported the establishment of the Medicare hospice benefit as part of the Tax Equity and Fiscal Responsibility Act of 1982. The initial benefit was designed to serve patients with 6 months or less to live. The benefit was limited to 210 lifetime days, based on the findings from the National Hospice Study (Mor & Kidder, 1985), which found that 95% of the patients were enrolled in hospice fewer than 210 days before death, and cost savings were associated with shorter lengths of stay.

Electing to receive hospice care substantially changes both the type of services team members provide to the terminally ill patient and how services are delivered and managed. Hospice care includes medical and psychosocial care and is provided by a Medicare-approved public agency or private company. It is available to individuals of all ages during their final stages of life. There are many differences between the objectives and delivery of hospice and traditional medical care. Given that the primary goal of treatment in hospice is palliative rather than curative, individuals electing hospice care must sign a waiver to forgo traditional curative measures and care. Once enrolled, the hospice provider assumes all risk for the patient (Harris, Dunmore, & Tscheu, 1996). Medicare pays the hospice service provider a predetermined daily rate to cover all health care costs for the dying patient. Four different levels of care are available through the Medicare hospice benefit: routine home care, which represents the majority (87%) of Medicare hospice payments (Medstat, 2000); continuous home nursing care (1% of hospice payments); inpatient respite care; and general inpatient care, which represents 11% of Medicare hospice payments. For older adults eligible for Medicaid, 48 states currently offer a hospice benefit under their state plan for providing Medicaid services (Center for Medicare and Medicaid Services, 2005).

Prognosis of Community-Based Chronic Care Service Delivery   Over the next 30 years, the United States will experience a tremendous increase in population aging as a result of low fertility, low mortality, and steady international immigration of young to middle-aged persons throughout the twentieth century (Bean, Myers, Angel, & Galle, 1994; Siegel, 1993). As the baby boom generation begins to turn 65 in 2010, the number of older adults is projected to increase from 39 million, or 13% of the U.S. population, to 65 million, or about 22% of the population (Macunovich, 2002). The fastest growing age group is the over-85 segment, with decennial percentage increases from 2000 to 2040. If low mortality rates keep pace with current estimates, there will be nearly 13 million older adults age 85 and above by 2040 (Martin & Kinsella, 1994). Given that the oldest old generally have some dependency needs and are the largest user of chronic care services, these estimates have significant social, economic, political, and public policy ramifications for the future (Lee & Skinner, 1999; Markides & Black, 1996; Moen, 1996).

The field of chronic care is seeing a number of dramatic changes. Central to these changes is a shift from an acute care approach to a chronic care paradigm, which integrates health, social, and housing services across a broad range of providers. The long-term care component of chronic care has been on the fringes of health care, and, to an even greater extent, nursing homes have been marginalized. Given the changing demographics, a well-developed, well-integrated, and effective repertoire of facility- and community-based services will be essential in the coming decades. Given the failure in the United States to ensure that all residents have access to acute and primary care, the challenge of ensuring access to high-quality long-term care services is even more daunting.

With the strong trend away from nursing homes toward other facility- and community-based options, there will likely be increases in four areas of facility-based care: (1) greater numbers of high end, elegant CCRCs and ALF; (2) increases in small freestanding care settings and intentional communities of individuals who live in supportive group housing that incorporates necessary services that are consumer-controlled and personalized (Thomas, 1996, 2004); (3) increases in special care units designed to serve people with dementia; and (4) increased medicalization of skilled nursing facilities to serve short-stay rehabilitation patients and long-stay people who need skilled nursing services that continually blur the distinction between acute and long-term care services. The number of assisted living facilities is growing at an extremely fast pace; as a result, this type of care is capturing some of the traditional nursing home market. With the expansion of both options, people with more money can purchase long-term care services that keep them out of nursing facilities, thereby increasing nursing facility reliance on Medicaid-eligible individuals and those at risk for spending down to Medicaid. It is not clear how regulations will deal with the increasing diversity in facility-based care options.

Chronic care has the potential to continue to stretch its identity through expansions on the HCBS side as well. Efforts such as the *Olmstead* decision have put more emphasis on the development and linking of additional home- and community-based services. This suggests that there could be expansion in the range of home and community options and, it is hoped, an improvement in opportunities to identify and access these services. Information technology offers consumers who can use the Internet better information on the services available and how to access them. Efforts to integrate the assessment process using electronic records should also help reduce fragmentation if privacy safeguards are adequate. The extent that services will be available to all regardless of their ability to pay is an unanswered question.

A number of states have Medicaid waiver services, but these do not reach an extensive market. In addition, because these services must be cost-neutral, they cannot offer the attendant care needed by people with advanced dementing illnesses or other illnesses that require 24-hour care. Unless there are dramatic breakthroughs that reduce the types of illnesses that require 24-hour care, facilities will remain an essential component of the chronic care continuum for many years to come.

EVIDENCE-BASED INTERVENTIONS AND PRACTICE GUIDELINES: FACILITY-BASED CARE

NURSING HOMES

As total care environments, nursing homes have the potential to affect residents' functioning in a variety of areas: management of chronic conditions, mental health treatment, and daily physical functioning. As such, research has focused on interventions that slow the rate of decline, maintain health, or optimally improve physical and mental health functioning. Targeted nursing home intervention studies have shown success in improving residents' overall functioning through rehabilitation regimens (Yeh & Lo, 2004), as well as performance on three key ADLs: toileting, mobility, and dressing (Feldman & Kane, 2003). One study that trained nursing assistant staff to help residents with moderate exercise and frequent incontinence care improved residents' functional abilities and reduced acute care costs in the nursing home (Schnelle et al., 2003). One negative aspect of this intervention is its labor-intensive requirements of nursing assistant staff, which could lead to staff burnout and turnover. In terms of mental health treatment, management of depression is a key issue in the nursing home. A recent review of the literature reported that both pharmacological and nonpharmacological treatments were effective in reducing residents' depression, with antipsychotic treatments showing the most consistent improvement (Snowden, Sato, & Roy-Byrne, 2003). Staff stability and empowerment also have effects on the well-being of nursing home residents (Barry, Brannon, & Mor, 2005). Nursing homes also have focused on improving quality of care by using standardized assessment tools and quality instruments. Hawes and colleagues (1997) found that upon implementation of the Resident Assessment Instrument, several problematic practices such as use of restraints decreased and positive practices increased (e.g., completion of advance directives and increased social activities), leading to better client outcomes.

Although studies suggest that specific interventions improve functioning and hence quality of care in the nursing home, a fundamental element for any long-stay nursing home resident is maintaining and improving quality of life (Degenholtz, Kane, Kane, Bershadsky, & Kling, 2006; R. A. Kane, 2001; Thomas, 1996). Quality of life is generally measured by client satisfaction instruments using Likert scales. Researchers acknowledge that quality of life is a multidimensional construct, incorporating items such as comfort, cleanliness, and food service (Mostyn, Race, Seibert, & Johnson, 2000), personal respect, emotional support, and involvement of loved ones (Ryden et al., 2000), and autonomy, activities, and dignity (Norton & Lipson, 1998). Recently, Rosalie A. Kane (2003) created a measurement that focused on 11 quality of life elements in psychosocial domains not explicitly identified in the Minimum Data Set instrument, such as functional competence, privacy, individuality, and spiritual well-being. Their analysis of this scale is that quality of life can be affected in the nursing home through both process and structural interventions. This work was expanded by Degenholtz and colleagues (2006), who found that self-reported quality of life based on this new measure was negatively correlated with several resident characteristics, including physical disability, visual impairment, depression, and being bed-bound, and positively correlated with social engagement. Facility-level factors that were negatively associated with quality of life were sanctions for not addressing resident needs and not providing a safe and clean environment. These results suggest that both resident- and facility-level factors are relevant in assessing and addressing quality of life in the nursing home.

ASSISTED LIVING

Assessment of ALF outcomes is difficult due to extensive local and state variation, diverse services, different models of care, and lack of common definitions or standards (C. D. Phillips et al., 2003; Zimmerman et al., 2003, 2005). Indeed, some states (18 in 2002) do not even have a licensing category that uses the term "assisted living" (Mollica, 2002). Unlike many community-based services, which are publicly funded, ALF have largely developed through market demand. Funding typically is covered by out-of-pocket payments, resulting in a great deal of variability (Chapin & Dobbs-Kepper, 2001). Choice is a key component of ALF as staff and administrators confront the challenge of balancing independence in a comfortable homelike living environment with residents' needs for functional assistance and medical care (Stefanacci & Podrazik, 2005). Whereas federal Medicaid regulations include coverage of care in nursing facilities for those who meet the level of care and the requirements of low income and low assets, ALF do not enjoy this same payment mechanism because they are not considered health care. Therefore, states wishing to include ALF as a Medicaid-funded program must have a waiver approved by the Center for Medicare and Medicaid Services. By 2002, 41 states had waivers to cover payment for some ALF under Medicaid for about 100,000 of the more than 900,000 people in this setting (Mollica, 2002). For those who do not meet Medicaid eligibility, ALF have proven to be financially beyond the reach for many older adults and their families, who must pay out of pocket.

Given that research on ALF is in the early stages of development, many studies compare and contrast ALF to nursing homes, and evidence-based intervention studies are rare. Therefore, this section focuses on what is known primarily from descriptive surveys. In a comprehensive nationwide study of assisted living, Hawes and colleagues (2003) assessed a representative sample of over 1,000 U.S. facilities. They found that ALF residents, in general, had greater privacy and choice of accommodations than nursing home residents, although the majority of ALF were categorized as having few services and low privacy. In terms of specific services, they found that nearly all ALF provided 24-hour staffing, room and board (three meals a day), and housekeeping, with about two-thirds offering assistance with some ADLs. More than half (55%) had an RN on staff, but only 11% offered what the authors considered to be a high level of nursing care service: 40 hours or more of RN coverage and additional nursing staff provided by the facility.

Another comprehensive examination of ALF was conducted as part of the Collaborative Studies of Long-Term Care, which examined ALF and nursing home care for over 2,000 residents in 193 diverse facilities in 4 states: Florida, New Jersey, Maryland, and North Carolina (Zimmerman et al., 2003). The authors also found that ALF offered more privacy and more choice than nursing homes, but had higher levels of residents' behavioral problems even though ALF residents tended to be less functionally and cognitively impaired. This possibly occurred because in most states AFL staffing requirements are minimal compared to nursing home coverage (Mollica, 2002). The study found differences across types of ALF as well, noting that the boundaries between types of care are increasingly blurred (Zimmerman et al., 2003). Hedrick and colleagues (2003) compared residents across facility types, including adult family homes, residential care, and ALF, and found differences in resident characteristics but similar health outcomes over a 12-month period. Similarly, a related study that examined different types of ALF based on traditional or new models of care and facility size found no difference in medical outcomes, transfer to nursing facilities, or functional decline among residents of large or small ALF (Rosenberg et al., 2006). Surprisingly, however, the study found that residents of newer ALF, developed as part of the surge in the ALF model after 1987, actually showed more functional decline and social withdrawal than residents in traditional facilities. The authors conclude that no single ALF model defines good outcomes and that regulations should be based on the benefits and problems associated with various models rather than using a one-size-fits-all approach.

In addition to those comparing different types of ALF, a study in Kansas identified characteristics of residents who were unlikely to be admitted or retained in ALF (Chapin & Dobbs-Kepper, 2001). These included two core types: (1) behavior problems or high level of cognitive impairment requiring 24-hour mental health supervision and (2) need for high levels of health care such as 24-hour skilled care, and needing help with mobility, extensive transferring, and exiting the building. Another study that targeted a random sample of assisted living facilities in central Maryland found that declining health, chronic pain, appetite changes, and being widowed increase the risk of transition from ALF to a nursing facility, whereas dementia and neuropsychiatric symptoms were not associated with a nursing facility placement (Rosenblatt et al., 2004).

Aging in place has been identified as an important ALF goal. Many facilities offered support for ADLs, yet Hawes et al. (2003) found that almost one-third (29%) of ALF did not have a licensed nurse on staff. Moreover, many AFL discharged residents who had behavioral problems, difficulty transferring, and moderate cognitive impairment. Using the same data, C. D. Phillips and colleagues (2003) found that the odds that a resident would be transferred to a nursing facility were related to resident characteristics that indicated needing more care—decreased functional status and cognitive functioning and facility characteristics that suggested more care was available—whether or not the ALF had a full-time RN. Residents who had access to a full-time RN were about half as likely to transfer to a nursing facility as those in facilities without this level of skilled nursing. To support aging in place, some state regulations allow residents to sign negotiated risk contracts, in which they agree to accept responsibility for outcomes related to the ALF level of care. These contracts allow residents to remain in the facility when their needs indicate that they are eligible for the level of care provided in nursing homes (Zimmerman et al., 2005), such as hospice services.

Zimmerman and colleagues (2003) examined differences between ALF and nursing homes and found that both facility types have problems that affect quality of care including difficulty with staff retention. Findings that organizational culture has a strong relationship to staff satisfaction, values of teamwork, and workers' attitudes toward their job (Sikorska-Simmons, 2005) support culture change movements that are seeking to impact a variety of types of facility care. Since approaches such as the Green House model, Wellspring, and the Pioneer Network are relatively new, comprehensive and systematic evaluations of their efficacy and replicability are lacking (Callahan, 2005).

SPECIAL CARE UNITS

Special care units have flourished in the past 2 decades, largely due to public demand for better residential care for people with dementia. Public support emanated from family caregivers and advocacy organizations who witnessed poor care inflicted on their loved ones by insensitive or poorly trained nursing home staff. Ideally, SCU are distinctly different from traditional care settings. However, determining what is "special" about SCU is challenging given that there is no universally accepted definition of this facility type (Ohta & Ohta, 1988; Sloane et al., 2001) and no national quality of care standards relating to treatment of dementia (Zimmerman & Sloane, 1999). Experts have disagreed on which design and programming features are necessary for a basic-level SCU treatment, leading to few states developing minimum guidelines (Gerdner & Beck, 2001). This inconsistency negatively impacts both family caregivers seeking care for their loved one and researchers attempting to evaluate program effectiveness. Many researchers and policy analysts have raised the concern that the SCU label may be used as a marketing ploy, creating a mechanism for existing facilities to charge higher rates for the same level of care as residents in their general population (Boling & Gwyther, 1991; Davis et al., 2000; Gerdner & Buckwalter, 1996; Ohta & Ohta, 1988; Sloane et al., 2001; U.S. Congress, Office of Technology Assessment, 1992; Zimmerman & Sloane, 1999).

Although residents with dementia may be able to function better in a specialized care setting, the potential for SCU to effectively improve functioning is challenging given that the severity and behavioral expression of dementia is different across individuals (Sloane et al., 2001). Recent estimates suggest that over 50% of the nursing home population has dementia (Sloane et al., 2001; U.S. Congress, Office of Technology Assessment, 1992). Without specific ways to define a priority group of individuals with dementia based on their cognitive impairment or functioning levels, SCU admit residents based on the facility's own criteria, which minimizes the ability to evaluate SCU effectiveness across different programs.

Very few states have created statutes or even operational guidelines on SCU (Gerdner & Beck, 2001). Lack of state oversight exists for several reasons. The first is that SCU do not have clear or consistent objectives for their specialized treatment. In fact, several models across states use strategies and treatment protocols that are in direct conflict with each other (Day, Carreon, & Stump, 2000; Gerdner & Beck, 2001; U.S. Congress, Office of Technology Assessment, 1992). For example, SCU do not have a consistent or regulated staff-to-patient ratio. Although some units offer higher staffing levels than traditional care facilities, SCU must adhere to the regulatory standards of the particular auspices where they function. Assisted living facilities have a lower staff-to-resident ratio than nursing homes and generally can employ unlicensed or uncertified staff as care providers. Also, existing facilities with SCU adjuncts sometimes rotate staff through the unit in an effort to maximize the care provider labor pool and diminish additional staff burnout (U.S. Congress, Office of Technology Assessment, 1992). Some programs are employed to reduce staff burnout, such as staff support networks and specialized training on managing residents with dementia. However, there are no mandatory training requirements for dementia-specific content or the number of training hours received.

Overall research has been inconclusive regarding the effectiveness of SCU to uniquely serve individuals with dementia. First, the lack of uniformity across SCU regarding whom they serve and how they operate negatively influences both the quality and the generalizability of research efforts (Chappell & Reid, 2000; Ohta & Ohta, 1988; U.S. Congress, Office of Technology Assessment, 1992; Zimmerman & Sloane, 1999). Second, it is impossible to assert that the special features in SCU embedded in larger facilities are beneficial only to those individuals with dementia (Chappell & Reid, 2000; Gerdner & Beck, 2001). Most nursing home residents benefit from features such as staff training, avoiding use of restraints, and flexible care routines (Chappell & Reid, 2000), which neutralize the need for special consideration for those with dementia. Additionally, many special features, such as environmental modifications, are often lumped together as one large intervention, making it difficult to separate the impact of some features compared with others (Day et al., 2000).

EVIDENCE ON COMMUNITY-BASED MODELS OF CARE

This section begins with a brief review of the effectiveness of community-based services to substitute for a delay in nursing home use. We then review specific evidence related to the effectiveness of case management, adult day care, and hospice to provide therapeutic and compensatory support to older adults with chronic conditions. A key feature of all three models of community-based care is their focus on coordinating and connecting services for clients and their caregivers across a vast health and social services continuum.

Several demonstrations were conducted to test the extent to which community-based options actually offered alternatives to facility-based care by improving health status and reducing health care costs through integration and coordination of health care and supportive services. Some programs showed that alternatives were cheaper, but more careful research showed that people in nursing homes were in general more impaired then people living in the community. William Weissert (1976) was among the first to conduct randomized controlled studies comparing the rate of nursing home placement among people who used adult day health care services compared to those who did not. His findings suggested that these programs complemented but did not substitute for nursing home care. Later research showed that those who used community-based services in general needed and benefited from them, but they did not have lower rates of nursing home admission, and use of community-based care actually raised overall health care costs (Weissert et al., 1988). Weissert also reported that when there was reduction in nursing home utilization, the savings were usually small, and community services had a limited effect in producing changes in health status.

CASE MANAGEMENT

Case management is an emerging supportive service that facilitates access to appropriate health and social services for high-risk older adults and their caregivers through assessment, counseling, and advocacy (Raiff & Shore, 1993; Scharlach, Giunta, & Mills-Dick, 2001). A major strength of case management is its ability to transcend traditional health care boundaries by coordinating and linking services across medical, behavioral, and social service environments. Yet despite the prevalence of case management practice, there has been little evidence of efficacy and effectiveness in application of these models. What studies do exist on case management models with older adults often lack rigor or contain methodological weaknesses that result in questionable findings (Lee & Tuljapurkar, 1998). In the past few years, several studies on the efficacy of case management with older adults have been conducted using experimental designs with randomized control groups (Boult et al., 2000; Engelhardt et al., 1996; Fordyce, Bardole, Romer, Soghikian, & Fireman, 1997; Gagnon, Schein, McVey, & Bergman, 1999; Leveille et al., 1998; Marshall, Long, Voss, Demma, & Skerl, 1999; Morishita, Boult, Boult, Smith, & Pacala, 1998; Naylor et al., 1999; Schore, Brown, & Cheh, 1999; Weuve, Boult, & Morishita, 2000). These projects aimed to improve health and daily functioning, reduce medical service use, decrease rates of depression, and increase client satisfaction, among other goals. Results of these studies are consistently inconsistent; some reported decreased rates of service use (Leveille et al., 1998; Naylor et al., 1999), and others reported no difference in or increased service use for those receiving this service (Boult et al., 2000; Fordyce et al., 1997; Gagnon et al., 1999; Long & Marshall, 1999; Schore et al., 1999). Similarly, levels of satisfaction and functioning for the case management group were also inconsistent across studies (Gagnon et al., 1999; Marshall et al., 1999; Morishita et al., 1998). Moreover, none of the studies measuring depression level were actually able to impact depression through their interventions (Engelhardt et al., 1996; Leveille et al., 1998; Naylor et al., 1999).

Current Models of Case Management   The most prevalent case management models serving older adults with chronic conditions utilize managed care systems to achieve their goals of improving quality of care and quality of life and cost savings. Here we summarize findings on a number of these models, including the PACE program, S/HMO, and case management models that link managed health care with community agencies.

The premise of the PACE model is that through monthly fixed payments from Medicare and Medicaid (for those dually eligible) or through private pay, services can be expanded beyond what is traditionally provided by either Medicare or Medicaid alone (Eng, Pedulla, Eleazer, McCann, & Fox, 1997). The combined fixed payments allow for the additions of community service provision, such as homemaker, respite care, home-delivered meals, and other community-based services. The evaluation of the PACE model revealed reductions in use of institutional care and rates of short-term hospital use compared to the overall utilization by the Medicare population (Wieland et al., 2000). These changes in service use contributed to the overall cost-effectiveness of the model (Eng et al., 1997). While these results are impressive, to date the PACE model is almost exclusively focused on serving the dually eligible, limiting the applicability of this model to the majority of Medicare recipients.

The S/HMO was implemented, in part, to determine whether additional coverage for long-term care with associated case management could produce sufficient savings to allow plans to offer chronic care benefits without increased cost to Medicare. Although studies shortly after implementation of the model were inconclusive, a recent study found significant reductions in nursing home use among those in the S/HMO (Fischer et al., 2003).

Within traditional Medicare managed care services, Kaiser Permanente has developed several innovative solutions to improve patient outcomes for members with chronic conditions including geriatric care management and disease management. The geriatric care management program uses a social case management approach to assist patients by coordinating care in both the health care and community-based service systems (Enguidanos et al., 2003). This service is mostly administered at the health care facility but has some provisions for home-based assessments. The disease management programs provide telephonic, disease-focused management and support to members. Both of these programs have demonstrated positive outcomes for individual diseases but lack the ability to manage multiple chronic conditions and their related acute episodes.

Another case management model linked to managed care, the Care Advocate Demonstration Program, was developed to collaborate across medical and social service delivery systems by offering a social care management intervention to high-risk older adults enrolled in a Medicare managed care health plan (Shannon, Wilber, & Allen, 2006; Wilber et al., 2003). This program used a brokerage model of case management, in which case managers individualized referrals within a service delivery network that, for the most part, lacked formal coordination of providers (Scharlach et al., 2001). Care advocates assessed participants' psychosocial and functional needs to identify immediate and long-term service needs, offered individualized information, and provided direct links to HCBS and medical services as appropriate (Alkema, Reyes, & Wilber, 2006). Findings indicated that characteristics associated with particular HCBS use varied extensively depending on the service provided. Age, sex, social support, living situation, education, specific functional impairments, heart conditions, and sensory impairments at baseline significantly predicted utilization in the six different HCBS categories (Alkema et al., 2006). Also, those who participated in the 12-month case management intervention had significantly lower levels of mortality than a comparable control group, increased primary care physician visits, and reduced hospitalization (Alkema, Wilber, Shannon, & Allen, 2007; Shannon et al., 2006). This coincides with previous studies that found decreased mortality when high-risk older adults participated in integrated community-based programs (Albert, Simone, Brassard, Stern, & Mayeux, 2005; Chatterji, Burstein, Kidder, & White, 1998; Shapiro & Taylor, 2002) and comprehensive geriatric assessment programs (R. L. Kane & Kane, 2000; Reuben, 2002), both of which used case management as a central intervention component.

Project IMPACT (Improving Mood—Promoting Access to Collaborative Treatment) is another successful collaborative project that used case management as the bridge between primary care and mental health services (Unützer et al., 2002). This multisite study used case managers, physicians, and psychiatrists in primary care clinics to provide clinically integrative treatment and support to community-based older adults with depression. Results found that those in the intervention group reported a significant reduction in depression score, improved physical functioning, and improved quality of life compared to usual care patients. Given that older adults generally receive mental health treatment from primary care physicians rather than specialized psychiatric services, this project's potential for successful replication in other primary care venues to reduce depression in older adults is high.

Adult Day Care

Several national studies examined characteristics of participants and the outcomes associated with ADC participation (Hedrick, Rothman, Chapko, Inui, Kelly, & Ehreth, 1991; Mace & Rabins, 1984; Von Behren, 1989; Weissert et al., 1989). Much of the research has examined the ability of ADC programs to substitute for nursing facility care and the extent to which these programs are cost-effective (Capiman & Gregory, 1984; Weissert, Wan, Livieratos, & Katz, 1980). Focusing on participants with dementia, Gaugler and colleagues (2003) found that those who used small amounts of ADC and those who used large amounts had a higher likelihood of placement. For those with moderate amounts, risk was reduced. More recent studies have indicated that ADC participants with Alzheimer's disease have an increased risk of institutionalization (McCann et al., 2005). Yet even with increase risk for nursing home placement, ADC results show significant positive effects on well-being and dementia symptoms (Zank & Schacke, 2002). Those in ADC stabilized or improved on various measures, whereas the untreated control participants worsened. Follow-up data showed a significant decline in health for the control group compared with ADC participants.

In addition to supporting older adults with functional or cognitive disabilities, ADC also offers respite to caregivers by providing supervision (Family Caregiver Alliance, 2003; Kirwin, 1991; Zarit, Stephens, Townsend, & Greene, 1998). Studies assessing the ability of ADC to reduce caregiver stress over a short- and long-term treatment length showed decreased depression and role overload measures (McCann et al., 2005). Zank and Schacke (2002) evaluated the ability of German adult day care programs to affect caregiver outcomes. Caregivers did not show a significant change on caregiver affective measures, but anecdotal reports acknowledged reduced burden, especially related to freedom from supervision responsibilities. Quayhagen and colleagues (2000) similarly found that caregivers whose spouse participated in a short-term day care group reported significantly decreased hostility toward their spouse. Research has indicated that ADC reduces caregiver stress and burden, potentially making it easier for families to continue caregiving at home.

Hospice

Since the initial conception of hospice as a Medicare benefit, it has generally been accepted that Hospice care results in improved care for terminally ill patients at reduced cost. This assumption is based on evidence arising primarily from prospective and retrospective studies. Numerous studies have documented the ability of hospice care to improve satisfaction with medical care among terminal patients and their family members (Baer & Hanson, 2000; Greer et al., 1986; Miceli & Wojciechowski, 2003; Teno et al., 2004), with one study finding that families felt that they received greater benefits from hospice care with longer enrollment prior to death (Rickerson, Harrold, Kapo, Carroll, & Casarett, 2005). In a study comparing end-of-life experiences among family members of decedents, Teno and colleagues found that family members of those receiving hospice care were more satisfied with the physical and emotional comfort received. Compared to patients who died at home receiving home health care, in the hospital, or in the nursing home, family reports among those receiving hospice were overall more favorable in terms of pain control, emotional support, and quality of care. These findings were also consistent among family members of nursing home residents, where family members receiving hospice reported improved quality of care and symptom relief following hospice care (Baer & Hanson, 2000).

Hospice use has also been associated with reductions in aggressive care in the terminally ill (Baer & Hanson, 2000; Greer et al., 1986). Although data from the National Hospice Study, a randomized controlled trial, did not find that hospice improved quality of life (Greer et al., 1986), subsequent analysis of the data set found that hospice care did improve quality of death (Wallston, Burger, Smith, & Baugher, 1988). Additionally, a retrospective cohort study suggested that hospice may be associated with longer survival time (Pyenson, Connor, Fitch, & Kinzbrunner, 2004). Hospice care has also been associated with increased likelihood of dying at home, a preference held by the majority of Americans (Brazil, Howell, Bedard, Krueger, & Heidebrecht, 2005; Townsend et al., 1990).

Although the evidence of the effectiveness of hospice is equivocal, there is a considerable body of literature that attests to the need for better care at the end of life. A recent report card on "Death in America" rated each state in terms of its ability to provide adequate patient care at the end of life (Robert Wood Johnson Foundation, 1999). Specifically, the report illustrated that no state excelled in enrolling at least half of decedents over 65 in hospice before death, and only one state (Arizona) came close.

The evidence for hospice care is also mixed in terms of cost effectiveness, but qualitative and quantitative research supports improved patient and family outcomes associated with receipt of hospice care. In line with these findings and thorough and extensive documentation attesting to the need for improving end-of-life care, the majority of current research on new models of end-of-life care have focused on developing and testing palliative care programs and models. Palliative care programs are largely built on the interdisciplinary model and the palliative (e.g., pain and symptom relief) goals of the hospice model, while providing services earlier upstream (greater than 6 months) prior to death. Preliminary data arising from these models support both improved quality of care as well as potential cost savings. Specific examples of community-based palliative care programs are the In-Home Palliative Care program and the CALL program.

IN-HOME PALLIATIVE CARE

Through reallocation of existing resources, Kaiser Permanente developed the In-Home Palliative Care program that provides comprehensive, multidisciplinary in-home care to terminally ill patients with the intent of enhancing comfort to and improving the quality of a patient's life, as opposed to attempting to achieve a cure (Brumley, Enguidanos, & Cherin, 2003). The goals of this intervention are pain control, symptom management, quality of life enhancement, and spiritual and emotional comfort for the patient and family. Unlike hospice, patients do not have to forgo curative care for palliative care services; they may elect to continue curative treatment while also receiving symptom control, education, and bereavement services. The core team (physician, nurse, and social worker with the patient and family) is responsible for coordinating and managing care across all settings and providing assessment, evaluation, planning, care delivery, follow-up, monitoring, and continuous reassessment of care. Physicians conduct home visits and are available along with skilled nursing services on a 24-hour on-call basis. In addition, advanced care planning is provided that involves patients and their families in making informed decisions and choices about end-of-life care. Studies have found that the In-Home Palliative Care model is successful in reducing both emergency room visits and hospitalizations, resulting in costs that range from 37% to 45% less than terminally ill patients receiving traditional care (Brumley et al., 2003; Brumley & Hillary, 2005; Enguidanos, Cherin, & Brumley, 2005). Further, patients enrolled in the palliative care program had improved satisfaction with care at 30 and 60 days following enrollment, compared to no change among those receiving traditional medical services. Palliative care patients were also more likely to die at home than those receiving usual care (Brumley et al., 2003).

COMPREHENSIVE, ADAPTABLE, LIFE-AFFIRMING, LONGITUDINAL PALLIATIVE CARE PROJECT

The premises of this model are that

> end of life care must encompass the larger context of the dying person's life; that life is lived in the community, not within the health care system; and that excellent medical care and symptom management are necessary but not sufficient in helping the patient and the family experience good end of life care. (London, McSkimming, Drew, Quinn, & Carney, 2005, p. 1215)

To accomplish this, the Comprehensive, Adaptable, Life-Affirming, Longitudinal (CALL) Project team developed care plans for patients following a comprehensive assessment. An array of services were tailored specifically to the needs of the patients and their families and were provided both within and outside of the traditional health care system, following patients as they transitioned through various levels of care. These services included coordination of health care visits, education and support, advance care planning, in-home support and assistance, a volunteer companion, bereavement follow-up for families, and connection to other health care and community-based resources as needed (London et al., 2005). Results of a longitudinal study revealed that those enrolled in the CALL program had low hospital admissions (29% of the sample), 48% were enrolled in hospice prior to death, and 38% died at home.

Case Study and Evidence-Based Practice Applications

Mrs. C, 78, was a recent widow who had been diagnosed with diabetes and congestive heart failure. After hearing Mrs. C's dog barking throughout the night, a neighbor checked in on her in the morning and found her on the floor unable to get up. When the paramedics arrived, Mrs. C could not accurately answer questions about her age, birth date, or where she lived. She had always been fiercely independent, but since the death of her husband she had struggled to pay her bills, keep her apartment clean, and adequately prepare food for herself. She told the paramedics that she has plenty of money to pay for her care as she was related to the king of England and had a grandfather in Montana who willed her money. However, Mrs. C did not remember if she had eaten in the past few days. Her companions, two parakeets and a small dog, appeared to be hungry and thirsty.

The paramedics called an ambulance and Mrs. C was taken to the emergency room, where her immediate medical condition was evaluated. She was admitted, her condition was stabilized, and her daughter, who lived in another city several hours from Mrs. C's apartment, was notified. When she arrived at the hospital Mrs. C's daughter was told that after she became stable, Mrs. C would be discharged to a skilled nursing facility for short-term rehabilitation. While she was in the facility, a member of Mrs. C's church arranged for the care of her pets. Mrs. C's physical and cognitive condition improved over the next several weeks at the skilled nursing facility; she was able to participate in self-care, and her diabetes seemed to be better controlled. She was discharged from rehabilitation to custodial care. Unlike the rehabilitation care, which was covered by Medicare, Mrs. C now had to pay out of pocket for her care. After 2 months of paying, Mrs. C had depleted her assets, making her eligible for Medicaid. Her functioning continued to improve and she resolved to leave the facility, but she had lost her apartment. Concerned about Mrs. C's ability to live alone, her daughter insisted that she live with her.

Mrs. C's daughter, who had a full-time job and was a single mother with two teenage children, suddenly found herself responsible for the care of her mother, a dog, and two birds. Neither Mrs. C's physician nor the staff at the nursing facility could make recommendations for services; however, the social service director at the nursing facility suggested that a case manager might be helpful. To find an appropriate case management service, Mrs. C's daughter took a sick day and spent it making multiple phone calls to a variety of providers. Eventually she located a case manager from a local senior center who was able to make a home assessment. The case manager discussed ways her home could be made more elder-friendly and referred Mrs. C to a community agency that offered Medicaid-waivered services that included adult day care for continued monitoring and social support. Mrs. C enjoyed the adult day care program, and the program provided peace of mind to her daughter while she was at work, reducing her stress from the demands of caregiving.

Over time her daughter noticed that Mrs. C was becoming increasingly confused, disoriented, and agitated. Despite the support from the day care service, Mrs. C's daughter found it increasingly difficult to manage her job, her parental responsibilities, and the care and attention her mother required. After the social worker at the day care program suggested that Mrs. C might need more care than they could provide, a comprehensive assessment was arranged, which indicated that Mrs. C has an irreversible dementing illness. Fortunately, she lived in a state where Medicaid covered assisted living, and the care manager helped locate several possible facilities for her daughter to visit and choose from. She decided on a facility that included a special care unit where Mrs. C was permitted to take her birds. Mrs. C. adapted well to the facility and the homelike environment. She seemed content, and her daughter was pleased that her mother was happy and well cared for. However, about 8 months after moving to the facility, Mrs. C was diagnosed with untreatable liver cancer. Her daughter worked with Mrs. C's physician and the case management agency to arrange for hospice care in the facility. Three months later, Mrs. C died peacefully in the assisted living facility with family by her side.

EVIDENCE-BASED POLICY RECOMMENDATIONS AND FUTURE RESEARCH DIRECTIONS

Community- and facility-based care providers work hard to provide high-quality service to their clientele, yet often do so independently of each other. Lack of service collaboration exists both *within* and *between* the health care, supportive services, housing, and transportation arenas. Each agency determines its own specific service eligibility, creates a unique assessment and care plan, and keeps separate records. Older adults and caregivers may have difficulty identifying, accessing, and arranging for services. Conversely, they may receive duplicative services, including engagement from multiple case managers who inquire about the same basic information and provide similar interventions. For those who need services from many agencies, this process becomes tedious and time-consuming. It is particularly inconvenient for working family caregivers who must arrange time to attend each individual assessment. This confusing mass of disconnected programs results in service gaps, duplication of services, budgetary and human capital inefficiencies, and ultimately frustration from consumers, caregivers, and administrators (Alkema, 2003).

Multiple and often competing forces contribute to service fragmentation, including the following:

- Heterogeneous consumer needs
- Various provider types and models
- Differing professional perspectives on appropriate care
- Numerous and mutually exclusive funding streams
- Disconnected bureaucratic authority with programs under numerous auspices
- Lack of an integrated information system for service provider and consumer use
- Incompatible federal, state, and local level regulatory requirements
- A variety of geographic service areas and capacities (Alkema, 2003)

Solutions to these issues necessitate the system's changing in the following eight areas (Alkema, 2003):

1. *Consumer-directed care:* Older adults have clearly expressed a desire to navigate and participate in the service delivery system, with the support of professional expertise if needed (Squillace & Firman, 2002). Several sites of the Cash and Counseling Demonstrations have shown that consumers are very satisfied with having greater control over hiring and training of personal care workers, without increased costs to the state (B. Phillips & Schneider, 2002). When consumers cannot directly participate in this model due to physical or cognitive limitations, this consideration should be extended to family caregivers acting as proxies. State and local agencies should revise current programmatic structures to maximize consumer-directed care and consumer choice to the extent possible.
2. *"No wrong door" approach:* A system should be created that has true or perceived seamless service delivery from the consumer's perspective. This proposal requires redefining service delivery from singular, unconnected programs to a broad, holistic service continuum that embraces older adults at all functional levels (Figure 17.1). Collaborative linkages between departments and programs should ensure that consumers connect with any service they need, regardless of what entity they encountered first.
3. *Enhanced collaboration between aging and disability networks:* The aging and disability networks both have constituencies that are consumers in the long-term care service delivery system. Both groups, using the *Olmstead* decision as a launching pad, should collectively advocate for eliminating institutional barriers to collaborative, community-based service delivery, such as disconnected information systems, rigid eligibility requirements, and individualized funding streams.
4. *Improved end-of-life care:* Given that Medicare and Medicaid will most likely remain the largest hospice payers in the country (Fox, 1999; Lynn, Wilkinson, & Etheredge, 2001; Medpac, 2002), restructuring the current hospice benefit may be necessary to increase access for those with diverse medical conditions and those residing in facilities. However, Huskamp, Buntin, Wang, and Newhouse (2001) found that simply expanding the current benefit structure will not be sufficient in addressing the gaps in end-of-life care. Smits, Furletti, and Vladeck (2003) recommend that centers for Medicare and Medicaid services (CMS) and the Agency for Healthcare Research and Quality support palliative care research to gather evidence for the effectiveness of new, innovative end-of-life care models. Education and training of our current and future health care providers must also be a critical part in improving care for the dying (Vladeck, 1999). Thus, the role of policy makers in end-of-life care reform must include advocating for increased funding and support for research and demonstration projects. Further, incremental reforms in Medicare and Medicaid are needed so that end-of-life care will be better integrated into clinical practice and not relegated to the last months or even days of life.
5. *Ongoing consumer evaluation of older adult service delivery systems:* Due to a variety of factors, the future cohort of older adults will be considerably

different from previous and current cohorts. To ensure appropriate programmatic development for current and future cohorts of older adults and stimulate corrective action when needed, consumers must partake in evaluation efforts at local and state levels. This suggestion implies responsibility by both governmental bodies and consumers themselves to evaluate and amend service structures. This means applying a continuous quality improvement approach to all levels of organizations involved in older adult services.

6. *Integrated information systems:* Collaborative efforts require an integrated information system to gather, coordinate, and share the appropriate level of information among all stakeholders. Problems such as incompatible systems, lack of a standardized data across programs, and inaccurate data collection have been cited as barriers (Newhauser, Brady, & Seligman, 2003). Essential elements include a consumer-friendly, Web-accessible information and assistance portal, uniform assessment and monitoring tools among providers, and data storage and tracking in the same or compatible format used for reporting and program evaluation. A recent article on promising practices in California suggested that integrated information systems should (a) include a comprehensive array of programs and services, (b) have the capacity to serve the needs of diverse users, (c) integrate multiple layers and levels of information, (d) standardize information from multiple diverse sources, (e) operate in real time, and (f) meet all requirements for privacy and confidentiality (Shugarman, Nishita, & Wilber, 2006).

7. *Collaboration between state, county, and local providers:* Multiple funding streams, duplicative regulatory requirements, and complex bureaucratic structures grossly inhibit integrated systems development. All levels of government should work collaboratively to simplify administrative processes both within and between themselves and develop a virtually seamless system of care to benefit consumers, family caregivers, and providers. Each entity must be willing to compromise and relinquish some turf to achieve the higher ideal of creating a consumer-friendly service delivery system.

8. *Horizontal and vertical collaboration:* This practice involves not only establishing collaborative networks between the state and local entities, but also working together across departments and agencies at the same institutional level. Changing systemic processes is the responsibility of both state-to-local and local-to-local efforts. Each bureaucratic unit should challenge its sphere of influence to employ operational changes, such as creating integrated information systems and incorporating consumer-directed care into their service model.

CONCLUSION

This chapter has addressed the background, service delivery elements, and current evidence base for several key programs and services in community- and facility-based care. As demonstrated by the historical and current evidence presented, this arena is complex and largely uncoordinated. There is, however, a growing body of evidence to support some pilot models for effective service delivery in both community- and facility-based care. Unfortunately, most of these models are not incorporated into standard practice, creating large variation in practices and care models. Further efforts are needed to improve integration and collaboration as well as to build the body of evidence of effective models. Additionally, initiatives from both the governmental and private sector are critical to support the continued translation of evidence-based models into standard practice across the spectrum of chronic care service delivery.

REFERENCES

Abramovice, B. (1988). *Long term care administration: The management of institutional and non-institutional components of the continuum of care.* Binghamton, NY: Haworth Press.

Addams, J. (1912). *Twenty years at Hull House.* New York: Macmillan.

Albert, S. M., Simone, B., Brassard, A., Stern, Y., & Mayeux, R. (2005). Medicaid home care services and survival in New York City. *Gerontologist, 45*(5), 609–616.

Alkema, G. E. (2003). *Statement of findings: Planning and system design.* Sacramento: California Commission on Aging.

Alkema, G. E., Reyes, J. Y., & Wilber, K. H. (2006). Characteristics associated with home- and community-based service utilization for Medicare managed care consumers. *Gerontologist, 45*(2), 173–182.

Alkema, G. E., Shannon, G. R., & Wilber, K. H. (2003). Using interagency collaboration to serve older adults with chronic care needs: The Care Advocate Program. *Family and Community Health, 26*(3), 221–229.

Alkema, G. E., Wilber, K. H., Shannon, G. R., & Allen, D. (2007). Reduced mortality: The unexpected impact of a telephone-based care management intervention for older adults in managed care. *Health Services Research.* Available from OnlineEarly Articles, doi:10.1111/j.1475-6773.2006.00668.x.

Anderson, G., & Horvath, J. (2002). *Chronic conditions: Making the case for ongoing care.* Baltimore: Johns Hopkins University and Partnership for Solutions.

Arno, P. S. (2002, March). *Economic value of informal caregiving.* Paper presented at the annual meeting of the American Association of Geriatric Psychiatry, Orlando, FL.

Arno, P. S., Levine, C., & Memmott, M. M. (1999). The economic value of informal caregiving. *Health Affairs, 18*(2), 182–188.

Baer, W. M., & Hanson, L. C. (2000). Families' perception of the added value of hospice in the nursing home, *Journal of the American Geriatrics Society, 48,* 879–882.

Barry, T. T., Brannon, D., & Mor, V. (2005). Nurse aide empowerment strategies and staff stability: Effects on nursing home resident outcomes. *Gerontologist, 45*(3), 309–317.

Bean, F., Myers, G., Angel, J., & Galle, O. (1994). Geographic concentration, migration, and population redistribution among the elderly. In L. G. Martin & S. H. Preston (Eds.), *Demography of aging* (pp. 319–355). Washington, DC: National Academy Press.

Benjamin, A. E. (2001). Consumer-directed services at home: A new model for persons with disabilities. *Health Affairs, 20*(6), 80–95.

Boling, K., & Gwyther, L. (1991). Defining quality of care for nursing home residents with dementia. In P. D. Sloane & L. J. Mathew (Eds.), *Dementia units in long-term care* (pp. 3–22). Baltimore: Johns Hopkins University Press.

Borrayo, E. A., Salmon, J. R., Polivka, L., & Dunlop, B. D. (2002). Utilization across the continuum of long-term care services. *Gerontologist, 42*(5), 603–612.

Boult, C., Rassen, J., Rassen, A., Moore, R., & Robinson, S. (2000). The effect of case management on the costs of health care for enrollees in Medicare Plus Choice plans: A randomized trial. *Journal of the American Geriatrics Society, 48*(8), 996–1001.

Brazil, K., Howell, D., Bedard, M., Krueger, P., & Heidebrecht, C. (2005). Preferences for place of care and place of death among informal caregivers of the terminally ill. *Palliative Medicine, 19*(6), 492–499.

Brumley, R. D., Enguidanos, S., & Cherin, D. (2003). Effectiveness of a home-based palliative care program for end-of-life. *Journal of Palliative Medicine, 6*, 715–724.

Brumley, R. D., Enguidanos, S., & Hillary, K. (2003). The Palliative Care Program. *Permanente Journal, 7*(2), 7–12.

Brumley, R., & Hillary, K. (2005, September). *Developing an outpatient based palliative care program.* Paper presented at the National Hospice and Palliative Care Organization, Management and Leadership Conference, Hollywood, FL.

Callahan, J. J., Jr. (Ed.). (1993). *Aging in place.* Amityville, NY: Baywood.

Callahan, J. J., Jr. (2005). What's new about the new politics of aging? *Gerontologist, 45*(5), 700–704.

Campbell, P. R. (1996). *Population projections for states—By age, sex, race and Hispanic origin: 1995–2025* (No. PPL-47). Washington, DC: U.S. Census Bureau, Population Division.

Capitman, J. A., & Gregory, K. L. (1984). *Supplemental report on the adult day health care program in California: A comparative cost analysis.* Sacramento, CA: Office of Long-Term Care and Aging, Department of Health Services.

Carlson, M. (1995, October 30). Back to the dark ages. *Time, 146.*

Centers for Disease Control and Prevention. (2002). *The burden of chronic diseases and their risk factors: National and state perspectives.* Washington, DC: U.S. Department of Health and Human Services.

Centers for Medicare and Medicaid Services. (2005). *Medicaid at a Glance: A Medicaid Information Source.* Washington, DC: U.S. Department of Health and Human Services.

Chapin, R., & Dobbs-Kepper, D. (2001). Aging in place in assisted living: Philosophy versus policy. *Gerontologist, 41,* 43–50.

Chappell, N. L., & Reid, R. C. (2000). Dimensions of care for dementia sufferers in long-term care institutions: Are they related to outcomes? *Journals of Gerontology: Social Sciences, 55*(4), S234–S244.

Chatterji, P., Burstein, N. R., Kidder, D., & White, A. (1998). *Evaluation of the Program of All-Inclusive Care for the Elderly (PACE) demonstration: The impact of PACE on participant outcomes* (Final report prepared for HCFA). Cambridge, MA: Abt Associates.

Coleman, B. (2001). *Issue brief: Consumer directed services for older people.* Washington, DC: American Association for Retired Persons Public Policy Institute.

Coleman, B., & Pandya, S. (2002). *Fact sheet: Family caregiving and long term care.* Washington, DC: American Association for Retired Persons Public Policy Institute.

Copeland, J., Chen, R., & Dewey, M. (1999). Community-based case-control study of depression in older people: Cases and sub-cases from the MRC-ALPHA study. *British Journal of Psychiatry, 175,* 340–347.

Curry, L. A., & Wetle, T. (2001). Ethical principles. In C. Evashwick (Ed.), *The continuum of long-term care* (pp. 261–273). New York: Delmar.

Davis, K., Sloane, P. D., Mitchell, C., Preisser, J., Grant, L., Hawes, M., et al. (2000). Specialized dementia programs in residential care settings. *Gerontologist, 40*(1), 32–42.

Day, K., Carreon, D., & Stump, C. (2000). The therapeutic design of environments for people with dementia: A review of the empirical research. *Gerontologist, 40*(4), 397–416.

Degenholtz, H., Kane, R. A., Kane, R. L., Bershadsky, B., & Kling, K. (2006). Predicting nursing facility residents' quality of life using external indicators. *Health Services Research, 41*(2), 335–356.

Doty, P. J., Stone, R. I., Jackson, M. E., & Drabek, J. L. (2001). Informal caregiving. In C. Evashwick (Ed.), *The continuum of long-term care* (pp. 132–151). New York: Delmar.

Dunn, S., Sohl-Kreiger, R., & Marx, S. (2001). Geriatric case management in an integrated care system. *Journal of Nursing Administration, 31*(2), 60–62.

Dychtwald, K., & Zitter, M. (1991). *The role of the hospital in an aging society: A blueprint for action.* San Francisco: Age Wave Press.

Eng, C., Pedulla, J., Eleazer, G. P., McCann, R., & Fox, N. (1997). Program of All-inclusive Care for the Elderly (PACE): An innovative model of integrated geriatric care and financing. *Journal of the American Geriatrics Society, 45*(2), 223–232.

Engelhardt, J. B., Toseland, R. W., O'Donnell, J. C., Richie, J. T., Donald, J., & Banks, S. (1996). The effectiveness and efficiency of outpatient geriatric evaluation and management. *Journal of the American Geriatrics Society, 44*(7), 847–856.

Enguidanos, S., Cherin, D., & Brumley, R. (2005). Home-based palliative care study: Site of death, and costs of medical care for patients with congestive heart failure, chronic obstructive pulmonary disease, and cancer. *Journal of Social Work in End of Life and Palliative Care, 1,* 37–56.

Enguidanos, S. M., Gibbs, N. E., Simmons, W. J., Savoni, K. J., Jamison, P. M., Hackstaff, L., et al. (2003). Kaiser Permanente Community Partners Project: Improving geriatric care management practices. *Journal of the American Geriatrics Society, 51*(5), 710–714.

Family Caregiver Alliance. (2003). *Fact sheet: Benefits of day care.* Retrieved October 21, 2003, from http://www.caregiver.org/caregiver/jsp/content_node.jsp?nodeid=886.

Feldman, P. H., & Kane, R. L. (2003). Strengthening research to improve the practice and management of long-term care. *Milbank Quarterly, 81*(2), 179–220.

Fischer, L. R., Green, C. A., Goodman, M. J., Brody, K. K., Aickin, M., Wei, F., et al. (2003). Community-based care and risk of nursing home placement. *Medical Care, 41*(12), 1407–1416.

Fordyce, M., Bardole, D., Romer, L., Soghikian, K., & Fireman, B. (1997). Senior Team Assessment and Referral program: STAR. *Journal of the American Board of Family Practice, 10*(6), 398–406.

Fox, P. D. (1999). *End-of-life care in managed care organizations.* Washington, DC: American Association for Retired Persons.

Fox-Grage, W., Folkemer, D., & Lewis, J. (2004). *States' response to the Olmstead decision: How are states complying?* Washington, DC: Forum for State Health Policy Leadership, National Conference of State Legislatures.

Gagnon, A., Schein, C., McVey, L., & Bergman, H. (1999). Randomized controlled trial of nurse case management of frail older people. *Journal of the American Geriatrics Society, 47*(9), 1118–1124.

Gaugler, J. E., Jarrott, S. E., Zarit, S. H., Stephens, M.-A. P., Townsend, A., & Greene, R. (2003). Adult day service use and reductions in caregiving hours: Effects on stress and psychological well-being for dementia caregivers. *International Journal of Geriatric Psychiatry, 18*(1), 55–62.

Gaugler, J. E., Zarit, S. H., Townsend, A., Stephens, M., & Green, R. (2003). Evaluating community-based programs for dementia caregivers: The cost implications of adult day services. *Journal of Applied Gerontology, 22*(1), 118–133.

General Accounting Office. (1998). *California nursing homes: Care problems persist despite federal and state oversight.* Washington, DC: Author.

Gerdner, L., & Beck, C. (2001). Statewide survey to compare services provided for residents with dementia in special care units and non-special care units. *American Journal of Alzheimer's Disease and Other Dementias, 16*(5), 289–295.

Gerdner, L., & Buckwalter, K. (1996). Review of state policies regarding special care units: Implications for family, consumers and health care professionals. *American Journal of Alzheimer's Disease, 11*(2), 16–27.

Germain, C. B., & Gitterman, A. (1996). *The life model of social work practice: Advances in theory and practice* (2nd ed.). New York: Columbia University Press.

Gold, D. (1991). A descriptive typology of dementia units. In P. D. Sloane & L. J. Mathew (Eds.), *Dementia units in long-term care* (pp. 50–61). Baltimore: Johns Hopkins University Press.

Gonzalez-Salvador, M. T., Arango, C., Lyketsos, C. G., & Calcedo Barba, A. (1999). The stress and psychological morbidity of the Alzheimer patient caregiver. *International Journal of Geriatric Psychiatry, 14*, 701–710.

Greer, D., Mor, V., Morris, J., Sherwood, S., Kidder, D., & Birnbaum, H. (1986). An alternative in terminal care: Results of the National Hospice Study. *Journal of Chronic Disease, 39*(1), 9–26.

Harris, N., Dunmore, R., & Tscheu, M. (1996). The Medicare hospice benefit: Fiscal implications for hospice program management. *Cancer Management, 3*, 6–11.

Harris Interactive Inc. (2000). *Chronic illness and caregiving: Survey of the general public, adults with chronic conditions and caregivers.* Baltimore: Partnership for Solutions.

Hawes, C., Mor, V., Phillips, C. D., Fries, B. E., Morris, J. N., SteeleFriedlob, E., et al. (1997). The OBRA–87 nursing home regulations and implementation of the resident assessment instrument: Effects on process quality. *Journal of the American Geriatrics Society, 45*(8), 977–985.

Hawes, C., Phillips, C. D., Rose, M., Holan, S., & Sherman, M. (2003). A national survey of assisted living facilities. *Gerontologist, 43*(6), 875–882.

Hedrick, S. C., Rothman, M. L., Chapko, M., Inui, T. S., Kelly, J. R., & Ehreth, J. (1991). Adult day health care evaluation study: Methodology and implementation. *Health Services Research, 25*, 935–960.

Hedrick, S. C., Sales, A. E. B., Sullivan, J. H., Gray, S. L., Tornatore, J., Curtis, M., et al. (2003). Resident outcomes of Medicaid-funded community residential care. *Gerontologist, 43*(4), 473–482.

Henry, R. S., Cox, N. J., Reifler, B. V., & Asbury, C. (2000). Adult day centers. In S. L. Isaacs & J. R. Knickman (Eds.), *To improve health and health care* (Vol. III). New York: Robert Wood Johnson Foundation. Available from http://www.rwjf.org/files/publications/books/2000/?gsa=1.

Herrmann, N., Black, S. E., Lawrence, J., Szekely, C., & Szalai, J. P. (1998). The Sunnybrook Stroke Study: A prospective study of depressive symptoms and functional outcome. *Stroke, 29*(3), 618–624.

Hoffman, C., Rice, D., & Sung, H. Y. (1996). Persons with chronic conditions: Their prevalence and costs. *Journal of the American Medical Association, 276*(18), 1473–1479.

Huskamp, H., Buntin, M. B., Wang, V., & Newhouse, J. P. (2001). Providing care at the end of life: Do Medicare rules impede good care? *Health Affairs, 20*(3), 204–211.

Institute of Medicine. (1986). *Improving the quality of care in nursing homes.* Washington, DC: National Academy Press.

Institute of Medicine. (2001). *Crossing the quality chasm: A new health system for the 21st century.* Washington, DC: National Academy Press.

Kaiser Family Foundation. (2002). *The wide circle of caregiving.* Menlo Park, CA: Kaiser Commission on Medicaid and the Uninsured.

Kane, R. A. (2001). Long-term care and a good quality of life: Bringing them closer together. *Gerontologist, 41*(3), 293–304.

Kane, R. A. (2003). Definition, measurement, and correlates of quality of life in nursing homes: Toward a reasonable practice, research, and policy agenda [Special issue]. *Gerontologist, 43*(2), 28–36.

Kane, R. A., Kane, R. L., & Ladd, R. C. (1998). *The heart of long-term care.* New York: Oxford University Press.

Kane, R. L., & Kane, R. A. (2000). Assessment in long-term care. *Annual Review of Public Health, 21,* 659–686.

Katz, S., Ford, A., Moscovitz, R., Jackson, B., & Jaffe, M. (1963). Studies of illness in the aged: The index of ADL—A standardized measure of biological and physical function. *Journal of the American Medical Association, 185,* 914–919.

Kaufman, S. R., & Becker, G. (1996). Frailty, risk, and choice: Cultural discourses and the question of responsibility. In M. Smyer, K. W. Schaie, & M. B. Kapp (Eds.), *Older adult's decision-making and the law* (pp. 48–70). New York: Springer.

Kemper, P., & Murtaugh, C. (1991). Lifetime use of nursing home care. *New England Journal of Medicine, 324*(9), 595–600.

Kirwin, P. M. (1991). Adult day care. In P. M. Kirwin (Ed.), *Adult day care: The relationship of formal and informal systems of care* (pp. 48–117). New York: Garland.

Kutner, G. (2001). *AARP Caregiver Identification Study.* Washington, DC: American Association for Retired Persons.

Lake v. Cameron, DC Circuit Court 364 F2d 657 (1966).

Lawton, M. P., & Brody, E. M. (1969). Assessment of older people: Self-maintaining and instrumental activities of daily living. *Gerontologist, 9,* 179–186.

Lee, R., Miller, T., & Edwards, R. (2003). *The growth and aging of California's population: Demographic and fiscal projections, characteristics and service needs.* Berkeley: California Policy Research Center.

Lee, R., & Skinner, J. (1999). Will aging baby boomers bust the federal budget? *Journal of Economic Perspectives, 13*(1), 117–140.

Lee, R., & Tuljapurkar, S. (1998). Uncertain demographic futures and social security finances. *American Economic Review: AEA Papers and Proceedings, 88,* 237–241.

Lesperance, F., Frasure-Smith, N., & Talajic, M. (1996). Major depression before and after myocardial infarction: Its nature and consequences. *Psychosomatic Medicine, 58,* 99–110.

Leutz, W., Greenlick, M. R., DellaPenna, R., & Thomas, E. (2003). A prototype for 2005. In W. Leutz, M. R. Greenlick, & L. Nonnenkamp (Eds.), *Linking medical care and community services: Practical models for bridging the gap* (pp. 210–226). New York: Springer.

Leutz, W., Greenlick, M. R., & Nonnenkamp, L. (2003). Situational analysis: Challenges and opportunities, strengths and weaknesses. In W. Leutz, M. R. Greenlick, & L. Nonnenkamp (Eds.), *Linking medical care and community services: Practical models for bridging the gap* (pp. 186–209). New York: Springer.

Leveille, S. G., Wagner, E. H., Davis, C., Grothaus, L., Wallace, J., LoGerfo, M., et al. (1998). Preventing disability and managing chronic illness in frail older adults: A randomized trial of a community-based partnership with primary care. *Journal of the American Geriatrics Society, 46*(10), 1191–1198.

London, M. R., McSkimming, S., Drew, N., Quinn, C., & Carney, B. (2005). Evaluation of a Comprehensive, Adaptable, Life-Affirming, Longitudinal (CALL) palliative care project. *Journal of Palliative Medicine, 8*(6), 1214–1225.

Long, M. J., & Marshall, B. S. (1999). Case management and the cost of care in the last month of life: Evidence from one managed care setting. *Health Care Management Review, 24*(4), 45–53.

Lynn, J., Wilkinson, A., & Etheredge, L. (2001). Financing of care for fatal chronic disease: Opportunities for Medicare reform. *Western Journal of Medicine, 175*(5), 299–302.

Mace, N. L., & Rabins, P. V. (1984). *A survey of day care for the demented adult in the United States.* Washington, DC: National Council on Aging.

Macunovich, D. (2002). *Birthquake: The baby boom and its aftershocks.* Chicago: University of Chicago Press.

Magni, G. (1991). Pain and depression in the population. *Nursing Times, 87*(33), 49.

Markides, K. S., & Black, S. A. (1996). Race, ethnicity, and aging: The impact of inequality. In R. H. Binstock & L. George (Eds.), *Handbook of aging and the social sciences* (4th ed., pp. 153–170). San Diego, CA: Academic Press.

Marshall, B. S., Long, M., Voss, J., Demma, K., & Skerl, K. P. (1999). Case management of the elderly in a health maintenance organization: The implications for program administration under managed care. *Journal of Healthcare Management, 44*(6), 477–493.

Martin, L. G., & Kinsella, K. (1994). Research on the demography of aging in developing countries. In L. G. Martin & S. H. Preston (Eds.), *Demography of aging* (pp. 356–404). Washington, DC: National Academic Press.

McCann, J. J., Hebert, L. E., Li, Y., Wolinsky, F. D., Gilley, D. W., Aggarwal, N. T., et al. (2005). The effect of adult day care services on time to nursing home placement in older adults with Alzheimer's disease. *Gerontologist, 45*(6), 754–763.

Medpac. (2002). *Report to the Congress: Medicare beneficiaries' access to hospice.* Washington, DC: Medicare Payment Advisory Commission.

Medstat. (2000). *Important questions for hospice in the next century.* Washington, DC: U.S. Department of Health and Human Services, Office of Disability, Aging and Long-Term Care Policy, and Urban Institute.

Mendelson, M. A. (1975). *Tender loving greed: How the incredibly lucrative nursing home "industry" is exploiting America's old people and defrauding us all.* New York: Vintage.

Metropolitan Life Insurance Company. (1999). *MetLife Juggling Act Study: Balancing caregiving with work and the costs involved.* New York: National Alliance on Caregiving and National Center on Women and Aging.

Metropolitan Life Insurance Company. (2002a). *MetLife market survey of assisted living costs 2002.* Westport, CT: Author.

Metropolitan Life Insurance Company. (2002b). *MetLife market survey of nursing home and home care costs 2002.* Westport, CT: Author.

Miceli, P. J., & Wojciechowski, S. L. (2003). Impacting family satisfaction with hospice care. *Caring, 22*(11), 14–18.

Miller, E. A., & Weissert, W. G. (2000). Predicting elderly people's risk for nursing home placement, hospitalization, functional impairment, and mortality: A synthesis. *Medical Care Research and Review, 57*(3), 259–297.

Moen, P. (1996). Gender, age, and the life course. In R. H. Binstock & L. George (Eds.), *Handbook of aging and the social sciences* (4th ed., pp. 171–187). San Diego, CA: Academic Press.

Mollica, R. (2002). *State assisted living policy: 2002.* Portland, ME: National Academy for State Health Policy.

Mollica, R. (2003). Coordinating services across the continuum of health, housing, and supportive services. *Journal of Aging and Health, 15*(1), 165–188.

Mor, V., & Kidder, D. (1985). Cost savings in hospice: Final results of the National Hospice Study. *Health Services Research, 20,* 407–421.

Morishita, L., Boult, C., Boult, L., Smith, S., & Pacala, J. T. (1998). Satisfaction with outpatient geriatric evaluation and management (GEM). *Gerontologist, 38*(3), 303–308.

Mostyn, M., Race, K., Seibert, J., & Johnson, M. (2000). Quality assessment in nursing home facilities: Measuring customer satisfaction. *American Journal of Medical Quality, 15*(2), 54–61.

Moxley, D. P. (1989). *The practice of case management.* Thousand Oaks, CA: Sage.

National Association of Social Workers. (1992). *NASW standards for social work case management.* Washington, DC: Author.

National Center for Health Statistics. (2005). *Health, United States, 2005, with chartbook on trends in the health of Americans.* Hyattsville, MD: U.S. Department of Health and Human Services.

National Hospice and Palliative Care Organization. (2005). *NHPCO facts and figures.* Alexandria, VA. NHPCO.

Naylor, M., Brooten, D., Campbell, R., Jacobsen, B. S., Mezey, M. D., Pauly, M. V., et al. (1999). Comprehensive discharge planning and home follow-up of hospitalized elders. *Journal of the American Medical Association, 281*(7), 613–620.

Netting, F. E., & Williams, F. G. (1999). Implementing a case management program designed to enhance primary care physician practice with older persons. *Journal of Applied Gerontology, 18*(1), 25–45.

Newcomer, R., Harrington, C., & Kane, R. L. (2002). Challenges and accomplishments of the second-generation Social Health Maintenance Organization. *Gerontologist, 42*(6), 843–852.

Newhauser, F., Brady, H., & Seligman, J. (2003). *Planning for a comprehensive database on aging Californians: Meeting public policy and research need for better information.* Berkeley: California Policy Research Center.

North Carolina Department of Health and Human Services. (2006). *History of Dorothea Dix.* Retrieved February 22, 2006, from http://www.dhhs.state.nc.us/mhddsas /DIX/dorothea.html.

Norton, S. A., & Lipson, D. J. (1998). *Public policy, market forces, and the viability of safety net providers.* Washington, DC: Urban Institute.

O'Connor, D. W., Pollitt, P. A., Roth, M., Brook, C. P., & Reiss, B. B. (1990). Problems reported by relatives in a community study of dementia. *British Journal of Psychiatry, 156,* 835–841.

O'Hara-Devereaux, M., Falcon, R., Li, J., & Kristensen, H. (1999). *Fault lines in the shifting landscape: The future of growing older in California—2010.* Menlo Park, CA: Institute for the Future.

Ohta, R., & Ohta, B. (1988). Special units for Alzheimer's disease patients: A critical look. *Gerontologist, 28*(6), 803–808.

O'Keefe, J. (1999). *People with dementia: Can they meet Medicaid level-of-care criteria for admission to nursing homes and home and community-based waiver program?* Washington, DC: American Association for Retired Persons.

Olmstead, Commissioner, Georgia Department of Human Resources, et al., v. L.C., 527 U.S. 581. (1999).

Parmelee, P., Thuras, P. D., Katz, I. R., & Lawton, M. P. (1995). Validation of the Cumulative Illness Rating Scale in a geriatric residential population. *Journal of the American Geriatrics Society, 43,* 130–137.

Penninx, B. W., Guralnik, J. M., Ferrucci, L., Simonsick, E. M., Deeg, D. J., & Wallace, R. B. (1998). Depressive symptoms and physical decline in community-dwelling older persons. *Journal of the American Medical Association, 279*(21), 1720–1726.

Penninx, B. W., Leveille, S., Ferrucci, L., van Eijk, J. T., & Guralnik, J. M. (1999). Exploring the effect of depression on physical disability: Longitudinal evidence from the established populations for epidemiologic studies of the elderly. *American Journal of Public Health, 89*(9), 1346–1352.

Phillips, B., & Schneider, B. (2002). *Moving to independent choices: The implementation of the cash and counseling demonstration in Arkansas.* Princeton, NJ: Mathematica Policy Research.

Phillips, C. D., Munoz, Y., Sherman, M., Rose, M., Spector, W., & Hawes, C. (2003). Effects of facility characteristics on departures from assisted living: Results from a national study. *Gerontologist, 43*(5), 690–696.

Pyenson, B., Connor, S., Fitch, K., & Kinzbrunner, B. (2004). Medicare cost in matched hospice and non-hospice cohorts. *Journal of Pain and Symptom Management, 28*(3), 200–210.

Pynoos, J., Nishita, C. M., & Perelman, L. (2003). Advancements in the home modification field: A tribute to M. Powell Lawton. *Journal of Housing for the Elderly, 17*(1/2), 105–116.

Quayhagen, M. P., Quayhagen, M., Corbeil, R. R., Hendrix, R. C., Jackson, J. E., Snyder, L., et al. (2000). Coping with dementia: Evaluation of four nonpharmacologic interventions. *International Psychogeriatrics, 12*(2), 249–265.

Quinn, J. (1993). *Successful case management in long-term care.* New York: Springer.

Raiff, N. R., & Shore, B. K. (1993). *Advanced case management: New strategies for the nineties.* Newbury Park, CA: Sage.

Reuben, D. B. (2002). Organizational interventions to improve health outcomes of older persons. *Medical Care, 40*(5), 416–428.

Rickerson, E., Harrold, J., Kapo, J., Carroll, J. T., & Casarett, D. (2005). Timing of hospice referral and families' perceptions of services: Are earlier hospice referrals better? *Journal of the American Geriatrics Society, 53*(5), 819–823.

Robert Wood Johnson Foundation. (1999). *State initiatives in end-of-life care: Advances in state pain policy and medical practice.* Princeton, NJ. Community-State Partnerships to Improve End-of-Life Care.

Roberts, R., Kaplan, G., Shema, S., & Strawbridge, W. (1998). Does growing old increase the risk for depression? *American Journal of Psychiatry, 154*(10), 1384–1390.

Rosenbaum, S. (2000). The *Olmstead* decision: Implications for state health policy. *Health Affairs, 19*(5), 228–232.

Rosenberg, P. B., Mielke, M. M., Samus, Q. M., Rosenblatt, A., Baker, A., Brand, J., et al. (2006). Transition to nursing home from assisted living is not associated with dementia or dementia-related problem behaviors. *Journal of the American Medical Directors Association, 7*(2), 73–78.

Rosenblatt, A., Samus, Q. M., Steele, C. D., Baker, A. S., Harper, M. G., Brandt, J., et al. (2004). The Maryland Assisted Living Study: Prevalence, recognition, and treatment of dementia and other psychiatric disorders in the assisted living population of central Maryland. *Journal of the American Geriatrics Society, 52*(10), 1618–1625.

Ryden, M. B., Gross, C. R., Savik, K., Snyder, M., Oh, H. L., Jang, Y. P., et al. (2000). Development of a measure of resident satisfaction with the nursing home. *Research in Nursing and Health, 23*(2), 237–245.

Scharlach, A., Giunta, N., & Mills-Dick, K. (2001). *Case management in long-term care integration: An overview of current programs and evaluations.* Berkeley: University of California, Center for the Advanced Study of Aging Services.

Schnelle, J. F., Kapur, K., Alessi, C., Osterweil, D., Beck, J. G., Al-Samarrai, N., et al. (2003). Does an exercise and incontinence intervention save health care costs in a nursing home population? *Journal of the American Geriatrics Society, 51*(2), 161–168.

Schoevers, R. A., Geerlings, M. I., Beekman, A. T., Penninx, B. W., Deeg, D. J., Jonker, C., et al. (2000). Association of depression and gender with mortality in old age: Results from the Amsterdam Study of the Elderly (AMSTEL). *British Journal of Psychiatry, 177,* 336–342.

Schore, J. L., Brown, R. S., & Cheh, V. A. (1999). Case management for high-cost Medicare beneficiaries. *Health Care Financing Review, 20,* 87–100.

Schulz, R., O'Brien, A. T., Bookwala, J., & Fleissner, K. (1995). Psychiatric and physical morbidity effects of dementia caregiving: Prevalence, correlates, and causes. *Gerontologist, 35,* 771–791.

Scudds, R. J., & Robertson, J. M. (1998). Empirical evidence of the association between the presence of musculoskeletal pain and physical disability in community-dwelling senior citizens. *Pain, 75*(2/3), 229–235.

Scudds, R. J., & Robertson, J. M. (2000). Pain factors associated with physical disability in a sample of community-dwelling senior citizens. *Journals of Gerontology: Medical Sciences, 55*(7), M393–M399.

Shannon, G. R., Wilber, K. H., & Allen, D. (2006). Reductions in costly health care service utilization: Findings from the Care Advocate Program. *Journal of the American Geriatrics Society, 54*(7), 1102–1107.

Shapiro, A., & Taylor, M. (2002). Effects of a community-based early intervention program on the subjective well-being, institutionalization, and mortality of low-income elders. *Gerontologist, 42*(3), 334–341.

Shugarman, L., Nishita, C. M., & Wilber, K. H. (2006). Building integrated information systems for chronic care: The California experience. *Home Health Care Services Quarterly, 25*(3/4), 185–200.

Siegel, J. (1993). *A generation of change.* New York: Russell Sage Foundation.

Sikorska-Simmons, E. (2005). Predictors of organizational commitment among staff in assisted living. *Gerontologist, 45*(2), 196–205.

Singh, D. A. (2005). *Effective management of long-term care facilities.* Sudbury, MA: Jones and Bartlett.

Sloane, P. D., & Mathew, L. J. (1991). Characteristics of residents with dementia. In P. D. Sloane & L. J. Mathew (Eds.), *Dementia units in long-term care* (pp. 65–89). Baltimore: Johns Hopkins University Press.

Sloane, P. D., Zimmerman, S., & Ory, M. (2001). Care for persons with dementia. In S. Zimmerman, P. D. Sloane, & J. K. Eckert (Eds.), *Assisted living: Needs, practices and policies in residential care for the elderly* (pp. 242–270). Baltimore: Johns Hopkins University Press.

Smits, H. L., Furletti, M., & Vladeck, B. C. (2003). *Palliative care: An opportunity for Medicare.* Mount Sinai, NY: Institute for Medicare Practice.

Snowden, M., Sato, K., & Roy-Byrne, P. (2003). Assessment and treatment of nursing home residents with depression or behavioral symptoms associated with dementia: A review of the literature. *Journal of the American Geriatrics Society, 51*(9), 1305–1317.

Squillace, M., & Firman, J. (2002). *Myths and realities of consumer-directed services for older persons.* Washington, DC: National Council on Aging and the National Association of State Units on Aging.

Starr, P. (1984). *The social transformation of American medicine: The rise of a sovereign profession and the making of a vast industry.* New York: Basic Books.

Stefanacci, R. G., & Podrazik, P. M. (2005). Assisted living facilities: Optimizing outcomes. *Journal of the American Geriatrics Society, 53*(3), 538–540.

Stone, R. I. (2000). *Long-term care for the elderly with disabilities: Current policy, emerging trends, and implications for the twenty-first century.* New York: Milbank Memorial Fund.

Tedesco, J. (2001). Adult day care. In C. Evashwick (Ed.), *The continuum of long-term care: An integrated approach* (pp. 83–96). Albany, NY: Delmar.

Teno, J. M., Clarridge, B. R., Casey, V., Welch, L. C., Wetle, T., Shield, R., et al. (2004). Family perspectives on end-of-life care at the last place of care. *Journal of the American Medical Association, 291*(1), 88–93.

Thomas, W. H. (1996). *Life worth living: How someone you love can still enjoy life in a nursing home—The Eden Alternative in action.* Acton, MA: VanderWyk & Burnham.

Thomas, W. H. (2004). *What are old people for? How elders will save the world.* Acton, MA: VanderWyk & Burnham.

Townsend, J., Frank, A., Fermont, D., Dyer, S., Karran, O., Walgrove, A., et al. (1990). Terminal cancer care and patients' preference for place of death: A prospective study. *British Medical Journal, 301,* 415–417.

U.S. Congress, Office of Technology Assessment. (1992). *Special care units for people with Alzheimer's and other dementias: Consumer education, research, regulatory and reimbursement issues.* Washington, DC: U.S. Government Printing Office.

Unutzer, J., Katon, W., Callahan, C. M., Williams, J. W., Hunkeler, E., Harpole, L., et al. (2002). Collaborative care management for late-life depression in the primary care setting. *Journal of the American Medical Association, 288*(22), 2836–2845.

Vitaliano, P. P., Russo, J., Young, H. M., Teri, L., & Maiuro, R. D. (1991). Predictors of burden in spouse caregivers of individuals with Alzheimer's disease. *Psychology and Aging, 6,* 392–402.

Vladeck, B. C. (1999). The problem isn't payment: Medicare and the reform of end-of-life care. *Generations, 23*(1), 52–57.

Von Behren, R. (1989). Adult day care: A decade of growth. *Perspectives on Aging, 18,* 14–19.

Wallston, K., Burger, C., Smith, R., & Baugher, R. (1988). Comparing the quality of death for hospice and non-hospice cancer patients. *Medical Care, 26*(2), 177–182.

Weissert, W. G. (1976). Two models of geriatric day care: Findings from a comparative study. *Gerontologist, 16,* 420–427.

Weissert, W., Chernew, M., & Hirth, R. (2003). Titrating versus targeting home care services to frail elderly clients: An application of agency theory and cost-benefit analysis to home care policy. *Journal of Aging and Health, 15*(1), 99–123.

Weissert, W. G., Cready, C. M., & Pawelak, J. E. (1988). The past and future of home- and community-based long-term care. *Milbank Quarterly, 66*(2), 309–388.

Weissert, W. G., Elston, J., Bolda, E., Cready, C. M., Zelman, W., Sloane, P. D., et al. (1989). Models of adult day care: Findings from a national survey. *Gerontologist, 29*(5), 640–649.

Weissert, W. G., Wan, T., Livieratos, B., & Katz, S. (1980). Effects and costs of day-care services for the chronically ill. *Medical Care, 18,* 567–584.

Wells, K. B., & Sherbourne, C. D. (1999). Functioning and utility for current health of patients with depression or chronic medical conditions in managed, primary care practices. *Archives of General Psychiatry, 56*(10), 897–904.

Weuve, J. L., Boult, C., & Morishita, L. (2000). The effects of outpatient geriatric evaluation and management on caregiver burden. *Gerontologist, 40*(4), 429–436.

Wieland, D., Lamb, V. L., Sutton, S. R., Boland, R., Clark, M., Friedman, S., et al. (2000). Hospitalization in the Program of All-Inclusive Care for the Elderly (PACE): Rates, concomitants, and predictors. *Journal of the American Geriatrics Society, 48*(11), 1373–1380.

Wiener, J. M., Illston, L. H., & Hanley, R. J. (1994). *Sharing the burden: Strategies for public and private long-term care insurance.* Washington, DC: Brookings Institution.

Wilber, K. H. (2000). Managing services for older adults. In R. J. Patti (Ed.), *Handbook of social welfare management* (pp. 521–533). Thousand Oaks, CA: Sage.

Wilber, K. H., & Alkema, G. E. (2006). Policies related to competency and proxy issues. In B. Berkman (Ed.), *Handbook of social work in health and aging* (pp. 893–901). New York: Oxford University Press.

Wilber, K. H., Allen, D., Shannon, G. R., & Alongi, S. (2003). Partnering managed care and community-based service for older adults: The Care Advocate Program. *Journal of the American Geriatrics Society, 51*(6), 1–6.

Williamson, G. M., & Schulz, R. (1992). Pain, activity restriction, and symptoms of depression among community-residing elderly adults. *Journal of Gerontology, 47*(6), P367–P372.

Wu, S.-Y., & Green, A. (2000). *Projection of chronic illness and cost inflation.* Santa Monica, CA: RAND Corporation.

Yeh, S.-C. J., & Lo, S. K. (2004). Is rehabilitation associated with change in functional status among nursing home residents? *Journal of Nursing Care Quality, 19*(1), 58–66.

Yelin, E., & Trupin, L. (1999). *California Work and Health Survey, 1999: Work, retirement, and health of Californians—A mixed story.* San Francisco: University of California, San Francisco, Institute for Health Policy Studies.

Zank, S., & Schacke, C. (2002). Evaluation of geriatric day care units: Effects on patients and caregivers. *Journal of Gerontology: Psychological Sciences, 57B*(4), P348–P357.

Zarit, S. H., Reever, K. E., & Bach-Peterson, J. (1980). Relatives of impaired elderly: Correlates of feelings of burden. *Gerontologist, 20*(6), 649–655.

Zarit, S. H., Stephens, M., Townsend, A., & Greene, R. (1998). Stress reduction for family caregivers: Effects of adult day care use. *Journals of Gerontology: Social Sciences, 53*(5), S267–S277.

Zarit, S. H., Stephens, M. A. P., Townsend, A., Greene, R., & Femia, E. E. (2003). Give day care a chance to be effective: A commentary. *Journals of Gerontology: Psychological Sciences, 58*(3), P195–P196.

Zimmerman, S., Gruber-Baldini, A. L., Sloane, P. D., Eckert, J. K., Hebel, J. R., Morgan, L. A., et al. (2003). Assisted living and nursing homes: Apples and oranges? *Gerontologist, 43 (Special Issue II),* 107–117.

Zimmerman, S., & Sloane, P. D. (1999). Optimum residential care for people with dementia. *Generations, 23*(3), 62–68.

Zimmerman, S., Sloane, P. D., Eckert, J. K., Gruber-Baldini, A. L., Morgan, L. A., Hebel, J. R., et al. (2005). How good is assisted living? Findings and implications from an outcomes study. *Journals of Gerontology: Social Sciences, 60*(4), S195–S204.

CHAPTER 18

Elder Abuse

PATRICIA BROWNELL and GINA R. ROSICH

E LDER ABUSE IS a complex and significant social and public health problem. There are neither easy explanations nor firmly established methods for examining, assessing, or ameliorating it. Despite over 30 years of research, policy implementation, practice, and public awareness efforts, there is still little consensus among researchers and policy-makers about definitions and measures (Chalk, 2000). However, professionals from a wide variety of disciplines continue to make progress in understanding the many forms of elder abuse that occur and evaluating the effectiveness of practice, program, and policy interventions intended to prevent and ameliorate this troubling social phenomenon.

This chapter examines the scope of the problem of domestic elder abuse and presents an overview of theoretical perspectives on elder abuse and mistreatment. Evidence-based interventions found in the professional literature and practice guidelines with vignettes are intended to assist professionals with ways to help victims of elder abuse. Finally, recommendations are made for policy initiatives and future research.

TRENDS AND INCIDENCE

In spite of over 30 years of public debate about elder abuse, there is no definitive answer to the question of how many cases of elder abuse occur in a given year. Research prevalence estimates have ranged from 3% to 10%, and the latest incidence study estimated that 820,000 to 1,860,000 older adults are abused each year (Tatara, Kuzmeskus, Duckhorn, & Bivens, 1998). These data are disputed by other experts in the field as representing undercounts (Thomas, 2000). There are many reasons for a discrepancy in estimates: methodology, samples used, and how the definition of elder abuse was operationalized. The earliest researchers in the field experienced conflict regarding these questions, and to this day, there is still some disagreement (Choi & Mayer, 2000; National Center on Elder Abuse [NCEA], 2006; Quinn & Tomita, 1997; Wolf, 1996). Variations in definitions used by policy makers, researchers, and practitioners compound the difficulty of achieving accurate estimates of incidence and prevalence, as well as identifying emerging trends.

Elder abuse can take many forms, but generally speaking, it can be broken down into six major categories:

1. *Physical abuse,* which involves the use of physical violence that induces pain or impairment and may or may not result in bodily injury (hitting, slapping, striking with objects).
2. *Sexual abuse,* which includes nonconsensual sexual contact of any kind with an elderly person.
3. *Emotional or psychological abuse,* which inflicts pain, distress, or anguish through threats, intimidation, insults, humiliation, harassment, and other forms of verbal aggression.
4. *Financial and material exploitation,* which involves the illegal or improper use of an elder's funds, property, or assets.
5. *Neglect,* which includes the deliberate or unintended failure on the part of a caregiver to provide a dependent elderly person with necessities such as food, medication, bathing, and social contact.
6. *Self-neglect,* which is failure on the part of the elderly person living independently to provide for himself or herself, threatening the health and safety of the individual (Choi & Mayer, 2000; NCEA, 2006).

These categories are generally accepted by researchers, having been adopted early by pioneers in the field such as Pillemer and Finkelhor (1988), who conducted the first large-scale prevalence study of elder abuse and neglect, and who continue to be cited in the literature.

The disagreements that arise in comparison studies of Adult Protective Services (APS) laws and in prevalence and incidence studies of elder abuse generally fall into practical and theoretical realms. Practically speaking, abuse definitions and mandatory reporting laws vary across the country by state and between researchers, among reporters, and in the understanding of the general public. Some do not use the term "abuse," and others distinguish between self-neglect and neglect by others. Adult Protective Services agencies also do not use the same terms when documenting reports and do not always collect the same type of data (Choi & Mayer, 2000; Goodrich, 1997; Hudson & Carlson, 1998; Jogerst et al., 2003; Wolf, 1996). Theoretically, some researchers are interested in broader categories, such as violation of rights (e.g., forced institutionalization or removal of personal property) and abandonment. Questions arise as to whether self-neglect should be included as a form of elder abuse as it is conceptually different from abuse and neglect by others, even though interventions may be similar for both situations. Still others distinguish between cases of accidental and intentional neglect or abuse when considering both criminal prosecution and interventions to help the elder person and the abuser (Choi & Mayer, 2000; Hudson & Carlson, 1998; Wolf, 1996).

These differences have made it difficult to compare research findings, develop assessment instruments, count the incidence and prevalence of elder abuse, and develop causal theories. Despite this, some impressive research has been conducted. As stated earlier, Pillemer and Finkelhor (1988) conducted the first large-scale random sample survey of elder abuse and neglect. They interviewed 2,020 elderly persons residing in a metropolitan community in Boston regarding their experiences of physical abuse, psychological abuse, and neglect. Financial abuse and self-neglect were not included. Their results indicated a prevalence rate of overall maltreatment of 32 per 1,000 elderly persons (age 65 and up). Physical abuse was reported most often, and spouses were found to be the most likely abusers (58%), followed by adult children (24%). They found no difference in number of incidents by sex, although women seemed to suffer more serious abuses than men. They also found the frail elderly to be the population at greatest risk for maltreatment.

In a study by Pavlik, Hyman, Festa, and Dyer (2001), case reports received during 1 year in a centralized computer database maintained by the Texas Department of Protective Regulatory Services—APS Division were reviewed. Texas is the largest state to have a centralized reporting system, and it has the largest protective service data repository in the country. Cases of physical abuse, emotional abuse, sexual abuse, neglect, medical neglect, and exploitation for clients age 65 years and older were tracked, with neglect differentiated by self-neglect and neglect by others. The study found that 80% of allegations reported were for neglect and that the risk of being reported to APS nearly doubled with each 10-year increase in age. They also noted that older women were 40% to 300% more likely than older men to be reported for abuse or neglect. They suspect that women are at higher risk than men for abuse by others; in terms of self-neglect, however, the ratio of men to women was close to 1:1.

Choi and Mayer (2000) conducted a study using data from intake and assessment files and case managers' progress and termination notes from 370 cases from the Erie County, New York Protective Services for Older Adults unit between 1992 and 1997. Their article includes a rich literature review on elder abuse. The study itself identified self-neglect (including self-endangering behaviors, poor financial management, and environmental hazards not involving others) as the largest problem facing their sample (51.9%). The remaining 48.1% of the sample were neglected, abused, and/or financially exploited by others; 37.6% (18.1% of the entire sample) were in the financial exploitation-only group, and of this group, most were victimized by perpetrators unrelated to them, such as neighbors, tenants, guardians, and others who initially came forward as "helping hands" but were overcome by greed. In addition, 10.7% experienced abuse only, and 2.2% experienced abuse and neglect; 15.7% experienced neglect and financial exploitation.

Choi and Mayer (2000) found that those who had acute or chronic illnesses were 62% more likely to have been abused, neglected, or exploited by others, and those who had alcohol or substance abuse problems were 70% more likely to have been self-neglecting. Neglect, psychological abuse, and financial exploitation were more commonly reported and substantiated than physical abuse. However, neglect was the highest reported problem (including self-neglect). Multiple forms of abuse and neglect are also found to occur simultaneously. Elders were less likely to be abused, neglected, or exploited by others if they lived alone and had social supports, but more likely to suffer self-neglect if they had difficulties with activities of daily living and substance abuse problems. Those with acute or chronic illnesses were 62% more likely than those without illnesses to be abused, neglected, or exploited by others. Elders living with others (mostly family members) faced the greatest likelihood of being physically and psychologically abused and neglected.

Both prevalence and incidence data on elder abuse to date are considered by many experts to be vastly underreported because of a lack of self-reporting by victims and perpetrators, the relative invisibility of the elder population, the lack of awareness of the problem on the part of the general public, and the lack of adequate assessment tools for professionals (Quinn & Tomita, 1997). This has led to the popularization of the "iceberg theory," which posits that substantiated incidents of elder abuse represent only the tip of the iceberg, with the largest number of cases identified by professionals but not reported to authorities, and a smaller percentage of cases both unidentified and unreported (Cyphers, 1999).

The most recent research study on incidence of elder abuse was the first national survey of state APS programs by the National Center on Elder Abuse (Tatara et al., 1998), which found that approximately 450,000 elderly people in domestic settings in the United States were the victims of some sort of abuse or neglect. This number increased to 551,000 when the category of self-neglect was added. Tatara et al. also reported the following findings:

- Female elders are abused at a higher rate than males, after accounting for their larger proportion in the aging population.
- Our oldest elders (80 years and over) are abused and neglected at 2 to 3 times their proportion of the elderly population.
- In almost 90% of the elder abuse and neglect incidents with a known perpetrator, the perpetrator is a family member, and two-thirds of the perpetrators are adult children or spouses.
- Victims of self-neglect are usually depressed, confused, or extremely frail (p. 12).

The findings of this national study were controversial. When results showed lower than expected numbers of incidence, advocates and agencies worried that funding for elder abuse research and services would not be prioritized (Thomas, 2000). However, with population trends showing an increase in the proportion of people age 65 and up with the aging of the baby boomer generation, and research showing that older people who are mistreated are 3 times more likely to die during a 3-year period than those who do not experience abuse, those concerned about elder abuse should caution against dismissing or minimizing it (Lachs & Pillemer, 2004).

Although APS statutes are state- and county-based and differ from one jurisdiction to another, the Older Americans Act (OAA) Amendments Title VII presents a national definition that frames elder abuse, neglect, and mistreatment in a human rights context (OAA, 42 U.S.C. section 3001 *et seq.*, 2000). Here, abuse is defined as "the willful infliction of injury, unreasonable confinement, intimidation, or cruel punishment with resulting physical harm, pain, or mental anguish or deprivation by a person, including a caregiver, of goods and services that are necessary to avoid physical harm, mental anguish, or mental illness" (42 U.S.C. section 3001 *et seq.*, 2000). This definition is intended to guide state and area agencies on aging in developing programs and services for preventing and protecting adults age 60 and above from experiencing family mistreatment.

The OAA defines elder abuse in broad terms, but agencies and services funded by the OAA do not have the enforcement powers of APS agencies, which are mandated by state law and regulation to provide involuntary services if deemed necessary to protect abused, neglected, and self-neglecting adults, including older adults, from harm, assuming they lack the mental or physical capacity to protect themselves from harm.

ETIOLOGY AND PROGNOSIS

Multiple theories have emerged to explain the phenomenon of elder abuse and shed light on possible preventive and intervention measures. Theoretical perspectives cited in the literature range from individual characteristics of the victim and abuser to structural theories that reflect societal and cultural factors (Anetzberger, 2005). Vulnerability and psychopathology theories suggest that elder abuse and mistreatment can occur as a result of individual characteristics such as victim high care needs (Steinmetz, 1990) or abuser psychopathology (Brownell, Berman, Salamone, & Welty, 2002). Situational theory (Grunig & Disbrow, 1977), vulnerability theory (Penhale & Kingston, 1997), role theory (Soeda & Araki, 1999), and ecology theory (Schiamberg & Gans, 1999) all suggest that interactional effects among individual circumstances and environmental contexts can lead to elder abuse and neglect. Social learning theory (Wolf, 2000), symbolic interactionism (Steinmetz, 1990), and functionalism (Powell, 2001) provide frameworks for understanding the impact of cultural values and norms on abuse of older adults by family members and significant others. Feminist theory (Nerenberg, 2002) explains the abuse of older women in terms of structural inequities in societies that disadvantage women and girls.

EVIDENCE-BASED INTERVENTIONS

Interventions can include preventive strategies as well as interventions intended to minimize or stop abuse or neglect of a vulnerable older adult. All interventions must start with good assessments, which include identification of risk factors and diagnosis and prognosis. The goal of screening and assessment of elder abuse is to identify the target (victim) of abuse or neglect, reduce or eliminate the continuation of mistreatment, and protect the victim. Health care workers are often the first to observe the physical manifestations of elder abuse and neglect but may misidentify the causes or choose to ignore them. Self-reporting of abuse or neglect is uncommon and unreliable; the stigma of abuse may make older adult victims and family members uncomfortable about disclosing it (U.S. Department of Health and Human Services, 2006).

ASSESSMENT

Research on assessing older adult victimization is far behind that of interpersonal violence in adolescents and young adults. Some researchers (Acierno, Resnick, Kilpatrick, & Stark-Riemer, 2003) have questioned whether valid methods for assessing elder victimization should be based on those used with youth and researched whether telephone screening could be used to assess psychopathology. However, the reliability and validity of telephone interviews (versus in-person interviews) has also been raised. In one study of elder abuse and neglect by family and caregivers and criminal violence (assault), researchers found no significant differences in observed rates of victimization (recent and distant past) for either form of assessment or in assessing psychopathology. In testing the feasibility of interview types, no difference was found in hearing problems, fatigue during the interview, or elevated distress from the interview questions. Telephone interviews were found to be significantly shorter, and elderly participants expressed a great deal more comfort with telephone interviews; however, these were informal assessments. In-person interviewers can provide more empathy and support. Conversely, telephone interviews may capture people afraid to allow someone into their home to conduct the interviews.

The use of explicit, behaviorally specific closed-ended event questions, contextually orienting preface statements, and simultaneous assessment of both assault by strangers and abuse by family members and caregivers are applicable to assessing victimization with older adults. These types of questions were able to detect various types of interpersonal violence as well as outline violence-related assault and perpetrator characteristics.

Fulmer, Guadagno, Bitondo, and Connolly (2004) provide a comprehensive overview of different types of assessment screening instruments. They included an overview of theoretical models for the occurrence of elder mistreatment (EM) and problems with underreporting and inconsistencies across fields and locations. They divided screening and assessment instruments and protocols into four types: checklists and guidelines, qualitative assessments, quantitative assessments, and combined qualitative and quantitative. They demonstrated how different screenings might be used in different settings (e.g., short forms in hospitals, longer forms by APS workers) and discussed some of the difficulties in distinguishing EM from normal signs of aging.

One study that evaluated a screening procedure for assessing elder mistreatment, emphasizing elder neglect, also examined how expert neglect assessment teams assess and diagnose cases of suspected elder neglect (Fulmer et al., 2003). Key themes identified in the study that must be understood by expert team members to determine if neglect should be suspected or confirmed include the underlying health status of the elder and caregiver dyad, the socioeconomic and life circumstances of the dyad, the credibility of data collected by others, and consequences of the assessment outcome.

Reis and Nahmiash (1998) sought to validate the Indicators of Abuse (IOA) as a screening tool for elder abuse and neglect. The tool was based on studies guided by theories of abuse that included "nonnormal" abusers, dependency, caregiver burden or stress, transgenerational violence, and social isolation. The researchers wanted to know which items from their 48-item checklist discriminated abuse and nonabuse cases. They also asked which of the indicators do not discriminate abuse and nonabuse and sought to develop a theoretical model of the problems that are abuse indicators.

The study successfully isolated a subset of 29 key items from the original checklist of 48 that discriminated the "abuse likely" and "abuse not likely" cases. Primary predictors were marital and family conflict, mental and behavioral health problems of the caregiver, and past abuse of the elderly person receiving care. Other indicators specifically about the caregiver included poor relationships with others, failure or difficulty understanding the care receiver's medical condition, reluctance to provide care, alcohol or drug addiction problems, unrealistic expectations on the part of the caregiver, inexperience in caring for an elderly person, financial dependence on the elderly person, and if the caregiver was a blamer. Lack of social support and poor current caregiver-receiver relationships were also indicators. Variables that did not signal cases of abuse, but that might still be problems experienced by the elderly person receiving care, included requiring help with activities of daily living, financial difficulties other than dependency, physical or cognitive impairment, the desire of the caregiver to institutionalize, and caregiver stress. The study partially supported theories of dependency, transgenerational violence, and social isolation as causes of abuse. Ultimately, the IOA was validated as a screening tool and identified as having potential as a teaching tool.

DIAGNOSIS

Diagnosis in the context of elder abuse and mistreatment is complicated by the necessity to identify the presence of abuse, neglect, or financial exploitation in a family situation, in addition to identifying physical, psychological, substance abuse, and other factors reflecting personal characteristics of the victim and abuser. Diagnosis of elder abuse and neglect depends on good assessment (Quinn & Tomita, 1997). Elder abuse may be difficult to detect if the signs are ambiguous and the victim is unwilling or unable to disclose the abuse.

Medical and social assessment tools have been developed, as discussed earlier, yet symptoms of abuse may be misattributed to chronic disease or cognitive impairment (Merck Manual of Geriatrics, 2000). Recognizing high-risk situations is critical for health practitioners as well as other helping professionals to ensure the safety and protection of a vulnerable older adult. Older adults may agree to share their home with family members who have substance abuse problems or serious mental disorders, and family members may have been discharged from a psychiatric or other institution to the home of an older adult without having been screened for risk of harm (Brownell et al., 2002). Physicians and social workers should pay particular attention to those situations in which an older person is discharged with high care needs to a family situation that may be unable to support that level of care (Merck Manual of Geriatrics, 2000).

Abused elderly people are at high risk of death through maltreatment or even homicide (Brownell & Berman, 2004). In one New York City study, female homicide victims 75 or older were more likely to be strangled, bludgeoned, or burned to death by adult children, grandchildren, or siblings than women under 75. One longitudinal study found a threefold higher mortality rate for abused patients over a 3-year period after the abuse than for nonabused patients during the same period of time (Merck Manual of Geriatrics, 2000). Prognosis is poorer for older patients whose caregivers have chronic medical and functional problems than for those with adequate care-giving supports.

SERVICE INTERVENTIONS

Although possible risk factors for occurrence of elder abuse have been identified in the literature, most interventions have not been subjected to systematic evaluation (National Research Council, 2003). Intervention research in elder abuse is in its earliest stages, and intervention models have been developed to address different types of elder abuse and neglect without rigorous testing for outcomes. The next stage in elder abuse research is to begin more rigorous investigation into the models' effectiveness in preventing or ameliorating the occurrence or effects of mistreatment on older people who may be traumatized or cognitively impaired. It is essential to educate university-based institutional review boards on elder abuse so that research can move forward (National Research Council, 2003).

Elder abuse and mistreatment is a complex social phenomenon, and interventions must be designed to address very specific factors related to individual situations. For example, different interventions are needed for frail, care-dependent older adults with impaired cognitive capacity and for mistreated older adults who are cognitively intact, live independently in the community, and sometimes serve as caregivers for their abusers (Brownell & Heiser, in press). Financial abuse may require different strategies from psychological or physical, including sexual, abuse. For elder abuse victims who choose not to separate from their abusive family members, a family preservation program is recommended (Bergeron, 2002). This model, adapted from child abuse practice models, was evaluated by a reexamination of data from a 1996 exploratory study in New Hampshire. Following are examples of programs targeting specific forms of elder abuse that have been described as representing best practice models in the literature.

INTERDISCIPLINARY TEAM INTERVENTIONS

INTERDISCIPLINARY TEAM MODEL

An interdisciplinary team (IT) model was developed in Wisconsin to address cases of elder abuse on county APS caseloads that have one or more of the following characteristics: chronic intractable case, case with ethical issues, case needing specialized expertise, caseworkers denied access, abuser or victim refuses services, and case with victim and family members facing serious environmental problems representing health and safety problems. A manual was developed for use by county APS offices, based on assessed need for IT services (Abramson, 2005).

CASE MANAGEMENT PROGRAMS

An intervention program for elder abuse victims using case managers was developed in Hamilton, Ontario, to help victims set long- and short-term goals, supporting victims in decisions as to whether or not to take action against their abusers, explaining harm-reduction options, and involving others in care plans. Outcomes for the program, which was targeted to mentally competent older adults living in the community, included a success rate of eliminating abuse in 35% of cases serviced and improving situations in another 31% of cases (Vladescu, Eveleigh, Ploeg, & Patterson, 1999).

FINANCIAL ABUSE

FIDUCIARY ABUSE SPECIALIST TEAM PROGRAM

Malks, Schmidt, and Austin (2002) presented a case study of a rapid response team in Santa Clara, California, that was created in the wake of a rise in caseloads from financial abuse. In their literature review, the authors reiterated the widespread problem of inaccuracy in counting the exact number of cases of elder abuse (in this case, specifically involving financial exploitation) because cases often are not recognized or reported. The authors found financial abuse a particularly underreported crime, and stated that family members and in-home caregivers accounted for 60% to 90% of perpetrators. They cited the 1996 national study, which revealed that around 40% of the 551,000 verified reports of elder abuse involved some form of financial abuse.

Elders are likely to hide abuse to protect children; victims of financial abuse may feel embarrassed for being exploited; and financial abuse may not be as easily recognized as bodily harm. Also, as noted earlier, due to a lack of federal statutes to regulate elder abuse, it has fallen to the states to develop guidelines, and those definitions are thus extremely varied. Malks et al. (2002) outline the Fiduciary Abuse Specialist Team (FAST) program, which involves a multidisciplinary team, a referral process, emergency response, and litigation efforts on behalf of victims. They cite the program as being very successful, with the greatest challenges being an unanticipated demand and unwillingness on the part of victims to press charges. A FAST program sponsored by the County of Los Angeles provides expert consultation and training to APS and other agencies using a team approach with consultants in both the nonprofit and private sectors (Aziz, 2000).

For many older adults, their most important form of equity is their home. A number of fraudulent schemes have been developed by con artists, some supported by banks and other reputable institutions, to manipulate older adults into unwittingly sign over their home or take out mortgages with monthly payments that they cannot afford. The Volunteer Legal Services Program of the Bar Association in San Francisco was designed to address home equity fraud against older persons. This program initiated a two-pronged approach against home loss: a training program to instruct attorneys how to review loan documents for truth-in-lending violations and other fraudulent practices, and a community outreach component aimed at linking trained lawyers to community agencies and their clients (Alfonso, 2000).

PHYSICAL ABUSE

VULNERABLE ADULT SPECIALIST TEAM

The Vulnerable Adult Specialist Team (VAST) provides medical consultation to agencies serving vulnerable older adults in Orange County, California, who may be victims of abuse or neglect resulting in a serious medical condition. The VAST can also assess older adult victims who may have an underlying medical condition that requires treatment, or contributes to their inability to care for or protect themselves against harm, or requires specialized care unavailable in the household (NCEA, 2006).

Physical abuse of older adults can be defined as a caregiver training or respite service issue, or as a criminal matter. For those cases of physical abuse that rise to the level of a possible criminal offense, investigators with special training in forensic work are critical to ensuring the protection of the elderly victim. The Elder Abuse Forensic Center, established in Santa Ana, California, is headed by a geriatrician and is the first national center to provide interdisciplinary expert consultation for APS and other agencies serving older adults who may be victims of family mistreatment (Cook-Daniels, 2003).

PSYCHOLOGICAL ABUSE

Psychological abuse may co-occur with other forms of elder abuse and is a particularly painful form of mistreatment that can lower the self-esteem of older adults and older women in particular (Podnieks, 1999; Seaver, 1996). Group interventions have been identified in the literature as among the most effective interventions for addressing this form of abuse (Podnieks, 1999; Vinton, 1999; Wolf, 1998). Enhancing the Health of Older Women, a psychoeducational support group for older women victims of abuse (Brownell & Heiser, in press), and Women's Empowerment in Later Life, an empowerment training and support group for older female abuse victims, are two models that have been pilot-tested using an adapted curriculum developed by Nova House Shelter in Canada (Schmuland, 1995).

TRAINING INTERVENTIONS

The City of New York, with the Department for the Aging as the lead government agency, developed and tested a training curriculum on elder abuse for law enforcement, prosecutors, and court personnel. A pre- and posttest evaluation found it to be effective in increasing knowledge on elder abuse among the target professionals in the criminal justice system (Brownell, Berman, & Salamone, 2005). The entire curriculum with modules can be downloaded from the City of New York website (http://www.nyc.gov/html/dfta/pdf/elderabuse_courtcurriculum.pdf).

Westley (2002) provides a module for educational information related to elder abuse. It was developed for use by health care professionals and includes an overview of abuse with definitions, profiles of "typical" abusers and victims, inpatient and outpatient case studies, a chart listing signs of abuse, and a posttest on the information provided. It also provides graphics with percentages on the types of domestic elder abuse and of reporters of domestic elder abuse, with a brief discussion of mandatory reporting and specifics on the law in the state of Virginia.

EVIDENCE-BASED PRACTICE GUIDELINES

Jogerst et al. (2003) evaluated the impact of differing state APS legislation on rates of investigated and substantiated domestic elder abuse. By 1985, every state had instituted some type of APS program, and as of 1993 all states had enacted laws addressing elder abuse in domestic and institutional settings. As noted earlier, state laws related to elder abuse are extremely diverse, and this has had a major impact on the study of incidence and prevalence rates.

Jogerst et al.'s (2003) study was thought to be the first of its kind, as no similar studies were found in the literature. Four dependent variables were used and 19 independent variables. (*Note:* APS statutes for all states and Washington, DC, were obtained through the Westlaw legal database http://web2.westlaw.com.) The study found that higher investigation rates were associated with a mandatory reporting requirement and the presence of a statute clause regarding penalties for failure to report elder abuse. States requiring public education about elder abuse also had higher report rates of abuse, suggesting that public awareness has a positive impact on increasing reports. Where there were more individual definitions of abuse in the regulations, there were also higher substantiation rates and ratios. These definitions may assist APS workers to better identify various forms of abuse. This was also true for states with separate caseworkers for child abuse and elder abuse investigations. Lower substantiation rates were associated with locations that had a larger proportion of elderly people in their population. The substantiation rate nearly tripled when reports were tracked. When reports are required to be tracked, APS workers and their supervisors are forced into a higher degree of accountability, and worker intervention efforts and successes can be monitored.

Elder abuse is a complex phenomenon, involving a range of abusive and exploitive behaviors and consequences for abuser and victim. It is also complicated by the multiplicity of potential relationships between victims and abusers, ranging from elderly parents and adult children and grandchildren, siblings, aunts and uncles, nephews and nieces, to spouses and partners. Old age as a variable can also complicate the picture, with age correlating with disabling impairments like Alzheimer's disease, which can trigger abusive behavior (Paveza et al., 1992).

Although physical abuse is the most dramatic and highly publicized type of elder abuse, it is also among the least common (Vida, Monks, & Des Rosiers, 2002). Financial exploitation and psychological abuse often co-occur, and a case example is offered that illustrates these forms of elder mistreatment.

Case Study and Evidence-Based Practice Application

Mrs. R is a 78-year-old woman who lives with her 42-year-old son, M. The son has been diagnosed as suffering from paranoid schizophrenia, but refuses treatment.

Mrs. R suffers from diabetes and has one amputated foot. She requires a special diet and depends on M to shop and cook for her. M cashes Mrs. R's Social Security check but spends most of it on marijuana, which he uses habitually. Mrs. R has been hospitalized several times for treatment of bleeding related to her diabetes, but always requests that she return home, stating that M is her preferred caregiver. She expresses fear that M will not be able to maintain himself alone and will come to harm without her in the household.

Intervention

A multidisciplinary team approach is the most effective form of intervention for cases like Mrs. R and M, where there is financial exploitation of an older adult co-occurring with chronic illness on the part of the elderly victim, and mental illness and substance abuse on the part of the abusive family member. A team consisting of a physician, social worker, and psychiatrist can evaluate the physical, social, and financial management needs of Mrs. R, while assessing the mental capacity of M, including the possibility of involuntary hospitalization, treatment, and medication. The social worker on the team would be responsible for developing and implementing a care plan that includes emergency home care, Meals on Wheels, and possibly social day dare for Mrs. R, as well as an assessment for eligibility to receive financial management. M could be assessed for eligibility to receive Supplemental Social Security, Medicaid, and adult day treatment. Whether involuntary services would be needed through APS and a court order for guardianship, or voluntary services could be provided through the area agency on aging service network would depend on the level of cooperation and compliance of both Mrs. R and her son in accepting the service and treatment plan developed by the multidisciplinary team.

Interdisciplinary teams have been identified as the most successful form of interventions for elder abuse in the community (Nahmiash & Reis, 2001). Project CARE studied intervention plans for 83 cases, which included 473 intervention strategies. These were designed and implemented by a specially trained interdisciplinary team based in a health service agency providing in-home services to older adults. According to this study, the most successful strategies were concrete assistance, nursing, and medical care, as well as in-home assistance, followed by empowerment strategies such as support groups for abused older adults, information about rights and resources, and volunteer peer support.

According to Nahmiash and Reis (2001), the least successful strategies were referrals to general community activities and programs. Caregiver abusers benefited most from counseling, education, and training, and abuser interventions were not only accepted, but successful in changing abusive behavior (Nahmiash & Reis, 2001). Brownell et al. (1999) found that elder abuse victims of impaired adult child abusers were more likely to accept services if services were also offered to their abuser. This was particularly the case if the abuser was a substance abuser or mentally ill.

An evaluation of short-term outcomes related to a client-centered case management program for elder abuse victims found that elder abuse was completely eliminated in a third of the cases and ameliorated in another third. Dimensions of the intervention that appeared effective included helping the victim set short- and long-range goals, providing information on legal rights, explaining options to decrease abuse (a harm reduction technique), supporting the victim in deciding whether or not to take action, and involving others in the care plan (Vladescu et al., 1999).

EVIDENCE-BASED POLICY RECOMMENDATIONS

The National Action Agenda 2002 emerged from the National Policy Summit on Elder Abuse held in Washington, DC, in December 2001 (NCEA, 2001). Top priorities included the following recommendations: Support a national elder abuse act, mount a national education and awareness effort, strengthen elder abuse laws, develop and implement a national elder abuse training curriculum, ensure appropriate mental health services are available to elder abuse victims, and increase awareness of elder abuse within the justice system.

In response to the national action agenda and legislative testimony from experts in every field related to gerontology, criminal justice, and elder mistreatment, the Elder Justice Act was first introduced in Congress by Senators Breaux and Hatch in 2002 and reintroduced in 2003 and 2005. Now in its 4th year as pending legislation in the House of Representatives and Senate, the Elder Justice Act (S. 2010) has an impressive array of congressional sponsors. With active public and professional support through the Elder Justice Coalition, it represents one of the strongest examples of evidence-based policy bills related to elder abuse on the federal level in the United States.

The Elder Justice Act is an omnibus bill that reflects several years of testimony by some of the country's leading experts in elder abuse and gerontology. It incorporates a balanced perspective on elder abuse that links justice, aging, and APS approaches with community- and institutional-based prevention and intervention mandates. Although it stops short of mandating reporting of elder abuse, a state-level policy issue, it does provide a definition of elder abuse and neglect that can assist in standardizing the definitions codified in state and local laws. It also recognizes that more research is needed on the incidence, prevalence, and best practice interventions for elder abuse, and that a dedicated source of federal funding would greatly strengthen state and locally funded (and underfunded) APS programs. The current legislative strategy in enacting the Elder Justice Act is to work with lawmakers to review its content and seek to include some components of the bill in the Older Americans Act reauthorization, with other components—most notably the APS provisions—in separate legislation (Robert Blancado, national coordinator, Elder Justice Coalition, personal communication, March 17, 2006).

Financial exploitation of older adults has increased dramatically in the past 20 years (Rabiner, Brown, & O'Keefe, 2004). Although much financial abuse and exploitation is perpetrated by older persons' family members, a significant portion occurs through abuses of powers of attorney, guardianships, unauthorized transfers of property, and fraud, thefts, and scams. Financial abuse of the elderly is addressed in the 2000 reauthorization of the Older Americans Act, and in state law and regulation, but there are still an estimated 5 million older victims of financial abuse and exploitation a year, according to the NCEA (2006). Policies that ensure improved protection of older adults against financial abuse, as well as legislative initiatives to promote prevention strategies and programs, are needed to improve the safety and well-being of older adults.

The 2000 reauthorization of the Violence Against Women Act (VAWA) addressed a gap in the original VAWA legislation by including a section on older women and abuse. The focus was primarily on the need for older women to have access to domestic violence services and both residential and nonresidential care that are age-appropriate. The U.S. Department of Justice, through its research arm, the National Institute of Justice, has provided limited funding for demonstration projects and evaluations to examine how best to serve older women domestic violence victims. The 2006 reauthorization continues the commitment to include abuse of older women as an area of concern. Under Title II: Improving Services for Victims of Domestic Violence, Dating Violence, Sexual Assault, and Stalking (Violence against Women and Department of Justice Reauthorization Act, 2006, Pub. L. No. 109-162, 42 U.S.C. section 13925), based on the National Elder Abuse Incidence Study, elder abuse perpetrators were defined as primarily family members.

The most recent VAWA reauthorization identified barriers for older victims wishing to leave abusive domestic relations as lack of ability to support themselves, ill health necessitating dependency on an abusive member, fear of being removed from their home in the community to a nursing home, and lack of relevant responses from traditional domestic violence programs and law enforcement (Pub. L. No. 109-162, 42 U.S.C. section 13925). Section 205 (Training and Services to End Violence Against Women in Later Life) supports the creation of multidisciplinary collaborative community responses to elder abuse and neglect and exploitation for victims who are at least 50. It also provides for the creation of cross-training for victims service and governmental agencies, courts, law enforcement, and nonprofit nongovernmental organizations serving victims of elder abuse (Pub. L. No. 109-162, Section 205).

Glendenning (1999) reviewed the literature on institutional abuse, wherein agency practices, the general environment, and rules become abusive. The author discusses research primarily in the United States and the United Kingdom, although he mentions research in Sweden and South Africa. He sites early studies in the 1980s that found physical abuse and physical neglect, as well as Medicaid fraud and theft, medication abuse, and undernutrition and malnutrition. Public policies that emphasize institutionalization of the elderly over community-based care may lie at the root of elder abuse in institutions. Other possible causes of abuse and neglect in nursing homes are job stress, time pressures, low pay, and lack of adequate training for aides and nursing assistants, and burnout. The Elder Justice Act addresses elder abuse from a domestic as well as an institutional perspective, and currently includes some provisions for encouraging criminal background checks of nursing home personnel (Robert Blancado, national coordinator, Elder Justice Coalition, personal communication, March 17, 2006).

The 2005 White House Conference on Aging (WHCoA) considered several resolutions on the federal government's need to address elder abuse as a serious public policy issue. A resolution to create a national strategy for promoting elder justice through the prevention and prosecution of elder abuse was ranked number 15 out of 50 resolutions passed by the 1,200 WHCoA delegates (Aziz, 2006). Included in this resolution were recommendations to enact and fully fund comprehensive elder abuse legislation, increase the capacity of state-based APS agencies to more effectively address elder abuse at the state and community levels, and issue a first-class postage stamp to promote elder abuse awareness (Aziz, 2006).

An international framework for policy change related to elder abuse and neglect is outlined in the Political Declaration and Madrid International Plan of Action on Aging (United Nations, 2003) that emerged from the Second World Assembly on Aging held in Madrid in 2002. Under the section "C. Priority Direction III: Ensuring Enabling and Supportive Environments, Issue 3: Neglect, Abuse and Violence" (pp. 43–44), the plan outlined two objectives. The first was to eliminate all forms of neglect of, abuse of, and violence against older persons by sensitizing professionals and the general public on elder abuse; enacting legislation and strengthening legal efforts to eliminate elder abuse; encourage cooperation between government and civil society in addressing elder abuse at the community level; and minimizing risks to older women, especially in emergency situations. Objective 2 called for the creation of support services to address elder abuse by establishing services for victims and rehabilitation arrangements for abusers; encouraging health and social services professionals, and the general public, to report suspected elder abuse; including training on elder abuse for the caring professionals; and establishing information programs to educate older persons about financial abuse, including fraud (United Nations, 2003).

EXAMPLE OF A STATE/LOCAL COALITION-BUILDING PROJECT UTILIZING EMPIRICAL RESEARCH

Project 2015, published in 2000, is a collaborative project between the New York State Office of the Aging (SOFA) and the State Society on Aging (SSA) of New York. It had its genesis in 1998, with the shared concern of SOFA and SSA that the baby boomers would begin entering old age in 2015 in New York State, and there had been no efforts on the part of state or local governments to anticipate the issues that might arise at this future time (Dr. Joanna Mellor, past president, State Society on Aging of New York, personal communication, May 7, 2006).

In spite of budgetary limitations, SOFA and SSA decided to collaborate on a series of papers on 24 key topics related to the aging-out of the baby boomers, including long-term care, transportation, and elder abuse. Experts in academia and agency-based practice were invited to contribute papers on these topics, which were compiled and printed in a briefing book by SOFA. New York's Governor Pataki then asked each of his state commissioners to respond to the articles by drafting a plan for how each gubernatorial agency would be ready to respond to the stated issues by 2015. This resulted in a publication of white papers, which became a road map for state government to use in anticipating the impact of the aging of the New York State population. The Project 2015 publications and a report on the demographics of aging are posted on the SOFA website (http://www .aging.state.ny.us.explore/project2015/index.htm).

This collaboration between academics and state government officials was perceived to lend legitimacy to the policy-making process, first at the executive branch level, and later at the legislative level. In collaboration with SOFA, SSA identifies one topic from Project 2015 as the focus for its legislative town hall meeting at its annual conference. This has resulted in an opportunity for ongoing dialogue among academics, practitioners, government officials, and legislators, providing increased access and opportunity to advocate for policy changes and exchange of ideas and information (Susan B. Somers, assistant commissioner for Adult Protective Services, Office of Children and Family Services, New York State, personal communication, May 5, 2006).

Two years ago the New York State Governor's Office, with over 30 nonprofit agencies and other governmental departments, hosted an elder abuse summit, which used as the framework for beginning dialogue the article on elder abuse from Project 2015 (Caccamise & Mason, 2004). During the 2005 WHCoA, the New York Governor's Office and SOFA and state delegates effectively strategized to vote a resolution on elder abuse number 15 in a list of 73 resolutions, giving it national prominence (Susan B. Somers, assistant commissioner for Adult Protective Services, New York State Office of Children and Families, personal communication, May 7, 2006). Three important U.S. public policies—the Older Americans Act Reauthorization (Title VII), the Elder Justice Act (still a bill), and the 2006 amendment to VAWA—all address elder mistreatment at the national level, and all were the result of local and state coalitions advocating for public policy change at the national level. The Madrid 2002 Plan of Action on Aging represents a similar effort on the international level.

EXAMPLE OF INTERNATIONAL PROMOTION OF PUBLIC POLICY TO ADDRESS SENIOR ABUSE

The Madrid 2002 International Plan of Action on Aging (Elder Abuse and Mistreatment section) establishes objectives and action steps to promote public policies and programs in nations around the world. This plan emerged from the Second World Assembly on Aging in April 2002, 10 years after the First World Assembly on Aging was held. The Madrid 2002 International Plan of Action on Aging (MIPAA; "Priority Direction III: Ensuring Enabling and Supportive Environments, Issue 3: Neglect, Abuse and Violence") includes the following objectives:

Objective One: Elimination of all forms of neglect, abuse and violence of older persons

Objective Two: Creation of support services to address elder abuse (Brownell, 2003; the plan can be found at http://72.14.203.104/search?q=cache:ERHapFZRBAAJ :www.globalaging.org/waa2/documents/international)

Currently the United Nations plans to monitor the implementation of the Madrid Plan in a process named Madrid Plus Five (or 5 years after the promulgation of the plan of action in 2003). This will be a grassroots, bottom-up review, with the assumption of the availability of top-down support. Governments can decide what part(s) of MIPAA to monitor; however, nongovernmental organizations (NGOs) must advocate with governments for what part(s) of MIPAA to include in their monitoring plan. First, NGOs and older adults must advocate for government to participate in the review; second, they must advocate for governments to include the elder abuse objectives as part of their review. The UN secretary-general will support and provide technical assistance through two offices: the Department of Economic and Social Affairs and the Department of Public Information.

The UN General Assembly will oversee the hearings on Madrid Plus Five through the Commission on Social Development, which will oversee the Madrid Plus Five Monitoring Plan and Implementation, based on the following timetable:

- *2006:* Nations that signed onto MIPAA must decide which sections to include in their monitoring plan.
- *February 2007:* The Commission on Social Development will request member nations to report on laws passed, programs established, and so on, since MIPAA (without outcome analyses), and on what aspects of MIPAA they have decided to review.
- *During 2007:* Bottom-up action review appraisal will begin on those aspects of MIPAA selected for monitoring.
- *February 2008:* Governments will present to the Commission on Social Development their responses to what they have found regarding:
  —Impact of policies, programs, and other initiatives.
  —Outcomes for older adults.
  —Direction of future social welfare policies.

There is an important role for elder abuse advocates, NGOs, and academic institutions in determining what constitutes "good" and "bad" laws, how to balance older persons' rights against intrusive "protection," and how to ensure adequate funding to implement the new laws.

To date, draft recommendations on the review methodology have been distributed to the member nations by the Department of Economic and Social Affairs (to be finalized shortly). The Commission on Social Development has approved the modality for the first review and appraisal and endorsed the schedule to start global review in 2007 and report back in 2008; has established the theme for first review at a global level: "Addressing the Challenges and Opportunities of Aging";

and has *recommended* a format for the 2008 review: plenary debates and a series of panel discussions and events.

The World health Organization, the NGO Committee on Aging, and the International Network for the Prevention of Elder Abuse are taking the lead in promoting global awareness of elder abuse through educational programs and the United Nations World Elder Abuse Awareness Day project, to be held on June 16 of every year starting in 2006. The Committee on Aging, which is an umbrella for over 45 NGOs with an aging focus, supports education and awareness about senior abuse. For example, during the past year it sponsored two programs on elder abuse at the United Nations in New York City. Speakers included Jill Hightower and Dr. Henry Hightower, who spoke in March 2006 on issues related to older women victims of family mistreatment, and Dr. Jordan Kosberg, who spoke in April 2006 about issues related to the abuse of older men. The International Network for the Prevention of Elder Abuse has undertaken an environmental scan on elder abuse, which will provide critical information on elder abuse from a global perspective, to complement government reports on MIPAA social policy responses to senior abuse. This is an example of an international policy implementation process that utilizes research as the basis of developing and monitoring implementation of social policies intended to prevent elder abuse and increase the safety and well-being of older adults, not only locally and statewide, but nationally and internationally as well (Brownell, 2002).

FUTURE RESEARCH DIRECTIONS

Both the National Action Agenda that emerged from the National Policy Summit on Elder Abuse and the Madrid International Plan of Action on Aging included recommendations for research. Priorities 8 and 9 of the National Action Agenda note that the lack of information on the scope of elder abuse and the ability of service systems to respond adequately hamper efforts to prevent and respond to elder abuse. By establishing a national elder abuse research and program innovation institute as part of the executive branch of the federal government, it is hoped that a coordinated and comprehensive national response to serve vulnerable older adults will be developed and evaluated. Other topics for research include cultural diversity and patterns of abuse, effective intervention methods, development of uniform definitions and standardized reporting criteria, and best practices for training APS, health, law enforcement, and social service professionals to better serve victims of elder abuse (NCEA, 2001).

The Madrid 2002 International Plan of Action on Aging recommends that further research be undertaken into the "causes, extent, seriousness and consequences of all forms of violence against older women and men and widely disseminate findings" (United Nations, 2003, p. 44). Research, including evaluation research, is identified as critical to improving preventive and protective services for older victims of abuse around the world, as well as providing "essential evidence for effective policies" (p. 49). As noted earlier, in 2007 the United Nations is planning a 5th-year review of the implementation of the recommendations included in the Madrid Plan. Nongovernmental organizations, including the Committee on Aging, recognized with consultative status at the UN, will take a leading role in this review. The motto of the NGO community at the UN is *Think globally. Act locally.* This provides another opportunity and forum to advocate for needed research to support changes in policy and practice in the United States and globally.

In one early study of APS practice, Staudt (1985) discusses how APS laws were originally designed to protect an elderly person's property more than their personal care and well-being. In the 1960 and 1970s, research into protection of older persons focused on demonstration projects and legislation. The primary focus of early APS research, however, was on the rights of older adults to self-determination, in particular framing the service debate in terms of an elderly person's right to receive services in the least restrictive setting possible. The ethical dilemma of elder rights to protection and self-determination is still a relevant research question, especially as mandatory reporting for elder abuse is still a debated policy issue in some states.

Clearly there is a critical need for intervention research (Chalk, 2000). Whether intended to provide preventive or protective services, most elder abuse interventions have not been subjected to rigorous review, and this hampers progress in developing effective prevention and intervention strategies, as well as advocating effectively for policies and funding to address elder abuse and neglect. Outcome research is also needed on clinical interventions, testing the effectiveness of therapeutic modalities through partnerships with practitioners and researchers (Tomita, 2006).

The field of elder abuse has expanded tremendously since the late 1970s and early 1980s, when elder abuse first came to public awareness as a form of domestic violence. There are now movements to both elevate its visibility to the national policy level and to critically evaluate the needs of elder abuse victims and the interventions that have evolved to address those needs. This is consistent with the evidence-based practice model that requires practice to be grounded in empirical evidence so that it is likely to result in outcomes that are predictable, effective, and beneficial to clients (Roberts & Yeager, 2004).

REFERENCES

Abramson, B. I. (2005). Wisconsin's experiences with elder abuse give rise to an interdisciplinary team manual. In J. M. Otto (Ed.), *Abuse and neglect of vulnerable adult populations* (pp. 14-29–14-36). Kingston, NJ: Civic Research, Inc.

Acierno, R., Resnick, H., Kilpatrick, D., & Stark-Riemer, W. (2003). Assessing elder victimization. *Social Psychiatry and Psychiatric Epidemiology, 38,* 644–653.

Alfonso, H. I. (2000). Mortgage fraud prevention program: Volunteer legal services program of the Bar Association of San Francisco. *Journal of Elder Abuse and Neglect, 12*(2), 75–78.

Anetzberger, G. J. (2005). The reality of elder abuse. In G. J. Anetzberger (Ed.), *The clinical management of elder abuse* (pp. 1–25). Binghamton, NY: Haworth Press.

Aziz, S. J. (2000). Los Angeles County Fiduciary Abuse Specialist Team: A model for collaboration. *Journal of Elder Abuse and Neglect, 12*(2), 79–83.

Aziz, S. J. (2006). Elder abuse captures attention of White House conference on Aging. *National Center on Elder Abuse Newsletter, 8*(3), 1–2.

Bergeron, L. R. (2002). Family preservation: An unidentified approach in elder abuse protection. *Families in Society, 83*(5/6), 547–557.

Brownell, P. (2002). Elder abuse intervention strategies: Social service or criminal justice? *Journal of Gerontological Social Work, 40*(1/2), 83–100.

Brownell, P. (2003). Madrid 2002: Global aging and violence against older persons post 9/11. *New Global Development, 19*(1), 15–25.

Brownell, P., & Berman, J. (2004). Homicides of older women in New York City. In A. R. Roberts & K. R. Yeager (Eds.), *Evidence-based practice manual* (pp. 771–778). New York: Oxford University Press.

Brownell, P., Berman, J., & Salamone, A. (2005, November). *Model training curricula on elder abuse for the criminal justice system in New York City.* Poster presented at the Gerontological Society of America annual conference, Orlando, FL.

Brownell, P., Berman, J., Salamone, A., & Welty, A. (2002). Elder abuse and the mentally ill abuser. In G. Landsberg, M. Rock, L. K. W. Berg, & A. Smiley (Eds.), *Serving mentally ill offenders: Challenges and opportunities for mental health professionals* (pp. 193–214). New York: Springer.

Brownell, P., & Heiser, D. (in press). Psycho-educational support groups for older women victims of family mistreatment: A pilot study. *Journal of Gerontological Social Work.*

Caccamise, P., & Mason, A. (2004). Policy paper: New York State Summit targets elder abuse, "The time to act is now." *Journal of Elder Abuse and Neglect, 16*(4), 41–61.

Chalk, R. (2000). Assessing family violence interventions: Linking programs to research-based strategies. In S. K. Ward & D. Finkelhor (Eds.), *Program evaluation and family violence research* (pp. 29–53). Binghamton, NY: Haworth Press.

Choi, N., & Mayer, J. (2000). Elder abuse, neglect and exploitation: Risk factors and prevention strategies. *Journal of Gerontological Social Work, 33*(2), 5–25.

Cook-Daniels, L. (2003). *Two new innovative services announced* (Woodbridges). Retrieved January 29, 2006, from http://www.woodbridges.net/elderabuse/interventions.

Cyphers, G. (1999). Elder abuse and neglect. *Policy and Practice of Public Human Services, 57*(3), 25–30.

Fulmer, T., Firpo, A., Guadagno, L., Easter, T. M., Kahan, F., & Paris, B. (2003). Themes from a grounded theory analysis of elder neglect assessment of experts. *Gerontologist, 43*(5), 745–752.

Fulmer, T., Guadagno, L., Bitondo, C., & Connolly, M. (2004). Progress in elder abuse screening and assessment instruments. *Journal of the American Geriatrics Society, 52*(2), 297–304.

Glendenning, F. (1999). Elder abuse and neglect in residential settings: The need for inclusiveness in elder abuse research. *Journal of Elder Abuse and Neglect, 10*(1/2), 1–11.

Goodrich, C. (1997). Results of a national survey of state protective services programs: Assessing risk and defining victim outcomes. *Journal of Elder Abuse and Neglect, 9*(1), 69–86.

Grunig, J. E., & Disbrow, J. (1977). Developing a probabilistic model for communications decision making. *Communication Research, 4,* 145–168.

Heller, J. (2005). Prevalence: An examination of elder abuse reports and data collection systems across the United States. In J. M. Otto (Ed.), *Abuse and neglect of vulnerable adult populations* (pp. 1-1–1-12). Kingston, NJ: Civic Research Institute.

Hudson, M., & Carlson, J. (1998). Elder abuse: Expert and public perspectives on its meaning. *Journal of Elder Abuse and Neglect, 9*(4), 77–97.

Jogerst, G., Daly, J., Brinig, M., Dawson, J., Schmuch, G., & Ingram, J. (2003). Domestic elder abuse and the law. *American Journal of Public Health, 93*(12), 2131–2136.

Lachs, M. S., & Pillemer, K. (2004). Elder abuse. *Lancet, 364,* 1263–1272.

Malks, B., Schmidt, C., & Austin, M. (2002). Elder abuse prevention: A case study of the Santa Clara County Financial Abuse Specialist Team (FAST) program. *Journal of Gerontological Social Work, 39*(3), 23–40.

Merck Manual of Geriatrics. (2000). *Chapter 15: Social issues—Elder abuse.* Retrieved January 29, 2006, from http:www.merck.com/mrkshared/mmg/sec1/ch15/ch15g.jsp.

Nahmiash, D., & Reis, M. (2001). Most successful intervention strategies for abused older adults. *Journal of Elder Abuse and Neglect, 2*(3/4), 53–70.

National Center on Elder Abuse. (2001). *National Action Agenda, 2002.* Washington, DC: National Policy Summit and Elder Abuse.

National Center on Elder Abuse. (2006). *Promising practices in elder abuse detail.* Retrieved January 29, 2006, from http://elderabusecenter.org/default.cfm?p=promisingpracticesdetail.cfm&vppid=7007.

National Research Council. (2003). *Elder mistreatment: Abuse, neglect, and exploitation in an aging America* (R. J. Bonnie & R. B. Wallace, Eds., Committee on National Statistics and Committee on Law and Justice, Division of Behavioral and Social Sciences and Education). Washington, DC: National Academies Press.

Nerenberg, L. (2002). *A feminist perspective on gender and elder abuse: A review of the literature.* Retrieved February 4, 2006, from http://www.elderabusecenter.org/pdf/publication/FinalGenderIssuesInElderAbuse030924.pdf.

Older Americans Act Amendments: Title VII, 42 U.S.C. § 3001, 106th Congress, 2nd Session (2000).

Paveza, G., Cohen, D., Eisdorfer, C., Freels, S., Semla, T., Ashford, J. W., et al. (1992). Severe family violence and Alzheimer's disease: Prevalence and risk factors. *Gerontologist, 32*(4), 493–497.

Pavlik, V., Hyman, D., Festa, N., & Dyer, C. (2001). Quantifying the problem of abuse and neglect in adults: Analysis of a statewide database. *Journal of the American Geriatrics Society, 49*(1), 45–48.

Penhale, B., & Kingston, P. (1997). Elder abuse, mental health and later life: Steps toward an understanding. *Aging and Mental Health, 1*(4), 296–304.

Pillemer, K., & Finkelhor, D. (1988). The prevalence of elder abuse: A random sample survey. *Gerontologist, 28*(1), 51–57.

Podnieks, E. (1999). Support groups: A chance at human connections for abused older adults. In J. Prichard (Ed.), *Elder abuse work: Best practice in Britain and Canada* (pp. 457–483). London: Jessica Kingsley.

Powell, J. P. L. (2001). Theorizing social gerontology: The case of social philosophies of age. *Internet Journal of Internal Medicine, 2*(1). Retrieved February 4, 2006, from http://www.ispub.com/ostia/index.php?xmlFilePath=journals/ijim/vol2n/age.xml.

Quinn, M., & Tomita, S. (1997). *Elder abuse and neglect: Causes, diagnosis, and intervention strategies.* New York: Springer.

Rabiner, D. J., Brown, D., & O'Keefe, J. O. (2004). Financial exploitation of older persons: Policy issues and recommendations for addressing them. *Journal of Elder Abuse and Neglect, 16*(1), 65–84.

Reis, M., & Nahmiash, D. (1998). Validation of the Indicators of Abuse (IOA) screen. *Gerontologist, 38*(4), 471–480.

Roberts, A. R., & Yeager, K. R. (2004). Systematic reviews of evidence-based studies and practice-based research: How to search for, develop, and use them. In A. R. Roberts & K. Yeager (Eds.), *Evidence-based practice manual: Research and outcome measures in health and human services* (pp. 3–14). New York: Oxford University Press.

Schiamberg, L. B., & Gans, D. (1999). An ecological framework for contextual risk factors in elder abuse by adult children. *Journal of Elder Abuse and Neglect, 11*(1), 79–103.

Schmuland, F. (1995). *Shelter support groups for abused older women: A facilitator's manual.* Selkirk, Manitoba, Canada: Nova House Women's Shelter.

Seaver, C. (1996). Muted lives: Older battered women. *Journal of Elder Abuse and Neglect, 8*(2), 3–21.

Soeda, A., & Araki, C. (1999). Elder abuse by daughters in law in Japan. *Journal of Elder Abuse and Neglect, 11*(1), 47–58.

Staudt, M. (1985, May/June). The social worker as an advocate in adult protective services. *Social Work,* 204–208.

Steinmetz, S. (1990). *Duty bound.* Thousand Oaks, CA: Sage.

Tatara, T., Kuzmeskus, L., Duckhorn, E., & Bivens, L. (1998). *The National Elder Abuse Incidence Study: Final report.* Washington, DC: National Center on Elder Abuse, American Public Human Services Association.

Thomas, C. (2000). The first national study of elder abuse and neglect: Contrast with results from other studies. *Journal of Elder Abuse and Neglect, 12*(1), 1–14.

Tomita, S. (2006). Mistreated and neglected elders. In B. Berkman (Ed.), *Handbook of social work in health and aging* (pp. 219–230). New York: Oxford University Press.

United Nations. (2003). *Political declaration and Madrid International Plan of Action on Aging* (DPI/2271—February 2003-20M). New York: United Nations Department of Public Information.

U.S. Department of Health and Human Services. (2006). *Out of the shadows: Uncovering substance abuse and elder abuse.* Retrieved January 20, 2006, from http://pathwayscourses.samhsa.gov/elab/elab_4_pg2.htm.

Vida, S., Monks, R. C., & Des Rosiers, P. (2002). Prevalence and correlates of elder abuse in a geriatric psychiatry service. *Canadian Journal of Psychiatry, 47*(5), 449–457.

Vinton, L. (1999). Working with abused older women from a feminist perspective. *Journal of Women and Aging, 11*(2/3), 85–100.

Violence against Women and Department of Justice Reauthorization Act, Pub. L. No. 109-162 (2006).

Vladescu, D., Eveleigh, K., Ploeg, J., & Patterson, C. (1999). An evaluation of a client-centered case management program for elder abuse. *Journal of Elder Abuse and Neglect, 11*(4), 5–22.

Westley, C. (2002). Elder mistreatment: Self-learning module. *MEDSURG Nursing, 14*(2), 133–137.

Wolf, R. (1996). Elder abuse and family violence: Testimony presented before the U.S. Senate Special Committee on Aging. *Journal of Elder Abuse and Neglect, 8*(1), 81.

Wolf, R. S. (1998). *Support groups for older victims of domestic violence: Sponsors and programs* (Grant No. 90-AM-0660). Washington, DC: National Committee for the Prevention of Elder Abuse.

Wolf, R. S. (2000). The nature and scope of elder abuse. *Generations, 24*(11), 6–12.

CHAPTER 19

Health Decisions and Directives about the End of Life

JAY WOLFSON and REBECCA MORGAN

PEACE OF MIND is something most people hope to achieve during the end of their life. Most people, if asked, would probably say that they would prefer to die peacefully, without pain, and with minimal economic and emotional trauma for their loved ones. Despite this obvious, nearly universal intent, the certainty of death is often masked in our society by a Peter Pan-ish belief that we will live forever anchored in a fundamental loathing of the prospect of death. As a consequence, planning for end-of-life-related events is often avoided or engaged without sufficient forethought and detail. It is natural for people to avoid planning for things they don't want to deal with. Yet the consequences can be disappointing if not difficult or even tragic for family members and friends left behind.

A panoply of economic and political factors has raised end-of-life planning to a level of personal, family, and social imperative. These include the costs associated with the long-term provision of skilled or life-sustaining health care services and the effects of a failure to clearly designate one's intentions regarding how end-of-life decisions should be made, or who should make them in the event of incompetence. The worst-case scenario is the years of legal struggle in the Theresa Schiavo case between the 1990s and 2004, during which her parents fought against their son-in-law over the right to determine the health care fate of a severely brain damaged woman.

The "age wave"—the largest single cohort in history—is making its way toward retirement, through early bouts with the "standard" chronic illnesses of diabetes, hypertension, cardiovascular disease, and certain cancers. This population is facing the challenge of living longer than their parents and grandparents and experiencing a broader array of illnesses and diseases, including neurological disintegration, bone structure weakening, organ system failure and dysfunction, and even HIV/AIDS, as sexual activity stimulated by Viagra becomes a possibility rarely before enjoyed.

In this chapter, we discuss the modern history of end-of-life health-related planning and decisions, often categorized as the "right to die." We review specific options that people and their families should consider when they plan end-of-life decisions. The purpose of planning end-of-life health-related decisions is to ensure that the express intentions of individuals are honored regarding the kind of health care services they wish to receive, how they die, when they die, where they die, and who has authority to make decisions about them. Included in this discussion are options regarding postdeath matters, such as burial versus cremation, autopsies, and donation of bodies or body parts.

HISTORY

DOCTRINE OF INFORMED CONSENT

The law is built on the concept of precedent;[1] that is, the law wants to decide like cases alike, and thus will look back at prior decisions to determine how to resolve current issues. But in the category of cases popularly named the "right to die," which did not come into existence until the late 1970s, how could the law look back at prior decisions? The courts looked at the doctrine of informed consent.[2]

As early as 1891 the U.S. Supreme Court in the case of *Union Pacific Railway v. Botsford*[3] discussed the issue of bodily integrity. Although concerned with what today would be termed a "personal injury" suit, the case is instructive in the seriousness with which bodily integrity is treated. The only issue before the Court was the power of the court to order a plaintiff to submit to a surgical examination for the purpose of determining the extent of the injuries for which the plaintiff had sued.[4] The Court held that "no right is held more sacred, or is more carefully guarded by the common law, than the right of every individual to the possession and control of his own person, free from all restraint or interference of others, unless by clear and unquestionable authority of law."[5] That is, quoting Judge Cooley, "The right to one's person may be said to be a right of complete immunity; to be

---

[1] Precedent is defined as "the making of law by a court in recognizing and applying new rules while administering justice . . . a decided case that furnishes a basis for determining later cases involving similar facts or issues. . . . In law a precedent is an adjudged case or decision of a court of justice, considered as furnishing a rule or authority for the determination of an identical or similar case afterwards arising, or of a similar question of law." *Black's Law Dictionary* (2004). See also stare decisis: "the doctrine of precedent, under which it is necessary for a court to follow earlier judicial decisions when the same points arise again in litigation. . . . The rule of adherence to judicial precedents finds its expression in the doctrine of stare decisis. This doctrine is simply that, when a point or principle of law has been once officially decided or settled by the ruling of a competent court in a case in which it is directly and necessarily involved, it will no longer be considered as open to examination or to a new ruling by the same tribunal, or by those which are bound to follow its adjudications, unless it be for urgent reasons and in exceptional cases." *Id.*

[2] Doctrine of informed consent from *Black's Law Dictionary* (2004): "a person's agreement to allow something to happen, made with full knowledge of the risks involved and the alternatives . . . a patient's knowing choice about a medical treatment or procedure, made after a physician or other health care provider discloses whatever information a reasonably prudent provider in the medical community would give to a patient regarding the risks involved in the proposed treatment or procedure."

[3] 141 U.S. 250 (May 25, 1891).

[4] Botsford at 251.

[5] *Id.*

let alone."[6] Some years later, a New York Appellate Court followed up on the idea of bodily integrity in *Schloendorff v. the Society of New York Hospital*,[7] where the plaintiff sued the hospital and others for allegedly performing surgery without her consent and for subsequently ensuing complications. The doctrine of informed consent can be seen clearly in the court's opinion; the court, citing to two earlier decisions, noted,

> Every human being of adult years and sound mind has a right to determine what shall be done with his own body; and a surgeon who performs an operation without his patient's consent, commits an assault. . . . This is true except in case of emergency where the patient is unconscious and where it is necessary to operate before consent can be obtained.[8]

This idea of bodily integrity, then, stands for the proposition of informed consent: that one has control over one's body and a touching without one's consent is an assault.

An exception to the doctrine of informed consent falls in the category of an emergency, referenced in the *Schloendorff* case. In the emergency exception, if the elements of the exception are met, then medical professionals can provide health care to the patient without his or her consent. Roughly described: The patient is in an emergency medical condition and as a result is unable to provide consent; time is of the essence, and no one (family or someone with authority to provide consent) is available or willing to provide consent.[9]

How does one jump from informed consent to medical procedures to applying the doctrine of informed consent to end-of-life cases? The U.S. Supreme Court answered that question in the case of *Cruzan v. Director, Missouri Department of Health*.[10] Reviewing *Botsford* and *Schloendorff*, the Court noted that bodily integrity is an integral component of informed consent.[11] Implied in the right to consent, the Court reasoned, "is the right not to consent, that is, [the right] to refuse treatment."[12] In many of the decisions involving the right to die, the courts based the right on the doctrine of informed consent or informed consent and the constitutional right of privacy.[13] Informed consent, then, is generally viewed as

---

[6] *Id.*, quoting Cooley, Torts, 29.

[7] 211 N.Y. 125 (N.Y. Ct. App. 1914).

[8] *Id.* at 129–130, citing to *Pratt v. Davis,* 224 Ill. 300 (year) and *Mohr v. Williams,* 95 Minn. 261 (1905).

[9] See, for example, *Shine v. Vega,* 709 N.E.2d 58 (Mass. 1999), n. 15 citing to Prosser & Keaton on Torts: "(a) the patient must be unconscious or without capacity to make a decision, while no one legally authorized to act as agent for the patient is available; (b) time must be of the essence, in the sense that it must reasonably appear that delay until such time as an effective consent could be obtained would subject the patient to a risk of a serious bodily injury or death which prompt action would avoid; and (c) under the circumstances, a reasonable person would consent, and the probabilities are that the patient would consent." W.L. Prosser & W.P. Keeton, Torts §18, at 117 (5th ed., 1984).

[10] 497 U.S. 261 (1990).

[11] *Id.* at 269.

[12] *Id.*

[13] *Id.* at 271.

including the right for a competent patient to refuse medical treatment,[14] which necessarily includes life-prolonging procedures.

THE RIGHT TO DIE

The issue of removal of life-prolonging procedures from a patient is relatively new, having come to the fore in 1976 in the case, *In re Quinlan*.[15] The facts of the case bear review: Karen Ann Quinlan, at age 21, for reasons unknown, stopped breathing for two 15-minute periods. Subsequently diagnosed as being in a persistent vegetative state, she was on a respirator and had a feeding tube.[16] Her father sought to have the respirator removed, positing a number of claims that would justify the removal of the respirator.[17] The Court's focus was on the constitutional right of privacy as a basis for the removal of the respirator.[18] The Court identified the applicable state interests as preservation of life and protection of the ethical integrity of the medical profession.[19] Because the Court was examining a constitutional right of privacy as the basis for the right to remove life-prolonging procedures, a certain analysis was required. Noting the amount of bodily invasion and the prognosis for Ms. Quinlan, the Court determined, "We think that the State's interest Contra weakens and the individual's right to privacy grows as the degree of bodily invasion increases and the prognosis dims. Ultimately there comes a point at which the individual's rights overcome the State interest."[20] Because Ms. Quinlan was incompetent at the time of the decision, the Court had to address the issue of whether the right was lost by virtue of her incompetency.[21] The Court determined that the right was not lost by virtue of incompetency; instead, it would simply be exercised for the patient by another.[22] The final question for the Court was whether a decision of this type could be made outside of the court system.[23] The Court identified a framework for resolution that involved the family, health care providers, and a consultative body:

> Upon the concurrence of the guardian and family of Karen, should the responsible attending physicians conclude that there is no reasonable possibility of Karen's ever emerging from her present comatose condition to a cognitive, sapient state and that the life-support apparatus now being administered to Karen should be discontinued, they shall consult with the hospital Ethics Committee or like body of the institution in which Karen is then hospitalized. If that consultative body agrees that

---

[14] *Id.* at 277.

[15] 70 N.J. 10 (1976).

[16] *Id.* at 23–25.

[17] The claims included free exercise of religion, cruel and unusual punishment, and the right of privacy. *Id.* at 35–40.

[18] *Id.* at 38–42.

[19] The court actually describes these as "preservation and sanctity of human life and defense of the right of the physician to administer medical treatment according to his best judgment." *Id.* at 40. Over time, the state interests have been described as preservation of life and protection of ethical integrity of the medical profession.

[20] *Id.* at 41.

[21] *Id.* at 41–42.

[22] In this case, it would be her family and guardian. *Id.* at 41.

[23] *Id.* at 48–52, 54–55.

there is no reasonable possibility of Karen's ever emerging from her present coma-tose condition to a cognitive, sapient state, the present life-support system may be withdrawn and said action shall be without any civil or criminal liability therefor on the part of any participant, whether guardian, physician, hospital or others.[24]

The following year, the Massachusetts Supreme Court further clarified the process for handling end-of-life cases in *In re Saikewicz*.[25] Mr. Saikewicz was pro-foundly mentally retarded, with an "IQ of ten and a mental age of approximately 2 years and 8 months,"[26] meaning that in the eyes of the law, he was never compe-tent to make a legally binding decision. Mr. Saikewicz was stricken with leukemia, and the court was faced with the question of whether he should un-dergo chemotherapy.[27] On appeal the court further refined the *Quinlan* analysis by expanding the applicable state interests to four: preservation of life, preven-tion of suicide, protection of innocent third parties, and protection of the ethical integrity of the medical profession.[28] The court echoed the *Quinlan* court, that the interest is not lost by virtue of the patient's incompetency, and determined that the substituted judgment doctrine would be used to make the decision that the patient would make.[29] Under the substituted judgment doctrine, the decision maker would make the decision the patient would make, if the patient could for a moment come back to consciousness, be apprised of the diagnosis, prognosis, and treatment options, and then make the decision. In other words, the decision maker stands in the patient's shoes and makes the decision the patient would make if capable of doing so.

In 1990, some months after the U.S. Supreme Court issued its opinion in *Cruzan*, the Florida Supreme Court issued its opinion in *In re Browning*.[30] Unlike most cases involving removal of life support, Estelle Browning was elderly and had actually made not one, but two living wills.[31] After the patient suffered a massive stroke, a gastrostomy tube and, subsequently, a nasogastric tube were in-serted.[32] Her guardian sought removal of the nasogastric tube.[33] The trial court, after examining the wording of her living will and the statute applicable at the

---

[24] *Id.* at 54.

[25] 370 N.E.2d 417 (Mass. 1977).

[26] 370 N.E.2d 417, 420 (Mass. 1977).

[27] *Id.* at 417–423.

[28] *Saikewicz* at 424–428. These state interests are fact-specific. They are not an exclusive or exhaus-tive list, and in fact there may be other state interests that apply, depending on the facts of the case in question. For example, in the case of *Washington v. Glucksberg*, 521 U.S. 702 (1997), the court iden-tified more state interests applicable to the question of legalizing physician-assisted suicide. As noted by the Florida Supreme Court in *Public Health Trust v. Wons*, "The state interests . . . are by no means a bright-line test, capable of resolving every dispute regarding the refusal of medical treat-ment. Rather, they are intended merely as factors to be considered while reaching the difficult de-cision of when a compelling state interest may override the basic constitutional right[ ] of privacy" (541 So.2d 96, 97, n. 13 (Fla. 1989)).

[29] *Saikewicz* at 750–753.

[30] 568 So.2d 4 (Fla. 1990).

[31] *Id.* at 8.

[32] *Id.*

[33] *Id.* at 8–9.

time, determined that the feeding tube could not be removed.[34] The statutory requirement (death is imminent) had not been met, because death would occur between 4 and 9 days after removal of the tube, and that was not considered imminent.[35] On appeal, although the Florida Supreme Court agreed that the Florida statute was not applicable to the case, the court determined that the state constitutional right of privacy (Article I, section 23) was the source of the right to refuse life-prolonging procedures.[36] The Florida Supreme Court began its analysis by referring back to the concept of autonomy, "begin[ning] with the premise that everyone has a fundamental right to the sole control of his or her person," and noting that the main element to self-determination

> is the right to make choices pertaining to one's health, including the right to refuse unwanted medical treatment. "We can conceive of few more personal or private decisions concerning one's body that one can make in the course of a lifetime . . . [than] the decision of the terminally ill in their choice of whether to discontinue necessary medical treatment."[37]

Unlike previous court opinions, the *Browning* court chose to not make any distinctions between the types of treatment or the patient's condition, instead finding that the right covers all medical choices.[38] Because Florida is a "substituted judgment state," the court addressed the application of substituted judgment, noting that although the doctrine is not without flaws,

> unfortunately, human limitations preclude absolute knowledge of the wishes of someone in [such] . . . condition. However, we cannot avoid making a decision in these circumstances, for even the failure to act constitutes a choice. That choice must be the patient's choice whenever possible. The right of privacy requires that we must safeguard an individual's right to chart his or her own medical course in the event of later incapacity.[39]

After discussing the "four state interests," the court then created a framework for decision making in end-of-life cases and set out what types of challenges would be appropriate.[40] The Florida Supreme Court opinion is significant, not so much for the decision-making process set out in the opinion, but because

---

[34] *Id.* at 9.

[35] *Id.*

[36] *Id.* at 9–10.

[37] *Browning* at 10, quoting *In re T.W.*, 551 So.2d at 1192; and referencing *Public Health Trust v. Wons*, 541 So.2d 96 (Fla. 1989).

[38] *Browning* at 11–12. "We conclude that a competent person has the constitutional right to choose or refuse medical treatment, and that right extends to all relevant decisions concerning one's health. . . . Courts overwhelmingly have held that a person may refuse or remove artificial life-support, whether supplying oxygen by a mechanical respirator . . . or supplying food and water through a feeding tube. . . . We agree and find no significant legal distinction between these artificial means of life-support" (citations omitted), and n.6: "We see no reason to qualify that right on the basis of the denomination of a medical procedure as major or minor, ordinary or extraordinary, life-prolonging, life-maintaining, life-sustaining, or otherwise" (citations omitted).

[39] *Id.* at 13.

[40] *Id.* at 15–17.

the court found the state constitutional right of privacy as a basis of the right to make health care decisions, including the right to remove life-prolonging procedures.[41]

BASIS OF RIGHT

As discussed earlier, the basis of the right to remove life-prolonging procedures has been found by many courts to be that of informed consent. However, as also noted, there are other bases of the right, including state statutes, state constitutions, and federal constitutions.

It is misleading, however, to categorize the state statutes as providing a basis for the right to remove life-prolonging procedures. All 50 states and the District of Columbia have statutes that allow adults to make some kind of advance directive (see later discussion). The focus of these statutes is narrow and can be summarized as follows: the creation of the directive, triggers for when a directive would become effective, and limitations of liability (professional, civil, and criminal) for those honoring the directives in good faith. What are generally missing from these statutes, when viewed from the patient's perspective, are enforcement mechanisms to have the directives honored.[42]

A few states besides Florida have state constitutional rights of privacy that are the source of the right to remove life-prolonging procedures. These provisions are important from the patient's perspective, because they provide a greater protection for the patient to have his or her wishes honored.

As noted initially in *Quinlan*, the federal Constitution provides the basis for the right.[43] Although the early decisions by state courts assumed that the federal constitutional right was based in privacy under the 14th Amendment, as the *Cruzan* Court determined, it is based in liberty.[44] Most frequently, however, the right is based on the doctrine of informed consent. If the doctrine of informed consent requires consent (absent an emergency) to treatment, then it stands to reason that implied in the right to consent is the right to not consent, that is, to be silent, and the right to refuse. Thus a patient can take positive action (consent to treatment), remain neutral (neither consent nor refuse—just not decide), or take negative action (refuse treatment or direct the withholding or withdrawing of life-prolonging procedures).

How the Right Is Exercised

As important as the basis of the right is, if not more so, is how the right is exercised. To understand the actual application of the right to a specific patient, one must first determine the condition or category of the patient vis-à-vis making a

---

[41] *Id.* at 9–12.

[42] The closest to an enforcement mechanism might be a section that requires a health care provider to transfer the patient to a provider who will honor the patient's wishes if the health care provider (usually for conscientious objection reasons) refused to honor the patient's directive.

[43] 70 NJ 10, 38–42.

[44] 497 U.S. 261 (1990).

health care decision. Generally speaking, patients can be divided into four categories (at the time of the decision to refuse life-prolonging procedures): the competent patient; the once-competent, currently incompetent patient; the never-competent patient; and the minimally conscious patient.

The competent patient is conscious and capable of giving informed consent. Therefore, for these patients, there is no need for a surrogate decision maker and no need for court intervention. Absent some concern about the patient's ability to give informed consent or the legality of the patient's direction, or, perhaps, the health care provider's concern about liability because of an unconventional wish of the patient, the patient's decision controls. If the patient chooses to exercise her "right to die" by having life-prolonging procedures withheld or withdrawn, then the patient's choice should be honored.

The most common category of patient is the patient who was once-competent, but at the time to make the health care decision is no longer competent. Most of the patients in the right to die decisions fall in this category, including Karen Ann Quinlan, Nancy Cruzan, and Estelle Browning. For this patient, there must be some surrogate decision maker and the application of the appropriate surrogate decision-making standard (most states apply the substituted judgment doctrine). The problem so often with these patients is that so few have made their wishes known or designated a surrogate. Most commonly, the patient may have made some statements in the past, but not in conjunction with his or her specific health condition. Therefore, the patient's wishes must be discerned as best as possible, and it may be necessary for a court to determine whether there is sufficient evidence of the patient's wishes before life-prolonging procedures can be withdrawn.

The never-competent patient is the patient who, although legally an adult based on age, in the eyes of the law has never had the ability to make legally binding decisions or to give informed consent. These patients suffer from severe mental retardation (note that some people can suffer from developmental disabilities or mild mental retardation and still be able to make legally binding decisions and give informed consent) and generally have the IQ of a very small child. For these patients, it was never possible for them to make advance directives or to state their wishes regarding life-prolonging procedures. For these patients, it is necessary to have court involvement to some degree, whether to appoint a guardian for the patient with the authority to make health care decisions, including end-of-life decisions, or to order the removal of life-prolonging procedures. For these patients, the court must look at factors such as health condition, treatment, ability to cooperate with the treatment, and side effects. An example of the court's analysis of factors to consider in such cases is contained in the *Saikewicz* decision.[45]

The whole area of jurisprudence in the right to die is driven by the advances in medical technology. So too is the fourth category of patient, the patient who is minimally conscious. These patients have some awareness and interaction with their environment and may be able to engage in rudimentary communication, such as answering yes or no questions with repeated prompting using assistive communication devices, eye blinks, and so on (Giacino et al., 2002). The challenge in these cases is the reliability of the communication. There is no real way to

---

[45] *In re Saikewicz*, 370 N.E. 2d 417, 430–432.

know whether the patient understands the question and whether the answer is truly a reflection of the patient's conscious decision. One of the more graphic examples of the issues faced in cases of patients who are minimally conscious is the case of Robert Wendland,[46] who was not comatose or terminally ill, nor was he in a persistent vegetative state.[47]

Think about how the category of patient affects the patient's right to refuse life-prolonging procedures. One tool that patients can use, but often don't, is the advance directive.

ADVANCE DIRECTIVES

Decisions about various health care issues at the end of life should be addressed in advance to avoid ambiguity or legal challenges. We review next some of the most common decision categories, generally referred to as "advance directives."

Advance directives are expressions by individuals, made while they are legally competent, about how they want certain health and medical procedures to be done for or about them in the event of disability or incompetence. Disability and incompetence can come in two forms: physical and mental. For example, following an accident, injury, or illness, a person may not be able to independently provide for many of his own daily living needs, such as preparing meals, driving, bathing, or caring for his own health care needs. Or patients may lose the capacity to speak and easily convey their wishes. In the event somebody becomes physically disabled or incapacitated, on a temporary or permanent basis, what guidelines should be used to provide care and services for him? What scope of care and services would that individual want?

The matter is more challenging when there is a mental disability or incapacity. Persons born with these incapacities have provisions made for them in the law, wherein guardians are appointed to make decisions on their behalf.[48] But what happens if, as a consequence of an illness or injury, a person loses substantial mental capacities and is no longer able to make decisions or convey information about his intentions?

Once a person has become incompetent, he is no longer legally capable of making certain decisions, and his intentions may not be carried out unless he has stated them in advance, according to the guidelines of specific state laws. As we noted earlier, living wills and health care surrogates took root during the 1970s.

Generally, these advance statements are written documents, which may have to be witnessed and notarized, and in some states, a particular form may have to be used or followed if the document is to conform to the law. But this is not universal. Some states accept as evidence verbal expressions of intention—but proving these up can be difficult and certainly costly if there is a challenge.

For example, assume that a wife claims that she had been told by her husband that he did not want any form of life-prolonging care in the form of a respirator, nutrition/hydration tube, heroic measures to resuscitate, or even antibiotic

---

[46] *Conservatorship of Wendland*, 26 Cal. 4th 519, 529–530 (2001).
[47] *Id.* at 524–526.
[48] See, for example, Florida Statutes, 744.3115.

therapy. But their child disagrees with his mother's statement of intent and believes instead that his father should be allowed to receive heroic, life-sustaining interventions at all costs. Families face disagreements every day around these issues. Most of these are worked out through the auspices of a social worker, hospice counselor, or therapist. But guilt, bad family relations, honest differences of opinion, and other factors can and do get in the way of a seamless end-of-life process. The consequences can be devastating, not only for family members who may literally feud, but for the incapacitated person who may be subject to prolonged periods during which his or her wishes are not being fulfilled. And we are not referring here to the physician-assisted suicide cases involving Dr. Kevorkian but to cases like Elizabeth Bouvia[49] or *Satz v. Perlmutter*,[50] where competent patients had to get court orders to have their wishes honored; and cases like *Quinlan* and *Cruzan*, the once-competent, currently incompetent patients, where the decision to remove life-prolonging procedures was contested; and more recently, the cases of *Wendland* and *Schiavo*, where the dispute was among the family members. (Mr. Wendland was clearly minimally conscious. There was a dispute between the parties about Mrs. Schiavo's condition. Her husband/guardian took the position that she was once-competent, currently incompetent, but her parents argued that she was minimally conscious, or more accurately, severely disabled.)[51]

By executing an advance directive, ambiguity can be reduced and conflicts between family members mitigated, although having an advance directive doesn't guarantee that there will be no dispute. Furthermore, physicians and hospitals greatly prefer to have advance directives in place because it reduces for them the challenges of having to negotiate with patients or family members about what the expectations and intentions are. Because the law requires that hospitals offer patients information about advance directives at the time of admission, patients cannot claim a lack of knowledge.[52]

Advance directives also may specify a person's wishes about participating in experimental research regimens for his or her disease, or they may provide for the donation of all or part of the person's body for use by others, for scientific research or for public display. For example, since 2000, a new technique called plastization has made it possible for people to have their body preserved using a polymer injection process and to be displayed for public or research uses.

Any advance directive can be easily modified or destroyed if a person changes her mind. In fact, many attorneys recommend revisiting advance directive documents and preferences every couple of years, just as one might revisit one's will or trust documents. It is also recommended that these documents be shared openly with family members, physicians, and one's attorney so that everybody knows where they are and what they say.

Advance directive are generally classified into the following categories of action or documents:

- Health care surrogates or durable powers of attorney for health care
- Living wills

---

[49] *Bouvia v. Superior Court*, 195 Cal. App. 3d 1075 (1987).

[50] *Satz v. Perlmutter*, 379 So.2d 359 (Fla. 1980).

[51] *Wendland*, op. cit.; *Guardianship of Schiavo*, 916 So.2d 814 (Fla. 2d D.C.A. 2005).

[52] 42 U.S.C. SS 1395cc, 395mm, 1396a.

- "Do not resuscitate" (DNR) orders
- Organ and tissue donations

The advance directive process can include express reference to how a person wishes to have her body treated once she dies. This relates to intentions regarding burial, cremation, and donation.

Health Care Surrogate or Durable Power of Attorney for Health Care   Although living wills may be the most familiar term associated with advance directives, they are not necessarily the most important or even the most useful. Rather, the designation of another person who is legally authorized to make medical and health care decisions can be far more valuable. These documents are called health care surrogates or durable powers of attorney for health care.

Each state has provisions that allow individuals to expressly name another person to make decisions about their health care. The scope of the designation can be very limited or very broad. It can refer to limited periods of incapacity, for example, during surgery or anesthesia, when a person is not able to make decisions for herself; or it can refer to periods following an accident or serious illness that might occur in the future, during which a person is similarly incapacitated. It can be a broad-based granting of authority in the event of general incapacity, either physical or mental (i.e., dementia). It can refer to specific types of medical decisions (such as surgery, administration of certain medications, experimental procedures), or it can reference authority to make decisions to withhold heroic measures or technological means of maintaining life.

It is prudent for a person to make a primary and a secondary designation for surrogacy. The primary designee will have the responsibility for making the specified decisions, but in the event that the primary is unable or unwilling to serve, the secondary surrogate assumes the responsibility. Selecting the persons to serve in these capacities is an important and serious decision. Some people feel that they are obliged to name their eldest child or their spouse, even though they will confide that they are not convinced that person would always make decisions in their best interests.

Some people also wish to select more than one primary surrogate, forming a team of decision makers. This has certain advantages when there may be a need for caring loved ones to discuss the realistic options and come to a consensus for the benefit of all. Multiple surrogates can also be valuable if more than one person is named and *either* individual is empowered to make decisions. This has particular value when surrogates do not live near the patient, or when one is not easily accessible during a time when a decision must be made.

But naming multiple surrogates can be an invitation to confusion and complexity, especially if it is done for the purpose of avoiding bad feelings among family members.

It is recommended that multiple, original, signed surrogacy documents be created and that copies be provided to the patient's primary care physician, attorney, and those who will be named as surrogates. Often, documents are executed and then placed in a safe deposit box or in an obscure drawer where nobody even knows they exist. Once a person is incapacitated according to the terms of the surrogacy and the state law, the document should be shared with physicians, hospital personnel, and others so that there are no mistakes about the intentions of the person. Many hospitals now encourage patients to formally file their surrogacy documents upon admission, even for simple procedures.

The surrogacy is considered by many to be the most important of the advance directives because it formally, legally, and expressly places a person's health decisions under the responsibility of a specific person. It helps up front to eliminate ambiguity and questions about who should make what kinds of decisions in the event of an incapacitating event. Figure 19.1 is an example of a surrogacy document.

Living Wills   Living Wills are probably the best-known form of advance directive, but they are not always the most useful or effective. Living wills are general statements about *how* an individual wants to be treated in the event that a life-threatening or terminal condition afflicts him. Living wills should generally be used *after* a surrogacy document, and in the event that there arises a question about what the person's wishes really were about certain end-of-life issues.

Most states provide that individuals may choose to withhold or remove certain medical care in the event of a terminal condition. "Terminal" refers to conditions for which no reasonable medical recovery is likely, and include persistent vegetative state, dementia, and other conditions. Each state law should be consulted for the specific conditions that apply. *Often patients do not realize that their living will is not effective unless those conditions are met.*

Living wills allow individuals to state that they want to be kept alive at all costs, regardless of their medical condition and regardless of the reasonable likelihood of recovery. More commonly, however, the living will reflects a decision by an individual not to be kept alive in the event of certain conditions or circumstances.

Figure 19.2 on page 533 is a sample living will document that provides a set of options for the person executing the document. It is important to appreciate that the living will should, to the extent possible, mirror the expected decisions that the health care surrogate will be making on behalf of the incapacitated person. Appointing a surrogate who will not uphold the intentions expressed in the living will is an invitation for disaster and legal expense. The surrogate should be fully familiar with the expectations in the living will and should be comfortable carrying them out. If not, the wrong surrogate may have been chosen.

Physicians, nurses, and health care organizations are in the business of keeping people alive and healthy as long as possible. Although physicians have not tended to view themselves as agents participating in decisions to end life, tacit understandings often existed between family members and physicians regarding end-of-life decisions. They were just not announced or memorialized in writing. When patients were very sick and in a terminal state, physicians would often let them, if not help them, transition into a peaceful death.

Again, specificity is important to avoid ambiguity and controversy. The particular form of the living will document is also important. In most jurisdictions, it must be signed, witnessed, and notarized. In some jurisdictions, it must follow a particular format and reference state law. Not all jurisdictions will honor the living will of another state. Persons who travel frequently or who have residences in more than one state should determine how each state requires living will documents to be created.

STATE OF

FLORIDA

COUNTY OF HILLSBOROUGH

DESIGNATION OF HEALTH CARE SURROGATE
FOR

_____

(Printed Name)

In the event that I have been determined to be incapacitated to provide informed consent for medical treatment and diagnostic procedures, I wish to designate as my surrogate for health care decisions, the following person, to act on my behalf:

Name: _____

Address: _____

In the event the above person, _____, is unable or unwilling to serve as my health care surrogate, I wish to designate the following person to act on my behalf:

Name: _____

Address: _____

I fully understand that this designation will permit my designee to make health care decisions and to provide, withhold, or withdraw consent on my behalf; to apply for public benefits to defray the cost of health care; and to authorize my admission to or transfer from a health care facility.

I further affirm that this designation is not being made as a condition of treatment or admission to a health care facility. I will notify and send a copy of this document to the following persons other than my surrogate, so they may know who my surrogate is.

Name _____

Name _____

Signed _____ Date _____

Witnesses: Name _____   _____

                                                                            Signature

Address _____

Name _____   _____

                                                                            Signature

Address _____

(continued)

Figure 19.1 Health Care Surrogate Template. Adapted from Florida Bar Templates, http://www.floridabar.org/tfb/flabarwe.nsf/840090c16eedaf0085256b61000928dc /b954f12053a410ec85256e28005bd4a0?OpenDocument.

STATE OF FLORIDA

COUNTY OF HILLSBOROUGH

The foregoing instrument was acknowledged before me this _____ day of _____ 200_, by _____ who is personally known to me or who has produced Florida State or _____ State Driver's License, Number _____ as identification and who did take an oath, and that the affiant's signature was witnessed by _____who is personally known to me or who has produced a Florida State or _____ State Driver's License, Number _____ as identification and who did take an oath and by _____ who is personally known to me or who has produced a Florida State or _____ State Driver's License, Number _____ as identification and who did take an oath.

Executed this _____ day of _____ 200_.

_____ Seal

My commission expires:

Figure 19.1   *(Continued)*

No legal document regarding a person's life or health should be signed without carefully considering the implications of that document and without consulting family and loved ones. Executing a health care surrogate or a living will without telling anybody about them is likely to create controversy and chaos. There are a variety of commercial and not-for-profit options that are available for people to use as repositories for their surrogate and living will documents. While a personal attorney, trust banker or friend/relative can serve as the holder of the document, some may prefer another third party.[53]

The Living Will Registry is a private company that seeks to provide national virtual storage and access services for persons who wish to file their living will documents in a central repository. But somebody still needs to know that you have located your document with their service.

Some jurisdictions will accept video statements of intent regarding health care surrogates and living wills. Some jurisdictions will accept verbal, unwritten evidence of a person's intent, usually subject to a hearing and the presentation of evidence. But to avoid confusion and ambiguity, written, signed, witnessed, and notarized documents are the only reasonable assurance that a person's intentions will be carried out.

The Robert Wood Johnson Foundation has funded the development and distribution of a the Five Wishes program, which is administered by Aging with Dignity, a Florida organization. Five Wishes is a document that offers a stepwise approach to helping people and their families ask and answer questions about end-of-life decisions.[54] The categories of issues addressed in the Five Wishes document include who will make decisions, the kind of care and treatment to be provided, the level of comfort or relative pain a person agrees to experience, and

---

[53] See for example, The Living Will Registry line at http://www.uslivingwillregistry.com.
[54] www.agingwithdignity.org.

LIVING WILL DECLARATION

_____
(Printed Name)

I, _____ voluntarily make this declaration on _____ 200_. I recognize that death is natural and is but a phase of the cycle of life. I do not fear death as much as I fear the indignity and futility of deterioration, dependence and hopeless pain. If there is no reasonable medical expectation of my recovery from a physical or mental disability, I do not wish to be kept alive by artificial means or heroic measures.

Therefore, if my attending or treating physician and another consulting physician determine that there is no reasonable medical probability of my recovery from any of the following conditions, I direct that life-prolonging procedures be withheld or withdrawn when the application of those procedures would serve only to prolong artificially the process of dying, and that I be permitted to die naturally with only the administration of medication or the performance of any medical procedure deemed necessary to provide me with comfort care or to alleviate pain, even if it hastens my death:

- I have a terminal condition caused by injury, disease or illness from which there is no reasonable medical probability of recovery and which can be expected to cause my death if not treated;
- I am in an irreversible end-stage condition that is caused by injury, disease or illness that has resulted in severe and permanent deterioration, indicated by my incapacity and complete physical dependency, for which treatment would be medically ineffective to a reasonable degree of medical certainty;
- I am in a persistent or permanent vegetative state characterized by permanent and irreversible unconsciousness and/or brain injury in which there is an absence of voluntary action or cognitive behavior of any kind by me, with an inability to communicate or interact purposefully with others in the environment around me.

In any of the situations described above, I direct that the following medical interventions that I have initialed be considered life prolonging procedures which I hereby direct not be administered to me:

_____ Placement on ventilator or other mechanical devices
_____ Surgical procedures and blood transfusions, except as needed to prevent or alleviate suffering
_____ Placement in an intensive care unit except as an absolute necessity to relieve suffering
_____ Chemotherapy or radiation therapy, unless there is a substantial medical probability my condition will materially improve
_____ Resuscitation efforts in the event of arrest of my heart or breathing
_____ Active treatment of a new reversible condition, such as a newly discovered cancer, heart condition or pneumonia
_____ Artificial nutrition and hydration (providing food and water through tubes)

I intend that this declaration be honored by my family and my physicians and health care institutions as the final expression of my legal right to refuse medical or surgical treatment or care and to accept the consequences for such refusal. I understand that my wishes may place a heavy burden upon others, and so I make this declaration to assume sole responsibility for my decision and to mitigate any feelings of guilt that my wishes may cause.

(continued)

Figure 19.2 Living Will Template.

I am emotionally and mentally competent to make this declaration, and I understand its importance.

_____

_____   _____ 200___

This declaration is witnessed by us in the presence of the declarant:

_____   _____
Witness   Witness

_____   _____
Address   Address

_____   _____
Telephone   Telephone

State of Florida   /
                        /
County of Hillsborough   /
_____ /

The foregoing instrument was acknowledged before me this _____ day of _____ 200__ by _____, who is personally known to me, and was witnessed by _____, who is personally known to me or produced a valid Florida Driver's License, and by _____, who is personally known to me or produced a valid Florida Driver's License, after all of them did take an oath.

_____
                                        Notary Public
_____   State of Florida

Figure 19.2   *(Continued)*

what and when people should be told about them when they are going to die.[55] The 11-page document can be acquired through www.agingwithdignity.org.

ETHICS CONSULTS

Both the *Quinlan* and *Browning* courts developed frameworks for deciding end-of-life cases outside of court intervention. Many times, a hospital ethics committee is involved in the review of the case and the proposed course of action. A hospital ethics committee is usually an interdisciplinary committee that looks at the case from a number of different perspectives, including, as the name implies, an ethical perspective.[56] This consultative body can provide guidance, make sure all the right questions have been asked, and affirm the appropriateness of a particular course of action. Ethics committees are generally composed of physicians, nurses, nonclinical persons, and often a clergy member, and at least one member of the

---

[55] *Id.*

[56] See an example of an ethics committee handbook, the University of Kansas Medical Center, at http://www.kumc.edu/hospital/ethics/ethics.htm.

committee is trained in medical ethical decision-making issues and processes. The purpose of the ethics committee is to place a variety of complicated clinical decisions about care, treatment, death, and dying within a well-balanced, orderly process. The entire palliative care movement to assure a comfortable, humane, and desirable (by the patient) end of life has been one of the vital forces behind the creation and operation of hospital ethics committees (Fins, 2005).

Do Not Resuscitate Orders   Do not resuscitate (DNR) orders are formal medical orders issued by a physician that carry instructions about resuscitating the patient. There are two types of DNR orders: the in-hospital DNR order, which is entered in the patient's chart, and the out-of-hospital DNR order. Generally, the latter relates to resuscitation in the event of an accident or a heart attack, stroke, or other sudden threat to life that occurs outside of the hospital. Physicians will issue a DNR order upon the request of a patient and after counseling if the patient suffers from chronic, terminal, and life-threatening conditions and the patient does not wish to prolong her life in a possible coma or vegetative state or in profound disability. Such orders are agreed to between the physician and the patient and signed by the physician.[57] The order is formally recorded in the patient's medical record. It should also be posted in an obvious place in the patient's home, such as on the refrigerator, and it can also be worn on a medical alert bracelet or necklace to alert emergency medical personnel.

The DNR order is a serious and important document that, unlike other advance directives, requires a physician's formal prescription. Enforcing the DNR order can sometimes be tricky, because the nature and severity of a potential life-threatening event can be a subjective matter. During an emergency, for example, well-meaning and well trained clinicians or others may automatically seek to provide CPR or some other life-saving function because they are not aware of the DNR order, because they don't believe that the event is sufficiently serious to cause potential long-term adverse effects, or sometimes because they do not support the idea of a DNR order. Some states have statutes or regulations that specifically address the out-of-hospital DNR order. Some require that the order be on a specific color of paper and have specific language and other requirements. In those states, a DNR direction contained in a patient's advance directive is not effective.

When an advance directive or the patient's wishes are not honored because a caregiver or health care provider refuses to honor the directive or disagrees with the patient's wishes, this can create a set of clinical, legal, and ethical dilemmas. Directives may not be honored for a number of reasons: there may be no knowledge of the directive's existence; a traveling patient may have left the directive at home; or the health care provider disagrees with the patient's directions.[58] Advance directive statutes generally contain conscientious objector clauses, which allow the health care provider to transfer the patient to another health care provider if the original provider disagrees with the patient's decision to refuse life-prolonging procedures on conscientious grounds (such as religious or moral beliefs). Beyond those clauses, a caregiver or health care

---

[57] See, for example, Florida Administrative Code 64E-2.031 and Florida Statutes, 401.45(3)(a).

[58] See, for example, *Will Doctors and Hospitals Recognize My Advanced Directive?* http://www.abanet.org/publiced/practical/directive_recognition.html.

provider who unilaterally decides to not honor the patient's wishes violates the patient's rights as well as the doctrine of informed consent. Problematically, however, it may be hard to know when an advance directive is being ignored, because most patients in this situation are not conscious and competent. And assuming discovery, what is the appropriate remedy? Removal of the life-prolonging procedures as expeditiously as possible? Absolutely. But what about the medical bills that have been incurred by the continuation of the life-prolonging procedures against the patient's wishes? Is it fraud if the patient's insurance is billed for this unwanted treatment? Can the patient's representative recover money damages for the disregard of the patient's wishes? These are difficult questions that are offshoots of the bigger issue of honoring the patient's wishes. In addition to the problem of discovering cases where the patient's wishes are not being honored is determining with necessary certainty that the patient truly wished the procedures withdrawn, the provider or caregiver knew it and intentionally decided to ignore it, and putting a dollar value on extra days of life. The advance directive statutes may contain penalties for those who willfully ignore a patient's directive, but discovery and proof continue to be a problem. For examples of these types of issues, see *Grace Plaza v. Elbaum*[59] and *Anderson v. St. George Hospital.*[60]

The American Bar Association is an especially helpful source of information about state-by-state legal options and requirements regarding health care surrogates, living wills, and other advance directive issues. Their website (http://www .americanbarassociation.org/rppt/public/living-wills.html#whyhavehd's) is an excellent portal to background and technical information.

Organ and Body Part Donations   Medical technology has successfully evolved to the point where there is a high demand for the recycling of body parts. Kidneys, hearts, lungs, corneas, body tissues, and bones are all now potentially reusable through transplantation. Throughout the United States organ procurement organizations (OPOs) have blossomed by acting as the intermediary by which persons in need of a new heart, lung, or kidney, can find and receive one from somebody who has died. The OPOs nationally coordinate their efforts through a series of organ data bank systems and local and regional priority lists for the receipt of specific organs.

This topic is of relevance here because the decision to donate body parts is an advance directive, or can become a family decision made while a patient is about to die. Decisions to donate can be made well in advance of death, but to make use of an organ it needs to be removed very soon after death. So timing is a very important issue for those seeking organs.

A decision to donate body parts can be made in several ways. Most states now have provisions that allow persons to designate their intention to be an organ donor through the driver license system of the state. The prospective donor's license is stamped with a code that provides notice to health care workers and others that the person has agreed to be an organ donor. Most states have computerized

---

[59] 82 N.Y. 2d 10 (1993).
[60] 77 Ohio St. 3d 82 (1996).

systems that can be accessed by OPOs and health care institutions to verify the donor's intentions. This means that in the event of an accident, injury, or serious illness, if a person is brought to a hospital there is advance notice to the hospital that the person may become an organ donor.

Other opportunities for advance statements of intent regarding organ donation include reference within the living will and even the general last will and testament. For specialized cases, such as cornea donations, the Lions' Eye Banks can be contacted in advance and permission given to extract that body part.

But the OPOs and persons seeking organs for transplantation do not rely solely on advance directives and driver license programs. Representatives from OPOs often have offices at major hospitals and may be alerted to cases of patients who are terminal and about to die. This is the delicate part: The OPO representative may then approaches the patient (if conscious and competent) or the family and seeks to get permission to obtain organ donations as soon as possible after death occurs.

Nationally, the organ acquisition process is managed by the United Network for Organ Sharing (UNOS). This organization was created in 1984 by Congress and is charged with administering the Organ Procurement and Transplantation Network. The UNOS describes its activities as including collecting and managing data about each transplant (harvesting and use) that occurs in the United States; facilitation of organ matching and placement; and linking medical professionals, recipients, and donor families for the purpose of maintaining an organ transplantation policy. More information is available at www.unos.org. The UNOS coordinates and monitors the activities of the individual organ procurement organizations throughout the nation.

Burial Cremation Options   Even if organs are being donated or if a person is contributing her body to a medical school, a decision usually has to be made about how the body will be finally treated. This usually means one of two options (other than permanent plasticized display): burial or cremation.

As with other decisions about the end of life, it is prudent to express intentions in advance about how the body will be finally treated. Within the two major categories of burial and cremation, there are myriad options. Some can be elaborate and expensive, such as custom burial crypts and specially designed coffins. But we are concerned here with the advance planning and options that should be considered.

When it comes to burial and cremation decisions, there is a nexus of state laws and religious customs that come into play. Some religions require burial of the body within 24 hours; some prohibit embalming. Some states require internment within a certain number of days of death (unless the body is maintained in a refrigerated facility). Many people die in a geographic location far from where they wish to be buried or cremated, and arrangements must be made to ship the body or the cremains.

There are burial and cremation societies nationally and locally, and most funeral homes will write advance contracts for the management of the deceased (body pickup, funeral, grave site or column burial location preidentified). Most churches, synagogues, mosques, and temples also have arrangements for taking care of the business aspects of burial or cremation in advance. Advance planning for the cremation or burial is important to avoid confusion, miscommunication, and even feuds among family and friends.

THE QUANTITY VERSUS QUALITY DEBATE

How long and under what circumstances should somebody be kept alive? Advances in medical technology and pharmaceuticals have made it possible to sustain life and life functions. At one level, this would seem to be exactly what medical science should strive to accomplish. But there are competing issues related to the maintenance of life and life functions: quality of life versus quantity of life as against cost of maintenance, and the rights of persons to make decisions or be involved in the making of decisions about end-of-life options.

In a nutshell, these competing issues are grounded in value systems and personal and religious beliefs regarding the value of the individual, the extent to which autonomy and personal decisions should play a role in life and death matters, and how much society is willing to pay for health and social services.

The cases of Nancy Cruzan and Terri Schiavo, as well as *Roe v. Wade*,[61] brought these value-based matters directly into the courtroom as well as the living rooms of America. The case of Theresa Schiavo captured many of the social, economic, philosophical, and clinical issues that define the challenges in death and dying decisions. It was as much about the tragedy of a single family, where the parents battled with their son-in-law for control over the fate of a severely brain-damaged woman, as it was about our national value compass as it emerges in the twenty-first century.

The Schiavo case catapulted a single, unconscious person into international limelight in a health care system that many analysts believe is fundamentally broken. The system itself has insufficient resources to provide adequate care and services to those in need, and it is not geared toward prevention. The more than $100,000 each year that was spent to maintain Ms. Schiavo in her hospice, it has been argued, could have been deployed to provide food, medications, and access to care for younger, healthy people or for seniors in need of additional social and medical care.

There are growing numbers of communities across the United States without neurosurgeons or obstetricians, and the cost of medical malpractice insurance has pushed many physicians out of practice. Medicare and Medicaid, federal programs that pay for the aged and the poor, are facing very real shortfalls in revenues and have devised means by which care can be more aggressively rationed through managed care and benefit reduction policies.

As people live longer and are certain to require more care as they age, how will decisions be made in our communities to provide one person or group with life-maintenance services costing $100,000 per year, versus the myriad other needs that present themselves?

This is the heart of the value question relative to life and death decisions. As resources become increasingly scarce, how will decisions be made to provide people with specific care and services? And what are the trade-offs that communities will face? An individual's choice to be kept alive at all costs or to be allowed to pass without any intervention has social and economic consequences—especially if society is helping to pay for the care.

Yet do we not, each of us, have an absolute right to enjoy our life completely and fully as long as we are capable of being kept alive? How do we balance our personal intentions against broader social value and good?

---

[61] *Cruzan*, op. cit.; *Schiavo*, op. cit.; *Roe v. Wade*, op. cit.

As medical science and technology provide means by which to maintain or extend life, many ethicists and clinicians ask how far it is reasonable to extend life, especially in cases where active, conscious interaction may be limited or nonexistent. But there is a substantive difference between choosing not to extend a life and assisting in its termination.

It is precisely the assistance in life termination that has become a major international policy issue. European nations have begun to sanction physician-assisted suicide,[62] and in the United States, the State of Oregon passed the Oregon Death with Dignity Act, permitting physicians to prescribe lethal doses of drugs to persons who have been diagnosed as terminally ill with no reasonable hope of recovery and who are in the last months of their life. This law was challenged in federal court by the attorney general of the United States (*Gonzales v. Oregon*), and Oregon won.[63] The federal government sought to regulate the use of controlled substances by physicians for purposes of assisting in death. The characteristics of persons taking advantage of the law appear to reflect the intentions of the people of Oregon in creating the law by referendum. Since the law was enacted in 1997 and physicians were permitted to prescribe lethal doses of medications, the State of Oregon has carefully tracked the data on persons electing to participate in physician-assisted suicide. Data published in 2006 are generally reflective of the state's experience:

> Compared to all Oregon decedents in 2005, PAS [physician-assisted suicide] participants were more likely to have malignant neoplasms (84% versus 24%), to be younger (median age 70 versus 78 years), and to have more formal education (37% versus 15% had at least a baccalaureate degree). During the past 8 years, the 246 patients who took lethal medications differed in several ways from the 74,967 Oregonians dying from the same underlying diseases. Rates of participation in PAS decreased with age, although over 65% of PAS users were age 65 or older. Rates of participation were higher among those who were divorced or never married, those with more years of formal education, and those with amyotrophic lateral sclerosis, HIV/AIDS, or malignant neoplasms. . . .
>
> Physicians indicated that patient requests for lethal medications stemmed from multiple concerns, with eight in 10 patients having at least three concerns. The most frequently mentioned end-of-life concerns during 2005 were: a decreasing ability to participate in activities that made life enjoyable, loss of dignity, and loss of autonomy.[64]

THE FUTURE

LESSONS LEARNED FROM *SCHIAVO*

If history serves as a guide, the lessons associated with the *Schiavo* case should provide a beacon of information to direct end-of-life decisions. Ms. Schiavo was a 27-year-old woman who had been married for 6 years before collapsing in her St. Petersburg, Florida, apartment in spring 1990. Following heroic efforts to bring

---

[62] www.assistedsuicide.org/suicide_laws.html.

[63] 126 S.Ct. 904 (2006).

[64] Oregon Department of Human Services, *Eighth Annual Report on Oregon's Death with Dignity Act*, March 9, 2006, p. 5, http://www.Oregon.gov/DHS/ph/pas/docs/year8.pdf.

her back and keep her alive, her parents and her husband spent years battling in court over who should have the authority to make decisions about her health care services, and in particular, the decision to discontinue artificial life support in order to allow her to die.[65]

Ms. Schiavo, like most Americans, did not have a written health care surrogate or living will document. Florida and federal law were tested to the extreme as every branch of state and federal government became very actively involved in what became the most litigated end-of-life case in U.S. legal history. In the end, Ms. Schiavo's husband, Michael, was permitted to withdraw her feeding tube, and she died. But not before the governor of Florida, the Florida legislature, the president and Congress of the United States, the Supreme Courts of Florida and the United States, and Pope John Paul II had weighed in on the case.[66] In the process, hundreds of thousands of dollars were spent on legal fees, and America and the world discussed death with dignity, freedom of choice, and the role of government in personal decisions.

Theresa Schiavo's end of life raised the importance of health care surrogates and living wills to a new high. Ms. Schiavo did not have any advance directives—something most young people would not generally think of creating. But her case caused hundreds of thousands of people of all ages to realize that advance directives are essential parts of any adult's legal portfolio. Estate planning attorneys advise families to discuss advance directives with all of their adult members and to encourage all to express their intentions in writing. As we noted earlier, these can always be modified. But if they do not exist, any family can find itself in the kind of expensive, heart-wrenching dilemma faced by the Schiavo and Schindler families.

MEDICAL SCIENCE AND RELATED OPTIONS

With or without organ donation, individuals have the option of determining that they want their body to be made available for scientific use. This can take several forms. Medical schools always need cadavers for their anatomy labs; this is one important way that young medical students learn about the body. Most public and private medical schools have formal donation programs.

Since 2000, a new process has made it possible for bodies to be literally plasticized[67] for the purpose of medical education and for museum display. Yes, museum display. What has become a popular, though highly controversial technique allows bodies to undergo an expensive treatment that includes complex, artistic autopsy. The bodies can then be used in medical training or they can be placed in public museum display programs.

---

[65] Wolfson, J. *In Re, The Matter of Theresa Marie Schiavo, A Report to Governor Jeb Bush and the 6th Florida Judicial Circuit,* Pursuant to the requirements of H.B. 35-E (Chapter 2003-418, Laws of Florida) and the Order of the Hon. David Demers, Chief Judge, Florida 6th Judicial Circuit regarding the appointment and duties of a Guardian Ad Litem in the matter of Theresa Marie Schiavo, Incapacitated, December 2003.

[66] *Id.*

[67] http://english.people.com.cn/200401/10/eng20040110_132296.shtml.

CONCLUSION

A combination of medical technology, economics, political, and social forces affect individual and family health-related decisions and directives about the end of life. In the United States at the beginning of the twenty-first century, there are profound differences of opinion about how, when, and by whose hand decisions to terminate life should be made. This applies to cases of infants born with disabling conditions; persons with terminal illnesses, regardless of their age; and aged persons at the "end" of their "natural" life period. While dying is a part of the life cycle, many people feel uncomfortable speaking about it, let alone planning for it. Failure to plan often results in expense, frustration and emotional pain for those left behind. End-of-life decisions can, and should, be integrated into the panoply of life management decisions, such as asset management and estate planning. Resource allocation imperatives in health care alone will likely drive public policy around end-of-life interventions, especially where public monies are involved. The costs of providing care and maintaining terminally ill people will be balanced against the costs of preventive and other services for the general population. Individual prerogatives about how one will be treated and cared for when ill or disabled and how and where they would prefer to die can only be honored if these intentions are expressly gleaned and made clear, unambiguous, and in conformance with the law.

REFERENCES

American Bar Association. (n.d.). *Will doctors and hospitals recognize my advanced directive?* Available from http://www.abanet.org/publiced/practical/directive_recognition.html.

Black's Law Dictionary (8th ed.). (2004). Rochester, NY: Thomson West.

Fins, J. J. (2005). *A palliative ethic of care.* Boston: Jones and Bartlett.

The Florida Bar. (n.d.). Available from http://www.floridabar.org/tfb/flabarwe .nsf/840090c16eedaf0085256b61000928dc/b954f12053a410ec85256e28005bd4a0 ?OpenDocument.

Giacino, J. T., Ashwal, S., Childs, N., Cranford, R., Jennett, B., Katz, D. I., et al. (2002). The minimally conscious state: Definition and diagnostic criteria. *Neurology, 58,* 349–353.

PART V

CONCLUSION

CHAPTER 20

Global Challenges for an Aging Population

JEANETTE C. TAKAMURA

T HE SIGNIFICANCE OF population aging as an emerging global phenomenon captured the attention of many policy makers, demographers, economists, and other social scientists during the second half of the twentieth century. Organizations such as the United Nations Economic Commission for Europe were among the first to examine the long-term effects of the rapidity of aging within its member nations. Interest increased as the multisectoral implications of a "graying world" became more evident. In particular, the Organization for Economic Cooperation and Development (OECD) and others took note of the demographic revolution's impact on national security, national budgets, economic rates of growth and competitiveness, and systems of social provision, health, and long-term care. For example, economists from the defense community were concerned—long before 9/11 and the Iraq War—about competition for scarce resources by aged populations on one hand and aged defense infrastructures on the other (Gouré, 2000; Peterson, 1999).

Today, most of the global community of 271 developing and developed nations remain significantly more knowledgeable about (and interested in) issues associated with children than they are about population aging as an unfolding and complex twenty-first century reality (United Nations, 2002a). Some of this is likely due to the persistent ageism that gerontologists have been battling for decades. It is probably also due to the constraints that nations anticipate because of projections about the enduring nature of the longevity revolution. Compared, for example, to threats to infant mortality that persist in various parts of the world, aging-related issues are relatively new phenomena. Thus, although the Internet and other modes of communication have disseminated information to far-flung people and communities, we have not yet reached a universal tipping point concerning global aging.

A much longer work than this chapter would be required to do justice to the differential rates of aging and country-to-country variations, including social, economic, and political structures and trends, a fully informed discussion of global longevity, its multiple dimensions, and the various policies, programs, and interventions. Nonetheless, in this chapter I attempt to do three things. I present and analyze the demographics of global aging, recognizing that the ongoing longevity revolution is occurring in complex environments. I identify and discuss three sets of policy and program challenges. Finally, I argue that evidence-based approaches to policy and program development as well as clinical intervention may be ideal, but note the unevenness in research resources and capacities that can be brought to bear in both developing and developed nations.

To provide an initial comparative perspective, I examine China in comparison to the United States. In some instances, I also provide a comparative view of Japan's response to the fact that 25% of its populace will be 65 years old and older by 2020 and 38% will be over 60 in 2050 (United Nations, 1999).

THE DEMOGRAPHICS OF GLOBAL AGING

Overview

Today, there are an estimated 6.5 billion persons in the world (U.S. Census Bureau, 2006b). In mid-2005, about 1.2 billion persons resided in the more developed world, with nearly 15% age 65 or older. This was significantly less than the 5.3 billion persons 65 or older (about 5%) in the developing world (Population Reference Bureau, 2005). Of this, 605 million persons are 60 or older; an estimated 483.3 million persons (7.46% of the world's total population) are 65 or older. By 2025, it is expected that 1.2 billion persons will be 60 or older. In 2050, the number of persons 60 and older is expected to rise to almost 2 billion. At that point, the size of the older adult population will exceed that of children (0 to 14 years) for the first time in human history (HelpAge International, 2002).

Approximately 3.3% of the U.S. population of 3.3 million persons in 1990 was 65 or older; 100,000 were 85 or older. By midcentury, the number of persons over 65 had grown to 12.3 million, and by the beginning of the twenty-first century, the elderly population in the United States had mushroomed to approximately 35 million older adults out of nearly 300 million persons (12%), 4.2 million of whom were older than 85. The Federal Interagency Forum on Aging-Related Statistics (2000, 2006) projects that in 2050 there will be 86.7 million persons 65 and older and 20.9 million who will have reached age 85 or older.

In the United States, the equivalent of one small town (about 7,918 persons) turns 60 each day (U.S. Census Bureau, 2006a). Regardless of how dramatic this sounds, the rapidity of aging in the developing world is staggering. In 2000, for example, the world's entire elderly population (60 years and older) numbered 600 million, with the population of 374 million elders in developing countries growing at an astonishing rate of about 795,000 persons per month (Kinsella & Velkoff, 2001). By 2030, 75% of the world's elders or 1 billion persons will be in developing countries. In comparison, the number of older persons in developed countries is likely to reach 362 million in 2030 (HelpAge International, 2002).

Approximately 27.4% of our global population is 0 to 14 years of age. In comparison, 65.2% of the world's people are 15 to 65 years old. Confronted by dramatic population aging, Japan, Sweden, and other nations have developed societal responses that may provide policy makers and professionals in the United States with an expanded notion of policy and program possibilities.

According to the Population Division of the United Nations (2002a), the oldest of the old—persons 80 or older—are increasing in number at twice the rate of the 60+ cohort. Not only will this subpopulation grow rapidly in 2050, those 100 and older will increase 18 times between 2000 and 2050 (from 180,000 to 3.2 million).

AGING IN DEVELOPING AND DEVELOPED NATIONS

The proportion of older persons to total population in the developing world is approaching 66%, up from 59% (249 million) in 2000 (Kinsella & Velkoff, 2001). This trend should continue through the decades ahead as the growth of the 60+ population in currently developing nations will dramatically outpace the growth in today's developed world. In less than 2 decades, developing nations will lay claim to 75% of the world's elderly population, with the number of older persons rising most dramatically in Asia and Latin America. In fact, individuals 80+ will represent the fastest growing age segment in the developing world (World Health Organization [WHO], n.d.).

The greatest share (54%) of the world's elderly persons is in Asia. Second is Europe (24%), where 24 of the world's oldest populations reside (United Nations, 2002a). Japan, the sole non-European nation with a significant proportion of its citizenry 65 and older, expects that its elders will represent more than 27% of its population in 2025, up from 14.6% in 1995 (Ibe, 2000). By 2030, more than 40% of elderly Japanese will be 80+; demographers expect that Japan will have the "largest number and proportion of centenarians" by 2050 (United Nations, 2002a, p. 25). In comparison, the United States is a relatively young country, ranking 32nd in the proportion of older persons to total population. Africa is home to the youngest aging countries.

Demographers forecast a huge rise in the number of elderly persons in China, estimated presently to be 88 million out of a population of 1.3 billion of all ages. By 2020, one-third of all persons in Shanghai, China's most cosmopolitan and modernized city, will be 60 and older. By 2050, China will have 331 million older persons—nearly equal to the total projected population of all persons of all ages in the United States. For comparison purposes, the older U.S. population, currently 35 million, will grow to 86.7 million by 2050 (U.S. Administration on Aging, 2005).

Although the rise in the sheer number of elderly Chinese will be astounding, Singapore (372%), Malaysia (277%), Colombia (258%), and Costa Rica (250%) will see extraordinary increases between 2000 and 2030 (Kinsella & Velkoff, 2001). With few exceptions, the most significant growth in the elderly population will be in the developing world. The aggregate rate of growth of the total world population will be half that of the elderly population in the developing world. Similarly, the developed nations' aggregate growth rate for older persons will be less than half that of their counterparts in the developing world (Kinsella & Velkoff, 2001).

The economic status of older persons in the United States and other OECD countries is significantly different from the rest of world's aged. About 9.8% (approximately 3.6 million) of older persons in the United States were at or below the poverty line, and 6.7% (2.3 million) of older Americans were between the poverty line and 125% of it in 2004. As with many women around the world, a larger number of older women in the United States were impoverished (12.0%) than older men (7.0%). Similarly, more older persons (17.9%) living alone were poor than were older persons who were living with their family (5.7%). Older African American and Latina women who lived alone were also more likely to be impoverished (U.S. Census Bureau, 2005). In contrast, most elderly persons in developing countries live lives of impoverishment and deprivation (HelpAge International, 2002).

Gouré (2000) and Petersen (1999) are among those who have seen population aging as generating burdens hazardous to economic and national security. Gouré cautioned that the ability of developed nations to rebuild an aging military infrastructure, counter the shortage of active recruits, and otherwise add to military spending in the United States will be seriously constrained by the anticipated budgetary requirements of Social Security and Medicare and the exodus of the baby boomers from an already less than robust workforce. The same scenario is expected in Europe, China, and India. Petersen's and Gouré's observations were made, of course, prior to 9/11, the war in the Middle East, North Korea's missile test in summer 2006, and similar events that reverberated throughout the global community.

BOOMERS AND AGING

Assuming that the United States will remain one of the most powerful sociocultural leaders in this century, envisaging the potential impact of the aging U.S. baby boom generation (born between 1946 and 1964) may help us to better address global aging in the future.

Unlike previous generations, the boomers will likely challenge the chronological age-based standard for retirement and "old age"—age 65—set in 1916 in Germany. Significant gains in life expectancy had not yet been realized worldwide during the 2nd decade of the twentieth century, nor had sufficient evidence been gathered about whether 65 should be viewed as synonymous with old age or whether it should demarcate a newly defined "middle age." In fact, findings from several recent studies suggest that chronological age-based definitions of aging and age-based criteria for retirement may no longer command the degree of concurrence that would legitimize their use. A 2000 survey of more than 3,000 adults of all ages in the United States concluded that many Americans regard discernible decline in physical ability, not chronological age, as the defining criteria for "old age" (National Council on Aging, 2000). A nationwide telephone survey of 1,000 adults of all ages found that definitions of "old age" appear to depend on the relative age of the respondent. Older respondents tended to define "old age" as older than did younger respondents (MetLife Mature Market Institute, 2005b).

In a study of retirement by a global financial institution, a sample of nearly 11,500 adults in 10 countries, there were also strong indications that neither age of retirement nor definitions of old age should be presumed to be linked to chronological age. It appears that both "retirement age" and "old age" are more commonly determined individually and personally, are often dependent on physical and mental capacity, and may depend on an interest in remaining actively engaged (Hong Kong and Shanghai Banking Corporation [HSBC], 2005). A follow-up 2006 study with a sample of 21,000 individuals and 6,000 employer organizations in 20 countries revealed a range of attitudes toward retirement and self-assessed retirement preparedness across countries (HSBC, 2006).

Using the criteria of the Older Americans Act, which defines old age as 60+, the leading-edge baby boomers became "older Americans" in 2006. However, most discussions presume that the first wave of boomers will come of age in 2011, when the cohort begins to reach age 65. At that point, baby boomer numbers in the United States will be more than twice the total population of Canada. This is hardly as dramatic as the number of boomers in developing nations, who will outnumber older persons in the developed world, in some cases by multiples of hundreds of millions.

Eighteen years separate the youngest from the oldest boomers, who were born between 1946 and 1964. Hardly a homogeneous generation, boomers have been differentiated by several observable differences and similarities. Gillion (2004) regards boomers born between 1945 and 1957 as distinct from the "shadow boomers" born between 1958 and 1963. Boomers can also be divided into market segments. "Younger boomers" born between 1956 and 1964 are purportedly less concerned about the future and are focused as consumers primarily on their children. "Older boomers," born between 1946 and 1955, are more concerned about the future, are more likely to try to protect themselves against future losses, but typically are also more self-indulgent, using more of their resources for vacations, homes, and clothing (MetLife Mature Market Institute, 2005a).

Within-group differences for individuals born between 1946 and 1964 are not limited only to the United States. In other countries, political developments, natural disasters, wars, epidemics, and the dynamics of the marketplace have created distinctive points of reference and differing resource expectations.

Boomers in the United States have a higher standard of living than did their parents. In spite of this, Hughes and O'Rand (2004) observed that boomers are characterized by more inequality in household incomes, home ownership patterns, and net worth. A MetLife study has estimated that the spending power of older boomers is about $1 trillion, compared to younger boomers at $1.1 trillion (MetLife Mature Market Institute, 2005a). Although boomers as a generational group have a declining overall percentage of persons in poverty—down from 9.5% in 1993 to 7.3% below the poverty level in 2000—more younger boomers were poor than their older counterparts. This may seem counterintuitive because of the spending power of younger boomers (MetLife Mature Market Institute, 2005a).

Trends for U.S. boomers' standard of living and economic diversity may be the same in most other developed nations as well. If the findings of two recent multinational studies with a U.S. sample are accurate, many adults as a whole and many boomers as a segment feel that they lack adequate knowledge about personal finance and investments to be confident about their financial security in retirement. In fact, retirement preparedness and knowledge of levels of financial capacity necessary in retirement were appallingly inadequate in 20 countries examined in 2006 (HSBC, 2006). Even well-educated boomers have said that they need more useful and usable information and guidance so that they can better plan for their older years in retirement (National Commission for Quality Long Term Care, 2005). These issues are in sharp contrast to economic security issues that are largely colored by the extensiveness of poverty among elders in many developing nations.

AGING IN RURAL AND URBAN COMMUNITIES

Urban and rural differences among older persons may be most readily observable by continent or region. Asian elders and older women tend to live in urban areas, whereas older Africans and older men tend to be residents of rural communities. About 74% of older persons in developed nations reside in urban settings. This is in sharp contrast to older adults in developing nations, many of whom now reside in rural settings, but more than half of whom will likely be affected by a push toward urbanization within less than a decade.

Policy makers worldwide have largely failed to bring the quality of life of persons in rural communities on a par with that of persons in large urban areas. Compared to more populous urban areas, rural communities tend to have poor (or no) public works, public health, and social welfare infrastructures as well as weak economic bases. With more poverty in rural communities, members of younger generations are less likely to remain in their ancestral villages, raising thorny issues of familial versus public support of aged rural members that spill over into urban communities.

Rurality is a variable that is typically synonymous with fewer resources and an outmigrating population. In China, existing household registration mandates discourage intranational relocations by disallowing access to government-sponsored programs in all but official communities of residence, regardless of how compelling the need for assistance. Elderly Chinese may be discouraged from moving away from resource-poor rural villages with their relocating offspring. If they choose to remain in ancestral villages, they must contend with the trials of living alone, lower standards of living, and fewer services and service providers and may expect to be without the economic and social support of family caregivers. If they move, they must adapt to unfamiliar urban environments in which government support is unavailable.

In Japan, a nation whose aging ratio will be the highest in the world within a few decades, health and aging policies have recognized the needs of elders and have provided for locally administered services. However, with younger offspring moving to urban areas, the need for formal caregivers and workers is acute. Unable to convince its own people to move for work to rural communities, Japan is cautiously opening its doors to a small number of immigrants, who may be able to fill formal care-giving positions.

GENDER AND AGING

The strength and influence of the world's older women should come to full bloom during the twenty-first century. In terms of sheer numbers, women outnumber men at age 65+, with a sex ratio of 1.0 women to every 0.79 men. The most dramatic figures in comparisons of women to men are observable when the 65+ group is further differentiated. For example, women outlive and outnumber men by 2 to 1 at age 80 and older—the fastest growing age segment in many countries across the world (United Nations, 2002c). Although men will presumably make gains in longevity in the decades ahead, women are expected to remain more long-lived and more numerous than men in all but a small handful of countries.

If childcare was one of women's leading social issues in the twentieth century, aging-related issues should be one of the most prominent concerns of younger and older women during the twenty-first century. Older women in developing countries are more likely to be poor and vulnerable, and the most vulnerable and the poorest among them are widows. More than 50% of women over 60 are widowed in many of the least resourced countries (HelpAge International, 2002). In the United States, older women who are widowed, living alone, and minorities are at the highest levels of risk for impoverishment. If they are single, women are placed at risk by the inequities meted out by the dynamics of our social structures.

Policy makers in the developed OECD countries have begun to focus on younger women because of the ramifications of global aging for economic competitiveness, growth, and productivity. International groups with members from developed nations have advocated for both pro-natalist and labor policies that encourage women to bear more children and enter the workforce (Center for Strategic and International Studies, 2001). Whether such policy directions would be acceptable to women and would result in altered dependency ratios in aging countries would depend on whether the policies can truly reverse disincentives to marriage inherent in long-standing labor, employment, and child welfare laws. They would also depend on the resiliency in developing countries and traditional societies of women's gender-role expectations, following on the introduction over the past 4 decades of more liberal Western models. In tradition-bound Japan, for example, growing numbers of women no longer accept the curtailment of their newly discovered right to exercise personal choice and enjoy individual freedom. To the alarm of policy makers, young Japanese women are postponing or refusing marriage and motherhood. So dramatic is the decline in fertility rates in Japan that it is referred to as "women's revenge" against male chauvinism (Japan Aging Research Center, 2000). Similar trends have been observed in China and other countries.

China's one-child policy has also generated ramifications that were unanticipated when it was institutionalized decades ago. The oversupply of men in China has resulted in a dramatic need for the repopulation of rural communities with women, where multigenerational family caregiving, farming, and other traditionally female responsibilities cannot otherwise be met. However, many Chinese women are simply unwilling to assume traditional roles and functions. Rather than remaining in rural communities and acceding to these expectations, greater numbers of China's women are migrating to urban areas to pursue lives defined more on their own terms. The implications of shifts in gender-role expectations such as the foregoing have generated considerable consternation among national and international commissions and organizations such as the Commission on Global Aging and the OECD. They have warned that robust national economic growth rates, fiscal solvency, raised standards of living, the ability of countries to meet national security requirements, and the internal stability of governments will depend on the availability of workers. As new policy directions are considered and legislated, the traditionally male cards of power and privilege may be reshuffled to benefit or assure equity for women, who ultimately are most profoundly affected by the aging demographic revolution.

Global aging will not occur in a vacuum. Social, economic, political, climatic, and other trends and forces, including the impact of extant policy provisions, are shaping the longevity revolution and the quality of life of older persons and their families in individual countries and the world community.

GLOBAL AGING POLICY AND PROGRAM CHALLENGES

The aging of the world's population has enormous implications for every facet of life in the twenty-first century. Social structures and societal processes will unquestionably require innovations and adjustments to meet the needs of the first large multigenerational population of older persons in history. Cross-national policy and research exchanges and collaboration will be essential, but will succeed only if there is a high level of interest and commitment by nations with differing immediate and long-term priorities.

Concerted international efforts to develop global consensus and implementation activities around policy priorities harkens back to the United Nations' 1982 Vienna International Plan of Action on Aging. The Vienna Plan failed to stimulate governments to address challenges and capitalize on opportunities associated with population aging. It ignored the countries of the developing world and was dismissed in turn by the resource-rich and rapidly aging developed nations. The plan failed to speak to the social and economic development of as well as human rights implications for older persons (United Nations, 2002b).

The 2002 Madrid International Plan of Action on Aging established a consensus aging agenda for nations worldwide. Issues and recommended action steps in three broadly encompassing areas presented in the 2002 plan corresponded to the concerns of older adults in both developing and developed countries. The three issue areas were "older persons and development; advancing health and well-being into old age; and ensuring enabling and supportive environments" (United Nations, 2002b, p. 7).

The Madrid International Plan's attention to the needs of older persons in developing nations is consistent with three of the eight United Nations Millennium Development Goals, all targeted for achievement by 2015. These are (1) the eradication of extreme poverty and hunger; (2) the promotion of gender equity/empowerment of women, (3) and combating HIV/AIDS, malaria, and other diseases (United Nations, 2005). The Madrid International Plan also embraces the five broad principles for older persons that are at the core of the 1991 United Nations Principles for Older Persons: independence, participation, care, self-fulfillment, and dignity (United Nations, 1999).

There is no shortage of global aging issues requiring the attention of world leaders. Two considered among the most pressing are the need for economic security and long-term care. In each of these, as with most aging-related issues, the particular vulnerability of women is a constant. A third issue that has been widely noted over the past decade is *active aging*. All are addressed in the Madrid International Plan and are examined in the following section.

ECONOMIC SECURITY

The United Nations Development Program defines "income poverty" as having individual earnings of under U.S.$1 per day. "Human poverty" is the presence of illiteracy, poor health, and malnutrition (United Nations, 2000). Countries in which human poverty is an everyday reality are obviously likely to have populations plagued by income poverty.

The between- and within-country differences in the distribution, dimensions, and causes of poverty and hunger and gender inequality can be vastly different in developed as opposed to developing countries. For example, 9.8% of the elderly population in the United States is at or below the income poverty line. In sharp contrast, the majority of the world's elders are impoverished (United Nations, 2000). Two-thirds of the world's poorest people live in rural sub-Saharan Africa and South Central Asia (Population Reference Bureau, 2005). Lacking adequate income, older persons experience food, water, and housing insecurity, all of which can deplete their ability and undermine their motivation to participate productively in the economic, social, and political sectors of their communities. This feeds further the cycle of income and human poverty.

Only 20% of the world's inhabitants have adequate social security protection, and less than 50% have any protection (Van Ginneken, 2003). Social security programs may insure no more than 10% of each country's total population in such developing regions and countries as Southeast Asia, Mexico, and sub-Saharan Africa. In China, a rudimentary "iron rice bowl" government protection program was established to offer five basic guarantees to needy elders in their advanced years: food, clothing, health care, housing, and funeral services (Wang, 2005). A number of factors, including elders' official, permanent household registration versus their actual community of residence, determine whether these guarantees can be accessed. Chinese residing outside of the communities in which they have their permanent household registrations tend to be marginalized and are unable to access health and social services.

In 1994, the People's Republic of China began the transition from the "iron rice bowl" to a "porcelain rice bowl" program. The iron rice bowl program was a socialist-based assurance of employment, with all of the accompanying benefits. In contrast, the "porcelain" program relies on private insurance, "social pooling," and individual retirement accounts to encourage the accumulation of adequate retirement resources. As with any option that depends on the private sector or personal responsibility, poor planning, an unfortunate circumstance, or a misstep can shatter the porcelain rice bowl and its promise.

The Madrid Plan recognizes that most national programs devised to eliminate poverty have typically ignored older persons. Noting the longevity and the nearly universal vulnerability of older women, it calls for the eradication of poverty and concomitantly emphasizes the magnitude of the importance of assuring gender equality in social protection schemes. The plan stipulates that a commitment to income security, social protection and social security, and poverty prevention programs is now crucial in an undeniably aging world. Consistent with the Millennium Goals, recent international discussions on the policy directions of poverty programs no longer cast effective antipoverty programs as solely in the realm of social welfare, but subscribe to the wisdom of reorienting economic development programs so that they empower the poor as a group.

In many countries around the world, the question that is debated is the wisdom of full to partial privatization of social security programs, not whether social security programs should exist. More important at this time is whether and how private-sector-based investment options should supplement traditional programs and whether the age of entitlement should be raised, scheduled benefits should be reduced, or scheduled revenues should be increased—the latter three being obvious mechanisms by which an entitlement program can be stabilized for the long term (Goss, 2005). The fundamental issues for policy development include the following:

- Goals of a social security program
- The roles of the market and the state
- Mechanisms that might assure the sustainability of social security protection
- A financing scheme that would best achieve long-term program goals

- The kinds and levels of benefits and their terms
- Whether and how social security programs might be better linked to social and economic growth and social entrepreneurship

These questions continue to be examined by OECD, the World Bank, and many other financial institutions.

In the United States, political perspectives and commitments around the future of the Social Security program are deeply divided and are driven by ideological convictions and economic interests. In June 2006, the U.S. Senate Budget Committee alarmed national aging organizations with its approval of Republican-introduced Senate Bill 3521. This bill would significantly modify federal budget laws, enabling the privatization of Social Security and the imposition of crippling cuts to the Medicare program. The bill calls for two commissions, each composed of nine members of the ruling party and six minority members. One commission is directed to study and propose unrestricted changes to Social Security, Medicare, and Medicaid. A second "sunset commission" is authorized to evaluate, summarily eliminate, or otherwise modify federal programs. These commissions may be mechanisms to facilitate the intentions declared in June 2006 by President Bush and members of the House Ways and Means Committee to privatize Social Security after the fall elections.

Pension systems and disability insurance require a much longer discussion than is possible in this chapter. They are complex topics and are best discussed as part of a comprehensive financing strategy that typically would include several pillars: savings, pensions, social security, and perhaps continuing employment. Unfortunately, pension and disability insurance programs in many countries are swiftly eroding and are frequently unreliable. In the United States, for example, a growing number of employers have ended or are in the process of or are planning to freeze or end underfunded defined benefit pension plans just as discussions are raging about the future of Social Security (Arnone, 2005). Recognizing the fragility of pension programs, the Madrid Plan articulated the importance of ensuring that pension schemes are characterized by fiscal integrity, solvency, and transparency. To that end, the OECD's (2006) recent guidelines adhering to the "prudent person" rule for pension fund management, that is, the care and skill with which investment fund decisions are to be made and risks are to be managed by individuals with fiduciary responsibilities, are particularly timely.

LONG-TERM CARE

Informal care by families is the primary mode of long-term care worldwide. In the United States, family members provide 80% of all long-term care of older persons informally. About 44 million family caregivers offer millions of hours of assistance valued at $257 billion annually for an average of 4.3 years. (For a comprehensive review and analysis of family caregiving in the United States, see Chapter 16 by Montgomery, Rowe, & Kosloski.)

Christakis and Allison (2006) found that caregivers in the United States suffer from health problems, depression, and, in the case of spousal caregivers, increased risk of dying prematurely. Many informal caregivers, an increasing number of whom are baby boomers, are twice as likely to be in poverty. Family caregivers must frequently modify employment arrangements in order to care for their relatives. Employment laws do not provide adequate relief to family caregivers, whose care commitments can extend beyond a year or two and be 24 hours a day. Support services are often not available and are frequently not affordable, accessible, or of acceptable quality. Lacking other care-giving alternatives, 9% of caregivers leave their job and 17% take leaves of absence.

The OECD (2005) recently examined the long-term care policies and programs in 19 of its member countries. A number of countries have laws that provide family caregivers of persons of all ages with varying types of assistance and benefits. Among the earliest to recognize and respond to the long-term care needs of their citizens, Sweden and Norway in the 1980s began to offer assistance to elders to enable family caregivers to sustain their roles in the workplace. The Scandinavian programs include institutional and home-based care options as well as cash benefits to caregivers. In Germany and France, social benefits are provided to help informal caregivers. Germany's long-term care insurance program pays for services provided by informal caregivers, home- and community-based services, and institutional care. Informal caregivers who provide significant assistance to frail and vulnerable elders also receive contributions to their pension funds.

In 1999, as a part of the Older Americans Act reauthorization process in the United States, the National Family Caregiver Support Program (NFCSP) was enacted, becoming the first U.S. national policy specifically dedicated to the special needs of caregivers of older persons. Federal funds allocated by formula and matched by the states have underwritten five sets of NFCSP services, ranging from information and assistance to caregiver education and respite. Unfortunately, as Montgomery, Rowe, and Kosloski note in their chapter, funding levels for the program have never been robust enough to meet documented needs.

China's emerging long-term care dilemmas and the factors that constrain its capacity to respond to those needs are unique. Following Confucian precepts, the family unit traditionally embraced filial piety and provided care to its elderly members. However, changes in the structure, composition, and expectations of the family have been in process since the Revolution in 1948. As of 2006, about 36% of China's elders are "empty-nesters." Sixty-four percent live with adult children, who presumably could be caregivers in the years ahead if these younger adults are not outnumbered by multiple generations of aged relatives, which would impose a tremendous care-giving burden.

Overpopulation resulting from China's adoption in the 1950s of the Russian "Hero Mother" model was followed in the late 1960s by the infamous one-child policy, which spawned the 4-2-1 problem. There is much discussion and great consternation in China over the anticipated emergence of a narcissistic society and the loss of filial piety as a fundamental value. This fear may be warranted as the sole, doting focus of four aged grandparents and two aging parents is the family's singular child (hence, 4-2-1). The reality is that China's one-child policy has significantly weakened the potential capacity of the Chinese family to provide long-term care support to its elders.

The Westernization of the Chinese lifestyle, from low- to high-fat diets to high levels of tobacco consumption, the replacement of physical activity with television watching as the most common activity among elders (Chang, 2005), and trends such as the nearly wholesale replacement of bicycles with cars as the primary mode of transportation, have given rise to a higher incidence of chronic disease. This does not bode well for the future with filial piety a vanishing ethic and the erosion of the traditional structure and composition of the Chinese family. Recognizing such trends in China, WHO recently lent its support to the development of a chronic disease and long-term care plan for 2005 to 2015. Community-based long-term care resources, such as private care homes and long-term care facilities, are only now beginning to appear in both urban and rural communities, although not at a sufficient pace. In addition, chronic disease prevention and control have been formally recognized as vital national activities through the establishment in 2002 of China's National Center for Chronic and Noncommunicable Disease Prevention and Control.

If China is just beginning to strengthen its social insurance program and develop formal long-term care resources, Japan has created universal pension and health insurance programs. After several rounds of policy and program deliberations, 1990 saw the creation of a Gold Plan for long-term care. The plan, a 10-Year Strategy for Health and Welfare for the Elderly, laid out a complex, comprehensive, multilevel blueprint for a national long-term care system. A decade later, Japan enacted the Long-term Care Insurance System (LTCI), a comprehensive public long-term care insurance program, which reversed the nation's earlier moves to finance long-term care services through private sector long-term care insurance. All citizens 40 years and older contribute to the LTCI. Community-based, domiciliary, and institutional services are dispensed at the local level using established criteria. Japan's long-term care policies have responded to evidence that informal caregivers both feel burdened and that their work roles have been disrupted (Clark, 1997). The system's policies acknowledge the dramatically altered composition of the family and anticipate the family's diminishing ability to provide care to disabled members in the future. Through a 2005 reform measure, a communitywide care system is being implemented to improve the quality of services, and communitywide support centers are offering consultations and care management to prevent the exacerbation of health risks.

Japan's drive to build a strong infrastructure of formal support services and programs is fueled by the demographic realities underlying the aging of its population. Fertility rates have plunged in Japan and, as noted earlier, many Japanese women are delaying or deciding against marriage. This pattern may not be confined to Japan. Similar trends are emerging in China, Italy, Greece, and other developed and developing nations. Many U.S. boomers and the generational cohorts following them are opting to delay marriage or not marry at all. These individuals may not be able to count on the availability of children, spouses, siblings, or other family members to participate in their care. To this group should be added the sizable number who probably will live alone.

In most parts of the world, it seems that reliable, usable information about long-term care is needed for effective life course planning. In the United States, the National Commission for Quality Long-Term Care (2006), the Henry J. Kaiser Family Foundation (2005), and others have reported on the lack of information and the confusion that families have concerning financing long-term care, services and resources, and family caregiving when older loved ones are no longer able to manage independently. Even long-term care researchers and experts find that "the theories [fall] apart" and that they are "unable to navigate the information, service, and program maze" (Kane & West, 2005) and negotiate on behalf of their parents. Information needs will escalate with the aging of the baby boom generation. Sending a sobering message to aging service organizations, the

American public have said that 59% would go to a family member or friend for information about nursing homes, 54% would go to their doctor, 25% would go to a community service agency, and only 23% would go specifically to a government program (Kaiser Family Foundation, 2005).

Active, Productive Aging

Active, productive aging has been promoted as a crosscutting, organizing theme in international discussions since the 1997 Denver G-8 Summit, when aging was first placed on the global policy agenda by Japan. The developed nations of the world, cognizant of declines in their worker-retiree ratios, have extrapolated from research evidence on social engagement, physical and mental activity, and economic and social productivity to emphasize the potential of older persons to contribute to the vibrancy of their nation's economy and "to create a social legacy of profound importance" (Center for Health Communication, Harvard School of Public Health, 2003, p. 9). They have come to understand that health and long-term care expenditures are likely to diminish if chronic illness and functional disability among older persons can be forestalled (WHO, 2002). Moreover, they recognize the gains that would accrue if each nation's elders were to add to the intellectual and other capital of their communities through lifelong learning.

As an organizing concept, active aging is in synchrony with the shift in the definition of and perspectives about aging described earlier. Most current and future elders in developed nations would agree with Germany's Count Otto von Bismarck, widely misrepresented as the proponent of age 65 as the chronological marker, that 70 years or older better approximates advanced age (Ferguson, 2004). Even when older persons have chronic illnesses, the presence of these illnesses is not necessarily disruptive of an active lifestyle.

As a concept, active aging reinforces the directions adopted by United Nations Millennium Goals. It supports economic development as a means by which poverty among older persons can be curbed and as a vehicle through which countries will be able to thrive and grow. The relevance of active aging to the development agendas of the developing nations has been affirmed on many fronts. An Inter-Regional Consultation on Aging, examining the findings of a 2000 Inter-American Development Bank–Pan American Health Organization Study of Older Adults in Argentina, Chile, and Uruguay, concluded that all three countries must make promoting an awareness of aging and achieving active, healthy aging a priority. In China, active aging is an organizing concept that meshes well with ongoing work to socialize citizens to the lifelong "right to learn" and to reverse creeping patterns of inactivity (Chang, 2005).

A 2000 Cornell Mid-Career Paths and Passages Study concluded that older baby boomers in the United States were typically projecting retirements at least 2 years earlier than the age of their parents' retirement. Younger boomers in turn were planning to retire 2 years earlier than older boomers (Moen, Plassman, & Sweet, 2001, quoted in Mellor & Rehr, 2005). However, these trends appear to be reversing themselves.

More elderly persons are engaged in full-time employment in the United States than in years past (Gendell, 2006). Several researchers have found that at least half of all workers reenter the paid workforce after retirement, even if for a short period (Moen, Erickson, Agarwal, Field, & Todd, 2002, quoted in Mellor &

Rehr, 2005). A report by the Federal Interagency Forum on Aging-Related Statistics (2006) notes that labor force participation rates for men and women 65 or older are on the rise. Over a dozen years, workforce participation by men 65 or older rose from one out of every four men to more than one out of three men (34%). Rates for women showed a similar rise, from 16% to almost 24% between 1993 and 2005.

With replacement rates down, fewer young people joining the workforce, and life expectancy extended, active aging and productive aging are organizing concepts that resonate within the public and private sectors as well as among middle-aged and young-old workers, many of whom are remaining in the workplace for longer than they had previously planned. Some countries, such as Japan, have successfully increased the statutory retirement age. Others, such as France, have increased the age at which mandatory insurance benefits can be accessed and have introduced a longer period during which contributions must be made in order to receive full pension entitlements (Sigg, 2005).

Vast differences exist in how nations are viewing and responding to their older citizens' economic security and long-term care needs—two examples of aging-related issues that are expected to rise further on domestic agendas worldwide. The foregoing discussion suggests that the social and economic development goals of the developing nations are as inextricably linked to their aging policy and program directions as they are in the developed world. Because of this, active aging is a concept that is being embraced as important to every nation's economy and the health and welfare of their citizenry.

EVIDENCE-BASED APPROACHES AND GLOBAL AGING

Global aging and evidence-based approaches to both health and social interventions and policy formulation have evolved along parallel tracks. Their intersection comes at a time when evidence-based approaches to policy and practice, although still controversial, are nonetheless gaining the endorsement of governmental and nongovernmental organizations, insurers, professional academies and associations, and leading foundations. The intersection is occurring as a significant number of countries are on the verge of crossing the threshold that distinguishes nations that are aging from others (12% of total population). It is also occurring at a time when the rapidity of aging in many developing nations will outpace their economic and social development. One sign of the confluence of the aging demographic revolution and the growing emphasis on evidence-based approaches was the call at the 2002 Second World Assembly on Ageing in Madrid for "comprehensive, diversified, and specialized research on aging in all countries, particularly in developing countries. Research, including age- and gender-sensitive data collection and analysis, provides essential evidence for effective policies" (United Nations, 2002b, p. 25).

There is no shortage of definitions of "evidence-based practice." Consolidating Roberts and Yeager's (2004) and the New York State Office of Mental Health's (2001) definitions, a strict rendering of "evidence-based practice" refers to practice that aims to achieve specific, measurable improvements in a particular condition that are attributable to the use of interventions deemed efficacious by systematic clinical research, provided that the interventions are consistently effective when evaluated against precise criteria. Other definitions run the full spectrum, from those insisting that "science-based" refers to a strict reliance on randomized controlled trials to those that accept findings from rigorously constructed and conducted qualitative research and professional observation studies, which some aver are most effective in documenting the client experience. A broad definition reported by the Institute of Medicine in 2001 simply suggests that evidence-based practice has three essential elements: best available research evidence, clinical expertise, and the consideration of client values (Institute of Medicine and the National Academy of Sciences, 2001), and helps us to appreciate more fully the value of best practices screened by consensus panels, competent professional judgment, and the importance of acknowledging the role of dynamic adaptation and the reinvention of interventions.

Although there is a desire to use evidence-based approaches, the Research Agenda on Aging for the 21st Century crafted during the Madrid World Assembly did not gloss over the range of research capacities represented in the global community. The sophistication of work in the United Kingdom (where the importance of utilizing sound evidence was first endorsed in the 1970s) should not be compared with beginning efforts to mount useful national research in developing nations, where reliable basic population data, large income and expenditure surveys for income poverty measurements, and other research staples may not be in place. Major research undertakings, such as the Pan American Health Organization's Study of Older Adults, must be launched in other parts of the world along with a host of other single-nation and comparative and international research studies, such as the initiative under way involving 12 developing countries an the examination of primary health-care-seeking behaviors of elders (United Nations, 2005). Significant work is also required in data-rich countries in which national, regional, state, and local data are often dissimilar, uncoordinated, and gathered to assure accountability instead of for social science research purposes, and thus cannot illuminate social or public health concerns. Accordingly, the Research Agenda on Aging acknowledges the breadth of the range of research capacity, noting the need to "assess the 'state of the art' of existing knowledge, as it varies across countries and regions" (United Nations, 2002a, p. 1).

In the United States, a national commitment to science-based policies and interventions was supported by significant funding increases to the National Institutes of Health. It was solidified in the early 1990s with the establishment and designation of the Agency for Healthcare Research and Quality (AHRQ). As the lead federal agency responsible for stimulating the improvement of the quality, safety, efficiency, and effectiveness of health care, AHRQ's focus has been on the promotion of evidence-based decisions and practice through rigorous services research.

To date, AHRQ's work on aging-related issues has been primarily with the National Institutes of Health, the Centers for Disease Control and Prevention, and the Centers for Medicare and Medicaid Services. However, Resolution 29, proposed during the 2005 White House Conference on Aging, urged the promotion of innovative evidence-based and practice-based medical and aging research and sought a systems approach to its promotion, coordination, and financing (U.S. Department of Health and Human Services, 2006).

Several interests underlie the race toward science-centered policy and practice. An observation readily generalizable to all realms of health and social welfare was articulated in the 1999 surgeon general's report on mental health: effective, empirically validated interventions are not widely known or used by professionals (U.S. Department of Health and Human Services, 1999). Thus, evidence-based approaches should be rooted in a moral and professional obligation to do no harm, to craft the most responsive policies, and to provide clients with the most effective treatment alternatives known. They reflect interest on the part of the federal government and private insurance plans in fiscal accountability around interventions, that is, reimbursements through Medicare and Medicaid for interventions that produce measurable results.

There is no question that science-based approaches are being promoted at the federal and state levels to stimulate changes in systems and procedures that have not been cost-effective. Fiscal and organizational accountability drivers enabled by the development of science and technology, the amassing of a critical body of research at the National Institutes of Health, and other research in the public and private sectors may help to rein in health care expenditures tied to aging. The Institute of Medicine has argued that the high incidence of medical errors, deaths and disabilities, waste, fraud, and abuse of resources can be curtailed with the routine employment of empirically sound interventions (Institute of Medicine and the National Academy of Sciences, 2001).

There are organizational and consumer-related drivers propelling evidence-based approaches. Where organizational effectiveness is valued, evidence-based approaches tend to support a culture of continuous learning. And evidence-based approaches may become the sine qua non in relation to clients with electronic access to information on the Web on health, social conditions, and treatments. With the baby boomers having achieved a higher level of educational attainment than any previous generation, a much more information-savvy older consumer can be expected (MetLife Mature Market Institute, 2005a; U.S. Census Bureau, 2000).

Despite the attention surrounding evidence-based approaches and the interest of many professional groups in the discourse and use of these approaches, it would be premature to claim that we are beyond the first generation of their design. The ambitious, if understandable, push toward these approaches is not without differing perspectives on the necessity and use of meta-analyses and randomized controlled trials. Nor is there a clear sense of how efficacious science-based interventions can be adapted in clinical practice for efficient use in real-world settings with diverse clientele. Although strictly defined evidence-based approaches appear to be ideal, their use becomes increasingly complicated as they are executed in contexts and under conditions dissimilar from those applied in trials. Moreover, the health and mental health conditions that typically afflict older persons are commonly complicated by comorbidities, which, in some instances, are only now becoming better understood. One simple reality has enormous implications for evidence-based approaches with older persons: The elderly population is far from homogeneous, and research on subpopulations and subgroups is still wanting in both developed and developing countries. This reality does not begin to address the additional need to be patient-centered and to attend to patient values and their roles in determining courses of treatment.

Rowan and Faul, Lightfoot, Park and Greenberg, and others who have contributed to this book are forthright in their assessment that evidence-based approaches for older persons are in their earliest stages. However, the work of the U.K.-based Cochrane Collaborative, which is engaged in the systematic review of evidence to determine the effectiveness and appropriateness of highly specified health care interventions and systems, and the Campbell Collaboration, which is dedicated to systematic reviews of high-quality evidence on education, criminal justice, and social welfare interventions and policies, offer cause for optimism that usable assessments will be produced, although over the long term. Optimism is warranted, again for the long term, as a consequence of the anticipated activity of Cochrane Centers in approximately 15 nations, the Collaboratives' beginning multinational investigation into the access to health services in low- and middle-income countries.

Some noteworthy progress has been made toward the identification of evidence-based interventions in specific areas of concern. For example, the Cochrane Collaborative has established the effectiveness of fall prevention interventions for older persons. Researched extensively by the Centers for Disease Control's Division of Nutrition and Physical Activity, the essential behavioral components of physical activity programs have been translated and are now being disseminated to state units on aging and community organizations through federally sponsored workshops and projects funded by private foundations. A study by the U.S. Agency for Healthcare Research and Quality (2004) concluded, based on systematic reviews, that a high quality of care can be achieved with specific end-of-life care interventions, most particularly for patients with cancer.

If evidence-based approaches are to be propelled forward with greater speed, a larger measure of professional commitment and significantly increased resources will be required at all levels (Bradley et al., 2004). The participation of professionals who are good by Reuben's (2002) standards will be key: They are respectful of patients, culturally competent, committed to continuous improvement, schooled in clinical studies, and able to work in teams. In the case of professionals who work with older persons, they must also understand the aging process, the diversity in the older adult population by generational cohort and other socioeconomic and other variables, and the complicated network of federal, state, and local aging policies, programs, and services.

CONCLUSION

Global aging presents opportunities and challenges that have never before been confronted by humankind. Although much of the literature has focused on the longevity revolution and its impact on the developed world, the greatest number of older persons will be in the developing world, where the pace of social and economic development is not expected to surpass the rapidity of population aging. Hence, income and human poverty are likely to continue to plague vulnerable populations, among them older persons. Although a significant body of research, conducted primarily in developed countries, can now be synthesized and analyzed to serve as the basis for policy, program, and practice interventions, much of the developing world does not have the luxury of large-scale population studies that can help to shape economic and social policies, nor do all developing countries have the cadres of professionals, the research capacity, and the studies conducted to enable the formulation of program and practice interventions informed by reliable, valid, and generalizable data.

There is no question that evidence-based approaches, already legitimized by many public and private sector entities, will continue to gain acceptance and will mature in the decades ahead. How quickly they are able to take root throughout the world will depend to some significant degree on whether the aspirations of the United Nations Millennium Declaration can become a reality. Aging policies and programs and social and economic development in both developing and developed nations are inextricably linked now and in the future.

REFERENCES

Arnone, W. (2005, May). *Developments in pensions and savings.* U.S. presentation at the National Academy of Social Insurance conference, Washington, DC.

Bradley, E. H., Webster, T. R., Baker, D., Schlesinger, M., Inouye, S. K., Barth, M. C., et al. (2004). *Translating research into practice: Speeding the adoption of innovative health care programs.* New York: Commonwealth Fund.

Center for Health Communication, Harvard School of Public Health. (2004). *Reinventing aging: Baby boomers and civic engagement.* Boston, Massachusetts: Harvard School of Public Health.

Center for Strategic and International Studies. (2001). *The challenge of global aging* (Report to world leaders of the findings and recommendations on global aging). Washington, DC: Author.

Chang, K. (2005, November 2). Professional presentation at the China National Committee on Aging, Beijing, PRC.

Christakis, N. A., & Allison, P. D. (2006). Mortality after the hospitalization of a spouse. *New England Journal of Medicine, 354*(7), 719–773.

Clark, R. (1997). *Active aging: A shift in the paradigm.* Washington, DC: U.S. Department of Health and Human Services. Retrieved July 5, 2006, from http://aspe.hhs.gov/daltcp/reports/actaging.htm.

Federal Interagency Forum on Aging-Related Statistics. (2000). *Older Americans 2000: Key indicators of well-being.* Washington, DC: U.S. Government Printing Office.

Federal Interagency Forum on Aging-Related Statistics. (2006). *Older Americans update 2006: Key indicators of well-being.* Washington, DC: U.S. Government Printing Office.

Ferguson, R. (2004, August 21). Blame it on Bismarck. *Toronto Star,* A–4.

Gendell, M. (2006). *Full-time work rises among U.S. elderly.* Washington, DC: Population Reference Bureau.

Gillion, S. (2004). *Boomer nation: The largest and richest generation ever, and how it changed America.* New York: Free Press.

Goss, S. (2005, May). *Can we afford social security when the baby boomers retire?* Presentation at the National Academy of Social Insurance Conference, Washington, DC.

Gouré, D. (2000). *The developed world's dual crisis of aging.* CSIS Conference on Global Aging, Paris.

HelpAge International. (2002). *State of the world's older people.* London: Author.

Henry J. Kaiser Family Foundation. (June 5, 2005). *Kaiser public opinion spotlight: The public's views on long-term care.* Retrieved January 24, 2007, from www.kff.org/spotlight/longterm/upload/Spotlight_June05_LongTerm.pdf.

Hong Kong and Shanghai Banking Corporation. (2005). *Future of retirement: In a world of rising life expectancy.* London: Author.

Hong Kong and Shanghai Banking Corporation. (2006). *Future of retirement: What the world wants.* London: Author.

Hughes, M. E., & O'Rand, A. M. (2004). *The lives and times of the baby boomers.* Washington, DC: Russell Sage Foundation and the Population Reference Bureau.

Ibe, H. (2000). *Aging in Japan.* New York: International Longevity Center.

Institute of Medicine and the National Academy of Sciences. (2001). *Crossing the quality chasm: A new health system for the 21st century.* Washington, DC: National Academy Press.

Japan Aging Research Center. (2000). *Aging in Japan.* Tokyo: Author.

Kane, R., & West, J. (2005). *Assisted living: What's in a name? Professionals with personal experience in chronic care.* Retrieved on January 24, 2007, from http:www.ppecc.org /stories/story_kanewest.htm.

Kinsella, K., & Velkoff, V. A. (2001). *An aging world: 2001* (U.S. Census Bureau, Series P95/01-1). Washington, DC: U.S. Government Printing Office.

Mellor, M. J., & Rehr, H. (2005). *Baby boomers: Can my eighties be like my fifties?* New York: Springer.

MetLife Mature Market Institute. (2005a). *Demographic profile: American baby boomers.* Westport, CT: Author.

MetLife Mature Market Institute. (2005b). *How old is old?* Westport, CT: Author.

Moen, P., Erickson, W., Agarwal, M., Fields, V., & Todd, L. (2002). *The Cornell retirement and well-being study: Final report.* Ithaca, NY: Cornell University, 2000.

Moen, P., Plassmann, V., & Sweet, S. (2001). *The Cornell midcareer paths and passages study: Summary.* Ithaca, NY: Cornell University.

National Council on Aging. (2000). *American perceptions of aging in the 21st century.* Washington, DC: Author.

National Commission for Quality Long-Term Care. (2006). *Out of isolation: A vision for long-term care in America.* Washington, DC: Author.

New York State Office of Mental Health. (2001). *Winds of change.* Albany, NY: Author.

Organization for Economic Co-operation and Development. (2005). *Long-term care for older people.* Paris: Author.

Organization for Economic Co-operation and Development. (2006). *OECD guidelines on pension fund asset management* (Recommendation of the OECD Council). Paris: OECD Insurance and Private Pensions Commission and Working Party on Private Pensions.

Peterson, P. G. (1999). *Gray dawn: How the coming age wave will transform America and the world.* New York: Three Rivers Press.

Population Reference Bureau. (2005). *2005 world data sheet.* Washington, DC: Author.

Reuben, D. (2002). Guidelines, EBM, and glidepaths: Talking the talk. *Journal of the American Geriatrics Society, 50,* 1905–1906.

Roberts, A. R., & Yeager, R. K. (2004). *Evidence-based practice manual: Research and outcome measures in health and human services.* London: Oxford University Press.

Sigg, R. (2005). Extending worklife: Policy challenges and responses. In R. Levinsky & R. McKinnon (Eds.), *Social security: Toward newfound confidence* (pp. 125–140). Geneva, Switzerland: International Social Security Association.

United Nations. (1999). *The 1991 United Nations principles for older persons.* Retrieved July 15, 2006, from http://www.un.org/esa/socdev/iyop/iyoppop.htm.

United Nations. (2000). *United Nations Development Programme poverty report 2000: Overcoming human poverty.* New York: Author.

United Nations. (2002a). *World population ageing: 1950–2050* (Department of Economic and Social Affairs, Population Division). New York: Author.

United Nations. (2002b). *Research agenda on ageing for the 21st century.* New York: Author. Retrieved January 24, 2007, from www.un.org/esa/socdev/ageing/ageing/ageraa.htm.

United Nations. (2002c). *Report of the Second World Assembly on Ageing: Political declaration and Madrid international plan of action on ageing.* New York: Author. Retrieved January 24, 2007, from www.un.org/esa/socdev/ageing/waa/a-conf-197-9b.htm.

United Nations. (2005). *Millennium goals.* Retrieved July 1, 2006, from http:/www .un.org/millenniumgoals.

U.S. Administration on Aging. (2005). *Older population by age: 1900 to 2050.* Retrieved July 15, 2006, from http://www.aoa.gov/PROF/statistics/online_stat_data /AgePop2050.asp.

U.S. Agency for Healthcare Research and Quality. (December 2004). *End of life care and outcomes.* Washington, DC: U.S. Government Printing Office.

U.S. Census Bureau. (2000, March). *Educational attainment of the population: 15 years and over by age, sex, race, and Hispanic origin.* Washington, DC: U.S. Government Printing Office.

U.S. Census Bureau. (2005, August). *Current population survey: Annual social and economic supplement, income, poverty, and health insurance coverage in the United States: 2004* (P60-229). Washington, DC: U.S. Government Printing Office.

U.S. Census Bureau (2006a, January 3). *Facts for feature.* Available from http://www .census.gov/Press-Release/www/releases/archives/facts_for_features_special_editions /006105.html.

U.S. Census Bureau. (2006b, June 8). *World population information.* Available from http://www.census.gov/ipc/www/world.html.

U.S. Central Intelligence Agency. (2006). *The world factbook.* Washington, DC: Author.

U.S. Department of Health and Human Services. (1999). *Mental health: A report of the surgeon general.* Washington, DC: U.S. Government Printing Office.

U.S. Department of Health and Human Services. (2005). *The booming dynamics of aging: From awareness to action* (White House Conference on Aging: Report to the President and Congress). Retrieved August 1, 2006, from www.whcoa.gov.

Van Ginneken, W. (2003). *Extending social security: Policies for developing countries.* Geneva, Switzerland: International Labor Organization.

Wang, D. (2005, November 2). Presentation at the China National Committee on Aging, Beijing, PRC.

World Health Organization. (2002). *Strengthening active and healthy aging.* Retrieved July 1, 2006, from http://www.who.int/hpr/ageing/ActiveAgeing.

World Health Organization. (n.d.). *Aging and the life course.* Retrieved July 1, 2006, from http://www.who.int/ageing/en.

Author Index

Subject Index